Editor of the *Sunday* ~~Te~~ ~~~~ ~~~~ ~~~~ has written for the *Wa*~~~~ ~~~~ *et Journal*, the *Financial Times*, the *Daily Mail* and *Standpoint* magazine. His first book, *Making It Happen: Fred Goodwin, RBS, and the Men who Blew Up the British Economy*, was shortlisted for the 2013 Financial Times/Goldman Sachs Business Book of the Year Award and won the Debut Book of the Year prize at the 2014 Political Book Awards.

'Fascinating . . . it is worth raising your eyes from the Brexit mud-slinging to read a new book on the history of the "Big Bang" financial reform . . . UK politicians should take heed of Martin's book.'
Financial Times

'As historical accounts of modern finance go, this is a corker.'
Breaking Views Reuters

'For anyone interested in finance . . . this is a readable history of how the City became the world's money hub.'
Sunday Times

'It is refreshing to read this lively account of a series of actions that add up to one of the undoubted, if not undisputed, successes of modern government action . . . a timely reminder of how the City of London got to where it is now'
New Statesman

'Martin's great trick in the book is his ear for echoes of the present in stories from the past, making the old City feel remarkably familiar today . . . Above all, Martin has a warmth for his subject, and its cast of characters, without excusing their feelings . . . With the journalist's eye for a good tale and a narrative style that rips along, Martin has turned an unloved part of British history about an unloved industry into a fascinating yarn.'
Philip Aldrick, *The Times*

'His book confirmed to me that the City is a financial centre like no other'
Literary Review

CRASH, BANG, WALLOP

Inside the Financial Revolution that
Changed the World

IAIN MARTIN

SCEPTRE

First published in Great Britain in 2016 by Sceptre
An imprint of Hodder & Stoughton
An Hachette UK company

First published in paperback in 2017

Picture Credits

© Getty Images: 12/Heritage Images, 29/Universal History Archive, 61/Icon
Communications, 76/Stan Meagher, 88/Steven Burton, 133/New York Daily
News Archive, 222/Maria R. Bastone/AFP, 249/Evening Standard, 277/
Shomos Uddin. © Copyright Guardian News & Media Ltd 2016: 268/photo
Sean Smith. © PA/Press Association Images: 149.
© REX/Shuttershock/Clive Limpkin/Daily Mail: 188. © Telegraph Media
Group Limited 1973: 79/photo Kenneth Mason. Excerpt from Serious
Money on p. 287 reproduced by kind permission of Caryl Churchill.

A CIP catalogue record for this title is available from the British Library

ISBN 978 1 473 62510 5

Typeset in Dante MT by Hewer Text UK Ltd, Edinburgh
Printed and bound by Clays Ltd, St Ives plc

Hodder & Stoughton policy is to use papers that are natural, renewable
and recyclable products and made from wood grown in sustainable
forests. The logging and manufacturing processes are expected to
conform to the environmental regulations of the country of origin.

Hodder & Stoughton Ltd
Carmelite House
50 Victoria Embankment
London EC4Y 0DZ

www.sceptrebooks.com

For William Martin

'The future is only the past again, entered through another gate.'

The Second Mrs Tanqueray, by Sir Arthur Wing Pinero (1893)

CONTENTS

INTRODUCTION

'We had a good day, we made money. That's what it's all about.'
Martin Pope, Hoare Govett & Co., 27 October 1986

In the beginning was Big Bang, but was it good? Thirty years on
from that moment of creation in the City of London in the autumn
of 1986, when a switch was flipped and the Stock Exchange was
opened up, liberalised and computerised, there is no consensus
about what it meant or on whether its impact was benign or malign.
Was the Thatcher government's Big Bang in the City inevitable,
almost an accident of historical circumstances, or a knowing innovation by ideologues? Did the changes to how the City worked
license an explosion of greed, selfishness and bonus-driven excess
in the Square Mile and beyond that contributed to the causes of the
crisis of the late 2000s and ongoing problems with the financial
system? Or was the financial revolution a creditworthy development essential to maintaining London as a leading financial centre?

That these questions do not have simple, pat answers suggests
that the real story of the City revolution in the 1980s is much more
interesting than the crude caricature of shouty men in red braces
guzzling 'shampoo' (champagne) by the gallon and waving their
wads (and worse) at the rest of us. But then, in Big Bang – when
foreign banks were allowed into the Stock Exchange, with old
British demarcations governing the City swept away – and in the
wider revolution of which that day was a key part, we too often see
what we want to see. It can be made to fit any version of history you
want, from Left to Right and all points of view in between.

For critics of finance, it is clear that it was a profoundly harmful development. Big Bang was emblematic of the wider liberation of markets and of international capitalism reasserting itself. Hubris abounded. Almost exactly a year afterwards came the international crash of October 1987. The new global architecture of open financial markets survived the shock and rebounded surprisingly quickly, making some people a lot of money for almost two decades, until the edifice came falling down in the crisis of 2008, at great cost to the rest of us. That's one version, in which the City is a demon. Indeed, the imagery associated with the City at points of crisis has become one of the defining motifs of the age. Whenever there is a tremor or full earthquake in the markets, when prices dip or a bank has done something it should not have, television crews are sent to film traders looking stressed about the trouble they have landed themselves and us in. Standing at desks shouting at their colleagues used to be standard procedure on these occasions. Now they are encouraged to look less agitated in front of the cameras and just sit there looking at their screens. It is the media cliché – of the trader as ruthless, overpaid arbiter – repeated like a pseudo-religious ritual when we want an explanation for why the economy is not doing what we want it to.

In that reading, Margaret Thatcher in the 1980s deliberately instigated this financial revolution and unleashed greed on a gargantuan scale. In attempting to outdo New York and Wall Street in terms of excess and selfishness, the Square Mile made itself a city-state cut off from the concerns of Britain's less affluent citizens. The two cities, New York and London, collaborated and competed frenetically until their combined efforts almost blew up the global financial system in 2008. That explanation can be heard on the Left and sometimes among traditional Conservatives too.

There is an alternative view, which holds that the reforms introduced were among the most positive of Thatcher's eleven years in office, and her defining international achievement outside the Cold War. Not only was the domestic City subjected to a welcome blast of meritocracy, in which the old school tie mattered a lot less than it used to, it was also reopened to the world, restoring it to the once dominant financial position it had enjoyed for the century leading up to the beginning of the First World War. This new 1980s openness was the modern equivalent of the bold British switch to free trade in the mid-nineteenth century. Just as happened then, British reforms inspired policy makers and financiers in other countries and the Thatcher approach to open markets and privatisation became the international norm. And anyway, most of what goes on in finance is nothing like the media caricature of screaming traders and massive bonuses. Pay for most City workers is not in the stratosphere. Post-Big Bang the place is an engine room of social mobility and opportunity. It is a British success story just as Wall Street is the humming motor of American capitalism. That is roughly how free market advocates see it.

For others, Big Bang represents the melancholy passing of a particularly English approach to capitalism, in which a gentleman's word was supposedly his bond and a decent lunch kicking off with gin and tonic followed by white burgundy, claret and port was a seemingly ancient birthright. Out went British ownership and dominance in the City; in came ever more of the hardworking Americans, ensuring that something intangible and peculiarly English was lost.

It certainly had another impact too, one that is entirely positive and often overlooked by men. Before the 1980s some women had begun to be employed in the Square Mile, but it was not until the Thatcher government's reforms that serious numbers of women started to make inroads. As recently as the 1960s it had been an almost exclusively male environment in which the employment of one woman on the floor of the Stock Exchange in Dublin could cause such a shock that the authorities in London took legal advice to protect themselves against anything of that kind happening in the City.

That glimpse of the financial universe pre-Big Bang illustrates that the changes of 1986 did not happen in a historical vacuum. While Monday 27 October was an emblematic exciting moment that encapsulated Thatcherism and the resurgent power of markets and those who work in them, there was plenty of life before it. Big Bang was just one development among many that marked London's re-emergence as a global financial centre over the course of several decades from the 1960s. That is a story with deep historical roots, which is why Part One of this book, 'Ignition', charts the origins and development of the ancient City of London from Elizabethan times, through centuries of war, fire and reconstruction, right up to the emergence of another equally ruthless leader in the late 1970s, Margaret Thatcher. In terms of how finance is regarded in the popular imagination, the transformation of the Square Mile has a claim to be the BC and AD moment. But a lot that matters happened long before. The modern City and finance make a good deal more sense if you understand where they came from, and also understand the interplay between London and other great global financial centres.

Part Two, 'Friction', tells the inside story of Big Bang and the people in politics and the City who engineered it. It deals not only with the City and high politics. The architecture, theatre, music, fashion, satire and media of the 1980s also feature. Indeed, London itself changed markedly in that decade, when a small group of property developers, public officials and financiers established a rival to the traditional City on the dockland wasteland in the East End. The City itself had to respond, by wiping away the grime and building higher in glass and steel. Part Two also includes an early appearance by a young journalist called Boris Johnson.

Part Three, 'Combustion', then deals with the crash of 1987, the serial scandals of the era, the dramatic growth of the City in large part thanks to the euro, the battle for supremacy with New York, and the disaster of 2008 and subsequent recovery. I close by assessing the City revolution – thirty years on – with the help of some of the most interesting players of the period. And I offer my own assessment. But what of the future? The Afterword assesses the challenges facing the City as it tries to come to terms with the UK's vote to leave the European Union, against the backdrop of the next financial revolution already underway. Politics, disruptive technology, and new digital currencies are about to reshape the City once again. That Afterword is entitled 'The Fate of the City and the Future of Money' – something we should all be concerned about.

Writing my last book about the collapse of RBS in 2008 and the wider financial crisis, it became obvious to me that a good deal of what I thought I knew previously about finance, politics and people had been wrong. I must confess that as a political commentator working on a leading national newspaper, I wrote about the financial crisis of 2007-2009 with only a limited understanding of many of the underlying concepts. That is why, a few years later, I sought as a baffled and furious taxpayer to understand the RBS failure, and to write about it.

Similarly, underpinning this book is an attempt to explain how and why the story of the West since the Second World War is to a large extent about an 'explosion of money'. This process has been driven by increasing debt, financial innovation, cross-border trade and the development of new technology making it easier to move that money ever faster around the globe. London is critical – and Big Bang was a decisive moment in the evolution of money – because a small patch of the British capital was used as a test site for a global experiment. We have all, in our different ways, been affected by the fallout and continue to be.

Crash, Bang, Wallop is not meant to be a dry, technical tale, however. It is told with the help of a remarkable cast of personalities, some of whom got into all manner of farcical scrapes and chicanery along the way. What became apparent, interviewing some of the key participants from the 1970s and 80s, and examining archive material, is that the architects of the financial reforms had no clear idea where it would all lead, or of the bonus bonanza and cultural conflict it would entail. 'I think the truth is that they didn't know what they were unleashing,' says a Thatcherite former cabinet minister. Sceptics will smirk at that. Didn't many of those involved go on to do very nicely in City boardrooms afterwards? That is true, of course, but there was, no matter what anyone might try to tell you, no one clear and dastardly plan for a financial revolution. Events proceeded at times chaotically, with the participants attempting to adapt to what we now think of as globalisation.

The bigger picture that emerges from the history of the City over almost five centuries is of invigorating innovation, openness to the outside world, frequent crashes followed by growth taking place in a peculiar environment, where generations of traders have usually resisted attempts at central planning or mapping the future. Indeed, the City's rise is the story of visionaries and rascals, and of the combined efforts of millions of souls trying to make themselves a living, constantly repeating the cycle of wealth generation, excessive excitement, panic, bust and renewal.

What is perhaps most striking about the City's development through those upheavals, in recent decades and over the centuries, is the strong retained sense of place, even though it has been burnt down several times and bombed to bits. Elsewhere, industries tend to rise on one spot and then, when trading patterns change, within a century or less they can be gone, leaving scrubland or a heritage site. One thinks of coalmining, or docks, or fishing, or ships, or car manufacture. In contrast, with varying degrees of success, what the City is doing it has essentially been doing for many centuries on one patch of ground. Trading in goods gradually developed from the sixteenth century into expertise learnt abroad in the art of trade financing, then into making money from money, always ring-fenced from the rest of us to an extent because of the City's secretive self-government that stretches back almost a millennium and was recognised by William the Conqueror. In that respect, the place has more in common with hallowed religious sites that draw their power from the physical connection to the past, reminding worshippers that there were people here before us and there will be others after we are gone. The City, with its evocative street-names, gothic rituals, baffling codes of behaviour, and temporal temples to mammon, looks to this visitor like the international financial equivalent of Harry Potter's Hogwarts.

To take a leisurely walk along modern Bishopsgate at the eastern end of the City, dodging the crowds of impatient workers rushing by on their way to a sandwich shop or a meeting, is to walk through history. Bishopsgate is named after a long-demolished three-towered medieval gate at the City Wall, which was paid for by foreign merchants from the Hanseatic League in the fifteenth century in return for their continental trading privileges. The heads of traitors were displayed on spikes on top of the gate. Later, the area was home to coaching inns serving visiting merchants, residents and 'stock men' driving animals to one of the many nearby stock markets. Walk past the church, St Helens of Bishopsgate, which was first consecrated in the twelfth century. That is where the merchant Sir Thomas Gresham was buried in 1579. St Helens miraculously survived both the Great Fire of London in 1666 and the attentions of the Luftwaffe in the early 1940s, although Gresham's altar tomb only narrowly avoided destruction when the church was badly damaged by two IRA bombs exploding in the early 1990s. Bishopsgate is also where Gresham, an Elizabethan trader and loyal friend of the Queen, had his London house. From there he travelled from Thames-side wharves to do deals in Antwerp, then the leading market or bourse in Europe. It is with the peripatetic Gresham, and a vital innovation he brought back from his travels, that this story begins.

Iain Martin
London, 2016

PART ONE
IGNITION

I

ON THE MAKE

'A public, or a private robber; a statesman, or a South Sea jobber.'
Jonathan Swift, to Mr Gay (1728)

Thomas Gresham – merchant, foreign adventurer, financial schemer, property developer, Royal advisor prepared to keep a rival of Queen Elizabeth I under house arrest[1] – was born to be one of the great figures in the history of the City of London. His wealthy merchant father became Lord Mayor, and grew the fortune of his well-established Norfolk family from London, where he became a supplier to Henry VIII and a witness to the turmoil of Tudor politics. Thomas – born in 1519 – was sent to Cambridge, but he was destined to follow his father by becoming a merchant, although he would soon eclipse his achievements and become an early archetype of what a smart, scheming trader can achieve with some chutzpah and an eye for the main chance. He also reshaped the City with a vital innovation.

To begin his career Thomas went first to the Square Mile, to become a member of the Mercer's Company, the exalted livery company or trade body that represented merchants. The City was the wellspring of wider London and already the centre of commercial power in England. The square mile or so of land on the north bank of the Thames had been colonised by the Romans, who built Londinium as a port protected by city walls. Abandoned after their departure, then repopulated from the ninth century and connected to a network of villages such as Westminster outside the walls, the City by Gresham's time was the centre of English trade in all its

*Sir Thomas Gresham – merchant, innovator, agent of the Crown – welcomed
Elizabeth I to name his Royal Exchange in the City in 1571.*

forms. On its wharves on the river, goods were loaded and unloaded. The stock markets – stock then meaning stall – were where for centuries butchers, fishmongers and others practised their trade. Through the streets, cattle were driven to market and produce carried to the herb markets. Some of the place-names in the City still reflect that comestible heritage: Poultry, Bread Street, Pudding (meaning offal) Lane, Milk Street and Honey Lane – the last two adjoining Cheapside (a medieval term for market). Since at least the Norman Conquest, the City had enjoyed a degree of self-government and autonomy within London, which remains the case today. As the medieval period gave way to the modern, and London continued to expand outside the boundaries of the Square Mile, the City of London remained distinct with its own customs, atmosphere, local government and legal personality. The City was of London but also apart from it.

But Thomas did not stay long. While he maintained a base in London, initially he went to the Low Countries and to what was then one of Europe's greatest trading centres and ports, Antwerp, where he developed his skills as a trader. It was where moneylenders, financiers and merchants of all varieties from across the continent did business. The Portuguese had begun to use Antwerp as an outlet for the sale of their spices from the East and the unrefined sugar sourced from its empire. German merchants and refiners were drawn like bees to the honey pot and the English had also established a trading house there in the early sixteenth century. The international flavour of Antwerp illustrated the extent to which the countries and city-states of Europe were bound together by money-making. In Antwerp's Bourse, the exchange where the traders gathered, Gresham became well connected.

That meant he was ideally placed to help when in the early 1550s the English monarchy got itself into yet another financial mess and the affairs of Edward VI, son of Henry VIII and half-brother of Elizabeth I, were unravelling. The problem facing the Royal Family in 1551, as so often, was the debts it had run up. As Edward VI's advisors at court squabbled over how to settle the young King's bills, new loans were taken out abroad, which only exacerbated matters. The rates of interest charged in Antwerp were ruinous. This is where Gresham came in most useful as the Crown agent. One of the solutions, Gresham concluded, was an early form of currency market manipulation. If he could, by hoarding currency and making it scarce, artificially drive up the value of the pound as it was traded in Antwerp, then the monarch's debts in other currencies would – proportionately – become smaller and easier to pay off. It took a couple of years, and several of his other schemes came to nothing, but it worked and the burden of royal debts was eased. A figure from a leading City of London family had arranged a bailout of the monarchy, rescued the royal reputation and bolstered his own connections at court.

Even then in finance you were only as good as your last deal. Favour could vanish quickly with a change of monarch. The advisors to Mary, Edward's successor, were suspicious of Gresham's influence. He was briefly excluded and had to work his way back. It took the elevation to the throne of the much cannier Elizabeth in 1558 for him to enjoy full royal favour again. It also helped there that Gresham's close friend was Sir William Cecil, who on the death of Mary became Secretary of State, principal advisor to the monarch. Gresham agreed to keep Lady Mary Grey, who had a potential claim to the Crown, under house arrest at his properties, and he was at Hatfield House in November 1558 for Elizabeth's first council as Queen. Even then, that day, he made the case that English merchants and moneymen deserved better protection from the Crown and complained that foreign traders had it too easy in London.

While the Elizabethan elite was in favour of trade, this should not be confused with free trade or open markets, concepts that would only gain credence two centuries later. Gresham and his fellow merchants operated in an era of mercantilism, a system in which the Crown guided economic policy and attempted to create trading monopolies protected by military force. The aim was for the country never to buy more from other countries than it sold because that way England might accumulate reserves of bullion and protect itself in war. Gresham was interested in innovation, however. And when he undertook an ambitious project designed to boost English finance and trade – first floated by his father[2] – the interests of a mercantilist monarchy and an ambitious merchant with a house on Bishopsgate were perfectly aligned.

Gresham's great innovation was the addition of what became the Royal Exchange, a bourse modelled on the institution in Antwerp and designed by a foreign architect with the City's livery companies paying for the land. In establishing this enterprise and overseeing its construction, Gresham was, in modern parlance, seeking to 'give something back'. His only son had died young and the opening of a bourse gifted to the City was an act of philanthropy, although, ever the man of business, he retained the leases on the shops overlooking the courtyard. The rents would enable him to recoup some of his outlay.

The spot he chose for that building – at what today is the busy junction at Bank – remains the financial City's polestar. Nearby Gresham Street runs into Lothbury Street, behind the Bank of England building. The Victorian iteration of the Royal Exchange stands on the original site of Gresham's Exchange, with a weathervane on the roof that is a golden grasshopper, representing the Gresham family crest. In the mid-sixteenth century, that early piece of City property development by Sir Thomas Gresham changed the face of the City. Previously, merchants and dealmakers transacted trade in a haphazard fashion on the street and in inns. This was the first time they would have a dedicated spot with proper protection from the elements, creating the potential for a multiplying effect by which traders on the make would know where to find their allies and rivals if they wanted to do a deal.

This innovation was deemed such an advance that the Queen was prepared to give it her royal imprimatur. On 23 January 1571, Elizabeth I left her residence at Somerset House on the Strand, accompanied by a guard with trumpeters heralding the monarch, and headed for a dinner in the City. Her short journey took her through Temple Bar, along Fleet Street, on to what is now Cheapside and Threadneedle Street, before she arrived in Austin Friars, near Bishopsgate, at the mansion of Sir Thomas. According to the account of Monsieur La Motte Fenelon, the French Ambassador who was at the table, there was playful discussion of the Queen's marriage prospects before, in the early evening, with dinner finished, a torchlit procession set off to open the first Royal Exchange. The historian John Stow, in his *Survey of London*, published in 1598, described what happened next: 'Her majesty returning through Cornehill, entered the burse on the south side; and after that she had viewed every part thereof above the ground . . . she caused the same burse by an herald and trumpet to be proclaimed the Royal Exchange, and so to be called from thenceforth, and not otherwise.'

The rising confidence and increased assertiveness of the Tudor merchant class is illustrated by the other attempts made by Gresham and his contemporaries to reduce the domestic influence of far stronger European rivals. It rankled with English merchants that London did not even have unhindered control of its own trade. On the site of what is today Cannon Street Station, the Hanseatic League (established in the fourteenth century) ran the Stillyard, a network of wharves by the Thames handling imports and goods for export to other parts of Europe. The power of the League, originating in Lubeck, Germany, stemmed from its mastery of cross-border commerce and control of trading routes. In Gresham's lifetime, the Stillyard or Steelyard still enjoyed privileges from the Crown in return for guarantees to help guard the City in the event of an uprising. The Liberal MP, author, playwright, soldier and spy, A.E.W. Mason, wrote in 1920 that 'the Stillyard was to the modern understanding, one of the strangest institutions which the world has ever seen. It took its origin from the debts of the early English kings and the money with which the German traders from the Baltic, the Easterlings as they were called, were able to provide them.'[3]

Gresham wrote to Queen Elizabeth deploring the existence of the Hanseatic League's trading house in the City: 'The Stillyard hath been the chiefest point in the undoing of this your Realm and the Merchants of the same.' A spasmodic crackdown had begun in Edward VI's reign, when the liberties of the foreigners with their trading empire by the Thames were removed. Queen Elizabeth banished them entirely in 1598 after Gresham's death, although under James I they were readmitted. The land was finally sold, by German owners, to a railway company in the 1850s. In those sixteenth-century squabbles involving Gresham and his friends, some of the major themes of the City's subsequent development – including notions of monopoly, skulduggery, foreign competition and the role of government – were already apparent. To what extent did London's trade have to be open to the outside world? Who did the City's senior figures truly serve other than themselves? How should London adapt to thrive?

There was a shady postscript to Gresham's career, however, that will sound familiar to those used to hearing about the misbehaviour of some modern financiers. An inquiry by the Crown into his dealings on its behalf found a number of apparent irregularities. Gresham could explain it all, he said. The lavish entertaining on expenses of foreign merchants was essential for the transaction of deals, and the high profits he had made in working on royal business were deserved, he claimed. Everything was accounted for, he assured the Queen. She was persuaded and Gresham was paid the last of what he was owed by the Crown. One of Tudor England's richest men, he died suddenly on 21 November 1579 on his way from a meeting at the Royal Exchange.[4]

Gresham may have given the City a commercial centre, to complement the ancient Guildhall from where the Corporation governed the City, but at the start of the seventeenth century in England the business of trading money, of making money from money, was underdeveloped. What was traded were principally real goods, such as cloth, timber, food, spices and jewels. At that point the notion of buying shares in companies and selling them to others was alien and the City of London was far behind where the Venetians had been centuries earlier, when by the early 1300s Venice had already begun to develop a commercial system capable of coping with the complexities and risks of long-distance trade. They had limited-liability joint-stock companies, with pools of shareholders; sophisticated markets for the trading of debt; mortgages; some education in business; bankruptcy laws; double-entry accounting; and a proper currency, Venice's ducat. The traders in Antwerp and other trading hubs had adopted and evolved these ideas, which had then been transmitted back out across Europe by merchants eager to diffuse risk and make more money. In the seventeenth century it was the Dutch, and only later the English, who exploited such innovations and became particularly good at the business of money.

It helped that London's Royal Exchange had an early boost following the sacking of Antwerp by the Spanish in 1576, an event that also caused the Low Countries to unite against Spain. The waning power of Spain then created a vacuum which the Dutch provinces filled in the late sixteenth and early seventeenth century. In the Dutch golden age that followed, Amsterdam became for a while the wealthiest and most innovative financial centre on earth. In war, at that point, the Dutch tended to best the English too, most embarrassingly in 1667 when the Dutch fleet sailed into the Thames estuary and at Chatham set a large part of the English fleet on fire before towing away two prized ships. Samuel Pepys, then Secretary to the Navy Board in Whitehall, wrote in his diary: 'Most sad to be sure. And, the truth is, I do fear so much that the whole kingdom is undone, that I do this night resolve to study with my father and wife what to do with the little that I have in money by me.'

It was a combustible period in the City. For Londoners the Dutch incursion looked like another God-given sign that the end of days was approaching, or at least that yet more tumult was on the way. In the Civil War, much of the City had backed Parliament, ostensibly out of resentment over the Stuarts' taxes and financial impositions. After all, the newly assertive merchant class of London was also used to a degree of self-government in the Square Mile. Even after that upheaval, there was no respite. On top of war and regicide came plague and then fire, against which the tightly packed pitch-covered timber houses were like dry tinder. In September 1666, when the Great Fire took hold, much of the City was burnt to the ground, including the first St Paul's Cathedral and the Royal Exchange. Pepys noted in his diary on 5 September 1666: 'The Exchange, a sad sight. Nothing standing there of all the statues or pillars.' Only the statue of Gresham remained, said Pepys and others who visited the scene.

Every disaster presents an opportunity, however. And in the rebuilding that followed and with the development of insurance, a new generation of men on the make took their chance. Those dwelling or working in the City lived permanently with such risks disrupting their activities and killing their customers. That being the case, sensible property owners and merchants needed ways to offset risk and to protect themselves against the possibility of further disaster after the Great Fire. One man in particular, Sir Nicholas Barbon, made it his business to exploit these opportunities to the full.

Barbon was the son of the puritanical Praise-God Barebone (his real name) and a physician trained in medicine in the Netherlands, an economist, a rapacious property developer, a Member of Parliament and a financial innovator. He was the archetypal financial adventurer in the late seventeenth-century style who not only began rebuilding the City from the ashes, buying up land at fire-sale prices and constructing rows of terraced houses made of brick. He also offered property insurance.

The idea of a contract, in which the businessman paid a premium for protection and payment if disaster struck, was not in itself new. Insurance contracts had existed in Genoa in the fourteenth century. But in the aftermath of the Great Fire, Barbon's mass-market application of the technique to houses was swiftly copied when its potential profitability became understood. His Insurance Office for Houses (later renamed Phoenix) operated from a building close to the site of the destroyed Royal Exchange and as many as five thousand homes in the rebuilt City were covered by his policies. Fire services were also launched by the individual insurance providers, although the resulting attempts at extinguishing blazes could be chaotic. The insurance companies would only put out the fires of their own customers, an approach not conducive to public safety.[5]

As well as leading the way on insurance, Barbon was also a pioneering writer on free market economics, and in *A Discourse of Trade* he dealt with interest rates, prices, currencies and the encouragement of commerce, describing the City of London as 'the Largest, Richest, and Chiefest City in the World, for Trade'. He died in 1698 or early 1699[6] at his country property, Osterley House in Middlesex. It was a house that had been owned by a previous City pioneer, Sir Thomas Gresham, more than a century before. Despite his success in building and insurance and in the development of economics, Barbon ultimately had less success in the other rapidly developing field of business that dominated the efforts of adventurous types in the City in the 1690s, namely banking. The developing English economy needed banks.

Once again, the requirements of the Crown played a key role in reshaping finance, when another monarch found himself short of money. England's new Dutch and Protestant monarch William III wanted to rebuild the navy and had to be able to borrow to pay for it. The emergence of the Bank of Amsterdam, and the founding of the first central bank by Sweden in 1688, suggested that the establishment of a Bank of England would provide a way to enable the government to borrow. A scheme proposed by a roguish speculator, the Scotsman William Paterson, was suddenly deemed attractive.[7]

The Bank of England was established in 1694, and offices on Walbrook were opened less than two hundred metres away from the Royal Exchange. From there it became the government's banker, the model central bank on which other nations based their own institutions. Privately owned, it was licensed by the government with a monopoly in England to issue notes. It eventually controlled the national debt and, in time, as they developed, the straightforward commercial banks would eventually be overseen by the Bank.

Other, smaller banks had developed out of the goldsmiths trade that thrived along the City's Cheapside. Goldsmiths had secure vaults, knew how to safeguard wealth and look after deposits, and some started to develop a sideline in banking and loans. In 1672, the goldsmith Richard Hoare founded the bank which later became C. Hoare & Co. He moved it to Fleet Street in 1690 and the bank is still owned by the Hoare family, trading on the same site. Barclays was on Lombard Street, where two Quakers – members of the radical, dissenting Protestant movement – set themselves up in business in 1690. John Freame and Thomas Gould financed Quakers launching new trading enterprises in the Caribbean and America, and backed the Welsh Copper Company and the London Lead Company. In Edinburgh, the Scots were also moving into banking, but in England banking was largely restricted to London at this stage, only spreading outwards across the country in the eighteenth century as commerce grew.

Then there were the joint-stock companies. The idea of companies with many shareholders owning a firm is common now and widely understood. It is how all manner of business household names and banks are structured, with financial institutions and individual investors buying tradable shares entitling them to a chunk of the profits, in the form of a dividend, in return. The model, though, has its roots in the mercantilist push for empire by England and then Britain from the sixteenth century on to the domination of India in the eighteen and nineteenth centuries, with a small group of investors putting up funds for adventure and exploration that might lead to trade.

The Muscovy Company of the 1550s had originated as the Mystery and Company of Merchant Adventurers for the Discovery of Regions, Dominions, Islands, and Places unknown, founded by three adventurers. A mission to Moscow was, mercifully, well received by Ivan the Terrible, and the building the Company used in the Russian capital still stands near Red Square. Other companies plied different trading routes, including the Levant Company, founded in 1581, which later merged with the Venice Company. These early adventurers and the Crown had struck a bargain. British explorers, in competition with foreign rivals, would claim new territory from which the Crown would gain revenue and global reach.

The Companies were not state-owned, although they operated with the encouragement of the Crown. The Elizabethan establishment of an American colony in Virginia, the first successful English colony, was exploited successfully later by the Virginia Company with its Royal Charter.

It was the companies established in Asia that changed the game, and once again the intense rivalry and colonial interplay between the Dutch and the English produced important innovation. England's East India Company was founded in 1600 to take on Dutch traders, who responded with the Dutch East India (1602). The Dutch, though, had a new weapon that spurred growth. Shares had been traded before in piecemeal fashion; now the Dutch East India built a stock exchange where they could be bought and sold alongside the bonds issued to raise debt. It introduced scale and the excitement of large amounts of speculation, meaning that in trying to outflank the English, the Dutch in Amsterdam had invented the modern stock market.

The English were slow to understand what was happening. The market for shares only developed gradually, as new companies such as the Hudson Bay Company and the Royal African were established. Their owners gradually learnt the possibilities and the joint-stock enterprises started to pay large dividends from plundering the New World. However, it was not until the late 1680s that shares were frequently traded in London, and this was driven by the Nine Years' War with France which meant that domestic merchants, their possibilities for overseas trade limited, looked for other outlets for their capital. When trading happened, there was a ready-made venue where business could be done, in the Royal Exchange alongside the merchants buying and selling goods and arranging shipments.

Buying shares was quickly understood to be perilous because the price rested on speculation about future profits, discoveries, lucrative new contracts or the commercial overspill from war and political upheaval. Perhaps for that reason, the stockjobbers and brokers started to develop a reputation as excitable types who thrived on rumour and made profits from hot air. It is perfectly understandable that early activities of the stockjobbers and brokers were seen as morally dubious, although there was a hunger for what they were selling. That contradiction is still apparent today, with clients complaining about the motives of those dealing shares or trading financial instruments while coming back for more in search of personal profit. In it, too, may lie the origins of contemporary complaints that the City does not produce anything solid or real, unlike manufacturers.

It didn't help in a deeply religious age that trading in shares or debt obviously involved selling and buying the inherently intangible, whereas a merchant selling a shipload of spice, grain or cloth could point to it or at least be held accountable if a consignment out in the field failed to materialise at the dockside. Stockjobbing was a seemingly magic trade, based on pieces of paper, promises and profits conjured from thin air, in an era when fears of sorcery and witchcraft still dominated in the popular imagination. Resentment of the stockbrokers and their black magic was already apparent in the aftermath of the joint-stock mania of 1693–5, during which there had been a flurry of trading as all manner of new manufacturing enterprises turned themselves into companies seeking investment. The frenzied activity looked a lot like gambling. In the parliamentary inquiry that followed, the commissioners investigated the 'pernicious art of Stock-jobbing'. Some of the unscrupulous and 'unjust' first subscribers, it was noted, sold the stock on for inflated prices to 'ignorant men' hungry for a quick profit.

Not for the last time, legislation was introduced aimed at regulating their activities. Stockbrokers had to be licensed by the Lord Mayor and take an oath to be true and faithful. They even paid a fee, and accepted a bond that would be forfeited in the event of bad behaviour. Their number was capped at 100, to curb the propensity to over-excitement and panic. In the Royal Exchange the joint-stock mania prompted a change too. Whether they were asked to go, or decided to leave of their own accord, it is unclear, but in 1698 the stockjobbers left the Royal Exchange and migrated to the streets nearby. The Royal Exchange had given them their first home. Next they congregated in Exchange Alley, or Change Alley, where they met in coffee houses such as Garraway's and Jonathan's. There, the new rules introduced by Parliament started to be disregarded and the throng of brokers and jobbers, both licensed and unofficial, grew with the market. The total amount invested in joint-stock companies was rising too. It is estimated that it rose from £4,250,083 in 1695 to £8,447,401 in 1703, at a time when the total industrial wealth of England was only in the region of £33m.

The stockjobbers of the early eighteenth century were operating in a city that had developed many – although not all – of the main constituent parts of a modern financial centre. In the Bank of England it had a national bank that could organise government debt; a busy trade in commodities based around the Royal Exchange; currency trading; gold trading; markets in insurance for property, business transactions and shipping; as well as the stockjobbers themselves. The City in which they worked had also been rebuilt in the decades after the Great Fire to become far more impressive. The new St Paul's Cathedral built to Wren's design was completed by 1710, and around it stone buildings and grand constructions replaced much of the timber-framed London of old. The energy and bustle were captivating for those who saw in the rise of the City the prom- ise of London becoming a global nexus.

The historian Peter Ackroyd has called eighteenth-century London 'voracious London', a vortex sucking in money, along with the needy, the greedy, the aspirational and the wicked. With three- quarters of English trade passing through the City, all roads point- ing to the capital, and its citizenry constituting one-tenth of England's population after the arrival of immigrants from Europe, it was as though London sat at the centre of an enormous web, spinning and casting out its thread ever further. The noise, the smell, the crush of crowds, the imprecations of the mob and the pressure always to make money, or just to survive, made it close to being bedlam. The City, where the money was, was the place during the day where the madness was most intense.

At the centre of the maelstrom stood the Exchange. For Joseph Addison, founder of the *Spectator* magazine, the place was a source of wonderment in the early eighteenth century.

There is no place in the town which I so much love to frequent as the Royal Exchange. It gives me a secret satisfaction, and in some measure gratifies my vanity, as I am an Englishman, to see so rich an assembly of countrymen and foreigners consulting together upon the private business of mankind, and making this metropolis a kind of emporium for the whole earth.[8]

That same year, in 1711, as Addison marvelled at the growing power of the City, a new joint-stock company was being formed that would soon create the greatest excitement of all among investors across England.

Debt was at the root of it, of course. The South Sea Company began with an argument about the size of the national debt when a new Chancellor of the Exchequer, Robert Harley, came to office. The cost of war and the over-reliance of the government on the Bank of England as a source of borrowing meant that a new source of funds was mooted. A state lottery was launched before Harley's brother Edward and his associates came up with what sounded at the time like a better idea. The £9m national debt would be consolidated and those who held it would get tradable shares in a new company, the South Sea. It would also have exclusive rights to planned trade in South America. Investors would be attracted to this public–private partnership and great riches would flow. There would be a human cargo too. The Company was one of those involved in shipping thousands of slaves from Africa to Jamaica.

That first incarnation of the Company was a flop when it became embroiled in political squabbles. It was in the second phase, with the Prince of Wales – the future George II – as titular head, and the political Establishment heavily invested in the venture, that a wild fashion for the South Sea Company in particular and investing in general took hold. Events in France fuelled the excitement, certainly.

The Scottish adventurer John Law, who escaped from prison in London after killing a rival in a duel, appeared to be working miracles with France's finances. He not only controlled the banking system; he had merged it with the Mississippi Company, which owned vast tracts of land in America. The speculation seemed to be renewing French national wealth. John Blunt and the other directors of the South Sea bought more of the national debt, almost £31m of it, and issued new shares.

In the City, in Change Alley, this was the moment of ultimate opportunity. The lure of speculation, easy profits and sudden wealth brought in crowds of investors. A newspaper described the scene: 'The greatest ladies thither came, and plied in chariots daily, or pawned their jewels for a sum, to venture in the Alley.' Not only the aristocracy put in their money. Anyone who could get their hands on a little money could travel to the City and take part. The immigrants that swelled the London population added to the throng, along with ambitious Scots who had travelled south in greater numbers after the Act of Union of 1707. The streets of the City around Change Alley were crowded with people of all religions seeking profit. The playwright William Chetwood satirised the scene in his play *South-Sea; or the Biters Bit.*

> **Plow:** A Stock-jobber! Pray, Sir, what Religion may he be of?
> **Scrape:** Religion! Why, they don't mind Religion in Change-Alley. But Turks, Jews, Atheists, and Infidels, mingle there as if they were a-kin to one another.

This was unsettling for some, considering the extent to which religion and fear of invasion by Catholic powers dominated thinking about politics. But not for the last time, a boom in the City was remaking the social firmament, breaking down barriers and creating opportunities for rapid advancement. It also obsessed those with capital or an interest. Edward Harley, one of those who had started the business, noted that even the most mundane correspondence in England at the time had to include talk of dividends and share prices. Gossip about stocks was the highly valued new commodity in London and beyond, as anyone with a little money to spare rushed to join in for fear of missing out. Inspired by the South Sea Company, a host of other ventures were launched, with companies embarking on all manner of schemes, from insurance to weird experiments in livestock breeding and waterworks that never transpired.

Not all of the activity was maniacal or ill judged. The amount invested in joint-stock companies rose from £20m in 1717 to £50m three years later, meaning that canny investors who bought and sold at the right moment did well, although such was the level of excitement that those trading with imperfect information, and without accurate data, were taking ever-larger risks as prices increased sharply. In early 1720 there was concern expressed in Parliament about the possibility of a crash. The so-called Bubble Act 'to Restrain the Extravagant and Unwarrantable Practice of Raising Money by Voluntary Subscription for Carrying on Projects Dangerous to the Trade and Subjects of the United Kingdom' became law in June. A crackdown on companies without official charters was attempted.

It was rather late in the day to attempt regulation though, and the speculation resumed in its intensity. In August of that year the price of a share in the South Sea Company peaked. The first great bubble in the City's history had been inflated. But bubbles do burst.

IMPERIAL CAPITAL

'Shares. O mighty Shares! . . ."Relieve us of our money, scatter it
for us, buy us and sell us, ruin us, only we beseech ye take rank
among the powers of the earth, and fatten on us!"'

Charles Dickens, *Our Mutual Friend* (1865)

The City was well used to plague, fire and war, but in the autumn
of 1720 came a new type of manmade catastrophe in the form of a
proper stock market crash. When the final efforts of the South Sea
Companies directors and their corrupt political allies in Parliament
to inflate the stock price were exhausted, the gravitational pull of
market forces exerted itself on investors, who realised too late they
had bought in to a fraud. From a high in the region of 1000, down
and down plunged South Sea shares, a dizzying process punctuated
by the occasional rally and rumours of salvation, until by September
the price stood at 175. Exacerbating the crisis, many of those who
had willingly allowed themselves to be duped had paid with
borrowed money, or promises written on paper, paying in instal-
ments, meaning that they owed huge amounts for shares they had
purchased on the assumption of ever-rising prices. The stock was
on the way to being almost worthless but they still had to make the
payments or be pursued by bailiffs.

Out in the country, as news of the catastrophe spread among
investors, anger turned rapidly to despair. On 27 September, a
William Windham wrote to his brother Ashe with an update of his
situation. 'There never was such distraction and undoing in any
country. You can't suppose too the number of families undone. One

*Bubble trouble: in William Hogarth, England had the perfect satirist
to capture the aftermath of the madness for shares which gripped
the country in the South Sea scheme (engraving, 1721)*

may almost say everybody is ruined who has traded beyond their
stock. Many a hundred thousand man not worth a groat, and it
grieves me to think of some of them . . . not a penny stirring.'

William was not the only Windham in trouble. Other members
of his family had also invested and James was almost wiped out.
'Poor Jimmy's affairs are almost Irretrievable', William wrote later
that year. 'Almost all one knows or sees are on the very brink of
destruction, and those who were reckoned to have done well yesterday are found stark nought to-day. These devils of Directors have
ruined more men's fortunes in this world than I hope old Beelzebub
will do souls for the next.'

The new newspapers that had sprung up, alongside invigorated
pamphleteers, hounded those in charge with an intensity bordering

on the vengeful. Not for the last time, there was also a vicarious pleasure to be had for readers in learning of the misfortune of others who had over-extended themselves in the rush for riches. Artists and satirists joined in too. An engraving from 1720 lists some of the 'bubbles' that had been inflated in the excitement generated by the South Sea Company, with companies established promising profits in all manner of areas, including in the coal trade of Newcastle, stockings, Irish sail cloth, a water engine, the bleaching of hair, sugar, insurance on horses, radish oil and the work of the Pennsylvania Company. Underneath an illustration of a ruined gentleman holding up a money bag, now empty, is a description of a previously wealthy investor cursing the 'pack of knaves' he had trusted with his fortune.

> Behold a canting miser who of late, For twice the value sold a
>   fair estate,
> To purchase South Sea Stock, in hope to grow as rich as
>   Croesus.

He was ruined 'among the rest', but had no one else to blame but himself, wrote the unknown author, because he had put his faith in the equivalent of 'games' and 'dice'. In this way trading in stock was presented as nothing more than gambling by the greedy, an image still invoked by critics of the City today.

William Hogarth, the greatest satirist of the period, also found his *métier* with his *South Sea Bubble*. Underneath the print, an inscription declared:

> See here ye Causes why in London,
> So many Men are made, & undone,
> That Arts, & honest Trading drop,
> To Swarm about Ye Devils shop.

In the 'Devil's Shop', in Change Alley itself in late 1720, as the denizens of the coffee houses digested the disaster, panic was followed by eerie calm when the crowds of profit-hungry investors disappeared. A ballad of the time[1] recorded the transformed scene: 'Change Alley's so thin, that man may now walk, and if he'll now listen may hear himself talk.' The action soon switched to Parliament, where in the Commons and Lords the government's enemies hoped to discredit the Whig Establishment. Members of the government had taken enormous bribes and free shares in the South Sea Company and there were calls for the directors, who included MPs, to be arrested and punished for their role. The financial destruction wrought on parts of the English, Scottish and Irish aristocracy by the bursting of the City of London's first proper bubble was certainly an insurrectionist's dream. The Duke of Montrose was exposed, Lord Londonderry was down £50,000 and the Duke of Portland was brought close to ruin. The Duke of Chandos, patron of the composer Handel, was one of the hardest hit. He had invested heavily and was left saddled with enormous debts. Only the financial acumen of his second wife, Cassandra, ensured that their position was not even worse.[2] She had also invested in the South Sea Company but had wisely diversified in time, putting at least some of her own money into assurance. After the Duke's death, the house he had built, Cannons, was demolished by his successor and the fixtures and fittings auctioned off, scattering artworks, along with the house's golden gates and its chapel, to other great houses. In Ireland, where the aristocracy had been keen investors, the Bubble produced a bank run in October 1720 and a decade of Irish economic stagnation.

For those further down the financial scale, those who lacked the connections and large amounts of land as collateral that would guarantee continued access to credit, the impact was often life changing. One anonymous investor, hitherto comfortably off, wrote a pitiful letter to his Member of Parliament explaining how his friend – a Mr S – had come to stay the night in the country and persuaded him and his wife to put all they had into South Sea stock, promising them riches. Now, three months later, they and their children were destitute and living in fear of the bailiffs. He beseeched

Parliament to help and pleaded for answers, without acknowledging that no one had forced him to mortgage his family's future in such a reckless manner.

Who, such correspondents wanted to know, had really caused this disaster? The directors and managers of the South Sea Company who had swaggered around the City and Parliament, hailed as alchemists, were certainly guilty. But they had not acted alone. The Westminster Establishment was complicit and an estimated four hundred and fifty MPs[3] had bought or been gifted South Sea stock at one point or another, along with more than half of the 200 peers in the House of Lords. The monarchy and its ministers had connived as though they ran a 'banana republic' at a time when everything was for sale for the right price, whether it was honours, government jobs, favours, insider information or justice. For that reason, with blame so widespread in the Establishment, the parliamentary investigations resulted in a great deal of noise and then a cover-up. The shameless scheming of the leading government minister, Robert Walpole, ensured that it was so. Yes, the most socially ambitious chancer from the Company, John Blunt, was stripped of almost all his wealth and banished to Bath. But his corrupt co-conspirator and assistant, Robert Knight, who fled to France with company papers (later 'lost' by the government) detailing the fraud and shady dealings, escaped with government help.

The bursting of the bubble was not a disaster for everyone who bought stock, of course. Such crashes rarely are. Those who had been smart enough to sell at the peak of the market did well. C. Hoare & Co, the private bank, records its partners making substantial profits for themselves and customers from speculation in the South Sea Company. Thomas Guy, a bookseller, who had begun with a shop near to the Royal Exchange, had made almost £250,000, and his fortune endowed a London hospital that carries his name still. But for understandable reasons, those who had been bankrupted or impoverished made more noise than those who had sold up in time. Their anger prompted action of a kind. On the same day that the House of Commons report into the South Sea Bubble was published in 1721, Parliament passed legislation to curtail stockjobbing.

The historian Stuart Banner describes the enduring legacy of the 1720s crystallising public opinion about stock markets. It defined attitudes about finance that crossed the Atlantic to the US in the eighteenth and nineteenth century, he says, and shaped much later arguments about regulation on Wall Street. 'Where one laid the blame for the bubble was important,' wrote Banner,

> because it dictated the kind of reform that would be necessary for the future. If a small number of dishonest stockjobbers was at fault, then they could be punished, and perhaps the market should be regulated so as to make it more difficult for similar dishonesty to prevail in future. But if the market itself was to blame – if securities trading was inherently bad, regardless of who the particular traders were at any given time – then a more drastic solution was necessary.[4]

That argument, about how much or how little markets should be regulated, rages still, and the same question – is it the City and Wall Street in general or just a few bad apples to blame? – is posed every time a bubble bursts.

There was another reason the British got over it relatively quickly after a period of fury and recrimination. Cheeringly, it was apparent that France had suffered a simultaneous disaster that overshadowed Britain's reverse. The collapse of John Law's schemes, and the exotic innovations that had helped inspire Blunt and his associates, produced an economic emergency in France in the autumn of 1720 that was even worse than that taking place in London. The Mississippi Company, based on inflated claims of the riches that would flow from Louisiana, had been merged with Law's bank and he was made finance minister of the tottering edifice. At the point of collapse Law managed to escape but France did not.

This humiliating national failure even helped create the conditions for the French Revolution that took place almost seven decades later. Post-Law, many of the French were left with a fear of paper money and shares and a suspicion of investment that hampered the development of banking, commerce and industry. Without adequate access to capital, innovations could not get sufficient funding and wealth remained excessively concentrated. The economy was tightly controlled by the bloated government and a vast royal household, pursuing a mercantilist policy that inhibited innovation and industry. The tax burden landed on the lower orders, who inevitably did not like it or the economic mismanagement. Eventually, revolution was the result in 1789.

The British experience in the eighteenth century was very different. After the South Sea experiment, old-fashioned land and solid property certainly came back into vogue because it seemed to have been proved much more reliable than the new-fangled paper money and share certificates, but attempts at restricting speculation and stockjobbing were largely unsuccessful. They presented too good an opportunity to make money. By the 1760s, the coffee houses of Change Alley such as Jonathan's were deemed insufficient for a growing trade, and the brokers leased a building of their own in Sweeting's Alley. The words 'The Stock Exchange' were inscribed above the door. In the aftermath of the South Sea disaster, the City had rebounded, not for the last time, as a result of ambition, determination and the tendency of the next generation of traders to push on and forget their predecessors' mistakes.

Empire also provided a vital impetus to the next period of expansion, as the East India Company plundered its way across Bengal. The word 'loot', for ill-gotten gain, was borrowed from Hindustani slang and entered the English language at this time. In the City, the East India Company's stock was a favourite investment. Trade obviously meant an increased flow of physical goods from the colonies passing through London's docks, goods which then flowed back out to Europe, producing profits for the merchants that they could then invest. The expanding commercial fleet needed insurance, and deals if they are to be done properly require lawyers and clerks to keep records.

How much of this came down to slavery? A considerable part of the trade that drove this growth was in people, in the slaves that were bought and kidnapped in Africa and then shipped to the Caribbean and to North America. Between 1750 and 1807 it is estimated that 2,307,986 slaves were exported by the English trade across the Atlantic[5], but in London, too, as many as 15,000 African slaves were bought and forcibly employed as domestic servants, often being treated appallingly. In Britain more widely, the building of new stately homes, the development of estates, spending on the art market, exploration, industrial development and the widening availability of sugar, tea and coffee came, in part, at the cost of epic African misery. The City was up to its neck in slavery. Men such as William Beckford (1707–70),[6] one of England's richest individuals, enjoyed fortunes built on the back of their plantations in Jamaica and elsewhere. Beckford was Lord Mayor of London twice and his monument stands in the Guildhall, the administrative centre of the City.

After the bursting of the Bubble, the South Sea Company continued to do business in a reduced form and from South Sea House on Bishopsgate its managers sent slave ships to Africa until the mid-1730s. Indeed, the Square Mile was peppered with other offices in which the slave trade was planned and conducted. The Royal African Company was based in Leadenhall Street, although it lost its monopoly when new rivals emerged to challenge it. The East India Company – part corrupt company, part political behemoth – was also based on Leadenhall Street and traded slaves via Madagascar in the Indian Ocean. Lloyd's insurance market in the Royal Exchange was where the slave traders and investors insured their ships and cargo. The City was also largely deaf to appeals of the campaign for abolition, apart from the Barclays who were Quakers and anti-slavery. David Barclay was exceptional in paying £3000 to free slaves and ship them to freedom in Philadelphia when he became the owner of a slave plantation in settlement of debts.

While the City's complicity in an abhorrent trade is not in doubt, it was not uniquely at fault. Many slaves were processed through other British port cities, notably Bristol and Liverpool. And neither were the British the only nation involved. The Belgians in Africa and the Dutch in their colonies had a deplorable record. What is disputed is the extent to which slavery was a defining factor that explains the City's rise, as is sometimes claimed by its most vehement critics. A study by the historian Nicholas Draper suggests that over a third of London's dock investors at the end of the eighteenth century, just before a long campaign for abolition was successful, were involved in the slave trade. Until they were moved eastwards, the docks were still in the Square Mile itself and the trade was enmeshed in the commercial life of London. As Draper says, while slavery was neither marginal nor dominant, it contributed materially to the foundation of the modern City.

Other powerful forces – financial innovation, the increasing economic weakness of rivals such as France, and hunger for profit – also drove its development. Even the reverse in the Americas, when British colonial arrogance caused a rebellion that led to independence, did not impede London's progress for long. Neither did the disruption of the French revolutionary and Napoleonic period. Britain had too many advantages, thanks to the beginnings of the Industrial Revolution in the north of England and the increasing sophistication of the financial system in the City. For all those reasons, Britain was becoming the world's most dynamic economy.

The Bank of England – which had been a prime mover in that transformation – was strengthening its position too as a model for the development of a strong central bank, which gave the state a usually reliable source of funding and monetary stability. After moving in 1734 to new premises on Threadneedle Street, next to the Royal Exchange, it expanded its footprint steadily and developed as the UK's central bank, attempting to satisfy the government's demand for money and managing a growing national debt that was increasing with every war that was fought. That debt was a trading opportunity, of course, because it could be bought and sold. Traders gathered in the Bank's new building – in the rotunda

– for that purpose, making such a racket that they were eventually expelled.

The City of London did not seed the Industrial Revolution that powered Britain's rise, however. Those funding the steam-driven inventions and industrial innovations in the West Midlands and the north of England often had to rely on more local sources of capital, and the limited interest that the City showed in funding domestic investment coloured the country's view of the City again. The City was certainly in Britain, but to its critics it seemed to stand apart, more interested in pursuing its own particular interests than in funding British enterprise. *The Economist* later observed drily that the City was more concerned during the Industrial Revolution with 'the course of events in Mexico' than with what happened in the West Midlands. That deep and enduring suspicion of the City, traceable to the South Sea Bubble, had continued to manifest itself in popular culture. In his bestseller *Every Man His Own Broker*, published in 1761, Thomas Mortimer explained the activities of those selling shares and castigated them for greed. The book was reprinted many times in subsequent decades.

Not everyone was put off, however. The City was becoming a fizzing entrepôt for the ambitious as the banks and financial businesses started to exert a magnetic pull, sucking in the aspirational in pursuit of employment. Recruitment for the Bank of England was still by recommendation of the existing directors and employees, although the report by a Bank Committee of Inquiry appointed in 1783 to investigate working practices reveals that applicants were from a surprisingly broad range of social backgrounds and experience, by the standards of the time, although they were all men and all Protestants.[7] The Bank preferred to recruit from the ranks of those who had left school at fourteen or fifteen, rather than looking for the university educated. These were the early stirrings of the City as the southeast of England's engine of social mobility, providing opportunities for advancement to clerks and managers prepared to tolerate painstaking and repetitive work. The clerks worked nine to five, although often longer, with the bosses getting away earlier when it was quiet. Mr Bentley told the Inquiry that he was 'seldom out of the office before 8 at night, if the business is heavy much later, & on a Saturday generally 'till 10 or 11 o'clock'.

The City was also a place that needed and welcomed hardworking immigrants from abroad. The Huguenot refugees fleeing persecution of Protestants in France in the sixteenth and seventeenth century had sought sanctuary in London and their churches peppered the City. Of the 45,000 or so Huguenots that moved to England, it is estimated around half settled in London, where in Spitalfields they manufactured silk. With the proceeds their anglicised descendants diversified and moved into finance and other City businesses. The French revolutionary period also drew other Europeans to London when continental bourses closed and the mainland succumbed to the chaos of war. The French occupation of Amsterdam in 1795 meant that brokers including Samuel de Zoete landed in London. Unrest in Germany also prompted Nathan Rothschild to leave Frankfurt and establish himself as a banker in the City. After the Battle of Waterloo in 1815, he is said to have made millions by cleverly learning and trading on the news of Wellington's victory over Napoleon ahead of the British government. Although a messenger overlooking the battlefield delivered the news back to London, the sums made that day as a result of it have certainly been exaggerated. Still, Rothschild and his fellow immigrants and their heirs brought a renewed continental perspective to the City.

When the economy recovered from the shocks of the Napoleonic period, and the debts incurred had been dealt with, London was the pre-eminent financial centre. The physical character of the City was changing too. The old wharves on the river within the City were inadequate and the water was too shallow for the new, larger ships. The first new docks were built further down the river and throughout the century trade pushed further eastwards until the docks dominated what became the East End, with its miles of wharves and warehouses. The City itself still had its markets serving London: food at Leadenhall, the wholesale meat market at Smithfield founded in the tenth century and the ramshackle fish market at Billingsgate. But increasingly financial affairs dominated the life of the City. When those food markets began to be served by the new railways, and the produce arrived at the City's stations near the markets, the old practice of livestock having to be herded and shepherded in from the countryside for slaughter diminished.

The streets of the City's financial heart were becoming cleaner as a result. The new buildings were growing grander, their motifs more imperial. The destruction by fire of the Royal Exchange, again, in 1838, meant that the architect Sir William Tite designed the imposing neo-classical building that is still there today, with a statue of the Duke of Wellington at its steps. Insurance companies, and Lloyd's the insurance market, occupied a large part of the space. Tite also designed numerous train stations in the capital and across Britain.[8]

The railway revolution in which Tite participated had another important impact on the architecture and atmosphere of the City. Not only did it mean large-scale demolition, to accommodate the new lines and stations; it also forced out the residential population as the land became more valuable for offices, now that the City was developing proper transport links that began to allow the clerks, bankers, stockbrokers and other workers to make their homes further away in the developing suburbs. The first rail terminus in the Square Mile opened in the City in 1841, at Fenchurch Street. The vast stations built south of the river – on cheaper land – such as Waterloo and London Bridge, with their lines stretching out across what was countryside to the southwest of London and towards Greenwich, made commuting increasingly feasible and popular for workers, who flooded into the City each morning. Not many of them worked in the Stock Exchange, however, which was very much a closed shop to which it was difficult to gain entry. In 1801 the brokers had moved to a new building in Capel Court, near the Bank of England, and from then on became much more efficiently organised, with an official list of prices.

Those involved still had a reputation for being interested merely in quick profits. The economist David Ricardo in 1814 described stockbrokers as attentive to their business, and hot on detail. They were not much interested in finance 'as a subject of science', preferring to 'consider more, the immediate effects of passing events, rather than their distant consequences'. There are regulators and contemporary chief executives of banks today, struggling to control more rapacious investment bankers and traders, who would say something similar about those chasing bonuses.

The members of the Stock Exchange in Capel Court in the nineteenth century were like their modern equivalents in another respect, in that they knew how to have fun, and booze-fuelled pranks were commonplace. Coat-tails were set on fire and the managers in charge had to issue warnings in an attempt to prevent the brokers on the Stock Exchange floor playing football or letting off fireworks. High-spirited City behaviour was not restricted to downtime between trades. In a succession of booms, new generations showed that the appetite for risk – essential in financial enterprises – could get out of control, but then, from the rubble of a correction or a crash, the market would restart and fresh, profitable innovations would be attempted. This is what happened in the railway investment booms of the mid-1820s and the 1840s, when there was a mania for steam and new possibilities. A hucksterish railway promoter such as George Hudson, who earned the sobriquet of 'Railway King' in the 1840s, could become exceptionally rich and then lose his fortune and the money of investors. But when the smoke cleared, and Hudson and others were penniless, the railway lines and a valuable national network that powered trade existed.

This also applied in the case of the so-called Foreign Funds, meaning the Foreign Exchange, which initially operated from the Royal Exchange and whose members were moved to the Stock Exchange in 1828. New states in Latin America wanted to borrow and there was a push to invest. In the most celebrated case, investors were duped by outright fraud, when General Gregor MacGregor (a Scot, who fought on the Republican side in the Venezuelan war for independence) claimed to be leader of the state of Poyais in Central America. It did not exist and the government bonds he sold were fake. He eventually returned to Venezuela and was given a state funeral in 1845.

The Latin American panic led to defaults and losses, of course. Reputations were ruined and fortunes lost, but London had extended its international reach yet again in a way that proved it was not insular, even if greed could on occasion cloud common sense. After all, openness to the outside world was the British way by the mid-nineteenth century when the country's leaders abandoned mercantilism and tariffs on goods and embraced the philosophy of free trade in a manner that split the Conservative Party. That extraordinarily bold decision, condemned by Conservative critics as contrary to the national interest, turned out to be one of the most important decisions of the century. The idea that free trade would increase prosperity in all territories, rather than disadvantaging native producers, was the origin of what in the late twentieth century came to be called globalisation. The Victorians got there first, and the City at the centre of this free trading imperial capital could only benefit when London's appeal as an open market increased.

The world was shrinking, offering even more opportunities for investment abroad. Technology surmounted distance and allowed prices or news that would once have taken a week to cross the Atlantic to reach London in minutes. The telegraph, invented in 1837, had already hooked up the London Stock Exchange to the regional stock exchanges that operated in Britain's major cities. Banks too now had access to much more information delivered speedily.

These improvements came at an obvious price. It was easier for shocks and bad news as well as good to be transmitted internationally from and to London. The panic of 1857 that began in the United States was the first such global crisis, and the effects were felt in Britain almost immediately. The slowdown in a booming US hit American railroad stocks and induced runs on the country's banks. British banks and financial institutions that had lent rail barons money were vulnerable and the British government had to relax banking rules to provide extra liquidity and prevent collapse.

The emergency also had an ideological impact. In that panic of 1857, Karl Marx detected the beginnings of the collapse of the capitalist model, although it turned out that he was wrong. Still, his analysis that capitalism and financial markets seem prone to surges of optimism and over-confidence – with excessive financial speculation creating a cycle of crisis after crisis – is hard to dispute. What his ideology blinded him to was the way in which for all the periodic setbacks and individual examples of venality and poor practice, over the course of the nineteenth century, banks, the Stock Exchange and the insurance industry grew and prospered, providing employment and the fuel for periods of further growth.

There were some attempts to introduce safeguards against recklessness. Business in the City in the mid-nineteenth century became professionalised as it increased in scale. Theoretically, this should have encouraged sobriety when successive governments sought to codify and construct a framework of law that might encourage economic activity while ensuring better conduct. It did not always work. Either appetites were too strong, or the oversight was too weak, and after the growth of English banking and government policies caused a credit boom, the bust in 1866 was even more spectacular than that of a decade before.

English banking had been way behind that in Scotland, where the Bank of Scotland and the Royal Bank of Scotland had from their formation been joint-stock banks, meaning they had a wide range of shareholders and access to more capital. The Banking Act of 1826 in England was introduced because the innovative Scottish banks were observed to have coped more effectively with the foreign crisis of the previous year. It enabled the creation of joint-stock banks on the Scottish model in England, and with the scrapping of the requirement that royal or parliamentary approval was needed, registering and starting a company became much simpler. The Limited Liability Act of 1855 also protected shareholders, ensuring that they would not be liable for the entire debts of a company if it went bust. This was a further incentive to invest. The new structures needed lawyers to arbitrate, and the need for reliable audits of larger companies spawned the accountancy profession. None of that prevented the crash of 1866, which was another classic financial smash of its kind that then contributed to a downturn in the wider economy.

At the centre of the crisis was Overend, Gurney and Company, a long-established bank and discount house, one of the key intermediaries in the City's financial system. In essence, the discount houses existed to lubricate the market. Banks could park spare money with them, earning a small return but being able to call it back at any time, while the discount house could then lend it out to others at a higher rate of interest. The discount house profited from exploiting the difference. All would be well, and credit would be increased, so long as the discount house was sensible and did not lend out too much. Overend, Gurney was gloriously reckless and the news of its troubles created a panic in London to match even that experienced in 1720 with the South Sea Company.

On Black Friday, at the height of the crisis, the editor of *The Economist*, Walter Bagehot, wrote to the Chancellor, William Gladstone, reporting: 'A complete collapse of credit in Lombard St and a greater amount of anxiety than I have ever seen.' Bagehot also identified why the public, or that part of it with financial interests, tended to be so shocked when an established firm such as Overend, Gurney went down. The British attachment to tradition seemed to have a hypnotic effect on customers. An old name, he wrote, held a 'magical potency over the multitude'. The breaking of the spell resulted in a downturn in the wider economy. But once again the crisis was not purely domestic; it was linked to foreign markets. Another player in the drama of 1866 had been Credit Foncier and Mobilier of England, a rackety outfit that sold dubious investments in companies in France and Italy. The perilous position of Italian financiers exacerbated matters.

What lessons could be learnt from the events of 1866? Inevitably, yet another inquiry was launched, the Stock Exchange was investigated, and attempts were made, and eventually ignored, to limit trading in the shares of bank themselves. A series of commissions of inquiry grappled with the question of how to improve regulation. Many critics thought the simple answer was to send financial miscreants to prison.

Bagehot himself made one of the most important and enduring contributions to the thinking about financial crises, in his classic work of 1873. In *Lombard Street: A Description of the Money Market*, he recommended that the Bank of England should act as the 'lender of last resort' to keep money flowing in an emergency. He was scathing in his criticism of the Bank's capabilities, and noted that training of directors needed to be introduced, especially now that the market was so much bigger and London was increasingly the pivotal centre in trading in foreign funds and international finance. In the City, and financial markets generally, he considered confidence key. Without it, the system would not function, and the Bank of England had a duty to maintain it more effectively. There was another problem, said Bagehot. Those working in the City tended to have short memories: 'Most men of business think – "Anyhow this system will probably last my time. It has gone on a long time and is likely to go on still." But the exact point is, that it has not gone on a long time. The collection of these immense sums in one place and in few hands is perfectly new.'

What was not new was the tendency to over-excitement and recklessness in a boom that offered seemingly easy profits. That questing spirit that had animated investors in the summer of 1720, and in 1866 in Overend, Gurney, was not unique to the City of London either. It was simply that London – as the great financial centre that profited most from the upswing – was particularly liable to suffer contagion in a crisis. No sooner had the lessons of 1866 been digested than an even greater panic was upon the markets. The emergency of 1873 started with the bursting of the stock market bubble in Vienna that May and migrated to New York in September. The international downturn hit London too. When markets fluctuated so regularly and publicly it is hardly a surprise that the greatest writers of the era chose to target the

City and the mores of those who populated it. In *Our Mutual Friend* in 1865, Dickens mocked the fixation with stock market speculation:

> As is well known to the wise in their generation, traffic in Shares is the one thing to have to do with in this world. Have no antecedents, no established character, no cultivation, no ideas, no manners; have Shares . . .Where does he come from? Shares. Where is he going to? Shares. What are his tastes? Shares. Has he any principles? Shares. What squeezes him into Parliament? Shares . . .

Anthony Trollope's masterpiece *The Way We Live Now* (1875) satirised a London in which everything was for sale, including love, family and friendship. He described a city gripped by greed and its wealthier citizens captivated by the chance to buy shares in a charlatan's railway project linking San Francisco and Mexico. In Augustus Melmotte, the novelist created the archetypal City rogue, the richest man in England whose wealth was of dubious provenance. A greedy Establishment desperate for a glimmer of reflected glory clamoured for tickets to his party and even put him in Parliament, before Melmotte's inevitable disgrace. To the Victorians it seemed as though the suspect ways of the City, its elevation of quick profit and its hunger for gossip and tips that could be turned into money, had somehow polluted wider society. Some argued it was the other way round. Perhaps the City of London was just providing a mostly profitable means by which the ever-present and legitimate human desire for financial advancement could be fulfilled, mostly legally.

What happened in the next few decades, particularly with the emergence of the Labour movement, proved particularly problematic for the long-term reputation of the City. The long slump, at the time termed a Great Depression, that ran through the end of the 1870s and through the 1880s following the 1873 panic, showed the British industrial and imperial powerhouse spluttering. How could it be that the wider economy would stagnate for almost two decades and unemployment could rocket while the City would barely feel the effects? How could the stockbrokers prosper while the country did the opposite? Were they only out for themselves? Such questions preoccupied a new, insurgent breed of left-wing politicians who thought the City's ways utterly abhorrent and unfit for the new century.

WEALTH, WAR AND WALL STREET

'Financiers in a fright do not make an heroic picture.'

David Lloyd George

Young aristocrats did not go to work in the City. None ever had until, in 1875, the Duke of Argyll's son announced that he had done something extraordinary. He had got himself a job. This development was thought so outlandish that society chatter centred on whether or not his father would ever permit him to take up the offer of a post with the stockbrokers Helbert, Wagg.[1] Charlotte Rothschild even thought the Duke might object to his son working for a Jew.[2] Not a bit of it. Lord Walter Campbell managed to persuade his father that stockbroking was a worthy career, bought his way in as a partner in the firm and became the first aristocratic member of the Stock Exchange.

Naturally, Helbert, Wagg's hiring was not motivated by charity. The firm wanted to develop its own private clients business and become less reliant on the Rothschilds for a stream of work. Having the son of a duke on the books helped to open the doors of class-fixated potential customers, and as a Christian he was able to transact business on the Jewish Sabbath, Saturday. Campbell's appointment was also an indication that at least a few in the aristocracy were attuning themselves to life in a country in which business and finance were becoming the main route to wealth following the Industrial Revolution. It soon might not be enough to own land and large estates alone, which had long been the principal source of income and status in Britain's upper classes. Opting to work in finance provided additional opportunities to arrange an injection of cash into grand but strapped families, alongside the practice of marrying wealthy Americans. In this period, small numbers of other aristocrats joined City firms, and after one was overheard saying that he felt on the Stock Exchange floor like an orchid in a turnip field, upper-class members were known for a while as turnips.

Even so, the upper reaches of the City remained for the most part the province of the powerful merchant classes. Their colleagues and staff were the aspirational southern middle classes and, in the less elevated roles, the upwardly mobile working-class men who had been lucky enough to have a little education and to know some-one who could get them a start as a messenger or junior clerk. Women barely featured in this highly stratified environment in which a great deal of the work, for those not on the floor of the Stock Exchange taking risks, was extremely dull and highly repeti-tive. The clerks and backroom staff across the City who transcribed the records daily and organised the ever-growing pile of paper were not having a racy time, at least not in the office.

For all that emphasis on procedure and politesse, the City could not shake the popular notion that it was a den of gamblers in which a fraudster could prosper. The scandals of the period saw to that. In the late nineteenth century, assorted rogues launched fake compa-nies that gulled investors, or pilfered from shareholders and fiddled the accounts. Barney Barnato was not a member of the Stock Exchange but he was a leading player in South African mining shares and deeply corrupt. He leapt overboard from the ship bringing him home from South Africa. Horatio Bottomley emerged from an orphanage, got a job as a messenger in a City legal firm, worked hard, learnt how to swindle, made a fortune, lost a fortune, became an MP, went bankrupt, helped to found the *Financial Times*, rabble-roused as a jingoist, went to prison and died broke. Whitaker Wright committed suicide in 1904 after being convicted of fraud over the collapse of his London & Globe Finance Corporation. The bad publicity was troubling for those in the upper reaches of the City, where the emphasis was on protecting the good name of the markets on which they depended. When the illustrious Barings Bank came close to collapse in 1890 as the result of reckless loans made in South America, a fund was organised by the Bank of England, with Rothschild taking part. It was deemed unthinkable that a firm of the standing of Barings could be allowed to go bust. As part of an exclusive network it had to be saved to maintain trust, even if its directors had been wilfully reckless.

Image was starting to matter more, as the democratic impulse spread. Outside the City, the tenor of political debate was changing, and while the socialist critique of the markets as the preserve of wealthy elites and unpatriotic gamblers was not yet widely electorally popular, or not among those men with the votes, the attack was beginning to resonate. The newly formed Labour Party even had a City Socialist Circle, which hosted Labour leader Keir Hardie at a celebratory banquet held in a restaurant on Fleet Street in 1900 after he won a Commons seat for the second time. Even the financial press that lived off satisfying the hunger of readers looking for news of deals, useful information and share issues, professed itself appalled by examples of wrongdoing and rampant cronyism. The *Financial News* was so agitated that under its 'muckraking' editor Harry Marks, who began his newspaper career in the US, the paper delighted in exposing dodgy share issues and presented itself as the investors' friend against an elite it suggested looked after itself. Alas, Marks himself ended up discredited, when it emerged in a series of trials and scandals that he had promoted shares in which he had a personal interest while posing as a crusader against sleaze.[3]

The combination of scandals, speculation and a noisy financial press trading gossip about markets that produced semi-regular crashes led *The Economist* in 1913 to criticise the short-sightedness and corruption of journalists on less elevated publications. There were, it said, degrees of depravity. Some financial journalists indulged in puff pieces about favoured stocks and blackmail, while others favoured abstaining from criticism that might offend advertisers. For all the criticisms, and the examples of wrongdoing, the City's grandees presided over a remarkable inheritance. The best firms had long histories and would go on to dominate the City for a large part of the twentieth century. Cazenove masterminded blue-blood stockbroking. Coutts in the West End, sitting outside the City but connected to it, served the banking needs of many members of the Establishment. Stockbroking names such as Panmure Gordon & Co. and James Capel were well established. Foreign firms had a foothold too. Lazard had been founded by five brothers emigrating from France to the US in the 1840s, and by the 1870s it had a related operation in London, which put it in a good position when later the US finance houses grew in importance in London.

With the growth of the joint-stock banks – such as Barclays and Lloyds Bank, serving more humble customers and businesses, and hundreds of other smaller banking and trading enterprises – and the world's leading insurance market at Lloyd's, London of the early twentieth century was home to the greatest conglomeration of financiers and moneymen on the make ever assembled. Their work was lubricated by a constant flow of gossip and international news, arriving by telegram and wires from abroad, and transmitted again verbally by men swapping inside information on their way to lunch. Most of all, the City immediately before the First World War was the beating heart of the British Empire. The vision of Sir Thomas Gresham more than three hundred years earlier, of his simple exchange trading goods and then financial contracts on a model pioneered on mainland Europe, had been realised a million times over. The City had mushroomed and spread until it was a teeming, seething, cacophonous moneymaking machine. This was the most powerful financial and trading centre in history, a manifestation of British imperial power and international clout.

The Rothschilds arguably had the most clout. They funded the purchase of the Suez Canal for Britain in the 1870s, securing a vital trading link, and later underwrote Cecil Rhodes' work in South Africa. Indeed, the City oiled the wheels of Empire and its architecture embodied the imperial impulse. Opposite the rebuilt Royal Exchange, which had been destroyed again by fire, was the latest incarnation of the Bank of England, designed by the architect John Soane, aping ancient Greece to emphasise the Bank's exalted status. The Mansion House, the residence of the Lord Mayor of London, completed the triptych, and underneath the busy crossroads ran the underground train lines that disgorged tens of thousands of workers every morning and transmitted them back to the suburbs in the evening. The lines skirted their way round the Bank's deep vault, which stored Britain's gold reserves, the largest in the world. In the surrounding Square Mile were the offices of every manner of City enterprise and the suppliers they needed to function, including printers, telegram companies, post offices, stationers, restaurateurs and publicans.

If the Stock Exchange itself had a somewhat rakish, raffish reputation, other City institutions sought to cultivate a sombre, more sober image. Good bankers, then like now, saw the value in pretending to be dull, perhaps because they knew that their inherently risky business rested ultimately on trust and making customers forget that in lending more than they took in they were creating credit and money from thin air. The other tribes in City life – the stockbrokers, the jobbers, the Bank of England staff, members of the insurance market Lloyd's, the lawyers and the accountants – each had their own private codes of behaviour and traditions, which were reinforced by the ancient City guilds and newer associations that met in gilded halls peppering the area. They may have been united by pride in being part of a wider, greater enterprise, with its own distinct government in the City Corporation, but they were discrete and they shunned outsiders. Some were freemasons and many more were members of livery companies. The City more broadly was a club, or a series of related clubs forming a commercial clubland.

The connection with that other male-dominated club Westminster, the seat of political power three miles away along the Thames, was strong, as it had been in the days of the South Sea Company. The smartest grandees of the Victorian City were often MPs and the House of Commons in its irregular hours accommodated the diaries of those who did business in the City in the morning, along with those lawyers who made their money in court. The Commons also started to include financiers who were, perish the thought, not Christians. Lionel de Rothschild was the first practising Jewish Member of Parliament, elected for the City of London Corporation. He only took the oath in 1858, following an eleven-year argument about non-Christians being sworn in as MPs. Those financiers with seats in the Commons served a useful function in Westminster. They could report the thoughts and shifting moods of those in the Square Mile and interpret their demands, fears and requirements. Much like the Commons, the City was steeped in tradition. It was viewed with suspicion for its role in periodic financial calamities but also respected by others for the way it made money from money. The place had a mystique.

Yet even at its Victorian height, at the moment of maximum power and reach, there were the first indications that London's pre-eminent financial position was starting to slip. These came during the Boer War, that unnecessary conflict fought partly over mining rights in South Africa and attacked by Keir Hardie, the father of the Labour Party, and his colleagues. Hardie's main preoccupation was the pay and conditions of industrial workers, but his robust opposition to the Boer War in South Africa was framed as an attack on the market system and on profit itself. 'The war is a capitalist war', he wrote in the *Labour Leader* newspaper. 'The British merchant hopes to secure markets for his goods, the investor an outlet for his capital, the speculator more fools out of whom to make money, and the mining companies cheaper labour and increased dividends.'

Throughout the conflict, in the House, as the members of the Stock Exchange called their building at Capel Court, there were wild declarations of patriotic commitment and community singing when news of key developments in the conflict arrived in London. The jingoistic jobber Charlie Clarke, a veteran of the Exchange, organised and led these noisy displays and the pro-war members celebrated victories and marked setbacks.[4] The Stock Exchange had good cause to be concerned about the Boer War. Investors had loaded up on South African mining stocks in what was known as the

'Kaffir boom', which briefly reached an intensity that would have been familiar to those caught up in the excitement of the South Sea Company's rise. Moreover, the South African mining boom had another unintended and damaging long-lasting consequence, because it drew in fresh interest and a surge of new members keen to profit. In the narrow street outside Capel Court, frenetic trading went on even after the House had closed for business at 3.30pm, in an echo of the early days in Change Alley. The boom in numbers meant that when the Kaffir boom ended, there was a glut of brokers who needed to protect their income.

The Stock Exchange had hardly been unrestricted in its practices. Admission was by election by the existing members and the public was not allowed over the threshold. But following the Kaffir reverse members established new restrictive codes that benefited those working in the City at the expense of customers or clients. Strict rules were devised on stockbrokers and stockjobbers, ensuring that the work of the two could not overlap. Stockbrokers dealt with outside clients – banks and investors – and advised them on the market. When the client needed to buy or sell shares he called in his stockbroker, who then had the firm's representatives on the Stock Exchange floor go physically to talk to the jobbers, with their own firms, to arrange and then make the transaction. The jobbers would become the centrepiece of the market – the so-called 'market makers' – because they took the stock from those seeking to sell it and held it (thus taking a risk) and then matched the orders up with willing buyers. The jobbers' profit came from what was termed the 'spread', the difference they could arrange between the buy and sell price for shares or other financial instruments.

After much consultation and discussion, minimum commissions were also introduced to protect the income of members from the possibility of insurgent rivals undercutting them. In introducing this new rigidity, the Stock Exchange was turning away from the spirit of outward-looking innovation that had defined its rise. Indeed, some of the rules would survive for more than seventy years, until the Thatcher government decided to act in the Big Bang era of the 1980s.

Although the changes of 1909 seemed small at the time, they were dark hints that a period of stagnation and relative decline was on the way, a process which accelerated dramatically in 1914.

As David Kynaston, the historian and author of the definitive four-volume modern history of the City of London, put it: 'The First World War was the worst thing that ever happened to the City.'[5] The impact of the European conflagration was felt even before the first shot was fired. By July 1914 a sell-off was underway as concerns about the international situation deepened. The Stock exchanges on the continental mainland experienced severe difficulties, and when war was declared in August the City was astonished.

In wartime, old enmities were put aside for a while. There was even help available for the government from the City titan Lord Rothschild, who had clashed with Lloyd George over the Liberal government's attempts in the so-called 'People's Budget' of 1909 to increase taxation on the rich in order to pay for increased spending aimed at tackling poverty. 'Really, in all these things we are having too much Lord Rothschild,' the Chancellor complained in a speech at the time, accusing his opponent in the City of trying to block social reform. But in the summer of 1914, Rothschild agreed to a meeting at the Treasury. It soon became apparent that Rothschild grasped the urgency of the situation and saw the need for fresh thinking. 'Lord Rothschild, we have had some political unpleasant-ness—' said the Chancellor, before Rothschild interrupted: 'Mr Lloyd George, this is no time to recall those things. What can I do to help?'[6]

More broadly, the Chancellor was unimpressed by the other City grandees. They were a jittery bunch in a crisis and seemed more worried about their own position than that of the country, Lloyd George concluded. Why did Lloyd George need their help? The government of the day had two financial problems, central to the task of conducting the war. Banks and brokers who had not thought that war would definitely come found themselves owed money from institutions and individuals in countries that were now enemy combatants. It fell to government ministers and the Bank of England to intervene and stall a run on financial firms and banks that would have destroyed public trust and damaged the economy at a difficult moment. The Bank of England and the Stock Exchange arranged for the rules to be suspended, so that bills did not need to be settled immediately, meaning that over-extended firms could survive rather than go under humiliatingly as they might have done pre-war. The government itself had needs too. It needed money to pay for the war, which meant eroding the gold reserves that underpinned the currency and borrowing from investors small and large, in issues administered by City firms and the Bank of England.

With war underway, Rothschild's patriotic advice on how to pay for military spending was straightforward. It is said that he declared: 'Tax the rich and tax them heavily.' For the City and its wealthiest scions, this presented obvious difficulties. It is little wonder that the grandees were worried. As the year came to an end, the atmosphere was one of gloom. A widespread hope that the war would be over by Christmas had turned out to be misplaced and the Stock Exchange did not reopen until the New Year. In the Exchange the mood also turned against outsiders. Understandable patriotism slipped into unattractive jingoism, although the City was hardly alone in that respect, with the popular press and the least attractive politicians of the time capitalising on the slaughter. A campaign was got up against German, Austrian and Turkish members of the Stock Exchange and bans were introduced to ensure that foreigners could not be members, rules that endured in a modified form long after the end of the war. There was a change in the outward-looking international character of the City, developed over centuries of history, sometimes balanced by domestic concerns, but usually expansive and open to profit wherever it could find it. The City was forced by war to withdraw in on itself and a complex system of transcontinental financial capitalism, funding investment, speculation and trade was all but shut down for more than four years.

Into the vacuum stormed New York's Wall Street, the ambitious upstart rival financial centre. Its financiers and investors had taken the model of modern financial capitalism created by the Europeans, and brought to its zenith by London, and were in the process of building something even bigger and more powerful. What had begun on the southern tip of Manhattan Island as a Dutch walled settlement became a slave market in the early eighteenth century and a place for financial dealings. By the late nineteenth century, with slavery gone, Wall Street was a financial market on the verge of making London look elderly and stuffy.

If London was the slow-moving imperial capital, Wall Street was the new, racier model. With the wealthy beginning to migrate to houses further north in Manhattan, Wall Street and the surrounding area were increasingly dominated by banks and financial traders of all types, occupying imposing offices that reflected the scale of American ambition. Vast profits were generated by the rise of US industrialists and hustlers turned magnates, through the railroad booms and busts, the exploitation of natural resources and the creation of epic enterprises in manufacturing that eclipsed anything even late imperial Britain could muster. Those US businesses needed vast capital markets to borrow from and invest in. They needed a large banking system. And their successes, tribulations and failures created a volatile market for shares, along with a popular appetite for profit and rapid advancement.

That era of seemingly boundless gigantism suited big personalities, and in the original J.P. Morgan (John Pierpont) Wall Street had the defining man of the age until his death in 1913. The publicity-shy tycoon was domineering in his business dealings, mesmeric even, and deployed his power to build the first $1bn company, when he bought out the Scottish-born Andrew Carnegie to create US Steel. Morgan was so well connected, with so many industrial and financial interests, that his critics cast him as the enemy of the worker and of democracy itself. When the US government was short of gold in 1895, Morgan was one of those who sold it what it needed, for a good price. In 1907, when share prices on Wall Street plummeted following a bout of reckless speculation by investors, Morgan corralled the other Wall Street banks and arranged the rescue. The family's tentacles extended abroad, where the outlets of the 'House of Morgan' in Europe included Morgan, Grenfell & Co in London. During the First World War, the second J.P. Morgan promoted the Allied cause, for a healthy profit, and in 1915 the bank arranged what was then the largest foreign loan in history, a $500m loan to France. The new plutocrats were owners of railroads, steel and financial interests on a scale that worried some Americans.

Louis Brandeis in *Other People's Money and How the Bankers Use It*, published in 1913, spoke of the American infernal 'curse of bigness', a theme that had been reflected in the agitation against the power of monopolistic big business by the progressive movement and, principally, President Teddy Roosevelt in the early years of the twentieth century. Yet Wall Street easily survived such assaults to become the symbol of thrusting, modern America, a great, glittering casino in New York where rich men multiplied their fortunes, the giant industrial combines bolstered their dominance and, theoretically, millions of Americans could invest, although it took a long time before investing became a mass participation sport. The movement was not all in one direction, and the swings and downturns could be as violent as anything experienced in London for centuries, as 1907 had demonstrated. Such concerns did not worry everyone, however. The trajectory was upwards and something of the audacious spirit of the Wild West permeated New York's financial dealings. Everything was bigger; there was more swagger than in self-satisfied London, and soon there would be more money too.

As power drained away from London, it surged in New York, Washington and Chicago. Not only had the New World come to the rescue of the Old when America entered the war in 1917, but it had cost the US a lot less than it cost Britain and France. Worst of all for London, the war represented the beginning of the end for sterling as the developed world's dominant currency and its replacement by the US dollar. The strict Gold Standard – which stipulated the value of the currency according to a fixed amount of gold, keeping the supply of money and prices stable – had had to be all but abandoned by the Bank of England and the Treasury in Whitehall during the war. There was higher inflation in Europe than in the US, which stuck to the Gold Standard. This made US goods cheaper, relatively speaking, and the Allies were hungry for natural resources to fuel the war effort. Annual American exports to Europe increased from $1bn to $7bn between 1914 and 1917. Simultaneously the Allies were funding their war in part by borrowing in the United States. It meant that while at the beginning of the war the US had been a debtor nation borrowing from Europe, by Armistice Day 1918 the position had been reversed and the US was a creditor nation.

Poor old Britain was close to being skint. Its national debt had soared from £650m to more than £7bn by 1918, or more than 130 per cent of GDP, in only four years. Victory had been extremely expensive for Britain and France, and not just in terms of the lives lost. Despite the British and the French being on the winning side, the financial future looked to be American. In the City immediately after the war the decline was not immediately apparent. This was the age before high-intensity bombing from the air, and while there had been raids by German airships, and a few bombs had fallen on the City, there had been little damage to the physical fabric of the place. The memorials erected to the war dead in the Bank of England, the Stock Exchange and the offices of firms across the City demonstrated that the workforce – messenger boys, members and the sons of partners – had contributed. But with the war over it was possible to imagine that business might resume as normal. A brief boom got underway.

There were portents, though, that the weather was changing. Not only was the surge in London short-lived because debt-ridden Europe succumbed to a post-war hangover; the ideological back-drop was threatening too. In the aftermath of a violent revolution in Russia, the old Liberal Party completed its death march and the socialist analysis grew in popularity, even if most of that creed's adherents in Britain were democrats and patriots opposed to insur-rection. The City, the Labour movement's rising stars suggested, was a relic of outmoded Victorian capitalism and a target for attack by those offering a new way of thinking about economics and soci-ety. In 1917, the young Herbert Morrison (grandfather of Labour politician Peter Mandelson) was particularly exercised about the self-government of the City and its perks and secretive ways: 'Is it not time London faced up to the pretentious buffoonery of the City of London Corporation and wiped it off the municipal map? The City is now a square mile of entrenched reaction, the home of the devilry of modern finance.'

The 'devils' of the City were facing these threats just as America's growth accelerated. After a brief recession, US gross national product rocketed from $72.99 billion in 1922 to $103.90 billion in 1929[7], wages rose sharply and the modern advertising industry emerged to satisfy the appetites of millions of new consumers. Simultaneously, Wall Street launched into an intoxicating boom of the kind in which London had once specialised. But while London and France had pioneered stock market crashes in 1720 with the bursting of the South Sea Bubble and the unravelling of John Law's schemes in Paris, America in the 1920s would soon prove that it could be equally innovative, and on a much grander scale, in a fashion that would reverberate in Europe. Visiting Europeans were intoxicated by Wall Street's dynamism in the 1920s and the seemingly magical possibilities for making new wealth, or replenishing old wealth, in the New World. Those members of the European elite lucky enough to have access to capital and contacts in North America joined in. Winston Churchill, the son of an American mother, was an enthusiastic investor.

By 1928 the party was in full swing, and even those who had expressed doubts were starting to believe that it was different this time: that most delusional state of mind in any seemingly endless boom. It appeared for a while as though America might be drunk, despite this being the era in which alcohol was banned nationwide by law. Prohibition, in force from 1920, far from encouraging sobriety seemed to induce recklessness and rule breaking. As the historian Thomas Fleming put it:

> Prohibition corrupted and tormented Americans from coast to coast. A disrespect, even contempt for law and due process

infected the American psyche. Rather than discouraging liquor consumption, Prohibition increased it . . . The 1920s roared with reckless amorality in all directions, including Wall Street. When everything came crashing down in 1929 and the long grey years of the Great Depression began, second thoughts were the order of the day. Large numbers of people pointed to Prohibition as one of the chief reasons for the disaster.[8]

Churchill turned up in New York, on his first trip across the Atlantic in almost three decades, shortly after he had lost his job as Chancellor of the Exchequer in 1929 and just as the boom in Wall Street was past its insane peak. He almost ruined himself, although he was saved from complete disaster by the action of Bernard Baruch, a Wall Street financier and advisor to presidents. Churchill, wrote William Manchester, was a great man. But he was not a great investor: 'He was a disaster.' He bought with alacrity at numerous outlets on Wall Street. When the market collapsed in October 1929 he stood in tears in Baruch's office in New York, convinced that all he had was lost. Chartwell, the house in Kent he loved, would have to be sold. His friend calmed him down and revealed that at least his trading on his account with Baruch's firm had not been calamitous. Baruch had left instructions with his staff for them to buy every time Churchill sold and to sell every time he bought. 'Winston had come out exactly even, he later learned, because Baruch even paid the commissions,' wrote Manchester. This somewhat mitigated Churchill's losses elsewhere.

Very few other investors were so lucky when the faltering boom turned to a spectacular bust on Black Thursday, 24 October, and then Wall Street had its worst day on Tuesday the 29th, during which all the share price increases of the previous year were obliterated. As J.K. Galbraith put it in *The Great Crash*, describing the cycle of despair: 'What looked one day like the end proved on the next day to have been only the beginning. Nothing could have been more ingeniously designed to maximise the suffering, and also to ensure that as few people as possible escape the common misfortune.'

Nothing so terrifying as the sound of crashing paper: a US newspaper reports on the whirlwind that hit Wall Street and the world economy in October 1929.

Endless ink has been spilt since on the question of whether the Great Crash of 1929 directly caused the Great Depression that followed it. How could a stock market crash which was restricted to a small number of investors, relative to the broader population, cause such a severe downturn in the 'real economy'? The debate is pointless and rooted in a misunderstanding of human frailties, the interlinked manner in which investment works and the psychology of an economic emergency. The crash of 1929 demonstrated again that when trust in stock evaporates it can, if the crash is serious enough, evaporate confidence in the wider economy and even weaken political institutions. It creates a justified fear – on the part of investors, manufacturers, employers, employees – that tomorrow will be worse than today, which alters behaviour, with obvious consequences.

In indebted Europe, the 1929 crash certainly created a feedback loop, causing loans from suddenly desperate American banks to be called in, in Germany meaning an intensification of political unrest.

In London the falls on the Stock Exchange were not as severe as in the US, but in the gathering gloom a momentous decision was taken for Britain to come off the Gold Standard to which the government had returned the UK after the First World War. A leading economy such as Britain was a cornerstone of the Gold Standard arrangement, the global exchange rate system in which countries fixed the value of currencies according to an amount of gold. If it prevented governments' bastardising or devaluing their currencies to get themselves out of trouble, it did limit flexibility in a crisis of the kind the global economy was confronting. On Saturday 19 October 1931, with a run on the pound underway, and the Stock Exchange busily trading, it was announced that Britain would come off the standard the following week, which necessitated a temporary closure of the Stock Exchange on the Monday. That month *The Economist* famously described the decision as 'the definite end of an epoch in the world's financial and economic development'. Other countries followed and although it eased the emergency in the UK, the change brought with it an outbreak of economic protectionism as, instead of coordinating policy, nations sought to guard their own industries from currency fluctuations. It was also an important moment because it highlighted so starkly Britain's shift from thinking of itself just a few decades earlier as the dominant global economic power – powered by Empire – to becoming one of a much larger number of economies blown around by the markets.

The impact in Britain of the economic crisis that followed the crash of 1929 and the subsequent recovery after devaluation depended very much on where you lived. The industrial heartlands of the north suffered as heavy industry was clobbered and unemployment rose to 2.5m in 1933. Other parts of Britain had a wholly different experience and by 1935 were booming. The new, modern industries producing chemicals, aeroplanes, washing machines and other household goods and manmade fibres prospered. The suburbs multiplied as 2.8 million houses were built in the decade. Bigger investment firms also prospered and became responsible for a larger and larger chunk of shareholdings and trading. The City was perfectly placed to exploit these brief few years of opportunity and growth as the European security situation deteriorated. There were even accusations of profiteering when Cazenove arranged the private placing of shares in Bristol Aeroplane shortly before the government announced in 1935 that the RAF was about to be increased in size rapidly.

With rearmament and another war on the way, in 1937 the City started to plan for it even if the Prime Minister and the government of the day were making strenuous efforts to avoid conflict. The Stock Exchange formulated a scheme, never implemented, to move to Pinewood studios in Buckinghamshire in order to avoid bombing. In preparation for the feared onslaught, London Stock Exchange firms were also allowed to move their office more than a quarter of a mile from the floor of the Exchange, but it was found that without the old set-up of firms operating within walking distance of each other that intimacy was lost and business could not be transacted with efficiency. It still very much required face-to-face encounters.

There was awareness that the City was an obvious target for German bombers because of its proximity to the Port of London's strategically vital docks, and arrangements were made for fire-watching and emergency plans as the country waited for war. The hope, as it was in the rest of the country, was that conflict with Hitler could be avoided. Indeed, there was celebratory after-hours trading in Throgmorton Street after the Exchange closed at the end of business on 28 September 1938, the day Neville Chamberlain waved his 'piece of paper' proclaiming peace in our time. The optimism did not endure long. Business gradually ran down in the months preceding the declaration of war in September 1939, which helped avoid a repeat of 1914 when so many financiers and traders had been caught out with positions open and money owing.

Staying put when hostilities opened meant that when the bombs fell the workers of the Square Mile found themselves in the front-line, alongside the population living around the docks in the East End. On the worst night of the Blitz, on Sunday 29 December 1940, the City was consumed by a Great Fire almost as intense as the conflagration that wrought such destruction in 1666.[9] A new generation described in letters and diaries the fight to save the City from the Luftwaffe. That night in December at Hoare's Bank on Fleet Street the staff manned the pumps, drawing water from the bank's private well as the bombs fell nearby.

At the Bank of England, senior clerk B.J. Rogers had a lucky escape.[10] After taking the tube from his home in Stanmore on the Sunday evening, to sleep in the office and be sure he was at his desk in the morning, he emerged from the tube station next to the bank and was almost killed by a bomb landing on Lombard Street. After dinner and a drink he went up on to the roof of the Bank of England and in a letter sent to his daughter recorded the scene:

> We were hemmed in by a wall of flame in every direction . . . The building next door to our dining club was alight and of course the churches and Guildhall are only a few yards from us. We could see St Lawrence Jewry already burnt out, glowing like an incandescent coal fire, while the Guildhall was burning furiously. In the distance was St Paul's standing out black in a ring of fire.

The conflagration consumed nineteen City churches and thirty-one of thirty-four guildhalls. A number of publishers went up in flames too, having been centred around St Paul's since the Reformation, when Protestant pamphleteers were encouraged to set up there. In the early hours of the morning a haunting image of Wren's great cathedral was captured by the photographer Herbert Mason and sent around the world. In what the *Daily Mail* described on its front page a few days later as 'war's most famous picture' the dome of St Paul's stood tall, glimpsed through the smoke. The picture was seized on as a symbol of the City and Britain's determination to withstand the onslaught.

But for all the talk of defiance, the cumulative toll of such raids was depressingly high. By 1944, a third of the entire area of the City had been flattened or so badly damaged that it was approved for redevelopment. Many of the oldest, historic buildings in the narrow alleyways had been swept away by bombing and fire, and warehouses, which before the war had taken up almost a quarter of the square footage of the City, had been burnt out along with famous landmarks. The previously unlucky Royal Exchange survived intact, remarkably, and did not need to be rebuilt this time, although it narrowly avoided destruction in January 1941, when a bomb landed on the road intersection at Bank and killed 111 people in the underground ticket station below, and on the stairwells and even the platforms. The Bank of England across the street took assorted hits throughout the war, as did the roof of the Stock Exchange in Capel Court. In nearby streets, bearing the names that told the City's story – Bishopsgate, Poultry and Gresham Street – lay the rubble of hundreds of years of history.

The other problem at the end of the war was that Britain's economy was not in much better shape either. For the second time in three decades, the country emerged victorious but in a perilous financial position. The national debt stood at almost 250 per cent of UK GDP, when little more than thirty years previously on the eve of the First World War it had been at well under 50 per cent. British industry, enterprise and productive capacity had been diverted into producing the instruments of war. Rationing was still in place. The American focus was on reconstructing Germany and Japan. Many financial markets in the City remained closed for several years and restrictions on moving currency out of the country were strictly enforced. Large parts of what had once been the thriving global centre of international capitalism, the fulcrum of an entire system of international trade, were a blackened wasteland.

From the ashes, might the City somehow rise again?

ROAD TO RECONSTRUCTION

'But what are we going to do if it doesn't work out?'

Sir Siegmund Warburg

If the Luftwaffe had failed to break the City of London entirely, despite doing a great deal of damage, it looked as though the new Labour government in 1945 might finish the job. That was certainly the fear in boardrooms and on the floor of the Stock Exchange when Winston Churchill was defeated in the general election held that year in July. Neither the scale of the landslide won by Clement Attlee, producing a Labour majority of 145, nor even the fact of the victory itself, had been expected. Indeed, the *Financial Times* editorial a few days later encapsulated the sense of dread among the denizens of the Square Mile. According to the paper's leader writer, the election result was 'the most serious reverse since the dark days of 1940'.[1]

The City now faced the prospect of a peacetime government committed to extending the collectivist centrally planned approach that had been adopted by the 1940–45 coalition government to build a war-winning machine. The war against poverty and for full employment would be won, Labour ministers said, only by nationalising industry, eliminating the inefficiencies of private ownership and reducing over-reliance on erratic financial markets and tarnished capitalism. To many war-weary Britons the new approach seemed like simple common sense, involving the application of the latest thinking on systems and efficient production to form a plan that avoided profiteering and duplication. It helped Labour that the folk memory of the

1929 crash and the distress and unemployment that followed in the Depression was also still strong. What socialism seemed to offer its adherents was modernity and a fresh start. In this brave new world, a secretive sector of the economy that had a long history of association with periodic bank runs, class-based cosiness and episodes of financial chicanery stretching back more than two centuries was always going to struggle to get a sympathetic hearing. Not only was much of the City in ruins; capitalism more broadly was about to come under attack as the new government got down to work.

The Bank of England was the first citadel to fall in 1946, although under government ownership it retained considerable operational independence and the Labour government needed its City connections to buy and distribute the national debt. It was more straightforward with the coalmines (taken into state ownership in 1947), road haulage and ports (1947), the railways (1948) and iron and steel (1950). The owners of the nationalised companies were compensated, and the Conservative government from 1951 put road transport and steel manufacturing back in private hands, but post-war Britain was collectivist in its outlook no matter which party was in power.

There are always some in the City who can spot an opportunity in times of crisis, and the shares of the soon-to-be-nationalised firms rose on the expectation that compensation would make funds available for investment elsewhere on the Stock Exchange in the shape of companies in newer industries. But the process of state control gummed up the basic workings of capitalism. Distressed companies that might have been bought over by new owners with fresh ideas, or gone out of business, or raised capital in London or on the regional stock exchanges to rebuild after the war, were subsumed into the expanding government sphere. The normal operation of the private sector was constrained, which meant fewer shares and less scope for what the City did, namely trading. The brief period when initial gloom faded and people in the markets were optimistic that the Labour government would not turn out to be as injurious to profits as they feared, came to an end with a devaluation crisis and a fuel crisis as ministers struggled to get the newly nationalised coalmines to function productively amid trade union demands and absenteeism.

State control impacted on the physical character of the City and its environs, too, although this only became apparent more gradually. The unions opposed modernisation and any job losses, which along with the introduction of the dock labour scheme regulating employment condemned the Port of London to a steep decline. Trade unions and government-controlled management were unable to agree on modernisation and automation, which led later to empty docks, as rival ports with waters deep enough took the new, much larger container ships. In this way, London's advantage as a centre for trading goods earned over centuries was surrendered in just a couple of decades. In the City itself, the destruction of the storage warehouses that had made up a quarter of the pre-Blitz Square Mile cleared the way for another transition. Rather than finance and the Stock Exchange being just one part of the area's economy, alongside the food markets, publishing trade and shipping, the balance shifted decisively. Although the rebuilding would take decades, and bombed-out sites were still visible years later, what filled the vast gaps were offices, often constructed cheaply in concrete.

Even there the early attempts at reconstruction brought conflict with the planners and with the modernising spirit of the era. Preparations had begun during the war for reconstruction, and in December 1943 government officials visited the chief engineer of the City of London Corporation – F.J. Forty – to study his plan for rebuilding.[2] The Corporation jealously guarded its autonomy and had declined offers of external help. The officials from Whitehall were appalled by what they found. The proposals were too traditional and lacking a vision, they said, because the Corporation envisaged rebuilding on the former street plan and putting excessive emphasis on office space and the needs of individual developers. 'We are not only disappointed, we are frankly alarmed', wrote a government official. 'Never since 1666 has there been such an opportunity to re-plan parts of the City, and, if the plans we saw are adopted, this opportunity will once again be missed.' The condemnation illustrates the extent to which the Corporation's outlook was at odds with the entire drive of national policy towards central planning by alleged experts, which was not surprising considering that the City was used to self-government and had evolved over centuries according to its own rhythms and tastes. Following a stand-off with Whitehall, the Corporation's plans were denied approval. There was redrafting and the Barbican development, opened in 1969, was one result of the new plan. But the more radical ideas were resisted, rapacious property developers moved in and the footprint of the financial City, around Gresham's Exchange and the Bank of England, and down Bishopsgate, largely retained its shape, although the architecture changed.

The secretive world around that hub appeared to operate much as it had done for decades. There were the stockbroking and jobbing firms, working in the Stock Exchange. The leading merchant banks nearby, such as Barings, Lazards, Kleinwort, Arbuthnot Latham, Schroder and Hambros, were members of the Accepting Houses Committee, the body with never more than 20 members that denoted established status and gave its members access to a pool of capital at the Bank of England on favourable terms. The merchant banks discretely served their clients' needs, advising firms during takeovers, recommending investments and commissioning work from the stockbrokers. The Bank of England oversaw the banking system and managing government debt, gold stocks and interest rates. A range of smaller markets operated with their own traditions, such as the London Metals Exchange. Lloyd's of London was based in Leadenhall Street, having abandoned the Royal Exchange before the war, while large insurance and assurance firms operated outside Lloyd's. All seemed relatively fixed.

In much the same way, it looked as though the traditional career structures would endure post-war. Even under a Labour government, recruitment in the City continued post-1945 for a while much as it had before. Ancestral ties, as well as the old school tie, counted for a lot. Sir Kenneth Kleinwort joined his family's bank after Eton and a French course in Grenoble.[3] His father and his uncle, Cyril, ran the bank, which before that had been run by their father, an astute figure marked out by his long, flowing white beard and habit of leaving the office on the dot and crossing Tower Bridge in his open-topped chauffeur-driven car at 3.30pm every day for an invigorating drive home to Sussex, no matter what the weather. The Kleinwort offices on Fenchurch Street featured a traditional high-ceilinged banking hall and a rabbit warren of wood-panelled rooms and corridors that gave the place a stately and paternal feel. Arriving in 1954, Kenneth was given six months to work out whether being a merchant banker appealed – it did, he loved the look of it – before he underwent a five-year traineeship, with spells in the key departments, and began his ascent through the organisation. Lord Rothschild, Jacob, also joined his family bank after Eton, and Oxford where he gained a first in history. But he quickly found the climate too stifling. He would learn more, he concluded, by spending several years in the outside world, first with an accountancy firm, then with Morgan Stanley in the US and a couple of veteran investors who taught him how the markets worked. Thus equipped, he returned to N.M. Rothschild & Sons in the early 1960s and, with his cousins, set about winning new business and replenishing the bank's coffers following decades of gentle decline. In 1960, aged twenty-seven, Bruno Schroder – Eton, Oxford and Harvard Business School, and a good friend of Kenneth Kleinwort – joined the bank started by his great grandfather, and was elevated rapidly following his father's death from a heart attack. Bruno had an accelerated journey to the board, although he was later eclipsed by his brother-in-law. In 1958 Bruno Schroder's sister Charmaine married George Mallinckrodt, an heir to an industrial fortune and a gifted banker. The German-educated George had started work at Schroder's four years earlier, and while Bruno stayed in the background, the arch-networker Mallinckrodt became the dominant force.

In stockbroking and jobbing, too, connections mattered. Nick Durlacher's father was the senior partner in Wedd, Durlacher and Mourdant, one of the largest jobbing firms, and it seemed natural that he would join too.[4] After a traineeship Nick graduated to the floor of the Exchange. It did not seem odd that there were no women, he said, because at school there had been none and at university there were very few either. Durlacher's father was an energetic player, in more than one sense of the word, and business was frequently carved up over drinks in the Angel Court Club, right opposite the Stock Exchange. Most decent-sized outfits also had a 'mess' or dining room providing lunch for the partners, and sometimes guests and managers. There was a degree of social mobility, as there had been throughout the City's history; it would be unfair to suggest there was not, but it took intelligence and considerable good luck to rise beyond what was seen as one's particular station. At Lloyd's of London, the insurance market, in among those wearing old school ties were plenty of members from less affluent backgrounds who had started straight from school and become successful. On the Stock Exchange floor, Brian Winterflood was a self-starter who had been born in East Ham, the son of a bus driver. Joining broking firm Greener Dreyfus as a messenger in the early 1950s he realised that with his humble background he was unlikely to prosper as a broker. He moved to the much less sedate jobbing firm Bisgood Bishop, qualifying as a jobber and becoming a partner in 1974. The Bank of England's Leslie O'Brien had also risen through the ranks and in 1942 was appointed as private secretary to Montagu Norman, the then Governor. O'Brien was a grammar-school boy rather than a product of public school and when he succeeded Lord Cromer as Governor, in 1966, it was an appointment in tune with the egalitarian tenor of the times. It also provided an echo of the recruitment practices in the Bank of England in the nineteenth century, when the managers preferred to recruit bright boys not from grand backgrounds. These were still exceptions, however. While the man – then, always a man – getting on the morning train from the suburbs or the less expensive parts of the Home Counties knew that he might get on through hard work, for the most part the upper echelons remained closed. For all but a few of those working in the City there was very obviously a ceiling on their ambition.

The individual institutions, operating like clubs, still functioned according to a clearly established social hierarchy. The larger broking and jobbing partnerships looked down on the lesser partnerships. The smarter merchant bankers regarded the clearing banks as dull and boring. The clearers were the high-street banks, joint-stock banks owned by a pool of shareholders, although most Britons did not have a bank account until the 1970s. If they were boring, perhaps it was their job to be boring. Building societies, and other mutuals, were thoroughly provincial and existed to provide mortgages. Back in the City, Mullens, as the government's stockbroker, styled itself as the grandest of the grand, although its status rested on handling the government's gilt business (issuing government debt for sale), which involved the ritual of its senior partner walking across from the Bank of England wearing a top hat to announce to the market any changes in the bank rate. If Mullens ever lost its privileges as government broker it wouldn't have much left.

The camaraderie, for those on the inside of any part of this strange world, could be intense. These stockbroking and jobbing firms – large or small – were partnerships, meaning that the partners shared the risks and the profits, giving the senior figures a strong personal interest in paying attention to what risks the staff were taking with their money. Even in the merchant banks such as Hambros that had outside shareholders, the companies were structured in such a way that the family retained effective control. There was a strange logic to the favouritism, the sharing of information and cosy deals, when the primary role of the City then was to manage the money and affairs of perhaps, at most, four or five hundred well-connected British families.

The sense of continuity in the decades immediately after the war was deceptive, however. The City was about to feel the disruptive force of an exceptionally gifted outsider, a German Jewish banker who had arrived as a young man in 1934 when he judged that there would not be a happy ending to the Hitler experiment. He had briefly been enthusiastic, because of the youthful energy he thought was being unleashed in his homeland, but a conversation ('a hint from heaven') with Hitler's first foreign minister, Konstantin von Neurath, convinced him to get out that day with his wife and move to London.[5] Alongside his new partner in business, Henry Grunfeld, another German Jew who had fled the Nazis and lost everything in the process, he formed the New Trading Company, which in 1946 was renamed S.G. Warburg.

Siegmund Warburg was an untypical British merchant banker in other respects. Although he was not the only one of his contemporaries with German lineage and connections, he was avowedly an intellectual on the German model who cared intensely about ideas and literature and corresponded – about politics – with the novelist Stefan Zweig, another German Jewish exile. The flat shared by Siegmund and his wife in Eaton Square, Belgravia, was filled with books and he preferred to avoid reading newspapers, as they were, he said, bad for the brain and not conducive to clear thinking.

Warburg also claimed not to be particularly interested in making a personal fortune, and he did not make much by the standards of what came later. Successful merchant bankers, he said, were not motivated primarily by money. They did it for the 'intellectual sport' and sense of constructive achievement, he claimed in a rare interview in the mid-1960s, with Joseph Wechsberg. Having seen the effects of the 1929 crash on Germany first-hand he stressed the need for wariness and encouraged his team to consider what would happen if their latest clever scheme flopped on contact with economic reality. 'What,' he asked, 'are we going to do if it doesn't work out?'

But Warburg's quixotic attitudes and ordered approach to business, with his pedantic fixation on details and employment of bright youngsters, was fused with an obsessive drive to win. In the late 1950s, from his office on Gresham Street, he wrought a transformation that introduced a much more cutthroat approach and earned him notoriety and a degree of fame on both sides of the Atlantic. The fine details of the Aluminium War of 1958 and 1959 do not matter much now. One of Warburg's clients – Tube Investments, run by Sir Ivan Stedeford – in league with an American company wanted to buy British Aluminium. Warburg organised the (secret) buying of shares and associated media manipulation to shame the members of the British Aluminium company's board, which was chaired by the august figure of Lord Portal, the wartime chief of the air staff. Even though Warburg's clients were making by far the best offer, the board of British Aluminium did not want the mere shareholders – the owners of the company – to know it. Warburg and Stedeford outwitted Portal and won control of British Aluminium, causing a sensation. In taking on the other merchant banks and the board of a large British company in this way, Warburg had defied the City's supposed code of ethics in which these matters were supposed to be dealt with quietly between friends and certainly beyond the purview of the press. He had only been admitted to the hallowed Accepting Houses Committee in 1957, when Warburg bought Seligman, yet here he was, soon afterwards, unleashing the first hostile takeover in the City's history. Critics accused him of lying, or at least of not being entirely frank in his dealings. Some rivals thought it was the absolute limit. Kenneth Kleinwort described it later as the moment when 'Americanised methods started to be applied in the City, and the atmosphere started to become less smooth, less gentlemanly than it had been in the past . . . the wave of toughness started to hit the City.'[6] Warburg was even described by others as a 'shit', which was saying something considering the low regard in which the rest of the City was held by many Britons.

The predations of the outside world, and the bad publicity from the Aluminium affair, which demonstrated how loftily shareholders were sometimes treated by the traditional City Establishment, did prompt the beginnings of a rethink though. Perhaps the City needed to explain itself a little better, particularly at a moment when the Establishment was under such scrutiny from satirists challenging the old conventions. When the BBC wanted to make a documentary series about the City – called *Men and Money* – cooperation was granted and the resulting films first aired in 1964.[7] The crew was allowed to film on the floor of the Stock Exchange and behind the scenes, and at the Bank of England the Governor, Lord Cromer, gave his first television interview. Cromer was a member of the

Baring banking family who had married a Rothermere, from the newspaper dynasty. In his interview for the documentary series he explained the workings of the Bank, and other episodes gave an insight into the Lloyd's insurance market and the world of economists, analysts and financial journalists. It asked if these experts really knew what was going on. Brokers at the sugar market, based in Plantation House, were also filmed shouting their orders promising to buy future contracts. At the Stock Exchange in Capel Court, the floor at work was recorded from a safe distance alongside the only women then allowed near it, who were guides in the public viewing gallery.

'Although the City is international, the romance of the market place is deceptive,' noted the scriptwriter Paul Ferris in 1964. 'In many ways it is a rigid little society, formal and exclusive.' The truth of that observation was illustrated in the same period in the disgraceful treatment of Lord Mancroft, a Conservative politician decorated during the war, who was forced to resign from the board of Norwich Union in 1963 because he was Jewish and newly powerful Arab investors abroad had threatened a boycott. When the Norwich Union board changed its mind, following an outcry in the newspapers, it was too late. Mancroft refused to return. As *The Spectator* put it in December 1963: 'He is quite right and he alone emerges with any dignity from this wretched affair.'[8]

While old attitudes remained – in the form of periodic outbreaks of anti-Semitism and the virtual absence of women – the key outsider turned insider launched an innovation that made 1963 a pivotal year in the fortunes of the City and in financial history. In the Eurobond, Warburg and his team produced something that was to have enduring consequences for the future of international finance and what came to be called globalisation. It may sound like a dry technical measure, but its introduction in London on 1 July 1963 turned out to have explosive consequences that did as much as anything – until the revolution of the 1980s – to open up London. The Eurobond (nothing to do with the euro, the European single currency, which came much later) was simply a way of companies raising money to finance projects and pay for expansion. It meant an Italian construction firm or a German car manufacturer could thereafter tap into the reservoir of dollars in London and elsewhere that had accumulated thanks to the dramatic increase in international trade in the aftermath of the Second World War and American spending on reconstructing Europe. The resulting Eurobonds – debt – could then be bought and sold by investors. The catalyst for this was a decision by President Kennedy to crack down on American financiers investing too much abroad rather than at home, when he introduced in 1963 what he termed an interest equalisation tax, which all but shut down US interest in speculation abroad.

Siegmund Warburg in his office in the City. A German immigrant fleeing the Nazis, in the 1960s he was a leading force in the re-emergence of London as a financial powerhouse.

S.G. Warburg spotted an opportunity and approached his friend Guido Carli, the Governor of the Bank of Italy, to request the name of any Italian firm that might want to try the Eurobond first. According to Peter Spira, then the most junior member of the Warburg team working on the project, Carli suggested the Italian steel company Finsider.[9] When complications meant that Finsider could not be involved, Carli next suggested Autostrade, which was looking to raise funds for the completion of the A1 motorway that runs from Milan to Naples. The resulting deal was managed by Warburgs, Banque de Bruxelles, Deutsche Bank and Rotterdamsche Bank and it was quoted on the Luxembourg stock exchange, for tax reasons. With that $15m deal, constructed in London with the help of City brokers, accountants and legal firms, the Eurobond was born. The business was swiftly copied by other merchant banks and grew rapidly, with London as the main centre and bonds issued in a wide range of other currencies and combinations. By the end of the 1960s, $3bn of Eurobonds a year were issued. In 1980 it was $26bn; in 1986 $185bn; in 1989 $224bn; and in 2013 $4 trillion.[10]

Warburg's initiative was visionary, and the result was not only the creation of a newly internationalised market which London came to dominate. The innovation and lure of profits also made the City increasingly attractive to foreign banks, principally those from Japan and the US. There had been small numbers of Japanese bankers in London in the late nineteenth century, when the Yokohama Specie Bank (later the Bank of Tokyo) opened in London in 1884, and a few more in the 1930s.[11] Following the cessation of hostilities in 1945, the Japanese returned with six banks opening London offices between 1952 and 1956 to facilitate trade with Europe for Japanese companies. A few more opened in the 1960s and there was considerable nervousness about dealing with the Japanese so soon after the end of the Second World War, but gradually relations eased and London became a key Japanese outpost. As a young girl, Huruko Fukuda had a unique perspective when she arrived in London in the early 1960s, thanks to her father's latest diplomatic posting to the London embassy as the representative of the Japanese finance minister.[12] The family's first glimpses of fog-laden London were not encouraging, but she settled, going to Cambridge to read history (where she booked the band Pink Floyd to appear at a ball). She became an expert on trade and then, initially ashamed to tell her wealthy family that she had lowered herself to stockbroking, embarked on a successful City career, first with Vickers da Costa and then with James Capel. Links between the London Stock Exchange and Tokyo had been forged from the early 1960s and in the mid-1960s the first Japanese bond in London was issued.

In 1964 there were only fourteen US banks with operations in London, yet by the mid-1970s there were more than fifty. America and Wall Street had serious advantages, and from the wreckage of the Crash, the Depression and the 1930s it emerged even stronger as the leading world economy thanks to the dominance of the dollar, the power of the American war production machine, the expansive corporate culture, advances in science and technology and the appetite of consumers. This created myriad opportunities on Wall Street, and in the smaller financial centres and cities across America where smaller banks and brokers plied their trade to local investors.

But London had a niche that made it once again a potential hub, or a bridge between other financial centres. As a result, the total number of foreign banks in London in the 1960s almost doubled. London – between New York and Tokyo – was in the perfect time zone for trading and it also had the English language, long-held expertise in foreign exchange and financing trade, and a framework of institutions in place stretching back several centuries. History and the promise of the future, in an increasingly international financial scene that would depend on technology and ease of communication, both favoured London. It looked as though it might be possible for that long process of isolation and decline – relative to Wall Street – that had begun in the shutdown of 1914 to start coming to an end. It was as though the City as an international centre and innovator was, tentatively at first, reconnecting with its eighteenth- and nineteenth-century roots. By the mid- to late 1960s it was possible to imagine that London might one day reclaim its status as the premier financial capital in the world.

For the new migrants from Japan, America or the European mainland, 1970s London could be a shock to the system. Henry Angest, an ambitious young Swiss banker, thought he was entering a Stygian world. 'It was a hardship assignment,' he says more than forty years later. 'The food in London was inedible for a Swiss. I noticed that the place was grimy and the streets were full of potholes. Many clever graduates went abroad in the brain drain and in Britain it seemed to take a year to install a telephone. It was a really backward country.' Charles McVeigh, arriving to set up shop for the New York securities house Salomon Brothers, had a slightly easier entrée. He and his wife purchased a home in Cheyne Walk, Chelsea, and settled in thanks to social introductions that came through the firm. McVeigh soon set about expanding Salomon in London, and Angest began a career that would lead to him buying and building up the private bank Arbuthnot Latham.

Left to right, Muriel Wood, Susan Shaw, Hilary Root, Anthea Gaukroger and Audrey Geddes, five of the first women members of the London Stock Exchange in 1973.

At the Stock Exchange, the battle for acceptance was hardest of all for women, until a campaigner, Muriel Wood, and several colleagues fought in the early 1970s for admission as members. A few worked for brokers and jobbers in the office, but without being members they could not rise to the rank of partner or trade on the floor of the Exchange. In keeping with the attitudes of pre-1980s society, a few of the old guard among the Stock Exchange membership excelled themselves when it came to the excuses offered as to why no woman should be admitted. Women would change the unique atmosphere. The Stock Exchange was more a private club than a conventional place of business, one letter writer to *The Times* claimed, a point contested by his pro-modernisation son who wrote to the newspaper to challenge his father's argument. This being Britain, others were particularly worried about the lavatory situation. The only woman to have ever walked across the floor was the Queen. What if, asked one member, one of the women needed to use the lavatory? There were lavatories nearby, responded the campaigners, who eventually won the day.

On Monday 26 March 1973 they started work, with the media on hand to record the historic moment. Susan Shaw was the first to go onto the floor, shortly after 9.30am, accompanied by Richard Bradshaw, her boss, who had backed the campaign to admit women. 'I didn't know what to expect. But actually it was amazing,' she said. 'People suddenly came up, and shook my hands, and said "Welcome, welcome" and "Well done", and I got kisses on the cheek from someone I knew.' Jane Partington, who worked on the floor shortly afterwards, found the environment much less congenial.[13] When she spoke sharply to a colleague, she was asked if it was the 'wrong time of the month'. The women had to be tough because, as Partington recalls, they were harassed by some of the brokers and jobbers and given unwelcome nicknames: 'I was the Night Nurse – there was Sweaty Betty, Super Bum, the Grimsby Trawler, the Road Runner, Stop Me and Pick One. They were very cruel.' The old tricks, the ragging and setting fire to newspapers, looked badly out of date and ludicrous in what was supposed to be a modern financial centre.

Elsewhere, 'voracious London' was sucking in new domestic entrants. At the American firm Salomon Brothers, where Charlie McVeigh worked, Valerie Thompson was one of the first of a new breed of potential traders. For her, the City represented escape and potential fulfilment after a difficult upbringing in Dagenham, Essex, which had been marred by poverty. With no exam qualifications she learnt to trade helping her greengrocer father, next got a job as a filing clerk for the stockbrokers Hitchens Harrison, and had the gumption to wangle a post as a telex operator at another firm, Vickers da Costa, despite not knowing how to operate the machine. Thompson learnt quickly, and when she was turned down for a post at Salomon she found out the name of the company's boss in London and called him direct. The job was hers. Thompson turned out to have an instinctive grasp of numbers and was eventually thrown into trading, after a stint making the tea. With no prior experience, she was suddenly the firm's Deutschmark trader in London: 'There came a point when I was taking positions in Deutschmarks and guilders and I had the idea that I would sell short and it went badly, horribly wrong. I sat there thinking, God! I've got to tell someone about this.'[14] Her boss was forgiving, and Thompson gained a valuable lesson about trading, namely knowing when to cut and run having made a mistake. In 1980 she was dispatched to New York, and along with her young daughter and nanny, was put up in an apartment in the Surrey Hotel on Fifth Avenue. It was a long way from Dagenham.

The City was not alone in feeling the impact of dramatic social changes during the 1970s, of course. Other British professions and walks of life were being opened up and exposed to outside influences. But the Stock Exchange itself seemed to have changed least of all, even if outwardly it had acquired a sheen of modernity thanks to the construction of the Stock Exchange Tower, opened by the Queen in 1975. The old Capel Court building, cavernous and forbidding, has been pulled down in 1966 and its replacement, at twenty-six storeys high, helped begin the move towards taller towers in the Square Mile that was initially resisted by traditionalists. But inside, despite the shiny space-age surfaces in fashionable cream and beige, the Stock Exchange still functioned according to a set of rules that looked increasingly obsolete. When Labour, under Harold Wilson, returned to office in 1974, rumours surfaced that the government had finally had enough and that reform was coming to the City.

The Wilson–Callaghan government of 1974–9 is often singled out for criticism, much of it justifiable, for the role it played in Britain's economic decline, but it is worth remembering the full technicolour horror of the inheritance left behind by Edward Heath's outgoing administration in 1974. A global oil shock in 1973 that put a rocket under prices and wage demands would have been difficult enough to contend with, but the Chancellor, Anthony Barber, had earlier embarked on a programme to liberalise lending, scrapping the ceiling controlling how much banks could lend and introducing a policy called Competition and Credit Control. Wilson commented that he did not realise Heath had a sense of humour until he appointed Barber as Chancellor following the sudden death of the widely respected Iain Macleod in 1970.

Even though O'Brien at the Bank of England had grave concerns that Barber and Heath did not know what they were doing, he was too slow to act. The money supply duly surged – meaning the amount of money in the economy rose dramatically as banks created credit and lent more – which propelled house prices upwards, at the rate of almost 50 per cent in one year in London, and created a stock market bubble based yet again on wild speculation. The outcome was a classic British smash in 1973 and 1974, featuring plummeting industrial profits, a series of strikes and the secondary banking crisis, in which small lenders had to be bailed out by the Bank of England and Slater Walker's Jim Slater, who had until then been the darling of the financial press, got into severe difficulties. The stock market crash was bad enough in Wall Street. In London, prices fell by 63 per cent in 1973/4 and there began a period of many months in which nothing moved and deals evaporated. The impact on employment and pay was severe.

It was in this difficult climate, with profits obliterated and the incoming Labour government increasing taxes at the uppermost level to 98p in the pound, that the City first faced demands for reform. The director of the Office of Fair Trading, Gordon Borrie, later a Labour peer, was particularly determined and made it clear to Wilson that there must be action. If other industries were subject to legislation aimed at tackling anti-competitive restrictive practices, and were subjected to necessary lectures on modernisation and innovation, then why should the City exist in its own bubble, defending cronyism and its own closed shop in the name of tradition? City elders sniffed class war in the air and when Sir Nicholas Goodison was elected chairman of the Stock Exchange in 1976 he swiftly had it confirmed that the government was going to bring the market's rulebook within the purview of restrictive practices legislation. At first the notion that the Stock Exchange faced potential prosecution by the government seemed faintly preposterous. Says one stockbroker of the period from an aristocratic, landed background: 'You must remember that the City kind of worked as it was. Don't ask me how or why. It just did, because it was a small group of people who would not stand for bad behaviour. The word would go round. That chap's dodge.' But wasn't it a cartel protecting the interests of a small elite? 'Yes, that was the problem. The City was for old British families protecting their wealth and looking out for each other.'

The contrast in that respect with mid-1970s Wall Street was stark. Reforms introduced there on May Day in 1975 destroyed the system of fixed commissions enjoyed by brokerages and gave investment banks such as Goldman Sachs and investment companies the chance to compete for more business. It sparked creative destruction, wiping out cartels and creating an increasingly go-go climate in which supposedly high-minded analysts at the brokers and in the banks had to start operating virtually as salesmen, identifying companies worthy of investment to attract customers and to generate deals. The potential for conflicts of interest only became fully apparent later, but in the late 1970s it looked simply as though New

York was gearing up for a new wave of innovation in the decade ahead. Shouldn't Britain follow suit? Goodison agreed that modernisation was necessary, but he and his members were concerned about the risks. He attempted to intercede with Roy Hattersley, the minister for consumer protection, and went to see him in his office in Whitehall to explain that a court case and a sudden judgment against the Stock Exchange could cause complete chaos. It would be impossible, he told the minister, to guarantee the stability of the markets. Hattersley was adamant that he would not countenance government intervention to halt any case, however. There must be no favours for the City.

By then the Labour government, led by Jim Callaghan following Wilson's retirement in 1976, had much bigger problems to contend with than the fate of the Stock Exchange. Hattersley was present on 1 December 1976 when the cabinet discussed what to do about the perilous position of the UK and the terms under which an emergency loan from the International Monetary Fund might be arranged. Various solutions were proposed to deal with Britain's woes, although the depth of despair is apparent in the Cabinet Secretary's note of the conclusions that day: 'A go it alone policy was not viable . . . rising unemployment was inevitable.' There was worse to come as the mistakes and mishaps of the previous decades by administrations of both major parties caught up with government. It had been Callaghan himself who was instrumental in blocking effective trade union reform in the late 1960s. Now the unions repaid him by destroying his government with a wave of strikes and unrest in the Winter of Discontent of 1978/9. Callaghan and the Chancellor, Denis Healey, attempted to bring some order and restraint to public spending, but the collectivist, paternalistic settlement that had come in with Attlee in 1945 was breaking up. It looked as though dilapidated old Britain was at risk of sinking quietly into the sea.

Much of the country's rather tired governing class seemed ill equipped to cope with the collapse of post-war certainties and the emergence of new ideas, as though it was scarred by the trauma of successive devaluations of sterling since the war and the decline in status this indicated. The final collapse in 1971 of the Bretton Woods Agreement, when Richard Nixon ended the system by which leading currencies were pegged to the dollar and physical supplies of gold in Fort Knox, was another change that seemed technical but its implications were revolutionary for countries such as Britain. Exchange rates would float, capital would begin to be much more mobile, moving to wherever investors saw a potential return, and the financial innovators of Wall Street were on the verge of inventing seemingly exciting products and ways of packaging and selling ever-larger amounts of debt for companies and countries. The future, the 1980s, looked to the alert as though it was going to be about openness to this coming tidal wave of money. Thanks to a long history of innovation, and its international outlook best expressed in the development of the Eurobond market by Warburg and others, the City of London was surely well placed to prosper.

First, though, the Stock Exchange would have to negotiate its way delicately around a new government headed by Margaret Thatcher, which came to office in May 1979. On 9 February, Borrie and the OFT had referred the Stock Exchange formally to the Restrictive Practices Court, setting in motion potentially years of legal action. Somehow the Stock Exchange needed to get out of this infernal court case. That shouldn't be too difficult. A woman – especially a Tory woman – wouldn't be too difficult to manage now, would she?

PART TWO
FRICTION

You say you want a revolution: accompanied by Sir Nicholas Goodison, Margaret Thatcher visits the London Stock Exchange in February 1979, three months before she won power.

DISCORD AND HARMONY

'I regret to tell the House that I cannot meet the request of the
Stock Exchange.'

John Nott, 23 October 1979

By temperament and outlook Nicholas Goodison was an unlikely
1980s revolutionary. As the author of *English Barometers 1680–1860*
(published in 1968), the chairman of the Stock Exchange was happiest
of all immersed in the study of furniture, clocks and music. His career
before the Thatcher era did not suggest insurgent tendencies either.
After Marlborough School and King's College, Cambridge, in 1958 he
joined the family City firm H.A. Goodison & Co., later Quilter,
Goodison, rising to become a partner four years later. Four years after
that, the same year his work on English barometers appeared, he was
elected to the Stock Exchange's governing body, the Council. As one
of several 'young turks', he did think the institution needed to liberalise, and he subsequently faced some resistance as chairman of the
Planning Committee from older members who did not think there
should be anything as racy as planning, but Goodison argued that
change should be evolutionary and carefully considered. The rules on
allowing members to trade overseas were relaxed somewhat, women
were admitted in 1973. Those who accused the Stock Exchange of
being a club were wrong in their diagnosis, thought Goodison. It was,
he remembers four decades later, 'very genial, very nice', with interesting people. 'But people didn't really appreciate what the Stock
Exchange was. Although it was a mutual understanding of 4,500
members, it was also the only regulatory body in the industry.'

Indeed, the City had its own delicate eco-system that had evolved over centuries. The Stock Exchange was the province of broking and jobbing firms, buying and selling shares and securities. It had no reach outside that realm of activity but beyond the Square Mile it had long been the most famous manifestation of the City. The Bank of England had no formal responsibility for the Stock Exchange or its dealings, but as the institution responsible for the issuance of national debt and its trading, the Bank relied on the Stock Exchange and kept a paternal eye out for excesses. The merchant banks, and the clearing banks, could not afford to offend the Bank of England either. It sat at the centre of a complex, inter-twined network of obligations and duties. The non-statutory Takeover Panel was also there from the late 1960s to police City takeovers and impose some order on companies and stockbrokers keen to do deals.

Having been elected as chairman in 1976, at forty-one the young-est occupant of the office, Goodison's attempts to explain the deli-cate nature of the Stock Exchange's role in this very British network to Labour ministers were a failure. Gordon Borrie, the head of the OFT, declined to agree a compromise, and many of Goodison's colleagues on the Stock Exchange Council felt that they must defend the existing arrangements. The old separation between brokers and jobbers offered the customer some protection from conflicts of interest, because the client knew that their broker had a sole respon-sibility to buy their shares at the best available price, and could not collude with the jobber. Customers feared that changes would mean competition and pressure on profits. If reform on the model of Wall Street was introduced – moving to so-called 'dual capacity' in which brokers and jobbers were effectively merged and scrapping minimum commissions on share trading – the customer might find their costs reduced, lowering profits.

Goodison and his colleagues were trapped. Realising with grow-ing horror how damaging and messy a potential court case would be if Borrie was allowed by the government to proceed, Goodison decided to try Sir Harold Wilson, by that time out of office. In

October of 1976 the newly installed Labour Prime Minister, Jim Callaghan, needing to give Wilson something to do, had asked him to chair a Committee to Review the Functioning of Financial Institutions, in an effort to examine how savings might be increased and industrial investment encouraged. Goodison suggested to Wilson that a new inquiry should be established to work out how to protect what was best about the City while introducing sufficient reform to satisfy the demands for change. 'Wilson was sympathetic,' says Goodison. 'Not at all hostile.' But the Stock Exchange chairman was wasting his time. There was no further inquiry and when Wilson's report was eventually published much later – in June 1980 – it was rendered irrelevant. By then the world had moved on, the era of Callaghan and Wilson was dust, and Margaret Thatcher was in Number 10. What mattered was persuading the Conservative leadership of the City's case.

This was to prove more difficult than it looked. Considering the scale of the changes that ended up being implemented by Thatcher's ministers, to the great benefit of many stockbrokers, jobbers and bankers, it is ironic that the Tory leader's initial early experiences in the Square Mile were not remotely conducive to friendly relations. Her official biographer Charles Moore records that on 4 February in the middle of the Tory leadership election of 1975, in which she defeated the incumbent Edward Heath, she went for lunch at N.M. Rothschild and had a tough time.[1] Several pro-Heath members of the Rothschild clan refused to attend and on the way back to Westminster she told the recently elected Tory MP, Norman Lamont, that she did not want to be taken 'to that red bank again'. The irony is that the Rothschilds and other merchant banks did extremely well later out of their role in arranging the Thatcher government's privatisation programme in the 1980s. But in the 'small c' conservative City of the mid-1970s she was not yet the warrior queen beloved of investment bankers and rapacious tycoons that she would become a decade or so later. In 1975 she was just the woman who had dared to cause trouble by taking on Ted Heath, the chap who led the Tory tribe, even if he was a chap who had presided over an economic cock-up of epic proportions in the early 1970s.

Thatcher's ideological re-engineering of the Tory Party had in the mid-1970s barely got underway. Although the think tank that she and Keith Joseph founded in 1974, the Centre for Policy Studies, was established to promote 'freedom and responsibility', it and the colleagues she trusted took time to develop a specific free market programme of policies. Her leadership was doubted by many of her old-school Conservative colleagues, and although a clear direction was apparent to her supporters, much of her time was spent seeking to reassure sceptical voters that she had the mettle to be prime minister. Following the calamities of the decade, and particularly after the Winter of Discontent, there was a sense of expectation in the City as the 1979 general election approached, and the Conservatives championed the urgent need for an economic renaissance and pro-business policies. Thatcher was received warmly in February that year when she visited the Stock Exchange and was given a tour by Goodison. That spring there was also a mini-boom in the market as share prices rose in expectation of a Tory win. Investors were also buoyed by the possibility that Britain's North Sea Oil deposits would make the years ahead easier to navigate, creating tax revenue for the Treasury and providing profits for investment. The Conservative manifesto put in front of the country in 1979 made no specific mention of the City itself, but it did emphasise the need for wealth creation, limiting taxes on capital and expanding share ownership.

Any hopes harboured by the City's senior figures of being given a smooth ride by the Thatcher administration did not survive early contact with the new government, however. On 22 May, with the government just eighteen days old, Goodison discussed the possibility of an exemption for the Stock Exchange with Sally Oppenheim, the new Minister of State for Consumer Affairs at the Department of Trade. Their conversation sparked an exchange of letters between the department and the Bank of England on whether or not Goodison's wish should be granted. That spring, John Nott, the no-nonsense Secretary of State for Trade, seemed unconvinced when they met several times in Whitehall. A colleague of Nott's remembers his scepticism: 'John thought Nicholas Goodison was looking to do a cosy deal. He wanted nothing to do with it.'

The truth is that Nott, a former merchant banker, had regarded a deal exempting the Stock Exchange as theoretically feasible, even desirable, but he felt it was now too late. On 30 May 1979 he wrote a long note to Geoffrey Howe, Chancellor of the Exchequer, detailing his thinking.

> We have, somewhat reluctantly, come to the conclusion that, if the legal proceedings before the Restrictive Practices Court had not already begun, following the rejection by Mr Hattersley (the former Labour minister) of the Stock Exchange's early request for exemption, it would have been right to exempt the Stock Exchange . . . However, the situation is very different now that the reference has been made.[2]

Any exemption would involve interrupting legal proceedings. Nott thus concluded: 'I do not believe therefore that we could justify giving special treatment to the Stock Exchange at this juncture.' Howe disagreed, and in a memo sent the following day from Number 10, the Prime Minister's staff advised Nott that the Chancellor wanted to discuss it as soon as possible after the looming Budget. Howe's view was that the Restrictive Practices Court was entirely the wrong forum to consider the future of the Stock Exchange. Could they not set up an ad-hoc committee or reconstitute the Monopolies and Mergers Commission?

Keith Joseph, the Secretary of State for Industry and one of the architects of free market Thatcherism, also became involved. He wrote to Nott on 6 June, indicating that he was not persuaded of the case for exempting the Stock Exchange and had no faith in the Monopolies Commission either. That summer, civil servants produced papers on the subject and by July, Howe, who was worried about the potential impact on the markets, was suggesting a compromise, in the form of either a stay of execution if the court

judgment went against the Stock Exchange or openness to sugges-
tions for reform. On 16 August, Nott wrote to Howe accepting his
suggestion. The result – the bottom line – of the discussions in
Whitehall was that the court case would go ahead, and Goodison
had failed to shift opinion. For all the myth of Thatcher driving
every aspect of government, the involvement of the Prime Minister
had been limited. In her handwritten note scribbled on a memo,
explaining that Nott would announce the next day that the Stock
Exchange would be allowed time to implement the judgment if it
lost, she said that she was content: 'Yes – it is a good compromise on
practical grounds.'

The disappointed Stock Exchange chairman was duly notified by
Nott, and in the Commons on 23 October 1979 the Secretary of State
confirmed it publicly, responding to questions from Tory MPs during
a debate on the competition bill.[3] There had been, he said, a great deal
of correspondence between Goodison's colleagues and ministers. 'I
regret to tell the House,' said Nott, 'that I cannot meet the request of
the Stock Exchange.' He defended the role of the Restrictive Practices
Court and indicated that the Stock Exchange would have a grace
period in which to make changes following a court judgment that
went against it. The implication was that the City was heading for a
kicking in court and had best get used to the idea.

Another factor was the quixotic personality of the Prime Minister
herself, frequently misread on the question of the financial revolution associated with the ideology carrying her name. One of the
great myths – fostered by the privatisations and reforms she introduced from which flowed great wealth to an old and new City
generation – is that she was always a natural supporter of the Square
Mile and its grandees, and deliberately designed a deregulatory
cornucopia of delights to please them. This was not the case. Says
an advisor to Thatcher from the early 1980s: 'Margaret looked at the
City and saw a self-satisfied old boys club that was rigid and stuck in
its ways.'

The grocer's daughter, the mercurial Methodist who had developed into a sophisticated political operator determined to shake

Britain out of its torpor, was hardly a natural ally of a bunch of men who had been in positions of authority during the UK's economic decline. They were judged undynamic; many of them had been to school together and sat on each other's boards; and now they were behaving like the leaders of an upmarket trade union. Her closest friend and most solid supporter was not of the City either. Her husband Denis was affluent industry, not City, and these tribal distinctions mattered, a lot, in the anthropological jungle of late 1970s and early 1980s Britain. Denis had taken over the family paints and chemicals business after serving in the Second World War, and when it was sold he served on the board of Burma Oil and several other firms involved in businesses such as waste management. His was the world of smart suburban golf courses, strongly held right-wing views, and gin and tonic with a stiff measure. As in a Venn diagram, the two tribes of City and British industry overlapped socially and commercially, of course. But the City – the Bank of England, the floor of the Stock Exchange and the network of brokers and jobbers – was not the natural terrain of the Thatchers.

The idea that Thatcher was actively seeking to do chums favours is not borne out by the correspondence of the period either. Goodison wrote to the Prime Minister on 6 November 1979 to express his regret at the decision by Nott, and to complain that he had not been consulted. His note gives an indication of how difficult the City was finding it to process a lack of cooperation from the leadership of a party that it had hitherto regarded as an ally. 'I really was astonished by the Government's failure to respond to our repeated requests for discussions before the taking of an adverse decision', wrote Goodison. 'As you know, I am a keen supporter of your Government. I am very sorry that I had to criticise it publicly for taking this decision without any consultation whatever with us. I had no choice, which was a very invidious position to find myself in.' An official wrote a covering note saying that Goodison's claim of a lack of consultation 'does not stand up'. Would the Prime Minister respond or would she like it passed to Nott? 'Alas, I shall have to reply', Thatcher scribbled. She sent a polite but firm response to Goodison. The Stock Exchange would have time to implement any changes, she wrote on 22 November 1979. Any suggestion that he had been ignored by ministers was not correct, she insisted.

The new government had more than enough to deal with without worrying about the bruised feelings of stockbrokers and jobbers. Indeed, the economic situation in which the UK found itself was dire. The Chancellor, not known for being excitable, had described it in stark terms in his first Budget in June 1979.[4] A depressingly familiar feature of the first Budget speech by new chancellors taking over after a change in governing party in the previous fifteen years, explained Geoffrey Howe, was that every one of them had found cause to complain, with more or less justice, about the pitiful state of their inheritance. 'The House will understand,' said Howe,

> in the light of the most recent evidence about inflationary trends, monetary growth, Government borrowing and the deteriorating trade balance – not to mention the post-dated cheques for public sector pay that I found on arrival at the Treasury – that I am certainly in no position to discontinue the tradition of my predecessors.

It was not only the fault of the previous Labour government, said Howe. Britain's decline had deeper roots, in the failure of the broad consensus that had existed between the two major parties since the Second World War: 'Are we not driven to the conclusion that the notions of demand management, expanding public spending and "fine tuning" of the economy have now been tested almost to destruction?'

The mild-mannered Howe announced measures aimed at restraining public sector spending, fighting inflation, controlling the money supply and reforming the taxation system. VAT was almost doubled, the standard rate of tax was cut and the top rate of income tax fell from 83p in the pound to 60p, giving a large boost to the take-home pay of the better-off in the City and industry and sending a signal that wealth creation – for some – would be the leit-motif of the Thatcher governments. As the economics commenta-tor David Smith put it: 'The 1979 budget was big and bold. Rarely has a government set out its stall, and its philosophy, so clearly.'[5] But the announcement that most merited such acclaim concerned the abolition of restrictions on taking money in and out of Britain. The decision would supercharge the changes underway in the financial markets. This was a revolutionary decision.

Inside the Treasury, officials had picked up one important clue during the 1979 election campaign about the transformative nature of what was coming. Before the election Nigel Lawson, as a member of the Conservatives' shadow Treasury team, had written a regular column for *Financial Weekly*, in which in his final contribution on 20 April 1979 he advocated the abolition of exchange controls – then the international norm – apart from in West Germany, where they had been scrapped by the pioneering finance minister Ludwig Erhard after the Second World War. In the UK's case, exchange controls were used to conserve the country's foreign exchange reserves and to improve the balance of payments, which restricted money leaving the country. It also hampered investment. Introduced at the outbreak of the Second World War, when the government needed all the currency, gold and securities it could lay its hands on, the most draconian restrictions were relaxed and then reintroduced from 1947, with certain controls reintroduced at points of crisis when the government judged that too much money was leaving the country. For the British tourist in 1979 this meant they were restricted in how much they could take out of the country on holi-day; for British companies it presented barriers to investing abroad; for foreign companies it made the UK highly unattractive, as once their money was invested it might be difficult to get it out; for the Stock Exchange it limited the scope for international trade.

Lawson was convinced that the economy needed to be more open to flows of money in both directions. British companies that invested abroad might prosper and reinvest profits at home or earn returns for their shareholders, he believed. Foreign investors would bring money, jobs and new expertise. When Lawson arrived at the Treasury in May as Financial Secretary, working for the Chancellor, he was surprised to be told that senior Treasury and Bank of England officials were expecting abolition of exchange controls, having attached too much authority to his article in *Financial Weekly*. Senior officials in the Bank of England agreed it was time Exchange Controls went, but in the Treasury the officials were opposed.

Like several of the boldest, defining acts undertaken by the Thatcher government, and ever since associated with her name, the exchange controls move was not actually her idea and she took some persuading that it was sensible. Howe had long been in favour theoretically and took the final decision, although he too had concerns about the practical implications. A quietly spoken and at times Eeyorish figure, Howe was capable of seeing a problem from eight different angles. In contrast, Lawson was much more 'Tiggerish'. After all, he had been a Fleet Street financial journalist and then an iconoclastic editor of the *Spectator* magazine from 1966–70.

Opponents feared that abolishing these controls would cause capital to flood out of the feeble UK economy as investors went in search of more prosperous climes, in turn causing a run on the pound. When Howe asked Lawson and officials to examine the possibilities, they judged that such a crisis was unlikely because the markets had faith in the new government and sterling was safe since its newly acquired status as a petro-currency made it more attractive, strengthening the pound. But Howe wanted to proceed in careful steps, with the first taken in the June Budget. The limit was raised on how much British travellers could take abroad and all investment by UK companies up to £5m was allowed automatically without the need for approval from the government. The following month, all restrictions on foreign direct investment were scrapped and investors – operating principally through banks and City firms – could invest in securities (stocks and bonds) abroad. In early October, Lawson pushed for full abolition, leaving Howe to persuade a 'hesitant' Thatcher. At the subsequent meeting of the cabinet, only the Environment Secretary, Michael Heseltine, objected, on the grounds that the wealthy would take the money out of Britain and buy nice houses on the Côte d'Azur. On 24 October 1979, Howe told the Commons that he was going for full abolition:

> There will from tomorrow be full freedom to buy, retain and use foreign currency for travel, gifts and loans to non-residents, buying property overseas and investment in all foreign currency securities . . . Portfolio investment will be wholly freed, and the requirement to deposit foreign currency securities with an Authorised Depositary is abolished. Foreign currency accounts can be held here or abroad. Passport marking for travel funds can now be abolished.

Howe's Labour opponents were appalled. Denis Healey, the Shadow Chancellor, responded that while there might be a case for some relaxation, abolition was a 'reckless, precipitate and doctrinaire' action which the government would soon regret. These concerns were understandable, if misplaced. The British were too used to exchange controls. In the Treasury, a team of 25 officials, and in the Bank of England 750 staff, managed and policed the restrictions. In many other countries something similar was then the norm and the notion of private money washing across continents, unimpeded by the intervention of government, seemed somehow illicit. Such a free flow was, of course, precisely what had happened in the late Victorian period, when the City and British investors sent a tsunami of capital abroad in search of profit, funding foreign railroads and industry. This time ministers hoped that capital would flood in from foreign investors, and that British companies would look abroad for opportunities.

Labour's opposition to the change persisted and in the party's 1982 pamphlet 'Investing in Britain', the City was singled out for criticism. 'Since the abolition of exchange controls, institutions have invested far too large a proportion of their funds abroad.'

Investments, the party said, had been insufficiently concentrated on the needs of the domestic economy, a theme which still surfaces periodically. In the party's manifesto for the 1983 election, dubbed afterwards the 'longest suicide note in history', Labour proposed the establishment of a Securities Commission to regulate the institutions and markets of the City, including the Lloyd's insurance market. Banks would have to submit detailed investment plans to the government explaining how they would help businesses of which the government approved, and if they did not cooperate they would be nationalised. Ironically, after Labour went on its long ideological journey following defeat in 1983, its leaders Neil Kinnock, John Smith, Tony Blair and Gordon Brown embraced the City and accepted that capital should be globally mobile, before the party ended up nationalising two banks, RBS and Lloyds, in the midst of the 2008 financial crisis. In the early 1980s, that calamity lay long distant in the future.

The warnings on Exchange Control abolition did turn out to have been overcooked though. Following a slow start – and a reverse during the economic convulsions of the early 1980s as industry was hammered by the effects of a strong pound and the high interest rates applied by the Conservatives to squeeze out inflation – foreign investment in the UK rocketed. Precise figures on inward investment have to be treated with caution, but the trend is clear. It is estimated that in 1975 total investment by foreign firms and investors was £260m; in 1979, £480m; 1985, £1.3bn; 1990, £3.2bn; 1995, £5.1bn; and 2000, £25bn.[6] Not all of this was down to the decision taken by Howe on exchange controls, of course. But taken together with what had developed in the Eurobond market in London since Warburg's innovations of the early 1960s, the abolition of exchange controls was one of the most significant acts of a British Chancellor in the twentieth century. The long deep freeze that followed 1914, when the free flow of capital was restricted and then frozen stiff between 1939 and 1945, was thawing.

Nicholas Goodison and some of his colleagues at the Stock Exchange grasped the significance of what Howe had done. He knew that if the UK was opening up to foreign investment, and foreign competition, then the City was bound to feel the effects. But how to harness this opportunity when any hope that a gentleman's compromise with ministers might be feasible had been abandoned and it seemed that Margaret Thatcher was content to see the Stock Exchange confronted in court?

That year, in September 1982, there was more pressure applied on the Stock Exchange when a brash new rival on the American model opened on a historic City site. LIFFE – the London International Financial Futures Exchange – took over the Royal Exchange building, on the site that Gresham had chosen for his Exchange in the sixteenth century. Under the roof topped with the Gresham-family gold-grasshopper weathervane, traders wearing bright multi-coloured jackets gesticulated and shouted their trades. The cacophonous enterprise was based on the Chicago-based futures markets, in which traders bought and sold futures contracts for commodities or shares, enabling suppliers and purchasers to insulate themselves from future fluctuations in price. An investor agrees to pay the seller if the price of a large consignment of a commodity – tea or coffee, say – falls below an agreed price. If the price goes above an agreed ceiling, the investor keeps it and makes a profit. It gives the producer certainty by reducing price volatility. The market soon broadened out beyond foodstuffs and into futures contracts on all manner of financial products. Assorted working parties from London had visited Chicago to discover how it worked, and Brian Williamson and John Barkshaw readied LIFFE in London. Unlike at the Stock Exchange, in which membership was hard to get and jealously guarded, LIFFE welcomed all comers, including banks and securities firms from abroad.

Nick Durlacher of the jobbers Wedd, Durlacher was one of those deputed to work at LIFFE when the firm decided that it should try this exotic new market. He was deeply disappointed to be leaving the Stock Exchange floor and, having never heard of futures markets, went off to the US to find out. What struck him most there was the noise, the jostling and the shouting. In the

London Stock Exchange you waited your turn. Not in a futures market. The night before the opening, there was a party in the Guildhall, the ancient seat of the Corporation of the City of London, at which the Bank of England Governor, Gordon Richardson, made a speech congratulating the innovators who had created LIFFE. He also rang the bell at 10am the next morning to get trading underway. Compared to the Stock Exchange, it was a bear pit. The new breed of traders tended to be young, below thirty-five, and the mix was, if not 50–50 male/female, at least close to that. Compared to the excitement at LIFFE, the long-established Stock Exchange round the corner risked looking like the genteel cousin or relic of a bygone age.

Inside the Bank of England, one of the most senior figures soon realised there must be a deal to be done on the future of the Stock Exchange. David Walker's early career gave him the perfect mix of experiences and contacts to be the bridge between the various outposts of the UK's financial and political Establishment. A grammar-school boy from Chesterfield, Walker joined the Treasury in 1961 with a double first in economics from Cambridge. During a period in Washington working for the IMF in the early 1970s, his views on Britain's economic situation hardened, and on his return to the Treasury he found himself working closely on the sterling crisis. Walker had been in the government car, briefing Denis Healey, on the infamous occasion in September 1976 when the Chancellor was on his way to Heathrow Airport. Healey was supposed to travel to the International Monetary Fund conference in Manila, but when they arrived at the VIP lounge, Healey and Walker discovered that the market pressures on sterling had intensified to such an extent that the Chancellor could not responsibly leave Britain. Gordon Richardson was also at Heathrow. They then had to get hold of Callaghan – with some difficulty as he was at the Labour Party annual conference – to update the Prime Minister. 'The whole thing was abandoned,' recalled Walker. 'I was invited to go back to the Bank with the Governor . . . on this day of great crisis he said well, perhaps we ought to talk about what we can do about the sterling balances. Let's have a quiet conversation and have some lunch.'[7] That conversation, and Walker's links with other officials, meant that in 1980 he was offered a post at the Bank of England, first running the economic intelligence department and then the 'lifeboat' for struggling companies that could not access funding from the commercial banks.

As an executive director of the Bank of England in 1981, Walker concluded that the City had to change. Here the Bank was in a curious position. Technically it had few formal powers and the Stock Exchange was self-governing as a membership organisation, but the senior figures in the Bank felt a general sense of responsibility for the City and perhaps wanted to extend their remit. The Stock Exchange firms also bought and sold the Bank of England's gilt-edged securities, the name for UK government debt. Walker's concern was that the City's firms were so badly under-capitalised, meaning they lacked the clout and resources of the larger American organisations to compete, that they would just die if nothing was done. If the court case went ahead, the City could be tied up in years of litigation and the malaise could damage London's reputation. Walker commissioned a young economist, Andrew Threadgold, to write a report that drew lessons from the liberalisation that had taken place in New York in 1975. When it was presented, Threadgold's initial 'Blue Skies' study was instrumental in coalescing opinion in the Bank of England and the Treasury. Walker and other officials were also concerned about a ruling by the European Court that appeared to suggest that single capacity – the separation of jobbers and brokers – could fall foul of European law.[8]

In the Treasury, the most senior official, Permanent Secretary Peter Middleton, and Geoffrey Howe were also discussing how to find a way forward, prompted in part by the work of the Bank. A meeting was convened at Number 11 Downing Street on 10.30am on 6 May 1983, three days before Thatcher went to the Palace to ask the Queen for a dissolution of Parliament and a general election. Around the table that day were Howe, Middleton, Gordon

Richardson, David Walker, and Arthur Cockfield, the Secretary of State for Trade. Cockfield was notoriously self-confident, an attribute that did not endear him to all of his colleagues. He ended up almost by accident being one of the most consequential and least mentioned figures in the Thatcher era. In 1984 she appointed him as a European Commissioner, where he played a leading role in driving through the single market, and in the process in Thatcher's eyes going irretrievably native in Brussels, to such an extent that he was not offered a second stint. At the meeting in Number 11 in May 1983, Walker saw that Cockfield was one who got the City and grasped what needed to happen. Cockfield advocated a potential compromise, centred on the abandonment of fixed commissions. It was agreed that this mess was at least partly down to the Stock Exchange's handling of the matter. There now needed to be private discussions with the Exchange, and the Treasury and Department of Trade were tasked with producing a negotiating brief. That meeting before the election was pivotal.

On the day after the 1983 general election when Thatcher was returned to office with a landslide, Goodison got encouraging news. Cecil Parkinson was appointed as Secretary of State for Trade and Industry and Goodison sent him a letter making a plea for talks. Would Goodison like to pop round to his office for a chat? He would. Parkinson had encountered the City earlier in his career as an auditor and while he recalled that he had been unimpressed and suspicious of the old set-up, regarding it as too much of an old-boy network, he saw the value in reinvigorating the City with a burst of reform and modernisation. The amenable Parkinson had consulted Nigel Lawson, newly appointed to take over from Howe as Chancellor, who told him that the compromise with the Stock Exchange was a positive development, as long as the promises of reform were real. David Walker found Lawson to be an enthusiastic advocate of change. The new Chancellor had the City in his blood. Lawson's father had been a tea broker in the City and his grandfather had been a senior partner in a stockbroking firm. As City Editor of the *Sunday Telegraph* in the 1960s Lawson had been there when Jim Slater was hired as share tipster, the same Slater who went on to have such a controversial career and then a sensational smash in the early 1970s when his Slater Walker empire got into difficulty. Lawson came to the job with few illusions about the City.

Goodison travelled to Parkinson's office and surprised the new Secretary of State by agreeing instantly to the outline of what was proposed. In a series of subsequent secret meetings they agreed the beginnings of a historic settlement. Fixed minimum commissions on share trading would be scrapped by late 1986, and further reforms would be introduced, including a system of appeals for those turned down for Stock Exchange membership to ensure that the 'old-boy network' could not block those it regarded as socially unacceptable. The question of dual capacity – abolishing the separation between brokers and jobbers – was parked for now, in recognition of the difficulties Goodison faced with traditionalist members of the Stock Exchange when it came to implementing any changes.

Parkinson next had to convince the Prime Minister that enough had been conceded by the Stock Exchange to merit the suspension of the potential legal action by the government. Writing on 12 July 1983, Parkinson deployed his considerable charm in a six-page memo in an attempt to persuade Thatcher that it was a good idea. 'New factors have now appeared. One is that Sir Nicholas Goodison has come to accept the necessity of some changes, and is prepared to negotiate.' That was a little harsh on Goodison, who had long accepted the need for changes but merely objected to the prospect of a difficult court case. But Parkinson was preoccupied with the Sara Keays affair, which was soon to be revealed in the newspapers, and it fell to Lawson to reassure the Prime Minister. On 21 and 22 July at the Stock Exchange Tower there were two days of closed discussions by the ruling Council, following a leak to the *Guardian* newspaper that suggested a settlement was being discussed. The Council voted unanimously in favour of settling.

At the final moment, the process was almost derailed when Willie Whitelaw, Deputy Prime Minister, expressed concerns in cabinet. Wouldn't it look as though the Tories were looking after their friends in the city, whose donations had helped the Tories to their recent election victory? Lawson had to make a strong case, explaining that it was not only the right course of action, it was also early enough in the Parliament for it to be forgotten later. That argument prevailed and the next day, on 27 July, Parkinson made an announcement to the Commons, in which curiously he said that while fixed commissions would go, separation between brokers and jobbers would for now be maintained, a position that did not endure for long. The reaction to the retreat of the Restrictive Practices Court, both from the Labour opposition and even from Tory-friendly newspapers, was scathing. It was, said Peter Archer, MP for Warley West, a slap in the face for the director of the OFT: 'Is the Secretary of State asking the House to accept that a deal between cronies in a smoke-filled room is a substitute for a full public inquiry into how public interest is affected by a major institution such as the Stock Exchange?' The *Daily Telegraph* on its City pages said that a government theoretically committed to competition had abandoned its own guardian of competition policy. The contrast with the destruction being experienced by British industry, which had its worst year since the Second World War as factory after factory closed, causing unemployment and distress, could not have been more pronounced. *The Economist* spoke of the Square Mile having been done a favour by its chums. But Tory ministers had, over four years of difficult negotiations, gradually arrived at a position where the City could rethink how it did business and open up to more outside competition. It might make it feasible for financial services to expand rapidly as the old manufacturers sank into the post-industrial wasteland. The City could be a beacon amid the gloom and national introspection. 'The truth,' says a Thatcherite minister of the period, 'is that I think they didn't know quite what they were doing. They didn't realise what they were unleashing.'

6

SELL

'We took the Concorde and were in the Merrill Lynch New York office by nine-thirty in the morning and by ten o'clock were back on the street, figuratively speaking, cheques in our hands for the unexpired terms of our three-year contracts. We took the twelve o'clock Concorde and were home for dinner.'

Sir John Craven

In the autumn of 1983 the partners in most City firms faced a choice. If they were lucky, the outfit which they had joined many years previously perhaps had an august name and a serious reputation rooted in many decades of trusted trading in shares or government gilts in the network of firms clustered around the Stock Exchange. Being a partner meant they were co-owners of the firm, a status which came with obvious advantages and disadvantages. They won when the firm did well. But their money, even their house, was on the line in a difficult year of trading, which made it sensible to pay attention if any of the firm's younger, racier types claimed to have discovered an ingenious way for the firm to make more money. If the theoretically bright youngster was badly wrong about his suggested technique or trade, the partner stood to lose a lot personally. The partner had a strong incentive either to pay attention when risky ideas were mentioned, or to foster a generally conservative approach and clearly established hierarchy so that his staff would not cost him his house in Surrey. But 1983 and 1984 were good years on the Stock Exchange, with prices rising. London was once again opening up to the world. The Americans and

Japanese who had arrived in the 1960s and 70s were scaling up their operations. The Stock Exchange stood to be transformed and while partners might be proud of their firm's high standing, tradition would only get you so far in the new era. But the firm they part owned had experience, contacts, wisdom and insight into the working of the markets at just the right moment when Wall Street and Tokyo were looking to London, partly because of its perfect position in the international time zone halfway between the two rival centres, and partly because of the early glimmer of reflected glamour from its trailblazing free market, reformist government. Suddenly, the old firm in which the partners had worked their way up was potentially rather valuable to new outside shareholders. And even if it were not, there was a chance it might seem convincingly valuable to potential purchasers for long enough for a foreign or a British bank to sign a large cheque for the partners. What would you do?

That was the question facing hundreds of partners in the second half of 1983 and in 1984. The City and its dining rooms and drinking dens buzzed with incessant gossip about who would be bought and for how much, as the senior figures tried to make sense of what was coming and ensure they made the right decisions. The confusion was understandable. It wasn't as though the agreement of July 1983 between Goodison and Parkinson, with the Bank of England guiding the way, laid out any detailed plan for what everyone involved should do next. The looming revolution posed an assortment of challenges, some of them bewildering. The best stockbroking and jobbing partnerships were targets and the merchant banks – which traditionally simply advised clients doing deals and placed customers' orders to buy shares or securities via independent brokers – were about to find themselves up against American banks that combined all these activities under one roof with much bigger resources. Merchant banks such as Warburgs, Schroder's, Lazard, Barings and others had to consider whether or not they wanted to buy stockbroking and jobbing firms, and integrate them into their businesses. But how might it be done? Who should they buy and for how much? The risk of getting it wrong could involve extinction and the premature death of a long-standing City firm. Get it right and a large villa on the Côte d'Azur and a mortgage-free existence was in prospect. There was going to be a lot of money to be made very soon.

What almost everyone in authority at the time could agree on was that the UK firms were under-capitalised for an increasingly international business. The fear was that they were way too small, with too little money, to compete with the Americans and Japanese. Where those in authority differed was over the extent to which British ownership mattered. At the Bank of England, that guardian of British economic prestige, David Walker in particular privately encouraged the British to be imaginative in dreaming up mergers and new agglomerations of firms, in the hope that several success-ful British champions might be formed to compete on equal terms with the Americans and Japanese. With Cecil Parkinson gone quickly – following his resignation from the cabinet in October 1983 over his affair with his secretary Sara Keays – the minister who pronounced publicly on such matters for the government was Alex Fletcher, the Minister for Corporate and Consumer Affairs. Ostensibly, Fletcher and his colleagues agreed. In an interview with the *Financial Times* published on 13 December 1983 he declared: 'If we want to maintain London as a prominent market, I think it is very important that the Stock Exchange and the majority of the institutions here should remain very firmly in British hands.'

In reality, these expressions of government concern were cosmetic. How could they be otherwise when Thatcherism rested on the idea of open markets and exposing institutions to competi-tion to produce dynamism? The government had spent several years refusing to intervene in defence of manufacturing industry, and it was entering a bruising battle with the miners and trade union mili-tants. It could hardly now try to prevent foreign takeovers at the Stock Exchange. In the Commons, when Fletcher was asked that year about the impact of potential mergers in the City he stressed that the market must take its course. 'It is a matter for the commercial judgement of the City and not for the government how the institutions best organise themselves to meet the future.'

One of the key figures in shaping how exactly the firms would organise themselves was the financier John Craven. For a firm that was to play a leading role in the birth of a new City of London, the name chosen – Phoenix Securities – was perfect. After all, the mythological bird rising from the flames – cited by the Ancient Greeks and the Romans and adopted as a symbol by the early Christians – represents reinvention, rebirth and resurrection. In the early 1980s, Craven certainly needed to resurrect his hitherto promising career. His professional life was suddenly looking cursed after he'd accepted a job at the US brokerage and wealth manager Merrill Lynch, to head their international operation based in London. It proved to be a huge mistake, although in the process Craven and one of his friends had gained a useful insight into how tough US bankers could be once the wooing was over and the new hire had turned up for work.[1] David Montagu (later the 4th Baron Swaythling) – a tough-minded and witty City aristocrat with a love of horse-racing, wine and winning in business – felt he and the younger Craven had been the victims of an American confidence trick by Merrill Lynch.[2] Montagu was already a City veteran, having chaired the family bank Samuel Montagu before it was sold to the Midland Bank in 1973. He then ran Orion, the joint-venture or consortium bank involving six foreign banks that briefly became a leading player in the European market. When he left he received thirty-six job offers, including one from Merrill Lynch. Both Montagu and Craven were led to believe that the other had already definitely agreed to join, Montagu as chairman and Craven as chief executive, and on that basis they signed up. It was a mission doomed from the moment they turned up for work in early 1980, with all of the authority residing in the New York headquarters and the culture of an American institution definitely not to their liking. Faxes containing irritating requests about office partitions, and other footling matters winged their way across the Atlantic. Montagu tended to throw the missives in the bin while Craven drafted rude replies.

The clash of cultures was even more apparent when Donald Regan, the chairman of Merrill Lynch in New York, announced that he wanted to visit London in 1980 to meet senior figures in the City and then go to Scotland to play golf. Regan was in line to become Ronald Reagan's first Treasury Secretary after the forthcoming US election, but was rather obviously out of his natural habitat on what may have been his first trip to London. A stellar Establishment guest list – including the Chancellor of the Exchequer and his wife, the Governor of the Bank of England and his wife, Arnold Weinstock of GEC, and Christopher and Mary Soames was assembled by Montagu and his wife for a dinner party at their home in honour of the Regans. 'It was,' said Montagu later, 'a spectacular disaster. Mr Regan barely opened his mouth.'³ The then rumour that he would be appointed US Treasury Secretary, which duly happened later that year, prompted Geoffrey Howe in his thank-you letter to the Montagus to say, 'if you're right about this man becoming Secretary to the US Treasury, then God help the Western world'. Montagu and Craven wanted out. 'After eleven months,' said Craven, 'we took the Concorde and were in the Merrill Lynch New York office by nine-thirty in the morning and by ten o'clock were back on the street, figuratively speaking, cheques in our hands for the unexpired terms of our three-year contracts. We took the twelve o'clock Concorde and were home for dinner.'⁴ Dealing with Wall Street and accommodating the American interest in doing a lot more business out of London was clearly not going to be straightforward.

An unemployed and worried Craven set up on his own, advising clients that included the Mexican government, the IMF and Canadian gold-miners. When he needed a name for his small business his wife suggested Phoenix. Hopefully, she told him, you'll rise from the ashes of your disastrous career at Warburg and Merrill Lynch. Luckily for Craven, his blend of skills and contacts left him ideally placed to advise City firms on how they might make sense of the changing landscape of international finance. He had seen how the Americans operated and he knew the City. His Phoenix Securities would act as advisor in more than two-thirds of the thirty marriages made by City firms as they raced to get ready for Big Bang, giving him and his small number of colleagues an enormous amount of influence in the process.

A Los Angeles bank, Security Pacific Corporation, moved first, even before the Parkinson/Goodison deal was announced. It bought a 29.9 per cent stake in the broker Hoare Govett. The rules were altered in stages to allow foreigners to buy larger stakes and then to take over British stockbrokers and jobbers. Among London's merchant banks in the early 1980s the most sophisticated players had been thinking ahead about this possibility already. At Warburg, the firm's guiding light flickered out in October 1982. Before Siegmund Warburg's death, the most influential British merchant banker of his generation had been amenable to the idea of Warburg's expanding its business, buying a stockbroker, and becoming what the Americans talked of as a fully-fledged investment bank. The old man's fear, his friends noted, was of excessive expansion and greed running riot. He had witnessed the economic and political impact of the Wall Street Crash on Germany in the early 1930s and seen the carnage it wrought. Men and women in the midst of a boom have a tendency to forget, but he could see the need for the firm he'd founded to adapt and change. In 1984, Warburg's parent company Mercury Securities bought a 29.9 per cent stake in Akroyd & Smithers, the leading jobbing firm, for £41m, a purchase followed by the government broker – Mullens, the men in the silk top hats – and the stockbroker Rowe & Pitman. The disappearance of Mullens – bought pretty much as a favour to the Bank of England, which did not want the firm that had traditionally handled the distribution of gilts humiliated – was another harbinger of change. The Prime Minister no longer wanted gilts – UK debt – to be handled by an exclusive arrangement via Mullens. It would be organised through a new office based inside the Bank of England. Warburg's purchases cost a total of £200m.

There was a further freedom that did not apply in the US. In Britain, without the separation between investment banks and retail banks that had been enforced, although gradually less assiduously, on Wall Street, there was also the possibility that the high-street banks could expand too and enter the securities business. A big British name, such as Barclays, NatWest or Lloyds, might buy a broker or two and seek to go beyond straightforward retail and business banking. Eventually, a small Scottish institution, the Royal Bank of Scotland, would (almost unimaginably) buy the much larger Nat West, expand its investment banking division and become, briefly, the biggest bank in the world before blowing up in spectacular fashion in 2008. All that lay far in the future.

Craven's phone was ringing with increasing frequency, as senior partners in other stockbroking and jobbing firms wanted advice on how they might sell themselves or establish new firms. Craven attempted to impress upon them that they should be careful and try to choose a suitor who might be a good match, rather than just falling for the buyer offering the most. They didn't always listen and many of the partners who stood to benefit from a sale had little expectation of staying on. They could pocket a million, or several multiples of that sum, and move on. To most of the population, a million pounds is still, today, a lot of money. In the mid-1980s it was undeniably a lot more money. It is estimated that more than 750 millionaires were created in the sell-off, with the total price paid for firms estimated as having been close to £1.5bn.

The process was complicated, partly because firms wanted to keep their discussions secret from each other. This meant it was also not always possible to get prospective buyers and targets in the same room. When Salomon Brothers in New York expressed an interest in possibly buying Wedd Durlacher, the Phoenix team suggested a fun trip to Wall Street, but it emerged that one of the most senior figures at Wedd Durlacher could not travel because he did not have a passport and had never left Britain, an unthinkable concept in finance thirty years later.[5] Wedd Durlacher was one of the leading jobbing firms, and had been run by Jack Durlacher, father of Nick Durlacher who had gone off to work at LIFFE. What Craven and his colleague Martin Smith helped secure eventually was a deal with Barclays, after talks with Kleinwort Benson got nowhere. The amount split between the partners for selling Wedd Durlacher was a pot of £100m. Barclays also purchased the stockbroker de Zoete, fusing it with Barclays merchant banking operation and creating the investment banking operation BZW. When the stockbroking firm Scrimgeour Kemp-Gee was bought by the American Citicorp, the price was £50m. The high-street bank NatWest purchased the jobber Bisgood Bishop, and the US bank Citicorp also spent £20m acquiring 29.9 per cent of Vickers de Costa, along with its operation in the Far East. N.M. Rothschild bought a chunk of Smith Brothers. The American firm Chase Manhattan swallowed Simon & Coates and Laurie Millman, two brokers.

Some firms found it difficult to decide because they had so many potential purchasers. Dundas Hamilton, the senior partner at Fielding, Newson-Smith, had to make the choice on behalf of his firm: 'At one time we had six different suitors,' he told an interviewer in 1988. 'They were American, a European bank and a London clearing bank . . . we thought we were quite a snip to be taken over. Ultimately we went to the National Westminster Bank and it turned out to be rather a tragedy.'[6] The UK merchant bank Morgan Grenfell could not make up its mind until it was too late and purchased a lesser jobbing firm, Pinchin Denny, for £21m. Already there were signs of trouble ahead, when senior Morgan Grenfell people briefed dismissively during the talks about their new purchase, describing the jobbers as looking like traders from a street market. The flaring up of class tensions between jobbers and brokers and grand merchant bankers did not suggest that a happy partnership was in prospect.

Goldman Sachs, Morgan Stanley and Salomon Brothers opted to hire staff to boost their own operations in London, rather than paying to buy an established firm, which may have been a better use of resources. Not all the old names allowed themselves to be swallowed up. Both Cazenove and Lazard decided to stand alone. Lazard stood back from the securities business entirely, choosing to remain as a merchant bank that solely advised clients, and Cazenove, the appointed stockbroker to the Queen, went its own way. The joint senior partner John Kemp-Welch, and other senior figures including David Mayhew, were determined to preserve the firm as an independent partnership. Clever old 'Caz' came up with possibly the most ingenious solution to the need for new capital, tapping twelve leading institutions for a loan of £32m that gave the investors zero influence on the firm but bolstered its position.

The sums seem small now relative to what followed in term of profits, losses and mega-deals in the next few decades, but the stakes at the time were high for a good reason. What only an insightful few understood at the time was that the entire basis of international finance and the business of money was changing dramatically, presenting new opportunities and challenges not just in shares, but also for those who traded in government and corporate debt, and increasingly from the 1980s, bonds made up of pools of mortgage debt. The roots of that revolution lay in President Nixon's decision in the early 1970s to uncouple the dollar from gold. Until that point, a dollar was worth a fixed amount of gold and was theoretically redeemable for said gold. The Americans had taken over leadership in the currency field from the British as the US economy surged to dominance in the twentieth century. Finally ending the connection to gold meant the dollar and other countries would be worth purely what the market decided. A central bank could print or create as much as it wanted, as long as (and this was a vital caveat) those in the market place buying and selling the debt – investors, traders – believed the government in question was good for it. This new post-gold approach facilitated a debt and credit explosion in the world's largest economy that was already well underway by the early 1980s. In 1970 the total debt of the US government stood at $370,918,706,949.93 (almost $371bn). By 1980 it was nudging $1 trillion at $907,701,000,000. By the year 2000 it was on its way to $6 trillion at $5,674,178,209,886. There was a brief flurry of excitement when it seemed under President Clinton and then in the early years of the George W. Bush first term that the US government debt pile might diminish or even eventually disappear. As I write, it is heading for $20 trillion.

Of course, that government debt fluctuates as a percentage of GDP – the output of the economy – as the economy grows or suffers a recession, and it is also eroded by bouts of inflation. Debt is necessary. It has been the fuel of economies, even before William III's allies established the Bank of England to lend the Crown money to rebuild the English navy. In good times and bad it can help power growth. The US economy has grown strongly since the 1970s despite its periodic detours into disasterville. But it wasn't just government debt that shot up. Private debt was growing sharply too, as homeownership was extended and access to credit cards went from being the preserve of an elite to a staple of life on main street. In the US, the government also underpinned home owner-ship through a network of state subsidies. There were attempts to check this debt expansion, such as when the tough-minded Federal Reserve chairman Paul Volcker, a Democrat appointed by President Carter in 1979 and reappointed by President Reagan four years later, instituted a credit squeeze in 1981 to reduce the money supply and bring down inflation. But while that initiated a lull it did not seri-ously impede the tidal wave of debt and opportunities for trading it.

Put that together with the innovations that had their roots in London in the Eurobond market – companies borrowing to fund expansion, restructuring or infrastructure – and the scope was immense for financiers buying that debt, distributing it and making a profit funnelling it to willing customers (the object of bond trad-ers' derision) who wanted the stream of income (the coupon) that a bond paid or the chance of selling when the price improved. Acting as the conduit between those who needed to sell the debt of govern-ments and companies, and investors seeking to buy them, put the hungriest firms at the apex of a rapidly expanding market.

The 1980s is often talked about in popular parlance as though the Reagan and Thatcher marketplace revolution was mainly about equities – stocks and shares in individual companies – but that was only part of it. Debt was a key element of the story. As the numbers got larger, the slice that firms and their traders could take and pay themselves got bigger too. In the early to mid-1980s the two would fuse together, debt markets and stock markets apparently in perfect harmony. Finance or debt was readily available for companies wanting to construct takeovers, and rumours or confirmation that a company might be in line to be bought pushed up its share price. This had long happened to an extent, but the scale was now mind-blowing. A Mergers and Acquisitions (M&A) boom in which household names would be sold or restructured – on borrowed money, leverage – was gathering pace. The junk bond business – which began with the aggressive trading of the high-risk low-grade debt of firms that traditionally had been looked down on by Wall Street because they were small and unglamorous – was also getting going in the US. On parts of Wall Street this climate produced quasi-criminal chicanery, and in some cases outright criminal behaviour in breach of the securities laws introduced in the 1930s. The scale of the money to be made in late 1970s and early 1980s New York increased the value of inside information about companies' intentions and tempted the greedy to trade it for gain.

Even on the legal side of the line, the Americans had understood the implications of the debt explosion earlier and better than anyone. In Michael Lewis's hilarious account of life at Salomon Brothers in the 1980s – *Liar's Poker* – he explains how bond traders became what the novelist Tom Wolfe later termed 'Masters of the Universe', cursing and shouting their way to mastery, crushing rivals and generally behaving like a highly unpleasant and money-obsessed version of the Muppets. Bafflingly, the sharp-eyed Wolfe was allowed onto the forty-first floor at Salomon Brothers in New York to undertake his research for the 1980s novel that would become *Bonfire of the Vanities*. We should be clear: the worst excesses of those he observed might have been reprehensible, but the men (mainly men) doing it weren't stupid. The governments of the Western world were taking a punt on debt, both public and household, and the bond traders and salesmen were responding rationally to the appearance of a giant gold-plated opportunity. American investors searching for higher returns were also becoming increasingly interested in the outside world and in buying up shares in foreign companies. American international pre-eminence in politics and culture was reflected in the internationalisation of its financial markets. The business of money was becoming less constrained by borders, which is illustrated by data from the US Federal Reserve. In 1965 the total US holdings of foreign corporate equities (shares in companies) were tiny, just $5bn's worth. In 1975 it was $9.6bn. By 1985 it would stand at $44.4bn. It kept on going, hitting $790.6bn in 1995 and almost $7 trillion in 2014.[7]

These epic forces were being unleashed as London got ready for Big Bang. Lewis, the unlikely bond salesman with a degree in art history, had, he acknowledged, lucked himself onto the graduate trainee scheme at a point when Wall Street was in transition. Banks and brokerages that had traditionally drawn much of their talent from the shop floor, promoting boys from the backroom, now wanted to hire as many high-achieving graduates from the leading American universities. This was not difficult. Such graduates had heard there was a lot more money to be made on Wall Street than in other industries, and fought to get themselves hired.

The firm Lewis had joined, Salomon Brothers, had had a relatively small operation in London since the 1970s, although in the 1980s under Charles McVeigh it was keen to grow. It was there that Lewis was posted, to a cramped office with a view of St Paul's Cathedral and not much else. It was Salomon that had also given Valerie Thompson, from a very different background, her break. Like the old-school traders on Wall Street, she had come up through the administrative route without formal qualifications. What mattered was that she was bright and ballsy with an instinct for numbers and the psychology of trading. Both graduates and the autodidacts of the trading floor could prosper, it seemed. What counted was ability, and profits.

In London, there was certainly suddenly a lot more money around and the pace of promotion, as well as excitement, was quickening. Davina Walter was in her early thirties when she was poached by Henderson in the mid-1980s to become a fund manager. On Wall Street, the stealing of staff and offers of vast salary increases was more aggressive at that point, as New York had a head start following its reforms in 1975. In contrast, Walter didn't want to offend her boss at Cazenove, who in the event was very civilised and understanding about her move. He was married to a Henderson. 'When I joined Henderson's I was employee one hundred and seventy-nine or eighty. Within two years there were over six hundred people.'[8] But not all poaching could be quite so polite. The booming jobs market created obvious opportunities for an innovative new generation of head-hunters who were prepared to be more audacious. Philippa Rose launched her recruitment agency in 1981 when she was only twenty-one. Rose had worked for less than two years in corporate finance at Kleinwort Benson and then for a recruitment agency. When she thought she might go mad interviewing any more secretaries she worked out how to start a business, and her employer invested £8,000 for 40 per cent of her new company, with Rose and her father scraping together the rest needed. Her targets were the brightest fellow youngsters who had joined the City, then realised that they were unsuited to their role and in need of a more lucrative challenge in another bank or firm. She offered to match them to the right institutions. The approach was daring and iconoclastic. Rose refused to deal with HR departments and went straight to department heads and CEOs, developing close relationships with them. In year one she made a profit of £11,000 and expanded her team. 'From there the trajectory was vertical for twenty years,' she recalls.

Ross Jones also enjoyed a rapid rise, though in his case it was through staying with the firm he had joined in 1977, despite having no real idea what it did. The answer was that Gerrard & National and the other discount houses provided liquidity to the market, as they had always done, lending it to the banks when they needed it and mopping up a profit, although they were also diversifying and turning themselves into fully-fledged investment houses that looked after more money for clients. Jones rose quickly and in 1984, on returning from a posting in Spain, he was appointed assistant director, making him senior to his former bosses. He was put on the gilts desk to learn and it was very exciting. His salary rocketed; he bought a flat and got his first car: a Porsche. Six months later, his salary was raised again and six months after that it more than doubled.

The head-hunters and fast-rising young professionals, traders and bankers would soon be known by a new word. In 1984 the term 'yuppie' was only beginning to enter the mainstream in the UK, although it rapidly became the catch-all nomenclature for young City workers, advertising executives, people wearing red braces, London estate agents or anyone who seemed to be suddenly earning a great deal of money and spending it ostentatiously on German cars, champagne and property. The yuppie as a species (meaning young urban professional) was first identified in the US in 1980 by Dan Rottenberg, an American journalist, writing a feature for *Chicago* magazine about the phenomenon of urban regeneration.[9] He noticed that affluent young professionals were declining to follow their predecessors to the suburbs, choosing instead to reclaim run-down but potentially valuable properties in the city. They sought urban excitement and were prepared, in numbers, to take over and renovate entire neighbourhoods. Yuppie was a good nickname that evoked an obvious contrast with the dazed, anti-materialistic ethos of the late 1960s and early 1970s hippie. A fair few yuppies in the US had been hippies first, before they got jobs and joined banks, or brokerages, or became architects or media executives.

In London, the word took on different class-based connotations, until there was confusion. Were City yuppies *arrivistes* or aristos on the make? The caricatures would overlap and by the middle of the decade it was a reliable, easy standby for any television news crew looking for a way to illustrate a package for the evening news about class, or the north–south divide, or the decline of manufacturing, to find a City wine bar and film the shenanigans. After hours it was not difficult to find people laughing and drinking champagne. Inevitably, their brighter colleagues declined to say anything. But some of the bolder and brasher types were prepared to burble on camera about how much money there was to be made.

This was one of the curious aspects of the period. On the one hand the smorgasbord of opportunity lent itself to largesse, celebration and intoxication, either to cope with the excitement or to come down afterwards. 'Some of my colleagues, not all, some, were coked up pretty much continuously,' is how one wealthy veteran, then a trader, remembers it. Simultaneously, it produced a shift to seriousness as the hours started to get longer in preparation for Big Bang and the need for a clear head when handling ever-bigger numbers became obvious. For that reason lunch had had it, or at least the old-school alcohol-fuelled lunch was on the way out. Not everyone drank pre-Big Bang, of course. David Mayhew, of Cazenove, decided in the 1970s that he would forgo alcohol during the working day in favour of clarity. But abstinence was not the norm. John Craven recalled lunches in Hambros' partners room before the 1980s: 'Partners would drift in and out. There was wine and port and no business talked at all. It was the atmosphere of a languid country-house lunch on a Sunday.'[10]

The old-school British moneymen already had long had a reputation among their American cousins for laziness, and those late starts and languid lunches were the nub of it. Never has the different meaning attached on either side of the Atlantic to the word 'pissed' mattered more. American firms pushing into London were not going to be very pleased – they would be pissed – if their staff went native and got pissed at lunchtime. Some Americans attempted to try the London way of lunching, although their efforts seem to have been driven as much by an anthropological interest in meeting the pickled specimens of the old City. Who really wanted to be 'out to lunch' when the office in New York rang demanding to know about a deal or a trade? When it was lunchtime in London the day was only kicking off on Wall Street five hours behind.

But that is not to imply the Americans were dull. Robert L. Hamburger had first arrived in 1971 with Chase, spending time in London and Rome, where in two years he dealt with the Vatican's account and while playing golf with the priest who ran the Vatican Bank said he learnt more about banking then than in the other forty years of his career combined. 'The American banker called Bob Hamburger. You couldn't make it up,' says one of the leading figures in London investment banking. Hamburger joined Goldman Sachs in 1979 and was part of the team in the 1980s that turned the institution from Goldman Who? – in London terms – into an investment banking behemoth. He later set up on his own as an advisor in M&A, bought a racehorse and subsequently published a number of erotic novels, including *Angels and Felons* and *My Saucy Wife*. There were many things that leading bankers or stockbrokers in London did pre-Big Bang, but writing erotic novels was not high on the list.

The adjustment to a more aggressive American approach was tricky for the Brits. Philippa Rose's clients who were placed with US banks in London could scarcely believe the difference in ruthlessness. They were shocked by how different the mentality was: 'The Americans were all about the deal. The British were about trying to offer the best advice. The Americans were "bugger that" we want the money.' A leading gilt-edged market maker of the period was most unimpressed with what he encountered: 'The morality – or the lack of it – of the American investment banks had to be seen to be believed. It was disgusting.' But the Americans did not arrive fully formed. As David Mayhew saw it, the Americans were still learning about the London outlook and the different attitude to risk. Although the Brits might have seemed more laconic and laid back, they were used to being a little more free-wheeling and unsupervised in their dealings. Unlike the Americans, the Brits were not – yet – locked in by the bureaucracy of risk managers and compliance people with which US banks and brokerages were well stocked, because so much American business was regulated by law, a legacy of public disgust over the Great Crash of 1929. The Brits, used to self-regulation and some insider trading masquerading as wisdom, liked risk more than they let on. And while all the chatter was of London needing an injection of American dynamism, where had the Eurobond market come from anyway? Not Wall Street. One of the single most important innovations in the markets in the second half of the twentieth century, which had mushroomed into an international multi-trillion dollar business, came from London in the 1960s. It had not happened within the Stock Exchange, of course, which added to the sense that Nicholas Goodison's colleagues had rather missed an opportunity. Now, the stockbrokers and jobbers had to get on and catch up.

At the Stock Exchange, Nicholas Goodison and his colleagues knew they did not have the luxury of time. What had sounded in July 1983 like a long-distant date – the three-year deadline for reform – was racing in. At the same time, a switch to screen-based trading was planned, moving trading from the traditional floor of the exchange face to face towards traders using the prices on their screen and buying and selling by telephone. George Hayter, head of the Exchange's information services division, and his team were trying to build something that could cope with the anticipated enormous increase in trading volumes. The original intention had been to start afresh, and construct a bespoke computer system. In 1984, Hayter explained why that would not be possible. 'There is a wide river to be crossed and time only to build a Bailey Bridge,' he said in a reference to the temporary structures favoured by Allied engineers in the Second World War.[11]

There would also be a D-Day, it was decided by the Stock Exchange Council: a single day, an appointed hour in 1986, on which it would all happen, rather than the switch to screen-based trading being phased in. Who first uttered the phrase Big Bang to describe it, in the context of the City rather than physics? Some credit Martin Jacomb (of Kleinwort Benson, a director of the Bank of England and later a director of Barclays). David Walker of the Bank of England thinks it was Douglas Dawkins at the Bank of England who first said: 'This is a cosmological event, a Big Bang.'

Either way it was agreed that it was best to do it all at once and create an impact. The wider financial revolution was also, if truth be told, already underway. The Thatcher government needed the City's help to implement what had grown from being a vague aspiration in opposition into a full-scale privatisation programme. And that meant shifting a lot of shares. In the summer of 1982 the government had announced its intention to sell British Telecommunications in 1984. The City had the venue, the expertise, the interest from American investors and the ability to move large amounts of capital in and out of the country since the abolition of exchange controls. The government had state-owned industries and billions of pounds in assets that it was ideologically committed to selling. Together, Thatcher's ministers, the merchant banks, stockbrokers and advertising agencies were about to push through some of the biggest sell-offs in the history of capitalism, in the process transforming the structure of the British economy and executing a manoeuvre that would be copied around the world.

OPPORTUNITIES

'If you see Sid . . . Tell him!'
Advert promoting the sale of British Gas shares to the public

Once it became clear that Mrs Thatcher's plans were going to be aligned with the interests of the dealmakers in the Square Mile, the scepticism among parts of the City's elite began to fade. The tricky negotiations on the future of the Stock Exchange were one thing, and Thatcher the outsider had needed to be assured in 1983 by her Chancellor Nigel Lawson that the agreement with Goodison and the Stock Exchange was not a stitch-up perpetrated by an old-boy network. But the Stock Exchange was not the City; the Exchange was one element, albeit an important element, of a much larger financial machine that the government needed to access. The Tories now required its help to implement one of the most daring and transformative programmes of the era, namely the privatisation of large parts of British industry and infrastructure.

Since the nationalisations undertaken during and shortly after the Second World War, the government on behalf of the taxpayer owned Britain's largest oil company, the airports, the national airline, a national steel company, gas, water, the telecommunications monopoly, British Rail, and much more besides. The workforce of the nationalised industries in the early 1980s was an astonishing 1.75m strong and between them they produced 10 per cent of national output. Several governments since the 1950s had attempted sell-offs, and there was limited denationalisation and then renationalisation, but state ownership seemed to be a fixed feature of the British landscape. A handful of Liberals and a few Conservatives explained that this was unhealthy. Despite David Howell MP, the future father in-law of Chancellor George Osborne, penning a Conservative pamphlet in 1970 in which the term 'privatisation' was first used, it remained a remote aspiration. The Heath government's subsequent failure all but killed off such thinking for a while and amid economic chaos Heath partly nationalised the air engine company Rolls-Royce and assorted shipyards. In 1975, following the return of Harold Wilson to Number 10 the previous year, the government had even acquired the controlling share of a large and broken-down car manufacturer in the form of British Leyland. The company rapidly became a byword for British decline. When the Prime Minister James Callaghan needed new official cars, two Rovers 3.5 were ordered from the company. Once thirty-four mechanical faults had been fixed and the cars had been made bomb-proof they were ready for Callaghan's use on official business. His advisor, Bernard Donoughue, recorded in his diary what happened when one of the cars was taken for a spin in the summer of 1978: 'He [the Prime Minister] decided to open the window for some fresh air and pressed the button which does this electronically. The result was that the window immediately fell in on his lap.'[1] Callaghan and his broken car window symbolise perfectly a late 1970s creeping national decrepitude that Thatcher was determined to address.

Despite the shortcomings, to many on the Left the continued existence of nationalised industries was a matter of pride, reflecting the dominance of collectivist thinking and the noble elevation of fuller employment above efficiency and the profit motive. To the small group of Thatcherites who won control of the Tory Party in 1975, excessive state ownership of industry was instinctively an abomination, a manifestation of government control giving customers a poor deal and hampering competition, investment and innovation. That said, they did not know how, exactly, to proceed. The first Thatcher administration arrived in office without a fully worked plan in May 1979, and during the run-up to the general election when Thatcher's shadow cabinet discussed the possibility of 'denationalisation' it was agreed not to make their early thinking public. Once in office, senior figures in the government, the Chancellor Geoffrey Howe and a handful of other ministers including Howell at Energy, John Nott at Trade, Keith Joseph, and Nigel Lawson working for Howe at the Treasury, were determined to push forward on the subject from the start.

Another much more junior but significant figure in the development of what became mass privatisation, someone who pushed the idea in Thatcherite circles, was John Redwood, then working in the City. While Redwood was academically highly gifted – a fellow of Oxford's All Souls no less – it is fair to say that he is not famed for his social skills. That other-worldly awkwardness gave him a remorselessly logical way of looking at the world that would later earn him the newspaper nickname of Spock. But it did give Redwood an advantage in one important regard, in that he did not care for convention. If the nationalised industries were unprofitable, creaking under the weight of their bureaucratic inefficiency, bedevilled by catastrophically poor industrial relations, then why not admit it clearly and sell them back into the private sector? That was the central premise of his influential book – a long forgotten text that endeared him to the Thatcherites – published in November 1980. In *Public Enterprise in Crisis: The Future of Nationalised Industries*, Redwood mapped out the beginning of a way to return such industries to the public sector by selling them, via the City. The Redwood link was important because he was at the merchant bank N.M. Rothschild, the bank that Thatcher had dismissed as 'that red bank' when she got a hard time during lunch there in 1975. That moment of awkwardness now forgotten, N.M. Rothschild would eventually become one of the institutions handling privatisations for Thatcher.

As it became apparent that Thatcher's ministers were serious about the scale of what was going to be attempted, the merchant banks and Stock Exchange firms readied themselves to assist. In that regard, N.M. Rothschild had several advantages. Not only was young Redwood – more Thatcherite than Thatcher – an evangelist for the privatisation message; more importantly, Evelyn Rothschild, the kingpin of the institution since his cousin Jacob had left N.M. Rothschild in a dispute over strategy in 1980, had hired the highly experienced and well-connected Michael Richardson from Cazenove the following year. Richardson had a direct Thatcher connection in that their sons had been at Harrow at the same time. His appointment was described by David Scholey at Warburg as the worst news he had received all year, because he knew it would bring Rothschild so much business.

With his charm and willingness to deal with some questionable figures such as the crooked media tycoon Robert Maxwell, Richardson was made for the high pomp of 1980s deal making. The City was the family business – insurance in his father's case – and when Michael bailed out of Cambridge after a few months he had gravitated towards money and markets, forging a career at Panmure Gordon in the 1960s, where he first represented Maxwell. That association led to him being ostracised when Maxwell's shady dealings over Pergamon were condemned to such an extent that Maxwell was judged famously in a Board of Trade inquiry as 'not a fit and proper person' to run a public company. The Maxwell connection did not put off Cazenove from hiring Richardson, and he was there until 1981 when he failed to make senior partner. Evelyn Rothschild swooped and offered him the post of Managing Director at N.M. Rothschild. Richardson was, according to Nigel Lawson, at first sight too suave and smooth to be true[2], but his courtesy and good manners made him an exemplary networker in business and politics, someone skilled in bringing in new business at just the right moment with the Thatcherites in the ascendency.

Not everyone in the City was impressed with Thatcher and anxious to assist. David Montagu, Baron Swaythling, was so appalled by the behaviour he witnessed at a meeting, and her rude treatment of officials and colleagues, that he declared he would have nothing more to do with her. At Cazenove there had always been more enthusiasm for Thatcher. Indeed, the firm had on the quiet helped finance her office in opposition when she was finding it difficult to raise funds. There was much enthusiasm for what she was attempting to achieve. David Mayhew, a rising star and future senior partner, felt that complacent old Britain was a poor country sinking into bedraggled irrelevance. Opening up the City to new capital and foreign investment and privatising the state-owned industries would, he was convinced, give the UK a chance of reinventing itself.

The great 1980s state sell-off began small. Initial minor steps towards what was then known only as asset disposal were taken in Howe's first Budget in 1979 in which £1bn of asset sales were announced. Thatcher also established a small cabinet committee to prepare more state enterprises for sale. Lawson emphasised the direction in a lecture in 1980 in which he identified British Airways as being among the first candidates, although only a small number of ministers were enthusiastic. Even the then head of the Number 10 Policy Unit – John Hoskyns – did not press the case initially, despite his reputation for bold thinking. The British Airways sale was eventually postponed until much later, because the airline was embroiled in a tricky legal case[3], but when Lawson was appointed Energy Secretary in the autumn of 1981, replacing Howell, he pushed through a number of sales. On 19 October it was announced that the government planned to sell its share in the oil-producing parts of British Gas and BNOC. Already the idea was germinating that Britain's entire electricity and gas industries should be sold off when the time was right.

None of this, even enthusiasts such as Lawson admitted later, was initially popular with the British public. Throughout, the *Daily Mirror* referred to it as 'the great Tory sell-off', and not in a flattering way. It did not help that two of the early, smaller sales went badly off course in different ways. The government-owned Amersham International, selling medical and industrial research radioactive isotopes, was sold too cheaply in 1982. N.M Rothschild and Morgan Grenfell were the advisors to the government and the company, and the low price meant there was a rush for shares – meaning they were over-subscribed. On the first day the shares traded at 40p above their offer price of 142p, leaving a rather large profit for investors at the public expense. The extent of the mistake compelled a horrified Lawson to hold an inquiry. Critics said that state assets theoretically owned by all were being sold off to investors too cheaply by the City. Such concerns would be highlighted relentlessly by the opposition parties and internal Tory opponents from the rival wing of the Conservative Party who saw the Thatcherites as reckless radicals prepared to risk national division in pursuit of ideological aims. When it came to the next sale – the much bigger Britoil – Lawson vowed to avoid a repeat of the poor publicity around Amersham, and the offer was under-subscribed.

It is not difficult to work out why these privatisations mattered so much to the generation of City leaders at banks such as Warburg, Rothschild, Kleinwort Benson and Cazenove. The government selling its stakes meant work, prestige and fees. The government would select City advisors, sometimes more than one merchant bank, to help it construct the business case, arrive at a valuation and handle the sale. Together a number could underwrite the offer for fees. They could also sub-underwrite the shares to hundreds of smaller City firms, dispersing the shares via the jobbers. There was another benefit. Even if they did not get such work themselves, it might help to generate a rising market, increased volumes and a sense of possibility and expansion. Rising optimism was certainly apparent in late 1982 and 1983. In Debbie Moore, the entrepreneur behind the dance studios and clothing line Pineapple, the Stock Exchange had its first ever woman to head a company being floated, on the smaller market (USM, the Unsecuritised Market). On the day itself in November 1982, Moore was pictured standing in the middle of the Stock Exchange floor, hands on hips, looking like the embodiment of go-getting early 1980s culture. Around her stood a crowd of mostly male workers and jobbers, surveying the scene and not looking entirely comfortable. Her success only ten years after women had first even been allowed on the floor itself was a vivid example of how much had changed. Here was an entrepreneur floating her own company, and in the 'leisure' and fitness business too, a type of activity that was emblematic of the self-improvement decade.

There were other advances for women. On 1 January 1983, Mary Baker became the first ever female member of the board of Barclays

Bank. In early 1983, the Unit Trust Association also got its first female chairman in Audrey Head of Hill Samuel. Unit trusts are a simple form of investment in which bundles of investments are bought from a money manager, with the hope that the manager can outperform the market in boom and bust. Their spread – there were 500 of them on sale from various companies by early 1983 – was more evidence that smaller investors were playing the expanding market. But what hooked the newspapers were the racier initiatives that had a populist twist, which might easily communicate this strange new world of investment and shares for a new generation of everyday customers, turning what was previously a minority sport into a mainstream concern. That year – in 1983 – even a football club, Tottenham Hotspur, tried floating itself, though in typical Spurs style it missed. Unimpressed investors sat on the touchline.

The privatisation of British Telecom was on an entirely different scale, however. Since the announcement in early 1982 that the government would sell more than half of the state-run company, it had been the prospect that most excited and worried the City, and for a while it looked as though nervousness about the scale of the task might make Thatcher proceed carefully, in stages. Government ministers such as Nigel Lawson venturing into the City encountered scepticism that it could be done, or certainly not in one go, because the amount of shares being sold – in the region of £4bn (the equivalent of at least £15bn thirty years later) – was so vast. If the offer was mismanaged, or priced too high leaving a shortage of buyers, or excessively low meaning investors got too much of a bargain at the taxpayers' expense, then the privatisation programme could be discredited as a racket benefiting the friends of the Tories. If it flopped it would be said that the entire concept of getting the state out of industry was doomed.

The job of ensuring the sale did not turn into a disaster fell to Martin Jacomb of Kleinwort Benson. He was assisted on BT by colleagues including David Clementi and James Rockley. This group was relatively unusual in believing that – at a push – the sale could be managed in one go, which helped win them the mandate in 1984.

Jacomb's family background was not in merchant banking and he had fallen into it almost by accident in the late 1960s through connections. After Eton, Oxford and National Service in the Far East he tried working for his father's wool-broking business in the City and found it insufferably dull. He tried the law (and in his spare time wrote about tax for the *Financial Times*, where he first formed a friendship with Nigel Lawson). Then, on holiday with Sir Cyril Kleinwort, he was asked to join Kleinwort Benson and liked the sound of learning to be a banker. Now, in the mid-1980s, one of the showpiece projects of the Thatcher era was in his hands. That meant he would have to contend with the Prime Minister taking a close interest in the preparations. Indeed, Jacomb and his team were soon treated to the spectacle of the Prime Minister playing what he termed 'cat and mouse' with her ministers (the mice) at regular meetings in Number 10. The problem – and opportunity – was that there would be so many shares that they could not rely on institutional investors such as pension funds and asset managers buying them all. They needed the public in large numbers to buy the shares too, along with some foreign investors. Here the interests of Thatcher's ministers, seeking to spread the notion of wider share ownership, were perfectly in tune with the interests of the City as organiser of the sale and distributor of the shares.

The general election landslide over Labour in 1983 emboldened Thatcher and her supporters, and while she was not yet in the period in which she would succumb to hubris, she did have command of the field. Her traditionalist Tory critics – the Wets – had largely been bested, and there were a greater number of reformist ministers in place who endorsed her approach to transforming Britain's standing and shrinking the size of the state. In 1984 they were not only engaged in a titanic struggle with the striking miners, designed to break the trade unions; Lawson, as Chancellor, was also redesigning the taxation system to encourage wealth creation. On the other side of the Atlantic Ronald Reagan was heading for re-election on the back of a booming Wall Street, economic rebirth and a recovery of national confidence. History was flowing in a free market direction.

*Cowboys and angels: President Ronald Reagan at the
New York Stock Exchange, March 1985.*

In the UK, that sale of British Telecom was the testing ground for an entire philosophy, of popular capitalism: the idea that the benefits of the market if properly brought to bear can increase prosperity and spread it widely. Ownership, the idea of a stake for the many rather than a narrow elite, appealed to Thatcher the Methodist and grocer's daughter almost as much as it suited her political aim to build a constituency of small investors who would not want the Left let back in to take what they had earned and accumulated. An advertising campaign managed to translate those populist instincts into marketing material that talked directly to Thatcher's people – the aspirational voters who had given her such a large parliamentary majority in 1983 – by creating the notion of scarcity and a rush for shares, an approach used even more blatantly in the later British Gas privatisation. For BT, along with the TV advertising blitz, much effort was put into wooing the press in the hope that if the sale was written about in a positive manner then the readers would apply for shares. At a press conference for several hundred hacks, the privatisation was duly carefully explained and it was stressed that the price would be low enough to make the shares attractive to the individual investor.

On the nuts and bolts of the deal, Jacomb and his team ran the operation from a 'war room' at Kleinwort Benson and talked of D-Day or Impact Day. On D-Day minus one, Lawson and Jacomb met in private at the Treasury to set the price, and on 16 November 1984 it was announced that more than three million shares would be sold at an offer price of 130p, bringing in almost £4bn for the government. In another sign that bankers were learning how to utilise the techniques and showmanship of another 1980s boom-time business – advertising – the price was unveiled with the dropping of a giant banner outside the Kleinwort Benson office. Jacomb's team then had a nerve-wracking wait of several days to find out how many Britons, by sending in their applications to the operation located in warehouse outside London that Kleinwort Benson had hired for the processing of applications, had applied for shares.

The British Telecom sale was certainly ground-breaking in its ambition and success. Nothing like it had ever been attempted, anywhere. Such was the rush for shares that the issue was five times over-subscribed and 96 per cent of British Telecom staff who were eligible became shareholders in their own company. The British public had 39 per cent of the shares. Inevitably, some sold them almost straight away, taking the profit when the price rose. To critics this was 'get rich quick' capitalism in action, with publicly owned assets transferred to large institutional investors who could sell them to whoever they liked, even foreign investors. These concerns of short-termism dominated Labour criticisms of the programme, and the former Prime Minister, the Earl of Stockton, Harold Macmillan, famously in November 1984 criticised the privatisation programme. It was dubbed the 'selling off the family silver' speech by the press, although the former Prime Minister did not use that precise phrase.[4] It was a wounding attack by Macmillan, who for all his dexterity with a soundbite turned out to be wrong. Telecoms privatisation was a spur to future investment. One only needs to consider how a monopoly provider, owned by the government, would have coped with the subsequent emergence of the mobile phone and rapid innovation, to see that the UK's state-run model was best ended.

With shares and privatisation attracting all the scrutiny, another market boomed but got a lot less attention. Although the sums involved in the fast-expanding Eurobond debt markets were enormous, this was not a market whose existence was widely publicised outside the pages of the *Financial Times* and publications such as *Euromoney*. In 1985, turnover in the Eurobond market, dominated by London, was more than $1.5 trillion. This was the way of doing business that had been started by Warburg little more than two decades previously with a $15m transaction. Yet when compared to what was happening on the other side of the Atlantic, even the booming Eurobond market of the mid-1980s seems in retrospect rather orderly and British. In the stock market, Wall Street had a head start because of May Day 1975, when fixed commissions were scrapped. Just as important was the cut (28 per cent to 20 per cent) in capital gains tax made in 1981 by a Republican administration keen to encourage investors to take bigger risks which might grow the economy. By the mid-1980s, the US was well into a sustained outbreak of merger and acquisition mania that made all that had gone before seem somewhat sedate. The specialist firms of private investors – venture capitalists and private equity funds – had only really become significant following the seeding of the early growth of Silicon Valley in the 1970s, but the expanding volumes, availability of credit and favourable tax environment meant that they were able to undertake steadily bigger and bolder deals. The US investment banks had an obvious interest in these developments as potential advisors either to the target company or to the prospective buyer. These were also not necessarily corporate takeovers either, in which one established firm bought a competitor in the same field. It tended to be a firm of financial specialists buying an established manufacturing company, and deploying projected profits to pay the interest while the buyer put in very little money and set about restructuring or breaking up the purchase into sellable portions. Defenders saw private equity as unlocking value that had been hitherto unnoticed, which might then be invested to better use elsewhere in new investments. For critics, it was pure financial engineering that piled debts on previously healthy companies and caused factories to close. The era culminated with the leading private equity firm Kohlberg Kravis Roberts paying a then unfathomable $25bn for RJR Nabisco, a food and tobacco company in 1988. That year there were ninety-seven billion dollars' worth of leveraged buyouts in the US, when just eight years earlier only a couple of billion dollars had been involved. As the size of these markets and deals increased, the fortunes to be made obviously became commensurately bigger. It would be odd then, considering the lessons of financial history going back to the South Sea Bubble and the fall of France under John Law, if this excitement did not produce in some a change in behaviour and ethical attitudes.

Like all such previous booms, the M&A boom created new heroes, and in time villains, whose rise this time symbolised the spirit of buccaneering 1980s capitalism. In Michael Milken of Drexel

Burnham Lambert the movement had its marauding monarch. So valuable was the highly intelligent Milken's 'junk bond' unit to his Wall Street firm that the management allowed him in the late 1970s to take it to the West Coast, for family reasons, from where he and his small team perfected their new approach. Junk in this case did not mean worthless, it was the term given in the 1980s to the lower-graded bonds of many smaller companies that Milken argued were actually under-priced, and would eventually produce as good a return as those of blue-chip stocks. Milken not only convinced traditional US Savings & Loan companies to stuff their portfolios with his 'junk bonds', at the annual 'Predators' Ball', but he and his team also promoted their work as having a higher social purpose. They were enabling those who had until now been unable to access funding to profit.

With a vast new pool of capital swirling around, and bigger profits, the value of inside information about what might be about to happen rose too. An investment banker, if he (usually he) had lax morals or expensive tastes, might find it worth his while to discreetly trade on his own account on information acquired working for a client, depositing any profits in secret offshore accounts. Or he could pass the clandestine information on to other predators, either for profit or for future preferment. It was against this bewildering background that the authorities in London attempted to make sense of the changes that were coming to the capital and to answer questions to which they did not have anything like a clear answer.

With the City on the verge of further growth, bringing the opportunity for fraud as well as for fortune, how might finance be policed?

One of the modern nostalgic myths about the Big Bang era is that immediately before it began there were either no scandals or hardly any wrongdoing. This is demonstrably false. Disgust at the notion of some in the City making out like bandits with other people's money long pre-dated the mid-1980s. In a modern echo of the public outcry over City scandals in the nineteenth century, there were numerous failed attempts made by governments in the 1970s to make insider trading illegal and to crack down on those City workers who used information to make a profit from intelligence that was not publicly available. Insider trading, carrying a potential prison sentence in the event of conviction, was finally made a criminal offence by legislation passed under the Thatcher administration in the early 1980s following a further string of consumer protection scandals. It was later made more explicitly illegal in legislation in 1985. And no wonder. The City of London police in a 1980 report described fraud as the 'growth industry of the 1970s' because it had increased in the Square Mile fivefold in that decade. Between 1980 and the end of 1983, the amount involved in cases under investigation by the fraud squad rose from £30 million to £115 million. That was just what was known about.

In July 1981, ministers and officials at the Department of Trade had been so concerned that the then Secretary of State, John Biffen, appointed Professor Laurence ('Jim') Gower to produce a report. Gower brought to the task a formidable legal brain, a determination to improve consumer protection and a wealth of academic experience. During his war service he had been involved in the planning of D-Day at Wilton House in Wiltshire and he later wrote the essential work on company law. Yet even as he took evidence, a scandal unfolded that transfixed journalists. The revelation in 1981 of fraud in the Manchester stockbroking firm Halliday Simpson led to the exposure of Sir Trevor Dawson, a director of the merchant bank Arbuthnot Latham, who was known in the City and in racing circles as 'the Galloping Major'. His disgrace led indirectly to another City name being bought up and revived by a foreigner. The taint of association with Dawson left the venerable Arbuthnot Latham highly vulnerable and its grandee chairman, Sir John Prideaux, had to accept an offer from Dow Scandia. The Swiss banker Henry Angest, who had landed in London in the 1970s complaining about inedible English food, was one of those who arrived with the new owners. Piece by piece he bought Arbuthnot Latham for Dow Scandia. He then became the owner and rebuilt it as one of the last-remaining distinctly British small banks. In contrast, Dawson did not meet a happy end. Ruined after his role in the Halliday Simpson affair was confirmed by an inquiry, in March 1983 Dawson drank a glass of champagne and then killed himself in his flat in Eaton Square, ensuring that his estranged wife and disabled son would benefit from life insurance policies in his name.

When in 1982 Gower produced his initial findings about how to regulate the City, he was leaning towards recommending the establishment of a tough and independent Securities and Exchange Commission, with subpoena power and teams of investigators on the model that existed in the US. By the time his final report was published early in 1984 he had backed away from favouring that option, and it seemed as though the Department of Trade and Industry – by then run by Norman Tebbit – would have oversight rather than a new independent body or the Bank of England, which was seen as too much a representative of the City to be a potential adjudicator. Even this diluted version of Gower's initial thinking deeply worried some inside Number 10. John Redwood, then the head of the Policy Unit in Number 10, was particularly concerned that it would lead to the government having to assume responsibility for all the 'foibles and problems of the market place'. In a memo to the Prime Minister he described Gower's scheme as 'dangerous'. Redwood was not alone in expressing concerns that Gower was being heavy-handed. Richard Lambert, writing in the *Financial Times* on 13 March 1984, warned of the dangers of group-think. 'From Whitehall to Threadneedle Street everyone seems to have approved the Gower report', he wrote. 'But is it possible that they are utterly, completely, 100 per cent mad?' The proposals would create, in Stani Yassukovich's memorable phrase, 'an alphabet soup of acronyms and regulators' which could, in Lambert's view, prove confusing and unworkable. Thatcher herself was also concerned. When the banker and Thatcher admirer Walter Salomon (who had no connection to Salomon Brothers) gave a speech a few weeks later attacking Gower's recommendations, and sent a copy of it to the Prime Minister with a covering note, she scribbled on it an instruction to the civil servant Andrew Turnbull: 'Andrew, can you let me have a note on the Gower Report. WS is quite possibly right.'

Gower, Salomon said in his speech to his bank's annual general meeting, was a lawyer of 'very high standing and reputation . . . whose chastity has never been broken by any spell of practical experience'. The problem, he said, was that new rules would be a 'haven' for lawyers charging high fees for advice on the regulations. 'Whenever I hear of proposals for "self-regulating" authorities and suchlike I think of the opening remarks of the Prime Minister of Denmark at the World Bank Meeting in Copenhagen,' said Salomon.

> We shall to evolve
> Problem solvers galore –
> Since each problem they solve
> Creates ten problems more.

This was a very Thatcherite epigram, and the Prime Minister liked it so much she marked it with six strokes of the pen. 'Professor Gower's propositions', Salomon continued, 'are from a practical point of view 1) unworkable, 2) interfere with the rights of the freedom of the individual, 3) tremendously costly and 4) will build up a vast bureaucracy.' The risk of constructing a bureaucratic system patrolled by lawyers was that it would reduce the responsibility of the individual to pay attention when they made investments, he said. Salomon was by no means speaking as a typical member of the banking Establishment defending its privileges. He had fought a decades-long battle with the Bank of England, which regarded the German Jew who had arrived in 1938 as unsuitable for recognition in the City, perhaps on account of his direct manner. His outspoken criticisms of the Stock Exchange hardly endeared him to some of his contemporaries either. In any case, Salomon advised Thatcher that Gower's threat to undermine the club mentality of the City and its institutions would have unintended consequences. Her willingness to listen to a figure who stood outside the elite and advocated increased competition was another example of her being drawn to disruptors and rebels, even if for once he was resisting change.

This row about how to regulate finance would not be resolved quickly, and the Gower Report duly disappeared into the Whitehall machine. As Big Bang neared, a battle would be fought between assorted parts of government, the Bank of England and the various vested interests of the City over where exactly power and control should lie. All the while, the Labour opposition accused the Conservatives of favouring their friends. When Tebbit made a statement on 16 July 1984 about Gower, the Labour front-bench spokesman Bryan Gould demanded that the government go further on regulation to deal with wrongdoing.

What is remarkable though is that this period is still portrayed almost exclusively as an era of evaporating regulation. Of course there was the deregulation of Britain's building societies, when they were allowed from 1986 to compete fully with banks and demutualise, and the looming Big Bang opened up the Stock Exchange to competition, but the run-up to Big Bang was characterised by the introduction of regulation, or what is termed re-regulation, to markets that had previously operated with a club mentality. As the academic Steven Vogel put it: 'The gentlemen's luncheon was replaced by the power breakfast, civilised rivalry was replaced by cutthroat competition; and discrete self-regulation was replaced by a nightmare from America: the proliferation of regulatory bodies, the endless creation of rules, and an invasion of lawyers.'[5] On that point of a profusion of lawyers, one of the most senior City figures of the period gets right to the heart of it three decades later: 'The most significant American import was not the longer hours or even the bonuses. It was the importation of the American approach to regulation and law. It is a country built on law, with a strictly legalistic way of looking at decision making.' As America's second President, John Adams, described it, what should prevail is 'a government of laws and not of men'.

In contrast, the traditional City self-regulatory approach until 1986 was distinctively English. Although it was imperfect it did rest on a fixation with reputation, a fear of exclusion by the tribe, and greater room for consideration of whether a questionable action was ethically acceptable as opposed to simply within the rules that were written down and punishable in the event of an infraction. The shift in the City to the American way produced a complete culture change that is still not much understood, even though it was by far the most consequential part of the process. The old system in London appeared to be entirely rules-based but it was British in that it allowed for a considerable amount of personal discretion and moral suasion. Says a leading British banker: 'With the Americans came the idea that if something is legal then it is OK or right. That became the simple test: legal or illegal. The thought processes required are really quite different. That was what changed. That was the real revolution.'

Add to that the rapid ongoing destruction of the partnership structure in the mid-1980s, as jobbers and brokers were bought over, and experienced, older hands departed newly rich with their share of the proceeds to acquire estates in the Home Counties or châteaux in France. Stani Yassukovich was one of those who watched in horror as, along with the timeservers, the City was emptied of many of the newly wealthy and smarter partners who knew how the place worked.

At that crucial moment, with the City being re-regulated and reimagined, the Prime Minister was conflicted in one other respect. She was a tremendous fan of swashbuckling tycoons such as James Hanson, the canny corporate raider who built a business empire out of tapping the banks and markets and then restructuring and selling on businesses. Hanson was given a peerage in 1983. The billionaire James Goldsmith was a more intellectually complicated character, in that he began the period believing in the vision of open markets and transcontinental globalisation, but as the decade wore on he became increasingly sceptical and concerned about the risks to democracy and national identity. These tycoons were glamorous figures, who because they were buying up businesses abroad were worthy of celebration in Thatcherite terms. As Hanson's adverts put it, his was a company from over here doing rather well over there, a message that echoed the Prime Minister's rhetoric of national rejuvenation. But further down the batting order, others of questionable quality were emerging who were keen to become the next great tycoons. The Cypriot tycoon Asil Nadir became a City sensation with Polly Peck, a small textile company he used as a vehicle to acquire all manner of interests. The unlikely Polly Peck for a while became a FTSE 100 company, and its eventual fall would besmirch those politicians who had befriended him.

The other side of Thatcherite dynamism it seemed was dodginess and wide-boy sharp practice. This was reflected in television and popular music when the Thatcherite ethos was attacked in a manner that would only intensify post-Big Bang. The writers of Britain's most popular television comedy of the decade – *Only Fools and Horses* – affectionately celebrated the market-trader ethos and the sense of community in a working-class London neighbourhood. First screened in 1981, by the mid-1980s it was at the peak of its popularity, with a loveable hero – Derek 'Del Boy' Trotter – defined by dubious practices and shady dealings, even if he retained a strong devotion to family. Underneath the laughter, it looked like a hymn to self-reliance and corner cutting. Everyone is only out for themselves and their mates, seemed to be the message. As the old Fleet Street joke goes: Ethics is a county to the northeast of London.

There was a counterpoint though in Band Aid in December 1984 and Live Aid the following summer, when pop and rock stars on both sides of the Atlantic played a day-long concert – creating a 'global jukebox' – to raise funds to tackle the famine in Ethiopia. For all the pious self-congratulation of some of those involved, the ringmaster Bob Geldof's insight was astute. Rock concerts to raise funds for charity were not new. George Harrison put on his concert in New York for Bangladesh in 1971, and American television had long featured 'telethons'. But Geldof and his team fused satellite technology, the techniques of London's thriving advertising industry and the glamour of the international rock elite, to blur borders and turn globalised charity into a media phenomenon. If

Thatcher and members of her government seemed bemused by these developments, and by the outpouring of donations and public enthusiasm, it fed into the developing narrative that the Thatcherites – with their privatisations and enthusiasm for growing the City – were hard-edged, uncaring and only interested in money. In time, in both the US with the election of Bill Clinton and later with the emergence of New Labour in the UK, that crude caricature would become immensely powerful. In Britain, developments in the City, and in the newly privatised utilities where management salaries started to surge, were cited by Labour as evidence of what was going wrong.

Sometimes those helping themselves to more money really didn't help themselves in terms of public perceptions. The screening in 1986 of a documentary called 'The Fishing Party' in the BBC's 40 *Minutes* series involved four enthusiastic advocates of Thatcherism being done up like kippers. Their prattling was intercut with radio reports of famines, poverty and mass unemployment. The four were filmed at work in the City, at home and in Scotland fishing and shooting seagulls. As they did this they offered their views on class, politics, capital punishment, Africa, badly behaved children, public schools, marriage, money, privilege and police brutality ('stuff a grenade up his arse!'). None of this made for particularly sympathetic viewing and 'The Fishing Party' stands as a case study in why it is best never to agree to appear in a fly on the wall television documentary.

A reviewer concluded: 'Any left-wing playwright would be hard pressed to come up with a juicier collection of right-wing nitwits.' The four became, for a while, public hate figures and symbols of the arrogance and excess that critics of Thatcherism blamed on her policies. 'We were young, foolish, opinionated and should never have done it. But that's no excuse,' said Guy Cheyney, one of the participants, years later. They had been stitched up but they should have known better. One commodity broker who was invited on the fishing trip, but luckily for him was too busy to attend, was a young Nigel Farage.

The social distinctions and gradations could be confusing. Those who needed a guide to the demarcations on London's social battlefield could refer to the *Official Sloane Rangers Handbook* as a starting point. The bestseller, written by Peter York and Ann Barr, published in 1982, stemmed from a feature that ran in *Harpers & Queen* in 1975. The *Handbook* was a work of anthropological genius, identifying and affectionately lampooning the tastes and attitudes of the young upper-middle-class (aspiring to be aristocratic) tribe that resided in Chelsea and Fulham and regarded the television adaptation of *Brideshead Revisited* (1981) as an instruction manual. By the early 1980s the Sloanes had an undisputed leader in Diana Spencer, an aristocrat who married a Windsor and became the Princess of Wales. The yuppie was a more brazenly ruthless American import that arrived when the market took off in 1983–84, and could be found too in advertising and parts of the media, although there were clearly elements of overlap in Sloane and yuppie dress and behaviour. Those Sloanes or their partners who worked in the City and bought well in Chelsea or Fulham at the right moment had the best of both worlds, however. They could use the money earned in the thrusting Square Mile to recreate their English idyll by buying a country home for weekends and decorating it from Laura Ashley. The price of country houses along the M4, the motorway into London, began to rise sharply. Of course, many City workers played no part in the game playing and style wars; they were too busy getting on with their work and adjusting to earlier commutes. At a firm such as Smith New Court, the morning meeting for analysts and other key staff was shifted forward to 8.15am, meaning they had to be in long before 8am to prepare. For those who lived in the country it meant that the long journey to work started at 5am. The need for a week-time London pied à terre – and a bonus to buy it – became greater.

Among the sharpest observers of the Thatcherite tumult was a duo of unlikely pop musicians, the Pet Shop Boys. The singer and lyricist Neil Tennant had been a music journalist, while his inventive musical partner Chris Lowe, on synthesisers and baseball caps, appeared mute. Their 1986 number one single 'West End Girls' explored the theme of ambitious East End boys on the make colliding with upmarket girls from up west. A version of this Thatcherite intermingling was beginning to be enacted during daylight hours in the City, where graduates and aspirational street-wise traders worked and socialised alongside each other. In an earlier song 'Opportunities (Let's Make Lots of Money)' – first released in 1984, but re-mixed and re-released later – the band created an ironic anti-Thatcherite anthem.

It was as though almost everywhere you looked in London, and the wider southeast of England, across the classes, ambition and money itself was breaking free of its constraints, and not just in terms of the transactions arranged by entrepreneurs, companies, banks, traders, small business owners and market traders pushing knock-off Sergio Tacchini trainers. In dress, mores and willingness to talk about wealth, for those intimately involved it was an intoxicating moment of liberation. For those not invited, it looked rather different. Soon this style revolution would also acquire an architectural emblem fifty storeys high. In the east, three miles from the traditional City boundaries, a rival wrought in concrete and glass on London's docks was being planned by one of the leading Eurobond practitioners and his property consultant, an American by the name of Gooch Ware Travelstead.

WALL STREET ON THE WATER

'The place was a tip: 6000 acres of forgotten wasteland.'

Michael Heseltine

Gooch Ware Travelstead had an idea. In early 1985, the American property developer stood at the wharf-side of one of London's docks with Michael von Clemm, chairman of Credit Suisse First Boston's London operation. In front of them in London's East End lay the empty Canary Wharf warehouses where for decades fruit from the Canary Islands had been unloaded. 'That's big enough to take a trading floor?' asked von Clemm. Sure it is, responded Travelstead. There was certainly plenty of space and the government was in the middle of trying to redevelop the docklands area, although it was not sure how exactly, or what bigger businesses would consider moving there. You could certainly construct a trading floor, said Travelstead, but the problem was you would never get the traders to agree to move out of the Square Mile on their own, leaving behind their friends and their favourite pubs. The only way to make it work would be to move the entire Credit Suisse First Boston (CSFB) operation – the back office, the admin staff and the traders – into one big building, a tower, right there at Canary Wharf and encourage a few other banks to join in. It would be an exciting alternative to the traditional City, or at least an adjunct of it outside the ancient boundaries controlled by the City of London Corporation. Everybody needed space, Travelstead said. The pair got back into the car and agreed that with Big Bang coming they could create something here.

Thirty years later, what they envisaged and set about building has become a symbol of the power of cross-border capitalism and then, after the crisis of 2008, the striking backdrop for thousands of media graphics illustrating what went wrong with big banks. But that Canary Wharf exists at all is in large part due to Travelstead's vision. In 1985 the Kentucky-born and Baltimore-raised advisor had flown to London to help von Clemm find modern office space for expansion in preparation for Big Bang. Travelstead was a natural entrepreneur who had studied architecture at college and gone into the business of developing commercial real estate in Manhattan. He loved buildings and as the property advisor to the US bank First Boston he recommended to the group where to buy and what to build. With space in short supply in the City, von Clemm needed to locate an office in London large enough to house a computerised trading floor in the American style. Travelstead, working with his brother, had scoured the City, looking for anything suitable. They thought for a while that they had found the right place, on Lower Thames Street, down at the riverside in the City itself, but they calculated that by the time the necessary permissions were secured from the Corporation it wouldn't be worth it and anyway it probably wouldn't be big enough for what CSFB had in mind. It struck Travelstead immediately that the City of London Corporation had controlled the zoning and politics of the planning regime for too long. It presided over a situation that simply made no sense other than as a monopolistic racket that suited it and its contacts. With finite room within the City, property was expensive, or prices sometimes varied wildly from one side of the street to the other for reasons that were impenetrable to outsiders. Theoretically the foreign banks were told it was possible to keep the facades of listed buildings of the late Victorian and Edwardian period, and then to build new offices behind them, but in practice they were too narrow, and taking on such a project probably meant considerable hassle from planning officials and the press. Why not go somewhere else instead where space was not at a premium? But where?

*Castles in the air: property developer Paul Reichmann and Margaret
Thatcher examine a model of the Docklands redevelopment scheme.*

Travelstead and von Clemm had only considered Canary Wharf
by accident, following an earlier trip the banker had made to
Docklands on behalf of the Roux Brothers, the restauranteurs he
had helped get started in London in 1967 by arranging a loan. After
opening Le Gavroche, Michel and Albert Roux instigated a transformation in taste and quality in the London restaurant trade. In the
mid-1980s they were considering combining all their storage and
basic preparation operations in one spot. As chairman of their business, in addition to his duties at CSFB, von Clemm thought that
Docklands might be a suitable and cheap option, especially considering the rates holiday being offered by the government, available
to any business that might consider opening there. Von Clemm was
certainly one of the most glamorous and assertive figures in high
finance in London in the 1980s, someone who was well known in
banking as an early adopter of the mobile phone after the early
brick-like mobiles were first introduced in the UK (two years after
the US). The devices seemed to sceptical Britons faintly ludicrous
and destined never to catch on. The comedian Ernie Wise was hired

to make what was publicised as the first call in the UK on 1 January 1985, from St Katherine's Dock at a press event, to the Vodafone office in Newbury, which was stationed over a curry restaurant. The early phones cost around £2000 and had a battery life of as much as twenty minutes. Von Clemm was often to be seen with one of these phones clamped to his ear as he kept in touch with deals and market news on the move, in the days when it was enough of a novelty still to be a talking point. He was a highly confident extrovert who had been born into a privileged upbringing on the US east coast, studying anthropology, gaining a doctorate, spending a year living with a tribe in Tanzania and then working for a spell as a reporter on the *Boston Globe* newspaper. Following a move to London he became an early innovator in the Eurobond market in the 1960s at White, Weld, the American bank that was keen to pursue and profit from the possibilities of Warburg's innovation. Later, working with Stani Yassukovich, he originated what were known as Floating Rate Notes, creating a whole new Eurobond market in short-term debt that was tapped by developing economies. His interest in anthropology, says a friend, meant he was perpetually fascinated by tribal behaviour and the motivation of buyers and sellers. He loved to sell new products and when he wanted to push his team he had T-shirts printed with the slogan 'Buy Bonds'. That self-confidence marked him out, and even though his tailoring came from Savile Row, his lively approach stood out in London as decidedly un-English.

Perhaps that super-self-confidence was why he was not to everyone's liking. He twice clashed with John Craven, the boss of Phoenix Securities whose firm was instrumental in the post-Big Bang City. They fell out in 1978 when Craven felt von Clemm and others had negotiated a deal behind his back. Then they clashed over a house when von Clemm told their mutual friend, Charles McVeigh of Salomon, that if he ever planned to sell the Cheyne Walk property owned by McVeigh, he must tell him because he wanted it. McVeigh eventually ended up selling it to Craven instead, leaving von Clemm furious about losing out. It was the house that had once been owned by Sir Cyril Kleinwort, of the Kleinwort family merchant bank. The ownership of the townhouse illustrated the changing fortunes of the City elite, as the Chelsea residence stuffed with art and once owned by an old-school grandee was bought by the young American McVeigh and then sold to Craven, one of the British driving forces behind the Big Bang. At the other end of London, von Clemm's appetite for adventure would have long-lasting consequences. He liked Gooch Ware Travelstead's suggestion of moving the bank's entire London operation lock, stock and barrel to the Isle of Dogs so much that he gave him the go-ahead to try.

The docks that had provided so much employment in London's East End in the nineteenth and twentieth centuries, running from the Port of London beyond Tower Bridge seaward, had been dying slowly since the late 1960s. It was another story of British decline and disinclination to change. The wharves that had once teemed with men, unloading and loading consignments going to and from the British Empire, declined as the docks were blighted by clashes between management and trade unions over pay and technology. Amid those arguments the opportunity to adapt London's port was missed and deeper-water rivals such as Tilbury in Essex were better equipped to cope with the vast container ships that were increasing the amounts that could be shipped around the world. Since the 1970s, ministers and civil servants had talked about regenerating the docklands, and assorted studies were commissioned by the local authorities, resulting in several announcements made with good intentions, although almost nothing happened. This was even though the human need was pressing. Only three and half miles away from the Bank of England and the bustling environs of the Stock Exchange were deprivation, decay and unemployment around the docks on an appalling scale. A government report recorded that between 1978 and 1983 alone, 12,000 jobs were shed. Unemployment among adult males in the area in the early 1980s was estimated to be running at almost 20 per cent and many families had chosen to flee in the previous two decades, resulting in a net loss of 60,000 in the population of Tower Hamlets and 55,000 from Newham. About 100,000 people had left Southwark, south of the river, and in the parts of the boroughs immediately surrounding the docks itself there were just 39,400 residents left, although a larger population lived nearby. Only 5 per cent of the docklands residents owned their own properties and the place had, a government study revealed, few amenities, no proper transport links and not even a decent cinema.

In *The Long Good Friday*, the gritty, grimy, glamorous British gangster cinematic classic released in 1980, some of the best action takes place against this decaying docklands backdrop. Although it was a dramatic representation for the cinema screen, in terms of ambience the film's portrayal of the Isle of Dogs was judged by film critics and those familiar with the place to be absolutely on the money. This was the London of empty docks, rusting cranes, poverty and pubs, supposedly featuring cockney punters who claimed to have known the Kray Twins, even if they hadn't. *The Long Good Friday* was quite prescient too in its depiction of what lay ahead in the 1980s. Even though Margaret Thatcher was not in office when the film was written or shot, the protagonist Harold Shand, played to perfection by a young Bob Hoskins, is a Thatcherite archetype, even if his methods of business would not have been remotely to her liking. In the film, the cockney mobster Shand dreams of redeveloping the West India docks and of building a sports arena there with the help of American mafia contacts he is keen to impress. In this way he hopes to go 'legit' in the decade ahead and graduate from gangsterism to property development, although his schemes are subsequently jeopardised by gangland warfare and the murderous attentions of the IRA.

The task of regenerating the real docklands fell to Reg Ward, a public servant who was even more ambitious for the area than the fictional Harold Shand. As a law-abiding official he faced a similar if less violent problem to that encountered by Shand, in that he needed his schemes to be taken seriously when the idea of redeveloping an area so vast and deprived still sounded outlandish. The extraordinary Ward was one of the pivotal figures in the saga, someone who fizzed restlessly with ideas for schemes and struggled to contain his excitement about the possibilities. Arguably, this made him perfect for a difficult job that might have daunted a figure with a more conventional and dull approach. When he scouted around for potential investors, and invited von Clemm to take a look at the possibilities in Docklands, it started a chain reaction.

Ward, originally from Gloucestershire, was a product of the grammar-school system and as the son of a miner had been the first in his family to go to university. In a string of jobs in the public sector, he earned a reputation for being visionary but sometimes difficult if others failed to implement his bold ideas. He was appointed chief executive of the newly formed London Docklands Development Corporation (LDDC) in 1981, after Ward was said to have impressed an interview panel of civil servants with his rare enthusiasm for the project, which had manifested itself in him spending three days before the interview walking around the deserted docks painting pictures of what it might eventually look like with the application of some innovative thinking and invest-ment.[1] Some daring was just what Michael Heseltine wanted to see in relation to Docklands. The dynamic and ambitious Environment Secretary in the newly elected government led by Thatcher had introduced legislation to establish the LDDC. In his memoirs, Heseltine described what had motivated him to push ahead where other schemes had failed. Flying into London over the East End one day early in his tenure he was appalled by the view of what he termed immense tracts of dereliction and vast expanses of polluted land left behind by modern technology: 'The place was a tip: 6,000 acres of forgotten wasteland.'[2]

The chief executive and his team got down to transforming the wasteland, and despite an early attempt to remove Ward over his unorthodox management style, began planning what to do with eight and half square miles of London. The scheme for a tube or subway system linking the area with the centre of London was deemed too expensive and work got underway on a light railway system instead. Ward suggested building City Airport on the Royal Docks and it was approved. Trees were planted, 10,000 of them in year one, and 60,000 in the first four years, to 'give the impression of action' as the LDDC put it, and to make the place a little more appealing to visiting potential investors who might think, on driving there from central London, that they had arrived in a post-apocalyptic wasteland.[3]

From the beginning, the politics on the ground were poisonous, partly because the Labour Party locally was opposed to the redevelopment on the grounds that developers would benefit too much. More should be done directly to help the locals, it was said. To make matters more complicated, these wrangles took place during the bitter infighting in a Labour Party that had shifted sharply to the left after its defeat by Thatcher. Ward's deputy chairman at the LDDC, Labour's Bob Mellish, had been the MP for Bermondsey since 1950 and in the front-line of Labour's internal wars against the hard Left. He decided not to stand again and in 1983 there was one of the most viciously fought by-elections in British political history, with Mellish supporting a non-Labour candidate against the gay rights campaigner Peter Tatchell. Allegations of homophobia dominated the campaign. The infighting and conflict came at a price. Just when the LDDC needed a good working relationship with local Labour councillors, the climate was not conducive to cooperation. There was also a vocal campaign established by locals who feared opportunism on the part of developers and the consequences of disregard for the people who had lived in Docklands for generations. The place had been bombed heavily by the Luftwaffe in the Second World War, rebuilt afterwards and then slowly destroyed by a combination of neglect and failure to adapt to economic reality. By the mid-1980s some locals felt after Ward's early efforts as though they had been living on a vast building site for years, and now there were rumours circulating of a plan for an enormous development for the benefit of Americans. Were the remaining residents about to become outsiders in their own neighbourhoods, overshadowed by tower blocks built for Thatcherite financiers? Not all those complaining that this was the case were disaffected, unemployed dockers. Indeed, many of the dockers simply moved to other parts of London or out to

counties such as Essex. All manner of other associated trades that
were associated with the docks had also been sunk, and the social
disruption was the London East End equivalent of what happened
in the early to mid-1980s in the parts of Britain that lost heavy
industry and coalmining. Deindustrialisation had started long
before 1979 and Thatcher's election, but it accelerated in the 1980s
and 90s. In 1975, 28.2 per cent of British workers were in manufacturing, by 1985 it was 23.9 per cent, and by 1993, 19.9 per cent.[4]
Across the North of England and in Wales and Scotland the adjustment was extremely painful.

In London, Ward and others at the LDDC struggled to convince
the remaining locals that the era of the docks was gone for good
and nothing like it would be coming back. The nature of employment was changing, the LDDC pointed out politely. Locals would
not necessarily be able to find work on their doorstep but the transport links being built should allow them to travel into the centre of
London or beyond to seek other types of work. That might be true
in time; then, to opponents of the development, it seemed, and still
seems, that the security of tenure and class solidarity in the docks
when they were open had been traded for temporary work and low
pay for too many locals. It also looked as though the sceptics warning that this was an idea that would never get off the ground had a
point. As late as 1985 it wasn't clear to the public or the government
what would fill most of the space at Docklands or form the centrepiece of the development. Of course, there was room for a great
deal of housing, and the first businesses to take up the government's
incentives were light-industrial firms and medium-sized businesses
looking for affordable accommodation. The Billingsgate fish market
moved from the City in 1982 to an ugly new building close to Canary
Wharf and the Westferry Printworks, printing titles that included
the *Daily Telegraph*, had opened nearby in 1984. But the government
that had established the organisation Ward ran wanted much more.
That is why Travelstead's proposal arrived at the perfect moment.
Just when the Prime Minister was keen to see the traditional City
opened up to the forces of competition and fresh thinking in Big

Bang, the American property developer turned up saying that the Establishment in the Square Mile was too old-fashioned and he would build London 'a Wall Street on the water', giving foreign banks an alternative to negotiating with the stuffy cartelised City Corporation.

Following von Clemm and Travelstead's initial conversations, a consortium was formed in the summer of 1985 involving Morgan Stanley, CSFB and First Boston's property company. Travelstead – who had a 20 per cent stake – rented an office in Mayfair for his team, which was soon full of architects' drawings and models of the initial seventy-one-acre site and plans for eight million square feet of trading floors and offices. On such a large project facing considerable public and press scepticism, the endorsement of the government and a deal on building the transport links was essential. Travelstead was summoned to see Nick Ridley, the Thatcherite Secretary of State for Transport, at 11.30pm one night in the department when the Commons was sitting late, and found himself transfixed as Ridley smoked a cigarette right down until it disappeared between his yellowing fingers.

After further discussions, the consortium agreed to contribute £50m to the transport costs. Travelstead's introduction to the Prime Minister herself came from Alistair McAlpine, the Conservative Party Treasurer and a close ally of Thatcher. Born in the Dorchester Hotel, into the McAlpine construction dynasty, the Tory leader's friend and 'bagman', or party fundraiser, was fiercely devoted to her interests. The iconoclastic McAlpine guessed correctly that Canary Wharf would appeal to Thatcher, and at Travelstead's subsequent meetings, several in Downing Street and one at Chequers, she was highly supportive of the bankers' scheme. When Travelstead was worried that the planned light railway would not include sufficient capacity or stations, leaving potential commuters or workers to try to get to the Isle of Dogs from other parts of London by taking long bus or taxi journeys through the East End, and creating traffic jams and transport chaos, he told Thatcher that it could derail the building of Canary Wharf. He recalls her being clear in her advice, suggesting that for all her anti-statist credentials she was a

pragmatist who had an impeccable understanding of how government functions. Build Canary Wharf, she told him. Don't worry
about traffic jams. Create a mess, she told the developer, and then
government will feel compelled to clean it up. That's how it works.

Ward and Travelstead formed a close working partnership, which
caused the chief executive of the LDDC problems when critics
accused him of doing too much to please the American banks. But
the pair remained convinced – when few others were – that there
would soon emerge one of the largest developments in the world.
Not every senior investment banker agreed, and one attempt in
1985 to explain the vision was a failure, thanks to a typical London
traffic jam. At Salomon, Charles McVeigh, like von Clemm, was
looking for a space for a large trading floor and could not find it in
the Square Mile. The irascible chief executive of Salomon's, John
Gutfreund, was interested in resurgent London because it was
perfectly placed for further expansion due of its position in the time
zone. When he took an interest in the search for property, von
Clemm persuaded Gutfreund to drive with McVeigh down to
Docklands. They had the drive timed as taking just twenty minutes
from the City, von Clemm assured the visiting American. Three-
quarters of an hour later, with the group stuck in traffic somewhere
between Wapping and the mooted Canary Wharf site, von Clemm,
pointing out of the window at another part of the wasteland,
explained that the LDDC planned to build a lot of low-cost housing.
Low-cost housing? Gutfreund was astonished. Why the hell would
he care about plans for low-cost housing?

After the visit, Salomon decided not to join the Canary Wharf
project, instead choosing an office block more centrally located
above Victoria Station, near Buckingham Palace. There they set
about constructing the largest trading floor in Europe, at a rumoured
cost of £25m, and even installed some ornate panelling in the executive suites upstairs overlooking the vast trading floor, because the
management was convinced that visiting major clients would expect
a bank in London to look at least a little as though it had heritage.
Valerie Thompson, the trader from Essex who had risen to become

a star and the first female director at Salomon, was one of those who moved onto the new trading floor below. When she was appointed manager of the London syndicate department on 10 July 1986, Gutfreund sent a memo via telex to all employees announcing it. A female colleague scribbled a note of congratulations: 'This is super news . . . there is hope for women at the Brothers.' The move to Victoria Plaza was not to her liking, however. It was too anonymous and excessively big, with row upon row of trading terminals. It seemed like a vast zoo. Who were all these people she didn't recognise? Another Salomon employee who made the move, who Thompson did know, was bond salesman Michael Lewis, already working part time in the evenings as a journalist, which would lead him into writing *Liar's Poker*, the inside account that later destroyed the reputation of Gutfreund and would forever associate the name of Salomon with excess and egotism. When a superior tried to threaten Lewis over a deal, he put it in the hands of the email syndicate manager, who he described as a brilliantly connected 'alley cat'. To Lewis's amusement, she managed with a few phone calls to nix the bully's promotion at Salomon.

In early 1986 that decision by Gutfreund to move to such a vast space at Victoria was not yet widely seen as an indicator of looming disaster at Salomon. It was deemed another blow to the ancient City Corporation and an indication that its geographical monopoly was finished. Two Corporation men who understood very well the implications of Gutfreund's move and the Canary Wharf plan were Michael Cassidy, the chair of the planning committee, and Peter Rees, the head of planning. Cassidy was a lawyer who was fascinated by the City, and in his role in the early 1980s working for the Post Office pension fund – then Britain's biggest – he saw how markets and trading were being changed by technology. His MBA, completed part time, was on Big Bang and when he was chosen as a councillor to be deputy chairman in 1985 and then chairman of The Corporation's Planning Committee in 1986, he was convinced that the City had to modernise and rebuild rapidly or it would continue to see banks and other firms look elsewhere. There was already some innovation underway, of course. Lloyd's of London, the insurance market, moved in 1986 to a strange custom-built building designed by Richard Rogers that had been begun in 1978. In the fashionable style of the time, the lifts and pipes were on the outside of the building, making it look like an overblown coffee machine. The arch-traditionalist architectural critic Gavin Stamp described it as 'that naive, posturing intrusion into the City'.[5] When the Queen opened it in November that year she was more diplomatic and praised the design. In her speech she made oblique reference to the difficulties Lloyd's had suffered earlier in the decade, when an embarrassing scandal over investor protection had exposed a group of underwriters siphoning investors' money into their own offshore accounts. The Chairman of Lloyd's, Peter Miller, said at the opening of the building that Lloyd's was trying to move on and the new structure was 'an exciting contrast to so much of the boring modern architecture of this city'. He noted that it would prove practical for trading purposes. 'If it is controversial, let it never be said that Lloyd's cannot take a risk.' That was one way of putting it. Later in the decade it would became apparent just how rapacious the appetite of some of those at Lloyd's had been for recklessness and risk with other people's money.

On the site of an old station, work also started on the thirty-two-acre Broadgate development in 1985, on its eastern extremity bordering Bishopsgate. Invited by the developers Godfrey Bradman and Stuart Lipton, on 31 July Thatcher herself clambered aboard a JCB earthmover and scraped a patch of ground. Afterwards, in the marquee, or 'this great tent' as she described it, she gave a speech in which she invoked the original Victorian builders of the railways and urged the developers to be inspired by history's example to remake the City. 'We are drawing back the curtain of the future,' as she put it.[6] The Prime Minister also used a saying that sounded Methodist but which actually comes from Goethe: 'That which thy fathers bequeath thee, earn it anew if thou wouldst possess it.' The development would maintain and enhance the reputation of London as one of the greatest centres of trade and industry, she said. 'And that is the reputation I like to keep going.' She returned the following year for one of the topping-out ceremonies, and when Broadgate Circle was completed one of the signature post-modern developments of the Thatcher era was revealed. It had clean, curved white lines that imitated the amphitheatres of the Ancients, and space for cafes in which financiers wearing braces and double-breasted suits – and that was just the women – might sit sipping Italian coffee.

Across from the Royal Exchange and the Bank of England, another piece of landmark post-modern architecture was given the go-ahead in 1986, after earlier plans in the 1970s for a tower had been blocked, following complaints led by the Prince of Wales, who loathed architectural developments that altered the character of London or eclipsed the streets in which they sat. The developer Peter Palumbo tried again and the architect James Stirling designed a triangular building, clad in pink and yellow limestone cake-like stripes. Construction was then delayed for six years because of a row over the demolition of Victorian listed buildings and an architectural dig during which the Museum of London thought it might have found the origins of the founding of Londinium.

Peter Rees and his team in the mid- to late 1980s realised that it would take far more than a handful of high-profile developments to rebuild the City. Cassidy had hired Rees in 1985, as deputy head of planning, although he was quickly promoted and his more conservative predecessor removed. Rees was only in his thirties and full of energy and ideas about how the City should look. There was no point thinking in romantic terms of repopulating the place with more flats or apartments, he said. He and Cassidy were convinced that the City needed much better offices for banks, insurance firms, lawyers and accountants, and much bigger buildings to accommodate the commuters that were the place's lifeblood. They ripped up the plan for modest redevelopment and, in the face of considerable opposition, and with close votes and the help of leaks to the financial press, Cassidy and Rees pushed through developments and relaxed Corporation rules. There would be no restrictions on basements, meaning developers could go down as far as they wanted to put in the workings of a modern building. The plot sizes were increased to allow large floors to accommodate traders, and they tried to plan ahead as the City's streets were dug and dug again to take ever more of the cables that were needed to funnel new technology into the buildings. They set aside extra space in the trenches for future fibre-optic expansion. Within five years a third – a third – of the Square Mile's office space was replaced.

The City had been slow to start rebuilding ahead of Big Bang, and was soon catching up. This meant intense competition with the rival Canary Wharf crowd, although thirty years later Cassidy contests the suggestion that it amounted to all-out war between Travelstead's team and the Corporation. Travelstead is not so sure. When the American went to the Guildhall, invited by Cassidy, to explain his plans, there was plenty of scope for cultural confusion, and in trying to convince the councillors who ran the Corporation that Canary Wharf would be a success he may have left them with the impression that the new arrivals thought the City itself was past it, which did not go down well with the audience. Either way, Thatcher and her ministers had got what they wanted, a highly competitive race to build and adapt London to suit the requirements of those operating in global markets. The City – spurred on by threats to its position – had become once again a great, expansive, international centre open to investment, as it had been in the Victorian and Edwardian period. Another figure who was supportive of Travelstead's scheme was the Prince of Wales. The American was invited by an equerry to Kensington Palace for a discreet conversation with the heir to the throne. On his arrival he encountered two children running around naked chased by a nanny. It was William and Harry. Charles said that he was in favour of Canary Wharf, but given his reputation for getting involved in rows about architecture he realised it might not help if he said so publicly. 'Sir,' said Travelstead, fearing a fresh outbreak of hostilities between the Prince and the architect profession, 'it is probably better if you don't say anything.'

Back on the Isle of Dogs in 1986 it was war of a different kind. On the ground, the network of community activists stepped up their campaign when Travelstead's plan was published and models were displayed for investors and residents to examine. The protests by the Association of Island Communities against Canary Wharf itself are captured in the documentary *Hardworking People*, made by the film-maker Woody Morris in 2013. It includes images of the day in July 1986 when the activists decided to storm the ceremony marking the turning of the first sod at Canary Wharf, attended by assorted senior bankers, dignitaries and Reg Ward. Compared to highly policed contemporary events, in which even the most humdrum press conference tends to be patrolled by security guards and a battalion of press officers who fear the sack if so much as the tiniest detail goes wrong, the Canary Wharf protest of 1986 was a thing of wonder.

The artist and activist Peter Dunn was one of those who watched the dignitaries assemble. He told Morris: 'They arrived in their big limousines . . . they had their sunglasses on, they looked like a whole series of mafia bosses to be honest. They had models of what Canary Wharf would look like in their marquee.' At the agreed signal, a whistle was blown and banners were unfurled declaring that 'Canary Wharf condemns the community' and demanding on behalf of locals the right to have a better say. Their banners were just the overture. Joining the protests were those in charge of Mudchute Farm, a community farm nearby that feared it would be closed down or threatened as part of the wider redevelopment of Docklands. They hired a lorry and, having filled it with sheep, drove to the ceremony uninvited, approaching from the other end of the dock. The lorry trundled towards the marquee and the podium, where the sheep were duly let loose to the bemusement of the guests and the horror of the organisers. With sheep wandering about, and some eating the flowers around the base of the podium, at one point Ward tried to be conciliatory. He took over some cham-pagne to the protesters, which seemed not to go down very well with the representatives of the banks, who wanted to know why champagne was being handed out to the enemies of progress with the press watching. As it was, the protest received little more than a few passing mentions in the next day's newspapers and would have been lost to history but for the efforts of the activists and local historians.

Even better than the sheep, the team from Mudchute unloaded a beehive in front of the podium and took off the lid as the Governor of the Bank of England attempted to make his speech. But Robin Leigh-Pemberton was unflappable. Not only had he been in the Grenadier Guards, serving in Palestine after the Second World War, but it also emerged that in his spare time he was a beekeeper, so he was untroubled when the bees were released near him. Many in his audience of the great and good, and not so good as the protesters saw it, were less relaxed and fled the bees by moving into the marquee to take shelter and have a drink. With the bees buzzing about him, and with his elite audience gone, Leigh-Pemberton kept going for a while with his speech before good-humouredly giving up.

It was all very British and as the protesters packed up it might have seemed as though any property consortium that presided over such a farcical occasion could not possibly be capable of creating and filling the largest development in Europe. Neither Ward nor Travelstead would complete the project, and von Clemm had already moved on in January 1986, when he suddenly resigned from CSFB. But they had forced the City to respond, to think about how new towers would be built and the Square Mile reshaped. What Travelstead, von Clemm and Ward envisioned and started at Docklands would grow. Out of the desolation, new temples to mammon soon began to rise.

9

BANG

'These theories were based on the hypothesis that all the matter in the universe was created in one big bang at a particular time in the remote past. It now turns out that in some respect or other all such theories are in conflict with the observational requirements.'

Astronomer Fred Hoyle, speaking in 1948

Thatcherism hit its peak in 1986. Within that year were clustered a series of events that might be considered remarkable enough individually. Taken together they amounted to the opening of the final act, the first intimations of the cavalcade of carnage that closed the decade and helped define the Tory Party's divisions for several decades. On 9 January, the Defence Secretary Michael Heseltine walked out of the cabinet in a row over the Westland helicopter company, heading to the backbenches from where he waited for an opportunity to challenge Margaret Thatcher for the Tory leadership and the premiership. She narrowly avoided ruin over Westland and Heseltine himself waited more than four years to strike. Although he was not to know it at the time, he would be aided enormously by Thatcher's doomed flagship policy, the Community Charge. Following many months of internal arguments, it first appeared formally in public in 1986, on 28 January, with the publication of a 'green paper' entitled 'Paying for Local Government'. The replacement of local rates with a charge – quickly dubbed a 'poll tax' by opponents – was the work of Kenneth Baker, the Environment Secretary, and William Waldegrave, the Minister of State at Environment, with Thatcher's enthusiastic backing. They were assisted by outside 'expert' Lord Rothschild, who had been appointed chairman of N.M. Rothschild, then specialising among other activities in privatisation. Victor, the third Baron Rothschild, had led an extremely eventful life. At Cambridge he was close friends with Philby, Burgess and Blunt, three of the Cambridge spies, an association which later caused him to be accused (wrongly) of being a Soviet spy. During his wartime service with MI5 he won the George Cross, and as a Labour peer and one-time backer of Ted Heath he ended up as an enthusiastic supporter of Thatcher and a trusted advisor. That is how he came in January 1986 to help unintentionally plant a slow-ticking poll-tax-shaped bomb under the government. As Lawson later put it in his memoirs: 'Rothschild prided himself on having no political judgement. He was above that sort of thing. William Waldegrave seemed to regard this as an advantage.'

The following month, the Single European Act was signed by the twelve members of the European Community, to make it easier to scrap physical, technical and fiscal barriers to trade. It led to the single market, in which European Union members agreed to abide by common regulatory standards and traded freely within the boundaries of the EU. This landmark measure in 1986 had been agreed only with some difficulty, and Lord Cockfield – the former Trade Secretary who, with David Walker, behind the scenes just before the 1983 general election had seen the way to a deal with the City and Nicholas Goodison – was one of the driving forces behind a programme designed to increase commerce within Europe, overseeing the White Paper ('Completing the Internal Market') that led to the Act. Thatcher wanted free trade and in return she agreed to an expansion of the European Community's power, only a little later realising the full extent of what she had conceded. Yet even in 1986 Cockfield was deemed by Thatcher to have become too pro-European, meaning he was not given a second term in post in Brussels. That did not matter, one term was enough for him to put a large dent in European history. The Act he helped instigate turned out to have two massive impacts on

Britain and Europe. It ushered in integration that eroded national sovereignty – because there was no longer a requirement for unanimity among the member states – and it eventually riled Conservative Eurosceptics. Rows over Europe helped split Thatcher's administration, contributing to her fall. But the effect on the City would also turn out to be enormous in that the single market helped London accelerate away from other European financial centres to become the undisputed hub in Europe, from where global banks could do business across Europe.

That same year, the Financial Services Act, overhauling regulation of the City and banks, also became law. Thanks to another piece of legalisation enacted that year, humble conservative-minded building societies (British savings and loans companies) were allowed to demutualise and compete with banks. Meanwhile, the government prepared the biggest privatisation of the lot: British Gas.

And all the time the clock ticked down to the day of Big Bang, scheduled for 27 October. At the Stock Exchange, much of the responsibility for preparations rested on George Hayter, the director of technical services. His team were attempting to construct a computer system that could handle the Stock Exchange's switch to an entirely electronic marketplace. Transactions would be expected to happen at high speed and not on the traditional floor face to face, although not all of the elements were new. Since the 1960s there had been a rudimentary electronic system for displaying prices, and in 1978 the more sophisticated Teletext Output of Price Information by Computer (TOPIC) was introduced. The FTSE 100 index of prices of the top 100 British listed companies, developed as a joint project with the *Financial Times* and then owned by the Stock Exchange, had replaced the FT 30 index. It gave anyone needing to get a sense of the direction of the market a good feel for it, with its red and green flashing icons. It was also faster, being updated every minute. The Exchange Price Information Computer (EPIC) held a database of the prices, but it depended on prices being observed physically and reported by staff on the floor of the Exchange. Even small delays meant that prices could have changed in either direction, and what really mattered in the old system was what the brokers and jobbers said to each other as they quoted a price and did a trade. For Big Bang to deliver an improvement, it all had to happen in real time or as close to it as possible, so that the numbers on the screen were not just a reflection of what had been the position very recently. The data seen on the terminal by the new generation trader would be the real price at that moment, based on the most recent trades, not an approximation. This was more than a minor spot of computer modernisation. It was a different way of looking at the world, in which flashing numbers on a screen came alive and the underlying data moved ever faster, way too fast for the human eye to see. The electronic prices would become not just a reflection of reality but the reality itself.

Hayter was unfazed by the practicalities. As he saw it, he had worked on larger projects, particularly the BOAC airline reservation system in the 1970s. Big Bang, though, was more difficult because it was akin to working in a goldfish bowl. Or it was, he told an interviewer, a little like swimming in a heavy sea. 'Every time I thought we had the project under control, we were hit by another roller.'[1] Satisfying every firm – the entire securities industry and every trader in the Square Mile – would prove impossible, but with time tight, Hayter's skill lay in finding a way through the internal politics of the Stock Exchange, and its ruling committees, to create a workable compromise. The ideal option of starting from scratch was not available, and when international shares started to be traded in significant quantities by foreign banks in London away from the Stock Exchange it brought additional pressure. Those firms doing it wanted a price system that suited their needs and if Hayter's team didn't build it, someone else might. Hayter and his team had to construct something quickly that would please sufficient members of the Stock Exchange and firms outside it that the Exchange wanted to attract. The answer was Seaq (Stock Exchange Automated Quotation System), on which all firms selling a particular share listed their prices, so that other firms could pick the best price quickly. The results of those trades, and their prices, then flowed automatically into a version of TOPIC in which a screen displayed the top 100 shares with pulsing red and blue lights, giving the trader a very quick feel for what the market was doing. If it was all red, that was not good. Seaq International also provided a bridge between New York, London and Tokyo, allowing brokers to see prices instantly elsewhere, creating a twenty-four-hour market. The way of conducting business that had existed for centuries was being abolished and in its place the Stock Exchange would become simply an electronic marketplace. Charging for access to the flow of information and controlling the platform on which buyers and sellers traded was what the new Stock Exchange was going to be about.

As Hayter and his programmers grappled with making their computers work, Parliamentary Under-Secretary at the Department of Trade and Industry Michael Howard was locked in early 1986 in a series of meetings with those who represented the firms that would come under the aegis of the proposed regulatory system. The experience was a little jarring for both sides, including for Stani Yassukovich. He was the son of a White Russian and a leading City figure who had arrived via Harvard and the US Marine Corps. He had been at White, Weld from 1961 and had become a Euromarkets pioneer in 1960s London. He was now chairman of Merrill Lynch Europe. When he and his colleagues encountered Howard, the government minister who had been given responsibility for steering the Bill through the House of Commons, they felt that for all his undoubted intelligence he was, as a non-financial person, having some trouble grasping the intricacies of how trading worked. But that sounds like market manipulation, Howard told them, when Yassukovich explained a manoeuvre (called a Greenshoe), a mechanism by which brokers arranged the orderly handling of a share issue to stabilise the price. Howard said he might have trouble convincing his colleagues that this was acceptable. From Howard's point of view, he was attempting to educate the City's senior figures in the realities of politics and public perception. If high finance was on the rise then it could expect a good deal more scrutiny and would have to be able to explain itself clearly. They were, he made clear, now going to be accountable .

The role of Howard the lawyerly minister was to turn the competing claims of financiers, the Stock Exchange, the foreign players in the Eurobond market – such as Salomon and Nomura – the Bank of England and the Treasury, into a coherent, workable piece of legislation. The Gower Report had begat a government White Paper, the establishment of a network of self-regulatory bodies under a new Securities and Investment Board (SIB) appointed by the government, and then the bill itself. Labouring, as the *FT* put it, under a portrait of Gladstone and his cabinet, Howard pushed it through in several months, dealing with complaints along the way and trying to get the right amount of regulation with the opposition shouting for more and the City for less.

But the battle fought in 1984 by John Redwood and others against Gower and statutory regulation of one form or another had been lost. The free market Redwood's recommendation of minimal regulation – via reliance on the common law and simple rules imposed by the City's own institutions – ended up being rejected in favour of the creation of a regulatory bureaucracy. The Bank of England's David Walker and the Treasury were convinced that the increasing complexity of the market made this inevitable and desirable. Thatcher herself seems to have understood little of these nuances. In the words of her biographer, Charles Moore, the Prime Minister's involvement in the details of City reform were 'seldom more than marginal'[2] and she was simultaneously deeply involved in foreign affairs, particularly in the thawing Cold War and in arguments over how to deal with the Apartheid regime in South Africa.

Howard had to deal with fresh complaints late in the process in the summer. He was astonished when Britain's clearing banks suddenly woke up and realised that the legislation might have implications for them if they sought to expand their activities out of straightforward banking. The accountants were also unhappy. In August, Derek Boothman, representing their professional body, went to see Howard and said that accountants must have immunity. As the *Financial Times* reported: 'At some point auditors may be expected to "shop" rogue clients to the Bank of England or the SIB, a prospect that is causing considerable heart-searching.' Howard rejected the special pleading. That did end up having an unintended consequence, in that it contributed to the reduction of choice in London. Only the biggest accountancy firms could afford the professional liability insurance that would be needed to audit the accounts of banks and larger financial companies. It was an added spur to the growth and dominance of a small number of giant firms that audited the big banks on rotation. As banks grew in size and diminished in number, the firms auditing them got much bigger too.

The clashes and compromises meant that the Financial Services Act 1986 was no purist piece of Thatcherism. It was pragmatic; it was a fusion. Simplistic talk of 1980s *laissez-faire* financial deregulation, as though Thatcher ordered all controls to be swept away, is daft. That is not what happened. The Thatcherite fondness for the term deregulation, and the way critics used the term with contempt, caused it to be fixed in the public imagination as a period in which ancient, strict rules were swept away in favour of libertine licence. Yet it was not the introduction of a free-for-all. The intention was to formalise regulation while safeguarding enough of the City's independence, with various interested parties pushing all the while for their version of regulation to be adopted. The Governor of the Bank of England pushed for some of the old City culture to survive, particularly the so-called reliance on 'the Governor's eyebrows', the phrase meaning that historically a raised eyebrow from the Bank of England should be enough to compel reckless firms to rein it in. Robin Leigh-Pemberton explained his position:

'I, and others speaking on behalf of the Bank, have stressed that such regulation is seen as a means to the greater end of continuing to attract international business to London as an open but well-regulated financial centre. The City has a long tradition of regulation by consensus and the principle of being bound by the spirit of the rules as much as by their letter. I would like to see this tradition survive the move to a statutory framework and the influx of firms from different cultures.'[3]

This was all very well, and there was much that would go wrong with the importation of more of an American-style system, but at that point (as Bank of England and senior Treasury officials understood) the government was under sustained and justified attack because of excesses in the City. For the most part, compared to what came later, the cases involved were small time. But the steep increase in the amounts involved in cases of financial fraud and the gradual exposure of a web of corruption at Lloyd's, the insurance market, was ammunition for enemies of the City. At Lloyd's, shady underwriting practices – and the failure to make it clear that claims for asbestosis would hit the market hard – left some 'names', investors, exposed. It would get worse. But most of the new wealth elsewhere in the City was legitimately and legally earned. The contrast with the situation in poorer areas of Britain was obvious. While in 1986 parts of the country were only just beginning to recover from decline and degeneration, the populous southeast boomed. And its most visible manifestation was the City, which sucked in talent, provided opportunity, put rocket boosters under house prices and became the source of footage for eager TV journalists needing images that embodied the freewheeling spirit of the Thatcher era.

It was just about possible for defenders of high finance to claim that there was no more fraud or wrongdoing than there had ever been. Perhaps the law was only catching up. But the sums to be made – even by the mid-1980s – were already much bigger, and by such a magnitude that it would be odd if there had not been a commensurate increase in temptation. Indeed, outside the City, the merger mania, pay-outs to partners and the beginnings of higher salaries and bonuses had been noticed by the British voters, MPs and media. Combined with reports of fraud and sharp practice, accusations of greed could be used to make the case against Thatcher. In the Commons it was observed by the opposition parties during the passage of the Financial Services Bill that many Conservative MPs were serving or former stockbrokers and City lawyers, accountants and insurance types, the strong implication being that they wanted to shield their colleagues from full statutory regulation or more stringent scrutiny. This meant that the ethics of the City and risks of greed were back being discussed, as they had been periodically in the eighteenth and nineteenth century on the floor of the House of Commons by the leading politicians of the day. In a debate instigated by Labour in the House of Commons on 12 March 1986, in which the motion called for proper regulation to crack down on City fraud and misbehaviour, the attack was led by Roy Hattersley, who as Labour Minister of Consumer Affairs a decade previously had refused to exempt the City from restrictive practices rules. Hattersley, a skilled polemicist with a gift for a turn of phrase, was coruscating:

> Unemployment now stands at between 3.5 million and 4 million, manufacturing trade is in deficit and real interest rates are at record levels. Each of those individual catastrophes has been intensified by the Government's enthusiasm for economic policies which benefit the City but damage the rest of the economy. We have today a Government of the City for the City and, by far too large an extent, by the City.

Paddy Ashdown, then a young Liberal Democrat MP and future leader of his party, said the City had become far too dominated, although not all of it, by 'the short term, the turn of a quick buck by tomorrow'. Unlike in the UK's competitor nations, he said, it was far too often uninterested in investing in the future, and in industry. He was appalled by the sums being earned:

> Young men, not yet 30, in the City are earning £60,000 or £80,000 a year. I see that the chief executive of Guinness has had his salary raised to £195,000 a year and has received shares worth more than £1 million. As the Big Bang approaches, such frenetic activity to buy people will get even more frenetic.

The Tory MP who attacked most ferociously was Geoffrey Rippon, a former Heathite who disliked Thatcher and was disliked in return.

Nonetheless, his comments about the culture of takeovers and egomania were cogent.

> What is happening in the City today in the sphere of mergers is utter madness . . . No one can stop takeover bids and no one would want to, but the message should go out to the City: 'For heaven's sake cool it.' A distinction must be made between mergers by agreement which stimulate organic growth and hostile bids that are designed to promote egomaniac empire building.[4]

Rippon was not referring to takeovers in the Square Mile itself, of brokers and jobbing firms. His target was the frenzied effort to facilitate and encourage lucrative takeovers of established retailers or manufacturers by the empire-building entrepreneurs, usually acting with borrowed money sourced from the City. The Labour MP Tam Dalyell praised Rippon's contribution and said that there was deep concern about the deals and spiralling salaries: 'There is real worry in the country . . . if there is another scandal, or series of scandals, the top will come off.'

The Cabinet Secretary agreed with enough of those criticisms to send a note five days after that parliamentary debate to the Prime Minister's private secretary Nigel Wicks. 'I do not know whether you are having the same experience but I am finding, among people who work outside the City of London but whose activities bring them into touch in some degree with the City, that there is increasing disquiet about the things that people think are going on in the City', he said.

> I do not just mean the levels of remuneration; a lot of people, including some from inside the City, think that it is a bubble that will be pricked in a year or two. They think more about the way in which corners are being cut and money is being made in ways that are at least bordering on the unscrupulous. It tends to be summed up by the people saying that they doubt whether it really

is good enough any more to leave the policing of the City to self-regulation. I'm afraid that all this is pretty vague and unspecific; but I find it sufficiently prevalent to be concerned.

The tone was strikingly different from that adopted the previous year in memos sent by John Redwood, when he had hailed Big Bang and urged Thatcher to take her share of the credit for what was coming. Redwood then left the Policy Unit to rejoin N.M. Rothschild as a director, responsible for overseas corporate finance and selling expertise on privatisation to governments outside the UK. He was joined there later by another member of the Policy Unit, Oliver Letwin. David Willetts, who stayed on in Downing Street, was notably more cautious than Redwood, and the tenor of discussions about Big Bang inside Number 10 changed with the great day drawing close. While free market theorising was all very well, the cold, hard implications for the government of it potentially backfiring were now considered in detail. At that point Thatcher was still, just, for all her reputation for being unyielding, a canny assessor of political risk. On the afternoon of 5 June 1986, she met to review Big Bang with the Chancellor, Nigel Lawson; the Secretary of State for Trade and Industry, Paul Channon; the Governor of the Bank of England, Robin Leigh-Pemberton; the Treasury's Permanent Secretary, Peter Middleton; John Caines from the DTI; David Walker from the Bank, and Professor Brian Griffiths of the Number 10 Policy Unit. Ahead of their discussion, Griffiths and his colleague David Willetts encapsulated the concerns in a note to the Prime Minister: 'If Big Bang goes off successfully, it will be seen as a showpiece for Government policy on deregulation and increased competition; if it leads to scandals and liquidations, it will be labelled the unacceptable face of unpopular capitalism.' They posed some good questions. Will there be boom and bust? Will there be fraud? Might the Americans and the Japanese dominate London? Is the regulatory regime right? Will the technology be ready?

Lawson opened the meeting by agreeing with Thatcher that there were risks and that inevitably there would be mistakes. Yet change was essential if the City was to remain competitive, he said. In the discussion that followed, the opportunities for fraud were a particular concern. 'The temptation to fraud, or to unethical behaviour, would be increased by the competitive pressures', an official wrote. Those present were encouraged that some financial institutions had hired compliance directors to ensure their colleagues stayed within the new rules that were on their way, although it was also observed that firms were increasing the scale of risks they carried off balance sheet. The new regulators would need to cooperate closely with their counterparts in other leading countries, although it was claimed the regulators were also finding it difficult at that stage to attract top-quality staff. Lloyd's the insurance market got a mention too, thanks to the assorted ongoing investigations into corrupt practices. When it came to Big Bang every effort must be made, it was agreed, to promote the benefits to the wider economy. Otherwise, 'there was a risk that people would only look at the high salaries and the deal-making' (this turned out to have been something of an understatement). Thatcher closed by requesting a further report to be circulated in mid-September, a month or so before D-Day.

There were portents of trouble ahead for British firms that summer, with several of the institutions that had paid large amounts for jobbing and broking firms still struggling to resolve the culture clashes that had resulted from takeovers and mergers. At BZW, the Barclays concoction created by the merger of Barclays merchant bank, de Zoete & Bevan and Wedd Durlacher in the hope that it would become a truly British rival to the major American investment banks, they were still stricken by internal warfare more than a year after the formation of BZW. This was despite the best efforts of chairman Martin Jacomb, formerly of Kleinwort Benson, who used to tell his team that challenging Goldman Sachs and Merrill Lynch 'is within our grasp'. One of the senior executives recalls it being a doomed venture: 'I'm afraid it was the worst type of British disaster. Many good staff and ideas. A lot of amateurishness. And a fair amount of strutting about.' As his colleague, Martin

Vander-Weyer, then a Barclays merchant banker and later a journalist, said: 'This was supposed to be the sexy side of finance, while high-street lending to personal customers and smaller businesses – the area in which Barclays had real expertise in depth – was an unglamorous poor relation.'[5]

Another esteemed British merchant bank was not making good progress either. The efforts by some of the management at Morgan Grenfell in 1986 to inject some dynamism and aggression produced a culture that was robust bordering on the nasty. As in other firms, the recruitment of outsiders caused resentment and some badmouthing of existing staff. Geoffrey Collier, who would be in the headlines very soon, and not in a good way, ran the new securities team in a particularly lively manner. Other British Establishment names dealt with the coming change differently. Barings opted not to partner with an outside investor, thus continuing family control. Hambro went in the other direction, when the family – Jocelyn, and his three sons, Rupert, Richard and James – departed in early 1986. Lazard, the merchant bank that was tied closely to its American and French counterparts of the same name, had stayed out of the securities business entirely. And stockbroker Cazenove would carry on as before, having not bought a jobbing firm or sought to change its business model.

There were further growing pains at the Stock Exchange, where Nicholas Goodison, with the help of Stani Yassukovich, was attempting to deal with a row that had the potential to jeopardise Big Bang, or at least to render it a damp squib over the next few years if it was not resolved soon. The original Gower proposals and the government's proposals for reform had been written almost as though the Eurobond market had not been invented. But this was the largest capital market in the world, so it must come within the scope of any new regulation, surely? Yassukovich, as a leading Eurobond practitioner, had become embroiled in trying to resolve the dispute, so that the regulation of Eurobonds (which were issued and traded beyond the remit of the Exchange) and the regulation of the Exchange itself might be merged. There was much opposition to the Exchange having control, particularly from Ian Steers of Wood Gundy, one of the biggest operators. It was only in September, with the 'Treaty of Throgmorton Street', that a compromise was agreed. The International Securities Regulatory Organisation (ISRO) merged with the Stock Exchange and Yassukovich became deputy chairman of the renamed International Stock Exchange. After almost two and a half decades in which it had attempted to act as though Eurobonds did not exist (the Eurobond market was the much bigger international market), they were now working together.

At the Conservative Party conference that year in Brighton, the Prime Minister was in a highly optimistic mood on the domestic front – not necessarily about Big Bang, but about the wider programme of which it was a part, a mission she termed a 'popular capitalism crusade' to enfranchise the many in the economic life of the nation. 'Millions have already become shareholders. And soon there will be opportunities for millions more, in British Gas, British Airways, British Airports and Rolls-Royce. Who says we've run out of steam? We're in our prime!'[6] The Conservatives under her, she said, were returning power to the people. 'That is the way to one nation, one people.' If she felt that she was now in control of events and in command of the battlefield at home, a jolt was delivered a few days later. At the Reykjavik summit between President Reagan and the Soviet leader Mikhail Gorbachev on the 11th and 12th, the American leader got carried away and proposed scrapping all nuclear weapons within ten years, a suggestion which terrified Thatcher. Persuading Reagan that his idea was impractical, and a threat to Western European security, occupied much of her time from then until her trip to Washington in November, where she succeeded in correcting American policy. Big Bang would not get much attention from Number 10 until after it had happened.

In October 1986, as the day approached, George Hayter continued to have difficulty convincing older London firms that the changes were going to succeed. Some well-established firms simply could not believe that the days of face-to-face trading were going to be over. Will George's computers work? they asked Goodison. They will work, Goodison said repeatedly. Even so, unconvinced market makers also wondered whether computers could entirely replace human contact on the floor of the Exchange. The sceptics had lobbied successfully for the installation of screens above the floor itself, at a cost of £2m, and they demanded increasing amounts of space. Twenty-eight firms declared they wanted to keep a pitch for face-to-face trading. Smith New Court was convinced it would need several dozen traders on the floor itself. It was as though they could not quite compute the disruption that was coming.

The full implications of London's expansion were beginning to be understood abroad, however. In Florence, the week before Big Bang at a conference of analysts from European financial institutions, the theme was 'towards an integrated European financial market', an aspiration that was fashionable in the light of the creation of Europe's single market and the determination of Europe's major governments to push for more trade, in finance as well as in goods.[7] The danger for other European financial centres, it was admitted, was that they were about to be left behind by London. A German analyst, Jochen Neynaber, warned about the impact: 'Frankfurt, Milan and Zurich will be provinces, particularly if we continue to be unable to synchronise our dealing and settlement mechanisms.' Patrick Lanney, a Brussels stockbroker, said that stock exchanges on the European continent must modernise urgently to keep up. From the US giant Morgan Stanley, Archie Cox – who ran its then still relatively small operation in London – made it clear that London would extend its lead. The future was big firms and big banks that would operate as 'global financial supermarkets' in which customers could access all the services they needed in one stop. Those giants would gravitate towards, and put their headquarters in, where most of the action was, he said. The strong implication was that London would be it. To underscore the point, a member of the Stock Exchange Council in London somewhat cheekily urged the members of other European Exchanges to come and play in the City.

There was a little less confidence on the ground as the City prepared for its first full rehearsal. Hayter's team had been testing the systems for months, but it was only on 18 October, nine days before Big Bang, that everyone tried it together for real. There was grumbling from some firms that there had been insufficient support and guidance from the Stock Exchange, although such complaints were dismissed by Goodison and Patrick Mitford-Slade, chairman of the Information and Communications Committee. If the newly merged firms had not invested enough in computer firepower then that was their fault. The Stock Exchange could not do everything.

It had been more than twenty years since the City stopped trading on Saturdays but for the rehearsal that old Victorian custom was resumed on a one-off basis. The *FT*'s reporter recorded the scene as work began early in the tower blocks and offices of the City. 'At 7.30am rows of strip lighting started to come on, shining through the mist and low cloud, as the newly integrated firms . . . prepared to log on for the first time to Seaq.' In the Christopher Street IT office, the computers were ready for early trading at 8am; shortly after that, the first attempts at buying and selling began. At 8.45am seventeen transactions per second were being processed, against a capacity of forty transactions per second, with the market on track to hit a deadline of 30,000 share prices having been accurately updated by 9am. But then problems developed, and not just because of the computers. 'It was very noisy,' recalls one participant. 'There was suddenly a lot of shouting across the desks and people standing up.' In the offices of dual-capacity firms, where former jobbers and brokers were now working together across from each other, within the same operation, it would take time for a smooth working partnership to develop. At the first real test with the market live, there were misunderstandings when cultures clashed. The brokers with clients on the telephone wanted their favoured customers dealt with first and let their colleagues know when they were unhappy or thought the service was too slow. The jobbers were too used to effectively being in charge.

The Bank of England's problems were simpler. A fire in a lift shaft at lunchtime meant the building had to be evacuated, although Eddie George and his team running the gilts operation had some trouble convincing staff that this was not a drill. Only when there was smoke in the corridors did the building empty for half an hour, disrupting the trading of gilts. While the central gilts office, which housed the Bank of England computer that settled all the deals in UK government debt, also went down for ninety minutes, Eddie George and his team were not concerned. Elsewhere the results of computerisation were mixed. Tim Coghlan, the BZW head of equities, said that there had been a 'fair feeling of depression' when the computers seemed to 'clog up'. But it picked up as the day went on, he said. Wood Street Securities suffered worse malfunctions, and there were problems too at Akroyd and Smithers, Kitcat & Aitken, Scrimgeour Vickers, Wood Mackenzie, W. Greenwell and Hoare Govett. The complaints were dismissed at a press conference given by Patrick Mitford-Slade at the Stock Exchange Tower at 5pm on the Saturday evening. He said that most of the problems were caused by the companies themselves and not by Hayter's team. There was even a suggestion that in some firms staff had overloaded the systems earlier in the day because they hoped to get away early, although it is more likely that there was a rush of excitement from those keen to try the new systems. As a result, a few firms declared that they would have to attempt further intensive rehearsals in the week ahead.

The fear of failure and embarrassment in public was accentuated by the sudden increase in interest from the international media, although not all of it was entirely serious in tone. American journalists in particular seemed to relish the concept of British City gents in bowler hats having to make it into the office before 9.30 in the morning. The *New York Times* put Peter Rawlinson, a partner in Schweder, Miller & Company, on its front page, in a photograph in which he was engaged (in a bowler hat, wielding a rolled umbrella) in the apparently remarkable act of going to work early. Phillips & Drew, a London broker, had even taken to providing a full English breakfast of eggs, bacon, sausages, mushrooms, 'the works', now that their staff were in before 8am. There was considerable mockery from Americans on Wall Street, who seemed in contrast so energetic that they might as well have got up before they went to bed, so eager were they to get into the office and begin trading. As usual, behind the headlines, the caricature of sleepy London and dynamic New York was not entirely fair. The smarter Wall Street types understood that the creation of the International Stock Exchange, and its merger with ISRO, was a threat, especially when added to London's exceptional cocktail of advantages: time zone, language, proximity to mainland Europe's markets, global links and centuries of financial innovation.

The reality of London's decades-long return and rise was also captured in the exhaustive pull-out in the *FT* on the morning of Big Bang. Such strong interest from the media resulted in a full house on the morning of Monday 27 October, when Hayter readied himself for launch. The risky notion of making the switch in one go on that morning as the London markets opened for business, and calling it Big Bang, had seemed like a good idea several years before. Now, shortly before 8am as Goodison surveyed the floor of the Exchange crowded with foreign television crews and curious journalists, he was a little apprehensive. After so much hype about the possibilities, and difficult negotiations with Margaret Thatcher's ministers, together with efforts to persuade the more conservative elements in the City that the revolution was really necessary, Goodison and his team were about to find out if the new computing systems would work when real trading started. Had the IT team in which Goodison had put so much faith to deliver the most widely advertised change in the City of London's long history done its job properly?

On the floor of the Exchange that Monday morning, some of the journalists – shepherded by the Stock Exchange's head of press Luke Glass – were waiting to find out the answer while explaining to each other why they were there. Sheila MacVicar of the Canadian Broadcast Corporation told the *Financial Times* that it was obvious

Toronto would be interested in Big Bang because Canadian financiers (living in the long shadow of New York) were keen to plug into the new global market. There was also interest in the implications for class-conscious Britain, she said. Canadians wanted to see 'how bowler-hatted gentlemen with rolled umbrellas who lived stable lives with their dogs in the country' would adapt to the computer era.

A producer for the West German TV station, ARD, explained that he and his crew had almost not made it along to watch Big Bang. The previous day – on Sunday – a British tabloid had exposed the Tory politician and novelist Jeffrey Archer. The order from Germany was that the ARD crew should drop plans to cover the Stock Exchange in London to go after a seemingly bigger bang, namely the story of Archer handing over money to a prostitute in Victoria Station and resigning as deputy chairman of the Conservative Party all the while proclaiming his innocence. Archer pledged to sue for libel. His denial echoed down the years, triggering a chain of events that took him many years later to prison for perjury. The man from ARD decided to ignore the demand from Germany to switch attention to Archer and turned up at the Stock Exchange on the Monday morning regardless. 'Knowing what I do about news editors I decided to go ahead anyway in case they changed their mind and asked for the pictures,' he said. This was to prove a sensible decision, considering what happened next.

As the journalists prattled and poked their noses around the hexagonal trading positions on the Exchange floor they were watched from the sidelines by traders waiting to get on with it, some of them impatient and annoyed at the presence of the media. They did not have long to wait. The computers warmed up, feeding information back to the offices of firms around the City, and at 8am the market opened formally. For almost fifteen minutes all was well. Then it started to go wrong.

John Scannell, the chief engineer, was in one of the operation rooms. He later described the system becoming overloaded with requests from curious firms eager to try it out:

Eight o'clock comes and the systems all come up. And we're looking at the page response request and it goes up to 1.7 million immediately which is a little bit bloody worrying. Then it crept up to sort of two million, three million, and four million. What's going on? This is quarter past eight. Then it got to five million, then everything is going berserk. Bells, and whistling, and ringing, and popping and banging.[8]

At 8.25am the older and more basic TOPIC system, Teletext Output of Prices Information by Computer, was approaching full capacity. At 8.29, more warning lights came on and the much-vaunted Seaq system went down. Seaq, the Stock Exchange Automated Quotation, was the new part of the system that was supposed to supply almost instantaneous, accurate prices to brokers, many positioned in the new, enormous trading floors built in offices across the City and beyond. Sitting in front of computers at new, expensive trading positions, they would do their deals with each other on the telephone, all fed by a continuous perfect stream of information in real time flowing from Hayter's computers. That was the theory and already it wasn't working. It looked to the watching media as though the revolution had gone phut and splat instead of bang. It was all rather embarrassing and very British.

Sir Nicholas Goodison decided that the best approach was not to panic. Far better to deploy some good old-fashioned dry English humour when the journalists gathered around him demanding an explanation for the difficulties. There was too much strain on the system, he told them, because every trader, carried away with the novelty, was trying it out. 'If you put a new monkey or dodo in the zoo,' he said, 'people will queue up to see it.'[9] For the sceptics among the old hands suspicious of the claims made for Big Bang, use of the term dodo – a bird that had been doomed to early extinction because it could not fly – sounded highly appropriate. How could computer screens with flashing lights and bleeping terminals ever be more effective than old-style stockbrokers and jobbers, often acquainted for years, looking each other straight in the eye and drawing on intuition and decades of experience? Here, on day one, was proof that the revolution was a flop. The computers had crashed.

Out in what the *Financial Times* referred to as 'the provinces', where the sister exchanges were hooked up to the mothership in London, confusion reigned among stockbrokers looking at blank screens. In the Stock Exchange Tower, parts of the system would work for a few minutes and then get overloaded again. Hayter and his team battled throughout the day, introducing patches and doing the equivalent of turning off the computer and turning it back on again. There were mocking headlines in the next day's newspapers, inevitably. 'Computer snafu derails London's new Stock system', was how the *Los Angeles Times* put it. The technical problems looked like a classic British balls-up, involving a Heath Robinson contraption resting on little more than the high hopes of gentlemen amateurs.

Such sniggering cynicism was deeply unfair. Hayter and his team were skilled professionals working under pressure who had devised something that stood a good chance of working, once the initial embarrassment faded and the TV crews disappeared. By the close of business on day one they had stabilised the situation. One of the brokers, Martin Pope of Hoare Govett, shrugged off the difficulties and gave the classic City response that could have been uttered for centuries: 'We had a good day, we made money. That's what it's all about.'

By the end of the week the system was functioning with only a few restrictions. Seaq started to work in harmony with TOPIC, and the volume and speed of trading grew rapidly. Like one of the first successful flying machines, bumping along the ground before only slowly gaining a little height and then beginning an ascent, they were up and away. The positions, the old booths on the floor of the Exchange, were not needed either. Goodison went down to look a few days after launch and the place was deserted because the brokers were all back at their offices with their colleagues, using screens and doing business by telephone. The old floor would not be needed. Big Bang had not brought the House down after all. It had cleared the way for an ambitious new computerised era. The City was ready for the future.

Margaret Thatcher, whose name is bound irrevocably with Big Bang, even though she had little to do with the intricacies of the measures, was not there that day. She did turn out two days later to another opening that encapsulated the can-do side of Thatcherism and the possibility-laden spirit that dominated then in the southeast of England. The completion of the final stretch of the M25 finished the orbital motorway around the capital that had first been proposed in 1905 and begun in 1973. Now cars would theoretically be able to whizz around the capital at high speed, in the motoring equivalent of the money revolution that had been launched a few days earlier. On the morning of the opening, 29 October, the Transport Secretary, John Moore, was taken over the route in a helicopter with officials to check that all was well before the Prime Minister turned up to cut the ribbon and make a speech. She was photographed striding out alone across the empty lanes, clutching her handbag, looking like Elizabeth I crossed with Elizabeth II. In her speech she said the M25 and the skills of the construction firms that built it symbolised Britain's 1980s revival. Then she returned to her increasingly weari-some complaint that criticism was running down the country: 'Now some people are saying that the road is too small, even that it's a disaster. I must say I can't *stand* those who carp and criticise when they ought to be congratulating Britain on a magnificent achieve-ment and beating the drum for Britain all over the world.' The M25, variously termed 'the most hated road in Britain' and the 'road to nowhere', soon became so busy and so essential to the economy of the capital that it was difficult to imagine a time when it had not been there.[10] It also presented illicit opportunities for those with sports cars to race at night, as part of a mysterious group termed by the media the 'M25' club. Police in Enfield said they had uncovered a dastardly plan for illegal road racing. Sergeant Eric Lock said: 'It is a rich race, with Ferrari [sic], Porsches and the very high-perfor-mance cars. We are pretty sure the race will be around the M25 in the early hours. We shall have extra patrols watching out and of course we have surveillance cameras dotted around the motorway. As well as all this all the drivers will have to stop at the Dartford Tunnel so we shall be ready for them.' The claims of the existence of a London equivalent of Hollywood's Cannonball Run, with yuppies and traders speeding around the orbital in their Ferraris, were first reported by a young journalist then working for *The Times*. His name was Boris Johnson.

GUINNESS IS GOOD FOR YOU

'If it was just insider dealing, it's not a proper crime like stealing.'
Scilla, in Caryl Churchill's *Serious Money* (1987)

By 30 October 1986 Nicholas Goodison had had more than enough of the press writing cheeky stories mocking the initial misfiring of his Big Bang. In a letter to the editor of *The Times*, the chairman of the Stock Exchange defended the launch and said the problems had been resolved.

> For four days now your columns have carried lurid and emotive words like 'fiasco', 'utter confusion', 'shambles' and 'collapse' – and <u>not a single word</u> about the huge improvements in the operation of the market. Whilst we are aware of our outstanding problems, and are working hard to solve them, I think you should be aware, Sir, that your packaging has been garish and your contents deficient.[1]

Goodison felt that the media saw it all as a tremendous lark in the long-established tradition of good old-fashioned British bungling. And he was right to feel aggrieved, in that the achievement of Hayter and his team was remarkable, especially given the pressures on time and the spotlight under which they were working. Trading had been moved largely successfully off the floor of the Exchange and the computers had worked 97 per cent of the time with £2bn worth of business (a normal amount) transacted each day. Within a few days many of the remaining glitches would be dealt with, the

A pair of 1980s yuppies, of the London variety.

trading floor at the Exchange would be left all but empty, trading volumes would soar, and the execution of Big Bang would be hailed as an achievement, even if the ethical implications would remain a subject of dispute outside the City.

That autumn, the Prime Minister was certainly keen to celebrate what had been achieved. In her annual speech to the City's grandees at the Mansion House on 10 November, she praised Goodison by name, and his colleagues, for their foresight and hard work in the face of 'teething troubles' and 'a good deal of knocking copy'.[2] The carping obscured an injection of youthful energy and dynamism, she said. 'The City's growing confidence and drive owe a good deal to young people. Its vast new dealing rooms are run by the young. People who made it not because of who they know or what school tie they wear, but on sheer merit. That is the kind of society I want to see. Gone are the controls which hampered success.' Once again, the Thatcherites were talking in terms of control being abandoned. Even though Thatcher went on to explain in her speech that the government had established a new legal framework, the greater and more excited emphasis was put on the liberating aspects of techno-logical change and the virility of younger traders. It is little wonder that this rather than the truth about regulation became the domi-nant narrative. Nevertheless, she added that the City's prosperity depended on its reputation for probity and fair dealing. 'The Stock Exchange has long had an impressive motto: "My Word is My Bond". That principle is not only part of its history, it is the basis of an even more successful future.'

Earlier that day, before Thatcher's speech in the evening at the Mansion House, someone senior who had betrayed that 'My Word is My Bond' motto resigned at Morgan Grenfell. Geoffrey Collier, head of the securities division, had been caught trading on inside information and funnelling the proceeds into an offshore account under another name. Until August 1985, Collier ran the Vickers de Costa operation in New York, before he was poached by Morgan Grenfell ahead of Big Bang. His signing-on fee, buying out his interests in the US, was a tax-free £250,000 and in his first year in his new position he earned £125,000. Even so, he traded on his own account without informing his employer, in breach of the rules, losing £30,000 in October 1986 when a tip he had about Cadbury Schweppes went wrong and the share price dipped unexpectedly. In early November he met with Robert Maxwell who was seeking to purchase an engineering group. Collier tried again and, through a contact in the US, secretly bought himself £144,000 of shares, giving him a profit of £15,000 when the news of the takeover offer became public. The management was alerted quickly by suspicious staff at the broker he had used, Scrimgeour Vickers. Not only was Collier in breach of company rules, which dictated every personal trade had to go through the company's own broker so it could be scrutinised; he had also broken the law. Collier – whose tough talk before Big Bang faded when it became clear he was a quiet family man facing potential ruin – was fired that day and a police investigation was launched. Several days later, Christopher Reeves, the chief executive of Morgan Grenfell, assured the press that such activity was not widespread: 'Mr. Collier clearly breached staff rules. This is something we are not prepared to tolerate, however senior the man.' It was an isolated incident, said a spokesman.

Following this setback, the year which had begun so promisingly at Morgan Grenfell was about to get a good deal worse. Reeves was regarded as one of the best bankers of his generation and after taking over the aged merchant bank in 1980 he had built it into a formidable machine. When it floated some of itself on the Stock Exchange in the same year as the run-up to Big Bang, raising more than £150m, demand was high and the offer was five times oversubscribed. But the aggressive push made by Morgan Grenfell turned out to have come at a cost, as was revealed by the exposure of Collier, and then a few weeks later by the emergence of the much bigger Guinness scandal. Although it had nothing to do directly with Big Bang, and its origins preceded the autumn of 1986, the illicit dealing and share support that were suddenly revealed were an extreme manifestation of the takeover mania consuming British business and finance in the 1980s. Indeed, Morgan Grenfell's testosterone surge that got it into such trouble was rooted in its aggressive expansion in that area. In 1986 it was the leader in London, seeking out, suggesting and advising on 111 takeovers. The revelation that the Guinness deal was suspect came via an investigation by US regulators that exposed a network on Wall Street of insider trading and share ramping by elite investment bankers supplementing their already vast incomes with trading on the side. Ivan Boesky, a tough operator who had used his wife's wealth to found his own stock trading firm, had made a fortune of several hundred million dollars by gambling on company takeovers. In November 1986, with Boesky cooperating with the SEC investigation in the US (he had even turned federal agent) he offered the information, almost as a throwaway, that Guinness in London had invested $100m with him. When news of this connection was passed to investigators at the Department of Trade and Industry in London, it led to an inquiry into the bid for Distillers. On 1 December, with Ernest Saunders, chairman and chief executive of Guinness, at work at his desk in London, two DTI officials turned up unannounced in reception at 9.30am. Their arrival caused panic.

In the US it was a tiny part, incidental even, in the uncovering of the multi-billion dollar racket in which the ringmasters were arbitrageurs such as Boesky. Eventually the much bigger fish – Michael Milken on the US West Coast – would fry too. In the UK, however, Guinness turned into the biggest corporate scandal of the decade. The transatlantic nature of the dealings and the sums involved demonstrated the increasingly interconnected nature of fast-moving markets, which was attributable to the spread of technology and the presence of the Americans in London and Tokyo. Although dynamism brought benefits, it also increased the potential for cultural contagion, not just in terms of market panic if stocks crashed, but also in the manner in which serious sums could be diverted almost instantly and the way in which corruption might spill across continents when borders were blurred. To critics of the City, it looked then as though an American virus had been injected into the British bloodstream, especially when figures such as Boesky were prepared to make the following statements: 'Greed is all right, by the way,' he told the 1986 graduation of UC–Berkeley's business school. 'I think greed is healthy. You can be greedy and still feel good about yourself.' Even if you think that, and you shouldn't, it is unwise to say it in public. There was another plausible interpretation, of course: that it had always gone on and the new generation was just more blatant and less embarrassed.

What was Saunders accused of in December 1986? During the takeover battle for Distillers that began in late 1985, he had organised a share support operation to keep the Guinness share price high and stiff the rival bidders, the Argyll Group run by James Gulliver. Those under investigation protested that this technique was hardly unknown in the City, even if the sums involved this time (as much as £300m) were large. The money invested with Boesky had landed after he bought Guinness and Distillers shares heavily. He was operating alongside a small group of investors and favoured speculators in London and Switzerland who were invited into the secret operation and given payments and an indemnity against any fall in the price of the shares they bought secretly on behalf of Saunders' team. Literally, they could not lose. 'They were greedy but they were caught in between eras, when one era ended and another began,' says a leading banker of the time, referring to the changes in regulation and the government's hardening attitude. 'It was that point when the music stops in musical chairs, and some people are left standing.'

Saunders was not the only person left exposed. Soon it became clear that some of the City's smartest names – including Cazenove – had been involved in arranging these trades, although they protested that they were innocent of wrongdoing. As an advisor to Guinness, Morgan Grenfell was implicated and Reeves – whose friends claimed he had known little directly about what had gone on – came under pressure from appalled officials at the Bank of England. On 30 December, amid a blizzard of revelations in the press, Morgan Grenfell resigned as advisors to Guinness. That day

Roger Seelig, the Morgan Grenfell takeover specialist who had handled the Guinness deal, was sacked. In mid-January, Saunders himself was fired by the board of Guinness, and at Morgan Grenfell on 20 January, Reeves resigned along with Graham Walsh, the corporate finance director. Rarely, since the scandals of the nineteenth century, had there been such a casualty list in a financial scandal, and the investigation had only begun.

Somewhat awkwardly, the City authorities and the government were then caught between hoping that the incidence of white-collar crime and insider trading was extremely low, while also wanting to advertise that the place was being energetically cleaned up. Both could not be true. Says one leading banker of the time on the question of insider dealing: 'It would not be legitimate at all to say that everyone was at it but it was a significant minority I think.' Says a former jobber: 'Some people had thrived for years on that "fill your boots" mentality, running their little sidelines. Most of it was pretty small. You have to remember that before the law changed the City ran anyway on inside information, on price-sensitive information that if you were attentive you picked up on the way to lunch or to the pub. You ran into someone and they said, "I'd take a look at X, very interesting. They've just had some good news that's not public yet; going to be good for the share price." People being what they are, some didn't abuse that. Others did.' One infuriating and baffling aspect, as far outsiders were concerned, was that as the City grew, financiers and traders such as Collier at Morgan Grenfell were already – legally – making large amounts of money. Yet still it seemed not to be enough and some made illicit trades in addition. How much more did they really need? As someone who has spent a lifetime in the City and worked on many of the biggest deals of the period puts it thirty years later: 'I'm sorry, it was greed. Big Bang let a lot of the crooks in. There you have it.'

That may be an exaggeration. George Blakey, in his history of the Stock Market, explained that there was nothing new about encouraging institutions and large individual investors to support a share price during a takeover attempt. It was merely a question of discretion and scale. It had usually been done by a nod or a wink over lunch at the Savoy Grill, or in the evening in clubland in St James's. 'Until this point, no authority would have been expected to question seriously the conduct of the City's leading merchant banks, stockbrokers and their clients. What the Guinness/Morgan Grenfell/Cazenove case did was to shatter the belief that the customary test of legitimacy was who you were, not what you did.'

The government's unease about these events was understandable. In all other respects Margaret Thatcher was extremely well placed ahead of an anticipated election in 1987. The economy under Nigel Lawson was growing strongly – at 3.2 per cent in 1986 and picking up speed – while unemployment had started in January 1986 to fall from stubbornly high levels. On the industrial front, the violent Wapping print dispute rumbled on over that winter, when thousands of activists fought with police outside the print plant that had been built in London east of Tower Hill to end the 'Spanish practices' that bedevilled the newspaper business.[3] After the Miners' Strike of 1984–5, Wapping marked the death of the power of the militant side of trade unionism. Indeed, the Tory leader recorded in her memoirs later that she felt at the end of 1986 as though it was all coming together. The reforms she had put in place were embedded and the privatisation and liberalisation of financial markets would soon be copied abroad. The Thatcherites had won.

The only economic blot, even in the parts of the country well disposed towards Thatcher, was the strong whiff of corruption wafting over from the Square Mile. In mitigation, the Prime Minister could point to the privatisation of British Gas in December 1986, centring on an advertising campaign bearing the catchphrase 'If you see Sid, tell 'im.' Sid was supposed to symbolise the British 'punter' being let in on a valuable secret. Although the tone was jocular and patronising, irritatingly so, the intent was deadly serious. There remained widespread public scepticism about privatisation (a word even Thatcher said in public that she did not much care for) on the grounds that it involved selling what many taxpayers thought they already had collective ownership of through their government. When the advertising agency Dewe Rogerson drew up its initial report planning the sale, it warned that overcoming voter hostility would require a television, radio and press advertising campaign that presented it as a not-to-be-missed opportunity for small investors. It was the creative agency Young & Rubicam that came up with the everyman Sid. It worked. With six weeks to go until the offer, there had been almost two million enquiries made to the telephone hotline, and polling suggested that there was a 74 per cent awareness of Sid among adults. When the final adverts were made, the agency wanted to give Sid a good send-off. He was cast as a climber disappearing into the clouds at the summit, as the final message reminded Britons not to forget to apply for shares in British Gas. In early December 1986, in a buoyant market, more than five million people did just that. 'British Gas', the Energy Secretary, Peter Walker, told the Commons, would have 'the largest number of shareholders of any company in the world'. Some 85,000 employees of British Gas, 99 per cent of the workforce, had applied, he added. A sale raising £5.6bn was used by the government to hymn the success of the concept of 'popular capitalism' and the extension of ownership. The opening up of one-time state monopolies to outside investment could not have been done without the help and expertise of the City.

There was not much time for ministers to celebrate, however, as early in the new year the focus was straight back on the flow of revelations and resignations resulting from the Guinness scandal. On 22 January 1987, Thatcher attempted to make it clear in the Commons that she would not tolerate any nonsense from the City, a line of defence that did not impress Labour MPs. 'I remind the House that this Government is fully committed to rooting out financial wrongdoing wherever it occurs,' she said. 'Because this Government made insider trading a criminal offence and provided that upon conviction it should carry a prison sentence.' On 28

January, Cazenove was cited in the Commons over Guinness. With the protection of parliamentary privilege, Labour's Robin Cook accused the firm of ramping up the share price. Sir Alex Fletcher, a Tory MP who as former Minister of Consumer and Corporate Affairs had enjoyed a small walk-on part in the preparations for Big Bang, spoke of dark deeds, although he was a consultant to Argyll, the rival to Guinness in the Distillers battle. He said that Price Waterhouse, the accountants tasked with examining the accounts of Guinness, 'might find evidence of cash payments for which there are no invoices that were probably made in plain brown envelopes and made to members of the professional criminal classes'. What a combination: 'might find evidence . . . cash payments . . . brown envelopes . . . the criminal classes'. Even Tory business-minded MPs were upping the rhetoric. The government was so concerned by the furore that Norman Tebbit even went as far as to invoke Conservative trade union reforms to illustrate the determination to tackle insider dealing and other illegality: 'We cleaned up the trade union movement and we'll clean up the City,' he said in early 1987.

Here there were a number of difficulties. At the time, the Secretary of State for Trade and Industry was Paul Channon. Being a Guinness he had to recuse himself during the investigation, even though he was not directly linked to the management of the company.[4] The association was unfortunate in the middle of a clean-up, even though he was blameless. Worse, the phrase self-regulation in terms of the City had become fixed in the political media and public imagination as the root of the problem. The Thatcherite emphasis on the term deregulation meant that there was no chance of getting a hearing for the notion that the rules were being tightened or that for the first time there was a statutory, legal framework. Sir Peter Tapsell MP, who had worked in the City, summed up how it looked: 'To the average citizen, defending self-regulation sounds like letting the privileged protect their own. Nobody blames the US Republicans for Boesky because Wall Street is regulated by the SEC. If Britain had a similar body, the Conservatives could no more be blamed for this than for the Great Train Robbery.'⁵ The Labour Party was even more blunt in its pre-election criticism of the government's handling of Guinness. 'The scandal shows how easily the unscrupulous and shameless reward themselves in Mrs Thatcher's Britain,' said John Smith, the party's trade and industry spokesman. This line of attack infuriated government ministers. To Michael Howard, who had steered through the Act mandating re-regulation of the City that became law in November 1986, it made no sense whatsoever. They were cracking down hard, weren't they? The DTI launched another four investigations into insider trading in the weeks after the Boesky and Saunders revelations and there were some signs that the DTI investigations were beginning to have the cooling effect that the government desired, at least ahead of the election. There seemed for a while to be a pause in the take-over boom. Why would aggressive takeover artists risk poor public-ity and worse with the government under pressure to show it was not soft on the City? In mid-January, the corporate raiders BTR dropped a bid for Pilkington, the long-established British glass-maker. Amid concern on the government side, and with members of the Labour front bench revving up to attack City greed and corporate vandalism, it was not the ideal moment to attempt a controversial takeover of a prominent British company. The lull was short-lived, however, and contrary to much of the reporting in the early part of that year, 1987 set a new takeover record in the UK.⁶ There were 1,125 such deals to a value of £15.4bn. In 1984 the equivalent figures had been 568 acquisitions to a value of only £5.5bn. Merger mania was not over yet, and it would take some-thing else other than Guinness to reduce the pace and restore a sense of proportion.

First, there was the 1987 general election to prepare for. In Lawson's Budget on 17 March, the Chancellor cut the basic rate of tax (by 2p to 27p) and taxes on small business were reduced in a package that was received warmly by Conservative backbenchers looking to hold their seats. It was popular with those in the market too, and the FTSE continued its rise. The stock market was only the most public manifestation of exuberance and rising confidence in the City's position. London's clout was also demonstrated by the increasing commitment of the American and Japanese houses to the UK capital. Between 1984 and 1986 the American firms – CSFB, Goldman Sachs, Merrill Lynch, Shearson Lehman, Drexel Burnham Lambert and John Gutfreund's Salomon Brothers – had more than doubled their staffing in London, from 2,311 to 5,519. The Japanese staffed up too. This was encouraging, although there was a drawback. As the economist John O'Matthews put it: 'The result was to add capacity to markets with existing overcapacity.' The foreign firms were also there for access to the Eurobond markets, and to make money from the dramatic increase in Euromarket activity. The volume of new issuance increased by almost 400 per cent from 1983 to 1986, in which year it hit $191.7bn. The total turnover of the Eurobond market, three-quarters of which was in London, stood at $2 trillion. Again, this received little attention. It was simpler by far to concentrate on the glamour of takeovers, and the hypnotic graphs on television news programmes that showed share prices for household names rising, and footage of confident young men (and increasing numbers of women) looking serious on the telephone while making millions and then taking the edge off it with a glass of champagne in one of the City's wine bars in the evening.

London's confidence was by no means all chemical-fuelled hubris, however. It was well positioned to prosper from what had begun (in the early 1970s) as a veritable explosion in money, in how it could be moved, traded and imagined. It seemed as though the US was losing its advantage. Japan's securities houses had been growing so rapidly – fuelled by money from booming Japanese industry – that they now dwarfed their American counterparts. Nomura had a market cap of $33.6bn at the end of 1986, against $5.9bn for the aggressive Salomon and $4bn for Merrill Lynch. London, with its historic advantages, was in the process of becoming the global crossroads where all these firms needed to be. In the spring of 1987, in international terms, despite the scandals and disgrace, Britain was back. Thatcher sought a third term looking forward to further reform and innovation, and Lawson made it clear to the Prime Minister that he would be part of it. He wanted to stay on as Chancellor after the election because his ambition was to complete his overhaul of the UK's tax system, and to bring down those taxes substantially.

Later in the same week as the March 1987 pre-election Budget, a play opened at the Royal Court theatre in London that sought to encapsulate London's financial revolution and to capture the essence of Big Bang's afterglow. The playwright Caryl Churchill's *Serious Money* was a satire on trading in which the new City was presented as being simply a cruder version of its ancient predecessor. In the text there are echoes of those plays written in the eighteenth century in the aftermath of the South Sea Bubble, and in particular of William Chetwood's *South-Sea; or the Biters Bit*. ('Plow: A Stock-jobber! Pray, Sir, what Religion may he be of?') Churchill and the cast – which included Gary Oldman, Alfred Molina and Meera Syal – visited the floor of LIFFE to familiarise themselves with the colourful, noisy futures market operating out of the Royal Exchange Building. When the play opened, the theatre critics were, as is usually the case, divided.[7] Martin Hoyle, of the City's own *Financial Times*, hated what had been done by Churchill and the director Max Stafford-Clark, the artistic director of the Royal Court. Stafford-Clark had been, along with David Hare, one of the founders in the 1970s of the socialist alternative theatre company, Joint Stock, which shared a name with the term used to describe early capitalist companies, the joint-stock companies such as the South Sea. An unimpressed Coveney described Churchill's writing in *Serious Money* as witless and facetious, churned out in doggerel, 'neither Restoration couplets nor Victorian panto poesy but a broken-backed jumble of varying rhythms, metre and rhyme that the author shoves into the ragbag from one moment to the next . . . Insiders may well enjoy the play. Outsiders may experience a numbing boredom.'

Some critics had perhaps missed part of the point, in that *Serious Money* was meant to be noisy, bawdy, uneven, cunning, silly, fun and fast-paced, just like the City, mirroring a trading session at LIFFE or a spot of stockjobbing in Change Alley in the eighteenth century. Churchill had produced an era-defining classic. Michael Billington in the *Guardian* rightly judged that she and Stafford-Clark, and the cast, had set out to produce a critique, a 'socialist play about a capitalist pleasure' as the *Listener* magazine called it. Yet they had ended up, in Billington's words, as fascinated by the City's frenzied energy as they were by its moral unscrupulousness. The critic from the *FT* was prescient in one sense, in that it was the insiders who loved *Serious Money* most. Tickets soon became coveted by dealers; indeed, they were that summer a tradable commodity. The City journalist Neil Collins in the *Daily Telegraph* described the excitement: 'Designed by Ms Churchill as a savage attack on the City, the same rough-edged dealers have flocked to see it in their hundreds, organising parties, taking the whole office, and having fun identifying themselves on the stage.' Max Stafford-Clark insisted that he was pleased the traders liked their portrayal: 'If you capture accurately enough the world of the people you are depicting, then it's very flattering and they will come and see it, just as people did in the Restoration.'

The success of the play had demonstrated one of the paradoxes of the period. Those in the vanguard of the financial revolution – the new generation of fast-rising traders who were questioned and increasingly mocked by middle-class journalists for their ethics, their accents, their behaviour or their taste in clothes or cars – were not ashamed. And why should they be in the circumstances? Their heroine, the Prime Minister, presented their ambition as a force for good, banishing memories of national decline. And who were the upper middle classes in particular to call the socially mobile traders vulgar anyway? In the City, as partners, the officer class had taken the money and run away at high speed during the carnival of largesse when old firms were bought up by Americans and other firms pre-Big Bang. Now that the Bang had boomed why shouldn't the troops see some of the action too?

The drama was not over, though. As spring turned into summer, it looked to outsiders as though levels of smugness on pay and status were going through the roof. As far as Thomas Sutcliffe was concerned, writing in the *Independent* that summer on the City dealer fashion for going to the theatre to see Caryl Churchill's play, the enthusiasm had got completely out of hand. The traders flocking to *Serious Money* were spoiling things for the rest of the audience, he wrote. 'It's now a little like going to see *The Resistible Rise of Arturo Ui* with a coach party of SS men.'

HIGH SUMMER

'I don't think we're going to see any more scandals on a very large scale. I think people have learnt their lesson.'

Ian Harwood, Warburg Securities, June 1987

On Friday 12 June 1987, the day after Margaret Thatcher's third general election victory, the BBC sent the presenter Joan Bakewell across to the City in search of jubilant traders at lunchtime. Let's go, said David Dimbleby, the forty-eight-year-old anchor of the Corporation's rolling election coverage, to an aerial shot from the airship the BBC had hired for the day: 'Looking down over the Big Bang . . . those huge towers that have gone up over the last few years . . . where the yuppies live, the people who drive down there between half past four and half past seven in the morning in their Porsches we're told and make a lot of money.' Signalling the relief of traders who did not want a Labour government, the stock market opened up strongly that morning in response to the news that the Conservatives had been re-elected with a majority of 102 seats.

It had been a scratchy contest defined by infighting in the Tory high command over how best to take on Neil Kinnock and see off Labour's slick but ultimately unsuccessful campaign. Once the camera crew with Bakewell had got its pictures of brick-like mobile phones and champagne flutes outside a bar, she asked a group of traders wearing the coloured jackets of those who worked at LIFFE whether they were going to become even richer now the Tories had got back in. They demurred at the idea that they were rich at all. So why were they celebrating? 'Why am I so pleased? Because I'm standing out here drinking champagne, basically,' said one. If Bakewell was looking for triumphalism among Thatcher's children, what she found instead was calm reflection and an eloquent explanation from several of the traders that the result would not make them any better off. Labour's high taxes, they said, would have made both them and the country worse off. But, asked Bakewell, what about the unemployed and the homeless? Unemployment would go down now, hopefully, one of the traders said: 'It's the safest and steadiest the country's been for years. Keep it on an even keel.' 'We've never had it so good, as they say,' said his colleague. 'Yeah,' said the first trader, taking a swig of champagne, 'Harold Macmillan. Where is he?'

The answer was that Harold Macmillan was no longer with us. The former Prime Minister had died in December the previous year at Birch Grove, his country house in Sussex. Macmillan's death represented the passing of a particular kind of patrician twentieth-century Toryism. The old 'actor-manager' was born in the late nineteenth century; he had fought and was wounded five times in the First World War; his career had been rescued and reinvented thanks to his appointment by Churchill in the Second; and as Prime Minister he hosted President Kennedy at Birch Grove in 1963. While he was opposed to Thatcher's approach to economics, it would not be true to say that Macmillan lacked understanding of aspiration. Far from it. He was introduced to an earlier version of social mobility when he lost his northern parliamentary seat, Stockton, in 1945 and switched immediately in a by-election to the safe seat of Bromley in Kent, where the Old Etonian encountered the rising, southern part of the lower middle classes working in new industries and in offices. He was curious about those who came from a different background to him, as he had been in the trenches. 'I am always hearing about the middle classes', he wrote to the director of the Conservative research department in 1957. 'What is it that they really want? Can you put it down on a sheet of notepaper, and then I will see whether we can give it to them?'[1] Thatcher needed no such guidance in discerning what Middle England voters wanted out of life; she was of striving Middle England herself and her instincts accorded perfectly with those voters she needed to reach to win. She was helped to that final electoral victory in the summer of 1987 by the opposition forces remaining divided too.

What had most troubled Macmillan and other so-called 'one nation' Conservatives about thrusting 1980s Thatcherism was that it seemed to have divided the country itself, between south and north and haves and have-nots. Such opinions were hardly unusual in the British Establishment in the 1980s, and indeed they formed the main thrust of the account the *Sunday Times* had already published of the Queen's concerns about the style and policies of the Prime Minister. The Conservatives certainly won a thumping majority in 1987, but in large parts of the country they had few or no seats. In Scotland, they were down to only ten constituencies and unlike in the US, where the Reaganite revolution was far more evenly spread geographically, pro-market Thatcherism was by this point a phenomenon that was in electoral terms largely (although not exclusively) restricted to the populous south centred on London and to parts of the Midlands. This puzzled Thatcher no end, especially in relation to Scotland, from where hailed the eighteenth-century father of market economics, Adam Smith. Her polite attempt to explain all this enraged her opponents when she later made the 'Sermon on the Mound' speech to the General Assembly of the Church of Scotland in Edinburgh in 1988, extolling the virtues of capitalism and giving the Scots credit for originating free market Thatcherism via Smith. The Tory leader's remarks went down that day in much of Scotland about as well as a request for a glass of Pimm's and a copy of *Tatler* in a Glasgow bar.

The other source of Macmillan's concern about the state of mid-1980s Britain in the years before his death was less well advertised, although it was linked to his condemnation of privatisation that was being achieved with the assistance of bankers and brokers. Macmillan had long retained an intense suspicion and dislike of the City, which was rooted in his experience of the late 1920s and the failures of finance that then caused large-scale unemployment. Anti-Semitism may have played a part. In private, Macmillan even used the term 'banksters' to describe bankers, according to Nigel Lawson, who knew him and in 1963 was drafted in to improve Macmillan's speeches. Macmillan had resigned by the time Lawson arrived and he found himself working for his aristocratic successor Alec Douglas-Home instead. In the mid-1980s as Chancellor, Lawson was pivotal in unravelling the Macmillan approach to economic management, rejecting the old Keynesian nostrum of delivering full employment through demand management and government involvement in industry. The Thatcherite programme so hated by opponents at that point and celebrated by its advocates as a British rebirth was not conservative in the usual sense, even if it involved going back to open markets, mobile money and the concept of London as a leading international trading hub as it had been at its Victorian and Edwardian peak. The Thatcherite impulse involved the sudden unleashing of such powerful disruptive forces in terms of class and attitudes to money that it made supporters and opponents alike aware that there was a revolution underway.

In such potentially combustible circumstances, with large parts of Britain unpersuaded and sympathetic to the colourful charges made by Labour that the Thatcherites were empowering spivs who cared only for cash, it would have helped if everyone in the City had behaved themselves that summer of 1987. Unfortunately that was not the case, and with a four-year bull run reaching its culmination, optimism tipped into outright greed and recklessness. Those in the markets pushing up prices on the FTSE 100 – up almost 25 per cent in 1986 and up 46 per cent in the first seven months of 1987 – did not have the benefit of hindsight, although those who cared to look could have found plenty of indications of what might be around the corner if they had examined the history of financial markets during periods of exuberance. There had also been a warning in another part of the market that what goes up can come down. In late 1986 and early 1987, the Floating Rate Note market – in the Eurobond market – experienced extreme turbulence. At Salomon Brothers in

London there was an inquest. Many of those selling in other firms had no experience, it was noted in memos. They were youngsters earning a lot of money with no understanding of the destructive power of a sudden change in conditions for the worse. Bosses were obsessed with getting their firm higher up the league tables, which meant reckless over-expansion. They had collaborated to ramp up the market, and investors who had grown careless had now been driven away when they realised they were being exploited.

Elsewhere, among traders there was comfort in knowing that the rises were replicated and even exceeded in the international centres. It was the Japanese who seemed to have taken complete leave of their senses, and if there was a correction due it would surely be worst there. Tokyo's Nikkei 225 index, bigger by total value than the US stock market for much of the 1980s, rocketed almost 11,000 points in the twelve months before October 1987, and it soon recovered from a tumble that June and July.

There was also a brief dip in the FTSE 100 in July after it hit a peak for the year on the 16th of 2443.4 points. The correction suggested share prices were coming back into line with the reality and that after this sensible adjustment there was no need for anything more dramatic. There were other positive signs too that the British were adjusting to life after Big Bang. After the excitements of the winter, one of the City's biggest names seemed to be in the process of sorting itself out. John Craven – of Phoenix Securities – had been drafted in that spring as chief executive at Morgan Grenfell to clean up after Collier and Guinness. That summer when he joined he reassured the press and investors that although Morgan Grenfell may have been bruised by scandal it was fundamentally sound: 'It's a hell of a good business that happened to have a couple of nasty setbacks recently.'[2]

It was possible to think post-election that all was set fair. Another talking head used by the BBC on election day plus one was Ian Harwood of Warburg Securities, who explained to the interviewer Nick Clarke the prospects for the years ahead. His remarks stand as a pretty good epitaph for the era, as well as being an example of the age-old tendency to excessive optimism in a boom. What, asked Clarke, about all the scandals? 'I don't think we're going to see any more scandals on a very large scale,' said Harwood. 'I think people have learnt their lesson.' That hopeful statement about lessons learnt could have been made in one form or another at pretty much any time since the 1720s and the mopping up after the bursting of the South Sea Bubble.

The denouement of the Geoffrey Collier case on insider dealing came on 1 July, when the former Morgan Grenfell man was sentenced. A media scrum outside the Old Bailey greeted the Oxford-educated Collier and his wife, although inside he got a more considerate reception. Collier had made a terrible mistake and he felt deep remorse, his wife Barbara said. This was echoed by his QC, Sir Robert Alexander, who, by a remarkable coincidence of the kind then not exactly unknown in the City, had recently been appointed chairman of the Takeover Panel, the voluntary body that policed mergers and acquisitions. The large house the Colliers owned in the Kent countryside had been traded in for something much smaller in Sevenoaks and the judge acknowledged that the experience of the trial had been crushing. He spared Collier a jail term, handing down a twelve-month suspended sentence and an order to pay £32,000 of fines and costs. During the trial his QC pointed out that Collier was a talented young man who would now struggle to find employment worthy of his abilities. He and his family subsequently moved to the United States and, based in Connecticut over several decades, he worked his way back legitimately working for a French bank.

With Wall Street enthralled and terrified by the ongoing SEC investigations, and Boesky awaiting sentencing by spending the summer enrolled at the Jewish Theology College in Manhattan studying Hebrew and the Talmud, it seemed as though the American taste for sudden and swift retribution was kicking in. In the UK, where the treatment of financial wrongdoing had traditionally been less robust, or handled with possibly too much discretion, the authorities were getting tougher. The investigation into the Guinness scandal continued, and the Department of

Trade and Industry also finally confronted the reality of fraud in Barlow Clowes, a non-City firm run by Peter Clowes that had promised extraordinary returns to investors while Clowes bought a château in France and private jets. Since Clowes was based outside the City, it was not the DTI's responsibility. He was supposed to be licensed by the DTI, and the rackety bond-buying business he had begun in Manchester was registered in Jersey. In the excitement of 1987 he attracted City attention by trying to go legitimate through buying other firms and attempting to list them on the Stock Exchange.

There was another striking example of peak boom behaviour that summer, although this time it was entirely legal, when the fledgling development at Canary Wharf in London's Docklands changed ownership in July. Michael von Clemm had already left Credit Suisse First Boston the previous year and the other bankers involved in the consortium gradually came to the view, in property developer Gooch Ware Travelstead's words, that they did not want to be developers and builders of the biggest property development in Europe. A buyer would have to be found for the land and the plan. This is not unknown in such projects, as the originators and initial investors decide to sell to a developer with deeper pockets or greater appetite for risk. But publicly it looked for a while as though the sceptics were right and Travelstead's vision of creating a rival or an extension to the City in the east would not be realised.

In early July the banks pulled out and the project was up for sale, prompting considerable press speculation about potential embarrassment for the government. The press did not know that Travelstead had been negotiating with Paul Reichmann, a Toronto-based property tycoon who was expanding his business rapidly. The UK – revived by Thatcherite reform, as he described it – was a place to invest big. Travelstead and Reichmann discussed the potential of Docklands as an international financial centre and on 17 July it was announced that Reichmann's family company – Olympia & York – had bought complete control of the £3bn project. At a drinks reception held a few days later to celebrate the deal, Reichmann forecast that the first phase of five million square feet of Canary Wharf office space would be ready within two years. If the locals remained unconvinced and community activists continued to put up billboards saying Docklands regeneration promised only 'jam for the developers, traffic jams for us', the organised opposition had started to wane after Thatcher's third election victory. Labour councils realised Canary Wharf was going to happen. On 30 July the Docklands Light Railway was opened by the Queen. She was taken by boat from Greenwich across to the Isle of Dogs, and by train to Poplar and then Tower Hill.

The Reichmann deal also meant two visionaries departed the scene. Reg Ward, the unorthodox but brilliant chief executive of the London Docklands Development Corporation, was levered out in murky circumstances. Gooch Ware Travelstead went voluntarily too from his beloved project. In doing so he claims he faced one of those life-changing binary choices, when for his 20 per cent of Canary Wharf Paul Reichmann offered him cash then or a five-year unsecuritised note from Olympia & York potentially paying out far more. Travelstead, to his eternal regret, took the note and only a little cash up front. In a decade of deals, the Reichmann trade turned out to be not as good as it seemed at the time, although in mid-1987 the atmosphere was so relentlessly go-go that the prospect of an imminent market crash or a serious reversal in the property market seemed distant enough to take the chance.

The atmosphere was most exuberant in the area of pay, as a survey of earnings published by *The Times* in 1987 demonstrated.[3] With firms competing to recruit the best, an investment dealer could expect £102,613, made up of £65,984 in basic pay and £36,629 in bonus. A chief Eurobond dealer earned a total of £84,133; a director of corporate finance £62,402; and a manager of forex dealing £42,719. These were averages for specific tasks and it was possible to gain the wrong impression from such surveys when the overwhelming majority of staff were not earning large salaries. As had long been the case, the City functioned thanks to the hard work of an army of staff who did not attract high pay or publicity. Even so, the rates of pay at the upper and middle end were rising fast, along with bonuses across firms that all staff benefited from. This was at a time when the average wage in the UK was a little over £11,000 and pay rises in parts of the public sector were held to a minimum after years of freezes. In the years before the television deals that transformed the English game, a footballer playing in the top English division in 1987 earned on average £62,400, although large bonuses could be earned on top of that.[4]

The London Banks Personnel Management Group also kept score in the City. In one of its regular surveys in 1987 it noted that typical pay outside finance had risen 45 per cent between the end of 1981 and late 1986. Meanwhile, general banking staff in London had enjoyed an average increase of 57 per cent in the same period; pay for foreign exchange dealers and Treasury specialists had increased 74 per cent and for management in investment banking and the capital markets the rise was 176 per cent in just five years. Simultaneously, interest rates fell from 14 per cent in 1985 to 9 per cent by 1987 and house prices climbed correspondingly when it became easier to borrow and confidence rose. A typical London property bought in 1983 for £50,000 was worth £95,559 by 1987. Although the average figures in the rest of the UK were lower, the rate of increase was similar. It was clear that if you were in work in the UK, your financial position was improving. If you were in work in the City and had serious responsibilities you were doing very well indeed.

Philippa Rose's City headhunting business was booming in mid-1987, and what she had started on her own aged twenty-one was now in such demand that clients were competing to persuade her to work for them. It was a glamorous and exciting time, in which she darted around Europe, staying in the best hotels and never having to worry about expenses, working direct for chief executives or other senior bankers, finding them the best, brightest young talent as business grew. There was a reason some people in the City were now earning loads more money, of course. London had long been underpaying for senior roles compared to Wall Street, and in the new dispensation the gap was suddenly transparent and unsustainable. As the *Guardian*'s Maggie Pagano, surveying the City employment market, described it: 'It was clear that employers would eventually have to pay the guy dealing in equities in London, earning perhaps £20,000 five years ago, the quadrupled salary level his equal in New York would be earning.' That being the case, no wonder ambitious youngsters wanted in.

By mid-1987 the City and finance more broadly had acquired an increased allure. In the US, Wall Street firms and management consultancies had increased their efforts from the early 1980s to recruit top graduates from the leading colleges, spending money on dominating recruitment fairs and marketing themselves to elite undergraduates. This was mirrored in the UK, where the share of new graduates in the UK going into banking, finance and insurance rose from 13.8 per cent in 1983 to 17.7 per cent in 1987. A skills shortage pushed up starting pay for gifted graduates, and the profusion of increasingly complex forms of trading and computer-based work meant that mathematicians and computer wizards were suddenly in demand. Modelling became the fashion and firms that had previously relied exclusively on the instincts and experience of their partners and senior staff, quite often working with inside information, now hired a new kind of financier.

'Peter, aged 27, is a classic example', wrote Pagano. 'He finished his PhD in nuclear physics about two years ago. He is now writing computer programs for the options trading desk and working on new products for one of the US's biggest investment banks based in London.' It could cause tensions and the infusion of technology did not always produce positive results. One trainee – being taught how to recommend stocks on the strength of minimal analysis, lunch and gut instinct – remembers his superiors mocking the nasal, mockney tones in which their new programmer, who had been hired from British Telecommunications, talked about his 'model'. 'How's yer model?' they asked him repeatedly. The 'model' and the recommendations it made turned out to be completely unsuited to stockbroking and worse than useless. Not every initiative worked,

although a large part of the future belonged to those who understood numbers and computers.

Just as there had been on Wall Street earlier, there was a boom
in demand for skilled analysts, who had long researched and
compiled reports on individual companies and market trends for
their broking firms or fund managers. Increasingly their work
would become fused with the sales force that existed to sell to
clients. Theoretically, there was supposed to be no blurring of the
line between what analysts recommended to customers and what
suited the company for which the analyst worked. Yet there was an
obvious risk of the customer being ill served by businesses that
were becoming more cutthroat and driven according to targets.
The old, clear division between brokers placing orders on behalf of
the client and jobbers in separate firms no longer existed. In many
post-Big bang firms it all came together under one roof with bigger
potential rewards.

Loyalty to an employer and colleagues suddenly counted for a lot
less in 1987, which was not simply down to the prospect of higher
pay. When the partners sold their firms, only a few firms adequately
shared the largesse with those in the executive tranche below – the
so-called marzipan layer – who were not partners but often did a
great deal of the work. 'We in the old guard were pretty selfish, yes,'
says one of them now. 'I regret that too late.' Why should an ambitious employee commit to one of the new conglomerations for life
when the older generation of partners had enriched themselves and
shown no loyalty to the heritage of their own firms? It all combined
to make employees much more willing to move jobs for the right
package, which imported something of Wall Street's ruthlessness
and its hire-and-fire culture, pay by results, big bonuses and macho
posturing.

Language coarsened too. There had always been a certain amount
of colourful talk in the City; now it acquired a cutting edge. In this
language you hadn't been ripped off or treated poorly by a rival in a
deal, you had been 'raped'. In London, the mingling of Wall Street-
style bond trader bragging, upper-middle-class uber-confidence and

Essex-boy-and-girl market-stall-trader straight talking produced a strange fusion, rich with possibility for satirists.

There was also an explosion of colour and sartorial extravagance in the hitherto buttoned-up City. Braces (suspenders in the US) had long been a City staple, or certainly among partners and senior management, but the dress code had always stipulated muted colours, along with plain white shirts and regulation suits. Now there was an eruption of colour on trading floors, in the form of brightly coloured braces, and the striped shirt, which would once have been considered a vulgar non-starter in the better firms, now became ubiquitous. The increasing number of young women being hired by banks and broking firms also had available a new palette of style choices thanks to the emphasis on power dressing. It blended aspects of the extravagant New Romantic fashions favoured by young clubbers in the capital earlier in the decade; the shoulder-padded sheen of American soaps such as *Dallas* glamorising ruthless businesses practices; and the increasing popularity of Italian designers such as Giorgio Armani. That burst of fresh colour in London and Wall Street did not extend to skin colour, however, other than in Japanese banks that employed Japanese staff sent to London. On trading floors, in backroom settlement operations and in banks, the staff remained almost exclusively white. There was an alteration in the balance of the classes, although so rapid was the cross pollination that it was sometimes hard for outsiders to work out where the street smart types – the barrow boys – ended and where the alleged 'Hooray Henrys' recruited from universities or the army began.

What everyone involved agreed on was that time itself was now a precious commodity, which was a remarkable change in a country which had little more than a decade earlier taken such a lax approach to industrial relations and productivity that power shortages led the government to introduce a three-day working week. The attitude was self-consciously American; with longer working days and so many deals to be done there was no time to waste. Time or the lack of it was the new signifier of status; the less you had of it the more important you were. This is where the Filofax came in. The Filofax was – and is – a personal organiser, a small leather cover containing neat removable sheaves of notes, diary and addresses. The concept had actually been launched in the US in 1910 and the UK in the 1920s, but like so many elements of 1980s fashion it was an old favourite updated and adapted for a brasher age. It became so popular in Britain that by 1987 it, and the inserts filled with useful information (making it the smart phone app of its day), were stocked in 1250 stores across the UK. The company had a turnover of £12m and was floated on the USM, the Unlisted Securities Market.

The Filofax was *de rigueur* for the 1987 go-getter who wanted to emit the signal that he or she was so incredibly busy planning take-overs and making reservations – or calling their PA to request reser-vations – at fashionable restaurants such as Le Caprice or Terence Conran's Bibendum. The latter opened in 1987, as did the River Café and Harvey's starring Marco Pierre White. If you were well-paid enough, your Filofax could sit on the passenger seat of your Porsche 911 turbo, or your BMW 5 Series, as you drove to one of those restaurants or back into the City at dawn. Indeed, fast cars, and foreign-produced cars particularly, were part of the package. Even if a sports car was out of reach, manufacturers such as Volkswagen used the advertising techniques and stylistic signifiers of the period to pitch to the mass market well beyond London. In a reflection of the changing balance of consumer power, the advertis-ing for cars also started to be aimed directly at women for the first time. In David Bailey's 'Changes' television advert for the VW Golf in 1987 the model Paula Hamilton was dressed as an immaculately coiffed and tailored Princess of Wales character, walking away from a mews house and an unreliable man to find solace and happiness in her VW Golf. In fashion, too, the yuppie style revolution was pack-aged for millions of consumers, particularly by the chain Next, where an affordable version of the 1980s dream – including City chic – was sold to millions of consumers. Inevitably, the style revo-lution was repeatedly parodied on shows such as *Spitting Image*, perhaps best of all in a spoof of the Dire Straits song 'Money for Nothing', complete with references to Filofaxes, Laura Ashley blinds and GTi's (the latter supposedly a favourite of Fergie and Lady Di's).

There was something distinctively British and class-fixated about this mockery, though. As the historian Graham Stewart put it, in the US the aspirational yuppie was sometimes mocked a little but in films such as *Trading Places* – a riches to rags to riches tale starring Dan Aykroyd and Eddie Murphy – the accumulation of money on the commodity markets was celebrated as representing a victory of the young over the old, and in the case of Murphy's character of the bright ghetto hustler, over entitled Establishment snobs. In large parts of the British media, particularly in the BBC, in which liberal arts graduates predominated, there was little sympathy for the Thatcher experiment and there were very few positive expressions in British popular culture or the arts of the benefits of markets.

This tension was highlighted when Caryl Churchill's *Serious Money*, which had been such a hit with City traders, transferred to Broadway later that year. The theatre critic of the *New Yorker* thought the work was a success in Britain because it appealed to the prejudices of the liberal-Left members of the audience even more than it appealed to traders. 'It's easy to see why this play was such a big hit in London', Mimi Kramer wrote.[5] Not only did it involve actors swearing, pulling down trousers and pretending to vomit, which was always going to appeal to the Brits, it combined all that with 'a confirmation of many of the British intelligentsia's most dearly held beliefs: that privatisation and free enterprise are bad things, the "the British Empire was a cartel", that foreigners buy Burberrys, that money is somehow something that one is better off yearning for than having'. In Britain, open ambition was unpleasant and impolite, she said. The play was simply an attempt to cash in on 1980s ethics and yuppie fashion. The Americans would be unimpressed, she thought. That is not to say that in New York there was no fun poked at the super-rich of Wall Street, especially in a city with such noisy tabloid newspapers. John Gutfreund of Salomon Brothers and his much younger wife Susan, a former Pan Am air hostess turned interior designer, made themselves targets. 'It's so expensive being rich,' she is reputed to have said. Infamously they had a crane hoist a twenty-two-foot Christmas tree into their Manhattan apartment. But the underlying assumption in America, in contrast to the UK, remained that, joking aside, it was better to make a lot of money than not.

By the late summer and early autumn of 1987 in the UK some City veterans had a nervous feeling that it was all running too fast. Ben Wrey was by then the boss at Henderson Global, a money manager that had expanded too quickly, going from 146 employees in 1983 and £1.1bn under management to 525 employees and £9.75bn by September 1987. He said later that he kicked himself for sensing that autumn what was wrong but failing to realise the full extent and not ordering a different course. David Mayhew of Cazenove, who had been dragged into the Saunders scandal and was backed all the way by the senior partners in protesting his innocence, felt a shudder of premonition but had Guinness hanging over him: 'Everything was flying. It was a rip-roaring bull-market.' Numerous others speak decades later of the sense that the numbers were so large that they no longer made any sense. Wanting so badly to be wrong, few of those involved changed their behaviour in time.

How wrong could it go? The answer came from the US that autumn, where Ronald Reagan's joke that the US budget deficit (the gap between income in tax receipts and government spending) was 'big enough to take care of itself' was no longer funny. Nigel Lawson and some economists had been warning for several years that the US was storing up problems. A falling dollar prompted fears of an international economic slowdown. There was also concern that Wall Street's reliance on electronic trading systems had introduced an extra layer of risk. The software had never been tested in a crash. On Monday 12 October the *Wall Street Journal* reported fears that a problem could 'snowball into a stunning rout for stocks'. Then, on

Wednesday the 14th, there were two pieces of news that sounded ominous to traders fearing higher interest rates. The news wires revealed that the US Congress was seeking to crack down on takeovers by tightening tax loopholes and the Department of Commerce posted trade figures that were worse than anticipated. This caused a judder on the markets. And then the bubble really burst.

PART THREE
COMBUSTION

GREAT STORM

'Earlier on today, apparently, a woman rang the BBC and said she heard there was a hurricane on the way . . . well, if you're watching, don't worry, there isn't.'

Michael Fish, BBC weatherman, October 1987

Hurricanes hardly ever happen in the Home Counties. Yet at 2am on 16 October 1987 hurricane-force winds were exactly what hit southern England. Nineteen people lost their lives in the carnage, a wind speed of 149kmph was recorded at Heathrow Airport, much damage was done to the foliage at the Kent estate of the Governor of the Bank of England Robin Leigh-Pemberton, and the town of Sevenoaks lost six of its famous trees. During the clear-up operation, BBC weatherman Michael Fish was widely ridiculed for his television broadcast made the previous evening as the storm wheeled its way towards the British coastline. Ever since, Fish has said that he had been misunderstood, and that his dismissal of a hurricane being on the way referred to the question of whether one was due in the Caribbean. He had warned of high winds in the southeast of England in the expectation that the worst would pass through the English Channel and subside. The Met Office was operating with rudimentary satellite technology and only one weather ship thanks to government and EC cuts.[1] Something as awkward as the truth was not going to prevent the misleadingly edited clip of Fish's hurricane comment being re-run in countless documentaries and news reports ever since.

Blow me away: the value of your investments can go down as well as up.
A US trader contemplates the chaos during the October 1987 crash.

That Friday morning the storm caused chaos in commuter land, and with train services cancelled, and roads blocked, very few staff in the City made it to their desks. Some battled through, among them Brian Winterflood, who was one of the proud few who kept trading. The Stock Exchange was open for business, although the Seaq computer system was not working and after a few hours the FTSE was suspended for the day because so little was being done. The timing of this day of disruption could hardly have been worse. Entirely unrelated to the chaos in England, Wall Street's falls on Wednesday and Thursday were followed by further volatility on Friday. It was exacerbated by traders in a hurry to get out of stocks and swamping the market for futures options. By the time the markets closed it meant that the S&P 500 had lost 9 per cent of its value in a week, making it one of the worst results in more than a decade. This timing mattered because in Tokyo and London executives, analysts and traders now had all weekend to call each other and worry about how bad it might be on Monday morning. The weekend newspapers also carried appropriately gloomy commentary about the prospects, and many of those making decisions finished their weekends knowing they would have to get in sharp the next morning and begin selling right from the start. Even so, the force of what followed came as a shock. In the words of Ben Wrey at Henderson Global, when it hit the City that Monday it hit 'like a hurricane'.

In their offices, with the screens running red, traders did their best to hold on tight. There was shock, awe and panic all around. Many of the younger traders who were earning comparatively large salaries had known little but rising share prices and optimism since they signed up a few years previously. Some were witnessed crying. The Eurobond specialists might have had an apprenticeship in market chaos the previous winter, but those who dealt in shares had enjoyed, with a few deviations, one of the great bull markets in history. Now prices were collapsing in a terrifying orgy of selling. Indeed, prices fell so much for the simple reason that it was all but impossible to find buyers.

The situation deteriorated when the US opened, and again the attempts of arbitrageurs to profit from the volatility caused confusion. At 10am in New York, some specialist firms did not trade for the first hour. Many of the top stocks – eleven out of thirty on the Dow Jones Industrial Average – opened late, causing traders to rush into the futures market to buy options.[2] Then the stocks opened lower than the arbitrageurs had anticipated. The result was chaos and wild selling, at which point the chairman of the Securities and Exchange Commission, the US regulator, proceeded to unintentionally make it much worse. Speaking at the Mayflower Hotel in Washington, David S. Ruder, relatively new to the post, said: 'There is some point, and I don't know what point that is, that I would be interested in talking to the New York Stock Exchange about a temporary, very temporary, halt in trading'. This was a logical development of the position he had outlined earlier that month, in his speech to the Bond Club of Chicago. There he mused on the risks from volatility in derivatives markets, of products based on options, or baskets of options linked to indexes, increasing the potential for confusion among traders and regulators. It might make sense to introduce a system to halt the market temporarily for thirty minutes or so to allow the restoration of order during an emergency, he had suggested in Chicago. Such rational concerns made sense in a quasi-academic speech. Those views, repeated initially without the full quotes, in a garbled fashion, a few weeks later on the day of a real live stock market crash, only intensified the panic. At 11.41 a wire report flashed up: SEC HAS DISCUSSED TRADING HALT. NOT NOW. Thirteen minutes later, there was an update: RUDER ON HALT. ANYTHING POSSIBLE.[3] 'Anything possible' are not words financial speculators like to hear during a panic. Rumours spread that the New York Stock Exchange (NYSE) would close completely for the day, worrying traders who feared they were about to be stuck with stock they didn't want that would be marked right down if the markets closed for a pause and then reopened later. Selling increased as traders raced to offload whatever they could. At 1.04pm the Dow Jones News Service published the full Ruder quote from a few hours earlier. In the confusion it looked as though this was Ruder's second comment within two hours, when it merely repeated his earlier remarks. The Dow Jones report was the trigger for more hysteria. It rippled right out across the US, as smaller stockbrokers tried to explain to their small investor clients what was happening. The next day, the *Wall Street Journal* reported a stockbroker in Pittsburgh answering the phone as 'John End-of-the-world-Posterato', telling a client: 'Oh no! Shut up and listen to me . . . You're in bad shape. I told you guys to get out, but you don't listen. What should you do now? Pray a lot.'[4]

For the young Christopher Tomkinson at his trading desk at Fulton Prebon in London, the drama gave him his first lesson in the power of panic and markets going berserk. His early trades in London left him exposed when the US market fell. The market in London went (twice) into what was termed 'fast market' status.

That meant that prices were not held. He had committed to the trade but the outcome depended on where the prices ended up later. It was, he told *Financial News*, too late to extract his orders. 'I could only watch and wait. We smoked a lot . . . I dared not trade anything else. I felt like an amateur juggler faced with eight flaming torches.'[5] An hour after the US markets shut he discovered that, thanks to that day's volatility, what should have turned in a $900,000 profit was actually a $122,000 loss. When London closed on Monday, the FTSE had fallen 11 per cent, or a record fall of 183 points. All manner of big companies were now worth a lot less than they had been twenty-four hours previously, not least of which was Rupert Murdoch's media business, down $1bn in value.

In the chaos, worsening news sometimes took a while to filter through. Before the age of the smart phone, it was possible (incredible as it might seem) for even senior people to be out of touch for an hour or two when they made the commute home. Ben Wrey knew it had been bad that evening, but when he got home and turned on the *Nine O'Clock News* he saw it was even worse than he feared. The Dow had fallen more than 500 points. In response he almost fell off his armchair. It had been a day of records, and not in a good way. In New York, the Dow fell 508 points in the end, closing at 1738.74, a 22.6 per cent slide and worse than any single day of the crash of 1929. More than 600 million shares were traded, which was a huge surge in volume. It was, wrote Chris Huhne, then the economics editor of the *Guardian*, 'a brutal reminder of how elemental and untamed economic forces still are. As in 1929, the financial tempest was unheralded.' The speed of the collapse also meant that a central weakness of the system was exposed when a multi-billion-dollar chain broke down. Part of the problem was that investors buying a futures contract lodged a sum as security with the broker. The broker lodged a portion of that with the exchange. In normal conditions this worked to create liquidity and to encourage trading. If the contract deteriorated, they had to post more security before the market opened for business the next day. When the market fell as fast as it did on Black Monday, the margin calls

– the calls to post ever more security on contracts that were losing value – were ten times the normal level and many firms looked as though they would have to cease trading. Phelan at the NYSE had to contact the Federal Reserve to plead for assistance in encouraging the biggest banks to extend large lines of credit to investors and brokers. According to the Fed's investigation, Citigroup's lending to securities firms that day was reported to have hit \$1.4 trillion as against \$200m to \$400m on a normal day. The Federal Reserve, keen to avoid a repeat of 1929, let it be known that it would do whatever it took to help the banks and the markets. When the markets closed, the ex-Marine chairman of the New York Stock Exchange, John Phelan, held a press conference in which he was frank: 'I call it the nearest thing to meltdown I'm ever likely to see . . . If it wasn't a meltdown it was certainly as hot as I want it to be.' Phelan had warned trading firms for a while about their over-reliance on electronic trading and derivatives such as stock index futures. He believed these had the potential to exacerbate the panic, since only a handful of traders understood the concepts and technology well enough to use them safely in a crisis. In an emergency, many others were just guessing.

In London terms this crash amounted to the worst experience since the secondary banking crisis of the early 1970s and this was much more concentrated, fast paced (thanks to technology) and high profile because of media attention. Suddenly London's geographical position seemed not to be such a boon either. What had been perceived as an advantage around Big Bang, in good times, of the glamorous market that never sleeps running on an almost continuous global loop, with Tokyo and other markets in the East leading off, London following and then New York and Chicago kicking in five hours after that, now seemed a year later like a carousel out of control. A bad session in one time zone influenced behaviour in the next, and round and round it went. How could you stop the world's markets and say I want to get off? The answer was that you could not. At the close of Black Monday, the Chancellor of the Exchequer watched developments with some trepidation. Nigel

Lawson's first concern was to prevent a complete collapse in confidence in Britain's boardrooms. He felt it was his job to project confidence, certainly much more confidence than he felt, in the hope that a crash in the markets was not followed by a dip or worse in the wider economy. 'Privately, I wasn't sure which way it was going to go,' says Lawson thirty years later.

There was little clear guidance from senior figures in the Reagan administration, with splits at the top of the government over how to respond, and the Treasury Secretary, James Baker, indicating that he was relaxed and did not think US interest rates should have to rise to deal with the dollar problem. It fell to America's central bank, and governor Alan Greenspan, to offer reassurance to the markets. 'The Federal Reserve, consistent with its responsibilities as the nation's central bank, affirmed today its readiness to serve as a source of liquidity to support the economic and financial system,' Greenspan said on Tuesday the 20th. In essence, he pushed banks to keep on lending and to extend lines of credit, assuring them that the government would stand behind them if needed. This reassurance came at a price, it would transpire much later. Greenspan's spraying of liquidity during any emergency came to be expected by those who operated in the markets. Might the confident assumption that they and the system would always be saved make them a little friskier when it came to risk and willing to take bigger gambles? The answer with the benefit of experience of the aftermath of the sub-prime crisis of the mid- to late 2000s seems to be 'yes'.

Black Monday and the following week was not a disaster for everyone. Ross Jones and the team at Gerrard & National, the discount house, were transfixed by the turmoil and then retreated on the evening of the 19th to a Lord's Taverners dinner at the Savoy Hotel where they had booked a table. One of their colleagues – Roger Gibbs – arrived late with the news that 'Wall Street's down seven hundred points.' Gerrard & National were less exposed than many others, because they traded in fixed incomes – bonds – although the following day they pondered nervously what to do, until a member of their board phoned in to point out that they were in an extremely good position. There would now be a 'flight to quality' and the relative security of bonds. 'The 1987 crash was terrific for us,' says Jones. They made a lot of money that week. Elsewhere, almost immediately, the crash had produced a change in atmosphere and outlook. The young head-hunter Philippa Rose noticed first the quietness and seriousness that descended on the City in the days following Black Monday. And that the phone rang only with banks saying that all hiring was suspended.

What the merchant banks and securities houses wanted suspended most of all was the British Petroleum privatisation, which by unfortunate timing was underway right in the middle of the market emergency. The British government's attempted £7.2bn sale of its remaining 31.5 per cent share in BP was, as Lawson said, 'the largest share sale the world had ever seen'. On the morning of 15 October, when those initial tremors were hitting the global markets, Norman Lamont (the government minister dealing with the privatisation programme and reporting to Lawson) and the chairman of BP, Peter Walters, announced the price of the sell-off (330p per share). By the morning after Black Monday, those who had agreed to underwrite the BP deal for a fee decided to ask the government to cancel, which Lawson and Lamont refused to do. The scrapping of the sale would not only have punched a hole in the government's accounts for the year, it would have suggested that institutions that had done very nicely out of privatisation wanted to be bailed out when market conditions were not in their favour. Lawson did, though, order the suspension of advertising, as in a falling market the government did not want to encourage any small investors to put their money into BP.

At that point, the chief smoothie from N.M. Rothschild, Michael Richardson, attempted to persuade Lawson to pull out. Richardson was an arch-networker – a City grandee and Freemason – who was used to being able to talk his way out of trouble, although this time he would have only limited success. On Friday 23rd he told Lawson that the seventeen British banks leading the underwriting were meeting to examine invoking a clause in the contract enabling them to withdraw and not purchase any unsold shares. Incredibly, and to the fury of Lawson and Thatcher, the Bank of England then took the side of the merchant banks. Lawson decided not to concede, and while he and the government offered to put a temporary floor under the price – buying back shares below an agreed level – the issue went ahead.

While these awkward discussions over BP continued, history played one of its tricks on the architects of Big Bang. The week after Black Monday, the Stock Exchange had arranged an anniversary conference on Monday 26 October 1987 to celebrate the success of their venture. At a press conference Goodison and other prominent figures made presentations on Big Bang before being questioned about the crash. Goodison acknowledged that the circumstances were not ideal, although he defended London and accused Washington policy makers of incompetence. 'The cause of the fall has not been the markets,' he said. 'It has been the decisions taken, or not taken, by world governments, particularly the United States of America . . . My view, and the European view, is that something needs to be done with the US fiscal deficit. One of the sad things about the present scene is that the U.K. is an outstanding country at the moment economically.' And the reformed London Stock Exchange was holding up during the crisis, he said. The next day's *Washington Post* summarised Goodison's explanation as follows: 'The computers didn't crash, the exchange did not close, and no one jumped out of a window.'

That day in the House of Commons, on Monday 26th, Labour MPs were far less sanguine. There was uproar as news of further falls on the markets filtered through from the City. The Shadow Chancellor John Smith, who had been appointed a few months earlier, demanded an urgent statement from Lawson and offered to scrap a debate on education to accommodate a full discussion of the market turmoil and the BP row. Lawson, it was explained to MPs by a Tory frontbencher, could not be in the Commons because he had to fulfil 'an existing engagement in the City'. That involved him speaking at Goodison's conference on what a brilliant success the previous year's Big Bang had been. Labour MPs went quite wild at this explanation and Brian Sedgemore MP described Lawson in such unparliamentary language – 'the arrogant bastard' – that the Speaker who presides in the Commons forced him to withdraw. The sharp-dressed cockney wit Tony Banks, another Labour MP, got further when he said that the 'fat bounder' of a Chancellor should be dragged to the Commons in a tumbril to explain himself. The Speaker, Bernard Weatherill, objected to the term 'fat bounder'. A vintage Commons exchange followed.

> Speaker: 'I dislike that expression.'
> Banks: 'Right. Corpulent gentleman.'
> Speaker: 'Almost as bad.'
> Banks: 'All right. Rt Hon corpulent gentleman.'

For John Smith and Labour, the crash was the first good news they had had in a while in their battle against a Tory government with a large majority. It was not that the Opposition wanted the value of Briton's pensions and investments to fall, but here was some evidence that the value of free market reforms, much like a share price, could go down as well as up. Labour spokesmen had used the City scandals of recent years to suggest that what had been unleashed was inherently corrupt, with the Conservatives creating a suspect set-up to suit their rich friends. Now the modernised City and global capitalism had delivered a crisis.

The press reaction to these events revealed contrasting perspectives. The *FT*, its journalists presumably mindful that there had been crashes throughout history and would be crashes again, dialled down on the hysteria and a week after Black Monday was almost relaxed in its analysis. The *Daily Mail*, a newspaper that had, and has, such an instinctive feel for the hopes and fears of southern England, was much more direct. The further falls a week after Black Monday caused the paper to get stuck into the authorities. Over two pages on Tuesday 27th the headline ran: 'It was relentless . . . down, down, down . . .' Another item mocked Goodison's Big Bang anniversary conference, declaring that there had been 'smoked salmon' but 'no signs of suicide'. The front page was even more to the point, taking up Lawson's theme about failure by the Reagan administration and urging action by the Americans. The waspish splash headline – 'Don't just sit there . . . do something!' – was a clever play on Reagan's famous non-interventionist small-government dictum that it was often better for government to just sit there (don't do something) rather than making matters worse.

Few had seen the October crash coming. The father of Zac Goldsmith, Jimmy Goldsmith, the swashbuckling businessman and corporate raider with a complicated private life straight from the pages of a thriller, was one of those who did. Ahead of the crash he sold every share he had. Only a few others did likewise and the usual recriminations, and calls for inquiries, observable in most crashes down the ages, then played out. In Washington the Reagan administration urgently wanted answers and turned to Nicholas F. Brady, an experienced financier, Yale athlete, WASP and friend of George H. Bush, then Vice President. On 8 November 1987, President Reagan issued an executive order establishing a task force led by Brady to report within sixty days on why the crash had happened and what might be done to prevent a repeat.

Brady stands out as one of the most fascinating Wall Street and political players of his generation. He was largely responsible for an improvement in the fortunes of the investment bank Dillon, Reid & Co. in the 1980s, although he was solidly unfashionable. He was sceptical about the takeover boom, spent some time in the US Senate, and later, under Bush, became Treasury Secretary. Brady bonds, the ingenious invention which allowed the restructuring and reduction of debt in developing countries in the late 1980s and early 1990s, carried his name. Contrary to expectation, the Brady Report on October 1987 when it landed the following January was an impressive piece of clear-sighted work. The assorted markets that had developed – in stocks, in futures, in swaps – were not set up to operate as 'one market' and, on the day, confusion had been the defining feature. The clearing systems – by which trades were logged and transacted – were not good enough and computerised programme trading introduced risks that should be mitigated, it said. Brady's team suggested the introduction of so-called 'circuit breaks' that could be used to pause trading and prevent a repeat of overly drastic falls in prices. Some of these conclusions were contested, particularly by more free market types who feared that the response would require greater bureaucracy, rather than allowing the Exchanges in New York and Chicago to adapt and find their own solutions.

Regardless of such concerns, the report formed the basis of reforms made in the US, and it and other reports encouraged regulators and policy makers to cooperate more closely with their counterparts in other major countries. Indeed, the crash had shown how quickly developments in markets in the Far East could work their way to London and then New York and back again. The transmission speed of a shock could now be measured in seconds rather than hours, days and weeks. That being the case, there was a need for much closer cooperation and international standards in markets that had become far more global. Later, Brady attributed the events of October 1987 in large part to the increased clout of the Japanese. Their traders had started the crash, over fears about the US economy and the dollar, and the powerful Japanese finance ministry and biggest firms had halted it. It was a seeming testament to the erosion of American power and to the increasingly interconnected nature of markets, or rather the speed at which shocks and corrections were transmitted between trading centres. 'The real trigger', said Brady,

was that the Japanese came in for their own reasons and sold an enormous amount of U.S. government bonds and drove the 30-year government [bond] up through 10 per cent. And when it got through 10 per cent, that got a lot of people thinking, 'Gee, that's four times the return you can get on equity. Here we go, inflation again.' That, to me, is what really started the 19th—a worry by the Japanese about the U.S. currency.[6]

When the markets crashed, the Japanese government encouraged the country's biggest securities houses – Nomura, Daiwa, Nikko, and Yamaichi – to prop up the market, which halted the slide in Tokyo and produced (for a few days at least) a relative respite in the US and in the UK.

The comprehensive nature of Brady's response in the US was in contrast to what happened in the UK. The Governor of the Bank of England, Robin Leigh-Pemberton, acknowledged in a speech in February that the British had been criticised for not having much to say about the causes of the crisis. Leigh-Pemberton did then make a stab at offering a cogent analysis of the crash. He explained just how big the bubble had been: 'In London, prices began to rise in a sustained way in early 1982, when the FT 30 share index stood at around 550. Over the succeeding five years or so, to the middle of 1987, the index moved up, to about 1850, an increase of almost three and half times.' Allowing for inflation, the real terms increase in prices was still in the region of 170 per cent. That had inflated profits and pay at securities houses and they would now feel the strain. It was not complacency, however, to claim that in difficult circumstances the trading systems in London had worked, he said. They had functioned relatively well under extreme pressure. And no amount of technology could ensure that everyone who wanted to get out of a market in an emergency could do so without suffering ill effects. 'So far, at least, the financial system seems to have weathered the storm passably well.'

These were lame Establishment excuses according to those who had expressed scepticism about the City revolution, the rising salaries of traders and the concept of increased share ownership. Wasn't Black Monday and its aftermath evidence that the hyped global financial revolution had encouraged greed and brought destruction? Those who thought so could get a dose of righteousness, and a hugely entertaining ride through boom-time Manhattan, by reading Tom Wolfe's *The Bonfire of the Vanities*, which was published in October 1987. Wolfe's central character, Sherman McCoy, was a greedy bond trader who crashed in his Mercedes and was propelled into a race row that landed him in the tabloids and the dock.

Alternatively, concerned citizens on both sides of the Atlantic could go to the cinema at the end of 1987 to see a film that had been made with the Boesky insider-trading investigation in mind but which now looked like a perfectly timed indictment of an entire era. On 11 December, Oliver Stone's morality tale *Wall Street* was released. The lead character was the corporate raider Gordon Gekko, a new-generation Wall Street titan with slicked-back hair, braces and a beach house full of modern art. He and his protégé Bud Fox, a hungry young trader who sells out his heritage in search of wealth, were from different angles archetypes of the age. In the film, Fox is so greedy for 1980s success that he is drawn into insider dealing and persuades Gekko to purchase the airline for which works Fox's blue-collar father, played by Martin Sheen. Stone presents the resulting scandal as a collision between honest toil and rampant greed. In the most famous scene, Gekko explains his philosophy to the shareholders of a paper company that is struggling. He explains how he can unlock value and make the discontented shareholders money. Hidden value, squandered or overlooked by corporate bureaucrats and managers, can be liberated and put into the pockets of the owners. At a mass meeting of hundreds of shareholders of Teldar Paper, his Michael Milken-esque polemic is a popular message. Greed should be embraced, Gekko tells the audience. It is nothing to be ashamed of, he says – Greed is good, Greed is right, Greed works; indeed man's fundamental progress as a species is down to Greed.

A week after the release of *Wall Street*, Ivan Boesky was sentenced to three years in prison for his part in the insider-trading scandal, for conspiring to file false stock-trading records. He admitted buying inside information from Dennis Levine, an investment banker. Levine was already in prison. Marty Siegel, formerly one of the leading corporate merger specialists on Wall Street, had taken $700,000 from Boesky for illicit information on deals. Siegel also pleaded guilty to criminal charges. The greed of Boesky and his accomplices made it seem that the cinematic representation of Wall Street was a fair reflection of real life in investment banking and on trading floors. Here Oliver Stone cleverly pushed some extremely old buttons too. The G-word – greed – was transgressive, an old testament taboo, a deadly sin, that all but the most extreme capitalists and coked-up traders would recoil from. While wealth creation and ambition are one thing, and rampant greed is another, the extravagant behaviour in the years leading up to October 1987 and the way in which it was portrayed by a novelist and a film director helped blur the distinction in the public imagination.

In Britain, rather typically, as has been the case for centuries, the artistic response to a crash and the forces that created it was primarily satirical and amusingly silly. In early 1988, the comedian Harry Enfield unveiled the character 'Loadsamoney', a brash plasterer waving about his wad of 'dosh' on Channel 4's 'alternative' comedy show *Saturday Live*. It was much more effective to satirise Thatcherism and condemn an obsession with acquisition by using a plasterer as opposed to a pension fund manager. But mortifyingly for the satirists, the vulgar Loadsamoney promptly became extremely popular and even had a hit single that took him onto *Top of the Pops*. The joke for a while was on Enfield, although the royalties may have eased any embarrassment. Indeed, there was something a little rich about alternative comedians – many from privileged and extremely affluent backgrounds – being so snooty about others, from places such as Essex, getting a shot at rapid advancement. Enfield had to kill off his creation when he became concerned that too many viewers relished his boasting and rudeness towards the poorer regions of England, although not before Labour leader Neil Kinnock deployed Loadsamoney as an example of all that his party asserted was wrong with Thatcher's Britain and the City.

Was that fair on those who had enjoyed such rapid accumulation of wealth? The rewards and the excitement had produced a surge of excessive confidence that this would not end. Like many other practitioners of his generation, Ben Wrey felt that the youngsters who had flooded Wall Street and the City were too optimistic and had become intoxicated by the market climbing ever higher. 'My view of markets was a different one, that they were tough . . . I mean they just make you look like a fool so often.' Such criticism was understandable and Wrey's was an astute observation born of experience, but who had allowed them to act like that? It was the elders of high finance on Wall Street and the City who had sanctioned the construction of the post-Big Bang machine, with its aggressive assumptions about the power of technology and the possibilities of rocketing pay. It was hardly surprising that some of those who had been recruited to man the machine were naive about its defects and blasé about the potential for disaster. But then the crash of 1987 wasn't a sustained disaster, or at least not one that seemed to endure in the couple of years immediately after the Great Storm, either in the City or on Wall Street. What was remarkable after such an intense episode was how quickly the markets recovered. The falls were reversed within months, so that Lawson could later describe October 1987 as an economic non-event. It seemed not to spread much into what the media referred to as 'the real economy' and it would not create a repeat of 1929. Growth was strong in 1987 and 1988.

There was a lot more to it than that though. There had been what amounted to an explosion of money in the decades since the 1960s, a revolution that facilitated bigger debt markets, new forms of trading, new products, changed markets, and computerisation that shrank the Western world and increased transaction speeds dramatically. At home, the Reaganites and Thatcherites had also enabled easier access to credit and the creation of a property bubble that would eventually result in overheating and the recession of the early 1990s. The seemingly inexorable rise of Japan would soon be halted, and in the UK and the US politics was about to transformed by leaders who accepted the framework of expanded markets and nascent globalisation. Simultaneously, the aftermath of the crash caused considerable carnage in the City, when it exposed how unprepared for competition were the firms that had been bashed together ahead of Big Bang. More scandals and explosions were on the way too. The City's trajectory was up and up, again, but not in a straight line.

CLEANING UP

'Go for the jugular.'

George Soros, Black Wednesday, 1992

Nicholas Goodison had more than done his time as chairman of the Stock Exchange. In November 1988 he went off to spend more time with his clocks and barometers, but he also constructed a portfolio of City directorships to go alongside his membership of boards in the art world. If during his busy tenure Goodison had failed to please everyone in the City – an impossible task, akin to herding cats – he and his team of technologists had brought the institution through the most extraordinarily intense and rapid period of change in the Square Mile for centuries, although there was more upheaval and innovation on the way. The London Stock Exchange was one of the institutions that would at points struggle to cope.

Nonetheless, the view of Ranald Michie, a leading financial historian, was that what had been achieved in London by the late 1980s in the creation of a new securities market was remarkable. It was not very British to boast about success, but London was once again a global marketplace, where big banks from around the world, in the right time zone, in their offices, traded by telephone based on current prices that were displayed on a computer screen. All of this was now done under a regulator and stamped with the brand of the London Stock Exchange. 'The New York Exchange had failed to achieve this in the 1970s,' pointed out Michie, and indeed there had been little innovation on the NYSE itself since 1975.[1] The change there had come from new, rival electronic platforms outside the traditional exchange, such as NASDAQ. Not a single one of the exchanges on the continent, neither Frankfurt nor Paris, could rival London's scope. Throughout the decade the increasingly open flows of capital across borders and the transformation wrought by technology produced a surge in volume in major markets, but the increase was most stagger-ing in London. Over the course of the 1980s, trading volumes on the New York Stock Exchange increased fourfold. In Tokyo, volumes increased nine times. In London the figure was seventeen times.

Competition intensified, which meant that established City names and some habits – decent claret in the boardroom at lunchtime, family connections at all levels throughout organisations, knowledge of market history and personalities, the lustre of tradition and order – that had only a few years earlier equated to elite status, now counted for a good deal less. In the case of some stockbroking and jobbing firms from the Old World, those supposed advantages were now all but worthless. The partners who had left with the cash, to fill their cellars in the small country houses and rectories of England with even better claret and good burgundy, had made a smart move in leav-ing just as life in the City became tougher, faster and less congenial. In that respect, Big Bang in 1986 was the pre-ignition moment. What followed the crash of 1987 was accelerated creative destruction.

The main impact in the years immediately following Black Monday was that it helped expose and destroy many, not all, of the British merchant banks and brokers in a manner that was humiliat-ing for the City. Although share prices in London recovered to their early October 1987 level by August 1989, many established, experi-enced British firms in the City never recovered, either as standalone entities or under their new owners who had paid so much for them during the bull market. It had been clear to the observant even before Black Monday that there was excessive capacity, and too many people on high salaries chasing business on which the spreads – the difference between the sell and the buy price – had narrowed, as the bigger participants moved to drive out smaller firms. Everyone had to fight harder to get critical mass and they were all under pres-sure to chase recognition on the league tables that clients referred to when choosing which firm to use. There was no hiding in the event of failure or poor performance and the new owners were ruthless in closing down or stripping back the old City firms they had paid premium prices for just a few years earlier.

The historian David Kynaston estimated that a total of £4bn had been spent on buying established operations large and small, and equipping them with new technology and higher-paid staff in preparation for the revolution, only for their names to be retired or closed down a few years later. Messels was destroyed by Shearson Lehman; the brokers Laurie Millbank and Simon & Coates were butchered by Chase Manhattan. Security Pacific killed Hoare Govett. Vickers da Costa and Kitcat & Aitken also disappeared in the carnage. Even some of the super-confident American incomers suffered problems. Had the vast spaces the size of football pitches accommodating the recently enlarged operations been leased to accommodate an expanding staff and their egos, or had the staff been hired to fill the vast new spaces? It was difficult to tell sometimes.

As Valerie Thompson and some of her colleagues at Salomon had seen during the Floating Rate Note emergency in late 1986, too many of the new, younger staff had never experienced one market reverse, let alone two or three. Elsewhere after the 1987 crash, as volumes fell temporarily and weaker outfits became vulnerable, some of the new generation discovered just how tough the business environment they had entered could be. Layoffs began across the City and for a while hirings were on hold. An estimated 12,000 jobs were lost in the following year. One British bank that struggled was the high-street Midland, which had bought the broker Greenwell and bolted it together with its merchant bank, Samuel Montagu. It closed its equities unit in early 1989 and Midland was eventually taken over by HSBC.

The clearest evidence yet that the Brits were struggling badly in the face of competition came at Morgan Grenfell. Its reputation as one of the premier British merchant banks had been damaged by scandal and it was a business experiencing acute culture shock. Not that long previously, it had been an archetypal last-generation institution, populated at the upper echelons by well-heeled City archetypes who would have been recognisable figures at any point in the preceding century. As *Financial News* recorded, the old joke was that a clerk at Morgan Grenfell famously asked for a pay rise because he could not live on his salary. His superior was astonished: 'You live on your salary?'[2] In an attempt to modernise in the 1980s it had grown staff and its spending much too quickly, in an understandable effort to achieve parity with the Americans and become a global force. In 1980 Morgan Grenfell had in the region of a thousand members of staff. By 1987 it had around two thousand, seven hundred employees. The overheads had quadrupled since Goodison and the government did their deal in 1983. And it had expanded most aggressively of all in the securities business, in the belief that it could become an all-rounder, one of those global financial supermarkets that it was predicted would force out smaller banks and brokers in the years ahead.

By 1988 the acquisitions – of the jobbing firm Pinchin Denny and the brokers Pember & Boyle – that had been made during the pre-Big Bang buying spree were not working, and the Morgan Grenfell people, an employee remembers, didn't like the new people: 'We thought they lacked the right experience and were not sophisticated enough. We weren't very nice about it.' Morgan Grenfell managers were put in to manage the new unit and while all seemed as though it might be fine during the final run of the bull market, the October 1987 crash revealed that it was not. Soon the securities division that had been billed to investors as a great new source of world-beating profit was losing close to £1m per week. John Craven took the decision to close it down and concentrate on banking and corporate finance. This revelation was promptly leaked to the *Daily Telegraph* and published on 6 December 1988. Craven got in at 7am and shortly afterwards unofficially confirmed the bad news to staff, speaking over the loudspeaker and apologising for the distress. The decision to close the securities business within Morgan Grenfell with immediate effect was formally confirmed at a board meeting at 9am. More than four hundred and fifty people lost their jobs that day, and while media attention was fixed on those who earned hundreds of thousands of pounds, and had sports cars thrown in as part of their packages when they joined, along with them went many who earned a lot less doing the support work.

In City terms the Morgan Grenfell reverse was profoundly shocking and humiliating. One of the most esteemed British banks, with a 150-year history, had tried to take on the world and lost. It was then left in that most dangerous position in the City of being a medium-sized operator in a business that was increasingly dominated by large players. For a while it had seemed Morgan Grenfell might be sold to the French bank Indosuez – sold to a French bank, imagine – before Craven talked to Alfred Herrhausen, the chairman of Deutsche Bank. The German banker flew to London and secret discussions began between the Morgan Grenfell team and one of the most alluring figures in the West German Establishment.

A long-time advocate of German reunification, Herrhausen had another merger on his mind that autumn. On 9 November 1989, the crossings between East and West Berlin were opened, thousands flooded westwards and the fall of the Wall and Communism began. That month, Herrhausen was in regular contact with political leaders, including the Soviet leader Mikhail Gorbachev. The more mundane matter of Deutsche Bank's purchase of Morgan Grenfell was also resolved that month when it was announced on the 27th that the Germans would pay £950m for Morgan Grenfell. It was stated that London would retain operational autonomy – this is often claimed in press releases about takeovers, and the promise held for five years – and Craven was given the great honour of being invited to be the first non-German to join the board of Deutsche Bank.

There was a chilling postscript, however. Three days after the deal was announced, Herrhausen left his home outside Frankfurt for work at around 8.30am, in a three-car convoy which took a route he had not taken in several weeks. In the late 1980s, German bankers and industrialists still had to take their security seriously, with communist terrorist cells remaining active. Yet somehow, someone knew the route and on a bicycle parked by the roadside was a bag full of armour-piercing explosives. The detonation was triggered when the infrared beam was broken by the car carrying Herrhausen.

The Red Army Faction, a West German terrorist group, was initially believed to be behind it, but did they have the expertise in their depleted state? Then it was rumoured that the Stasi, the East German secret police, had organised the attack or at least assisted. Some pointed to Herrhausen's attendance at the secretive Bilderberg conference and his enthusiasm for debt forgiveness for developing countries, which apparently angered some American banks and the US government. The case was a conspiracy theorist's dream: the Stasi, allegedly irate Bilderbergers, mysterious American bankers, the CIA or a combination of all of them must have done it. Herrhausen's murder remains unsolved. It is a reminder that as recently as 1989 Germany was divided and a leading European financier could be blown up on his way to work in Frankfurt while statesmen and leaders grappled with the fall of Communism.[3]

Back in London that November, the question at Morgan Grenfell was more down to earth. Was the deal of which Herrhausen had been the architect still on? Craven sent a note to staff on the day of the murder assuring them that the other managers at Deutsche Bank wanted to press ahead in spite of the shocking news. 'I have conveyed my sympathies to the Board of Managing Directors,' wrote Craven, 'and we shall all have to work that little bit harder to ensure the relationship is as successful as I know it will be.'

The future these European institutions were chasing seemed to belong to institutions such as the American Merrill Lynch, Morgan Stanley or Goldman Sachs, or the Japanese at Nomura – the banks and securities houses that had the scale to cope even when they hit serious trading losses. Their recently graduated youngsters putting together deals, overseen by their elders who had survived the mid-1980s, needed quite particular skills, different from those of their trader colleagues who worked on a different floor. They had to be able to conceptualise what might work for their clients if it was bolted together, acquired or sold, then structure the deal in a clever way and marshal City lawyers and tax specialists to assist, taking as fees a percentage based on the final price. More and bigger deals meant bigger bonuses. The notion that the big American banks, particularly, operated according to their own allegedly reptilian code, ruthlessly rejecting sentimentality, sacking at will and focusing on the interests of the firm, is a complaint heard a lot from some older City types. Yet the City, and the government, had invited these people in and created the marketplace in which they could do their thing. It was a bit rich to act surprised when American investment bankers smashed the competition and behaved like American investment bankers.

For the young head-hunter Philippa Rose, running her own firm and finding talent for big banks in London, the complaints were nonsense. After a brief dip following the 1987 crash she was soon prospering again. Her approach involved refusing to deal with human resources departments, and she broke every HR rule in the book, believing that what mattered was finding brilliant people rather than merely 'ticking boxes'. She was in demand and the banks fought over her services. 'As the business grew we had a lot of people phoning up trying to get me and that made me a bit smug about life,' she recalls. Her greatest triumph was her company winning the business of Goldman Sachs when it decided in the early 1990s to make a major commitment to Europe and London, and to make the UK capital the centre of its operations outside the US. Assorted head-hunters sat an exam, testing their knowledge of finance and the identities of senior figures and fast-rising stars in the City. Rose's habit of quizzing clients to learn more about all areas of finance – 'what the fuck is a Eurobond?' – produced its dividend when she came top with 82 per cent. Goldman consumed as much as 40 per cent of her time as the bank filled its new international headquarters on Fleet Street, in the Peterborough Court building vacated by the *Daily Telegraph*, whose poor journalists were moved to the Canary Wharf development where there were as yet no pubs. And then Rose tried to leave, explaining that Morgan Stanley had hired her company. She went to see the chief executive of Goldman Sachs International and was told: you can't resign. She was driven home immediately to pack a bag and then to the airport for a first-class flight to New York, where Goldman Sachs installed her in the presidential suite of the Plaza hotel. Dinners and meetings ensued with the most senior people, who all but brainwashed her out of the notion of working for Morgan Stanley. She came back to London, told Morgan Stanley the bad news and was blacklisted by them for the best part of two decades.

The leader who had helped unleash those market forces – the ambition, the transatlantic deal making, the wooing of young executives for ever-larger sums, the ruthless hiring and firing – got the sack herself in November 1990 when the Conservative Party ejected her from Number 10. Thatcher's departure was no ordinary vacating of office, because she had been no ordinary leader. Most leaders being booted out are not usually treated to adulatory statements from the US President; the Japanese Prime Minister; former French President Valéry Giscard d'Estaing; Czech anti-Communist freedom fighter turned President Vaclav Havel; and members of the tottering Soviet leadership that she had done much to defeat. Among Britain's allies, only the German government – perhaps understandably, considering Thatcher's opposition to German reunification – did not join in. A spokesman asked for a statement said: 'We would find it rather difficult to do that.'

In Britain, there was even less unanimity. Labour's Tony Benn was coruscating: 'Mrs Thatcher did more damage to democracy, equality, internationalism, civil liberties, freedom in this country than any other Prime Minister this century.' A furious Ann Widdecombe MP disagreed and said the removal of her heroine would make the rest of the world think the UK had gone completely mad, while Keith Joseph, Thatcher's intellectual mentor, wrote to the departing Tory leader describing her as 'a giant – a beautiful giant'. Former cabinet minister John Biffen MP said generously of the leader who had cast him aside: 'She was a tigress surrounded by hamsters.' Outside Westminster, the tigress's opponents celebrated and her stunned supporters swore vengeance against the successors who had the temerity not to be her. The hotelier Rocco Forte waxed lyrical about the triple election winner: 'She was a lady sent to us on wings from heaven.' The entertainer Max Bygraves even composed a tribute song – 'So Long Maggie' – and went on LBC, the London radio station, to perform it to put-upon listeners:

They say a week in politics
Can be a long wait,
But you stayed on eleven years
And made Great Britain Great.

In contrast, the City was as unsentimental as ever. Business is business, after all. Share prices actually rose. Over the course of the week in which she was removed, the FTSE 100 went from 2068.30 to 2170.50. The market rose in 1991, 1992 and 1993, providing more evidence of the disconnect between the increasingly international City and distress when it occurred in the domestic economy. Out in the country, the 1990s began with the 1980s boom turning to a brutal bust, causing a property crash and a surge of repossessions.

It even took down the owner of the development at Canary Wharf Thatcher had championed as Prime Minister. Paul Reichmann's Olympia & York had spent in the region of £7bn on the development, but with the tube link that Thatcher had promised being delayed for a decade, and her gone, it was difficult to attract sufficient high-paying tenants to the newly opened tower and surrounding buildings. There was the light railway that took an age from the City, and river taxis. But who really had any appetite to sit on a boat from central London, getting seasick going down the Thames on a freezing cold February morning at 7am? Loaded with loans, in 1991 Reichmann's property empire went into meltdown; by spring 1992 it was bust. A new company was formed and Paul Reichmann eventually bought his way back in. The private, deeply religious man who had taken Travelstead and von Clemm's idea and made it manifest in concrete and steel lived to see it become a success. It was later sold – at too high a price – to another consortium before it was rescued by the China Investment Corporation in 2009 during the next property crash. If anyone in the mid-1980s had suggested this chain of events, pre-Tiananmen Square when China was not yet a market economy and Canary Wharf was a wasteland, it would have sounded insane. Or it might have been thought someone had got Japan and China mixed up. In the intervening years

Japan had become stuck in its debt-addled slough and China has risen to challenge Western dominance.

For the property developer whose vision on the dockside in 1985 had started the Canary Wharf adventure, the collapse of Olympia & York in 1992 represented a personal financial disaster. The unsecuritised five-year note Gooch Ware Travelstead had taken from Reichmann had been due to pay out later in 1992, but with Reichmann's empire bust he got almost nothing. It did not make Travelstead bitter and when he looks today at Canary Wharf he is proud: 'I was routinely taken to task by the press as a crazy American. In twenty years, I said, that's the way it's going to be. I'm incredibly proud of it. It became what we said it would become.' The Canary Wharf experience also led to other interesting work opportunities. The Mayor of Barcelona, who had visited Travelstead's Mayfair offices to view the model of Canary Wharf, got in touch and asked him to help with the redevelopment of the Barcelona waterfront. There he built the Hotel Arts, working with the architect Frank Gehry. The Thatchers – out of office – stayed as Travelstead's guest in Barcelona after the hotel opened.

In London, the hangover from the late 1980s was played out in a series of trials and travails. Of course, the most sensational of these court cases related to Guinness, in which Ernest Saunders, Anthony Parnes, Gerald Ronson and Jack Lyons each went on trial for theft and false accounting in relation to the share-price-ramping operation run during the takeover battle with Argyll for Distillers. All four were convicted in 1990. In the courtroom Saunders made what turned out to be a calamitous decision, by choosing to go into the witness box to give evidence in his defence. As the *FT* explained the day after his conviction, a trial that had not necessarily been going well for the prosecution was transformed by his spell under cross-examination. 'Unemployed and with nothing to distract him from his troubles, he had become obsessed with the need to vindicate himself.' His version of events stretched plausibility. 'He alleged a vast conspiracy that included the government.' Everyone but him was a liar, he seemed to suggest.

A subsequent trial of Roger Seelig, former head of corporate finance at Morgan Grenfell, and Lord Spens, another banker, collapsed. The case against David Mayhew, who had been backed throughout by Cazenove, was also scrapped, and he became senior partner at Caz. Saunders then infamously won early release from open prison, when it was claimed that he displayed the early symptoms of Alzheimer's. Gerald Ronson – who had been dragged into the share support operation by Saunders – was in the same prison as Saunders and had to endure regular visits to his cell by his nemesis. Ronson later claimed he was the first to think of the ruse that got Saunders out of jail. 'I joked, "Make out that you're mentally ill. It wouldn't be difficult for you because besides being a psychotic liar, you are mentally deranged . . . If you made out you've got Alzheimer's, nobody could ever prove it, because if they looked inside your head, what are they going to find?" '[4] That revelation confirmed the suspicions of those who thought that Saunders' 'recovery' was an act rather than a medical miracle. Friends and supporters of the convicted tycoons maintain they had only been caught doing what was commonplace in pre-Big Bang London, and furthermore they were targeted unfairly. Certainly, three of the Guinness Four were Jewish, and it seemed as though they had been pursued when non-Jews were not. The episode hardly reduced the City's reputation for anti-Semitism.

Next up was Robert Maxwell, although he cheated justice. The City had had plenty of warnings about the ebullient Maxwell, publisher, owner of the *Daily Mirror*, decorated war hero and a serial shyster. The satirical magazine *Private Eye* had battled him for years and his fellow tycoons knew he was deeply untrustworthy and corrupt. His credentials as a former Labour MP, and ownership of the Labour-supporting *Mirror*, meant that he was part of the Labour family, however. Given way too much licence by his board, he looted the pension fund of Mirror Group to the tune of £440m. Before this was revealed, but with it being reported that Maxwell was struggling to repay debts to banks including Goldman Sachs, on 5 November 1991 he fell, or more likely jumped, off the back of his yacht, the *Lady Ghislaine*.

Mirror, mirror: crooked Robert Maxwell could not have got away with it for so long without the help of some of the City's finest firms.

'Bob was always squeaky clean to me', was the much-mocked verdict of Sir Michael Richardson at N.M. Rothschild. Indeed, the City was up to its neck in Maxwell's activities, along with smart legal firms who cranked out libel writ after libel writ. Even Geoffrey Collier's undoing at Morgan Grenfell was down to intelligence picked up in talks with Maxwell. For a period, N.M. Rothschild's US operation – Rothschild Inc. – had had a close relationship with Maxwell, making $17m in fees from his battle to win control of the publisher Macmillan. Sensibly, the bank's owners then put some distance between themselves and the tycoon, with his closest advisor, Robert Pirie, pushed out. After Maxwell's death, Rothschild in London was summoned to help pick through the wreckage of Maxwell's companies.

The budget version of Maxwell was Asil Nadir, a charlatan puffed up and sold to the public with the assistance of a selection of eager politicians, investment bankers, brokers, lawyers and accountants. Nadir's company made no rational sense. It was a rackety creation. It had begun as a textile firm, moved into fruit packaging, more textiles, Japanese electronics and household appliances. The main purpose it seemed was to build Nadir into an international tycoon, and create a suitable impression by offering lavish hospitality and wooing politicians.[5] For a while Polly Peck was taken very seriously, and Nadir's acquisitions were funded and his deals trumpeted as the efforts of a man of vision, until the early 1990s recession exposed the Tory donor's looting of the company to the tune of £29m. Nadir was a crook but he was also just the latest incarnation of Trollope's Melmotte, the mysterious man on the make, welcomed and used by Establishment figures looking for entertainment and easy money, and then dumped in a hurry. Nadir fled the UK for Northern Cyprus, returning seventeen years later to attempt to clear his name. In 2012 he was sentenced to ten years in prison.

The culmination of the Blue Arrow affair was also messy. County NatWest, the investment bank operation of NatWest, had botched the sale of a recruitment agency in 1987. County NatWest had said more shares had been sold than had been, and unbeknown to investors it held on to 19 per cent and stashed the shares in a variety of accounts, hoping to sell them gradually and on the quiet. The deceit might have worked, but for the intervention of the October 1987 crash, which revealed what had gone on. The scandal damaged NatWest badly and inquiries dragged on for years. In 1993 the former chief executive Tom Frost was exonerated of leading a cover-up, and the fraud trial of three directors of NatWest who had resigned became a £40m shambles. They were later cleared by the Court of Appeal. Those in the City who wonder why their good, entirely legal work was often overlooked, should consider it from the point of view of the public, which became accustomed in those years to seeing on their screens news footage of a steady procession of prosperous men walking in and out of court.

The serial corruption by some at Lloyd's, the insurance market, at times made the rest of it look tame. Since the early 1980s the leadership at Lloyd's had been aware that claims for asbestosis were highly likely to cause large losses for insurers, although it was only almost a decade later that the Lloyd's Names, those who were invited to invest in pursuit of high returns, found this out. Being a Lloyd's Name had once been a badge denoting Establishment status, although in the search for funds agents had widened the search. The financial advantage was supposed to be that a Name did not hand over any money – he or she only undertook to write a cheque for their share in a year in which there were any losses – and they could simultaneously use their money to invest elsewhere outside Lloyd's, perhaps doubling it or making it work twice. There would not be any losses, would there? Lloyd's was as safe as the Bank of England. It knew what it was doing with money, surely; if it did not, who did? It turned out to be an extremely risky way to invest because the Names had unlimited liability, and in the early 1990s thousands of them were promptly ruined. Houses were sold and they had to appeal to the Lloyd's Hardship Fund, administered by Mary Archer, for living costs. Their stories were contemporary versions of the woes experienced by the upper middle classes ruined in the South Sea Bubble.

The court cases involving the Gooda Walker syndicates that had run up losses of £1bn revealed the full shabbiness of the affair, with staff testifying that the Names were being treated in a cavalier fashion and even fleeced. Meanwhile, Anthony Gooda and Derek Walker had prospered while piling their Names into appropriately named 'catastrophe syndicates'.[6] A run of disasters, including Piper Alpha in the North Sea in 1988 and the Lockerbie air disaster in 1989, increased claims and made the losses in the early 1990s worse. The striking exterior of the post-modernist Richard Rogers building from which Lloyd's operated might give the impression that the work inside embodied efficiency, mysterious power and the British financial inheritance updated for a new era. Inside, some of the underwriters had behaved with about as much decorum and good sense as Del Boy Trotter. As Julian Barnes explained it to American readers in a letter from London in the *New Yorker* in September 1993 – 'The Deficit Millionaires' – it had been revealed that one of the pillars of the Establishment was made out of Styrofoam.

Did this carnival of sleaze confirm that the Tories had unleashed corruption? Or had their reforms simply amplified what was already there and made its exposure possible? Certainly the roots of the Lloyd's scandal stretched way back before Thatcher's spell in office, and it was a product of a badly run cartel of the kind she detested. Maxwell was a crooked tycoon given houseroom by the Left. But there was no doubt that many of the other scandals involved miscreants being monstrously greedy, playing on a pitch that had been rolled by the Tories.

Thatcher herself was struggling in the early 1990s to adjust to life out of power, travelling the world making speeches, searching for a role, seeking validation, and becoming increasingly agitated by the ambitions of the nascent European Union. The aftershocks from the reinvigoration of markets that she had helped instigate kept on reverberating. One in particular knocked Thatcher's own party off its feet, even more than the scandals, in the process creating an opportunity for a Labour revival.

On 16 September 1992, her successor as Prime Minister, John Major, got a piquant lesson in the power of free-flowing international markets, when the UK was humiliatingly evicted from the ERM (the European Exchange Rate Mechanism). The ERM had been designed to lock in member currencies within agreed bands and to reduce instability. Thatcher's reluctance to join (she relented a year before she lost office) caused tensions with cabinet ministers who were concerned by her growing Euroscepticism. Meanwhile, Germany, France and others saw the ERM as a step towards a European single currency, which she feared. As Chancellor, then Prime Minister, John Major saw the ERM as a tool for reducing inflation, which had surged again. He invested all of his authority in keeping the UK in the ERM.

On the other side of the Atlantic, an international speculator called George Soros became convinced over the course of the summer that this would not work, and by the autumn had placed a series of big bets against the Bank of England. He and several other major investors gambled that governments would not be able to maintain exchange rates at their then levels, and that pressure from the markets would force ministers and central bankers to abandon their policy, leaving those who had bought and sold anticipating that outcome big profits.

Britain crashing out of the ERM on Black Wednesday turned out to be a great boon for the British economy, in that it enabled a devaluation, lower interest rates and a recovery, although all that many voters remembered was the Chancellor, Norman Lamont – who was not an enthusiast for the ERM, unlike his boss John Major – pushing interest rates up briefly to 15 per cent in a doomed attempt to convince those in the markets that they were prepared to do anything to stay in. The resulting farce was highly symbolic, and close to being the economic equivalent of the Suez crisis, in which the limits of British post-war power were demonstrated humiliatingly.

The government had been bested by Soros, who won $1.5bn over the course of September, and the Tory tribe that had spent many years telling its critics that you cannot buck the market had just had the adage proven. When an advisor to Soros said with the denouement approaching that he should build up their position gradually, Soros said no: 'Go for the jugular.'

That the eventual end result of the crisis was the bolstering of the UK's economic recovery initially seemed almost beside the point, with the television news full of footage of very highly paid young people in braces shouting at each other. The Liberal Democrat leader Paddy Ashdown for once caught the mood with a succinct observation on Black Wednesday about the government: 'They have lost control of the economic situation.' That was it. The Conservatives since 1979 had often suffered periods of extreme unpopularity between general elections, but they always came through on the assumption of enough southern voters that, broadly, they had the economy covered and heading in the right direction. As that trader interviewed by Joan Bakewell on the BBC the day after the 1987 election had said: 'It's the safest and steadiest the country's been for years. Keep it on an even keel.' Even keel and steady were certainly not words that came to mind in late 1992. The Republican Party also suffered a reputational collapse in the US election in November, and Bill Clinton became President. Soros, who was presented in the press as part Bond villain and part seer, was, it turned out, definitely not what he termed 'a free market fundamentalist'. Markets worked, he said, but the idea that they were perfection and needed no supervision was a fantasy.

All this had another impact at Westminster. The gusto with which hitherto Tory-supporting newspapers devoured Major and other ministers in the wake of the shambles taught the next generation of Labour leaders what seemed to be the central truths of the 1990s: those in markets wield the power, be nice to them in all but the most exceptional circumstances; and the media is a monster that can eat a government alive if the leading figures in it are insufficiently skilled at manipulating journalists, editors and proprietors.

Despite it being a moment of triumph for the power of the markets, this was not a happy period in the City. At the Stock

Exchange itself there was a technological cock-up, several years after the departure of George Hayter, steward of Big Bang, that brought humiliation. The advances made in computerisation and reorganisation during Big Bang were not followed up successfully, and the attempt to create a faster computer system – TAURUS, the Transfer and Automated Registration of Uncertified Stocks – was an embarrassing failure. In March 1993 the management cancelled the project, at a cost of £75m to the Exchange and £320m spent by member firms. The chief executive, Peter Rawlins, resigned and the Bank of England had to step in to help construct a replacement computer system.

The harm done by the IRA in the same period was much worse. The Irish Republican campaign against the UK had been relentless, with bombs set off in the capital and beyond for decades, targeted at shoppers, the transport network, the armed forces, police, politicians and the Royal Family. The City had received relatively little attention during the Troubles, but now that it had a much higher profile it was the ideal location for terrorist spectaculars and murder. Shortly before 10:30am on 10 April 1992, the day after a general election, the IRA parked a lorry containing a fertiliser bomb outside the Baltic Exchange, killing three people and all but demolishing the building where the market in shipping contracts was based.

Little more than a year later the Bishopsgate bomb was exploded on the morning of Saturday 24 April 1993, killing a photographer, injuring more than forty people and causing £1bn of damage. The scene that greeted staff and managers on their arrival as they rushed to their offices was dystopian. The facilities staff at Henderson, along with Ben Wrey, discovered that their building had had a lucky escape but climbed onto the roof to take a look. Wrey recalled looking across the skyline at buildings including the NatWest Tower and the Hongkong and Shanghai Bank: 'It was just astounding. There wasn't a single window left in place in those buildings. Everything was hanging out, falling out.' The curtains billowed and some of the millions of pieces of paper blown from the buildings, later shredded by the police, were found as far as two miles away. A so-called 'ring of steel' had to be constructed, with roads leading into the City narrowed and armed guards posted.

The impact of these attacks was more than monetary; the damage done to the City's historical fabric was significant too. The Bishopsgate blast almost destroyed Gresham's tomb in St Helen's, and demolished the medieval St Ethelburga's Bishopsgate, which had survived both the Great Fire of 1666 and the Blitz. It had to be rebuilt and reopened later as a centre for peace and reconciliation. The City had recovered from attacks before; of course it had. This time it would take a few more knocks to its prestige and then, via Europe, it would rise to new heights.

EURO VISION

'Frankfurt is not in the same league as London.'

Henrietta Royle, 2002

Siegmund Warburg had been, for a while, a great enthusiast for European political integration. Having experienced pre-war Berlin and the Nazis before he escaped to London – once there, helping fellow refugees recover what they could – it would be a surprise if he had taken any view other than to advocate greater European cooperation, trade and friendship. His Eurobond innovation in the 1960s, which was so enthusiastically adopted by the Americans and others, remaking London, was one of the most effective pieces of cooperation in the post-war period, providing capital and aiding investment. But the firm the great innovator built in London did not survive much more than a decade after he died. Warburg the merchant bank was taken over and integrated out of existence after his successors took a series of missteps.

It began when Warburg's attempted to do a deal with Morgan Stanley in 1994. David Scholey, the Warburg chairman, hoped that the combination would turn Warburg's bank into an operation with global clout. For their part, the Americans wanted to get their hands on Mercury Asset Management, the £100bn of assets, managed by Warburg's parent company. On 15 December 1994 a short statement revealed that the deal was off. One of the most curious aspects of finance is the way in which a failed takeover or merger attempt exposes the smaller party, because those in the market know that it tried to sell itself but something went wrong. It amounts to an admission that the firm cannot prosper on its own. Warburg had approached the Morgan Stanley deal with expansive confidence; now, having been jilted, it found itself vulnerable to the predations of outsiders. It withdrew from the Eurobond market and started to leak senior staff, who moved to rivals. In May 1995, Warburg was sold to Swiss Bank Corp for $1.37bn.

It was a sorry end for the business that had been built by Warburg, and the even more publicity-shy Henry Grunfeld. It is fortunate that Warburg himself – perceptive student of human foibles and the leading merchant banker of his generation – did not live to see it. His successors had conducted themselves precisely as Warburg had feared they would, pushing for scale and ignoring his view that what mattered were relationships and not just money alone. And for all the talk that he was a pragmatist who understood that eventually his bank would have to find a partner, this was a forced sale of one of the most innovative financial institutions of the modern period to a rather boring Swiss institution. Peter Spira, who had been the youngest member of the original Eurobond team in 1963, spoke for many when he said he was appalled at the outcome. Spira had left many years earlier and, following an unpleasant experience as finance director at Sotheby's, where he found the auction house business even less honourable than the City, he joined Goldman Sachs as vice-chairman. When Warburg's went, he could scarcely believe it. 'All my contemporaries who left, we all felt exactly the same: shame, sadness,' he told an interviewer.[1] He and his former colleagues felt as though it was like a club or regiment that they had helped to build up, and now it was gone.

But between the collapse of the Morgan Stanley deal and the Warburg's sale to the Swiss, there occurred a spectacular disaster that eclipsed all the reverses for the Brits and combined several of the themes of the City revolution. The historic British merchant bank Barings had, in trying to compete, moved into areas its owners and management did not understand. Barings was trying to make its own transition from the era of merchant bank to the whizzier world of securities trading, using the bank's own balance sheet to play the markets. Initially it had considerable success, particularly when Christopher Heath ran Barings Securities. In 1989 he was described by the press as Britain's best-paid man, earning more than £3m, a figure which caused resentment in the other parts of family-owned Barings. He was forced out in early 1993 and an attempt was made to bring the securities division under greater control. The new controls turned out to be worse than rudimentary and the bank's owners became ever more hooked on the seemingly magical profits that had started to flow in from its trading operation in the Far East. A young trader, not yet thirty years old, had been put in charge of a new futures operation in Singapore. His name was Nick Leeson.

Giving Leeson, who was enormously keen to become wealthy but not smart enough to do it legitimately, so much control and money stands as one of the most stupid decisions in the history of the City. How it was ever allowed to happen still baffles some of those involved when the collapse was revealed. A Bank of England veteran who was there that weekend says: 'I have thought about it ever since. Why did they keep sending the money to Leeson in Singapore? Greed for the returns is the only explanation I can ever come up with.' In Singapore Leeson had been allowed to control both the trading operation and the settlement operation. That meant that normal controls – where backroom staff would ask questions about his trades – simply did not apply this time. He employed a secret account (88888) to hide his losses. Even when questions were asked it resulted in no action. By February 1995 the losses totalled £832m and Leeson wrote a resignation letter and boarded a flight out of Singapore.

In London, Peter Baring went round to the Bank of England to break the news that Barings had been defrauded and was as a result somewhat awkwardly completely bust. An attempted rescue did not get very far. Salomon and others were contacted, but with little clarity on how much Leeson had really lost it was impossible for them to step in and buy it. Elsewhere in London Ben Wrey was one of many who got a call, in his case from one of his non-executive directors who had just heard the news: 'Ben, overnight your banker has gone out of business and I just wondered what you were doing about it?' Like many senior people in firms across the City that day, he rushed to the office along with IT people to work out how exposed they were, and which clients had money that might be locked in the collapsing Barings.

That weekend, there was a summit of the City Establishment at the Bank of England, at which the performance of the Barings team was quite extraordinary. Attempts to stick to the family line that they had been defrauded were weakened when the team explained that they had sent £800m to Leeson in the months before the losses were revealed. There were gasps around the table when this emerged. Barings was done for. The Bank of England concluded that its failure would not endanger the market, which turned out to be right, and in Tokyo and New York it got little attention. But the end of Barings provided the quintessential example of Britons grown greedy and flattened by forces they could barely comprehend. The Bank of England and regulators were also criticised for their failure to spot how lax Barings had become.

Warburg and Barings had each gone, joining the myriad brokers and jobbers that a decade before had seemingly been fixed landmarks on the City scene. Not all British firms did badly, however. Far from it. Out of the remaining British merchant banks Cazenove prospered, and Lazard stood apart. It was possible to make a new success out of an old business in London if it adapted, although in the case of Smith New Court even it ended up sold to the Americans eventually. The firm was run by Michael Marks, who had started straight out of school as a runner – delivering stocks and collecting cheques when it was still done by hand – at the stockjobber Smith Brothers; then he became a blue button at the Stock Exchange and in 1975 a partner and boss at Smith Brothers. When Smith New Court was created in 1985, part owned by N.M. Rothschild and chaired by Sir Michael Richardson, Marks was one of the pivotal figures that those needing to buy substantial chunks of companies could call on.

In 1995, when Smith New Court was bought for £526m by the Americans at Merrill Lynch, Marks became a leading figure in the company, continuing a career trajectory that proved that, for all Thatcherism had busted open cartels, there existed a much older London tradition manifest in the rise of Michael Marks. The City had only become so stratified along class grounds from the late Victorian period, whereafter merchant bankers looked down at brokers, who looked down at jobbers, who were the ones with the best understanding of personal risk because they had taken most of it, holding shares for sale on their books. Even when the place was more hierarchical, some people burst through, such as Marks, and the City would not have worked half as well without German immigrants. It had been an engine of social mobility and advancement for bright boys such as Marks – always boys – to varying degrees from its earliest days. It is just that Thatcherism and Big Bang made social mobility, for a while, an even bigger component of the City's personality.

In that respect, London in the mid-1990s was a land of opportunity, and the flood of money flowing through it meant you had to try quite hard in the City, or be unlucky or too greedy, to lose everything more than once. If a trader and his or her colleagues knew enough; if they were a certain type who enjoyed risk, had a feel for markets and did not get over extended; they could become extremely affluent by working themselves into the right place, putting in long hours, trading intelligently and skimming (legitimately) a little of the billions, trillions, that surged through the fibre-optic cables running beneath London's streets and flowed into their offices onto computer screens and back out again. Those little slices of a large sum, taken repeatedly as money sped through the system, soon added up to big numbers. In each area the profits on individual transactions might look small to those who benefited, because the turnover numbers they dealt with for their firms on a daily basis were so large. Bigger numbers, and bigger bonuses, might easily distort one's sense of self-worth.

The resentment at being asked to listen to these increasingly assertive City folk as though they had access to a superior form of insight and intelligence was expressed well by Neal Ascherson in the *Independent on Sunday*. The coverage on television news of almost any major event since Big Bang must it seemed, he said, be accompanied by interviews with rows of 'cream-faced young men' called analysts being asked for their opinions.

> They know a bit about money, in the sense of short-term speculation prospects. But their views on politics, so readily offered, are amateurish. Any of us, given a couple of whiskies and a read of that morning's *Independent*, could do as well. But they come from the City of London, and the City knows about money, and money is what politics is really about.

Trading – in shares, derivatives, foreign exchange or commodities – attracted most of the attention when the press or television examined the City at moments of crisis, perhaps because it was so telegenic and reminded the audience of what they had seen in films such as *Wall Street*. The loudest of the breed, the young working-class men out to make quick fortunes, were dubbed 'barrow boys' who after work in the City's newly busy bars consumed 'shampoo' (champagne) by the cellar-full. LIFFE was searched for drugs by police sniffer dogs, although somehow nothing was found. But there was a lot more to the new City besides aggressive trading. The decisions increasingly were guided by research analysts who studied the market and assessed the state of companies and wrote reports for their colleagues and clients recommending what should be bought and sold.

What had been a pretty rudimentary and unfashionable aspect of finance now became more glamorous, and listed companies had to undergo being grilled by research analysts from big banks and investment houses. The focus started to be on quarterly reporting by companies, meaning that not long after major manufacturers, supermarkets, retailers, airlines and high-street banks themselves had got through one explanation of how they were performing their team had to start preparing the next. The risk there was that while it brought a degree of increased professionalism, it could encourage short-termism and the cult of the leader inside the companies themselves and among some investors. It also required companies and big banks to build large internal bureaucracies dedicated to protecting the scrutinised chief executive, with the help of public relations experts and marketing people. Of course the share price had always mattered and the returns to shareholders too, but it and the CEO, chairman and finance director were now assessed with more regularity and in a less forgiving manner. There still existed plenty of investors, analysts and fund managers who wanted to take a longer-term view and who were genuinely motivated by the excitement of finding far-flung companies worthy of investment; however, there was no doubt that the pressure for short-term returns had increased.

One spot where the Brits really prospered in the 1990s was in building businesses that operated in the space between traditional well-known institutions struggling to cope with the competition and the ruthless foreign arrivals. Often best suited to the new dispensation were the entrepreneurial Brits who had first turned up for work in the 1980s. They had intellectually processed the explosion of money, landed in the City at the right moment and married their insight with a ruthless eye for the main chance. New firms such as ICAP (founded in 1986 as Intercapital by Michael Spencer) placed themselves at the international crossroads of finance, as inter-dealer brokers matching clients such as big banks with pools of shares and interest rate products, foreign exchange, commodities, emerging markets and credit, and trading for themselves too. In asset management, a company such as Aberdeen Asset Management, established by Martin Gilbert after a buy-out of an investment trust in 1983, could fill the need for investment opportunities and advice that came stripped of City insider condescension.

These businesses were tiny at first, and Aberdeen was one of the firms that later ran into severe difficulties for selling 'split-cap' investments to consumers as low-risk when they were anything but (Aberdeen was subsequently rebuilt by Gilbert and his team). But the swashbuckling tenor of the times suited the insurgents, who were unimpeded by having to reconcile themselves to accommodating traditions or form. They would grow quickly. Terry Smith was another such outsider who blossomed in a climate that suited the irreverent and the intelligent. Smith was a grammar-school boy from the East End, who after university became one of the leading research analysts. His approach rested on the extraordinary idea of telling investors the truth. Could this ever catch on? His frankness got him fired as head of UK company research at UBS Phillips & Drew in 1992 when he published *Accounting for Growth*. That incendiary document questioned the assorted ruses and creative accountancy that were employed by advisors and accountants to make some businesses appear more successful to investors than they were. The book sold well and Smith went on to make a fortune as a fund manager with a predilection for punchy comments about politics.

All this put the next generation of political leaders on the centre-Left in an odd position. The new leader of the Labour Party, Tony Blair, and the Shadow Chancellor, Gordon Brown, realised that they had to reconcile their party to many of the Thatcherite market reforms to win, and that meant stepping up what had started under their predecessors as a 'prawn cocktail offensive', wooing City types and convincing them that Labour had changed and was not about to nationalise the banks. The Blair–Brown view had been bolstered by visits to Washington to see Bill Clinton, who had won the Presidency in 1992 by not trying to refight the battles of the 1980s.

Standing in the way of success in the City or in business would only reinforce the old stereotypes that did not appeal to swing voters, it seemed. Some people were going to be paid a lot of money. But who? And what constituted proper reward or grounds for populist complaint? The criteria were unclear. Was the benchmark simply what you could get? The City pay boom in the mid-1980s, which accelerated again in the 1990s, had set an example, and ambitious executives in industry and commerce could see that some of the people advising them on deals, or moving around their company's reserves of foreign exchange, or trading corporate bonds, were being paid much more than the chief executives of major companies that were theoretically their clients. The phrase 'paying the market rate' became fashionable, and remuneration committees found themselves inundated by inflated evidence – from head-hunters and the like – that only by paying what was on offer in comparable jobs would they land or keep the best person.

This ostensibly had a certain logic, but the implications of this self-serving racket first became fully apparent during the infamous case of the chief executive of British Gas – Cedric Brown – who became in the mid-1990s the media's most unpopular person in Britain, hunted by the tabloids and branded 'Cedric the pig'. The Labour leadership proved itself adept at castigating him, to please the voters, while being nice more broadly to business and the City.

Yet Cedric Brown's story, like that of John King who had successfully privatised British Airways and taken a 116 per cent pay increase, might in another context have been considered an admirable tale of hard work and social mobility. When Brown became chief executive of the privatised monopoly, the American chairman of the company, used to US corporate largesse, approved a salary of £475,000, a £600,000 incentive deal, almost £1m worth of share options and a guaranteed £180,000 annual pension on his retirement five years hence. It represented a 900 per cent increase for that role over the course of a decade.

All of the contemporary resentments and accusations – about corporate pay, greed, privatisation, the property crash – came pouring down on poor (or not so poor) Cedric Brown's head.[2] He was accused by the press of a transgression deemed to be even worse in British terms than greed, however. His house was judged to be petty bourgeois and 'neo-Georgian'. In contrast, the chairman of British Gas, who was paid more than £400,000 for a three-day week at British Gas, got a lot less attention than his chief executive. He was self-made too but treated more leniently, having acquired the good taste to live in a flat in Cadogan Square, Chelsea, and own a nice property on the US east coast in the exclusive Martha's Vineyard.

In the US, on Wall Street, the equation tended to be much simpler. You secured high pay? Well done, good luck to you. Although it should not be forgotten that this had not always been the case. The original J.P. Morgan stipulated that no manager should be paid a salary more than twenty times the salary of the lowest-paid worker. Try getting that principle readopted by an American investment bank today. But in the UK it was more complex, partly because of the quirks of the class system and partly because significant changes that came with Thatcherism received inadequate attention at the time and produced effects that were only understood later. It was connected to the argument over financial regulation and the importation of an American approach (if it is legal, it is fine or right).

Combine the two – get paid what you can, it is the market rate; and it is all entirely legal – and you have created the conditions for the row that took place in 2016 about the offshore investments of David Cameron's late father. A partner at Panmure Gordon, he had established a vehicle in Panama through which family investments were routed, perfectly legally. But in 2012 Ian Cameron's son had condemned entertainers who avoided tax (rather than evaded it, which is illegal). Cameron Junior was accused of hypocrisy and the affair illustrated that one of the main contradictions of the Thatcher experiment remains unresolved. Imagine asking Harold Macmillan, or Gladstone or Disraeli, whether the law is all that matters in such circumstances. They would probably answer that while the rule of law is important, and without it we are sunk, there should be more to it than that. What of duty, restraint and setting an example to others? Cameron knew it too, which is why he later withdrew his comments about the immorality of comedians minimising their tax bills. And what of Thatcher, the Methodist? Whether one disagrees with her or approves of her record, she was clear that a moral and ethical impulse – reward for work, and without wealth there is nothing to help the weak – defined her approach to politics.

The New Labour leadership when it swept away the Conservatives had its own unique answer to these problems. Part of the skill of those who restored the party to power in May 1997 was that they initially so cleverly accommodated themselves to Thatcherism, on both sides of the Blair–Brown divide, and adapted it. They rarely attacked her in name because it was recognised that she had won three general elections and remained popular – as a promoter of aspiration – in much of the south where Labour needed to win seats. Peter Mandelson's quote, often used out of context with the second half lopped off, in which he said that he was 'intensely *relaxed* about people getting *filthy rich* as long as they pay their taxes', is much more revealing than the bowdlerised version, for it reveals the essence of the New Labour compact. The leadership now welcomed Thatcherite markets and unashamed wealth creation, and would use the proceeds to pay for progressive policies and higher spending on public services.

In such circumstances who, other than cranks or old-fashioned types who remembered that booms end, could object to the example of the City as a great British success story? It had spread out to Canary Wharf, where banks such as Morgan Stanley, J.P. Morgan and a resurgent Barclays occupied towers. Barclays was again building an investment bank, after selling the struggling BZW and launching Barclays Capital, led from 1996 by Bob Diamond. In the City itself, the remodelling instigated by Michael Cassidy and Peter Rees from the Corporation altered the skyline, and in 2004 the Richard Rogers building, christened the Gherkin, opened. The competition from Canary Wharf had after all compelled the Corporation to approve even bigger office blocks that could rival what was on offer a few miles away.

Another outpost of finance had also sprung up in London's West End, in Mayfair, where on Dover Street and in streets nearby emerged Hedge Fund Alley. Its firms were often boutique in scale, promising superior returns, owned privately with a relatively small number of staff investing borrowed capital. Private equity and venture capital firms abounded, injecting money into undervalued firms and sometimes loading them with debt while sucking out proceeds to invest elsewhere. In such inventive, expansive times some surveys in the mid-2000s showed that London pay and performance had overtaken New York. More than ever, the Americans had to be over here. The investment banking operation of Schroders was sold in 2000 to Citigroup; Robert Fleming went to Chase Manhattan; and even Cazenove under the leadership of David Mayhew was sold to J.P. Morgan in 2004.

It seemed at the time that the simultaneous expansion of Britain's high-street banks, several of which had tooled up to compete at global investment banking, made a kind of sense. These were starting to be talked of, usually by themselves, as potential world-beaters worthy of government endorsement. RBS became, briefly, the biggest bank in the world by balance sheet in late 2007, and a former building society called Northern Rock grew by borrowing money on the markets and repackaging – securitising – the loans, which was a terrific model as long as they could access sufficient credit on a daily basis. The denizens of the City sometimes deny any culpability for this madness. RBS was a Scottish Bank, HBOS was technically headquartered in Edinburgh, and Northern Rock was based in Newcastle. The truth is that the analysts pronouncing on banks'

Clever old Caz: David Mayhew in 2004 when the bluechip City firm Cazenove was one of the last to sell to an American giant, in its case J.P. Morgan.

prospects were based in the City, and they had a mixed record in spotting trouble. The asset managers who bought and sold shares in these and other banks loaded up with other people's money. Many of the accountants and lawyers who assisted the expanding banks were in London. And the securitisation employed by Northern Rock and so many others was merely a version of what investment banks had, they thought, perfected in the field of repackaging sub-prime US mortgages. The British banking boom of the 2000s was in part a creation of the Square Mile.

The media was hardly blameless in talking up all this activity and expansion in banking and other industries. The business sections of Sunday newspapers had long enjoyed the 'Friday night drop', in which companies or their public relations agencies 'dropped' stories to financial journalists. As the journalist Chris Blackhurst put it shortly afterwards:

> Stories that were being hailed as major scoops of journalistic endeavour were often nothing of the sort, involving little more than a phone call from a PR to a friendly, trusted reporter. The drop has all manner of uses. Poor results will be leaked to Sunday journalists in advance to soften the blow. In takeovers, agencies will dish the dirt on the opposition in a way they could not do in any official document. Speculation about next year's figures, even the private lives of the directors, will all be handed to a favoured journalist. The Sunday papers will be used to smoke out possible bidders, to trash business rivals, to bring about votes of confidence by putting pressure on recalcitrant boards.[3]

Were financial journalists breaking any rules? Jeff Randall, a leading observer of the Square Mile, a former City Editor of the *Sunday Times*, was convinced they were not. All they were doing was getting stories: 'In order to be guilty of insider dealing you have to deal,' Randall said. 'Knowing or having access to price sensitive information is not a crime. It is what you do with the information that counts. We are in the business of revealing to our readers price sensitive information. That is why they buy the paper.'[4]

It was a good point. Journalism in London or New York was hardly pure, far from it, before the financial revolution of the 1980s, but what had been created thanks to the increased reader interest in the markets, in the rise of the financial PR firm attempting to better control stories to the advantage of clients, was a bigger and more valuable market in information. Many of those practices in politics that are commonly attributed to the rise of so-called 'spin-doctors' in the 1990s, inflated press officers trying to mould their clients image and control the story, often in vain, were prefigured in the interplay between City PRs, large companies, investment banks and financial hacks that reached a zenith in the 1980s and 90s.

In Britain it had another effect, in TV news. As the scale and importance of the financial markets increased, and access to sophisticated insight and gossip about them became a more valuable commodity, so the stock of City journalists rose. In 2000, Randall was appointed as the first business editor of the BBC when its new director general, Greg Dyke, decided that the Beeb had taken far too lofty an attitude to moneymakers. The Corporation had traditionally preferred to have an economics editor, who covered business too when necessary. This was no longer good enough, Dyke told the Confederation of British Industry in a speech in early November 2000: 'Up to now we thought it was good enough to have the economics editor also being responsible for business coverage on the side. It was wrong.'[5]

The then economics editor was Peter Jay, who as Britain's ambassador to Washington in the late 1970s had been an early convert to monetarism and the concept of squeezing inflation out of the economy by getting the money supply under control. In the early 1980s Jay was one of the founders of TV-am, presiding over programmes informed by a 'mission to explain'. The ratings were dire, and Dyke was drafted in to rescue the situation in the spring of 1983. He promptly ripped up the formula, opted for ratings-friendly excitement and introduced a 'rapping' rat – Roland Rat, accompanied by a sidekick called Kevin – who is credited with helping to save the company. Much later, when Dyke hired Randall in 2000 at the BBC, he was implementing his own 'mission to explain', arguing that the BBC had to become much better at explaining markets and companies to its large audiences in terms they could understand. Dyke and Randall were defining media products of the Thatcherite 1980s, and even if Dyke was a Labour supporter, he shared with Randall distinctly meritocratic, anti-Establishment instincts. Their appointments at the end of the 1990s would have been unimaginable in the BBC of twenty years earlier, before the rise to fresh prominence of the City and the elevated position business was now accorded.

It did seem for a while as though there was a lot to celebrate. On 25 October 2006, two days before the twentieth anniversary of Big Bang, the guest speaker at the annual City of London Corporation dinner was someone from the anti-Blair side of the New Labour civil war. Ed Balls, the government's City Minister, had been Gordon Brown's closest aide and a major combatant in the fight to keep the UK out of the single currency.

Big Bang in October 1986 had been a tremendous success and decisive moment in the history of the City, he told the audience of financiers and politicians that evening: 'It confirmed that in financial services Britain would choose global integration and openness over protectionism and national ownership, competition and market discipline over discrimination and cartels.' He also disagreed, he said, with those who criticised the 'light touch' approach to regulation. 'To revert to more heavy-handed, detailed or mechanistic regulation which put process before substance would divert us from proper risk-assessment and stifle innovation. We do not intend to fall into that trap.'[6]

The following day there was a celebration at the Mansion House, with Nicholas Goodison acknowledging in a speech that he was surprised that so many of the old City firms had disappeared following the reforms. It was widely agreed that Big Bang had been a roaring success, though. In the intervening two decades, the value of traded shares in London had increased from £161bn in 1986 to

£2,496bn in 2006. The banking sector had boomed, with total assets up seven times to £5.5 trillion. The Treasury pulled in 26 per cent of its corporate tax receipts annually from the financial services industry. In the *FT*, John Kay eschewed boosterism and offered a more nuanced verdict. The greatest beneficiaries of Big Bang had been the partners of the firms that sold out when brokers and jobbers were bought at absurd prices by large banks in deals that almost all failed, he said. 'The partners retired to expensive yachts and exclusive villas: the marzipan layer of employees below resented the alien culture of their new masters.' And for all the celebration of success, Kay warned that the evolution of competitive markets always has unpredictable consequences. How right he was became apparent only a few years later.

This is not an account of the financial crisis of 2007–9 that followed. There is no shortage of volumes available already on that episode. An earlier book of mine charted the rise and fall of the Royal Bank of Scotland and its chief executive Fred Goodwin. Suffice it to say that on both sides of the Atlantic a lending surge, a mania for excessive scale, too much bad leadership, ineffective regulation, consumer hunger for goods and houses and a willingness to borrow to pay for it, all came together to produce a new version of an old story. The disaster was followed by a rescue operation and then a sustained campaign of ultra-cheap money, creating more lending and in the UK another property bubble in the south of England. Add to that QE, or money printing. A bubble was blown to get us over the bursting of the previous bubble.

But something else extremely significant and positive had happened in the City between 1986, that pivotal year, and the aftermath of the financial crisis. The launch of the European single currency, completed on 1 January 2002, turned out to be the making of the modern City when no one outside the City was looking, and even though the Eurozone suffered its own crisis. The success of the euro in London might be thought odd when one considers the successful campaign waged to prevent the UK joining what Germany and France created out of the ERM. At the time it was claimed by advocates of British entry that Frankfurt, which boasted the European Central Bank, would eclipse London as Europe's new financial centre. To anyone who had ever been there, this seemed unlikely.

As Henrietta Royle, deputy chief executive of British Invisibles, a body promoting the UK's financial services industry, told the BBC in 2002: 'It [Frankfurt] is not in the same league as London.' Michael Lewis (not the author, another Michael Lewis) had worked in Frankfurt and was unimpressed too. He told an interviewer: 'It is about the size of Reading but not as interesting.' London in the early 2000s simply had too many accumulated advantages, and too much had been invested there by American banks. The introduction of the EU single market, and 'passporting', which allowed banks to operate anywhere in the EU if they were adequately regulated in one country, meant that the UK was free to become the centre for trading of all types in euros. By 2013 its lead was enormous. Centred on London, the UK had 78 per cent of all foreign exchange trading in the EU; 85 per cent of all hedge fund assets; 50 per cent of fund management; 74 per cent of OTC (over the counter) derivatives trading; 31 per cent of equity market capitalisation; 19 per cent of all bank lending in the EU; 23 per cent of insurance premiums ; and 18 per cent of total EU financial services GDP.

The irony is that the Thatcher-era reforms had led to London dominating trade in the European currency the UK had decided not to join[7], ending a sixty-year shutdown in global securities markets that dated to 1914, and which had partially been reopened with the Eurobond in 1963. Even if Thatcher did not plan it – and it started before her, with technological innovation making it feasible – it was hardly pure accident. Key decisions were taken by her and her leading ministers which dramatically sped up a European and global financial revolution.

It turned out that the British abolition of exchange rate controls in 1979, allowing money to flow across borders seeking investment opportunity, had been a transformative act that became internationally highly influential. It was copied four years later by Australia and then by New Zealand. It eventually became standard in much of the world. Ten years after Geoffrey Howe, urged on by Nigel Lawson, removed the UK's exchange controls, even France followed. On 12 December 1989 the French finance minister, Pierre Bérégovoy, made the announcement confirming it. The previous weekend, at a summit in Strasbourg, the move had been urged by Mrs Thatcher. The European Community (the forerunner of the European Union) set a series of countries deadlines, and within a few years Italy, Spain, Portugal and Greece had complied.

That cross-border flow had another side effect on the British, who had once taken such pride in national ownership of their industry and commerce. It had not been uncommon for politicians and newspapers to talk of national champions and to oppose foreign firms buying up British assets, even when British companies were buying up so much themselves in other countries. The Royal Bank of Scotland was protected from foreign takeover by Margaret Thatcher's ministers in the early 1980s. But even if there was public disquiet when British brands went into foreign ownership – as in 1988 when the confectionery firm Rowntree was bought by Switzerland's Nestlé for £2.5bn – it started to become the norm and to attract a lot less comment. Some voices were raised asking if it made sense for water companies or electricity providers to be owned by French companies, but complaints rarely lasted long.

The English even accepted the principle – if not the reality, when it did not produce victory for their own team – of football clubs such as Chelsea, Manchester United, Manchester City, Liverpool and Leicester being owned by rich foreigners. The London Stock Exchange itself ceased to be a membership organisation in 2000 and it is now owned by a variety of international shareholders that in recent years have included the Qatar Investment Authority and the American investment giant Blackrock. Money follows money, and just about anything British – apart from the Queen – is for sale for the right price.

The Thatcherite privatisation programme, which could not have been carried out without the assistance of the City, was also exported and adopted widely. In India, Chile, Singapore, Brazil, France, Germany, Israel, South Korea, Norway, and many other countries, telecommunications, banking, airports, airlines, water, electricity, property, and much more besides were auctioned. Big Bang-style reforms were also implemented in stock markets across the world. In Tel-Aviv in 1986 the old exchange was rudimentary until Esther Levanon arrived from more than a decade working in computers for the Shin Bet, Israel's internal security service. 'At the time there were several dozen traders delivering orders,' she said, 'With battalions of typists inputting the data.'[8] She computerised the operation in a model that owed much to London. In the Paris Bourse and in the Amsterdam Stock Exchange open outcry was faded out. At the Frankfurt Stock Exchange, which eventually became Deutsche Börse, computerised pricing like London's was introduced from September 1987. Eventually, Amsterdam, Brussels and Paris grouped together, were sold to the Americans (NYSE) and then ICE, the Intercontinental Exchange.

But they did not – for now – rival London. How could they? With the rich and aspirational from America, Russia, France, the Gulf and beyond flocking to London – rocketing houses prices and creating a luxury goods boom – it attracted money, some of which was invested in changing the face of the place well beyond the Square Mile. The wealth disparities became ever more obvious, but the drabness and a lot of the grime was wiped away. None of it would have happened without the City and its pull. London was a magnet again, a global hub, voraciously sucking in talent, much-welcome investors, shady playboys, oligarchs laundering dirty money, luxury-obsessed layabouts, and the greedy and the needy. Its re-emergence was down to a most peculiar array of advantages, along with a dose of luck, and reforms that between the invention of the Eurobond and 1986 restored London. The City was back. Was this a good idea?

1986 AND ALL THAT

'I maintain it was not a good idea. I question whether it was necessary.'

Stani Yassukovich

Making my way across a large garden in central London, trying not to drop a tray bearing a pot of Earl Grey and two scones, I approach Sir Nicholas Goodison sitting on a bench in the shade. His remark that I would make a good butler may be a joke, but I am not entirely sure. Despite Goodison's physical frailty – he was born in 1934 – his sense of humour and powers of recall are fully intact. 'Why was it called Big Bang? Because everything changed.' We talk for several hours in the summer sun about the City and how quickly it changed in the 1980s. What is remarkable is that, aside from the cars and some of the architecture, those horrible office blocks put up in the decades immediately after the Second World War, the City of the early 1980s would have been essentially recognisable to a time-travelling worker flown in from the 1930s, or even from the 1880s. Many of the big names on brass plates were still the same towards the end of the 1970s when Goodison became chairman of the Stock Exchange. It had been that way for what seemed like forever. The Stock Exchange functioned largely as it had for decades; the Bank of England was the embodiment of financial power; the City of London Corporation ran the Square Mile (it still does) as a self-governing entity; the railways funnelled in commuters at roughly the same time each day as had been the case a century before; business was conducted face to face; and the sober modes of dress and

'Voracious London': the City's Royal Exchange, the Bank of England, the
Stock Exchange, and Thomas Gresham's old neighbourhood Bishopsgate,
now sit in the shadow of a new generation of temples to mammon.

less sober codes of behaviour were pretty constant. Within ten years
of Big Bang, the City looked quite different. Behind old facades new
bars opened serving the City new generation, some of them modest
and others unafraid to proclaim their genius, which was often
simply rooted in luck. Most of all the modern City became about

what went on in offices of big banks and investment firms in the Square Mile and at Canary Wharf, in equities, forex, interest rates, debt, derivatives, corporate finance, where during a much longer day London was hooked live to markets around the world moving money, trading, hustling based on information that blinked red and green on a computer screen. Trading and doing deals there had always required foreigners in the City. Now there are more Americans, still some Japanese, and lots of the French. Bonuses have boomed. If anyone played a leading role in creating this festival of moneymaking, it was Goodison. Thirty years after Big Bang, does he think it worked?

'We achieved making London the leading international centre. It is a more competitive market, but the Stock Exchange is simply one market among many and I didn't expect that. Things moved in ways I didn't foresee.' What does he think was lost? 'I thought the Stock Exchange was a brilliant informal regulator . . . tough. Now it has all become a matter of law and if something is a matter of law it is open to challenge.' It is now, he says, an international market in people. He simply cannot understand why such enormous fees are paid and he recommends more openness. 'Total disclosure on salaries and how they are made is where I would start.'

The Stock Exchange has changed considerably in the decades since he left. It demutualised in 2000, and is now owned by institutional investors around the world rather than members. It is based in nondescript offices near St Paul's Cathedral that could, really, be anywhere on earth where financiers do business, from New York to Singapore to Frankfurt. In the spring of 2016, the latest attempt to arrange a merger between the London Stock Exchange and Deutsche Bourse in Frankfurt began.

After hours talking through the late 1970s to the mid-1980s I worry that Goodison may be exhausted. Not a bit of it. It is time for a drink. Goodison sends me off to collect a Cinzano and soda and I return with the drinks, handing him his while sipping a glass of white wine as afternoon turns into early evening. 'I mean,' he says, 'supposing that the Stock Exchange had stayed as it was. It would have died.'

Since the 1980s, Lord Lawson has had to endure becoming almost as famous for his diet (he lost five stone after leaving office) and for his daughter being Britain's leading television cook[1] as he is for being a highly significant reforming Chancellor of the Exchequer from 1983 to 1989. He lives in France and commutes to the House of Lords, where we sit one morning discussing the financial revolution. Lawson liked the City from the start and made friends there when he began his career as a journalist in the 1950s. He was the *FT*'s Lex columnist for a while. 'The City was one of the better parts of the British economy, which doesn't say very much for the other parts of the UK economy. It was good at commodities and good at foreign exchange.' When he became Chancellor after the 1983 election, the Trade Secretary Cecil Parkinson was distracted by the Sara Keays affair and Lawson got involved in the discussions with Goodison. Thatcher was in favour of more competition but she took some persuading about the wisdom of a deal with Goodison. It was the united front presented by Parkinson and Lawson that he thinks convinced the Prime Minister to proceed in the face of doubts from her deputy, Willie Whitelaw. 'Her concern was how it would be interpreted politically. She was always in favour of more competition but she was not instinctively pro-City,' Lawson says. Although Lawson thinks thirty years later that Big Bang was entirely necessary for the City to become the global hub it is today, with hindsight he thinks it should have been accompanied by more safeguards. 'We should have had a Glass-Steagall,' he says, referring to the US legislation from the 1930s that used to prohibit high-street banks getting involved in trading. 'Look at the banking malpractices of 2008. A large part of that was the high-risk culture of the investment banks polluting the traditionally cautious culture of the joint stock banks.' But the City should not be derided, he says. 'As we have seen, the bankers certainly have feet of clay and we don't have to listen to them. But look, there are very few industries in which this country is undoubtedly world class. Banking and finance is one of them.'

Sir David Walker has seen it from inside government, the Bank of England and the boardroom. There are not many people who have had a better seat from which to view the financial revolution of the last fifty years. He was there as a young Treasury official when Denis Healey turned back at Heathrow Airport during the IMF crisis in 1976, before Walker played a critical role at the Bank of England preparing the ground for Big Bang. He was chairman of Morgan Stanley International, author of the government-commissioned review on corporate governance after the financial crisis of 2008 and then chairman of Barclays when it was struggling to recover from a wave of scandals. We meet at his office, where the seventy-six-year-old is non-executive chairman at Winton Capital. Did he think Big Bang was a success? 'Oh yes, absolutely. It was essential. I find it hard to see how the City would have survived as a major international centre without it.' He regards the claims of those who say that it was all better, and more gentlemanly, before 1986 as a 'rose-tinted' view that overlooks how much sharp practice there was. Insider dealing was not illegal at all until 1980 and then only definitively with fresh legislation in the mid-1980s. Before that the practices of 'front-running' shares (using inside information or analysts' reports to trade before letting clients in on the action) and exploiting nefariously obtained tip-offs were widespread in the old City. 'These weren't bad people. They were good people, but the barriers to entry were very high with an ancient set of restrictions. The original City coffee houses were designed to keep people out.'

There were drawbacks to the changes in the City, on Wall Street, and beyond, he says. Part of the problem was that as companies and banks became bigger and vastly more complex, relying on technology that had only recently been unavailable, operating across borders, they needed all manner of products, for foreign exchange, hedging to mitigate risk, and for swaps and ways of parcelling up debt. 'The pace of change accelerated alongside the globalisation of trade and the freeing up of capital flows. This explosion in the markets outstripped the ability of regulators to understand it. They found it very hard to keep up. Simultaneously, the fact it was possible to make a lot more money reduced discipline.' Walker became a regulator for a while, chairing the Securities and Investment Board (SIB) from 1988 and trying to disentangle the work of his predecessor Sir Kenneth Berrill, who had created a jumble of rules that could have filled several large rooms if piled up. Walker tried to return to some simpler 'principles-based' regulation that could be understood by those supposed to be obeying the rules. Several years later, after he had moved on, the incoming Labour government in 1997 introduced a tripartite system under Gordon Brown, in which, fatally, the Bank of England lost day-to-day control of supervision of the banking system. Regulatory failure may have contributed to the 2008 banking crisis, but there was not a shortage of regulation. Insufficient attention was paid to the potential instability of large financial institutions, and the perils of big banks being unable to access funding in an emergency. That credit crisis – triggered by concerns about who held sub-prime derivatives – mutated into a financial crisis and a run on the American and British banking systems, which had, once again urged on by politicians, lent too much on property.

As I prepare to take my leave of Sir David we discuss colourful figures now long gone – Michael von Clemm and Baron Swaythling, horse-mad David Montagu, the man who at Merrill Lynch had Don Regan to dinner and then got a note from Geoffrey Howe saying the Western world was doomed if Regan ever became US Treasury Secretary, which he did. All thirty years ago or more but really, underneath it all, are the people and issues involved now any different? Have ethics changed? Walker pauses to think. It is a very big question, he finally says, before acknowledging he doesn't have a definitive answer. Much of what happens in respect of credit and market risk, he says, isn't really new. It is all there, observable in one form or another, in the history of finance. The key differences now are the huge scale and complex global links of financial market activity which have greatly increased the vulnerability of the whole system to shocks.

The history can be downright wrong or misleading though. One sees it written into the record that the deal that ushered in Big Bang is the Goodison–Parkinson deal. But while Goodison persevered patiently to find a solution year after year, Parkinson inherited the idea, gave it a shove in 1983 with the help of officials and Lawson, and then departed shortly afterwards. But ground-breaking work done by the Bank of England was critical in advocacy of a deal. It was Walker who put the game-changing paper by the Bank of England's Andrew Threadgold on the table in Downing Street advocating a deal to reform the Stock Exchange, at the meeting held days before the 1983 election. Geoffrey Howe saw the sense of it and it was the soon to be ex-Secretary of State for Trade, Arthur Cockfield, who really grasped the scale of the opportunity, says Walker. Cockfield turns out to have been one of the most important figures of the Thatcherite era. Yet his name three decades later is unfairly all but forgotten. It was Cockfield as an EU Commissioner who worked on preparations for the Single European Act of 1986, producing a tariff-free EU which along with myriad directives that followed made it possible for the City to become Europe's undisputed financial capital. Major roles in Big Bang and the Single European Act constitute quite a record.

Michael Howard – now Lord Howard, then the minister who steered the Financial Services Act through the Commons – who became Home Secretary in 1993, then Conservative Party leader in 2003, played a significant role in the developments of 1986 too. He says that history has the regulation story quite wrong: 'I get quite cross when people say it was all about untrammelled free markets with no constraints. It was the first attempt to put financial regulation on a statutory footing, albeit on a self-regulatory basis.' The accompanying Big Bang that happened simultaneously, but which had been planned several years before, was an achievement, he says. 'Without it we would not have the world-leading financial services we have today.' But didn't it associate his party with wrongdoing and excess in the City? 'I suspect the Conservative

Party was associated with the City well before Big Bang.' The Guinness scandal was dealt with pretty robustly, he points out: 'No one can accuse us of being soft on the City.' For all the talk that the 1980s was a period of deregulation, the rise in costs demonstrates that the reduction of regulation is largely a myth. In 1986, the direct cost of UK financial regulation was estimated to be £20m; this rose to around £90m by 1992 and £673m in 2014.

What of the practitioners in the marketplace who lived it? To see David Mayhew of Cazenove, the most blue-chip firm of all that is now no longer independent and is embedded in J.P. Morgan, I go to the US bank's Thameside offices near Blackfriars. The look is clinical modern financial chic – I mean the offices, not Mayhew, who is terrifically entertaining and sharp as a knife. J.P. Morgan also has a tower at Canary Wharf and assorted operations elsewhere in the City and he remains involved part time having 'retired' in 2011. 'I don't think Big Bang, one day, properly describes what was happening. Until the abolition of exchange controls we were a little island, then we re-joined the financial world. That combined with the political push and technology were what drove it.' In contrast, according to Mayhew, the 1960s managed to be dull with short working days, punctuated with moments of great drama during takeovers over which there were no rules of combat and no protections for investors. The caricature of alcoholic excess is overdone, he says: 'They weren't all completely pissed.' If the changes had not been made in the 1980s he thinks London would not have had an international capital market, which he says has provided a very efficient provision of capital to Europe and the world. 'Downsides? Loss of morality? Too much money? There is a question as to whether the system has got it right.' Back in the 1950s there was not such an obsession with shareholder value alone. 'I don't want to pretend we're going to have Victorian values but the Americans are very good at giving money away as well as making it.' The whole capitalist system need defending, he says. 'Ain't any other systems that have done so well.' Mayhew is certainly correct that Americans give more once they make it. Giving is regarded as a duty. Even allowing for the difference in the size of population, the money given to churches, and the tax breaks that are built in to the US system, the gap is enormous. In 2014, total US giving by individuals, foundations, corporations and bequests amounted to $358.4bn (£248.3bn) against £10.6bn in the UK.[2]

Ben Wrey visits the City only rarely but at his home in Kensington we discuss the strange beauty and power of the historic corners of the place that have not been rebuilt in recent decades, such as in Austin Friars where Gresham's house stood in the sixteenth century. Ahead of Big Bang Wrey had seen the impact in the US of May 1975, when travelling for Henderson he glimpsed the way in which small brokers were wiped out by competition from big Wall Street firms because minimum commissions had been scrapped, reducing their income: 'There was this feeling in London that it wouldn't be that brutal here because we don't do things like that. They had underestimated the arrival of the big American banks. It was a pretty shocking experience but it was needed. It brought London right up.' The City now, he suspects, is not quite as much fun as it was but it had to change: 'I don't think it's sensible to be sentimental about the changes or the people. The old world was terribly inefficient.'

Philippa d'Arcy (née Rose) is no longer a head-hunter and left her firm to run a business outside London, opening her rather lovely home, which has its own church, for conferences and weddings. She thinks moaning about the downsides of what happened with rising salaries misses the point. The country was in a hole before the 1980s; the world was changing; it was free markets. 'One has to suck it up and move on.'

Sir Henry Angest, the Swiss immigrant who built up Arbuthnot Latham and became a major donor to the Conservative Party and to Eurosceptic causes, claims that regulation is now much too intrusive and that it advantages the biggest banks, the mega-banks, over the smaller institutions such as his. Big Bang and associated developments were worth it though, he says: 'There was huge activity with building, with cranes everywhere. Foreign restaurants and new chefs opened up. Celebrities came back. Life came back to London.' His Chief Operating Officer, Andrew Salmon, son of a stockbroker, joins the conversation in the Arbuthnot boardroom and says that the 1980s were overwhelmingly positive because the markets were opened up. It brought prosperity to the City. There was a flaw, however. 'For my generation it lured one in. The city is what has really boomed. It has sucked talent out of other parts of the UK. For a while the City became deified and the people became heroes.'

Others go much further in their criticism. Charles McVeigh III, formerly of Salomon, which was swallowed by Travellers, and then Citigroup, the Salomon brand disappearing down the plughole of financial history, is senior Advisor to Citi Private Bank and Vice Chairman of their European Advisory Board. He also chairs Rubicon, a successful London-based hedge fund. He is convinced that capitalism as currently constituted is in serious trouble. It is the capitalists who risk blowing up capitalism if they carry on as they are, he says. Part of the problem is that attitudes have changed and those coming into finance are too often not interested in the lessons of history. 'I'm an old fart. I'm asked regularly at Citigroup to meet with trainees, which I love to do. I look at the audience and they don't give a damn. They're bored. What matters to them is what's happening now and what's in it for me.' This is a disaster, he says, because they need to learn and everyone will suffer if they do not. 'I think capitalism in its current form is broken. The trillions of wealth created between 2008 and 2015', by cheap money and in asset bubbles, 'has gone to 4 or 5 per cent of the population. The companies hide behind the idea their job in life is to enhance shareholder value. Fine. But if we cannot take a long-term perspective we're in trouble. Capitalism is not too big to fail.'

Valerie Thompson, who loved working with Charlie McVeigh and Salomon in the 1980s and left to spend more time raising her daughters, agrees and thinks that the markets have become a toxic debt-laden soup. She enjoyed the intellectual challenge at the time and was extremely good at it, although she disliked the sexism of some of her other colleagues. She recalls the boss Gutfreund visiting London, and smoking a fat cigar, ordering her as she walked past, 'young lady, do a twirl'. It was a low point, and another was when she was jumped on by a man from corporate finance. At one point only one in ten of her colleagues on the sales side were women. Parts of Salomon were a get-rich-quick machine run on testosterone.

Stani Yassukovich is the most blunt of all about the shortcomings of Big Bang. He was Goodison's deputy chairman at the Stock Exchange, a childhood friend of the now departed Michael von Clemm, and a leading figure in the Eurobond revolution at White, Weld. He lives in the South of France, where he indulges his interest in the theatre. What happened, he says, was a tragedy, particularly when the best firms were snapped up pre-1986: 'The worst result of Big Bang was that most of the partners took the money and ran to buy estates in Gloucestershire, which meant a huge exodus of talent and experience. That changed the ethos and culture of the City for the worse. We saw the departure of people who had worried about the reputation of their firm rather than whether bonuses will be paid. It created a movement towards acquisition and to consolidation, which led to too big to manage and too big to fail.' Previously, he claims, the financial community provided an agency function serving other businesses. 'When finance became a business on its own it changed. The all-singing all-dancing financial services institution is a nonsense.'

That does not mean that what was achieved lacked worth. Sometimes members of one pre-Big Bang gang still get together and remind themselves that is the case. In September 2013, Yassukovich and some of the other original pioneers of the market instigated by Siegmund Warburg gathered in black tie at the Savoy Hotel in London to celebrate the fiftieth anniversary of the first Eurobond. Peter Spira spoke and Rupert Hambro said in his remarks that for all the talk of innovation in the 1960s the bonds that London had arranged for foreign markets in the nineteenth century surely counted as an earlier innovation. Gene Rotberg, the former Treasurer of the World Bank, told the audience that what had been achieved was socially extremely useful. It had funded and facilitated corporate expansion and trade from the 1960s onwards. It was an essential part of globalisation, which had brought developing countries such as India into the global economy and changed lives. 'You created access, you were the catalyst for globalisation and while you did not invent cross-border financing – you honed it, polished it, adjusted it, made it fit the circumstances and the demands of investors.' The result he said, had been a transformation in economic development and human prospects across the world. Said Rotberg that evening: 'No, it is not likely you will be remembered by name in a hundred years – that kind of immortality – but a little girl from Bangladesh, as yet unborn, one day will have dinner here returning from her studies at Cambridge or Oxford and she will one day do wondrous things. That will bring you a different kind of immortality.'

As someone who is pro-market, I endorse that statement, of course. Open capital markets are a boon to humanity, matching capital with ideas for business expansion, innovation or infrastructure. The attempt to live without them to varying extents, from the First World War until the abolition of exchange controls by Geoffrey Howe and Nigel Lawson, were a disaster. When successive governments combined closed markets with control of industry and excessive trade union power it turned Britain into a madhouse. In narrow terms, the Stock Exchange could not have been rebuilt if it remained a closed cartel either. Shamefully, women were largely shunned until the 1970s (although this was standard in many areas of industry and finance across the West) and the City operated too often according to connections rather than merit. Opening the Stock Exchange to outside capital and foreign ownership were simply a recognition of the economic reality that this was the way the world was headed. But it is no good me giving a Panglossian pro-market pitch and pretending that the financial revolution did not have some serious, deleterious effects for Britain. As Charlie McVeigh, who joined Salomon Brothers in 1971, the year I was born, correctly put it: capitalism is *not* too big to fail. Those – like me – who believe that open markets and trade hold the key to prosperity would be fools to pretend problems were not created.

The side effects of Big Bang were deeply damaging, so I will list them:

1) It eroded the vital idea of loyalty between the generations. When too many of the partners in long-established City firms took millions in the mid-1980s and cleared off, they sent a signal to those in less senior positions they left behind that what matters is what you can get and bugger the institution or your colleagues.

2) In the decades that followed, it encouraged corporate greed and discredited restraint. It is the morality of the modern football club. Of course most of us try to get paid what we can get paid, but the monomania that it induced and the way corporate larceny was discussed as though it was evidence of dynamism, usually in institutions when it was shareholders' money being taken, and other people's money and leverage being used, would have had those involved horsewhipped just about any time before 1970. One hears it said (approvingly) in certain sections of London society: 'Oh, X took £25m out of Barclays', or 'Y took £50m out of Goldman.' Take, take, take.

3) An American concept of law and compliance was imported, in which the sole question was often legality. In financial services in terms of dud products sold to customers this destroyed trust that will take many years to rebuild. The 1990s and 2000s revenue-raisers (Payment Protection Insurance and so on) that British banks have so far paid out more than £30bn of compensation for selling to customers were legal. Does that mean they should still have been sold, so that executives could take bonuses and depart, and now shareholders are fleeced to pay the bill? Does legality always make such behaviour acceptable? Of course not. There must surely be room for adults running companies to add a caveat at times – is it right? – to the legal test.

4) It encouraged merger mania and an obsession with scale in British banking, in which banks copied each other and City firms in bolting themselves together and becoming ever

bigger (and closer to government too) until they became wards of state in a manner that continues to distort the economy, warp incentives and keep the focus on pumping out consumer credit rather than finding and financing business innovation.

There is no point re-regulating the 1980s thirty years on, however. What makes more sense is to look at what is about to happen – is already happening – in finance and to ask how the lessons of London's extraordinary past can be applied to maximise future gain and minimise the pain. Even before the UK voted in the summer of 2016 to leave the European Union, the City was going to face serious challenges coping with the latest high-speed revolution tearing through global finance. That revolution is driven again by technology, innovation and creative destruction, and it seems likely to have consequences as far-reaching as the changes that took place between 1963 and 1986. Now, on top of that, the City has to cope with the destruction of the very settlement (out of the euro, but open and operating as the EU's unchallenged financial centre) that has brought such prosperity to the Square Mile in the first decades of the twenty-first century. Can the City do what it has done so often in the past and reinvent itself again for a new era?

AFTERWORD: THE FATE OF THE CITY AND THE FUTURE OF MONEY

Twenty-four hours after David Cameron announced that he intended to step down as the UK's Prime Minister, someone else resigned. Of the many momentous developments that took place in the hours, days and weeks after Britain voted in June 2016 to leave the European Union, the departure of Lord Hill (Jonathan Hill, Baron Hill of Oareford) as Britain's European Commissioner in Brussels was deemed particularly unexciting. Other than in the financial press it was reported as one resignation among many, seemingly a minor diplomatic curiosity destined to become a historical footnote when the whole, dramatic story of Brexit is written.

In part that is because Hill, a Conservative Peer, is neither bombastic nor well known. That obscurity is entirely deliberate on his part as he hates publicity, which is a highly unusual characteristic in a politician. When I once travelled to interview him in his Berlaymont office shortly after his appointment in 2014, he and his advisors were most pleased that he managed in the resulting conversation about financial services regulation to say nothing newsworthy, other than taking a mild-mannered pop at the UKIP members of the European Parliament he had seen tearing up the bars of Brussels.

Unfairly, Hill had even been dubbed 'Lord Who?' by his critics at home and abroad when he was appointed by Cameron to Britain's post in the EU Commission. The mockery was unjustified because although Hill had kept a low profile, he was an experienced operator who had been a key figure behind the scenes in John Major's Number 10 in the 1990s, and a veteran of the Conservative Party's collective nervous breakdown over the Maastricht Treaty in that period. Much later, as a successful schools minister and then Leader of the House of Lords under Cameron, he had a reputation in government for quietly getting business done, which is why he was sent to Brussels in the first place. When he landed that post of EU Commissioner for Financial Services, he had of course to represent the interests of the Commission, the powerful civil service of the EU, and the interests of all the other member states. Nonetheless, the financial Establishment back in London, in the Bank of England and the Treasury, and in banks and large institutions, knew it had an ally who wanted to protect the City's peculiar and unique deal in the EU, in which it is outside the euro while transacting the bulk of euro business for the rest of the continent.

When Hill resigned immediately it was the diplomatic equivalent of a bucket of cold water in the face for the British financial Establishment. Rather than attempting to remain in post and speak up while the UK negotiated its difficult exit from the EU, Hill left without ceremony, observing sadly that the City had lost its voice in Brussels. This was an understatement from an understated individual, but represented a dramatic shift that many in the City found troubling. As he headed for the last Eurostar out of Brussels-Midi station, he was instantly replaced by a Latvian who had previously had responsibility for dealing with the euro. The City had lost out within days of the UK voting. The consequences of the Brexit vote that much of the City had failed to anticipate started to unfold.

Even someone sceptical about the EU (as I am) should acknowledge that Europe, and the euro, played a part in successfully remaking the City to an extent that was not widely understood outside the Square Mile. With Big Bang providing a further springboard, on top of the benefits of history, language, time zone and attractiveness to American and Japanese financiers, the launch of the single currency propelled the City to new heights. Even the crisis of 2008, which took down banks and caused widespread economic distress in countries such as the UK, and the Eurozone crisis that followed three years later, only dented what had been built in London. The mechanisms for handling the epic amounts of debt that needed issuing and trading in euros, and for arranging the currency hedges and other manoeuvres that needed to take place, survived, even if the post-crisis tightening of regulation reduced trading profits and slashed bonuses. If you were an international bank or institution that wanted to be a proper player, you still needed to be located in London, sitting at the crossroads between the dollar and the euro.

Do these firms need to be in London for much longer? During Britain's bitterly fought EU referendum campaign, the City and its supporters certainly issued warnings about the potential impact of a change in the UK's status. The *Financial Times* estimated in June 2016 that fifteen global banks between them employed just shy of 70,000 staff in the investment bank divisions in their London offices, including 8,000 each at Barclays and JP Morgan, 5,500 at Goldman Sachs and 7,000 at Deutsche Bank.[1]. That is a lot of jobs and a lot of people paying tax. In total, the City of London estimates that financial services contribute £66.5 billion in taxes to the Treasury annually. That amounts to 11 per cent of the national total. The 2.1m working across the UK in banking, and other services such as accountancy, constitute 7.2 per cent of workers. The British may dislike banks, but the City is the powerhouse of a globally significant industry that the UK can ill afford to see damaged.

International rivals have long eyed London's dominance, the jobs it has created, and the tax revenue that flows from employees and corporate taxes. There has emerged again the prospect of the rise of alternative venues such as Frankfurt (home of the European Central Bank and a city sometimes sneered at in London), and politicians in Paris, Dublin and pro-EU Edinburgh in the summer of

2016 took the opportunity to woo banks and others that want to trade inside the EU. In a period of uncertainty, while the UK's trading arrangements with the EU were being sorted out, Parisian civic leaders attempted to rebrand their city as the new London. Even if the evidence is that American bankers would rather live and educate their children in London rather than move to Frankfurt and learn German, and even if France's labour laws make hiring problematic, the risks of a longer-term drift away of activity and personnel to Germany and France are impossible to ignore. Some of those large employers – including J.P. Morgan – committed to keeping a large presence in London, but they have legal entities in place in other countries that allow them to assess the options and then move positions at will.

Fundamental to the City's dominance has been the UK's so-called passport, which has allowed global financial institutions to base themselves in London, the great hub, and from there to do business in countries across the European Union. The efforts of the European Central Bank to insist that institutions should be sited within the Eurozone, rather than simply the wider EU, to settle and clear trillions' worth of transactions in euros, were blocked by a ruling of the Luxembourg-based General Court. It is possible – and a few analysts warned of this before the referendum – that even if the UK had opted to stay in the EU, the ECB and politicians in the Eurozone would have tried again and removed London's privileges anyway; we will never know. The UK chose to leave the EU, and for finance there will be consequences.

Complicating the British dilemma is the deep distrust that has long been felt elsewhere in the continent for the City and its way of doing business. Efforts have been made to regulate finance more aggressively since the last crisis. Hill and other British-born officials spent considerable time attempting to persuade officials and politicians from other parts of Europe that the super-charged Anglo-Saxon model of financial capitalism, as embodied by the modern City, is not the anti-Christ, or at least not quite as bad as they think it is. According to leading bankers, and the Bank of England, this produced a valuable dividend, in terms of measures that Hill and his team managed to mitigate or shelve by the use of quiet diplomacy.

That matters because a lot of modern finance – particularly since the crisis of 2008 – is about the game of managing the profusion of regulations, rules and licences – a boon to lawyers and expanded compliance departments. There is national regulation, and a country such as the US takes the primacy of its law in relation to anything that touches on the US, even if transacted abroad, extremely seriously. Any British or French traders facing investigations on market manipulation find that out pretty quickly.

Other markets such as Britain have their own national codes and rulebooks, and the UK's has been radically overhauled in recent years with two new regulatory bodies in place. There is an effort at coordinating international standards – via the Basel rules, produced by the Bank of International Settlements – and the post-crisis regulation was designed to shock-proof banks against bank runs in a future crisis. Basel III is not implemented across the board, though. As well as that, the European Union and the European Banking Authority has also pushed its own standardisation. The danger is that the UK will now be excluded from discussions and European rule-making that ends up having an impact on British banks attempting to do business abroad. There may even be a degree of retribution from those who have long wanted to nail the Anglo-Saxon financial model and were previously constrained.

Before the referendum, Hill had also been working on the EU's big idea, which sounds dull but which has the potential to power growth and create jobs in the decades ahead. The aim is to create what is termed a capital markets union (CMU). In essence, it will be an EU-wide scheme that will make it easier for companies to access capital. A company now too reliant on bank loans to fund its expansion, to build a new plant or purchase a technology platform, would be able with greater ease to issue shares right across Europe and attract investors. Moving money around Europe at high speed, often passing through London, is easy thanks to the changes of the last three decades, but tapping patient long-term funds for investment across borders could be made much easier. In addition, the over-reliance on debt, as opposed to attracting investors in return for equity, has arguably skewed the European economy, encouraging the creation of a model in which companies in countries such as Britain are criticised for relying too much on borrowing big. The CMU is meant to give companies and entrepreneurs access to cheaper finance from more reliable sources. The project will still go ahead post-Brexit, although the danger for London must be that it is no longer in a position to benefit as much as it might have done. In the worst-case scenario it is left locked out entirely in the final years of this decade.

This is all looking pretty grim for the City, then. As an exit from the EU approaches, the place is entering one of its periodic existential crises when for a few years its leaders wonder what is to become of them and their staff. As a shock to the system Brexit might not supersede David Kynaston's assessment that the First World War was the worst thing that ever happened to the City, because the outbreak of war in 1914 destroyed open capital markets and flows of investment and trade. But for pessimists it is possible to see what is coming with Britain's departure from the EU in the next few years in a similar context. Although it is a development not as bad as a war, it may produce a partial pulling down of the shutters, with a consequent impact on growth. London as a financial centre has thrived when it is free trading and open to outside influence, and now its status and the precise nature of its access to important markets is going to be at least in doubt for what is left of the decade.

There is another more positive way of looking at what comes next, however. Not just because for all the gloom-laden prognosis London is Europe's financial capital too. Europe relies on it and to damage it too much in the years ahead would be an act of self-harm by other European economies. Sensible voices may eventually prevail and a deal may be done to continue cooperation. If we look beyond Brexit too, the waves of digital disruption and innovation are already lapping around the ankles of the world's leading financiers, and the UK is in a good position potentially to benefit. Indeed, there are few areas of economic activity more ripe for being disrupted than banking and finance in the West, with its long-established institutions, powerful central banks, vast internal bureaucracies and closed networks of licensed operators gaming regulation and nursing political links. And it may already be happening.

In the City, and in New York, when it comes to assessing the impact of innovation, a great deal of attention a few years ago focused on the speed of specialist trades in High Frequency Trading (HFT), the way in which big banks and insurgent operators utilise ever-faster internet access, or microwave links, to gain minuscule advantages over each other that when scaled in a blizzard of trades adds up to profit. The automated nature of much of that trading is the logical evolution of the programmatic trading that helped cause difficulties in New York on Black Monday in 1987. Since then the technology on the trading side has changed the dynamics of Wall Street and the City. Where the high-speed infrastructure is most useful is in allowing investment banks to use the platforms of the London Stock Exchange and others to execute complex financial manoeuvres quickly and safely. That means a big investment bank in New York that wants to offset a large exposure – say $10bn of a particular financial instrument – by dispersing it to other banks, or swapping it for exposures which other banks have, can do it with the Exchange acting as the clearance and settlement house that both parties, and the regulator, can trust. Less than half of what the London Stock Exchange does now is about buying and selling individual shares. It is far removed from the days of the old Stock Exchange with its trading floor and noisy capitalist carnival. This is about providing a computerised platform for others to use.

In the US, in New Jersey where space is much cheaper than Manhattan, sit the data warehouses where investment banks store their orders and matches for such trades. The fibre-optic link with Chicago, and the derivatives and futures market of the Mercantile Exchange, is one of the key trading routes in the global economy. In the UK, the London Stock Exchange has its own facility and at Docklands, where goods used to be unloaded having taken weeks to cross the oceans, is the facility that handles foreign exchange trading. In Essex, in Basildon, the US Intercontinental Exchange (ICE) has its data operation, which handles the order matching for many of the trades. Slough, outside London, contains more such operations.

That aspect of high finance – the secretive high-frequency trading for trading's sake – obviously prompts ethical and practical questions. Is it any more than superfast, automated gambling, like a computerised equivalent of the transactions that took place in 'Change Alley in the City of the 1720s? No, not really, but the aim is to identify value and make profit that can then be recycled, reinvested and consumed.

Equally as interesting for the future of the City is the wider revolution that threatens to end the dominance of some existing retail institutions, and to change the way in which those of us outside finance experience and think about finance as consumers. Jonathan Hill, when he was in post, was astonished on a platform at Davos – the gathering of the global elite – to find himself taking part in a discussion sponsored by a major institution on whether or not the digital economy represents a threat or provides an opportunity for banks. It is here, now, he thought. Can't these people see what is happening to them? Traditional banking, or the part of it that does not adapt quickly, could be about to be eaten alive by fast-moving start-ups.

Think about how much has changed in the music industry, or how we watch television or order a taxi or a cab in London, New York or many other major cities. Our expectations of what we can do with an app have developed so quickly, since the arrival of smart

phones. The UK has a great advantage in turning these digital appetites into growth because it has embraced internet commerce more
enthusiastically than any other country. By 2016 the internet economy had almost doubled in the UK since 2010. It is expected to
provide 12.4 per cent of the UK's GDP (total economic output). In
South Korea it is 8 per cent; in China 6.9 per cent; in the US 5.4 per
cent; and in Germany 4 per cent. The British are making the transition to the internet economy fast.

Despite this, in Britain and across Europe many banks and other
financial services providers still function in terms of customer
service and technology not much better than they did a decade
ago. Having been built in the era when consolidation and scale
were fashionable, they have vast overlapping computer networks
that are sometimes ageing and difficult to manage. They have to
spend a lot – and use a lot of technical expertise – just to get simple
apps and online operations to work smoothly across the bank's
systems.

The contrast with those other fast-changing sectors is marked.
Forty-three per cent of Britons do some or all of their supermarket
shopping online for home delivery, according to a 2016 report by
Mintel, and a quarter use online exclusively for that purpose. On
prime-time sports television in the UK during advertising breaks, or
via social media, consumers are slickly marketed betting services
that allow live betting on every aspect of the game as it happens.
That approach – giving consumers what they want at the push of
an app notification – is creating highly demanding consumers. If
they use services such as Spotify for music they are used to accessing
a vast library in the Cloud, and services such as Netflix, Amazon
Prime and the BBC's iPlayer have attuned viewers to getting what
they want when they want it. Live television viewing has declined
since the arrival of the internet, and the young – with alternatives
such as gaming and social media available – show no sign of picking
up the TV habit.

Why would such citizens, who are used to instant access and
speed of service, put up for long with money being the one area of

consumer activity that operates according to an old set of rules? What happens to the existing providers in banking and investment if insurgent rivals are better able to create faster and more appealing products? You only need to pose the question to see the scale of the opportunity for new companies. As the authors of the Boston Consulting Group report on digital banking published in 2016 – *Banking on Digital Simplicity* – put it: 'FinTechs are beginning to erode the profitability of traditional banks' business lines – from lending to personal finance, payments, and retail investments – often by offering faster service, less expensive products, and a better customer experience.'

The UK and the City have made a good start in this field. Indeed, on some measures London is recognised as the leading centre in FinTech development. Although California employs more people – just – London and New York benefit from their traditional hub status and opportunity to cluster people who either know or care about making money out of money. The best example can be found at Canary Wharf in the tower built by the Reichmanns, where three floors (the twenty-fourth, thirty-ninth and forty-second) are now given over to the Level39 project. The owners of Canary Wharf set out in early 2013 to make it Europe's 'largest technology accelerator space for finance, cyber-security, retail and smart-city technology companies'. It benefits from proximity to the major banks based in Docklands. Where a new Wall Street on the water was created out of the idea of von Clemm and Travelstead in the 1980s, young coders and entrepreneurs launching start-ups are attempting to reinvent finance and London all over again. Elsewhere, in the clusters of tech developments in London's East End on the edge of the Square Mile, FinTech is also a strong presence developing products for investment and retail banking.

For consumers, new ways to pay (facial recognition instead of even a contactless card) are promised, together with new online banks that will make switching accounts so easy that it takes a matter of seconds to complete. The technologists and tech giants do not always get it right, clearly. Apple made much of the launch of its payment service, in which you wave your iPhone to pay. It has not taken off as expected, and the mainstream banks have instead made a success of contactless payments using the bank-card. Apps can do more than just checking your account. If others can hook up new technology and mobile apps with fresh thinking on how to sell shares to individual investors they may even be able to revivify the notion of a share-owning democracy. Officially only 12 per cent of the market in London is estimated to be owned by small investors, although it may be somewhat higher. Why not use this as an opportunity to encourage further direct participation by small investors?

What worries the Bank of England and its Canadian Governor Mark Carney, who has spent a considerable amount of time exam-ining FinTech and discussing it with his team, is whether or not all this highly encouraging innovation will translate into significant numbers of jobs in the next decade. The City's role since the nine-teenth century as a provider of mass employment could diminish, if what FinTech produces are profitable small businesses that invent products which can be sold to existing tech giants, or if they take very little human firepower to operate. With trading increasingly automated, and overseen by a smaller staff of technologically minded experts, and retail perhaps heading that way too, what is the niche for real people? It appears to be in inventing new financial products; regulating the machines; and providing wealth manage-ment and investment advice on deals to their fellow human beings with serious money to invest and who want more than to rely purely on an app on their phone.

What no one involved in the existing financial eco-system should be in any doubt about is the speed with which the technologists can have an impact. As the experience suffered by the news business demonstrates, the transformation once it starts can be extremely rapid. Facebook was only launched in 2004, and Google in 1998, yet between them they hoover up a reported 85 per cent of online advertising revenue between them. They dwarf the legacy news companies in terms of market capitalisation, and in under two decades they have disrupted one of the hitherto most powerful of all businesses and helped destroy hundreds of long-established newspaper brands across the US.

It would be ironic if some of those thrusting international financial behemoths that were built in part out of the creative destruction of the 1980s in London, when they subsumed and then buried so many old, smaller established London firms, found now that it is their turn and they are too bureaucratic to adapt. They must spend so much time managing regulation and their own internal structures. This is what capitalism should break up, of course. It is powered by creative destruction, as it was in the City of the nineteenth century when smart immigrants outwitted those who were too slow to adapt to the spread of technology and innovative ways of thinking about finance. Or as it was by Warburg in the Aluminium War of the late 1950s, when he outplayed the City Establishment to win, or when the American banks that were successful in London from the 1970s onwards flattened their rivals.

The biggest banks and securities houses should not be written off, however, even if they face disruption and the weaker among them die. After all, when it comes to the most audacious – and fashionable – FinTech innovation of all, the banks have invested heavily. The best-known proponent of blockchain is Blythe Masters, an English former J.P. Morgan financier now based in New York. When the underground digital currency Bitcoin was launched it was built using blockchain technology. All that underpins the currency is code, a mathematical calculation, that allows the virtual currency to be produced and traded in a way both sides can see and have total trust in. No government or central bank controls it and the transaction costs, unlike in traditional banking, are zero. The insight of the firm that Masters runs was that this could be taken mainstream, so that major banks could use the underlying blockchain methodology to move dollars, pounds and euros and make trades.

The original advocates of the cryptocurrency Bitcoin see this as a revolutionary moment in which they ignore conventional currencies, trade in Bitcoin and break the banking system apart. In contrast, the biggest global banks and asset managers see it as a way to reduce their costs and empty their back offices of staff to survive. They have something which the insurgents do not have, too. For all of their crimes and misdemeanours, the existing banks are a known quantity to governments and regulators. Governments need a secure and reliable network to buy and distribute their debt, otherwise they cannot spend (which would be problematic what with them lately spending a lot more than they take in in tax revenues). The global economy is really a giant debt machine, and the global banks are conduits for that debt, funnelling it to investors and trading it and repackaging it themselves. The world's largest central banks and governments are not, any time soon, going to allow their conduit to be smashed to bits and replaced by an anarcho-group of libertarian freelance currency visionaries who from small beginnings want to challenge the supremacy of the dollar and destroy the ability of government to manipulate and devalue currencies for their own short-term electoral ends. Expect governments to leap on the first proper scandal that comes from the world of cryptocurrencies, when something goes wrong and large numbers of people notice, or terrorists are involved, and then to assure everyone that blockchain and the like is now well within the sphere of robust government regulation.

Or a central bank will use the blockchain technology and invent its own digital currency as a rival to Bitcoin. And that is just what it seems the Bank of England is doing in partnering with a team of academics from University College London who have come up with RSCoin. It is claimed to be many times faster and more reliable than Bitcoin, but the most important respect in which it differs is that it can be controlled by the central bank and the state. This appals Bitcoin advocates, who say that the point of their revolution is it constitutes a liberation, denying government control of the financial system. The Bank of England's interest is in being able to manage the money supply and help the government ensure financial stability. If the UCL scheme works, and the Bank of England reinvents the notion of the central bank as arbiter of the digital economy, it will be an echo of its innovative origins.

Assisting the government – back then to borrow – was the original purpose of the Bank of England when it was established in 1694. Eventually it became the model central bank which others copied. Now, the building which houses the Bank – which has its first foreign Governor – sits opposite Gresham's Exchange, where few City traders are to be found any longer, unless they have popped in for an espresso at the bar in the centre of the floor or a glass of something expensive to celebrate a bonus. Others may have nipped in to buy a watch or jewellery from one of the boutiques clustered around the edge of the building, because the Royal Exchange – in its third architectural incarnation since Elizabeth I opened the original building – is now a smart shopping centre. LIFFE left ages ago, and the Stock Exchange which used to be very nearby is now more distant, over in Paternoster Square next to St Paul's. These changes – evolution at the Bank, leisure at the Royal Exchange and the transformation of the Stock Exchange – are quintessentially City. For centuries its leaders and workers have been good at building something new while maintaining old facades. Adaptability and ruthless reinvention are what it is about.

It is certainly true that the range of pressures and competing demands now is daunting. Technology is reshaping the future of money. There is going to be a battle over the nature and control of digital currencies. The financial regulatory empires and blocs – of which the EU is one – may soon look very out of date. Consumer behaviour will reshape and disrupt retail banking. But of all the global financial centres facing such challenges and opportunities, nowhere else starts with more natural advantages in terms of experience, language, time zone and history than London.

The evidence of its history suggests there is little point in trying to come up with a route map into the digital future or prepare any grand scheme. Even though decisions good and bad made by countless individuals have shaped the Square Mile, the place is stubbornly resistant to too much planning. Back in the 1980s the best informed and intentioned of those who pushed through Big Bang did not get it all right, or spot what came next. In 1986, at the time of Big Bang, no one would have predicted that the euro would get going so quickly after the fall of the Berlin Wall in 1989, and that the euro, even as it struggled, would help London play such a role in global finance. There is no reason to think that the next thirty years of life after Brexit and digital disruption will be any less eventful.

All that one can say is: the City will survive, and prosper. It usually does.

SOURCES AND ACKNOWLEDGEMENTS

Crash, Bang, Wallop is not an exhaustive, complete history of the City of London and it is not meant to be. David Kynaston's peerless four volume history, covering 1815–2000, is there for those who want that and I encourage readers to buy it. In the case of this account there will no doubt be those who think that their firm or bank, or their personal story, merited inclusion or more attention. I can only apologise for any oversights or omissions.

But rather than covering everything I have attempted instead to tell the extraordinary, exciting story of the City in the 1980s, and to set it in the broader historical context in a manner that makes it, I hope, enjoyable and useful for the general reader and the City specialist. If I have succeeded in that effort even in a small way it is down to those who gave their assistance so generously.

First, I am grateful to the British Library and the staff of the oral history department for permission to access and quote from its NLSC City Lives series. The founders of that project had the foresight to interview several hundred people about their careers in the City of London. Some of the subjects are now no longer with us, and having their recollections, hearing their voices, was an invaluable resource. City Lives is more than a financial treasure trove. The contributions make for addictive reading and listening. There is fun and wisdom involved. I spent many happy hours listening to and reading the City Lives contributions, and it made me more convinced than ever that similar efforts should be made now to record the testimony of those working in contemporary finance, politics and regulation so that lessons might be learned by future generations when the next crash or financial revolution comes as it surely will.

In some cases, the City Lives transcripts and recordings were the starting point for me interviewing participants as the 30th anniversary of Big Bang approached. Many other City and political figures gave generously of their time and agreed to be interviewed. Even now there were a few participants who were more comfortable speaking off the record, perhaps fearing that even thirty years later they might find themselves shunned for saying that perhaps Big Bang let some crooks in. In the text are a smattering of off the record quotes. But others felt the urgent need to testify publicly about what it – the 1980s financial revolution – meant. Most of the quotes are drawn from those interviews by me and archive material. The British press also did a particularly good job of recording what was going on in the City in the 1980s, and where I have drawn from contemporary accounts they are credited in the text or the endnotes.

I drew too on a wealth of insights in academic papers and books, which are credited in the endnotes and bibliography.

Friends and family who had to put up with me writing my last book managed somehow to pretend that writing another one was a good idea. I am eternally grateful for the love and good humour of Jack and Margaret Martin. Pretty ace too are Alistair Martin, Carla Matassa, Ilaria and Natalia; Jim and Pamela McJannet; Guy and Sylvia Chatfield, and Sofia and Oliver Chatfield; and Douglas McJannet and Neil Oughton.

I am grateful too for the support and encouragement of Jonny Patrick, Michael Donn, Alan Cochrane, Jenny Hjul, Bruce Anderson, Edward Lucas QC, Patience Wheatcroft, Andrew Neil, Rhoda Macdonald, Alison Gray, Gerald Warner, Simon Nixon, Con Coughlin, Ben Wallace, Andy Coulson, Will Lyons, Andrew Wilson, Andrew Roberts, Adam Bruce, Richard Muschamp, Tim Montgomerie, Angus Macpherson and John Boothman. My brilliant colleagues Susan Walton, Zac Tate, Rachel Cunliffe, Olivia Archdeacon, Nicole Gray-Conchar were patient and supportive beyond belief when I was spending time on Crash Bang Wallop. Thank you also to J.K. Rowling, who via social media decoded some of Margaret Thatcher's handwriting on a crucial memo from the National Archives. Xavier Rolet, chief executive of the London Stock Exchange, was also very generous with his time and his insights on the future of finance.

My agent Peter Robinson is simply the business and my editor Drummond Moir and his team at Sceptre have been terrific to work with throughout.

Most of all, I want to thank my wife Fi and son William for their endless patience. They both said never again after my last book, and then they relented, despite knowing what it would entail. I am glad they did, because it allowed me to immerse myself completely in a fascinating period. Until writing this book I thought of 1986 and the events of the years around it, my formative years, as being recent, barely history. Now, as it must, it is slipping into the historical middle distance and prejudices have hardened to the point that it seems the 1980s financial revolution can mean whatever you want it to mean, whether that be market-driven liberation or the dawn of a new selfishness. I hope *Crash, Bang, Wallop* demonstrates that what really happened and the complexity of what it meant is much more interesting than the myth.

BIBLIOGRAPHY

Books

Ackroyd, Peter, *London: A Biography*, Chatto & Windus, 2000.

Augar, Phillip, *The Death of Gentlemanly Capitalism: The Rise and Fall of London's Investment Banks*, Penguin, 2008.

Augar, Phillip, *Reckless: The Rise and Fall of the City*, Vintage, 2010.

Bagehot, Walter, *Lombard Street: A Description of the Money Market*, Henry S. King & Co, 1873.

Balen, Malcolm, *A Very English Deceit: The Secret History of the South Sea Bubble and the First Great Financial Scandal*, Fourth Estate, 2009.

Banner, Stuart, *Anglo-American Securities Regulation: Cultural and Political Roots, 1690–1860*, Cambridge University Press, 2002.

Barnes, Paul, *Stock Market Efficiency, Insider Dealing and Market Abuse*, Gower, 2009.

Blakey, George G., *A History of the London Stock Market: 1945–2007*, Harriman House, 2009.

Burgon, John William, *The Life and Times of Sir Thomas Gresham, Founder of The Royal Exchange: Including Notices of Many of His Contemporaries With Illustrations, Volume 2*, E. Wilson, 1839.

Burk, Kathleen and Alec Cairncross, *Goodbye, Britain: The 1976 IMF Crisis*, Yale University Press, 1992.

Burrough, Brian and Heylar, John, *Barbarians at the Gate: The Fall of RJR Nabisco*, HarperCollins, 1990.

Calomiris, Charles W., *Fragile by Design: The Political Origins of Banking Crises and Scarce Credit* (The Princeton Economic History of the Western World), Princeton University Press, 2015.

Carswell, John, *The South Sea Bubble*, Cresset Press, 1961.

Cassis, Youseff, and Cottrell, Phillip L., *Private Banking in Europe: Rise, Retreat and Resurgence,* Oxford University Press, 2015.

Coggan, Phillip, *The Money Machine: How the City Works,* Penguin, 2009.

Courtney, Cathy and Thompson, Paul, *City Lives: Changing Voices of British Finance,* Methuen Publishing Ltd, 1996.

Davenport-Hines, R. P. T., *Speculators and Patriots: Essays in Business Biography,* Frank Cass and Company Ltd, 1986.

Donoughue, Bernard, *Downing Street Diary: Volume Two, With James Callaghan in No. 10,* Pimlico, 2009.

Ferguson, Niall, *The House of Rothschild: Money's Prophets 1798–1848,* Penguin, 1999.

Ferguson, Niall, *The House of Rothschild: The World's Banker 1849–1999 Vol 2,* Viking, 1999.

Ferguson, Niall, *High Financier: The Lives and Time of Siegmund Warburg,* Penguin, 2010.

Floud, Roderick (ed), *The Cambridge Economic History of Modern Britain, Vol III, Structural Change and Growth 1939–2000,* Cambridge University Press, 2004.

Galbraith, John Kenneth, *The Great Crash 1929,* Penguin, 2009.

Gaskin, Margaret, *Blitz: The Story of December 29, 1940,* Houghton Mifflin Harcourt, 2006.

George, David Lloyd, *War Memoirs of David Lloyd George, Volume 1,* Odhams Press Ltd, 1938.

Gleeson, Janet, *Millionaire: The Philanderer, Gambler, and Duellist Who Invented Modern Finance,* Simon & Schuster, 2001.

Gresham, Perry, *The Sign of the Golden Grasshopper: A Life of Sir Thomas Gresham,* Jameson Books, 1995.

Groysberg, Boris and Paul M. Healy, *Wall Street Research: Past, Present and Future,* Stanford University Press, 2013.

Handley, S., Hayton, D.W. and Cruikshanks, E. *The History of Parliament: The House of Commons 1690–1715,* Cambridge University Press, 2002.

Harris, Robin, *The Conservatives: A History,* Bantam Press, 2011.

Hennessy, Elizabeth, *Coffee House to Cyber Market: 200 Years of the London Stock Exchange,* Ebury Press, 2001.

Hilton, Anthony, *City Within a State: Portrait of Britain's Financial World,* , Cambridge University Press. I.B. Tauris, 1987.

Ingrassia, Catherine, *Authorship, Commerce, and Gender in Early Eighteenth-Century England*, Cambridge University Press, 1998.

Kay, John, *Other People's Money: Masters of the Universe or Servants of the People?*, Profile Books, 2015.

King, Mervyn, *The End of Alchemy: Money, Banking and the Future of the Global Economy*, Little, Brown, 2016.

Kochan, Nick and Pym, Hugh, *The Guinness Affair: Anatomy of a Scandal*, Christopher Helm Publishers Ltd, 1987.

Kynaston, David, *The City of London: A World of Its Own, 1815–90*, Pimlico, 1995.

Kynaston, David, *The City of London: Golden Years, 1890–1914*, Pimlico, 1996.

Kynaston, David, *The City of London: Illusions of Gold, 1914–4*, Chatto & Windus, 1999.

Kynaston, David, *The City of London: Club No More, 1945–2000*, Chatto & Windus, 2001.

Lawson, Nigel, *The View From No. 11: Memoirs of a Tory Radical*, Bantam Press, 1992.

Lewis, Michael, *Liar's Poker*, W. W. Norton & Company, 2010.

MacFarlane, Charles, *The Life of Sir Thomas Gresham, Founder of the Royal Exchange*, Charles Knight, 1845.

Mackay, Charles, *Extraordinary Popular Delusions and the Madness of Crowds*, Richard Bentley, 1841.

Mason, A.E.W., *The Royal Exchange; A Note on the Occasion of the Bicentenary of the Royal Exchange Assurance 1920*, Royal Exchange Assurance, 1920.

Matthews, John O., *Struggle and Survival on Wall Street: The Economics of Competition Among Securities Firms*, Oxford University Press, 1994.

Michie, Ranald, *The London Stock Exchange: A History*, Oxford University Press, 1999.

Moore, Charles, *Margaret Thatcher: The Authorised Biography, Volume One: Not For Turning*, Allen Lane, 2013.

Moore, Charles, *Margaret Thatcher: The Authorised Biography, Volume Two: Everything She Wants*, Allen Lane, 2015.

Parker, David, *The Official History of Privatisation Vol 1: The Formative Years 1970–1987*, Routledge, 2009.

Parker, David, *The Official History of Privatisation, Vol 2: Popular Capitalism, 1987–1997*, Routledge, 2012.

Plender, John, *Capitalism: Money, Morals and Markets*, Biteback Publishing, 2015.

Reid, Margaret, *All Change in the City: The Revolution in Britain's Financial Sector*, Palgrave Macmillan, 1998.

Roberts, Richard, *Take Your Partners: Orion, the Consortium Banks and the Transformation of the Euromarkets*, Palgrave Macmillan, 2001.

Rogers, James Edwin Thorold, *The Industrial and Commercial History of England (Lectures Delivered to the University of Oxford)*, G.P. Putnam's, 1892.

Sherman, Sandra, *Finance and Fictionality in the Early Eighteenth Century: Accounting for Defoe*, Cambridge University Press, 1996.

Stamp, Gavin, *Anti-Ugly: Excursions in English Architecture and Design*, Aurum Press, 2013.

Stewart, Graham, *Bang! A History of Britain in the 1980s*, Atlantic Books, 2013.

Stewart, James, *Den of Thieves*, Simon & Schuster, 1991.

Stewart, Walter, *Too Big to Fail: Olympia & York: the Story Behind the Headlines*, Beard Books, 2000.

Stow, John, *A Survey of London, Written in the Year 1598*, Whittaker and co, 1842.

Thompson, Valerie, *Mastering the Euromarkets: A Guide to International Bonds, the Instruments, the Players, and the Game*, Irwin Professional Publishing, 1996.

Thorpe, D.R., *Supermac: The Life of Harold Macmillan*, Chatto & Windus, 2010.

Vogel, Steven K., *Freer Markets, More Rules: Regulatory Reform in Advanced Industrial Countries*, Cornell University Press, 1998.

Wechsberg, Joseph, *Trifles make Perfection: The Selected Essays of Joseph Wechsberg*, David R. Godine Publishers, 1999.

Williams, Richard J., *The Anxious City: British Urbanism in the Late 20th Century*, Routledge, 2004.

Articles

Draper, Nick, 'The City of London and Slavery, Evidence from the First Dock Companies 1795–1800', *Economic History Review*, 2 May 2008.

Inikori, J E, 'Measuring the Atlantic Slave Trade: A Rejoinder', *The Journal of African History*, Cambridge University Press, October 1978.

Pardo-Guerra, Juan Pablo, 'Creating Flows of Interpersonal Bits: The Automation of the London Stock Exchange 1955–90', *Economy and Society*, Volume 39, 2010.

Geoffrey Wood, Forest Capie, Frank Sensenbrenner, 'Foreign Investment in the UK: Flows, Attitudes and Implications', *Journal of Interdisciplinary Economics*, 2005.

Andrew Leyshon and Nigel Thrift, 'The capitalization of almost everything: The future of finance and capitalism', *Theory, Culture, Society*, December 2007.

NOTES

Chapter 1

1. Gresham assisted Elizabeth by agreeing to be jailer for Lady Mary Grey, keeping one of the three Grey sisters who had a claim to the royal succession under house arrest at two of his homes in the City and then at Osterley, west of London.

2. Indeed, the construction of the Exchange from 1566 represented a vindication for the Gresham family. His father Sir Richard Gresham (knighted by Henry VIII) had been Mayor of London and had attempted to get a similar scheme implemented decades before, although at the time the conservative City Corporation had rejected the idea. Merchants were told when Sir Richard's earlier plan was rejected that they must continue to do business in the open air on Lombard Street. Now, thanks to Thomas, London got its Exchange.

3. A Note on the Occasion of the Bicentenary of the Royal Exchange Assurance. A.E.W. Mason, Royal Exchange, 1920.

4. Gresham's tomb is in St Helen's, Bishopsgate, in the shadow of the Gherkin building, surrounded by the offices of modern City firms.

5. It was not until 1833 that the London Fire Engine Establishment was founded by ten fire insurance companies. The Metropolitan Fire Brigade was formed in 1866 when the insurance companies told the government that they could no longer bear the responsibility for fighting fires.

6. Barbon's will was received by his executors on 6 February 1699, although he may have died in late 1698. Will of Nicholas Barbon of Osterley, Middlesex. (National Archives).

7. The Bank of England's creation is sometimes ascribed to the poet, statesman and Chancellor of Exchequer Charles Montagu, later Earl of Halifax. Montagu subscribed money to the scheme (he was not alone in that) and

was involved in the passage of the legislation through the Commons. But see History of Parliament for an explanation of why claims made on Montagu's behalf appear exaggerated. The plan was Paterson's. He resigned from the Bank's board of directors following a disagreement and his reputation never recovered from the failure of his subsequent scheme, in which Scotland attempted and failed to colonise part of what is now Panama.

8. Joseph Addison in *The Spectator*, 19 May 1711.

Chapter 2

1. *The South Sea Ballad / Set by a Lady*, from the Baker Business Historical Collections – Kress Collection, Harvard Business School.

2. *Women's Agency in Early Modern Britain and the American Colonies*, Rosemary O'Day, p221.

3. *A Very English Deceit*, Malcolm Balen, page 321.

4. *Anglo-American Securities Regulation: Cultural and Political Roots, 1690–1860*. Stuart Banner, p66.

5. Estimate by J.T. Inikori, from 1976 in 'Measuring the Atlantic Slave Trade: A Rejoinder', published in the *Journal of African History*, Vol. 17, No. 4 (1976), pp. 607–627. A long-running academic argument has raged in recent decades over the numbers, with some contesting Inikori's estimates.

6. Not to be confused with his son and scandal-prone heir, William Thomas Beckford, the so-called 'Fool of Fonthill', the art collector and novelist who had a scandalous affair with William 'Kitty' Courtenay, from Courtenay's boyhood. With his fortune Beckford built Fonthill Abbey, which was later destroyed. There was little of the family fortune left by the time he died in 1844.

7. Anne Murphy, of the University of Hertfordshire, undertook a study for the Bank of England of working practices in the 18th and 19th century.

8. William Tite retired from architectural practice twenty years before his death in 1873. He became a Liberal MP and in the 1850s was a leading voice in the campaign to persuade the then Prime Minister, Lord Palmerston, that the building that is now the Foreign and Commonwealth Office should not be built in the Gothic style, as the architect George Gilbert Scott suggested. Tite won that battle in the war between neo-classicists and advocates of the Gothic style. Gilbert Scott designed the building in the Italianate style. Tite Street in Chelsea is named after him.

Chapter 3

1. The London Stock Exchange, Ranald Michie, page 101.
2. *City of London, the History*, David Kynaston, page 102.
3. For a good account of the career of Harry Marks and the *Financial News*, see Dilbert Porter's essay in *Speculators and Patriots: Essays in Business Biography*. Edited by R.P.T. Davenport-Hines. See also 'The war is a capitalist war,' *The Labour Party and the World*, Volume 1. Rhiannon Vickers.
4. Elizabeth Hennessy, page 86.
5. *City of London, the History*. Kynaston. page 273.
6. Lloyd George, war memoirs. Volume 1, page 70.
7. 'The Estimation of Pre-war GNP'. Nathan S. Balle and Robert J. Gordon, *Journal of Political Economy*, 1987.
8. 'Prohibition: A cautionary tale', Thomas Fleming. *The Wall Street Journal*, 3 January, 2010.
9. See M.J. Gaskin's outstanding study of the night of 29 December 1940.
10. Gaskin, page 259–60

Chapter 4

1. *Financial Times*, 7 August 1945.
2. See Professor Peter Larkham lecture on rebuilding London after the Second World War, July 2015. See http://bitly/29WSc09.
3. Sir Kenneth Kleinwort interview, NLSC City Lives.
4. Nick Durlacher interview, NLSC City Lives.
5. Warburg interview, from *Trifles Make Perfection*, essays by Joseph Wechsberg.
6. NLSC City Lives interview.
7. The full series of *Men and Money* is available to watch on the BBC's archive website. http://www.bbc.co.uk/archive/menandmoney/
8. *Spectator* notebook, 13 December 1963.
9. Peter Spira speech on the 50th anniversary of the Eurobond.
10. Bank of England Quarterly, November 1991, page 522.
11. Japanese banks in London, Bank of England Quarterly Bulletin November 1987 http://www.bankofengland.co.uk/archive/Documents/historicpubs/qb/1987/qb87q4518524.pdf
12. Haruko Fukuda interview, NLSC City Lives.

13. 'The ladies who toppled the London Stock Exchange', *Daily Telegraph*. Interview by Harry Wallop, 25 March 2013.
14. Valerie Thompson, NLSC City Lives.

Chapter 5

1. *Margaret Thatcher, The Authorised Biography*, by Charles Moore (pages 291–2).
2. Nott to Howe, 30 May 1979, National Archives.
3. John Nott, Hansard, 23 October 1979.
4. 1979 Budget speech, 12 June 1979.
5. David Smith, Something will turn up. http://www.economicsuk.com/blog/002127.html
6. *Foreign Direct Investment in the UK: Flows, Attitudes, and Implications*. Forrest Capie and Geoffrey Wood with Frank Sensenbrenner, Cass Business School, London.
7. David Walker interview, NLSC.
8. Bank of England archives, note from David Walker 4 May 1983.

Chapter 6

1. Sir John Craven interview, NLSC City Lives
2. David Montagu interview, 1993, NLSC City Lives. It is greatly to be regretted that Montagu never got to write his memoirs. His testimony to the City Lives project is endlessly entertaining and insightful. He had been a founder of London Weekend Television and ran Rothmans.
3. NLSC City Lives. The set-piece described by Montagu is worthy of being staged in the theatre as a farce.
4. Sir John Craven, NLSC City Lives.
5. 'The day Big Bang blasted the old boys into oblivion', *The Independent*, 28 October 2006.
6. Dundas Hamilton interview, NLSC City Lives.
7. US Treasury data.
8. Davina Walter interview, NLSC City Lives.
9. 'About that urban renaissance,' *Chicago* magazine, 1 May 1980.
10. Sir John Craven, NLSC City Lives.
11. George Hayter interview, *Financial Times*, 19 October 1984.

Chapter 7

1. *Downing Street Diary*, volume 2, Bernard Donoughue, page 354.
2. Nigel Lawson, *View from Number 11*, page 758.
3. British Airways, along with other established airlines, faced the prospect of court action over attempts to put the budget airline Laker Airways out of business.
4. Addressing the Tory Reform Group at the Carlton Club on 8 November 1984, Macmillan said: 'First of all the Georgian silver goes, and then all that nice furniture that used to be in the saloon. Then the Canalettos go.'
5. *Freer Markets, More Rules: Regulatory Reform in Advanced Industrial Countries*, Steven Vogel, 1996.

Chapter 8

1. See 'Reg Ward: the man who transformed London's docklands', written by Jack Brown for CapX in January 2016. Brown is writing what will no doubt be the definitive work on the remaking of Docklands and the building of Canary Wharf.
2. Michael Heseltine, *Life in the Jungle*, Hodder and Stoughton, 2000.
3. LDDC monograph – Learning to Live and Work Together, 1998.
4. OECD international sectoral database, 2002.
5. Gavin Stamp on Lloyd's of London in *Anti-Ugly: Excursions in English Architecture and Design*.
6. 1985 Jul 31 Margaret Thatcher Speech commencing construction of Broadgate, National Archives.

Chapter 9

1. George Hayter profile, *Financial Times*, 19 October 1986.
2. *Margaret Thatcher, the Authorized Biography volume II: Everything She Wants*, Charles Moore.
3. Robin Leigh Pemberton, Bank of England annual report, February 1986.
4. Rippon was a talented lawyer who did not achieve his political ambitions, although he was given responsibility by Ted Heath in 1972-73 for the negotiations that led to the admission of the UK into the European Community.
5. 'A lament for the bank I loved', by Martin Vander-Weyer, *Independent on Sunday*, 29 November 1998.

6. Thatcher party conference speech 10 October, 1986, Thatcher archive.
7. Minutes of 14th EFFAS Congress, European Federation of Financial Analysts Societies : Florence, 15/17 October, 1986 : 'Towards an integrated European financial market'.
8. Interviewed by Juan Pablo Pardo-Guerra, for 'Creating flows of interpersonal bits: the automation of the London Stock Exchange, 1955–90'.
9. *Financial Times*, 28 October 1986
10. As Joe Moran said in the *Guardian* on the 25th anniversary: 'The inauguration of the M25 was the last major road-opening to generate real public excitement. The queues at both ends of the final section were much longer than usual because drivers were itching to be the first to complete an orbit.'

Chapter 10

1. Letter to editor, *The Times*, 30 October 1986.
2. Thatcher mansion house speech 1986, Thatcher archive.
3. Anyone who doubts how crazy the situation was pre-Wapping need only read *Full Disclosure* by Andrew Neil, then editor of the *Sunday Times*. Or read *Notes From a Small Island*, which contains Bill Bryson's account of the restrictive practices and corruption of the print unions.
4. Paul Channon obituary, *The Times*, 30 January 2007.
5. *The Official History of Privatisation*, page 389. David Parker's two volume history.
6. Takeover activity in the 1980s, Bank of England Quarterly 1989.
7. Reviews from *File On Churchill*, by Linda Fitzsimmons.

Chapter 11

1. See *Supermac: The Life of Harold Macmillan*, by D.R. Thorpe.
2. Quoted in the *Financial Times*, 27 October 1986.
3. New Earnings survey, cited in Leyshon and Thrift.
4. Sporting Intelligence.com, English footballer pay 1961–2010 (2011).
5. 'Business as Usual', Mimi Kramer, *The New Yorker*. 14 December 1987.

Chapter 12

1. 'Romeo would have spied the storm'. *New Scientist*, 22 October 1987.
2. *A Brief History of the 1987 Stock Market Crash, with a Discussion of the Federal Reserve Response*, Mark Carlson, Board of Governors of the Federal Reserve, November 2006.
3. *Black Monday: The Stock Market Catastrophe of October 19, 1987* by Tim Metz, Beard Books, 2003.
4. *Wall Street Journal*, by Clare Ansberry, page 42.
5. 'Black Monday remembered, 25 years on', David Thomas, *Financial News*, October 2012.
6. Brady quoted by Daniel Burnstein, *Yen!*, New York: Simon & Schuster, 1988, p. 156.

Chapter 13

1. Michie, The Global Securities Market, OUP, 2008.
2. The Tally, *Financial News*, 26 November, 2014.
3. 'Superbomb mystery. The Herrhausen Assassination.' *Wired*, July 2008.
4. *Leading From The Front*, Gerald Ronson, Mainstream, 2009.
5. Nadir's company donated £440,000 to the Conservative party and in June 1993 it was revealed that when he was initially under investigation he had been gifted a watch by the Tory minister Sir Michael Mates, on which the MP had had engraved the following message: 'Don't let the buggers get you down.'
6. In May 1996 Walker was found guilty and fined by the Lloyd's Disciplinary Committee for conducting insurance business in a disreputable manner. His conduct had been reckless rather than deliberate, it was concluded.

Chapter 14

1. Peter Spira, NLSC City Lives interview.
2. 'Cedric Brown, fat cat in the dog house'. *Independent*, Monday, 13 March 1995.
3. 'How the City was spun'. Chris Blackhurst, *Management Today*, 1 February 2000.

4. 'That Friday feeling', *Guardian*, 27 September 1999.
5. 'Does Auntie mean business?' *Observer*, Paul Farrelly, 12 November 2000.
6. Speech by Economic Secretary to the Treasury, Ed Balls MP, at the City of London Corporation Dinner, 25 October 2006.
7. Many reports were written warning of the dire likely impact of the UK not joining the single currency. One such paper was 'Consequences of saying no: an independent report into the economic consequences of the UK saying no to the euro.' Chaired by David Begg, Imperial College Business School.
8. *Jerusalem Post*, January 2008.

Chapter 15

1. His daughter is Nigella Lawson.
2. For more information on giving in the US http://nccs.urban.org/nccs/statistics/charitable-giving-in-america-some-facts-and-figures.cfm and in the UK https://www.cafonline.org/docs/default-source/about-us-publications/caf-ukgiving2014

Afterword: The Fate of the City and the Future of Money

1. Staff numbers across all fifteen firms' investment banking divisions were as follows: BNP Paribas 2,500; Goldman Sachs 5,500; Bank of America Merrill Lynch 4,500; Nomura 2,600; UniCredit 800; Deutsche Bank 7,000; UBS 4,000; RBS 2000; Société Générale 2,800; Credit Suisse 5000; although not all of them in the investment bank division: Barclays 8,000; HSBC 5,000; Morgan Stanley 5,000; JPMorgan 8000; and Citi 7,000.

INDEX

Page numbers in *italics* refer to figures.

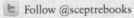
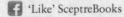
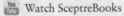

A Christmas Angel at the Ragdoll Orphanage

SUZANNE LAMBERT

PENGUIN BOOKS

PENGUIN BOOKS

UK | USA | Canada | Ireland | Australia
India | New Zealand | South Africa

Penguin Books is part of the Penguin Random House group of companies
whose addresses can be found at global.penguinrandomhouse.com

First published 2016
001

Text copyright © Suzanne Lambert, 2016

The moral right of the author has been asserted

Set in 12.5/14.75pt Garamond MT Std
Typeset in India by Thomson Digital Pvt Ltd, Noida, Delhi
Printed in Great Britain by Clays Ltd, St Ives plc

A CIP catalogue record for this book is available from the British Library

ISBN: 978–1–405–92691–1

www.greenpenguin.co.uk

What we have done for ourselves alone dies with us; what we have done for others and the world remains and is immortal.

Albert Pike, *Ex Corde Locutiones* (1897)

Contents

PART 2

Happy Endings

CONTENTS

CONTENTS

Dedication to the Sisters
of Nazareth

I wonder, are the paths we walk, the challenges we face, the heartache and the joys in each of our lives, preordained before we come screaming into this world? Some would lead us to believe that there is a higher being who ensures our journey here is set in stone, enabling us to achieve all that we came here to do. Is it possible that there is no such thing as coincidence and, when we find ourselves placed in challenging, strange and unexpected situations, we should pause to see how we feel in our hearts at that precise moment? Maybe it is in those moments that we are being guided to truly know why we are here and to understand our life's purpose.

When Victoire Larmenier was born into this world on 21 July 1827 she was to become one of the founders of the Sisters of Nazareth, who would dedicate their lives to the care of the elderly, infirm, vulnerable, babies and children. Victoire's father was a marine carpenter and wood trader and they lived in Liffré, France. Following the death of her father in 1838 and the remarriage of her mother a few years later, Victoire was sent to board at the Ursuline Convent at Vitré. After leaving school she worked as a secretary and bookkeeper in her stepfather's tailoring business in Liffré.

In 1845 Victoire left home and set up a small haberdashery business in Rennes. The shop was located in the parish of Toussaints. It was here that her religious vocation developed under the influence of Father Gandon, one of the curates. Through Father Gandon, Victoire became acquainted with the Little Sisters of the Poor and the great work they did and knew in her heart this was what she was meant to do. When she was twenty-four years old, with Father Gandon's encouragement, she entered the Paris novitiate of the Little Sisters of the Poor and became Sister Basile Marie Larmenier.

Her life's work had begun and, as one of a small party of four, she moved to London to establish a foundation. Within a few months she was appointed Superior, and the members of the community started gathering the poor and aged into their care. In 1861 the Holy See allowed the Hammersmith community to separate from the Little Sisters of the Poor and, three years later, the London Sisters were recognized by the Roman Catholic authorities as a diocesan religious community under the title Sisters of Nazareth. Victoire, now with the religious name Sister St Basil, was among the first of the group to make their profession in April 1864.

By the time she died, in June 1878, Victoire had founded eight more Nazareth Houses in England, Scotland, Wales and Ireland (one of which remained with the Little Sisters of the Poor in 1861). Sister St Basil's life had begun and ended but others would carry on with her good work.

The congregation of the Sisters of Nazareth was founded 154 years ago. They have seen two world wars, fought their own private battles, and seen both the best in human nature and the worst. They have held abandoned children in their arms, housed and taken care of them until it was time for them to step out into the world on their own, and they have opened their doors and hearts to care for the elderly, infirm and vulnerable.

Their hearts have been made heavy and their shoulders greatly burdened by those who chose to mete out anything other than kindness to the innocents of our world, may God forgive them.

The Sisters of Nazareth continue to do very similar work in the world today as they did in the early days. There are Nazareth Houses in seven countries. The emphasis is on care for older people, providing residential care, nursing care for those with more intensive needs, and looking after those with dementia or those in need of palliative care. In some regions there are retirement villages to help people live independently for as long as possible. The sisters also work with children and young people, running nurseries and other schools throughout the regions. They care for abandoned babies and run clinics for children orphaned by AIDS in South Africa, where they also run food programmes.

They have worked tirelessly, giving of themselves, so that others would not only survive but feel cared for. They battled through all the difficulties of the Second World War to open another four Nazareth Houses and were ready and prepared in 1945 to once more open their doors to those who needed them – and there were many.

No one was ever turned away from their doors. I know. I was one of them.

*

This book, therefore, is born out of a desperate need to bring to the world the stories that show how, in every corner of the world, there is a beauty and goodness that we know nothing about. Well hidden, maybe, but there all the same. When we hear these stories of kindness, with just a little sprinkling of magic thrown in, a spark ignites somewhere deep inside us, restoring our faith in humanity, if only for a moment.

I hope you enjoy these stories and that they bring a little comfort, especially to those of you who have known great pain and sorrow and whose challenges have, at times, seemed too hard to bear.

I am so very grateful to all those who have been brave and kind enough to share their stories, life challenges and thoughts with me – and now with you.

William Shakespeare wrote, 'some are born great, some achieve greatness, and some have greatness thrust upon them'.

To the Sisters of Nazareth

Enchanted clocks and mermaids:
Whoever would have thought
Such magic would take place there,
When first the house was bought?

Brick by brick they built it,
Families came and went,
The house stood still and waited
For children to be sent.

It knew somehow there were ahead
Not one but many goals:
To shelter, house, protect, hold dear
And soothe a thousand souls.

High up the wall the clock was hung
And by some magic trick,
Without the need for human hands,
The clock began to tick.

The chestnut tree stood tall and proud,
It whispered on the air:
'Be ready now and listen well,
The time has come. Prepare.'

At the bottom of the garden
The pond shone in the sun.
The reeds all swayed from side to side,
The magic had begun.

The clock ticked in the hallway,
The tree stood tall with pride.
The mermaids gently listened
As the doors were opened wide.

So stay awhile and listen,
And as each page is turned,
Read the stories to be told
And lessons to be learned.

I pray your heart is strengthened,
Your tears are ones of joy,
You feel the magic and the love
For every girl and boy.

I dedicate this book to you, with love and thanks.

This book is for those who you cared for, and care for still.

This is for those who, in the future, will know – if only for a moment – what it is to be held in your safe and loving arms.

PART ONE
Weathering the Storm

Memories

It was Christmas Eve and Nancy was sitting quietly in the room with Gemah curled up on her knee. Nancy looked down at her young granddaughter in her arms and pulled her even closer as she stirred and reached for her hand. Nancy was seventy-three years old and had never been more content.

Her daughter, Susan, walked into the room at that moment to close the curtains and stopped to look at them. It was a picture in her mind she would never forget. Neither her mother nor her daughter knew she was watching them, so engrossed were they in each other. Susan stood still for a moment and continued to watch them before crossing the room to close the curtains, pausing to look at the first flakes of snow which were now beginning to fall. *I was the child she got to keep,* Susan thought to herself. It had been a battle they had fought together and won. Mum had told her so many stories of Christmas that warmed her heart, made her laugh – and some that made her cry.

'It's time for me to make Christmas magic for you now, Mum,' Susan had told her earlier today.

'Oh, darling,' she had said, 'it already is. There's only one thing that will make it even better.'

3

'What is it, Mum?' Susan had asked.

'A cup of tea and a mince pie, love – and put the TV on while you're at it,' she had said, with a twinkle in her eye.

There were presents under the tree, and when Gemah woke from her nap there were two she would be allowed to open. Nancy smiled with excitement. It was getting dark in the room and Susan switched the lamp on. There was going to be a heavy snowfall tonight.

Later that evening, as the snow fell over Newcastle-upon-Tyne, Gemah excitedly opened her Christmas Eve gifts. Princess pyjamas, a beautiful pink dressing gown with a cream satin collar, and a video of *Cinderella*. As Susan busied herself in the kitchen, Nancy and Gemah curled up together once more on the sofa and set the video to play. Gemah's eyes opened wide as the film began. 'Perfect,' Nancy whispered.

Nancy and Gemah clapped, smiled and sang along, almost crying with delight when the pumpkin turned into the crystal carriage. As children do, Gemah asked to see the film again the moment it was finished. Susan reset the video and returned to the kitchen as they settled down once more to enjoy the magic and wonder of Cinderella falling in love with her prince and – Gemah's favourite moment of all – when the fairy godmother turned the pumpkin into a crystal carriage. Nancy smiled, knowing that the crystal carriage was to be delivered by Santa later that night.

Gemah looked up at her grandma. 'Will I be a princess one day, grandma?'

Grandma looked shocked. 'Well, goodness me, didn't you know? You already are,' she whispered.

Dear God forbid, Susan thought, *I will never get this child to sleep tonight.*

'So will I have a horse and carriage?'

'Well, of course you will,' Nancy told her, smiling. 'After all, princesses' dreams all come true,' and Nancy fervently prayed that they would.

'Grandma, will I marry a handsome prince?'

'Well, maybe if you are a very good girl,' she laughed.

'What do think he will be like, Grandma?' Gemah asked, her eyes shining.

As Nancy thought for a moment, Susan stopped what she was doing in the kitchen and listened.

Gemah never took her eyes off her grandma as she waited and *Cinderella* ended for the second time.

'Well, if God answers my prayers, he will be kind, thoughtful and love you always – as I do.'

'Will my dress be as beautiful as Cinderella's?'

'Oh, even more so,' said Grandma, 'and you will be even more beautiful.'

Susan's eyes filled with tears and one escaped and dropped amongst the bubbles in the sink.

Later that night, Nancy decided that, wonderful though the film was, even she could not face watching it again that day. 'Let's do something else,' she said to Gemah.

'Tell me more of your Christmas stories, Grandma,' the little girl said.

No problem there. Grandma's favourite subject.

Susan hurriedly finished the preparations for the next day. 'Wait for me!' she called. 'Don't start without me.'

It was only a few minutes later when she hurried back and sat beside her mum and smiled, knowing what was to come. Susan turned off the big light and switched on the Christmas tree lights that played festive music. Susan and Gemah looked up and waited.

As usual at this time of year, Nancy's mind wandered back to Christmas 1929. She was nine years old and her mother, Anne, had just died. It was one of the saddest times of her life. In early January, Nancy and her sister Margaret would be taken to Nazareth House Convent School in Jesmond, Newcastle-upon-Tyne. Her sister Mary, who was only a baby, would be sent to a baby home in Spennymoor, some twenty miles away. Her brothers Benny and Michael were old enough to stay at home.

'I have to go to work,' their father, Ernest, told them. 'It's the only way.' Injured in the Battle of the Somme, Ernest had a war pension that would pay for his girls to be looked after. 'You will live there and be well taken care of,' he promised them, 'and I will visit you as much as I possibly can.' Ernest's grief lay heavy on his shoulders. His Anne was gone and he must cope alone now and do the best he could for his children.

How cold it had been that day, Nancy remembered, as her father walked Margaret and herself down the long driveway, their feet and hands freezing cold. Nancy remembered how frightening the house had looked until she saw the statue of Our Lady of Lourdes in the grounds and, for some reason, had felt comforted.

Nancy looked down at Gemah snuggled tightly against her. It was warm in the room but Nancy shivered. She had never forgotten that day, so long ago now. Then, just as suddenly, she was warmed as her mind drifted back to all the children she had later looked after. The convent school had eventually become an orphanage and Nancy had stayed to look after the children in the nursery. Nazareth House Orphanage had become her home, and she loved it. So very many little ones – and she had cared for and loved each and every one of them.

It had been a constant battle in the early years to make each Christmas a time of magic and wonder for the children. The orphanage had been full the year she sat up all Christmas Eve making rag dolls for the girls, and never in all these years had she forgotten their faces when they woke on Christmas Day. It had brought a tear to her eye and a lump to her throat, and had almost made her late with breakfast. *Heaven forbid!* she thought, smiling. Nancy missed her sewing – she could mend or make anything until her stroke in 1990, and the crippling arthritis in her hands made it impossible to hold a needle now.

Where were the children now? she wondered once more. What were they doing this Christmas Eve? Did they remember with fondness being a child at Christmas? *I wonder, will anyone tell their stories?* she thought. *I do hope so.*

Praying for Strength

Nazareth House Orphanage, September 1939

The room was completely silent and the lone figure looked to be absolutely still. Her hands were in the prayer position, clasped tightly together to stop them from shaking, and her eyes were tightly closed. Mother Superior shivered. Never had she felt so alone or so very frightened. There was the fear deep inside her that refused to go away and the knowledge that she was the one who must be strong and hold them all together through whatever life was going to throw at them in the next few months. 'Let it be months, not years,' she whispered in prayer and lifted her rosary beads to her lips and held them there for a moment until once more her hands began to shake. It was hard to believe the news and the horror that was expected to follow. It was almost impossible to contemplate yet another war. There was to be an announcement later today. Maybe the news would be better than they all feared.

She looked out of the window and her eyes rested on the statue of Our Lady of Lourdes. She turned away from the window and made her way through the parlour towards the chapel. Her footsteps echoed as she walked slowly, head bent, down the long corridors and paused at the chapel doors. Stepping through them into the chapel, Mother felt immediately calmed by the sound of children's voices coming from somewhere in the distance. Closing the chapel door, Mother walked forward and stood looking towards the altar at the cross of Our Lord and felt tears sting her eyes. 'The children,' she whispered, 'what about the children?' Surely, they had suffered enough already.

Mother jumped as the chapel bell rang, calling the nuns to prayer. The sisters would be along very shortly. Mother took a deep breath. This was what she had been born to do; there was no doubt in her mind. It was up to her to lead the others, be strong, keep the fear at bay. Never once taking her eyes from the cross, Mother Superior slowly walked up towards the altar and knelt on the steps before the cross of Our Lord. 'Please help me,' she whispered.

Sister Mary Joseph was the first to arrive and saw Mother kneeling at the altar. She paused, then walked towards Mother and knelt beside her, smiled and bowed her head. Sister Mary Joseph had been sent to help out in the nursery and was often in more trouble than the children themselves. She had a silly way with her, Sister Veronica had said. Mother disagreed. Sister Mary Joseph had one of the kindest hearts she had ever come across, and she would hear no more.

Sister Mary Joseph placed her hand gently on Mother Superior's arm and whispered, 'Mother . . .'

'Yes, Sister.'

'What should we pray for?'

'The strength to forgive, Sister.'

'How can we forgive them, Mother?'

'We will have help, Sister.'

'Oh, of course,' said Sister Mary Joseph, smiling as she stood up. 'We have Nancy.'

That wasn't exactly what I meant, Mother thought as, once more, her eyes fell upon the cross. 'Nancy,' whispered Mother. The coldness inside began to be replaced by a feeling of warmth. Sometimes children had a way of stealing into your heart and making a permanent home there, and Nancy had moved into Mother's heart lock, stock and barrel from the day she had arrived as a young nine-year-old child. Mother couldn't imagine the house without her in the nursery. The children loved her, as did the staff and the nuns. A force to be reckoned with, yet one of the gentlest souls Mother had ever met.

Mother stood up and once more placed her now steady hands together in prayer. Of course, she wasn't alone.

She had Nancy.

Walls Have Ears

Nancy stood perfectly still, looking through the bars of the bathroom window in the nursery, and watched young Michael and his mother walk away up the long driveway. Mother and son, together once more. This was a sight that never failed to move her and touch her heart in a way she could never have explained to anyone. This was the way it was meant to be. 'Happy endings,' she whispered to herself. There were never enough of them.

Over the years Nancy had seen and heard it all. Her knees had been sat on by hundreds of children and she had wiped away tears with the edge of her apron whilst rocking, soothing and comforting, knowing that words would be lost on these little ones. There was only one thing that got rid of the cold inside, the fear and loneliness – and it wasn't words. 'Smile at them,' she told everyone. 'Smile at them and hold them, and when they feel better a sandwich and a drink of juice will do the job.' Nancy thought everything in the world could be sorted by food and a drink of juice – or if it was a problem of epic proportions, there was always a cup of tea.

Nancy was nineteen years old and her whole world revolved around her 'little ones', as she called them. The children who sat on her knee knew, quite simply, that here was someone who would fight their corner, take away that nasty feeling inside and replace it with a sense of comfort. Most of all they would be safe in her care and, sometime down the line, when the fear had eased, there would be laughter and fun and all would be well in their little world.

Standing at the window today, Nancy was thinking about not only the children but also the mothers and fathers – sometimes their tears were worse than the children's. Martha Harrison had been only nineteen when she was widowed and had placed her child into care until she found work and somewhere to live. When her son had been taken from her she had simply leaned against the parlour wall, slid slowly down into a crumpled heap and begun to sob at first, then scream – refusing to leave. Consoling words of 'There now, dear, it's all right' and gentle pats on the shoulder were to no avail.

Mother Superior slowly shook her head. 'I am so sorry, my dear,' she said, before turning to Sister Mary Joseph. They looked at each other and at the same time said, '*Nancy.*'

Purposefully Nancy had walked into the nuns' parlour and asked everyone to leave. She sat down on the hard floor and put her arms around young Martha's shoulders and sat with her silently until the sobs began to subside. 'Tell me about Michael,' she asked her gently.

For the next hour Nancy heard all about Michael – his favourite toys, how they played together every evening before bed, his favourite stories – and finally about Martha's husband, who Michael was named after. Nancy then helped Martha make plans for the future and talk about all the things she and Michael could do when they got back together. 'Hold those thoughts,' Nancy told

Martha, 'and you will be back here before you know it, ready for your new life together.'

When Sister Mary Joseph returned to the parlour, Nancy and Martha were chatting happily over a cup of tea. *How does she do it?* she thought to herself, smiling. It was a much calmer Martha who left that day with a lighter heart, knowing her son would be looked after by this lovely girl with the bright blue eyes. Nancy, as she so often did, walked up the parlour stairs, through the door into the nursery, then hurried back to the bath-room and watched Martha walk all the way up the long drive, turning only once to wave at Nancy at the bath-room window.

Now it was 1939. *Another story has found its ending,* thought Nancy. Martha faced a long road ahead of her, trying to bring up a child on her own with little family to help her. Nancy closed her eyes and prayed for them before turn-ing away from the window. There was, as always, lots to do today. Not for the first time she wondered how many people had paused at those iron gates at the top of the driveway and seen the words 'Nazareth House' before taking their first steps towards the house where their own unique stories would begin and end. Some happily – yet, so often, some not.

Nazareth House had become her home and she could never imagine leaving. The thought terrified her. This was where she belonged now. Mother Superior had promised she could take her Holy Orders soon, and Nancy was thrilled. Strangely enough, Mother herself could not imagine a life without Nancy. She was the heart of the nursery.

Nancy had a busy day ahead, yet she paused on her way down the long corridor. 'Walls have ears, so they say,' she said out loud to nobody in particular. Would the thoughts and emotions of all these souls stay somehow imprinted on these walls? Would future generations stand in this spot and feel not only the sorrow but hear the laughter and the children's voices echoing in the hallways and off the walls?

Nancy's smiled faded. 'Pull yourself together,' she said to herself. 'Honestly, having these fancies indeed!'

As she walked along the corridor to make her way to the nuns' quarters, Nancy's thoughts once more strayed to the children and she wondered to herself.

Will anyone ever tell their stories?

Storm Clouds

As the storm clouds outside gathered, Mother Superior very slowly placed the private telephone in her room back on its receiver, her hand shaking. She was sitting very still, looking out of her window, except for her busy fingers which were running over the rosary beads on her lap. Only a few hours ago she had switched the radio off and closed her eyes in disbelief. Another war. It was bad enough that it had happened once. Twice was unthinkable. There had been worried whispers in the corridor today and she had seen the nuns with their heads bent towards each other. She would need to put a swift stop to it. The children and staff would have to know soon enough about the changes that would have to take place, although how on earth she would tell them was entirely another matter. The children were to be moved to Nazareth House in Carlisle where they would be safe from German bombers. *Oh dear*, thought Mother, *they are not going to like this one little bit.*

Her gaze fell upon the grotto outside her window and the statue of Our Lady of Lourdes. She closed her eyes in prayer but could think of nothing to say. She would speak to Father and they would arrange Mass and pray together, that would be best. The children were not to be told yet, and – most importantly – they were not to be afraid. It must be dealt with sensibly. Mother would gather all the staff together this evening and talk to them. Nancy was another matter. Mother was more afraid to tell Nancy of the telephone call she had just received than to inform the staff of the necessary changes due to the impending war.

They had survived it once and they would survive it again – but at what cost? Wives would lose their husbands. Families that should have been would never be. Parents would exist rather than live, always remembering how old their sons would have been and no longer dreaming of the grandchildren they might have brought into the world. Photographs and medals on mantelpieces would take the place of the family portraits that should have stood there. Families would be ripped apart in grief. Yet out of it all there would come strength and courage. Mother would happily have forfeited this for peace. Far too many children would never get the chance to know their fathers, and that was wrong. That was not what this God-given world was made for. No matter how much she prayed for understanding, Mother Superior simply did not understand.

Maybe there would be some last-minute reprieve and it would not happen after all. The announcement on the radio earlier today made this seem very unlikely. So, once more, they would have to stand together and fight. Mother Superior shivered – 'fight' was not a word she liked one little bit.

How many years had she told her staff, over and over again, in everything that happened – good or bad – that there were lessons to be learned? 'Yes, well, as far as I am concerned, the lesson to be learned the last time was that this should never happen again,' she said out loud to herself.

Britain was going to war. In many corners of the world there would be private and personal battles to be fought; war affected not only those on the battlefields.

Mother had promised Nancy, and promises should never be broken. She knew of Nancy's love of God; it had been only a short time ago that the young woman had knelt in front of Mother and asked to be accepted as a Sister of Nazareth, wanting to dedicate the rest of her life to the children. Finally, the time had come and Nancy was preparing to take her Holy Orders. They were all thrilled. The phone call had ended all that. The Sisters of Nazareth were closing the doors on any further Holy Orders in response to the declaration of war.

As the storm finally broke and the rain began to pour down the parlour windows, Mother Superior once more looked out upon Our Lady of Lourdes, the torrential rain giving the impression that Our Lady was crying. 'As well you might,' whispered Mother.

And for the first time in very many years – in private, in pain – Mother Superior bent her head and wept.

Innocent Faces

Nancy thought she had seen and heard it all in the nine-teen years she had been on this earth but nothing could have prepared her for the sight before her eyes today, and nothing in the world could have stopped the tears that sprang into her eyes at the horror before her. Moment-arily stunned, she leaned against the wall for support. She thought she might stop breathing, but that would be ridiculous. So she closed her eyes and gulped, willing herself to become calm. Yet even with her eyes closed to blot out the scene in front of her, the tears insisted and continued to flow.

There was a gentle touch on her shoulder and the sound of clicking rosary beads calmed her somewhat. 'We must be brave, Nancy,' whispered Mother Superior.

'I don't feel brave,' said Nancy, finally wiping her tears and lifting her head to face Mother. 'I am angry, extremely angry, and horrendously saddened.' Nancy bent her head and, as her shoulders shook, Mother Superior put her arms around her and allowed the release of tears.

Mother looked up at the cross on the wall and closed her eyes in prayer. 'God help me,' she whispered, not for the first time that day. She would be called upon to hold them all together and they would survive this. They had to.

Nancy, as always, would find a way to make it fun for the children. She always did – and yet, was it asking too much? Nancy was nineteen years old. *Almost a child herself*, thought Mother. This was so unfair. A spark of anger rose to the surface and it took all her resolve to push it away. Anger and hate never did anyone any good, and it certainly wouldn't help now.

Mother continued to hold Nancy in her arms, remembering the day she had arrived, sad, stubborn and frightened. Nancy had grown up with the children and gradually taken over looking after them. It all came so naturally to her. The children looked up to Nancy and loved her. Somehow the nursery began to run like clockwork with Nancy around. There was laughter, noise, children singing – and tears and tantrums were swiftly dealt with. Today Mother was angry with herself for not remembering how young Nancy actually was. Just a young girl, a child herself, maybe she had given her too much responsibility. Mother Superior smiled. No, Nancy had done that herself, she knew her own mind and was well able to stand up and fight her corner. She had stood up to Mother on more than one occasion when she believed she was right. An angry Nancy often made Mother want to laugh, or smile at least.

Mother would never have voiced it out loud but she loved Nancy very much indeed, as did the other nuns – especially Sister Mary Joseph, who Nancy worked with. It took a great deal of pressure off her shoulders, knowing Nancy was there. Never wanting a regular day to go out, she would work her shifts around the children and take a day off when necessary. It was too much to expect Nancy to deal with the children without more help, especially now.

Nancy lifted her head and followed Mother's stare to the cross on the wall. 'I can't even think what to say to Him today,' Nancy said. 'What do we ask for, where do we start?'

'We start,' replied Mother, 'by asking Him to stand beside us, closer than He has ever been before, and pray for the strength to forgive.'

Nancy looked up at the cross, put her hands on her hips and said to Him, 'Yes, well, I will get back to You on that last one.'

'Nancy!' said Mother, shocked.

Suddenly Nancy straightened her shoulders. 'Well, it certainly isn't the first challenge we have faced, Mother, and I doubt very much whether it will be our last.'

Mother waited.

Then Nancy smiled. 'I know! Yes, that's it. We will tell them it's a holiday. A holiday, Mother, the children will love that,' she said, pulling herself together and wiping her eyes. 'We can tell them about the big cellar at Carlisle and how we can play hide and seek.'

Mother said nothing, simply continuing to watch Nancy as she began to make plans for their move to Nazareth House in Carlisle. *Only Nancy could turn this into an adventure*, she thought. Mother took Nancy's hands. 'Are we ready now?'

'We have to be,' said Nancy.

Together they turned and walked towards the children in the hall, gasping once more at the horror in front of them.

One by one, the children turned towards them. Every small face was wearing a gas mask, hiding those beautiful innocent faces. Nancy ran across the hall, forgetting her promise to show no emotion in front of the children. They immediately began gathering around her, pulling at her skirt, crying to be picked up and comforted.

Once more Nancy looked up to the cross, then turned to Mother Superior. 'Maybe I should pray for more arms,' she smiled.

Operation Pied Piper

On 1 September 1939 the sight of thousands of children making their way towards the trains that would take them away from home and the comfort of their parents' arms was one the world should never have seen. The children had labels around their necks like pieces of luggage. Letting their children go and be herded on to trains, placing them into the hands of strangers, was the biggest sacrifice any parent could make for their child's safety if the posters on the walls of Britain were anything to go by.

Long after the war was over, the events of those early days in 1939, the trauma and painful memories, would remain deeply hidden within so many people and would never quite be forgotten. Many of the young children simply did not understand where their families were. Feeling isolated and terrified, they wondered where Mummy was, why she was no longer there and if they would ever see her again.

The word most often whispered in the air on those four days in September 1939, when Operation Pied Piper began, was simply 'Mummy'. As Britain's brave men prepared for battle the children began their own personal battles – as did the mothers, who simply had to stand back and watch their children leave. Many heartfelt prayers were said during the war years, but none more so than on those four days. Even those that had never prayed before cried out in anger and fear and pleaded for their children's safe homecoming.

Nancy was sitting in her room. Her heart had never felt heavier; she did not, never could, understand the reasons for war. She walked slowly over to the window and looked out over the chapel roof to the silent bell that would not be rung again for some time. Leaning her head against the glass, Nancy prayed for it all to be over soon and for the safety of all the little ones. 'They have done no wrong,' she told Him. 'Please, God, do not let them suffer.'

Nancy looked around her room, taking in the sight of her bed and her favourite cream cover with the little blue flowers embroidered on it. Her dressing-table mirror looked strange and forlorn without the holy pictures stuck into its corners. There was nothing really different about the room – and yet, somehow, it knew. The wardrobes and drawers were empty, and there was a loneliness about it. The suitcase that stood in the middle of the room said it all, she supposed. It said, 'I am going away, I have no idea when I will be coming back and what life will be like when I return.'

They had tried so hard, all of them, to stay happy in front of the children, to keep life as normal as possible – especially after the demonstration of the gas masks, when the children had become frightened. Once one of them started crying, it had started them all off. 'I almost feel like joining in myself,' Nancy had said to Sister Mary Joseph.

They had stood strong and worked tirelessly during the evenings, long into the night, when the children were asleep, packing their bags. They had a long and tiring journey to Carlisle ahead of them. The older children – her sister Mary being one of them – had already gone, and tomorrow it would be Nancy's turn with four staff and eighteen children. Margaret, Nancy's eighteen-year-old sister, was to work in the munitions factory and her brothers would be facing the battlefields. As for Nancy, it was up to her to look after the children and keep them safe.

When Nancy heard the announcement on the radio of Operation Pied Piper it had immediately given her an idea. There was a book of Grimms' fairy tales somewhere, she thought, and after only a couple of minutes rummaging in the attic she had found it. She told the children all about the Pied Piper and his golden pipe with all the children dancing behind him, making the whole evacuation into a massive game for them all. They knew the story by heart now, bless them, and constantly asked for her to read it just one more time. Of course, in Nancy's version there were no rats, and the children were all led to a land made of sweets. 'Heaven forbid!' she told Sister Mary Joseph. 'No good begging for nightmares.' (It is unknown how many confused faces there were in later years on hearing the real story of the Pied Piper of Hamelin.) 'At least the children are with us,' Nancy said to Sister. 'They are not being sent to stay with strangers. God only knows what those little treasures taken from their families feel like.'

'I will pray for them,' Sister Mary Joseph said.

'Yes, well, ask for a miracle or two while you're at it,' Nancy said, sarcastically.

*

On an early September morning the children, unusually quiet, all stood close together as they walked down the nursery steps and then along the corridor into the nuns' parlour. The large oak doors were opened wide and Mother Superior and the Sisters of Nazareth stood and watched them with a smile on their faces that hid the heaviness and sadness in their hearts.

Nancy was at the front, her head held high. She walked forward towards Mother Superior, looking straight ahead, afraid of what she might do if she looked directly at her. She paused momentarily when Mother gently placed her hand on her shoulder. Nancy closed her eyes and reached up for a moment and squeezed Mother's hand. There was nothing to be said, they had said it all over the past few days, and Nancy had pleaded for no long goodbyes. 'They are simply dramatic and unnecessary,' she had said. 'Courage, that's what we need – and happy faces in front of the children.'

They began walking up the long driveway and Mother Superior stood there long after they had disappeared from sight. The great oak doors were closed and the sound echoed through the empty corridors.

Nancy walked along Sandyford Road in Jesmond, the children following closely behind. 'I hope we've got everything,' Nancy sighed, her mind turning to all things practical.

Suddenly there was a scream from one of the children, making everybody jump.

'Whatever is wrong, Jocelyn?' shouted Nancy.

'Oh, Aunty Nancy,' the girl cried, 'you've forgotten your golden pipe!'

And the Children
Refused to Sing

As the evacuation train gathered speed the children began to get fretful. They very quickly became bored with looking out of the train window, no matter how exciting Nancy tried to make it. Their tummies were rumbling and no amount of stories or songs were going to help. They were tired and hungry, but it would be at least another fifteen minutes before they got to Carlisle. Nancy and her young helpers started getting the children's coats on. They didn't want to play this game any more – some were crying, refusing to get ready, wanting their tea – and Norman was the first, but certainly not the last, to scream, 'I want to go home!'

Oh Lord, thought Nancy, *this is worse than I could have imagined*. No amount of shushing or cuddles could calm the children, and even though they had never been on a train in their whole life before, the adventure was wearing very thin indeed.

'I don't like the Pied Piper any more, Aunty Nancy,' Betty said, stamping her feet.

'Not over-keen on him myself at the moment,' Nancy said to herself as the train began to slow down.

Nancy had to shout above the noise so the staff could gather everyone together before eighteen tired and hungry children, with their gas masks slung over their shoulders, made their way on to the platform where they received their tuck bags. Greedily they delved in – and every one of the children had eaten their biscuits before they even left the platform.

It was a long walk from Carlisle station to Nazareth House and the staff took turns carrying the most exhausted of the children on their hips.

There was a sudden stab of pain in Nancy's knee and she almost lost her footing. *Oh, dear God, not now*, she thought. *Not again.* She had refused to believe there was anything wrong. There was no time for that sort of nonsense. 'I don't do being ill,' she whispered to herself. There was a long journey ahead of them, and Nancy stopped for a moment and pretended to be checking the children were all right, momentarily closing her eyes as the pain once more gained in intensity. Maybe she should have let the doctor look at it.

He had noticed her limping some months ago but she had managed to avoid him every time he came to the nursery by hurrying off to her room or the laundry building. Dr Graham was no fool; he had stood one day, arms crossed, outside Nancy's room, determined to speak to her.

Nancy jumped when she opened the door. 'For heaven's sake, Doctor, are you trying to give me a heart attack? Some doctor you are, skulking behind doors, frightening people. Now if you will excuse me, I have work to do. We don't all have time to hang about in corridors, thank you.'

'Nancy, wait, please don't go. You know we need to talk.' The doctor gently placed his hand on Nancy's shoulder, smiling. 'How about we go back inside your room? I am in great need of one of your wonderful cups of tea.'

Nancy smiled. 'Very well,' she said, inviting the doctor in.

Goodness, I have done it, Dr Graham thought, immensely pleased with himself.

Only a few minutes later, Nancy brought in a tray with a pot of tea and a plate of cakes. She placed them in front of the doctor and poured him a cup of hot, strong tea. Dr Graham selected a delicious-looking piece of cake and raised it to his lips.

'There now,' Nancy said as she marched across the room, 'enjoy your tea, Doctor. Some of us have work to do – I will close the door on my way out.'

And she was gone.

Dr Graham sat stunned for a moment, looking at the closed door, the cake still hovering in front of his lips. 'Oh, well,' he said to himself, smiling, 'it would be a shame to waste this cake.' He would speak to Mother Superior on his way out and make her aware of the problem.

Mother Superior was also no fool. She had noticed Nancy limping on more than one occasion. It would have to be dealt with; Mother would make Nancy listen and see sense. Unfortunately, before she found the time to speak to her, war was declared and all thoughts of Nancy's knee were forgotten.

It had been all right since then, thought Nancy, the pain now slowly subsiding. It was something or nothing, she had told herself. Until today.

'Is there something wrong, Aunty Nancy?' one of the children asked, tugging at her coat.

Nancy took a deep breath. 'Heavens, no!' she said. 'Come along, children,' and once more she took a deep breath and gritted her teeth. 'Not today,' she whispered. 'Please, not today.'

Nancy had begun to limp but insisted she was fine. *This is all I need now*, she thought again.

'Not far now,' Nancy called out to young Catherine at the back of the line of children. 'Keep them all together! Come on, children, we're nearly there.'

It was then it started to rain, and once more the children began to cry.

Nancy raised her eyes to heaven. 'And what have we done to deserve that?' she said angrily. 'Yes, I know we are to be challenged. Well, if You would be so kind, save any more challenges for another day, thank You very much,' she said. Then, softly, 'Please, God, just let me get these children dry, warm and fed as quickly as possible.'

Nancy's sister Mary had already arrived, and Nancy hoped she would get the chance to pop down and see her as soon as the children were settled – whenever that would be. At last, ahead of her, Nancy could see the house.

'Come on, children,' Nancy called out for the final time, 'we're almost there now. Who wants to sing a song?'

Unfortunately, for the first time in the history of the Nazareth House Orphanage, the children refused to sing.

It was worse than she could possibly have imagined. It had all been organized so quickly and the sisters hadn't been prepared. They had tried their best, of course they had, but there were not enough beds. The nursery children would be fine – they had found mattresses for them and heavy blankets – but the children downstairs were sleeping on the floor. More beds would be coming in a few days. In the meantime they would have to make do, they had been told.

Nancy's heart froze when she saw the bathroom. There were long pieces of marble with holes cut out containing basins to wash in. A bar of carbolic soap was provided, and small tins of salt for the children to brush their teeth. There were two tin baths but only a very small amount of hot water. Nancy wrinkled her nose at the thought of dirty children and leaned against the wall for support. *For the first time in my life I just don't know what to do*, she thought. *It's out of my hands.*

It was only when Norman shook her hand and looked up at her with tears in his eyes that Nancy felt annoyed with herself. 'It's all right, son,' she said. 'Believe me, everything is going to be just fine and we will be home in no time. Promise.' Nancy had never broken a promise in her life. She hoped fervently that this would not be the first time.

It was late that night before Nancy eventually crawled into the bed that had been provided for her and took three of the smallest children into it with her. 'We will do all we can, Nancy,' the nuns had said, 'we will ask for more help and blankets.' Nancy had smiled at them. Everyone was doing their best in an impossible situation, she thought to herself as she tried to sleep on a bed with no pillow.

Exhausted though she was, sleep would not come. Nancy was thinking about her little room with the set of drawers and the holy pictures that were stuck into the corners of the mirror on her dressing table, and tears stung her eyes. She was nineteen years old – wise beyond her years, they said. Able to handle any situation with dignity, sympathy and understanding. She could control a room full of children with just one look and soothe the most fractious child – not to mention calm any situation and turn a trauma into something fun and exciting.

That night, as Nancy lay looking out of the bedroom window, the stabbing pains in her knee became worse. For the first time in her entire life she was the one who wanted arms around her and to be held close, comforted and told everything would be well.

The Tea that Would
Never be Drunk

Eventually, as time went on, the children began to settle, and Nancy's organizational skills were the talk of the Carlisle home.

It was a Sunday evening and Nancy had settled all the children into bed and was hurrying along the corridor to share a much-needed cup of tea with the nuns in their small lounge. Nancy loved this room, with the comfortable chairs and the beautiful statue of the Madonna and Child which stood in the corner of the room. She had no sooner walked through the door than her knee gave way and she fell into the room. There was a flurry of activity as they all rushed over to help, ignoring Nancy's cries of 'Leave me alone, I just tripped!' Nancy was helped into a chair and given a cup of tea. With shaking fingers she lifted the cup to her lips, dropping it suddenly when the pain engulfed her once more.

As her eyes filled with tears Nancy hastily wiped them away. 'I have survived dragging the children from home all the way here,' she sobbed. 'I have told them more stories than I ever thought possible – just to keep their young minds from being worried or frightened – I have survived the horror of not having proper toothpaste, and I assure you I can survive this. Please, Sister,' she begged, 'I will be fine again in the morning. Just say a prayer for me –'

There was a knock on the door. The doctor who was on duty had decided to pop in to check all was well. A Sunday evening was an excellent time to call, as there was always tea and biscuits.

Sister looked at Nancy. 'Well, it seems my prayers have been answered,' she said, smiling.

The nuns left the room – and Nancy would have followed them, had she been able to. Her knee was red and extremely hot. 'Inflamed,' the doctor said.

'Well, yes, of course it is,' Nancy told him. 'If you spent as much time as I do on your knees tending to the children and cleaning floors, your knee would be a little bit red as well.'

No-nonsense Nancy was not used to being ignored, but Dr Wilson was having none of it. 'Rheumatoid arthritis and what looks like severe inflammation and swelling. I am having you admitted to hospital, young lady, and no questions asked. This must have been going on for some time, Nancy.'

'The children,' Nancy insisted, 'please, Doctor, I need to look after the children.'

'I am afraid it is you who is going to be looked after,' he said, standing up. He snapped his bag shut. 'I will make the arrangements. Now, enjoy your cup of tea.' Dr Wilson patted Nancy on the shoulder and then left, closing the door behind him. *So much for my cup of tea*, he thought.

Nancy sat in silence, then gently lifted her cup of tea on to her lap. The Madonna and Child looked on as her tears began to flow and each tiny drop fell into the tea that would never be drunk.

*

There was a flurry of activity the next morning and Nancy looked on whilst a bag was packed for her to take to hospital. No amount of pleading to just leave her alone until the pain passed was listened to and she was removed to Carlisle Infirmary, where she was informed she would need a knee operation. 'Nonsense,' she told them. 'Wrap it up, if you must, and let me get back to work.' But all to no avail.

'Well, at least you will get a bed to yourself,' Catherine, one of the young nursery helpers, had said, trying to lighten the situation when Nancy was preparing to leave for hospital.

Nancy had not been amused. 'I would rather share my bed with all the children piled on top of me,' she had cried. 'Please let me stay,' she'd said, over and over again, 'I won't be a bother. Just strap it up,' she had pleaded.

'I'm sorry,' Sister Mary Martha had said, 'it will be over soon, Nancy, and we will look after the children for you.'

Nancy did, indeed, have a bed to herself – in a hospital with clean sheets, where it was warm and she would be looked after. Nancy blamed herself. If only she hadn't been so selfish and asked for someone to take care of her, this wasn't at all what she had in mind. Well, they had best get on with it, she thought, and let her out of there – the children needed her. *It's only arthritis for goodness' sake*, she thought. She could see no need for an operation.

Apparently, it was a little more serious than that. But when the doctor tried to explain it to her Nancy didn't want to listen. 'Just do it, and then get me out of here,' she said, angrily.

*

Two weeks later, Nancy was sitting by her bed looking out of the window and struggling to see the home in Carlisle, in the distance. But she was too far away and there was nothing for her to see. Nancy had experienced many emotions in her life but never the cold loneliness that she was feeling now. It was three weeks before Christmas and everyone was saying the war would be over by then. It was all that kept her going. *Imagine*, she thought to herself. *Home with the children for Christmas*. Nancy began to plan it all in her mind.

They would get all the old paper out of the attic and make the longest paper garlands ever seen. Nothing was ever thrown away – last year Nancy kept all the Christmas cards that had been received and scraped the glitter off them. The children would have great fun making glitter decorations with her. Cook would bake cakes, and Nancy would see if the children could maybe help decorate the one for the nursery. What fun that would be. War or no war, there would be gifts for the children. Nancy could make something out of nothing, everybody knew that. Just three more weeks.

Preparations for Christmas 1939 were the only thing that kept Nancy from the deep depression that was threatening to engulf her. Each visiting time she would look hopefully towards the door only to find that, once more, nobody had come to visit. As Nancy looked out of the window beside her bed, for the first time in her life she felt abandoned. She had been wrong: nobody cared about her, she wasn't needed after all, and she had been forgotten. As darkness fell she cried bitterly as she held tightly on to her holy pictures – her only source of comfort.

She was wrong, of course. She was loved very much indeed by many people in her life. Catherine and Celia, Nancy's young helpers in the nursery, had asked for permission over and over to go and see her but they needed the bus fare and the nuns had no money to spare. Money was very tight indeed and was needed for the children. Mary, Nancy's younger sister – who was downstairs with the older children – had not been told her sister was in the infirmary for fear of upsetting her. Nancy was admired, looked up to and needed more than she could ever have known. Had she been at home in the Royal Victoria Infirmary, in Newcastle-upon-Tyne, it would have been a very different story indeed. Nancy was simply yet another casualty of war.

The days rolled by and it was Christmas Eve when Nancy finally gave up hope of getting back to Nazareth House in Carlisle, let alone home. The children were so young they might forget her. Nancy could bear anything but that. No one had come to visit. The Sisters of Nazareth had their hands full looking after all the children and doing everything they could to secure more food, blankets and beds for the children.

'There's a war on,' Matron told her.

'Yes, I know,' Nancy said, 'and if I hear those words one more time I will scream. I am perfectly well aware there is a stupid war on, but the children need me.'

Matron called the staff nurse over and told her to settle Nancy's bedding. 'No more nonsense now,' she said.

Nancy, who never held with rudeness, felt like throwing something across the ward.

The lady in the bed next to her leaned over and asked, 'How many children do you have, dear?'

Nancy crossed her arms and scowled at her. 'Eighteen,' she said, haughtily.

'Well I never,' said the lady as she turned her back on Nancy. 'No need to be rude.'

Meanwhile, the staff of the Carlisle home were having a hard time trying to make this Christmas as good as they possibly could for the children. 'We don't want to sing Christmas carols without Aunty Nancy,' the children said stubbornly. There was no time for visiting Nancy, they were told, but they could help look after her when she came back.

The nuns said surely the children would stop asking about her when the excitement of Christmas came along. They were wrong.

As Nancy sat looking out of the hospital window on Christmas Eve, crying for the children and praying to God that they wouldn't forget her, back at the Carlisle home Sister Mary Martha walked into the nursery.

Seeing the sad faces before her, Sister gathered them round her. 'Come along now, children, I know how difficult it has been. But it's Christmas Eve and I have heard there is to be a very special person coming to visit you when you are all fast asleep.' That was just what they needed, she thought, as their faces brightened.

There were cries of 'Oh, how wonderful!' and 'Thank goodness!' alongside squeals of delight.

Sister Mary Martha was very pleased with herself indeed. 'And can you even begin to guess, my dears, who that might be?'

The children jumped up excitedly and all began to shout at once.

'Oh, Sister Mary Martha, is it Aunty Nancy?'

Sister Mary Martha opened her mouth but couldn't think of a single thing to say.

The Saddest Christmas

At Nazareth House in Newcastle it was a good hour since Mother Superior had replaced the handset, and she was still very angry indeed.

The house had fallen silent after the children left and Mother hadn't liked it one little bit. She too had believed this would all be over by Christmas. The nuns had spent many hours making decorations, ready to welcome the children home. It had kept them busy and had helped raise their spirits.

Cook had stayed to look after them and had been busily preparing far too many Christmas cakes that nobody would eat. 'All this talk of rationing, indeed,' she had said. 'These cakes will keep forever. Don't you worry, Mother, there will be cake in this house for the little ones returning. Just you wait and see. A piece of my cake and they will be happy little ones again.'

'We are all happy eating anything you make,' Mother Superior told cook, who blushed and hurried away to the kitchen.

It was with heavy hearts they all realized that there would be no homecoming for the children and staff after all. They all tried to keep their spirits up on Christmas morning but their voices seemed to echo along the corridors, making the house seem even more empty. Mother told the nuns, after their far too quiet Christmas dinner, that she would call Nazareth House in Carlisle to ask after them all and wish them a Merry Christmas. No war would stop her doing that.

Mother was a little confused when, after talking for a good ten minutes, there had been no news of Nancy. Nancy was the heart of everything, so why was there no talk of the endless stories, sing-songs and decoration-making? On hearing Nancy had spent the last six weeks, including Christmas Day, in Carlisle Infirmary, Mother's heart froze.

For a moment she was unable to speak. It took a moment longer to find her voice again, and another moment to control it and subdue her anger. 'Excuse me, Sister, are you telling me that Nancy, our Nancy, has been in hospital for over six weeks?'

'Well, yes, unfortunately she has knee trouble. It had been going on for some time apparently, Mother – didn't you know?'

Mother ceased being angry at the Carlisle house nuns and immediately turned the anger on herself. Whatever had she been thinking? They should have insisted and looked after Nancy themselves. Mother reached for her rosary beads with her free hand and prayed for forgiveness.

'Are you there, Mother?' Sister Mary Martha asked. 'Is everything all right?'

'Yes, Sister, I do apologize. I am just shocked at the news. I would not have left her there alone – someone should have gone to see her. I would have visited.'

'Oh, we weren't allowed to, Mother, and it would have been too far for you to come.

'Sometimes,' Mother said, with a sharp edge to her voice, 'we must do what we think is right, Sister – with or without permission.'

Sister Mary Martha was shocked. 'Yes, Mother,' was all she replied.

Mother regained her composure and in a very controlled yet firm voice asked, 'Can you tell me, please, why I was not informed?'

'We have been busy, Mother. There's a war on.'

Those words again, Mother thought. Like Nancy, she was utterly fed up of hearing them.

It was an hour later that Mother began to feel as though she had been a little unfair. After all, they didn't know Nancy like she did. The nuns were dealing with an impossible situation, in a house filled with more children than it had ever been built for. They were doing their best. 'Oh, Nancy,' Mother said to herself, 'I would have come to visit myself, had I known. Never in a million years would I have left you there, alone, with nobody to visit.'

Mother Superior's job was to hold them all together – through whatever life threw at them – to never show weakness and to be strong always. Yet today there was nothing she could do to hold back the tears or rid herself of the picture in her mind of Nancy, alone, in the infirmary. This was, indeed, the saddest Christmas ever.

Later that evening, after Mass had been said in the chapel, each of the nuns walked forward and lit a candle for Nancy, each voicing their own thoughts to Mother.

'I am sure she will be back with us soon, Mother.'

'I bet she will be up and about in no time – you know how she hates fuss.'

'I bet she misses the children, Mother.'

'I bet she gave the nurses lots of laughs,' said Sister Mary Joseph.

Mother Superior smiled at them. 'Hmm,' she said. 'I bet she gave them a hard time.'

The Sewing Room

Nancy was returning to Carlisle today. 'And not before time,' she said, over and over again. Honestly, what nonsense this had all been.

She was now counting the minutes to getting out of hospital. She had forced herself to stand up without looking to all the world as if she might fall over at any moment. There would be no looking after children for a while, they told her. She would need to sit and rest – unless she wanted to be back in hospital again. *We will see about that*, she thought to herself. *Fuss about nothing*. It was only the threat of being kept in hospital that stopped Nancy from arguing back. She had risen at 6 a.m. and had been sitting, dressed and ready, beside her bed for best part of the day now, refusing any meals that were brought to her. Eventually, at three o'clock in the afternoon, she was taken in a wheelchair to the ambulance that would take her back to Nazareth House.

Nancy's heart was pounding. All the way back she thought about the children. Would they have grown in six weeks? What had they got for Christmas? Had they been all right without her? Nancy pushed the thought of the children forgetting her firmly to the back of her mind. Instead, she thought of all the children who had been sent away from their homes. *What had Christmas been like for them and their parents?* she wondered. *This has got to stop*, she thought, *it has simply got to end*. Nancy never, ever wanted another Christmas like this one. Next year she would make it up to the children and it would be the best one ever. The garlands would be bigger, the whole nursery would be covered in glittery decorations, they could have extra cake, and Nancy would make them all the most wonderful presents ever. The ambulance doors opened and Nancy looked around her excitedly for the children. *Any moment now*, she thought, as they wheeled her inside the doors and along the corridor.

'No, no,' she told the nurses, 'not this way. I need to go upstairs. I want to see the children!'

Catherine and Celia – the two older girls, who had been helping in the nursery during Nancy's absence – came hurrying down the corridor towards her. Nancy tried unsuccessfully to stand. She might be sitting but she drew herself up as straight as possible and looked at each of them.

'Hello, girls.'

'Hello, Aunty Nancy.'

'Where are the children?'

'Well, erm . . . you see . . . well, it's just, erm . . .'

'Let's start again, shall we? Catherine, Celia, where are the children?'

'Oh, Aunty Nancy, the infirmary said you could only come back if you had a job sitting down.'

'And what in God's name do they expect me to do sitting down might I ask?' Catherine's hands were shaking, and Nancy stretched her hand out. 'Come here, darling, I'm sorry, it's all right, just tell me. I promise not to get angry. Honestly.'

Catherine and Celia looked very doubtful indeed. 'You are to work in the sewing room,' they told her, nervously. 'We have to take you there now.'

Silence for a moment.

'Very well,' was all Nancy said. She might not be able to stand but she held her head high and showed nothing of the emotion she was feeling inside. It was bad enough being pushed around in this contraption, trying hard to hold on to her dignity. Honestly, what nonsense this all was.

Catherine pushed the wheelchair as Celia walked beside her. They opened the door and Nancy was wheeled in. They stood on either side of her and waited nervously.

It was quite a pretty room, all in all, Nancy supposed. Seeing the bags and bags of scraps, her eyes lit up. There was ribbon, all types of material, boxes of sewing needles, pincushions and many reels of different-coloured cotton. 'Well, now, this is a treasure trove,' she said to them.

Catherine and Celia were very pleased. It was all going much better than they had expected. Nancy seemed to be taking this very well indeed, yet somehow it all seemed to be a bit polite and strange. Celia just couldn't put her finger on what was different. She leaned towards Nancy, nodding her head, 'We can show you how to manage.'

'Yes,' said Catherine loudly, leaning in towards Nancy and shouting now, 'don't you worry about a thing.'

There was a pause.

Then Nancy tilted her head to one side and smiled. 'Thank you, girls, but I'm immobile. Not deaf or stupid, thank you very much indeed.'

There was just a moment's hesitation, then all three of them burst out laughing. And it was a good while before they pulled themselves together. It was all right now, the tension was broken – this was their Aunty Nancy, and things were back to how they should be.

Tea was brought in and Nancy looked around the room and began to plan what she would make for the children when she wasn't busy darning or mending clothes. Catherine and Celia watched her for a moment, then began to make their way back to the nursery. They'd only got as far as the door when they jumped at the sound of Nancy's voice.

'No, no, no, my darlings. I think not.'

'Is there something you want, Aunty Nancy?'

'The children,' she said. 'Down here. Now, if you don't mind.'

Nancy sat looking at the door and listened. Finally, there it was. The sound of lots of little footsteps thundering down the stairs. The door burst open and they ran to her, climbing up the wheels of her chair to get to her, and clambering on to her knee.

'Be careful!' shouted Catherine and Celia at the same time.

But Nancy was smiling and had tears in her eyes, which had nothing to do with the pain in her knee. The children were all talking at once, yet Nancy heard every single word they said.

'You missed Christmas, Aunty Nancy.'

'It never even snowed like you said it would.'

'Why did you leave us?'

'Sister Mary Martha told us if we were very good you would come and visit us on Christmas Eve, when we were asleep.'

'Why didn't you come?' they all asked.

'Ah, well now, I believe that was Santa Claus she was talking about.'

'Well, I don't think much of him,' said Betty, 'he didn't even stay and tell us a story.'

'My, my. Don't you know the story of the very first Santa Claus?' she said to them.

Automatically the children began to gather closer. Catherine and Celia joined them and they sat on the floor around Nancy.

Life had returned to normal.

All eyes upon her, Nancy settled down to tell them the story.

'Oh, goodness me!' screamed a very excited Betty. 'Look, Aunty Nancy, it's snowing.'

As they all looked towards the window, Nancy raised her eyes to heaven and smiled. 'Nice timing,' she whispered, then settled down to tell them the story of the very first Santa Claus. 'One day, a very long time ago, in a faraway land called the North Pole . . .'

Ridiculousness

'Ridiculous!' Cook shouted out loud as she slammed the dough on to the kitchen bench. The preparations for Christmas 1940 were well under way and she was very angry indeed. 'Nobody tells me what to do!' she shouted, and the dough was kneaded with renewed vigour and once more slapped on to the bench. There were angry tears in her eyes every time she thought about it. Rationing, indeed. 'Don't you dare mention that word to me again,' she had shouted at the walls. It was to be hoped that the walls were listening, as there was nobody else to hear her angry rant.

Cook had been preparing little treats for the children for weeks now. They were all in tins, hidden away in the larder, just in case the wee mites came home. Imagine a homecoming with no cake – what did they think she was? 'Ridiculous!' she shouted out loud again. Stop baking? Might as well tell her to stop breathing. It would be a sad world without cake, Cook thought, as she looked down and watched her tears drop into the dough that would be a complete waste and no use to anybody now it had taken such an awful battering. Cook wiped her tears and sat down on the chair, staring at the useless piece of dough which she knew would not rise.

She had asked to be allowed to travel to Carlisle, to see Nancy and the children, but had been turned down. 'We need you here,' Mother Superior had told her. 'I cannot allow you to be away for days on end, you are far too important to us. Dear me,' Mother had said, smiling and hoping to calm the situation down, 'can you imagine how we would manage without you?' Cook was having none of it and had marched down the corridor, slamming the kitchen door behind her.

'Ridiculous!' she said again to herself, sitting alone in the large kitchen. 'This war is simply beyond ridiculous. They should have been home a year ago.' This was the strongest word Cook ever allowed herself to utter. She looked around an empty kitchen with nobody but herself in it. The benches were gleaming and every pot and pan shone brightly. There was, after all, very little to do but clean. Cook was not used to having so much time to herself. Her day usually started at 5 a.m. and finished late every evening. She was happy and content, bustling around, ordering about the young helpers who came in from Jesmond and Heaton, teaching them to cook and bake and ensuring everything was always kept clean and tidy. Tilly was showing great promise. There should be hustle and bustle, the noise of children in the corridors, menus to be made and followed to the last detail.

Mother had asked Cook to take part in the Christmas Day evening Mass but Cook had refused. 'No, thank you,' she had told Mother, 'I will return to church when the children return home, and not before.' Mother had looked shocked, but Cook didn't care – she was too angry inside. She couldn't remember the last time she had cried. There had been no need for tears in her life, she was perfectly content and happy. Up until the last minute, Cook had believed that somehow the sisters' prayers would be answered and God would find a way to send the children home for Christmas. 'Well, I will return to You when You return them to me,' she announced to the empty kitchen and looked at the sad lump of dough that she would have to use up somehow, because waste was ridiculous.

At every Mass, Mother would turn her head, hoping to see Cook sitting on the bench at the back of the chapel where she usually sat. But to no avail. Mother had seen Cook earlier that afternoon walking down the corridor. She had seen her lift her head defiantly as she passed the church, marching straight past, refusing to look sideways. Mother Superior's heart had saddened. 'We must pray for her,' she had told the sisters.

As the months went by, they all settled into a new routine and Cook managed perfectly well. No amount of rationing would make any difference to her. There were a million different ways of baking and making meals, she told anyone who would listen – and indeed, Mother Superior and the sisters continued to eat delicious meals. 'Rationing, indeed,' she would say. Somehow, God only knew how, there was always cake. Nobody and nothing, including a world war, would stop Cook baking.

It was with great sadness as Christmas 1940 approached that it became obvious the children would not be coming home. However, as usual, the sisters looked forward to the special cake that would take pride of place on the table at teatime. Tea on Christmas Day always consisted of chunky sandwiches, cake and numerous cups of tea. They all remembered the year Sister Mary Joseph had mentioned triangle sandwiches and had received the coldest stare from Cook they had ever seen.

'Triangles, Sister Mary Joseph? Triangles? Not one bite in them, tiny useless little things. My sandwiches are proper sandwiches, to be eaten and enjoyed, thank you very much. Triangles, indeed. Ridiculous.'

Never since had anyone dared to say anything about Cook's delicious proper sandwiches. 'Door stoppers,' Nancy had called them, laughing – but it was thought better not to mention that. Cook always laid the table in the Mirror Room, off the parlour, and it would be absolutely splendid. It had been a tradition that cook was invited to share tea with the sisters on Christmas day, and it was always a very relaxed and fun part of the day. When it was all finished and the tea things cleared away, Cook would take her favourite chair over to the large range, put her feet up on the stool and snooze for as long as she wanted. There was never anything more to do on Christmas Day night.

Christmas Day 1940 was to bring the greatest shock Nazareth House had ever seen. Christmas Day dinner had been eaten and very much enjoyed. Cook had been invited to partake but had refused. After much thanks and appreciation, Cook smiled and together they all carried the dishes to the kitchen and the sisters retired for a much-needed rest after eating far too much food. Sister Mary Joseph had shed a few tears in the morning and said she was missing Nancy and the children far too much to eat anything, then had proceeded to eat twice as much as anyone else. Mother simply smiled and chatted. Not for one moment would she let them all know how much it broke her own heart not to have the children home.

As teatime approached the sisters began to freshen up and await Cook's delicacies. They gathered in the parlour and began to discuss their favourite part of Christmas Day: the Christmas cake. What would it be like this year? Last year it had looked as though it was covered in snow, with holly and berries and little people all made out of icing, although where on earth she had got all the ingredients from nobody quite knew or dared ask. Mother Superior joined them in the parlour and together they made their way to the Mirror Room for tea and excitedly walked in. They stood shocked to the core. Nobody spoke. Not one single person could think of a thing to say. Mother turned to look at the sisters, then back to the table, completely confounded. She opened her mouth to speak and found nothing would come out.

For the first time in the history of Nazareth House Orphanage the table was completely bare, and there was no Christmas tea.

Suddenly Mother Superior spoke. 'Cook must be ill,' she said and hurried out of the room, the sisters scurrying behind her.

Down the corridor they all went, without saying a single word, and then stopped outside the kitchen door. Sister Mary Joseph pushed forward and put her ear to the door.

Silence.

'What on earth will we do?' Sister said, with panic in her voice, and put her ear to the door again.

'I think,' said Mother, 'the sensible thing to do would be to go in, don't you?'

Sister Mary Joseph removed her ear from the door and Mother knocked. Gently at first, then louder.

No answer.

Mother paused, then slowly turned the door handle and entered the kitchen. There Cook was, sitting in her comfortable chair, looking 'bold as brass' as Nancy would have said. She looked up at them, as if to say, 'Speak to me, if you dare!'

Mother and the sisters simply stood and stared at her questioningly.

Cook stood up, folded her arms defiantly and said, 'Christmas tea will be served when, and not until, the children return home,' and with angry tears in her eyes sat back down. 'You may close the door on your way out,' she said and turned her head to face the oven. Nobody was going to see her cry.

Mother quietly asked the sisters to leave and walked over to Cook, placing her hand on her shoulder. Never had Mother Superior seen Cook so angry and, certainly, never had she seen her cry. Mother knew Cook would be embarrassed – and after all, what was there to say? Mother gently patted Cook's shoulder. 'Very well,' was all she said, 'we will wait until the children return.'

It was a sad and sombre evening as each of the sisters gathered round the radio with a cup of tea, and very few words were spoken.

Christmas night 1940, each of the sisters returned early to their rooms. A few tears were shed, many prayers were said and all hearts were heavy and saddened.

Sister Mary Joseph looked at the cross on the wall. 'Can you imagine?' she whispered. 'Christmas without cake. Ridiculous.'

The Loudest Prayers
in the World

On the first day of September 1941 the skies were filled with the sound of aircraft and one hundred bombs fell on Jesmond and the surrounding areas, some landing in the grounds of Nazareth House. The Sisters of Nazareth had taken cover in the basement and prayed, once more, not only for themselves but for all those affected by war. Mother Superior felt as though they should be doing more, fighting back somehow, although 'fight' was not a word she liked to use.

Had it really been two years since the children had left?

As the months rolled on, Mother began to think about Christmas once more. The house seemed to be a cold and lonely place these days. The silence was almost deafening. Mother was once more hoping for Christmas in a house filled with the sounds of children singing and the excitement that they spread everywhere they went. For the last two years the nuns had said to each other, over and over again, 'We will not be beaten. We will prepare for their homecoming. Every Christmas the decorations will be hung just in case.' For the Sisters of Nazareth – and Cook – it was their own way of coping. Their prayers in the chapel became even more frequent in December as they prayed for the return of the children, knowing that unless the war ended it was simply not going to happen.

On Christmas Eve Mother looked out of the window at what was quite a bright and sunny afternoon for December. It had even refused to snow. There was no sign of Christmas – either outside, in the grounds, or anywhere inside Nazareth House. There would, of course, be Midnight Mass as Christmas was, after all, about celebrating the birth of Jesus. Even so, Mother could not help imagining all the children busy in the chapel on Christmas Eve as they made the Nativity scene in the corner of the church. There was always straw – littered all over the church – Joseph, Mary, the ornamental animals, the cradle which held the baby Jesus. And, of course, each year one of the children was chosen to place the star above the stable. Year after year, the chapel had been filled with laughter on Christmas Eve. It was a magical time. It had been Nancy's idea, Mother remembered, to make this a tradition each year. Something else for the children to look forward to and to help them understand the real meaning of Christmas. 'Telling them about it isn't enough, Mother,' she had said. 'Let them be part of the story, then they will understand better.'

Mother closed her eyes, as she had done for the past two Nativities, and remembered Christmas Eve 1937. The chapel had never known such confusion and noise as it had that year. The children managed to get straw halfway up the aisle, as well as in the stable; Joseph had his head knocked off and had to be fixed with glue; Betty had got overexcited and been sick in the straw, and they had to start all over again. Nancy simply smiled. She was loving every single moment of it.

'It will be fine tomorrow, just you wait and see,' she had told Mother, and she had sent the nuns out of the chapel because they were getting in the way. At a look from Mother Superior Nancy had said, 'Erm . . . I mean, until it is all finished. More of a surprise that way.'

Mother had wanted to laugh but controlled herself and said, 'Very well, Nancy.'

Sister Mary Joseph's shoulders were very definitely shaking with laughter, Mother remembered, and smiled at the memory. Later that evening, when the candles had been lit and the Christmas-tree lights that had been donated were twinkling, Mother had led the nuns into the chapel. There was only one person there, kneeling at the altar, with an enormous smile on her face. Nancy. They had all walked forward and stood in front of the Nativity scene before them. Mother put her hands on Nancy's shoulder and they all drew close together to stand before Jesus in the crib. Joseph's head was slightly hanging off, the straw looked like it had been dropped from a great height, one of the donkeys had a leg missing, and the star was crooked. Mother Superior thought it was the most beautiful sight she had ever seen.

The chapel this year was empty, devoid of Christmas, and Mother Superior was very angry with herself indeed. 'We will not be beaten,' she said once more to herself. Whatever had she been thinking of? Mother hurried out of the chapel and gathered the nuns around her.

'What has been our thinking up to now?' she said.

'We will not be beaten!' called out Sister Mary Joseph.

'Then why is the chapel empty?'

'Well, because you said –' Sister Mary Joseph got no further.

'I was wrong,' said Mother Superior. 'So we know what we have to do.'

Long after darkness had fallen, the Sisters of Nazareth pulled out all the boxes from Nancy's attic of treasures and began to bring Christmas to the chapel. Joseph still had a wonky head, and the donkey was still minus one leg, but Mother Superior would not have had it any other way. Midnight Mass was a beautiful service – as good as it could be without the children, they all thought.

They had left the best until last. Moments before Midnight Mass started, Mother Superior and the Sisters of Nazareth walked together to stand before the crib and place the star above it, before taking their place on the chapel benches and praying that one day soon the children would return to place the Star of Bethlehem above the stable themselves.

Only a few days after Christmas, Mother knew that this war was not about to end any time soon – and no amount of prayers would change that. 'So this was meant to be,' she said to herself. 'I have to believe that somehow this is a God-given challenge that we have to face. It will make us stronger, we will appreciate life more and we will love and be grateful for that love more than ever. We will not be beaten,' she said to herself once more.

Mother's thoughts turned not only to the world and all the sorrows and challenges it was facing but to Nancy in the infirmary during Christmas 1939, alone and probably more frightened than she would ever admit. Her heart ached. She wanted Nancy home. She wanted all of them home.

On 29 December 1941, when she heard the sirens, instead of hiding away safely, Mother Superior marched purposefully towards the chapel and walked up to the altar. The nuns followed her.

'God will protect us,' Mother said. 'He has never let us down before and He won't today.' She looked up towards the cross on the altar and said out loud, 'We will not be beaten. We will not hide. We believe and trust in a God who will protect us.'

The skies over Newcastle-upon-Tyne were filled with the sounds of aircraft. The Sisters of Nazareth lifted their heads and began to pray.

Quietly at first.

The aircraft approached Byker nearby and the roar became louder.

Mother Superior began to pray more loudly and the Sisters of Nazareth joined in.

The aircraft were nearer now, the engines were louder and the first bomb was dropped.

The prayers in the chapel became even louder until the nuns were almost shouting.

As the bombs exploded, they became louder still.

The prayers of the Sisters of Nazareth drowned out any sound of the bombs that were falling. So mighty were their prayers that day, the house didn't move, the grounds remained as splendid as they had always been, and the Sisters of Nazareth stayed safe, held in the arms of the loving God who always had been and always would be there for them.

Finally, all fell silent and the nuns bowed their heads in hushed prayer.

Mother Superior once more looked up at the cross of Our Lord. 'We will not be beaten,' she whispered. 'Thank you, Lord.'

Summer Days

The children and staff at the Carlisle home were enjoying an extremely hot summer day and the children had been sent out to play in the grounds as soon as breakfast was over. Nancy had worked since early morning darning the children's clothes, which they seemed to be growing out of every single day. It only seemed a moment ago that they were babies – and here they were, growing up so fast. Watching them grow beyond five years old was a pleasure. The only problem was, it would be harder to let them go.

She had watched them change, growing from babies into young helpers who would often hurry down to the sewing room and sit with her, mending and sewing buttons on cardigans. Nancy had even taught them how to darn clothes. She had been so lonely without the children and had only got through each day knowing that, at some point, they would sneak out and run down to see her.

The staff at Carlisle worked hard to keep the children together and stop them from wandering the corridors on their own. But if any of the children went missing there was only one place to look. The sewing room. At any given opportunity the children would hurry down the stairs, run along the corridor and burst in on Nancy, who would immediately stop what she was doing. Nancy smiled, remembering the day Sister Mary Martha had burst into the sewing room shortly after her return from the infirmary saying they had found an extra bed. Would Nancy please come back upstairs to sleep in the children's dormitory so they could all get some proper rest? Nancy had looked extremely smug and very pleased indeed. She had not needed to worry at all. The children had never forgotten her and never wanted to let her out of their sight again.

Nancy recalled one Sunday morning when the children were being particularly difficult. Sister Mary Martha had left Catherine and Celia in charge. When Sister Veronica and Sister Angelica returned to say lunch was ready, they found a completely empty room. No noise. No children. The two sisters looked at each other.

'Are they playing hide and seek again, do you think?'

'What – all of them?'

'I found it rather tiring last time, and extremely undignified.'

'Well, we had better find them fast – lunch is ready.'

But the children were nowhere to be found.

When Sister Mary Martha came to find out what was going on, she discovered Sister Veronica and Sister Angelica on their hands and knees in the dormitory looking extremely flustered.

'Sisters, may I ask why you are on your knees looking under empty beds?'

'It's the children, Sister Mary Martha, they've disappeared.'

'Disappeared, Sisters?'

'We have looked everywhere.'

'Everywhere?'

'Yes, Sister,' they chorused, looking at her for inspiration as to where they might look next.

'You're absolutely sure you have looked everywhere you can think of?'

'Oh, absolutely.'

'I see – so you have already checked the sewing room?'

There was silence for a moment as the two sisters looked at one other before scrambling to their feet and hurrying downstairs to find the sewing room full of children being told the wonderful story of Rapunzel that held everyone spellbound. Sister Veronica and Sister Angelica crept into the room, forgetting all about lunch, and sat amongst the children and learned all about the young girl with hair so long you could climb up it. It was standing room only, and the little sewing room was crammed full.

It was a good fifteen minutes later that Sister Mary Martha made her way back to the dining room. Total silence. Not only had the missing children not returned, the staff were now missing too. This was beyond ridiculous and Sister Mary Martha began to feel very annoyed indeed. She was not used to having her orders disobeyed and made her way purposefully downstairs. She paused for a moment outside the sewing room and listened before turning the handle and making her way in, to find out what on earth was going on.

So engrossed were they, nobody even looked up. 'Oh, for goodness' sake!' said Sister Mary Martha out loud, and suddenly everyone turned their heads.

'Oh, hello, Sister,' said Nancy, smiling, 'do take a seat.'

Everyone continued to look at Sister Mary Martha – and waited.

'Oh, I give up,' she said, and Sister Veronica hastily jumped up to give her superior a seat.

'Start again, Aunty Nancy,' the children said.

'Very well,' said Nancy, and they all leaned forward. 'Once upon a time . . .'

That day, as war raged on, twenty-five dinners had sat cold and uneaten as Nazareth House in Carlisle felt Nancy's magic at work once more.

The summer of 1945 was hot and sunny and as Nancy sat outside in the grounds watching the children play, her thoughts once more turned to Nazareth House in Newcastle. 'Home,' she whispered to herself. Earlier that morning she had received a telephone call from Mother Superior, who called regularly to speak to Nancy – to ensure all was well, and to give her all the news from home. Nancy remembered roaring with laughter on hearing all about Cook's refusal to bake, and their conversation had cheered her up no end. In the early days, every time the phone rang Nancy would hope and pray that it was the call telling them to come home. Nancy closed her eyes momentarily. 'One day soon we will go home,' she said and prayed it was true. In the meantime, it was a beautiful summer's day today and she was enjoying the sunshine. The children were growing up so quickly, they had adjusted to all the changes even better than Nancy could have hoped for. Look at them, she thought, as they ran around the grounds chasing each other and playing with the toys the sisters had given them. It had taken longer than Nancy had hoped for her knee to recover but she had managed her duties in the sewing room alongside looking after the children without a word of complaint. As the sewing machine whirred Nancy always had one ear listening out for the children. She would stop and smile, then hurry on with her work so she could go and see them. How could she let them go? she thought suddenly. Usually, when the little ones were five years old, they went downstairs to the Junior Department, but this time she had watched them grow up and the bond was even greater. *I almost feel like they are mine*, she thought. Betty and Michael were bored with games and were sitting beside Nancy, reading a book. They had stopped asking to sit on her knee and be read stories, so Nancy was helping them to read books themselves. *I love them so much*, she thought, putting her arms around them. One day they would all go home and everything would return to normal. The Carlisle home was only a temporary stay and, although the nuns had been wonderful, and the children had been safe and cared for, Nazareth House in Newcastle was Nancy's home. Always had been and always would be.

'Oh, darlings,' she said to Michael and Betty, 'when we go home I promise I will get you some wonderful new books to read.'

They looked up from their books with a puzzled expression on their faces. 'What do you mean, Aunty Nancy? We are home,' they said.

They had forgotten.

Nancy thought the pain she had suffered in her knee was nothing compared to the pain in her heart right now, and she squinted up at the sun to hide her tears.

No matter how many stories of Nazareth House in Jesmond she told the children to help them remember, the truth for many of them was that Carlisle felt like home. Every Christmas they had practised their Christmas carols and Nativity play, and each year Nancy prayed she would be sitting watching it in the chapel at home in Newcastle. Yet they had forgotten, and Nancy's heart was heavy. The pain she had suffered from the debilitating arthritis that was now controlled by drugs was simply something to be dealt with. It could be forgotten. Nancy knew what it was, and how to deal with it – so that was that. Nothing and nobody would ever stop her from working with the children. And anyway, she was feeling stronger by the day.

The hot sun was making Nancy sleepy and when Sister Veronica came to play with the children Nancy drifted off to sleep. She was woken suddenly by Sister Mary Martha shaking her by the shoulders.

'In all that is holy, what on earth do you think you are doing, Sister?' Nancy said, stumbling to her feet.

'Oh, Nancy –'

'Yes, Sister.'

'It's a call.'

'A call, Sister?'

'A phone call.'

'Yes, I gather that,' said Nancy, laughing.

'No, you don't understand, Nancy, it's THE CALL!'

Nancy's heart began to hammer in her chest and she grabbed Sister Mary Martha's hand. Then suddenly she turned and ran as fast as she possibly could into the house, down the corridor, into the telephone room. She paused, straightened her clothes, patted her hair and then picked up the handset to receive the news she had waited for all these years.

They were going home.

New Battles

This was Britain and we were a nation of great courage and strength, we would stand tall and fight for what we believed in and no matter how many bombs fell, how horrific the destruction, the England we knew would one day return. The British fought back – as, of course, everyone knew we would.

The great became greater, the weak became stronger, the timid showed a bravery and courage they never knew they had. The British stood tall and proud to show the world what they were made of, in the belief that one day they would stand victorious.

The losses were worse than any living soul could ever have imagined, and it was six long years before it was finally over. There were many thousands of individual stories with happy endings taking place all over the world as fathers met their children for the first time and many parents once more held their sons in their arms, thanking God for bringing them home safely.

Yet for so many, new battles were just beginning. As homecoming celebrations went on all around, so many sat quietly and alone, knowing that their doors would remain closed. Their loved ones would not be returning home, and life would never be quite the same again.

There were readjustments to be made for those injured in battle, either mentally or physically. They returned to a very different world than the one they had left.

Children waited for fathers who would never return and wives cried for the planned futures that would never happen.

So many children would never know the joy of being thrown playfully up into the air, of being held in their father's arms or carried on his shoulders.

Many of the men prayed for the peace and quiet that coming home would bring them, not knowing that it was in the silence of the night that the roar of battle would be at its loudest, living on in their memories for many years to come.

For so many, new battles were just beginning. Many years in the future, these war veterans would still tell their stories with tears in their eyes and a heartfelt sadness for the futility of war.

Yet through all this there grew a strength, a coming together to give support.

'Rallying round,' Nancy called it.

Cake at Last

Mother was breaking all the rules and hurrying down the corridor as quickly as she could. She had just received a telephone call telling her the children would be returning home on Friday. Only three days' time. There was one person who needed to know immediately. This last year, Mother had become very worried about Cook – she had seemed to lose all hope. Mother paused outside the kitchen door, knocked and entered. Cook was snoozing in front of the oven where she was now to be found most days. It had been so long without the children, she was wondering if they would ever return. Mother hurried over and shook her.

Cook jumped up and asked what on earth she thought she was doing. 'Scaring people half to death, for goodness' sake. Really, Mother!'

'The children,' Mother whispered, hardly able to speak.

'The children, Mother?'

'The children. Oh, Cook, they are coming home with Nancy on Friday.'

'Friday?

'Yes, Cook, Friday.'

'This Friday?'

'Indeed.'

'The children,' Cook said once more and collapsed back into her chair.

There were a few moments of silence, then suddenly Cook spoke hurriedly. 'No disrespect,' she said, gently pushing Mother towards the door, 'but I need to be left alone. I have things to do.'

Within seconds, clouds of flour were being thrown into basins and cupboard doors were opened wide.

Mother sighed and held tightly on to her rosary beads that hung around her waist. 'Thank God,' she said. 'All is as it should be.'

For the next three days nobody dared even speak to Cook. The kitchen door was firmly closed and only opened when absolutely necessary to deliver meals and return dishes. Every time the sisters passed there were sounds of spoons being whisked around bowls, kettles whistling and even, at one point – much to everyone's amusement – the tuneless sound of Cook singing. Mother Superior thought it was one of the most wonderful sounds she had heard in the last few years. The sisters, who had been deeply deprived of cake for so long, would find excuses to walk past the kitchen, stick their noses to the door and deeply inhale the wonderful aromas of newly baked cakes. On more than one occasion Mother had told them to please act with a little decorum. And what on earth were they doing hanging around the kitchen when there was so much to be done for the children's return? Yet she had to admit the aromas pervading the corridors were beyond wonderful.

It was Thursday evening and nobody had seen Cook all day. Lunch had not arrived and there had been no response to any knocking on the kitchen door.

At 5 p.m. – just as Mother Superior decided that enough was enough and prepared to face battle to ask for food – a large tray was brought in.

The sisters all jumped up at once.

Then slowly all sat down again.

Still no cake.

'Let's be grateful for the sandwiches,' Mother said, smiling.

'Maybe when we have eaten the sandwiches there will be another tray,' said Sister Mary Joseph, hopefully. And they all nodded their heads.

It was decided that Mother Superior would take the tray back, along with Sister Lucy. They knocked and waited with anticipation. The smell of baking was unbelievably wonderful and they both unconsciously leaned forward and sniffed appreciatively. The door was suddenly wrenched open and Mother and Sister Lucy almost lost their dignity by falling flat on their faces. Cook took the tray, smiled and closed the door firmly.

'No cake, Mother.'

'No cake, Sister Lucy.'

Despondently they walked back to tell the others the sad news.

At 6 p.m. the chapel bell rang out. It was time for evening Mass and Mother Superior and the sisters took their places to give thanks for the children's homecoming tomorrow. Sister Lucy played the organ as they sang loudly in thanks.

There was a sound. Very faint, but Mother heard it even through the loud organ music and the nuns' voices raised in song. It was a sound she had waited for all these years. The sound of the chapel door being opened. Mother closed her eyes and began her whispered prayer of thanks. There was no need to turn round, Mother knew Cook was there.

It was a beautiful thanksgiving service and as Sister Lucy began to play the last hymn, Mother heard the sound again and knew Cook had left. It was so hard not to smile or laugh out loud from the pure joy in her heart at that moment. Nodding at each of the sisters, Mother began to walk up the aisle with all the nuns following her.

There was a gasp and they all stopped. The sisters stood still, unable to move, as one by one their gaze fell on the floor at the back of the chapel.

As the sun streamed through the windows of Nazareth House chapel on a beautiful summer's evening in 1945, it lit up the most beautiful sight for many a year.

Rows and rows of the most gorgeous little cakes any one of them had ever seen.

Mother slowly turned to see the Sisters of Nazareth with grins on each and every one of their faces. All dignity forgotten, Mother raised her arms to heaven and cried out.

'Cake at last!'

Homecoming

Nancy had recently turned twenty-five years old, and this was the best birthday present ever – they were going home, finally.

Nancy sat in the sewing room, where she had been helping make clothes for all the children and mending existing ones to make them last longer. They had been at Carlisle so much longer than she could ever have believed. When Nancy had told the children they were going home, she was saddened to realize that some of them couldn't remember home. Little Joseph had been two when they left and was now nearly eight years old. He would be going to school downstairs with the bigger children when he returned. Nazareth House in Carlisle was all he remembered.

It seemed like a long journey home on the train. The children were tired and confused, and Nancy just counted the minutes – waiting for that moment when she would see home again. Most of the children had nodded off on the train and Nancy watched them sleeping. They had been almost babies when they had marched up the drive, pretending to be following the Pied Piper. *Now look at them*, she thought, her eyes falling on each of them individually. How they had grown. Nancy knew all their little ways, their characters. Normally she would only have them in the nursery until they were five, but these children in her care were now aged between seven and nearly eleven years old. It had been wonderful to watch them grow. But now, of course, when they went home they would be going downstairs. *What would they become?* Nancy wondered. Michael loved anything to do with music, Theresa loved to read, and the others all had their own little talents and favourite things to do. Nancy had done everything she could to protect her children and hoped it was enough.

The train rattled into Newcastle Central Station and they all clambered off, the staff carrying the bags and trying to help the children assemble in an organized line to make their way home.

Nancy was no longer tired – she was so excited to be returning home. 'Come on, children!' she shouted. 'We're nearly home. Come along now, big smiles and happy faces.'

Finally, they reached the large iron gates of Nazareth House and Nancy paused for a moment before striding forward, down the drive, relishing the sight of the house before her. It took all her resolve not to run all the way.

It would be a long time yet before the effects of the war were no longer felt. But it was a beginning, and that was good enough for Nancy.

Mother Superior and the Sisters of Nazareth were more than ready for them. They had been ready for six whole years, and they had been hovering around the big oak door for hours now.

'Home!' Nancy called to the children, once more.

As they all hurried down the driveway, the great oak doors of Nazareth House were opened wide to welcome them home. Suddenly everywhere there was noise, activity, children shouting and staff trying to calm them all down. They were so excited to hear Cook had prepared a very special celebration supper for them – and there was to be cake!

Mother Superior smiled at Nancy, doing everything she could to maintain her dignity and not grab her and hold her in her arms. 'Are you well?' she asked with a smile.

'I am, Mother.'

Mother took Nancy's hands. 'Welcome home. Oh, Nancy, welcome home. Is there anything at all I can do for you?'

Nancy paused. Then, with a sparkle in her eye, she placed her hands firmly on Mother Superior's shoulders.

'Yes, you can burn that wretched book. I am never reading *The Pied Piper of Hamelin* ever again, as long as I live.'

All Grown Up

Nancy's heart beat faster as she shepherded the children upstairs to the nursery dining room where cake and a hot drink were waiting for them. It was nearly time for the moment she had waited for all these years. Firstly, though, it was time to see to the children who were all tired, hungry and far too quiet for Nancy's liking. It saddened her heart so much to think that this no longer seemed like home to some of the children. Nancy's heart ached as she watched them scramble to sit down in the first chair they found and tuck into their welcome home treat. Nancy could still remember where every child used to sit, but the children had forgotten. It brought a tear to her eye to see that the children could hardly fit into the tiny chairs and their knees were hitting the tables. They had only been aged between two and five when they left, crying all the way to Carlisle to be allowed to go home. The eldest were now nearly eleven years old and ready to join the older children. There were many casualties of war, and Nancy had been told the nursery would be full by early next week. Nancy had never had a nursery full of new children to deal with. It was usually a case of helping the new little ones to mix in with the others who were already settled. *This is going to be fun*, she thought, and then smiled. None of that mattered now, except being home.

It had all been so different from how she had imagined it. In Nancy's dreams, lying in Carlisle Infirmary, the children would come home, run up the stairs, burst into the playroom and find all their favourite toys, and she would sigh with relief. Reality had been quite different. At eleven years old, Norman no longer wanted to play with his favourite little blue train, and Betty was no longer interested in dolls. In fact, there had been no interest in the playroom at all. Cake was what they wanted.

It had been so wonderful, Nancy thought, to see them growing up. Nancy watched Celia and Catherine bustle about, helping the younger children, with pride in her heart. What wonderful girls they were, she thought. They had been twelve years old and sensible children and had therefore been chosen to help Nancy on the journey to Carlisle and to help with the younger children in the nursery when they got there. Nearly eighteen years old they were now, and would have to make their own way in the world. Nancy, of course, had insisted that they stay with her until a suitable place had been found for them to go. She wondered, not for the first time, what on earth she would do without them. To watch them grow from babies to adults, then let them out into a world they knew nothing about, was something Nancy would not allow. They must be helped, she insisted, and Mother Superior had promised.

At this moment the girls were giggling and laughing in the small staff kitchenette. Nancy had told them they had earned the right to use it. They were to have a hot drink and help themselves to cake, Nancy said. Catherine and Celia were thrilled. Never had they felt so grown up.

As they giggled and drank tea, Nancy turned her thoughts to organizing the dormitories. The girls and boys could no longer share, so it took some time to get everything sorted whilst she allowed them all to sit in the sitting room with books and games. By the time Nancy and the staff had got the bedding situation sorted, half of them had already fallen asleep on the sofa and the chairs. Finally, all the children were sent to bed for an early night – and not one of them complained.

At last it was time, and Nancy's heart began to beat faster. She went to the end of the corridor to retrieve her small battered suitcase and walked towards her room. She stood for a moment, hardly able to believe she was finally home, before slowly turning the door handle.

It was exactly the same as before. The room had waited for her and nothing had been changed.

Nancy walked around the room, running her fingers over the surfaces. *Not as clean as I would have kept it*, she thought, then dropped her suitcase and threw herself on to her very own bed in her very own room and looked out of the window at the chapel bell.

'We're home,' she shouted out loud. 'We're home!' Nancy leapt up and walked over to the suitcase, then placed it on her bed and opened it. 'Come on,' she said to the contents, 'let's get sorted and make this place look lived-in and loved again, shall we?'

The clothes were hung in the wardrobe and the drawers were filled. Then, finally, Nancy lifted her Bible out and opened it, gently removing her holy pictures.

'We made it,' she told them, then walked across the room and stuck them back into the corners of the mirror on her dressing table. Nancy lifted her head to listen as, once more, the chapel bells began to ring.

She smiled at her holy pictures. 'Welcome home,' she whispered.

The Calm before
the Storm

The noise in the house seemed to get louder every day. The children were once more adjusting to their move, but there had been many tears and tantrums over the last few weeks. Cook had more or less locked herself in the kitchen – and it was to be wondered whether she actually ever left to go to bed. The constant sound of Cook's tuneless singing could be heard all along the corridor, and never had Mother heard the Sisters of Nazareth sing so loud during Mass. The children were back, and life was returning to normal. Mother Superior was very happy indeed.

There had hardly been any time to talk to Nancy since the children's return but today Mother had arranged to see Nancy in her room so they could have a cup of tea together. Mother gently tapped on the door and entered. Nancy was looking out of her window at the bell on the chapel roof. Together they stood side by side, and Mother waited for Nancy to speak.

'When I closed my eyes, this is what I saw,' Nancy said. 'The view out of my bedroom window. I imagined I could hear the bell, and it brought me comfort. Only for one very short moment did I almost give up, I missed home so very much.'

'We were never told you were in hospital, Nancy,' Mother said. 'I would never have left you there alone, and

I have never forgiven myself for not insisting that you saw a doctor before you left. It won't happen again, Nancy. In future, if I have any concerns about you, I will deal with them – with or without your consent. Do you understand?'

'Of course, Mother,' Nancy said, smiling. 'My knee is very much better now and I have medication for the times it becomes a bother. On those days I'll rest my knee while I do the darning.'

'Yes, I hear you were quite wonderful in the sewing room, Nancy. I am not quite sure how they will manage without you.'

'This Christmas is going to be really quite wonderful, you know, Mother. We have talked about it and prepared for it, and I am literally counting the days. I can hardly believe we are back. We survived, Mother.'

'Indeed we did, Nancy. Now, how about that wonderful pot of tea I see you have prepared for us?'

For the next hour they chatted happily and Nancy told Mother all about the new children and how they were beginning to settle down. Mother watched Nancy and thought how wonderful it was to see the sparkle in her eyes. 'I am so proud of you, Nancy,' Mother said.

Nancy became quite flustered and began cleaning up the tea tray, saying it was time to get back to work. The children would be wanting their own tea soon.

Mother hurried back to the parlour with a smile on her face and joy in her heart. She gathered the nuns together and they chatted about how wonderfully settled every-thing was becoming.

Later that evening, in the chapel, Mother stood before the cross of Our Lord and thanked Him for bringing them all safely through challenging times.

'God bless Nancy,' she said. 'She has grown so much and she has learned the lesson of patience and how to take things in her stride. A calmer soul altogether.'

Mother Superior knelt at the altar and began her evening prayer, enjoying the calm before the storm that was about to break.

The Longest Paper Garland
in the World

It was no time at all before Nancy and the staff's hands were full with a new nursery of eighteen children as the months rolled on towards Christmas 1945. It took more than a few stories, cuddles and promises of Christmas to calm these little ones who were all struggling to adjust to their new circumstances, and Nancy lost count of the tears she had dried and the sleepless nights. But finally, as December drew near, the children began to settle, feel comforted and at home. Nancy had talked non-stop about all the Christmas decorations, telling them about previous years and the garlands they would make and how they could sprinkle glitter all over them. This year would be even more special. The garlands would stretch all the way down the long corridors.

'How long will they be?' the children asked.

'The longest paper garlands in the world,' Nancy told them, and the children became very excited indeed.

Many hours were spent singing Christmas carols whilst Nancy ironed in the playroom, and by mid-December the children's favourite carol was 'We Wish You a Merry Christmas', which they could sing loudly and – heaven forbid! – dance to. Nancy's dream was of her little angels standing perfectly still on the altar steps next to the stable, with white sheets and halos, singing 'Silent Night'. But that was looking very unlikely indeed. They were happy – that was all that mattered – and no wonder they were excitable, she thought. After all, today was a big day. That very afternoon Nancy was going up to the attic to get out her box of paper and glitter. It had been there for six years, waiting for this very special Christmas.

There had already been the kindest donations of toys and sweets for the children, and Nancy was glowing at how wonderful this Christmas would be, regardless of how difficult times were. Home was simply the best place in the world, she thought to herself, and not for the first time that day she wondered how Catherine and Celia were getting on. They had jobs in Newcastle and were living with relatives not far away. *Just as it should be*, Nancy thought, and yet felt the familiar tug at her heart when she thought of them. She missed them so very much. Pulling herself together and refusing to get ridiculous, she reminded herself of how thankful she was to be back in Newcastle and hurried up to the attic to have a wander round her treasures.

Nancy was shocked to the core. Things had been moved. Someone had been in her attic and meddled. Yes, that was the word. Meddled. She stood for a moment and took it all in. There were the boxes that held the summer toys, the boxes of May Procession dresses and veils, old clothes that could be used for rags, and a box of old toys. Yes, as she looked around at the crammed attic, she saw that everything was still there. She moved forward to the big box of straw in front of her. There was Joseph, still with his head half hanging off, a three-legged donkey and a very sorry-looking, wonky star. All there except for the very special box. Nancy, of course, knew exactly where she had left it. For over an hour she went through every single box, meticulously looking and checking, but her Christmas box was absolutely nowhere to be found.

Mother Superior and the nuns were in the parlour excitedly discussing the preparations for the Christmas service. They all heard the footsteps marching along the corridor at the same time. 'I don't like the sound of that at all,' said Sister Mary Joseph, and they all nodded in agreement.

Each of the nuns stopped what they were doing, paused and waited.

Nancy marched across the parlour with an expression on her face that told how extremely upset she was. Sister Mary Joseph and the nuns had suddenly jumped up from their seats, ready to run, but a glance from Mother made them stay where they were.

Mother Superior rose slowly and went to stand beside them. 'Safety in numbers,' she whispered, smiling. She spoke first, 'Hello, Nancy, what is it?'

'Someone has been meddling.'

'Meddling, Nancy?'

'Yes, meddling. In my attic, amongst my treasures.'

'Treasures, Nancy?'

'For the children's Christmas, Mother.'

'Nancy, we had to go up to your attic to get the Christmas stable. We put it up every year, hoping with all our hearts you would be coming home,' she said, trying to ease the situation.

'Well, we are home now, Mother. However, my treasures for the children are not.'

'Could you be more specific, Nancy?' asked Sister Mary Joseph, bravely.

'It was a big – or should I say, enormous – box, full of paper.'

Light was dawning on the faces of the Sisters of Nazareth.

'Oh, you mean the rubbish in the big box at the front of the –'

Sister Lucy quickly dug Sister Mary Joseph in the ribs, which Nancy did not miss.

No one dared speak.

'Rubbish? Did I hear you say *rubbish*? Well, just to be specific, that was a whole year's worth of gathering lefto-ver paper. There was so much of it, we were going to make garlands that would hang not only in the playroom and dining room but all along the corridors this year. There was a bag of glitter which I had spent hours scrap-ing off old Christmas cards.'

'Oh, I know,' said Sister Lucy. 'I got covered in it and . . .'

There was a moment of embarrassed silence. Everyone waited.

'Oh, that's fine, Sister Lucy,' replied Nancy, sarcastic-ally. 'Well, now, maybe you wouldn't mind just rolling down the corridors on top of the garlands for me.'

Sister Mary Joseph's shoulders were beginning to shake and she was terribly afraid she was going to laugh out loud. Nancy, on the other hand, was not amused in the slightest.

'So, just to be clear, Sisters, what exactly did you do with the box? Anyone?'

'We threw it out,' said Mother Superior bravely.

'So, let me get this right,' Nancy said slowly. 'Because you felt the need to meddle and clear up in my special attic, the children will have no garlands.' Nancy looked directly at Sister Lucy, angry tears forming in her eyes, then turned questioningly to each of the nuns.

The Sisters of Nazareth bowed their heads in shame.

Mother Superior was remembering why the house had been so quiet. For a split second she wondered if the war would have ended sooner if they had sent Nancy to the front.

Mother Superior stepped forward. 'Nancy, that is enough. It was a simple mistake and we are very sorry indeed.'

Nancy opened her mouth to speak.

But before she could, Mother Superior asked, 'Nancy, who is Mother Superior here?'

'Why, you are,' said Nancy. 'That is why I know you will take it into your own hands to come up with a solution,' she added, before turning on her heels and marching back to the nursery.

Mother and the sisters stood silently and watched her go.

'Oh, well,' said Sister Mary Joseph, 'that makes Judgement Day seem like a breeze.'

Later that evening there was a knock on Nancy's door. Knowing it would be Mother, Nancy stood up, straightened her apron and patted her hair before answering the door.

'Oh,' Mother,' she said, 'I am so sorry. But for six whole years, this Christmas is all I have thought about. We have talked about it and planned it for so long. We were going to make the longest paper garland in the world. And oh, Mother, the children were so excited.'

Mother Superior put her hands on Nancy's shoulders. 'Calm yourself,' she said. 'It has been difficult for all of us. You have been brave beyond words, Nancy. You have never complained – well, not much, anyway,' she said with a smile. 'You have held those children in your arms and your heart and seen them safely through the horrors of war and asked for nothing for yourself.'

Just at that moment the chapel bells rang out.

'Come to Mass with us, Nancy,' Mother Superior said, 'and we will pray for a solution.'

Their prayers were answered very quickly indeed. Father Michael, on hearing all about it, said he would ask his parishioners for help, and the following week more boxes of paper were brought to Nazareth House door than they could ever have hoped for. The longest Christmas garlands in the world would be hung along the corridors of Nazareth House, just as they had planned.

Christmas Eve found Nancy and her staff in total chaos upstairs in the nursery, getting eighteen two- to five-year-old children ready for their carol service. Joseph with a wonky head, Mary, Baby Jesus and the donkey with three legs were in the stable waiting for them. 'We have chosen who will put the star on the stable this year, Nancy,' Mother had told her. But to be honest, it was the last thing on Nancy's mind.

Eventually, the children were in twos, holding hands, making their way down the stairs and into the chapel to sit on the altar steps. The candles on the altar had been lit and Nancy had to take herself in hand and try very hard not to cry when the children began to sing. Suddenly, the chapel doors opened and Nancy turned round to see Catherine and Celia, who had been invited for the carol service, walking down the aisle to place the Star of Bethlehem upon the stable. It had been Mother's idea to invite them – to surprise Nancy, who was smiling from one ear to the other. The star was put in place and the girls walked towards Nancy and sat on either side of her.

Nancy thought her heart would burst with joy as she held their hands and they all stood up for the children to sing the final carol.

'Oh, how sweet do they look, Nancy?' Catherine whispered.

'Don't speak too soon,' she replied.

The children began to sing as loudly as they could. 'We Wish You a Merry Christmas' was sung more enthusiastically than it had ever been heard before, and Christine and Celia began to giggle when some of the younger ones began to dance.

'Told you!' Nancy said, smiling, not caring in the least.

Just over the wall, outside the chapel, people hurrying home to avoid the bad weather forecast for later that night stopped for a moment.

In the distance the children of Nazareth House Orphanage sang, more loudly than they had ever sung in their lives, wishing the world a very Happy Christmas.

Newcastle-upon-Tyne smiled. All was as it should be.

The Most Magical Christmas
Gift of All

There is no greater gift than to give of ourselves. How many times is the excitement of Christmas morning all about watching the faces of others, full of excitement and joy? The atmosphere around us seems to change at Christmastime as we look back on the year we have left behind and wonder what the one ahead will bring. We become emotional over the movies on television, and our hearts do a double flip when our children look up at Santa with that magical sparkle in their eyes. For many of us the sound of children's voices raised in song will bring a tear to our eyes. Parents the world over will sit in school halls and sob unashamedly as their children take their place for the school Christmas play. 'Christmas magic' Nancy called it.

On Christmas Eve 1947 Nancy was thinking how quickly the years were rolling by. Last Christmas had been a wonderful day, even though she had never made it to bed. She had eventually got the extremely excited children to sleep and was just reaching for the light when she heard the words: 'My friend at school is getting a rag doll for Christmas – can you imagine?' Nancy had felt a lump in the back of her throat and knew exactly what she had to do. Christmas, after all, was a time for miracles. She had gathered rags, buttons and wool and had sat up all night making rag dolls for the children. The look on their faces on Christmas morning was a sight she would never forget as long as she lived. Christmas truly was a time for magic.

This year the donations had been received early and the children would all get a small present each, as well as a bike to share and a doll's pram for the nursery. It was going to be absolutely wonderful – or at least, it would be when she had finished the mammoth amount of ironing waiting for her in the playroom, Nancy thought, as she hurried along the corridor. She paused as she passed the chapel and listened to the children practising their Christmas carols for Mass the next morning. It was going to be one of the busiest days ever, and she was already behind with the chores, yet she quickly pushed open the door and crept to a bench at the back, closed her eyes and listened. It didn't really matter whether they got it right or not – she thought it was absolutely perfect.

It was rare that Nancy got a moment to herself to sit down, so when Sister Lucy saw Nancy in the chapel she knew just what to do. "'Silent Night',' she whispered to the children.

They looked up and smiled at Aunty Nancy and began to sing. Nancy's eyes filled with tears. By the time she hurried away, knowing she was now even more behind than ever, her apron was extremely damp in one corner. Today was a big day, they had talked about it and dreamed about it. Nancy was determined that this would be a very special Christmas Eve, after all the children had been through. Once more it was time to hang the longest garland in the whole, wide world along the corridors of Nazareth House. This was becoming a new tradition, and each year the garlands seemed to get longer and longer.

So it was that twenty-two extremely excited children clambered along the corridors. Parts of the chain got torn as they dropped it and had to be stuck together again. The noise levels increased to 'screaming pitch' as Nancy would have called it. The overexcited children were fighting over who would hold which bit, Geraldine and Robert were trying to climb up the ladder together, and Sister Mary Joseph had to run to catch it before it toppled over. Sean was sitting on the floor crying and when asked why said he didn't know and decided to cry even louder. Nancy stood and watched them. 'This isn't exactly the way it was planned,' she said to Sister Mary Joseph, who was standing giggling at them all.

It was typical that when the chaos was at its worst Mother Superior walked up the corridor. 'This looks interesting,' she said to the children, who took no notice of her at all, far too engrossed in what they were doing. 'What are you making, Nancy?' she asked.

'Christmas magic,' Nancy said.

Mother looked on at the chaos in front of her and then saw what it was. The longest Christmas garland in the world. Mother smiled, remembering Christmas 1945. 'Christmas magic indeed, Nancy.' She smiled, and left them to it.

Nancy eventually managed to impose some kind of order but it took most of the afternoon to hang the garlands. As the afternoon became dark Nancy knew the time was getting on and there was still, as always, an enormous pile of ironing to get through – although this year the children's stockings were all prepared up in the attic. She gathered the children together at the end of the corridor and they stood and looked at the longest garland in the world.

'Look at their little faces,' Nancy whispered to Sister Mary Joseph. 'They will never forget this.'

The garlands were simply made out of old papers, nothing particularly colourful, but it was the children who had made them. They felt special, involved and very proud of themselves indeed. The smile on each of their faces and the sparkle in their eyes said it all.

'The afternoon helpers should be here any minute now,' said Nancy. 'Do take the children along to wash their hands and get ready for tea. I am going to start tackling the ironing.'

They hurried off as Nancy made her way to the playroom. But she was soon fetched by a harassed Sister Lucy who told her that both of the helpers would be late. Could she help in the dining room instead? Naturally, as it was Christmas Eve, the children had gone beyond excitement and were extremely tired. Young Sean was asleep with his face on the table. 'Oh, goodness!' said Nancy as she tried to wake him up and he started to cry. As soon as Margaret and Carol – Nancy's new helpers – arrived, they were rushed into the dining room to help out as Nancy hurried to the dormitories. She laid out all the children's freshly laundered pyjamas and dressing gowns before making her way back to the dining room to help clean up whilst the children were taken to the bathrooms to be washed and got ready for bed.

'Look, Nancy,' said Sister Mary Joseph, smiling, 'why don't you just leave the ironing for another day?'

'Leave the ironing. *Leave* the ironing?' said Nancy. 'Sister Mary Joseph, I have never left the ironing in my life. I've never heard the like.'

Sister Mary Joseph began to giggle and said, 'Oh, Nancy, you've gone pale at the thought.' Then suddenly they both began to laugh. 'I think we need a bit of Christmas magic ourselves, don't you?' said Sister Mary Joseph.

'Indeed we do,' said Nancy, and she hurried towards the playroom.

But she was called back before she even got there. The children were crying because the garland had fallen down at one end, so the ladders were retrieved and all was settled. It was later than Nancy had planned when they finally got all the children to bed, expecting them to go straight to sleep as they were so tired. Unfortunately, some of the children were overtired and couldn't sleep. After all, Santa was coming tonight, wasn't he? they said. How could they possibly be expected to sleep?

Nancy's fingers were itching to grab the iron and get started. But instead, she picked up a chair and turned the light off. She sat in the middle of the dormitory and began to tell the children stories until at last, half an hour later, they were all asleep and she was able to creep out of the dormitory to the playroom. Her eyes were heavy and her knee had begun to ache again.

Mother Superior was standing outside the staffroom as she watched Nancy walk down the dimly lit corridor, and her heart ached. She looked so very tired, she thought.

Nancy gave so much and asked for nothing in return. *Why on earth didn't we do something special for her this year?* Mother was no fool, she knew Nancy was still struggling with her knee, but all she would say was, 'It's all nonsense, Mother, I'm fine.'

Nancy smiled now. 'Hello, Mother,' she said, yawning. 'All asleep, at last,' and she made her way to the playroom, only to be called back by Mother Superior.

The staff, Mother said, were all invited to their own Christmas Eve supper in the staffroom. The table was laid and Cook had baked especially. They were waiting for her, Mother said, so Nancy once more left the ironing behind and did as she was told. It was a lovely supper and Nancy very much enjoyed the cake and tea. It was only ten minutes after they'd finished that Sister Mary Joseph looked over to see her fast asleep in the armchair beside the radio.

Mother sighed. 'I only wish there was something we could do for her, for a change.'

Sister Mary Joseph agreed. 'Maybe we could make her a present? I have some lovely soap from my sister, and I know Sister Angelica received some pretty hand-kerchiefs. We could all put something in and make her a gift.'

Mother Superior said she would think about it, but it was now time to clear up and get prepared for midnight Mass. Father would be here soon, and they must get his supper ready in the parlour. Mother hurried away and wondered if she should gather the nuns together to see if they could come up with something special for Nancy – and yet a gift of soap and handkerchiefs seemed not to be quite what she was thinking of. *But then, what do I want?* thought Mother, and could come up with no answers.

Mother had only just reached the door of her room when Sister Mary Joseph came running through the door at the top of the parlour stairs which led to the staffroom and nursery. She continued to hurry down the stairs, out of breath, and ran across the parlour to Mother, who held up her hand and asked what on earth she thought she was doing.

Sister Mary Joseph was trying hard to contain her excitement. 'Oh, Mother,' she blurted out, 'I have the perfect gift. It's everything Nancy has taught us about the joy of giving of ourselves. Oh, Mother, it really is perfect.'

Sister Mary Joseph waited.

'Would you like to share it with me, then?' said Mother.

Sister Mary Joseph nodded and began to tell Mother all about the very magical Christmas gift.

Immediately, Sister Mary Joseph was sent back upstairs to ensure that nobody woke Nancy. She was to be allowed to sleep in the chair until it was time for midnight Mass. 'It's your special mission,' said Mother. 'I do not want Nancy woken up.'

Sister Mary Joseph hurried back upstairs, crept along the corridor and gathered the staff together excitedly. They waited at the staffroom door as Sister Mary Joseph quietly closed it, before they all tiptoed off to prepare for midnight Mass.

Sister Mary Joseph was very pleased with herself, until she realized that she would have to be the one to wake Nancy – and she wasn't looking forward to that at all. But there was no need, as the staff all heard Nancy burst out of the room at 11.40 p.m., asking at the top of her voice why nobody had had the common sense to wake her up when there was so much to be done. The staff all scuttled off down the various corridors, muttering about 'too much to do' and they 'thought someone else had done it'. Nancy was left to ponder when on earth the ironing would get done.

It was a beautiful Christmas Eve service, as always, and Nancy thoroughly enjoyed it. There were cups of tea and cake afterwards, then everyone went their separate ways. Mother walked with Nancy to the nursery to ensure she did no more work – after all, it was now Christmas Day. The children's stockings were hung at the end of each of their beds with their little gifts, and Nancy finally crept into bed. *Honestly*, she thought, *after sleeping half the evening I will never get to sleep.*

She was wrong. Nancy was fast asleep the moment her head hit the pillow.

As the house settled down to silence, in the early hours of Christmas morning, very slowly along the corridors crept the nuns of Nazareth House, up the parlour stairs, from the dormitories and from the junior department downstairs. They gathered at the end of the corridor and were told what to do. Sister Mary Joseph stood silently outside Nancy's door and listened. No sound. The Sisters of Nazareth tiptoed along the corridor and began to make the very magical Christmas gift. In complete silence in the dimly lit room they all worked silently until five in the morning when, finally, the last part of the gift was complete.

Slowly, and totally exhausted, they crept back along the corridors, knowing there would be no time for bed as the church bells would ring out at 6 a.m. A cup of tea, a wash and a change of clothes was all there would be time for. Sister Mary Joseph could not have slept, anyway – she was counting the minutes until Nancy saw her magical Christmas present.

At six o'clock on Christmas morning the bells rang out and Nancy jumped out of bed wondering how on earth she had managed to sleep so long. Hastily, she grabbed her clothes and began to dress, hoping the staff were on their way to see to the children. Never, ever had Nancy not been the first one to the dormitories on Christmas morning to wake them. She quickly ran a comb through her hair, opened the door and stopped.

'What on earth?' she said, looking at all the nuns gathered outside her door smiling at her.

Sister Mary Joseph stifled a yawn.

'Been up all night, Sister?' Nancy laughed.

Mother took Nancy's hand. 'Come with us,' she said. 'Sister Mary Joseph had a rather wonderful idea, and we have something for you.'

'For me? What do you mean, for me?'

'Wait and see, Nancy.'

The all arrived at the playroom door and Sister Mary Joseph stood ready to open it. 'Close your eyes, Nancy,' she said, laughing.

'Really, Sister, I'm not two years old, you know.'

'Just do it,' said Mother, 'please.'

Nancy, for the second time in only two days, did as she was told and closed her eyes. She was led into the children's playroom, where the ironing board and iron always stood.

'Happy Christmas!' they all shouted.

And Nancy opened her eyes.

There was total silence as Nancy looked around the room. Hardly able to believe her eyes, she stood completely still for a moment. Then she walked slowly towards the ironing board and picked up a small card with a Christmas tree on the front. Inside it read: *To Nancy, Christmas magic from the Sisters of Nazareth*. Nancy lifted her head, looked around the room once more, and then quietly began to cry.

All around the playroom there were piles of freshly ironed clothes. The underwear in one corner, all the jumpers in another, dresses, trousers, cardigans all beautifully ironed and further separated into boys' and girls'. Hours and hours of ironing had been done for her. Nancy could think of no more wonderful present that she could possibly have received. The nuns had cared for her enough to do this, and for probably the first time in her life she was absolutely speechless.

The noise of the children began to filter through to the playroom and the moment was broken as the sisters began to gather round Nancy, telling her all about their night of ironing and how they had each helped to make it so special for her. Nancy knew at that moment that for the rest of her life she would never forget their magical gift of love and kindness.

It was a wonderful start to Christmas Day, and Nancy was bubbling with joy as she took all the children to Mass that morning. Everyone was talking about Nancy's gift, and she felt very special indeed.

Father was the only person who had not heard about it yet as he stood delivering his Christmas sermon. He thought he had done rather well this year. He had spent many hours working on it. But as he looked over at the front bench, he thought maybe he needed to work on his delivery.

There on the front bench in the chapel during Christmas Day Mass sat the Sisters of Nazareth – all fast asleep.

PART TWO
Happy Endings

Dolly with Her Head
in the Clouds

Five years later, all thoughts of the war firmly behind her, Nancy was now thirty-two years old. She was busy ironing a pile of clothes that never, ever seemed to come to an end whilst Dolly read fairy tales to the children from one of the many books that had been kindly donated. The children had been quietly listening and taking in every word that she said to them. Dolly had such a way with her, Nancy thought. Nancy would certainly have argued and tossed her head in indignation if anyone dared to accuse her of having favourites – and yet, there was definitely a small part of Nancy's heart that warmed when she saw Dolly, her youngest helper, with the children. Eighteen years old, Dolly had wanted to be a children's nurse but that sort of nonsense was not accepted in her family. It was her younger brother's college education that would be paid for first, when the time came. So at fifteen years old Dolly had come along to help out in the nursery under Nancy's supervision.

Nancy had given up trying to make Dolly as sensible as she felt she should be considering she was in a position of trust with the children.

'Dolly brings a sense of fun to the children,' Sister Mary Joseph would say.

'She lives with her head in the clouds,' Nancy replied.

Yet each time Nancy thought of Dolly, it made her smile. If Dolly Marshall wanted to believe in a lifetime of dreams and happy endings, then who was she to take that from her? Nancy had never believed in happy endings – not for herself, anyway. She was perfectly content with life. And that was quite enough, thank you, she would say to herself. 'No-nonsense Nancy' they called her, and yet there was that ever-constant twinkle in her eyes. She was the head of the nursery department, looking after more children than she could ever have imagined. Nancy could look at a child and simply know what was needed.

Sister Mary Joseph laughingly told all the children one day that Nancy had eyes in the back of her head. Then she quietly whispered to Mother Superior, 'Actually, you know, I think she really may have. No matter what they do, she always knows. Honestly, Mother, even I wouldn't dare lie to her.'

'One would hope that you would not lie to anybody, Sister Mary Joseph,' said Mother, smiling. 'I do know what you mean, though. She has that way of looking at you and somehow you just do as you are told – even me,' sighed Mother. 'And yet, she has a way of making you feel special too.'

Mother Superior had never forgotten the day Nancy had arrived, a quiet sensible little girl but with a deter-mined, no-nonsense attitude. She smiled, remembering the time Nancy's father had turned up to take her home and she had stubbornly refused to leave, simply told Mother Superior, 'No!' and returned to her work. It was the single and only time anyone had ever dared disobey Mother, and it still made her chuckle. Mother Superior had watched Nancy grow up and become the most won derful young woman. The children loved her so much; she knew how it felt to feel lonely, frightened and unsure, and she dealt with it perfectly. Nancy had the capacity to make every child feel loved and special without accepting any nonsense – or Dolly's 'ridiculous notions', as she would call them. Mother wasn't fooled. Nancy loved Dolly and had taken her under her wing.

'Dolly never thinks before she speaks,' Sister Mary Joseph frequently told the other nuns, with amusement. 'Honestly, it just all comes tumbling out. She is a constant source of laughter.'

That was until earlier today, when she'd blurted out, 'Ooh, Nancy, when you get married and have babies –'

Nancy had cut her short. 'Dolly Marshall, wash your mouth out with soap and water. I have never heard such ridiculousness!' Poor Nancy had turned beetroot red, and they had all been utterly shocked when they saw tears in her eyes. 'I have enough babies here,' she had stammered, and hurried from the room.

Dolly had run to her room and cried until her eyes felt red-raw, so horrified was she at upsetting Nancy. No matter what had happened, whenever children cried they were cuddled, knees were sat upon, stories were read. When the children were taken screaming from parents' arms and placed in Nancy's care they were soothed until they felt better. Dolly always felt so much for these little ones and would feel like crying herself. Not Nancy. 'Tears aren't going to help them,' Nancy would say. 'Get the storybooks out, take them to the playroom, play games. But no crying, Dolly.'

Nancy never cried – ever.

But Dolly was wrong. Nancy had shed many tears in the privacy of her own room, down the corridor next to the dining room, which is where she sat now. She had been so proud the day Mother Superior gave her this room of her very own. Her single bed with the pretty sheets and bed cover. A little brown set of drawers with a mirror on the top and a large wardrobe in the corner. Nancy was looking at the two small holy pictures stuck in the edge of the mirror as the pain struck her from nowhere. Other people had babies, she thought. Having children was something she had dreamed of as a child, always being the first one to offer to take the babies for a walk in the back lane. She had held her sister Mary and felt the wonder of holding a new baby. 'One day, that will be me,' she had said.

It was too late now, she knew. And then she blushed once more, thinking about the things her friend Tilly had told her about babies and men. Nancy had been utterly mortified. 'Oh, I don't think I would like that at all,' she'd said to Tilly, shocked to the core, and Tilly had roared with laughter. They had been the very best of friends since they were both young girls. Tilly had worked in the kitchen and had married the man she fell in love with on seeing him for the first time working in the gardens of Nazareth House.

All these thoughts were running through Nancy's head as she sat perfectly still, staring at her holy pictures. *Babies*, thought Nancy; even the word evoked so many emotions. Sometimes the ache of never holding her own child was simply too hard to bear. It was all right as long as there was a *maybe one day*. But maybe one day was not going to happen now. Happy endings, indeed. It was easier to pretend that these feelings didn't exist, that it didn't matter. After all, there were always Tilly's children – not to mention all the little ones in the nursery that needed her love. The little ones! Nancy jumped up and hastily wiped her eyes on her apron. What in God's name was she doing, blubbering away in her room? She took a deep breath, looked once more at her holy picture of the Madonna and Child. 'I'm fine,' she said to Our Lady as she stood and straightened her clothes then changed her apron.

The Madonna and Child looked on as Nancy closed the door behind her and made her way down the corridor to see Dolly. Nancy could never have imagined that her prayers would, indeed, be answered – in a way she could never have envisaged or dreamed of. Only a few miles away another story was beginning that Nancy did not know of. But it was one that would change her life completely.

Nancy tapped on Dolly's door and went in.

'Oh, Nancy,' Dolly said, 'I am so sorry.'

'Dolly Marshall, never apologize for something you have not done. You are a good girl, and I . . . well, I . . . oh, goodness me, I am babbling away.' Nancy put her arms around Dolly's shoulders. 'You are a good girl,' she said again, looking a little sheepish and embarrassed.

Dolly giggled.

'Come on, young lady,' said Nancy. 'Let's go and sort out the children's tea – or there will be more tears before bedtime.' Nancy was extremely embarrassed; displays of emotion were not her thing. There had been too much nonsense today already for her liking, but the tears in Dolly's eyes broke her heart. Nancy patted her hand. 'It's just that it is too late for me, you see,' she said to Dolly. 'And where would I find the time for a baby, when I have you to keep on the straight and narrow?'

Dolly hooked her arm through Nancy's. They walked back to the playroom, laughing together, and let Sister Mary Joseph leave to continue with her duties.

Immediately, all the children gathered around Dolly for another story. They sat cross-legged on the floor as she delved into the world of imagination and wonder, whilst Nancy set up the ironing board in the corner of the playroom.

It was a peaceful scene. The rain was still lashing against the windows and the branches of the old conker tree in the garden swayed in the wind and scattered leaves all over the playground. The playroom was quiet except for the sound of Dolly's voice. Nancy was busy and the iron was whizzing over the clothes that were needed for the next morning. She looked as though she was completely concentrating on the job in hand, but Nancy was listening and often glanced over at Dolly. Bless her, she didn't have a sensible bone in her body. She was bubbly, funny, had an incredibly naive nature and was one of the sweetest, kindest girls Nancy had ever met. When she told a story, the children listened; she could make the simplest tale sound exciting. Tonight the children's eyes were like saucers. A couple of the younger ones had actually fallen asleep on the playroom floor, and young David was fast asleep in the playpen amongst the toys, clutching an old blue train.

Nancy sighed. All back to normal, she thought. *What on earth was I thinking earlier? Letting things get the better of me.* Well, there would be no more of that today, thank you, she told herself as once more she attacked the ironing energetically.

'And so, they all lived happily ever after,' Dolly whispered, leaning in towards the children.

Happy endings, thought Nancy. *If only.*

Dolly looked up at Nancy, smiling. 'What's your happy ending, Nancy?' she said.

Nancy paused, then smiled back.

'Well, an end to this ironing pile would be nice.'

The Magical, Singing
Ironing Board

Autumn was nearly over and unusually there was an early threat of snow. It was a bright and sunny day yet absolutely freezing cold, Nancy thought, as she began to plan the busy day ahead. The Nazareth House Orphanage was full to brimming this year and Nancy had her hands full already without anything else coming along. She paused for a moment to put the heavy basket of laundry down and glanced out of the window that looked out on to the children's play area. Why did children's playgrounds look so desolate without the children in them? she thought. The enormous conker tree looked bare and the swings were swaying gently in the breeze.

Nancy had seen many winters and Christmas Days, had made and hung more paper chains and told more stories than anyone could ever imagine. The children and the Nazareth House nursery had become her life since arriving all those years ago. She had very quickly grown accustomed to the ways of the orphanage, and somehow – even as a small child – she was the one called upon to help the little ones. She was always ready with a cuddle, and was never too busy to read them a story. Where had the years gone? she wondered to herself, before continuing on her way to the playroom to iron while watching the children play.

There were hurried footsteps along the corridor behind her. Sister Mary Joseph was calling her. *What now?* thought Nancy.

'Now, Nancy,' said Sister Mary Joseph, 'I know you are busy today.'

'Understatement,' said Nancy with a smile.

'Yes, well, it's just . . . oh dear.'

'Please, Sister, I am very busy. Would you mind just telling me, so I can attempt to get the ironing done sometime before Christmas Day?'

'Nancy, I know the nursery is full,' Sister Joseph put her hands out and shrugged her shoulders, 'but what else can we do?'

'A new child, is it, Sister? Well, we will manage, I suppose. Heavens! That will make it twenty-three this year – and all under five years old. I hope Santa has kept up to speed.'

'More love to give out,' said Sister Mary Joseph, placing her hands on Nancy's shoulders.

Nancy smiled back. 'No, Sister, more ironing.'

The little boy was sitting in the parlour with the lady who had brought him here. He hadn't been at all frightened walking down the long driveway, seeing the enormous house ahead with all the windows, the wooded area to his left or the beautiful statue of Our Lady of Lourdes to his right. He had kept his eyes down, focusing on the stones and his feet as he counted out each of his steps. He had already cried more tears than any four-year-old boy ever should. He had heard them whisper the words 'alone in the world now' and didn't even understand what they meant. But he didn't like the sound of it at all. Mummy's voice was what he missed the most. Sometimes when he was in bed, if he concentrated hard, he could still hear her singing, but it hadn't happened for a long time now.

Nancy was determined to at least get the laundry into the playroom before she made her way down the stairs from the nursery to the parlour to meet her new young child. Oh dear, she thought, when she saw him. Quiet as a mouse with his head bent, eyes staring at the floor. Tantrums and screaming Nancy could deal with – had done so on hundreds of occasions now, she thought – they were natural, and she had a million and one ways of dealing with them. But this tore at Nancy's heart. There was something here that said, 'The pain is too raw, too deep, you cannot help me.' Well, Nancy hadn't been beaten yet, so she simply walked forward, knelt in front of the little boy and said, 'Hello, love, my name is Aunty Nancy. What is yours?' and waited.

'Timothy,' said the lady who had brought him.

'Thank you, I was talking to the child,' Nancy said, politely but firmly.

'What is your name, love?'

There was a very small whisper that Nancy only just caught.

'Timothy Brown.'

'Well, Timothy Brown, I think there are lots of people who would like to meet you. Come along,' she said, and took his hand. 'I will take him from here,' she said, nodding at the lady. 'If you wait here, Mother Superior will be along shortly to see you.'

Nancy chatted all the way back up the stairs into the dormitory, where she showed Timothy his new bed. She told him all about the playroom and the toys and said there was even the possibility, if it stopped raining, that he might get to play outside with the others in the playground. Still Timothy stared at the ground and his tears fell straight from his eyes, splashing on to the wooden floor. And it was then that Nancy heard his voice properly for the first time as the child began to cry. There were still no words, just the heartbreaking sound of a young child sobbing. Nancy stopped talking, simply picked the child up in her arms and held him as tightly as she could, rocking him gently backwards and forwards until finally he fell asleep. It was not the first time that she had done this – and would most certainly not be the last. 'Poor little soul,' she whispered as she kissed his forehead and put him down on top of his new bed. Then she left to ask Dolly to keep an eye on him. 'If I leave this ironing pile another day and it gets any higher, we will need a roof extension,' she said to Dolly, 'and the children will be running around in their vests.'

However, it was nearly lunchtime, so the ironing would have to wait – there were children to feed. She would give Timothy something to eat after his nap.

After lunch, Nancy once more looked longingly at the pile of clothes, and then out of the window. 'Oh, to pot with it!' she said. 'Get the children's coats on, Dolly, they need to have a run about.'

It was a job and a half, but eventually twenty-two noisy and excited children with their winter coats and shoes on clambered down the nursery stairs into the playground. Little Timothy was brought down by Sister Mary Joseph to play with the children. Nancy watched him very carefully. Still not a word. He sat alone under the conker tree, not even wanting to join in when Nancy and Dolly ran round the playground jumping on the last of the autumn leaves, making crunching noises, until the gardener came running from the bottom of the garden and asked Nancy and Dolly what on earth they thought they were doing, making such a mess for him to clear up.

Dolly and Nancy gathered the children around them and made their way back to the playroom, carrying a couple of the younger ones who were beginning to look very tired indeed.

'By some stroke of magic we may get them all washed before the tea bell rings,' Nancy said.

'Ooh, Nancy, do you believe in magic?' Dolly asked.

Nancy turned to look at Dolly, hands on her hips. 'Oh, yes, definitely,' she said. 'As much as I believe in the ironing fairy.' She popped her head round the playroom door. 'Nope,' she said, 'it's still there.'

Dolly looked at Nancy, then they both burst out laughing.

'You are funny, Nancy,' said Dolly.

But Nancy was no longer laughing. It was now nearly four o'clock, and she was no further forward.

Bath time was noisy and messy. After the younger ones had been put to bed, Nancy usually took the older ones into the television room, but tonight they were allowed back in the playroom.

'They can have their supper in here tonight,' she said, 'whilst I get on with my work. Finally!' Nancy switched on the iron but was stopped in her tracks when she looked across the room. There he was, Timothy, still sitting in the corner of the room. At least he was looking up now and watching the children play. Nancy's eyes stung. 'Oh, for heaven's sake,' she said to herself, 'there's no time for me to be getting all silly.'

It was then she had the idea. A ridiculous one, she thought to herself. And yet it might just work.

'Oh,' she said out loud to the children. 'Well, now, would you believe it?'

The children looked up from what they were doing. Aunty Nancy had her head on the ironing board.

Sister Mary Joseph, who was passing the door on her way to the chapel, paused and opened her mouth to speak, then changed her mind. 'I'm not even going to ask,' she said to herself as she hurried to evening service.

'Sssssh,' Nancy said to the children, '. . . listen.'

The children began to gather around the ironing board. Nancy, all the time, was looking out of the corner of her eye at Timothy. Yes, she had definitely got his attention.

'What is it, Aunty Nancy?' called Janet.

'I . . . I think the ironing board is singing.'

There were gasps and 'oohs' and 'aahs' from the children who were now very quiet indeed, so hard were they listening.

'Oh, Aunty Nancy,' said David, 'is it magic?'

'Well, indeed it is,' she said, her fingers crossed behind her back. 'Yes,' said Aunty Nancy as she straightened up and looked directly at Timothy, 'I do believe this is a magical, singing ironing board.' She bent down once more. 'What is it?' she whispered to the ironing board. 'Oh, I see. Well, it seems that before it will sing out loud *all* the children have to join in.'

'Oh, do join in, Timothy,' the children shouted.

There was a pause.

And, ever so slowly, Timothy began to walk towards the group of children around the ironing board and sat down.

'Oh, my goodness!' Nancy said, then began humming loudly and pretending she didn't know where the sound was coming from. 'Oh!' she said. 'Did you hear that, children?'

'Yes!' the children were shouting excitedly.

Imagination is a wonderful thing, thought Nancy, smiling.

'It wants us to join in,' she said. 'Quickly now, children, move in front of the ironing board so I can see you all.'

The children waited and little Timothy looked up at Nancy and saw the kindest blue eyes he had ever seen in his life. These eyes twinkled and said all would be well, and he believed them. He felt it happening all of a sudden, at the corners of his mouth, and then a bubbly feeling in his tummy. He looked around the room, then back at Nancy, and at long last gave her the most beautiful smile, which melted Nancy's heart. It was only the screams of the children wanting the ironing board to sing that brought Nancy back to herself.

For the next two hours, long after the children should have been put to bed, Nancy ironed with gusto – apparently, the faster the iron moved, the louder the ironing board sang and the louder the children's voices became. Nancy was hissing, humming and tapping her foot. The sounds of children singing drifted down the nursery stairs, echoing all along the corridor, and could be heard just inside the chapel downstairs.

Mother Superior looked questioningly at Sister Mary Joseph, who shook her head. God only knew what she was up to, thought Mother, her eyes raised heavenwards.

It was nine o'clock before Nancy eventually got to put the magical, singing ironing board away, all the clothes pressed and in piles for the next day.

Timothy immediately fell into a deep sleep, dreaming of the magical, singing ironing board and feeling the coldness that had lain inside him for days being replaced by a lovely warm feeling. As night fell and Timothy slept soundly, once more he could hear the soft sounds of Mummy's voice singing to him, and deep down somewhere inside him there was a feeling of being loved.

In the early hours of the morning, long before the children woke and Nancy's day was due to begin, there was a gentle tap on her door.

'Sister Mary Joseph, what on earth is it at this ungodly hour?'

'Sorry, Nancy, it's a little girl, an emergency. She is with Mother Superior in the parlour now. Can you come quickly?' Sister Mary Joseph had tears in her eyes. 'A very sad little girl, Nancy,' she said, her fingers clicking the rosary beads that hung around her neck.

Nancy quickly dressed and hurried along the corridor, glancing into the playroom as she passed.

'Oh, my,' she said, 'what on earth will I have to think of next?'

Enchanted Clocks
and Mermaids

The child who had arrived in the early hours of this morning was Lucy Jones, who was four and a half years old. The half was very important indeed, because it meant she was nearly five years old – and when that happened, she would be starting school. Mummy would be able to get a better job then, and they could move out of the one room they had been living in since Lucy was born. Lucy had Daddy's eyes, Mummy would tell her over and over again, and every time they thought of him it would bring him closer. Lucy wasn't sure it was fair that Daddy was with the angels – she would much rather have him here – but every time she asked questions, Mummy would look so sad that Lucy had stopped asking. Lucy had a small tin box and the only photograph she had of her mummy and daddy together was in there. It was her most prized possession. Her mother, Mary Jones, even after all these years, still felt the injustice of it all and missed Alfie every single day. Mary often smiled to herself; she had faced many battles in her lifetime but God had sent her Lucy and she thanked Him from the bottom of her heart every time she said her prayers.

'Mummy, maybe we should play our game tonight after tea,' Lucy had said.

So that night, huddled in front of the gas fire, Mary and Lucy had closed their eyes and played Let's Pretend. It was a beautiful sunny day and they lived in a cottage with flowers and trees. At the bottom of the garden was a magical lake with enchanted water where mermaids swam. There were always mermaids in Lucy's imagination after receiving the mermaid storybook Mummy had bought for her third birthday. She had listened to the story so many times now, she knew it off by heart. Theirs wasn't an easy life, but they had each other and were managing. And that was enough for now, Mary would say over and over again. Neither Lucy nor Mary knew that very soon there would be more battles to face – for both of them – and their courage, strength and love would be tested once more.

Mary woke up early in the morning, feeling very poorly indeed. She refused to let it get the better of her during the day, but at night Mrs Williams, the landlady, heard Mary's cries and called Dr Morton. Only five days after their last game of Let's Pretend, Mary was taken to hospital and Lucy was taken, screaming, from the mother she loved with all of her heart. Terrified and crying, Lucy had sat curled up in the corner of the room, clutching her tin box and storybook.

Her treasures were placed into an old brown suitcase Mrs Williams had spare. It had been filled with all Lucy's clothes, few as they were, and the tin and storybook – when they had been prised from Lucy's fingers – were placed on the top.

And so, another child took that long walk down the driveway wondering what life held in store for them. Lucy had not spoken at all to the lady who had collected her and told her all about her new home. There was no way of knowing how long the child would be left here. Polio could be a long job – and there was always the chance the child would have to be adopted, if the worst happened. The lady chatted happily, trying to cheer Lucy up, but the little girl wasn't listening. She had both her eyes and her ears closed on the journey to Nazareth House. It was, after all, the best way to play Let's Pretend.

It was very early in the morning when Nancy heard the knock on her door. Ten minutes later, after briefly hearing about Mary and Lucy, she was hurrying along the corridor, combing her hair and tidying herself as she made her way to the nuns' parlour, where Mother Superior was sitting with a very frightened and lonely child. 'Oh, my,' said Nancy to herself, 'here we go again. Poor mite.' Even after so many children, it never failed to twist her heart when she saw a child looking so lost. *Really*, thought Nancy, *they could save their words*. Both Mother Superior and the lady in the parlour were talking non-stop to Lucy. Any fool could see the child wasn't listening.

'Thank you. I will take it from here,' said Nancy.

Mother Superior looked relieved. 'Oh, thank goodness you are here, Nancy. Yes, all will be well now,' she said with a smile.

The lady and Mother Superior left to attend to the relevant paperwork. Nancy sat beside Lucy and took her hand.

The parlour was a huge space with a glass-dome ceiling and wooden floors. There was no sound at all, except for the ticking of the enormous clock which hung on the parlour wall. The pendulum swung from side to side, and

Lucy quietly sat and stared at it, her arms clutched tightly around her small brown suitcase.

Nancy leaned slightly closer to Lucy and whispered. 'Oh, I see, you must be very special indeed. Not everyone recognizes that the clock is magic.'

Lucy looked up at Nancy. 'Magic?'

'Oh, yes, absolutely, it is an enchanted clock.'

Nancy waited, looking straight ahead as the clock continued to tick. Then, slowly, she squeezed Lucy's hand. 'I could tell you all about it tomorrow, if you like. Come along now, Lucy,' she said in a firm but kind voice.

They climbed up the long staircase and Nancy didn't miss the fact that twice Lucy looked over her shoulder to glance at the enchanted clock. They made their way along to the nursery quarters, past the playroom to the dormitory where she would sleep. Nancy opened the suitcase, glancing at Lucy's storybook, and without any nonsense changed Lucy into her nightgown and tucked her up into bed.

Lucy grabbed Nancy's hand. 'Could I have my book and tin, please?'

Nancy turned to switch off the light as she left the dormitory. She saw Lucy curled up, clutching her tin and storybook. She hadn't missed the picture of the mermaids, and the seeds of an idea were beginning to take place in her mind.

Back in her room, Nancy wondered if she could grab another hour's sleep before it was time to get up and deal with a new day. Honestly, an enchanted clock! Whatever was she thinking?

*

The children were very excited when they woke to find a new little girl in their dormitory and it took Nancy some time to calm them all down. The morning staff came along and helped dress and wash the children before taking them all into the dining room for a very noisy breakfast.

Lucy ate almost nothing and said even less. It was an extremely busy morning, as always, when Dolly – the youngest of the nursery-staff – came to tell Nancy that Lucy kept walking around with her eyes closed.

'Well, maybe you could simply ask her why?' Nancy said.

'Oh, I have, she just says it's Let's Pretend.'

'Yes, well, let's pretend the washing has thrown itself into the washing machine and the mangle has squeezed it all dry and the fairies have popped along and hung it all up, shall we?'

Dolly burst out laughing. 'Oh, Nancy, you are funny. But you know quite well you have a way with the children. You ask her. Please.'

Nancy looked through the bars of the playroom window to the playground. Lucy was sitting under the conker tree reading her book – or was she? Her eyes were closed but her lips were moving. Nancy was thinking of the many children she had watched sitting underneath the big old conker tree, somehow getting comfort from sitting against the large tree trunk. Not for the first time Nancy thought the chores of the day would have to take a back seat as she made her way down the stairs into the garden.

It was a beautiful garden with a lush green lawn and to the right stood the enormous conker tree. At the bottom of the garden, on the left-hand side, was an orchard where the apple, pear and plum trees grew and, to the right, high iron gates behind which was a large pond surrounded by all types of green plants and home to many frogs and pond life.

Nancy walked into the garden and down to the iron gates. Some of the children followed her, as they always did. Nancy waved at Lucy as she passed and called out to come along and see the pond. Lucy bent her head and squeezed her eyes even tighter shut. Nancy paused, seeing the book in Lucy's hand, and smiled.

'Very well,' she said, 'of course if you don't want to see the mermaids . . .'

Nancy was counting in her head: one, two, three. Yes, there it was, the spark that said, 'What did you just say?'

'Well, if you change your mind,' Nancy said and turned away, smiling.

Lucy ran to her side, as Nancy knew she would, and she gathered the children around her, making them promise not to wake the mermaids in the pond.

'Hold my hand, Lucy,' Nancy whispered as all the children waited for Nancy to open the gate.

They had never been allowed into the pond area before, and there were excited whispers all round. Very carefully, they all stood in a circle around the pond with Dolly at one side and Nancy at the other.

Lucy looked up.

'What should we do, Aunty Nancy?' the children chorused.

'What do you think we should do, Lucy? Maybe you could tell all the children about Let's Pretend.'

'Yes, do. Go on, Lucy!' the children shouted.

'Well,' said Lucy, closing her eyes, 'the most beautiful mermaid in the world lives at the bottom of the deepest ocean and rides on the backs of the dolphins. She has long red hair and bright green eyes and everything she touches is enchanted and magical. She can swim faster than all the sea creatures in the world. And if you touch her, all your dreams come true.'

Nancy's eyes were stinging with tears on hearing this wonderful story. She knew only too well that Lucy's mum must have read her this story over and over again for her to know it by heart, and her description of the mermaid was beautiful.

That afternoon at the bottom of the garden, by the pond where the mermaids lived, Nancy, Dolly and the children danced around the garden of dreams, laughing and singing, as yet another young child felt Nancy's love work its magic.

Lucy's heart slowly began to mend during the coming weeks and months as winter turned into spring. The children often visited the enchanted pond, where they told stories of magical mermaids and enchanted lagoons. They whispered their hopes and dreams into leaves which they threw into the pond for the water fairies to take to the mermaids.

On sunny afternoons they sat around the pond with their feet in the water, splashing. Their toes tingled and they sang songs and felt the touch of the mermaids. It was, of course, only when you squeezed your eyes tightly shut and felt the tingling in your toes that you knew you had been stroked by a mermaid and, one by one, the children squealed with delight each time they felt the mermaid's gentle touch. It had nothing whatsoever to do with Nancy and Dolly stirring up the reeds at the bottom of the pond with a stick. Nothing at all. Honest.

One afternoon, all the children were found standing looking out of the playroom window with extremely sad faces as the rain lashed down. Nancy once more left the chores, pleaded with Barbara in the sewing room for scraps, and helped the girls make mermaid tails and the boys make pirate costumes.

The very next day, the garden was filled with noisy, happy pirates and mermaids, and the conker tree looked on and sighed. No lonely children today to sit in the shade of its branches. *All is well*, Nancy said to herself as she sat watching the children play. *Enchanted clocks and mermaids*, she thought, smiling before she made her way back to the laundry, praying that some enchanted elves might just have done the washing for her.

Bath time in the nursery was always noisy, and the children had to be prised out of their mermaid costumes to get washed – although Nancy was at a loss to explain why mermaids had to take their tails off before getting in the bath. They were in the dormitory, getting their night clothes on before tea, when Sister Mary Joseph knocked on the door.

'Nancy, quickly! We have a visitor.'

The lady stood at the end of the long corridor looking out of the window, her eyes resting on the pool at the bottom of the garden.

Very thin, very pale, yet very beautiful indeed. Nancy looked at her and understood perfectly. That beautiful red hair and those bright green eyes.

Nancy walked back into the dormitory where all the children were chatting and dancing about, waiting to be taken for their tea. She took Lucy's hand. 'I think you may have a very special visitor, darling.'

Lucy looked up at Nancy, then down the corridor, and gasped. It had been more than six months. For a moment, as the enchanted clock in the parlour paused, neither mother nor child moved. Until suddenly Mary dropped her case. And Lucy did something no child was allowed to do and ran full speed down the long corridor and threw herself into her mother's arms.

It was the end of the summer and the trees were rustling in the light breeze. Nancy watched Lucy dancing up the drive, telling her mother all about the enchanted clock, the magical pond, the singing, dancing and mermaid's tails.

Nancy was still watching when Mary paused halfway up the drive to turn round. Whether Nancy could see her or not she wasn't sure, but Mary brushed away the tears in her eyes and raised her hand to wave to Nancy. 'Thank you,' she whispered.

'Bless you both,' said Nancy as she turned away from the window and hurried along the corridor to give the children their tea.

Mary grabbed Lucy's hand. 'Oh, Lucy, do you know just how much I missed you?'

'Ooh, Mummy, did you know there were mermaids at the bottom of the garden?'

Attic of Treasures

Dolly had never been so excited in her entire life. As the skies became darker and darker on this late afternoon in December, she sat at the table sewing angel costumes for the children as Nancy went around all the rooms putting the big lights on. Nancy had patted Dolly on the shoulder and, in the most unusual display of emotion, had given her a hug and told Dolly what a wonderful job she was doing. 'You're a good girl, Dolly Marshall,' she had said to her. 'Excitable and head in the clouds,' Nancy had laughed, with a twinkle in her eye, 'but a good girl.'

'Dilly Dolly Daydream', Nancy had nicknamed her, and Dolly was thrilled.

For weeks now, Nancy and Dolly had gathered every scrap of material they could find, had torn up old clothes, begged and borrowed from Barbara in the sewing room, to make angel costumes for this year's Nativity which was to take place tomorrow afternoon in the chapel. Nancy had been teaching Dolly to sew since she had first arrived. Dolly's favourite times were when she and Nancy sat together in the evening, when all the little ones were in bed, and got the sewing basket and button box out. Nancy would make tea and sandwiches and, together, they would sit at the large table by the window and listen to the wireless in the corner of the room whilst darning and making clothes for the children. Nothing was ever thrown out, no matter what it was – a torn skirt, stained clothing, a ragged piece of cloth – it would be kept.

'Ooh, look, Sister,' Nancy had announced one day, looking overly pleased by an old battered basket in her hand which had surely seen many better days. 'This might come in handy one day.'

A stunned Sister Mary Joseph, her hands in the prayer position, leaned forward, paused and said, 'And may I ask, Nancy, in God's name, what for?'

'Well . . . something,' said Nancy, and turned on her heel, making her way to the attic where every piece of treasure, broken or otherwise, was kept for the day when a use would be found for it. 'And woe betide anyone who meddles with my useful treasure,' she had been heard to say on more than one occasion when a clear-out was threatened. She need not have worried – since the last meddling episode, nobody dared.

Dolly was extremely proud of her darning skills; even Sister Mary Joseph now brought all her small bits of mending to Dolly. 'You have a gift,' she told her. 'Your darning skills are simply wonderful,' she had said only last week. Never had Dolly felt so thrilled.

She looked up and watched the first flakes of snow begin to fall, remembering once more the day she had arrived here. All her dreams up until that day had been to qualify as a children's nurse, but it was to be her brother who would receive the necessary funding for further education, as Dolly was only a girl. The memory still stung, and a very angry Dolly had been sent to help out at the local orphanage to assist the staff and children. Dolly closed her eyes and thanked whoever – or whatever – it was that had sent her here and smiled to herself, remembering seeing Nancy for the first time.

'What are you smiling at?' Nancy asked Dolly, momentarily looking up from a particularly difficult piece of stitching work.

'I was thinking about the first time we met, Nancy.'

Nancy continued to sew, and she too remembered that day in October. It had been a cold and windy day, and a very bedraggled-looking young girl had stood before her, the redness in her cheeks having nothing to do with the howling gales outside. This was a very angry young woman, and Nancy had felt like laughing when she looked at her. Honestly, the girl actually looked like she was about to stamp her foot! Nancy had had to stifle a giggle. 'Hello, young lady,' she had said, 'you may just want to remove the leaves from your hair.' Dolly had shrugged her shoulders and stood quite still.

Nancy gently took Dolly to the large mirror over the mantelpiece in the television room and turned her round. They stood there together until Nancy could bear it no longer and burst out laughing. But she stopped abruptly when she saw the tears forming in young Dolly's eyes. 'Cup of tea and sandwiches in order, I think,' Nancy had said and, taking Dolly's hand, led the girl to the small kitchenette. 'Hardly enough room to swing a cat in,' Nancy had said, 'but it's where we can escape to when we are hiding from the world, to get five minutes' peace.'

Dolly had sat at the small table on a little wooden stool. Somehow, sitting in that little kitchen, with the kettle singing on the hob, watching Nancy cutting sandwiches and cake, Dolly began to feel a warmth, a sense that everything was going to be all right. Dolly sipped her hot tea and began to relax, watching Nancy bustling about and chatting to her non-stop.

Sister Mary Joseph knocked on the kitchen door and called out to Nancy.

'We've been caught out, Dolly,' Nancy whispered, making Dolly giggle.

Sister popped her head round the door. 'Sorry, Nancy, I have to go and find the gardener to tidy up the leaves in the garden.'

'Oh. I wouldn't worry about that, Sister,' said Nancy. 'Dolly Marshall has gathered most of them in her hair walking down the drive.'

Dolly roared with laughter. 'Oh, Nancy,' she said, 'it's going to be all right, isn't it?'

'Why, Dolly, why wouldn't it be?' Nancy replied.

Dolly had no answer for that and continued to drink her tea, feeling happier by the minute.

Yes, Dolly remembered that day well. For the next six years Nancy had taught her everything, and it had been a magical journey. On Dolly's sixteenth birthday she had been invited to live in and have her own room next to the children's dormitory. There would be one day and one evening a week off to visit her family. It was a real job, looking after children, and Nancy had promised Dolly that she could be the one to manage the children in the sick bay when necessary. All was perfect in Dolly Marshall's world, and she was very happy indeed.

'A cup of tea, I think,' Nancy said, breaking into Dolly's remembrances as she stood up to close the big heavy curtains.

'Oh, please don't,' said Dolly, 'it's just begun to snow, and I would like to watch it.'

Late into the night Dolly and Nancy sat and sewed, making the angel wings, halos and dresses out of some old white sheets – naturally, from Nancy's treasure store. 'You see,' she had told them when asked to make angel costumes, 'it was worth keeping those old sheets. Told you so.'

That night, just before Christmas 1953, as the children slept and the snow fell, Dolly Marshall was sitting with Nancy as midnight approached and, as sometimes happens, suddenly her eyes stung at the happiness she felt inside.

Until she jumped up and screamed. 'Oh, my goodness, Nancy, the crib!'

'Crib?'

'We forgot the crib.'

Both Dolly and Nancy paused and looked at each other. The needles stopped sewing, the enchanted clock in the parlour held its chime, the mermaids in the pond waited, and time stood still as the horror of the situation hit them both.

The radio suddenly began to play once more and the Cathedral Choir began to sing 'Away in a Manger'.

Nancy sighed and took up her sewing again. 'The basket, Dolly,' she said calmly.

'The basket?'

'The old basket in the attic. It will be just the job.'

Dolly sat back down. 'Oh, Nancy,' she said, 'how perfect.'

The last halo was finished just as the enchanted clock chimed midnight.

'Ooh, Nancy,' Dolly said, her eyes wide open, 'it's a sign.'

Nancy laughed. 'It's a sign all that tea has gone to your head, Dolly Marshall.'

Later that night, Dolly snuggled under the covers, dreaming of all the excitement of the Nativity play tomorrow and the beautiful little angel costumes she and Nancy had made together. She was very pleased indeed.

Nancy switched off the light and crawled into bed, and the smug look on her face would have greatly amused Sister Mary Joseph.

'Told you it would come in useful one day,' she said out loud to herself, thinking of her attic full of treasures and the old battered basket.

Nancy curled up under the covers.

'Told you,' she said. 'Told you so.'

Nativity Plays and Buckets and Spades

'Well, that went well,' Nancy said, trying above all else to hold her head high, and failing miserably. Honestly, she didn't know what was worse. The stifled laughter, or the shocked look on Mother Superior's face when Joseph and Mary decided to fight over who was supposed to pick up the baby from the crib and Joseph decided to smack Mary over the head with Baby Jesus. But not before Mary had pulled one of his legs off.

Nancy had decided to just close her eyes, blot the whole scene out of her mind, and pray to God for forgiveness. She had waved her hands, desperately signalling to Sister Angela to quickly start playing the piano for the next carol. There they stood, her little ones. They could not have looked more angelic if they tried, with their little white sheets tied around the middle with tinsel and their angel wings and halos. They sang beautifully, just as they had rehearsed, and Nancy was very pleased – except, of course, with Mary and Joseph who sat, arms crossed, in a huff on the steps of the altar with faces like thunder, looking as if they would begin to cry or fight any moment now.

Nancy crept quietly to the back of the chapel and began to give hand signals to speed up the proceedings. 'Hark the Herald Angels' was sung faster than the speed of light, confusing not only the children but everyone who was watching. Sister Mary Joseph prayed every moment for it to be over, so frightened was she that she might just scream with laughter in front of Mother Superior who sat unmovable in the front pew, her hands folded in her lap, showing no emotion whatsoever, except for maybe the tiniest smile which was beginning to tickle the corners of her mouth. She certainly would never have dared steal a glance at Nancy.

Nancy absolutely and totally refused to even think about Tommy Martin, who had decided to pick his nose in the middle of 'Away in a Manger', wiping it on the towels that made up his costume. And young Derek, who decided it was OK to swing the baby lamb by its tail round and round his head in time to the music, nearly knocking Madeline over. Then – God forbid! – little Michael decided he needed the potty and began shouting, 'I need a wee wee.' Nancy turned to look at Dolly, who was silently mouthing, 'I took him. I took them all before we got here. I did. Honest.'

Nancy smiled and looked straight ahead as she began shepherding the excitable and noisy children from the chapel as quickly as humanly possible, with a look on her face that said to everyone, 'Leave me alone and do not ask.'

It was not known whether the nuns' heads were all bowed in prayer or whether they were simply trying to maintain their dignified silence, holding themselves together as much as humanly possible to ensure they did not laugh in church. Nancy was sure she saw the slight shaking of shoulders as she walked past.

'Could have been worse,' whispered Dolly.

'Dear God, how?' Nancy replied. 'Go on, then, Dolly. How?'

Dolly had no answer.

It was certainly going to be one of those days, Nancy thought. The parcels of donations for the children's Christmas stockings had still not arrived, and they had been promised that the nursery toys would be there later that afternoon. *Here we go again*, thought Nancy, hoping that the toys would be here sooner rather than later. There was still so much to do, and she did not like being behind with her plans, certainly not on Christmas Eve.

Nancy's shoulders sagged when she heard the screams coming from the dormitory where Dolly and some of the staff were helping the children change out of their costumes and back into their play clothes. Nancy hurried along to the dormitory to help, then made the decision to let them all put their outdoor clothes on and run about in the garden. 'Let them blow off steam,' she told Dolly. 'Make snowmen ... make snowballs ... anything,' she told the staff. 'Just take them outside so I can organize the Christmas stockings.'

Only ten minutes later, Nancy shouted in frustration as she heard the children clambering back up the nursery stairs. 'What now?'

'Have you looked outside, Nancy?' said Dolly as she bundled all the very wet children into the playroom to look out of the window.

'Well, I did ask how it could get any worse, didn't I?' said Nancy, as all the children gathered around her, jumping up and down excitedly.

The blizzard had come from nowhere. It wasn't the pretty falling snow that had been forecast – you couldn't even see the playground.

'We wanted to play in the snow,' some of the children were sobbing. 'You promised.'

'Oh, Lord,' said Nancy, worriedly. And she prayed for the hundredth time that day that the Christmas toys would arrive in time.

But it was not to be.

The whole of Newcastle-upon-Tyne came to a standstill that day. No cars or vehicles of any kind would be travelling to Nazareth House Orphanage that Christmas Eve, bringing the much-needed toys for the stockings.

Nancy could have cried. She helped calm the children as much as possible and told the staff to uncover the large sandpit and let the children play in the sand instead.

'Nancy . . .' Dolly began to say.

But Nancy was gone, hurrying down the corridor to her room to sit down for five minutes and think about what on earth she was going to do. Letting the children down on Christmas morning wasn't an option. It would take more than rag dolls this year – more than half of the children were boys.

Nancy sat on the edge of her bed and looked at the little holy pictures stuck into the corner of her mirror – one of the Madonna and Child, and another of Jesus surrounded by children. 'Don't look at me like that,' she said. 'A helping hand would be nice if You don't mind, thank You. Oh, dear Lord,' she said again, 'now I'm talking to myself.'

The knock on Nancy's door was Sister Mary Joseph, who had come to tell her that the donations would not be coming. The car bringing them couldn't get through. 'What are we to do, Nancy?' she said, clicking her rosary beads nervously.

Nancy was beginning to panic just a little, and Sister Mary Joseph's constant clicking of the beads was not helping her mood in the slightest. 'Well, He could do with giving us a hand,' Nancy said, pointing at the holy picture.

'Nancy Harmer, that's irreverent,' said a very shocked sister.

'And so is watching twenty-three little children wake up on Christmas morning without a present,' said Nancy in a very sad voice.

Sister Mary Joseph took Nancy's hand and, together, they sat quietly whilst they said a prayer to God to help them.

'Come on, then,' Sister Mary Joseph said to Nancy's holy pictures, 'get a move on. We need help.'

'Ooh, Sister Mary Joseph, how irreverent,' said Nancy, sarcastically.

They would have laughed, but this was no laughing matter. They had got no further in their thoughts or prayers when Dolly knocked on the door.

'Sorry, Nancy, but I was trying to tell you the sandpit is empty – there are no spades or anything. Do you know where they are? The children are still crying and wanting to play in the snow.'

Sister Mary Joseph and Dolly both jumped with fright when Nancy leapt up and screamed. 'That's it, Dolly, that's it! Oh, my goodness, *that is it!* I could hug you, Dolly Marshall.'

Dolly stepped forward for her hug but Nancy ran straight past her and was thundering down the passage and up the attic stairs with Sister Mary Joseph and Dolly close behind her.

'Help me,' she was saying as she grabbed boxes, throwing them to one side.

'What are we looking for, Nancy?' they asked.

'A big box!' she shouted back at them.

Dolly and Sister looked at each other. 'A big box,' they mouthed, silently. There were hundreds of big boxes all over this crammed and jam-packed attic.

'It came in October – a donation for the children – and I put it away.'

'A clue, Nancy?' asked Dolly, tentatively.

Nancy shouted, 'Here it is! Here, Dolly, Sister, help me with this box.'

They clambered about the attic and, together, lifted down the massive battered box which sat on top of a heap of other boxes of all shapes and sizes. Nancy's face was lit up, and Sister Mary Joseph and Dolly tried to imagine what wonders could possibly be inside this huge box. Neither dared speak.

Nancy was removing the tape. 'It came too late for summer,' she told them quietly, 'and I put it away.'

As the blizzard continued to rage outside, there was total silence inside the attic of Nazareth House as slowly, very slowly, Sister Mary Joseph, Dolly and Nancy lifted up the lid of the box.

Had the picture of Sister Mary Joseph and Dolly's expressions been captured for all time, it would very possibly have been a world best-seller. Neither moved or took a breath.

There, in the box at the top of the attic, were a hundred brightly coloured buckets and spades.

'There, now,' said Nancy, with a gleam in her eye. 'What do you think of that?'

Unfortunately, neither Sister Mary Joseph nor Dolly could think of a single word to say.

Sandcastles in the Snow

A very confused Sister and Dolly carried the big box clumsily down the attic stairs into the television room. Nancy was chatting about tinsel, glue, glitter and bows. It was a good ten minutes before she paused for breath and looked up at her dear friends, who were looking at her with a million questions written on their faces.

'What's the matter with you two? Cat got your tongues?'

'Buckets and spades?'

'Sandcastles and stuff?'

'Really, Nancy, buckets and spades – what are we to do?'

As the blizzard continued to rage outside the television-room window, Nancy walked slowly over to the wireless. The Cathedral Choir was beginning the Christmas Eve carol service as she closed the heavy curtains. It was then that she told Sister and Dolly exactly what they were going to do.

Dolly was to rummage in cupboards, drawers and boxes, gathering every bit of pretty ribbon, glitter and tinsel she could find, along with the contents of a large box of broken Christmas decorations that Nancy had found in the attic, which was absolutely perfect.

'Told you we would find a use for it,' Sister and Dolly said to Nancy, laughing and making fun of her.

'Well, I have been proved right, have I not?' she said, with a toss of her head.

'You have, indeed,' they agreed.

And long into the evening the three friends sat decorating the buckets and spades, making snow buckets for the children. The enchanted clock chimed midnight and Nancy, Sister Mary Joseph and Dolly finally crawled into bed, covered from head to foot in glitter, glue and bits of tinsel.

'Thank you,' Nancy whispered to her holy pictures before finally turning out the light.

The children woke early next morning to find their stockings full of oranges and sweets; they were so grateful for the small treasures in their Santa socks. Dolly had been sent out into the garden for the very special job to be carried out that day.

Nancy told the children they all had to get dressed very quickly, because it seemed there was a very special surprise. Twenty-three little boys and girls aged between two and five were helped on with their outdoor clothes, wellington boots, thick socks, coats, scarves and hats. And finally, after a lot of noise and confusion, they were all led to the playroom and sat on the floor.

'Well,' said Nancy to the children, 'where are your special presents? I really thought they might be in here.'

The children looked around them, as though their special Christmas presents would suddenly appear out of nowhere.

'You know, Nancy, I do believe I actually heard Santa Claus outside last night, in the garden,' Sister Mary Joseph said.

The children all began to speak at once. 'Can we look in the garden, Aunty Nancy?' they said.

'Well, I certainly think we should, don't you?'

A chorus of children's voices were shouting, 'Please, Aunty Nancy, can we go outside and look?'

'Come along, then,' Nancy said, shepherding the excited children down the nursery stairs to the garden.

Nancy threw open the big doors leading to the garden and the children ran into the playground.

There they were, standing in a row in the deep snow. The very special Christmas presents that Santa had seen fit to leave in the garden. Twenty-three wonderfully decorated snow buckets and spades.

That Christmas morning the snow finally held off and the children of Nazareth House Orphanage laughed as they played happily in the deep snow, making snow castles, their noses red, their fingers freezing, and with a sparkle in their eyes brighter than any on their buckets.

'Dear God, snow buckets indeed,' Nancy whispered, raising her eyes to heaven before turning and retracing her steps to the nursery dining room to prepare for the children's Christmas breakfast.

Upstairs, Mother Superior stood alone in the long corridor looking out of the window. The scene below her was one that brought a tear to her eye. The children were squealing with delight as they dug into the snow with their spades, then turned their buckets upside down and tapped on them. Mother smiled at their delight on discovering they had, indeed, managed to make snow castles.

There was so much to do today, and she should be making her way downstairs to the chapel, yet still she stood and watched. Nancy suddenly reappeared in the garden, looked up and waved at Mother before running off once more to play with the children. Mother reached for the cross at the end of her rosary beads, lifted it to her lips and gently kissed it before making her way to the chapel. There was nobody there yet and Mother walked down the aisle to stand before the crib, smiling.

'Thank you for Nancy, Lord,' she whispered. 'Our very own Christmas Angel.'

Queen of the May

Lillian Edwards had never been so excited in her entire life, all four and three-quarter years of it. When she woke on that Thursday morning in May she kept her eyes tightly squeezed shut, almost afraid it might be raining – which would ruin everything, of course. It had to be a nice sunny day. In church, last Sunday, she had been a very good girl. She had knelt quietly and prayed that it would be a lovely, warm, dry day. Every year, the May Procession took place in the grounds of Nazareth House. It started with the church service, then they all walked around the grounds singing hymns until they reached the grotto with the statue of Our Lady of Lourdes.

That was when it happened. The most important part of all in Lillian Edwards's mind.

The crowning of the May Queen.

Lillian's heart skipped a beat as she remembered the moment she knew that, this year, it would be her turn. This would be her third May Procession and, as usual, all the girls would be dressed in white dresses, with white veils, the most beautiful little white gloves and a garland for their hair. Except, of course, for her this year it would be a crown. There was always great excitement when Aunty Nancy went to the attic and brought down the big brown boxes containing all the dresses, veils and garlands. The 'big ones' in the nursery (as the over threes were called) were allowed to help Aunty Nancy and Dolly carefully remove all the paper and straighten everything out.

At the beginning of May the gardeners worked extremely hard in the run-up to this occasion, ensuring that the lawns were cut to perfection and free of any stray leaves. Cook began her preparations for the menu that would be served to Mother Superior. And, of course, there were all the cakes to be baked. It was always a very special occasion.

Lillian had never actually taken that much notice of the crown, or the crowning of the May Queen, to be honest. All she could ever think of whilst walking around the grounds was the celebration tea afterwards, which was always wonderful. Cook spent hours baking cakes with all sorts of wonderful toppings, and last year they had actually had ice cream and jelly. It had been a talking point for weeks. This year, all Lillian could think about was that moment when she would stand in front of the grotto and be crowned Queen of the May whilst all the children were singing 'Bring Flowers of the Rarest'. She sighed once more, hardly able to believe that the day had finally arrived.

Lillian need not have worried. It was a beautiful spring day and the flowers had been gathered by the gardeners early that morning and placed all the way round the statue. There were a few chairs to either side of the grotto, draped with flowers, for Mother Superior, the nuns and some of the staff.

Cook had been up since 5 a.m. The cakes were baked and decorated, the sandwiches prepared and the big urns all scrubbed, cleaned and ready to be filled.

The grounds of Nazareth House this year were especially beautiful and the rhododendron bushes all down the driveway were blooming in what Mother Superior said were the most incredible colours she had ever seen. There were hundreds of crocuses in the little wood behind the bushes, and the whole area looked totally magical. The trees stood tall and majestic as the little wood waited in all its resplendent glory for the children to walk through it, their voices raised in song. The sun shone on Our Lady of Lourdes, who stood serenely in the grotto with a delicate garland of flowers placed on her head.

There was a calmness in the parlour as the enchanted clock in the hallway ticked on, the hands slowly moving towards the time of 11 a.m. when the service would begin in the chapel.

Upstairs, in the nursery, it was not quite so calm. Twelve girls, aged between two and three years old, and ten boys were being dressed. Nancy, Dolly and Sister Mary Joseph had been up since six o'clock to give the children their breakfast and get them washed, and they were now trying to dress the excited youngsters. Two garlands were already damaged, and Sean was screaming because Andrew had stood on his tie and it was dirty. Maureen was crying because she couldn't find her garland, and little William was screaming his head off for no reason whatsoever that Nancy could see. 'Ignore the noise,' Nancy shouted. 'Just get these children dressed!'

Dolly began to sing to calm the children down but, for once, it didn't work.

The enchanted clock in the hallway continued to tick. It was now ten thirty.

It was only when all the girls were finally dressed and ready to be presented to the world – or, at least, to Mother Superior – that two of the children decided they needed the toilet, then three, then four. Panic once more ensued. Nancy excused herself, to at least run a comb through her hair, she said, as Sister Mary Joseph began to line the children up in the corridor in twos.

Lillian decided that, as she was Queen of the May, she must be a very big girl now and had been the least trouble of all the children. She had stood quietly at the bottom of her bed, dressing herself, and had stood ever so still when Dolly brushed her hair. There was no garland for Lillian, oh no, she would be waiting until she stood before Our Lady of Lourdes, when all the children would sing the traditional hymn, 'Bring Flowers of the Rarest', and Mother Superior would place the crown on her head.

As the clock ticked towards eleven Mother Superior and the nuns were in the chapel waiting for the children. Sister Mary sat upstairs at the organ, her fingers poised.

With only five minutes to spare, there was no longer any sign of the chaos of the morning, the chapel doors opened and, slowly and quietly, the children walked down the aisle to the sounds of 'Ave Maria'. Beautifully turned out and well behaved, as usual. *How does she do it?* the nuns thought.

Mother Superior smiled as the children took their places, then raised a questioning look to Sister Mary Joseph that said, 'Where are Nancy and Dolly?'

Sister Mary Joseph's answering look said, 'Believe me, you do not want to know.'

There was a quiet calm in the chapel, as befitting the occasion, whilst the children took their places and knelt on the benches with their heads bowed and their hands in the prayer position. Mother Superior was very proud. But where were Nancy and Dolly? Father was looking at Mother, waiting for her indication to start the proceedings. Once more Mother stole a look at Sister Mary Joseph, who gently shook her head. Mother nodded at Father and the service began.

The crowning of the May Queen would take place at eleven forty-five.

The enchanted clock continued to tick.

Outside the chapel doors, up the stairs to the nursery and along the corridor into the dormitories, the scene was not quite so peaceful. Nancy and Dolly had both completely lost their composure and at this moment were throwing everything around the room. They were under beds, tipping out boxes, pulling the sheets off the beds.

All to no avail. The Queen of the May crown was missing.

'Stop!' screamed Nancy to Dolly. 'This is ridiculous. Panic will get us nowhere. It has simply got to be here somewhere.'

'But where?'

'Dolly Marshall, if I knew that, we would not be in this state.'

'Maybe we should pray.'

Nancy dropped to her knees. 'Dear God, where is the crown?' she shouted up at the ceiling.

Dolly burst out laughing, then stopped. 'Oh, Nancy, what are we to do? It's just not here.'

'Run along quickly to the parlour, Dolly, and see what time it is now.'

Dolly began to walk out of the dormitory and jumped when Nancy shouted, 'Run, Dolly, run!'

There were rules about running in the corridors of Nazareth House. Dolly broke them and ran all the way there and back.

The hands on the hall clock pointed to eleven fifteen.

The chapel doors opened and the children silently, in their twos, walked out of the chapel and into the grounds, each one smiling with their hands in prayer, ready to sing. Lillian was at the front with Mother Superior. Nancy would have been so proud of them. Mother Superior looked around, hopefully, but there was absolutely no sign of Nancy or Dolly. The sound of children's voices raised in song as they walked round the grounds of Nazareth House on that warm, perfect sunny day in May could be heard on Sandyford Road. People stopped to listen, as always.

The little wood was ready, the crocuses swayed in the gentle breeze, the trees stood tall and the air carried the scent of the rhododendron bushes all around the grounds.

All was as it should be. Well, outside in the garden, any-way. Upstairs, Nancy and Dolly stood in the dormitory surrounded by total and utter chaos.

'It's gone, Nancy,' said Dolly, with tears in her eyes. 'We will never find it in time.'

'Maybe we should ask the enchanted clock to halt time,' said Nancy, with a weak smile.

It was then that the sun glinted and reflected off some-thing in the middle of the room. No, unfortunately, not the Queen of the May crown. It was the wire ring of young Alison's garland after she had pulled all the artificial flowers off.

Nancy ran forward and grabbed the wire ring, then Dolly's hand, shouting, 'Garden, now!' Together they ran down the nursery stairs towards the chapel. Dolly stopped to genuflect as she passed, and Nancy grabbed her hand. 'We will pray for forgiveness later,' she said. 'Now, run!'

The enchanted clock continued to tick. It was eleven thirty.

Nancy and Dolly burst through the doors and ran towards the little wood from where the children were just emerging on their way to the grotto of Our Lady of Lourdes.

Nancy grabbed Dolly and pulled her behind the rhododendron bush.

'It's all right,' whispered Dolly. 'We weren't seen.'

But they were seen. Mother Superior, unbeknown to Nancy, also had eyes in the back of her head.

Nancy, on her way downstairs, had stopped only momentarily to run up the attic stairs and grab the necessary tools.

Furiously, they worked, cutting off the beautiful scarlet flowers from the rhododendron bush, Nancy trimming and curling ribbon to hang from the flowers, with a few crocuses also wound in. They didn't speak, just sat in the wood with their fingers working as quickly as they could as the hall clock continued to tick.

It was now eleven forty-two and they were finished.

Nancy and Dolly crept out from behind the bushes and slowly walked forward, side by side, to take their place behind the children at the grotto. Fortunately, everyone was looking towards Our Lady of Lourdes. Except, that is, for Mother Superior, who looked at them, closed her eyes just in case she was hallucinating, then opened them again.

'Mother of God,' she whispered.

There they were, Nancy and Dolly, standing facing her and looking to all the world like they had both been dragged through a hedge backwards. Their hair looked as if it hadn't seen a comb in weeks, their knees were dirty – and was that a bit of twig sticking out of Dolly's cardigan? And, dear God, could someone please tell her why Nancy, instead of the little bouquet of flowers that had been especially made for her, was holding a pair of gardening scissors?

Mother Superior closed her eyes once more and then opened them again. No, it was actually real. Nancy smiled weakly. Sister Mary Joseph turned her head to look, and gasped.

Mother immediately began to sing, and all the children joined in. 'Bring flowers of the rarest . . .'

The crowning of the May Queen was about to take place and Lillian stepped forward. Very slowly, Dolly walked up and presented Mother with the crown of flowers.

Realization was beginning to dawn. This was not the usual crown, and Mother suspected Nancy and Dolly had once more saved the day. It was absolutely beautiful. Mother paused and looked up at Nancy, who just shrugged her shoulders and smiled. She nodded at Nancy and smiled back, mouthing the words, 'Well done.' Mother glanced at Our Lady of Lourdes. Probably just a trick of the light, but for a moment there she looked like she was smiling too.

Lillian Edwards was crowned Queen of the May with the most beautiful handmade crown of fresh flowers anyone had ever seen.

For the rest of her life, Lillian would never forget this day.

And neither, dear God, would Nancy.

The Very First Baby

The screams in the Mother and Baby home in Scotswood, Newcastle, would have drowned out any noise in the Nazareth House playroom on this sunny day in June 1955.

Molly was refusing to push, knowing with all her heart that, no matter how hard she had tried not to, she loved this child before it was even born. The last time, Molly had pushed with joy – hardly able to contain the excitement of holding her first child in her arms. She had been surrounded by gifts, words of encouragement and advice. The little cot had been painted in the prettiest shade of yellow Molly had ever seen and there had been several smiling and happy people around the cot when she placed her daughter gently down. There were no smiles this time. Divorced now, she had been told simply to 'get on with it' – she was shamed, disgraced – and Molly's heart was breaking. No matter what they told her, she was this child's mother. She had carried the child, felt it move for the first time, felt it grow, and now it was time to bring it into the world. A world which Molly and the child would not be sharing. *What was it about mothers and babies?* she thought. *Before we have even seen them, we love them. We love them before we even know them or hold them.* And Molly was trying with all her might to hold on to her child for just a few moments longer, knowing they would try to take it away from her immediately.

One final push, and, as the house mother took the child to wrap it in a blanket, Molly screamed, 'Give me my child! She's mine, let me hold her.' Silently, with no signs of sympathy or care, the child was handed over and Molly looked into her daughter's eyes. Her tears spilled over, gently landing on the child's cheeks. Molly stroked the tiny face and whispered, 'Susan. I will call you Susan. It means "courage", I am told, and it's possible you and I are going to need a lot of that, my darling.' Molly held the child close and cried tears nobody saw and sobs no one heard.

It was only a few days later that Molly's screams, as they took the child from her, would have been heard as far away as Nazareth House in Jesmond, if anyone had been listening.

Nobody was.

Molly's life had changed forever and, as she walked slowly towards the waiting car, tears pouring down her face, she felt an emptiness she would carry with her for the next fifty years.

Once she had settled into the back seat of the car, her parents asked her gently, 'Are you all right?'

Molly didn't answer; she simply couldn't speak. Clutching a small bag that held the nightdress that little Susan had been wearing, Molly lifted it up and breathed in the scent of her young baby, then closed her eyes and prayed like she had never prayed before. 'I already know she will be all right,' she told Him. 'They are taking her to live with her father. They promised me that. It's just that I need to see her again one day. Hold her in my arms and tell her I love her.' As Molly held tightly to the last memory she had of her tiny child, she stared out of the car window, feeling totally numb.

There was no way of knowing, that day in June, that three lives were to change completely. Life would never be the same for any of them. Molly was, indeed, right. A great deal of courage would be needed, and there would be challenges to be met, heartache and fear, battles to be fought. A great many tears would be cried – and yet, there would be so much love and joy in all their lives.

Molly had packed her case and hadn't turned round to take a final look at the room where she had spent precious days dressing, bathing, feeding and loving her daughter. The empty cot that stood in the corner was the saddest thing Molly had ever seen in her life. She had closed the door behind her and, making her way along the corridor back to the outside world, she had prayed, 'God, please, if you're listening, could I at least see her again one day?' Fortunately for Molly, once more, God was listening. But it would be another fifty years before Molly and Susan finally found each other again and Molly got to tell her daughter how very much she loved her.

Molly's promise had not been met. As she prayed, two women were already walking down the long driveway towards Nazareth House.

They were carrying a tiny child who was to change Nancy's life forever.

Today the children in the nursery were all running noisily around the playroom while the grass in the playground was being mowed by the gardener. They were noisy and fretful, and Nancy kept looking outside, hoping to see that the grass was done so they could go outside. A nursery full of children playing inside on a hot day was never a good idea. They needed to be running around, chasing each other, playing games, letting off steam. Once more, Nancy looked hopefully out of the playroom window and saw the gardener resting for a moment in the shade of the conker tree. There was a scream from the corner of the playroom and Nancy turned to the children with promises of playing games outside, but all to no avail.

'Maybe they would be allowed to play in the big ones' playground today, Nancy?' said Dolly, hopefully.

Nancy paused. 'Now that, Dolly, is an excellent idea. I will run down and ask Mother for permission.'

Divine timing, I believe it is called. Nancy hurried down the stairs into the parlour, which was usually silent except for the ticking of the enchanted clock. But today she paused halfway down, hearing voices at the door. Nancy crept down a little further and quietly sat on the step, looking through the stairwell. There were two ladies at the door with Mother Superior and Sister Angela, and one of them held something that looked like a bundle of blankets in her arms. She caught the words, 'Nobody wants the child, we can't look after it. The parents are not married.'

It, thought Nancy. *It*. Oh, dear God, it was a baby, and a tiny one at that. Nancy crept down a few more stairs until she reached the bottom, and paused. Her heart was beating so fast she could hardly breathe.

She heard the words, 'I am so sorry, my dear, we do not take babies at Nazareth House. Our children in the nursery are between two and five years old.'

Nancy, for the rest of her life, never knew what made her do it. She hurried across the parlour, her arms outstretched. 'I'll have the baby, Mother, I'll look after it.' Nancy looked at Mother Superior. 'Well,' she said, with determination, 'it is a child of God, after all.' Her heart was now hammering in her chest.

There was silence as the two women at the door waited.

Nancy stood still, afraid to move. At this moment something inside her was screaming that this was meant to be. Suddenly, the child stirred and Nancy felt her heart glow as she stepped forward, her arms still outstretched. Mother Superior took the child and placed it into Nancy's arms. The child's tiny fingers reached for Nancy's hand.

'It seems God's will has been done,' said Sister Angela.

'Or Nancy's,' said Mother Superior under her breath. *Honestly, I don't know who is Mother Superior here, myself or Nancy*, she thought, but with a slight smile on her face. 'Come along,' Mother said to the women, 'there is paper-work to be completed.'

All thoughts of the children upstairs and the slacking gardener were gone completely and time stood still for Nancy. Slowly – very, very slowly – she walked across the parlour, past the enchanted clock and towards the nursery stairs, to a life that was to change forever from that very moment.

Mother Superior filled out the necessary forms and wondered, not for the first time, why she even bothered to make decisions with Nancy around. Nancy would make her own mind up, and stick to it. Mother Superior was already very worried indeed. She had not failed to see the look in Nancy's eyes. But this child was not, and never would be, her own.

Nancy, however, had other ideas.

Rock-a-bye Baby

It was almost like carrying nothing, was Nancy's first thought. The child was as light as a feather, wrapped in only a fine cream blanket. Nancy looked up at the nursery stairs and thought, for the first time, how steep and slippery they looked. She made her way through the door downstairs instead, which took her into the junior department. Slowly, never taking her eyes off the child, Nancy carefully walked along the long corridor, past the kitchen, and made her way up the back stairs. Very carefully, one step at a time, she carried the child and made her way through the door, back into the nursery.

Dolly was at her side immediately. 'Well, what did she say, then?'

Nancy, unusually, simply stood there without saying a single thing.

'What did Mother Superior say about the children playing in the big playground? Did you even ask?' Dolly was looking extremely worn out, hot and harassed. 'Nancy, what on earth is the matter? Oh . . . what's that?'

Nancy said nothing, just continued to look at the child.

'Nancy, it's a baby.'

'Well, thank goodness you told me. You know, Dolly, I was wondering what it was.'

'It's a baby.'

'Yes, I think we have established that, Dolly.'

'What are you going to do with it, then?'

It was at this point that the child began to cry.

'Well, I think feeding her may be a good idea.'

Dolly came closer and looked at the child. 'Ooh, Nancy, how tiny she is. What's her name?'

'Oh,' said Nancy, 'I never thought to ask. I am sure Mother will let me know. Look, Dolly, the gardener has got to be finished by now. Take the children outside with Sister Mary Joseph, and let me figure out what to do here.'

Nancy watched Dolly and the children clamber down the parlour stairs, and silence fell upon the playroom once more. There was something she desperately wanted to do. It was ridiculous, maybe, but all the same, Nancy could not wait to be on her own. Nancy looked around the room until her eyes fell upon the little pink doll's cradle that had been donated for the children to play with. Next, she found a doll's blanket and made her way over to the cradle. Ever so gently, she placed the child in the cradle and sat on the floor beside her, rocking the cradle as she soothed the little child. *Soon*, she thought, *I will do it soon.*

Whilst Nancy was in the playroom, there was a flurry of activity as the news reached the junior and nursery departments. The caretaker had been hastily called for and the cot in the sick bay, handy for the younger children, had been taken apart to be reassembled in Nancy's room. 'The baby will wake the other children in the dormitory,' Mother Superior had told Sister Mary Joseph. 'If Nancy wants to be responsible for the child, it must stay in her own room for now.'

The women had fortunately brought a bag with a few baby clothes, nappies, bottles, a soother and some baby formula. It would do for now, thought Mother, who was nervously making her way to her private telephone to inform the religious order of the new arrival. How on earth was she going to explain this to her superiors? Yet, in her heart, she knew she had made the right decision — or, at least, Nancy had, she thought once more.

How could anyone not want the child?

One Day, Maybe

Unwanted. It was an injustice to all the people involved.

Little Susan was only days old and was loved very much by at least three people.

The father could not bring up the child on his own, but he would never forget her and would always be a part of her life. It was 1955, and fathers simply did not raise their own children. And there were Grandma and Grandad Robinson to be considered, who steadfastly refused to have shame brought to their own door.

'One day, Billy, it might be different,' his mother told him, 'but today is not *one day*.' Grandma Robinson showed nobody the emotions she felt inside on hearing the news that her first grandchild had been born. Without even having seen the child, she felt a warmth of love flood through her. 'A granddaughter,' she had whispered to herself, with tears in her eyes, hastily wiping the evidence away on the edge of her apron. It was no good being sentimental, she told herself, nobody must know about the child. Not yet, anyway. 'One day, Susan,' she whispered.

One day, maybe.

Billy would visit Susan; he would contact Nazareth House next week. He could take her for days out, they would have fun, and he would be safe in the knowledge that she would be well looked after. His sisters had told him about the lady who had taken his child in her arms, and Billy felt a stab of pain. He hadn't realized that, from the moment his daughter was born, he would love her – regardless of the circumstances.

'One day,' he said to himself. 'I will go back for her,' he promised himself.

One day, maybe.

Molly had returned home with an emptiness inside that numbed the pain. Her arms felt useless and empty. Sarah, her eldest child, who was three years old, was thrilled to see her mum come home. Molly gathered her child in her arms, easing the pain, and held on to her so tightly, refusing to let go. She carried young Sarah upstairs to their bedroom and locked her door. Sarah and Molly cuddled up together in the big armchair. And then Molly, once more, began to cry – heartrending sobs that could be heard throughout the house. Molly cried for so long that, over fifty years later, Sarah still remembered her mum's heartbreaking sobs.

Molly had been married when Sarah was born. It had all been so different. 'You will forget about this baby, and move on,' they told her. But Molly did not want to forget and, for the rest of her life, 27 June was a day of great sadness. As each year rolled by, Molly continued to pray that, one day, she would see her daughter again – not only to explain why, but to tell Susan that she loved her.

One day, maybe.

Nancy loved the child from the moment it was placed in her arms, somehow knowing that this child was different. This would be *her* child, and God had answered her prayers. He had never let her down before. You couldn't possibly love a child this much after a couple of hours and bear the pain of it being taken away. Nancy hoped beyond hope that what she had been told was true, and nobody wanted the child – except her, of course.

One day, the world would know that this was Nancy's child.

One day, maybe.

The Mirror

What was it the women had said?

Nobody wanted the child.

Well, they were wrong. Nancy wanted the child, and somehow she would fight to keep it. *There must be a way*, she thought to herself. *A few hours in my life and she already feels like my daughter.* Nancy rocked the doll's cradle back and forth, closed her eyes and prayed.

'Dear God, please let me keep her, please, please.'

The sleeping child held tightly on to Nancy's finger, confirming everything she felt. Nancy was waiting for the special moment she knew would be coming soon. As she sat in the playroom, rocking little Susan to sleep, there was major activity going on in her room. People were bustling in and out, laying out baby clothes on Nancy's bed, preparing bottles of milk. And the caretaker was hammering in the screws, putting together the baby's cot.

Dolly had been sent to gather blankets and a hot-water bottle. 'Really, Sister,' she said, questioningly, 'a hot-water bottle? It's ninety degrees in the shade out there!'

'Well, I don't know what to do,' the nun said, anxiously.

'Don't worry,' said Dolly, 'Nancy will know exactly what needs to be done.'

Eventually, the room was ready and the excitement inside Nancy was bubbling and ready to explode – although there was nothing on her face to show this. Just a sweet smile as she sat silently rocking the baby, humming Brahms' Lullaby.

It was nearly time, and Nancy could hardly wait.

Nancy cradled the tiny child in her arms and carried her out of the playroom, down the corridor to her room. People wanted to look at the baby and were oohing and aahing over her. A baby, indeed! There had never, ever been a baby in Nazareth House. Nancy tolerated it for about five minutes. Then, as the baby began to cry, she shooed everyone away. It was not quite the moment she was waiting for, not yet.

Mother Superior was standing at the door. 'Nancy . . .'

'Oh, please, not now, Mother. The child needs feeding, and I still have the children to see to.'

Mother's heart was breaking. She had known Nancy since she was nine years old and could read her like a book. There was nothing she could say to her right now, but they would have to talk later. Mother saw the holy picture on Nancy's dressing table and momentarily closed her eyes. 'God help me,' she prayed. 'I don't even know what to ask for. If this is Your doing, then please take care of Nancy. Don't let her be hurt. Please.' With a heavy heart, Mother Superior turned to leave.

'Oh, Mother,' called Nancy. 'What's her name?'

'Susan, her name is Susan.'

'Susan,' Nancy whispered as she picked up the bottle, sat on her bed and fed the child for the first time. It wasn't as if she didn't know what she was doing. Her very best friend, Tilly, had four children and it was with Tilly's family that she spent every day off. They had been friends from the very first moment they met, when they were both nineteen. Tilly had been a cook in the kitchen and was simply the most wonderful person Nancy had ever known. Nancy had, of course, held and rocked each one of Tilly's children. But this was different.

Susan had been fed and changed. It was time. Nancy took a deep breath, stood up and walked across the room to stand in front of the mirror on her large wardrobe. 'Oh,' she gasped, looking at herself. 'Look at me! This is my daughter,' she said to the mirror. 'Isn't she beautiful?'

It was at that moment that Susan opened her eyes and looked at Nancy. 'Hello, Mum,' the big blue eyes said.

No-nonsense Nancy was moved beyond words. 'Hello, darling,' she whispered. 'Just look at us.' For fifteen minutes Nancy stood in front of the mirror, unable to pull her eyes away. There had never been that redness in her cheeks before, and her eyes had never looked more blue. This was how it felt to be a mother, to hold a child in your arms, knowing that, without doubt, you would spend the rest of your life fighting their battles, supporting, loving and caring for them.

Nancy glanced at the holy picture of the Madonna and Child tucked into the corner of the dressing-table mirror. 'I have looked after, and loved, many children – and will continue to do so, I promise. But this one is mine.' Carefully, Nancy placed the child in her cot, putting her arms through the bars as Susan instinctively reached out to wrap her fingers around Nancy's thumb.

The Madonna and Child looked on as Nancy began to sing lullabies to the tiny child.

The holy picture of Jesus that was tucked into the opposite side of the mirror also looked on.

'Very well,' He said.

A Very Shiny Present

For the first few days Nancy almost held her breath every time she held Susan in her arms, wondering how long it would be before someone came to take her away. Her heart beat faster each time the tiny hand wrapped itself around her fingers and she would look at the holy pictures tucked into the corners of the mirror and whisper, 'Don't forget, You promised.' She knew every feature of the child's tiny face and, within days, instinctively knew all her little ways. 'Nobody would ever know she wasn't mine,' Nancy said to herself.

She had hardly slept last night, for today was going to be a very special day. One that every mother looked forward to. In just a few more hours, it would be time. When you had wondered and dreamed about something for so long, knowing in your heart the dream would never become a reality, then it was all the more incredible when it did.

It stood there in the corner of the room. Nancy lay in her bed, smiling as she looked at it. Absolutely perfect. She glanced at the clock on her bedside chest of drawers. It was still only 4 a.m.

The baby stirred and Nancy put her hands through the bars of the cot. 'Are you excited too?' she whispered. 'Not long now, I promise.'

Nancy and her daughter slept holding hands, something they would do for many more years to come.

Yesterday had been a busy day.

Nancy was getting the children ready for their lunch when she heard the commotion on the nursery stairs. 'What on earth is that noise?' she shouted.

Sister Mary Joseph burst through the nursery door and said, breathlessly, 'Oh, Nancy, it's a present.'

'A present?'

'Yes. Close your eyes now.'

Nancy folded her arms. 'For goodness' sake, Sister, don't be ridiculous!' But she was smiling.

'You must close your eyes for a present, Aunty Nancy,' said Joseph. 'Everyone knows that.'

'Yes, go on,' the children began to shout, gathering around Nancy and getting involved in all the excitement.

Nancy sighed. 'Very well.'

There was a bit more shuffling and whispering going on and Nancy was just about to open her eyes when her hands were guided to a handle of some kind. There was a sudden silence all around – even the children fell silent – and then, slowly, Nancy opened her eyes.

'Oh,' was all she could manage. Somehow, her throat seemed to have closed up altogether.

The sisters all began to talk at once.

'It's not perfect –'

'It's a bit dirty and scratched –'

'The hood clip has broken off, but I am sure it can be mended . . .'

Then they all fell silent as they looked at Nancy and waited.

'I think,' she said eventually, 'that it is the most beautiful present in the whole world.'

And then, suddenly, they all began to talk at once.

For the rest of the afternoon Nancy washed and polished the bodywork of the pram, over and over again, until she could almost see her face in it. Dolly had taken some old sheets and embroidered them with Susan's name, and Nancy had been speechless. She picked the little sheets and blankets up and began to prepare her most beautiful present for their first trip out together, tomorrow morning.

How kind everyone was being to her.

Mother Superior was also awake early and, once more, Nancy came to her mind. Billy, Susan's father, could return any time he liked to take the child back. Indeed, that was the plan. Billy couldn't possibly look after the child himself but, one day, when he got married, he would come back for his little girl. Nancy fervently prayed that day would never come, and that Billy would stay single forever. But it was extremely unlikely.

When the chapel bell rang out at 6 a.m. Mother Superior had been awake worrying for hours, but Nancy jumped up and lifted little Susan out of her cot. 'It's my day off and we have a big day ahead of us, my darling,' she said as she fussed about, washing and dressing the tiny child. Nancy chatted non-stop, telling Susan all about the nearby park and how the sun was bound to shine today of all days.

It was only seven o'clock and far too early, so Nancy went along to the kitchen and made herself a cup of tea, carried it back to her room and waited.

At eight the sun began to stream through Nancy's window and bounced off the shiny bodywork on the very special present, which stood in the corner of the room gleaming.

Nancy walked over and very gently laid Susan down in the most perfect pram anyone had ever seen. Black shiny bodywork, gleaming wheels that showed not a single bit of dirt from the pavements outside. 'A few dints, maybe,' said Nancy, 'but that gives it character.' Susan gurgled happily and kicked her legs. 'There you are, you see, isn't it wonderful, darling?' Nancy's smile stretched from ear to ear and lit up her face.

The little embroidered sheets were tucked in, and they were ready to go. Nancy took a deep breath and opened her door. Then, for the first time, she pushed her daughter in the beautiful shiny pram along the corridors of Nazareth House until she reached the nursery stairs. And paused . . .

'Oh, now, I never thought of this,' she said, but Sister Mary Joseph and Dolly came to help and together they half bounced, half carried the big pram down the stairs. Goodbyes were said, and Nancy was on her own at last as she made her way up the driveway, pushing her daughter in the pram and looking to all the world like a new mother.

Sister Mary Joseph and Dolly had hurried upstairs to the window and stood watching Nancy walk up the driveway. 'Look, Sister,' Dolly laughed, 'you can almost see Nancy smiling from the back of her head.'

Mother Superior was also looking out of the window downstairs, clicking her rosary beads and praying. Had she done the right thing by taking the child in? The consequences could be horrific, and Mother did not want to see Nancy hurt. She could only hope that this was all part of God's plan. Mother picked up the cross that hung at the end of her prayer beads and closed her eyes. 'Please, God, don't let her get hurt,' she prayed, for what felt like the hundredth time.

As Nancy had hoped, the sun shone all morning, and she walked for miles, pushing her daughter in the pram, smiling at other mothers and stopping to chat about their offspring. It was in nearby Heaton Park that Nancy heard the words she had always dreamed of. The young girl was sitting on the bench next to Nancy when she turned and smiled.

'How old is your daughter?' Only five small words.

Nancy played them over and over again in her head as she walked back home.

Honestly, what on earth was everyone worrying about? Nancy wondered.

Life was absolutely perfect – especially when you had a wonderful, shiny, gleaming pram.

God's Promise

How long could she possibly hope to keep her? Nancy wondered. If she had known being a mother would bring so much pain, would she have done it? That was the problem – she hadn't thought at all, it had just happened. There had been no way of knowing when she woke that morning, on the day Susan had arrived, to a day like any other that, in a single moment, later that day her whole world would change forever. Making her way down to the parlour, there was no way she could have known what she would see and hear. How many times in the last year had she had a reason to walk through that door into the parlour?

Nancy would never forget that day as long as she lived. The tiny child in the lady's arms, and hearing the word 'unwanted'. It was what had made it seem like God's will at the time – but now? Nancy no longer knew. Maybe it was a new challenge that had been sent to her. A new test. Up until now, Nancy had believed that everything that happened in life had a reason and was God's will. *How smug was I? Dealing out words to people, without actually knowing what it really felt like*, she thought, as hot tears rolled down her cheeks. *How many children have I loved?* she thought, knowing she had lost count long ago. Love was very different to how she thought it should be. Up to now, it had meant giving all she had to give, wiping away tears, understanding and feeling joy in her heart when a previously sad child smiled. So what had gone wrong? Now all she felt was pain. A heart-wrenching terror of what life would be like if she lost Susan. Love wasn't meant to be painful, surely? There was no way she could ever imagine waking up in the morning without being able to reach out and take her daughter's hand.

Daughter?

Mother Superior had warned her from day one. 'Nancy, she is not – and never will be – your child. You may, of course, look after her, as you wish, until we can find a home for her. But I beg you not to get too attached.'

It was too late. From the moment the child had been placed in her arms, Nancy had felt the bond immediately. For some reason, she knew this child was hers to keep. Why would she feel that, if it wasn't true? So why was this happening?

They were doctors, apparently, who were coming today and wanted to adopt the child that Nancy had held in her arms for the first six months of her life. There wasn't a thing Nancy didn't know about this little child. Nancy was her mother in every sense of the word. She had pleaded, but had been told it was out of their hands. Apparently, no matter how much she had given, was prepared to give – even if it meant laying down her life for her, as dramatic as that sounded – Nancy must prepare to hand the child over.

Nancy had run to the one place where she could get comfort and had knelt on the altar steps and bowed her head in prayer. 'If this is a test to help me better understand how a mother might feel on leaving her child here, forget it!' she shouted at the cross above her. 'I will do everything

I can to help them, anyway. I don't need this extra test! Haven't I always carried out Your will? I offered up my life as a nun and that was taken away from me, only to find the children needed me, and I accepted that was Your will. I prayed for a child of my own and You placed one in my arms. So dear God, what have I done to deserve this?'

The door of the chapel opened slowly but Nancy did not hear it. Mother Superior was at a loss to know what to say or what to do. She had warned Nancy, over and over again, not to get too attached and blamed herself entirely for allowing this to happen. The child should have been turned away from the door. Mother sighed, knowing she could never have done that either. Sometimes there were simply no answers. Mother listened to Nancy's angry words, then watched as she began to sob. She walked down the aisle to the altar and knelt beside Nancy. There were no words that she could think of to say to her, so she simply prayed to God to find a solution.

Mother Superior took Nancy's hand and, together, they walked to the side of the chapel and lit a candle. No words were spoken. What, after all, was there to say? Billy, Susan's father, would be here by now. Mother left Nancy in the chapel where she would find solace. If there was any to be found.

Mother Superior made her way to her room, where the papers had been prepared and Billy and the social workers were waiting for her.

'It has been explained to you?' they asked Billy.

'Indeed it has,' he answered curtly.

'You are unable to look after the child yourself,' they said.

'So I am told,' he replied angrily.

'There are a couple wanting to adopt, and the papers have been prepared.'

Mother Superior bowed her head, unable to look at any of the people in the room. For the first time in her entire life, Mother wanted to cry out, 'Please, don't take her!' But, of course, she would do nothing of the sort. It was not her place to do so. She looked up at Billy and their eyes locked. *There is a pleading in those eyes. And pain*, Billy thought. Suddenly, quite simply, Billy understood. There was a very slight smile at the corner of his mouth that Mother Superior did not miss, along with a flash of anger in those very dark eyes.

The social workers didn't even look at Billy as they shuffled the papers on Mother's desk. Eventually, still without looking at him, they spoke.

'You will do the best for your daughter and allow her to be adopted.'

'Is that right?'

'It is for the best.'

'So you say.'

'You are ready to sign the papers?'

'I will have to hand over any right to see my daughter, is that correct?'

'Naturally.'

'I will walk away from here without seeing her again or having any right as a father over how she is brought up?'

'It is all for the best, Mr Robinson.'

Billy watched as they began to rustle the papers and find a pen to hand to him. He had been called here today for this, he thought to himself. As always, nobody listened;

everyone thought they knew best. Well, nobody had ever told Billy Robinson what to do, or how to do it, and they weren't going to start now. He looked up, caught the pleading look in Mother Superior's eyes again, and smiled.

'Are you ready, Mr Robinson?' they said.

'Absolutely.'

Mother Superior's heart began to pound and she never took her eyes off Billy. The pain was unbearable.

They handed him the pen.

Billy took the pen, looked at Mother Superior and winked. Then he drew a line right through the adoption papers and walked out of the room.

As the social workers tutted, Mother Superior smiled sweetly at them and quietly left the room. Once the door was closed, she hurried out and caught Billy just as he was leaving. 'Thank you,' she said.

Billy waved, got into his car and drove away.

Mother thanked God that, for once, a child put up for adoption would not be leaving. She then hurried along the corridor, quickly dipped her fingers into the Holy Water outside the chapel and prayed for forgiveness.

She hurried up the nursery stairs into Nancy's room, lifted the child into her arms and gently carried her back down the stairs towards the chapel.

What a difficult day this had been, she thought to herself. Then, for the second time that day, she opened the chapel door and walked forward to place the child back into her mother's arms where, it seemed, she belonged.

God had promised, and God never broke His promises.

Bouquet of Onions

It was one of the most beautiful places in the world, and it was Susan's favourite place to sit amongst the trees and flowers. The wood stretched all the way down the left-hand side of the driveway and in the summer was covered in a blanket of flowers of many different colours. Beautiful bluebells, lilac crocuses and enormous rhododendron bushes displaying blooms of every shade of pink. When the breeze gently blew through the trees, the flowers would sway and the colours seemed to merge into one another, almost creating a rainbow-coloured carpet. It was the fact that the flowers seemed to simply grow wild, without being tended, that made it so magical to look at. Nature had taken over and shown what she could do entirely on her own.

It wasn't really a wood, of course, Susan knew that. It was an enchanted forest, and over on the other side of the drive was a small field of clovers where she had spent many hours searching for the four-leaf clover that would make all her dreams come true.

Nancy watched her young daughter from the window. As always, she smiled, and her heart beat a little faster. She had loved Susan from the moment the child had been placed in her arms. It didn't matter that she hadn't given birth to her, Susan was her whole world. So many nights Nancy would come to bed and lie down, looking at her daughter in the little bed next to her, and thank God over and over again for giving Susan to her. Then, in the next breath, she would plead with Him not to let her be taken away. Nancy would watch her young child sleeping for a while, then get out of bed, pick her up and take her into her own bed. Mother and daughter slept, as they did most nights, with their arms wrapped around each other.

Nancy knew exactly what Susan was thinking today, without being told – it was a mother thing – she just knew, and it broke her heart. She watched as Susan kept looking towards the top of the driveway and jumping each time she thought she heard a car. Billy, her father, hadn't been able to come in the last few weeks, and Susan looked forward to his visits so much. *For six years I have loved her more than I ever thought it was possible to love anyone. Her every feature, the sound of her voice, the way my heart races when I look at her and my heart swells with joy and pride just thinking of her. I spend every waking hour of the day loving her,* Nancy thought. *There is nothing I wouldn't do for her – and yet, is it enough?* Hot tears began to drip down Nancy's cheeks on to her apron. *Always sensible, well known not to make a fuss. No-nonsense Nancy, they call me, and look at the state I get myself into when I worry about her loving me. Does she love her father more than me?* she wondered. *Maybe there is something in being the biological parent, after all. Could it be that no matter how much I love her, she will never really be mine?*

Susan loved the story that Nancy had told her so many times of being brought to Nazareth House. From when she was a tiny baby, Nancy would whisper the story to the sleeping child, telling her how special she was and how God had wanted them to be together. Susan had grown up listening to it and knew the story off by heart. She had asked very few questions about her parentage, thought Nancy. Susan just seemed happy to accept that Nancy was her mother. And Billy was her father who came to see her as often as he could. Nancy's heart always froze, watching Susan leave for a day out with her father, always worrying that one day she would not want to come back.

Nancy wiped away her tears as she turned away from the window. It had been such a lovely morning. When the flowers had arrived earlier for the Easter Service on Sunday, Nancy had gone downstairs with Susan to take them to the chapel.

'Ooh, Nancy, who's been sending you a bouquet?' one of the staff shouted.

'Yes, very funny,' Nancy had replied, smiling and carrying the baskets of flowers down the corridor. 'And who, might I ask, would be sending me flowers?' she laughed.

Once inside the chapel, Nancy had told Susan what all the flowers were called and, together, they began to smell the scent of each one separately. They spent a wonderful couple of hours decorating the church, ready for the Easter Service, and Nancy was very pleased with herself at how it all looked.

'There, now,' she told Susan, 'what do you think?'

But Susan had a puzzled expression on her face. 'Mum, what's a bouquet?'

Nancy sat Susan on her knee. 'Well, it's when you pick lots of different-coloured and beautiful flowers, like the ones on the altar, and you bunch them all together and tie a ribbon around the stalks.'

Susan thought it sounded absolutely beautiful.

*

Nancy forgot all about flowers as she took a deep breath and began to prepare the dining room for the children's tea and called Dolly to go and bring Susan in from the wood. Nancy had no more time for reflecting that day. There was tea to be served and cleared up, bath time and a mountain of sewing to do before her head would hit the pillow that night. And Susan was up to something, Nancy was sure of it. Susan kept smiling at her, beaming from ear to ear every time she looked her way.

'And what are you grinning at?' Nancy had asked her.

But Susan wasn't telling. 'Nothing, Mum,' she said, and continued to smile.

Nancy would find out later, no doubt. But for now there still seemed to be a million and one things to do. Dolly offered to put Susan to bed, saying she would tell her a story and then settle the children if Nancy would get the sewing kits out.

At half past seven Nancy set out the sewing box on the big table and put the radio on. Dolly came in from the kitchen with a pot of tea and two cups and they settled down for an evening of mending.

'Susan is already asleep,' Dolly said, unable to stop herself smiling and grinning.

'Dear God, not another one,' said Nancy, laughing.

Together, they sat late into the night until the mending pile was almost done. Many cups of tea had been drunk and they had chatted endlessly, as they always did when sewing. Nancy yawned and Dolly stretched as they began to sort out the piles and put the sewing kits back into the baskets.

'Get yourself to bed, Dolly,' Nancy said. 'I will clear up the teacups,' and she kissed Dolly's cheek.

Dolly grinned again.

'No more,' said Nancy, laughing, 'for goodness' sake, go to bed. Honestly! What on earth is all this grinning about?'

Dolly pretended to go to bed but hid just inside the dining room, next to Nancy's room, and waited. It had been so hard to keep the surprise from Nancy all night, and Dolly was very excited. It had been Susan's idea but Dolly had helped.

It was after 11 p.m. and Nancy was tired as she switched the night lights on in the corridor and made her way quietly to her room, where Susan would be fast asleep. The moment Nancy opened the door the smell hit her. She stopped for a moment, stunned. 'What in all of God's creation is that?' she said as the smell nearly knocked her out. There on the table, in the glow of Susan's little red night light, was what was causing it.

Nancy walked slowly over. There was a little piece of paper with writing in red crayon: *To my mummy a bokay of flawes Love Susan*.

Nancy felt the catch in the back of her throat and hot tears filled her eyes as she picked it up. A warmth and joy that told her just how very much her daughter loved her made her gasp. No crocuses or bluebells, or even blooms from the rhododendron bush, but onion flowers which were growing wild in the wood had all been tied together with one of Susan's hair ribbons. The whole room stank of onions. Nancy stood totally still for a moment, then lifted the bouquet up and roared with laughter.

Dolly, who was listening very carefully, was not sure this was quite what she had expected to hear. And then suddenly the smell began to reach her. Doubting that all had actually gone to plan, Dolly slowly crept past Nancy's room and along the corridor to her bedroom.

Nancy opened the bedroom window slightly and placed the flowers in a cup with a little bit of water on the window sill. Then she went over to Susan, picked her up in her arms and took her into bed with her, and they snuggled up together.

Nancy lay there for a long time, smiling to herself. And in the pretty glow of Susan's little red night light, the last thing she saw before finally closing her eyes was the most beautiful onion bouquet in the whole world.

Just in Case

It had been a wonderful summer and there had been lots of long, hot and sunny days but winter was in full swing now. The flowers in the wood were long gone and the trees and grass were covered in a blanket of snow.

As evening fell, Nancy wondered if this day would ever end. Honestly, if it could go wrong today, it had gone wrong. At lunchtime the rope on the hatch that was used to pull up the meals from the kitchen to the nursery had snapped. It had taken all afternoon for it to be fixed and in the meantime they were all running up and down stairs with trays. 'I should weigh six stone wet through,' Nancy called out, after hurrying downstairs to the kitchen with the last tray, and Cook had burst out laughing.

The children seemed to be very argumentative today – and even after bath time, when they usually began to feel tired and quieten down, there had been tears and tantrums. The mangle had jammed, one of the sinks had overflowed and, as Nancy had mopped it up, one of the children had slipped in it, got soaked and dry pyjamas had been sent for. Somehow, Nancy had been behind all day. It was unusual for her to feel so thankful when all the children were eventually asleep in bed.

Dolly had hurried along to the small kitchenette, ready for a much-needed cup of tea, telling Nancy that the children had not liked the story she was telling them and had taken simply ages to settle.

'It's the run-up to Christmas,' Dolly said. 'I was telling the children tonight all about Santa, how he creeps into the dormitories and brings stockings full of goodies which he leaves at the end of each of their beds,' she said, her eyes shining. 'I told them how hard Santa works to make sure they have a lovely Christmas.' Dolly's face was flushed with excitement as she sat sipping her cup of tea, then she looked up to see Nancy standing with her arms folded, looking at her.

'Dolly Marshall, are you saying you sat telling the children about Santa Claus and then expected them to go to sleep? No wonder they took ages to settle. Anyway, I will be having a word with the big man on Christmas Eve and telling him if he had to look after these little ones all year round, wipe their tears, keep them clean, play with them, sing to them, wash and iron all their clothes, then he would know what hard work was, instead of swanning in here for one night like the big I AM.'

Dolly roared with laughter, and it took Nancy quite a while to calm her down. They made another pot of tea and carried it through to the big table in front of the window, in the television room. Dolly turned the dial up on the radio and sat down, smiling at Nancy.

Nancy laughed, 'Oh, well, it's been one of those days, but all is well now.' She picked up the bag of buttons, which burst at the bottom, and hundreds of buttons spilled out and bounced all over the table and the floor.

Nancy closed her eyes and pointed at Dolly. 'I can see you laughing, even with my eyes closed,' she said.

It was a good half an hour later that the last button was retrieved from under the piano which stood in the corner of the room and an old brown box was found in the attic for the buttons.

The sewing didn't get finished that night. But there was always so much darning and sewing to be done, there was never going to be an end to it, anyway, Nancy said. She retired to her room early that night and looked through her buttons. So many pretty colours. If clothes ever became too old to repair, Nancy would cut the buttons off and keep them. 'Just in case,' she would say every time she hid away something that she might find a use for later. 'Waste not, want not,' she would say, over and over.

Old clothes were ripped into strips to use on the girls with long hair. Their hair would be twisted and the rags tied round to make the most incredible ringlets. Nancy was very proud of how her girls were turned out. The rest of the clothes were kept for cleaning rags.

Nancy held some of the small buttons in her hand.

'Where on earth did you get them all from?' Dolly had asked. 'It looks like there are hundreds of them.'

'Well, I cut them off things, don't I?' Nancy had said. 'Just –'

Dolly had burst out laughing and interrupted her. 'Yes, I know, Nancy. Just in case.'

Nancy remembered the night the rags and buttons had been used to make rag dolls for the children. Nancy's button box had done her proud. For the rest of her life, she would never forget the children's faces when they woke up on Christmas morning to see a little rag doll resting on the bottom of each bed.

'And now it's nearly Christmas again,' she sighed, and finally turned out the light after what had seemed like an extremely long day.

On Christmas Eve this year the staff gathered around the Christmas tree. They had decided to open their little gifts early, as Christmas morning was chaotic once the children woke. A pot of tea was in the centre of the table, along-side the best cups and saucers. Cook had made supper for them all and had excelled herself this year. The cake and sandwiches looked absolutely wonderful. The staff gath-ered around, chatting and enjoying their treat very much indeed. The gifts were exchanged and there were choruses of 'thank you', 'oh, how wonderful' and 'just what I wanted'.

Then Nancy was handed one of her gifts, which was from a grateful parent.

'What is it?' Dolly said.

'Well, not having the gift of being able to look through wrapping paper, I just can't guess,' Nancy said, and every-one laughed. 'It's round,' she said, 'and very prettily wrapped.'

'Oh, for heaven's sake, get it open,' Dolly said.

Slowly, Nancy opened the parcel.

'Oh, how lovely!' everyone said. 'A tin of Quality Street.'

'Mmm,' said Sister Mary Joseph, 'I love Quality Street . . .'

The room became quiet when everyone realized Nancy was not speaking, just staring at the little tin of sweets.

'Something wrong?' asked Sister Mary Joseph.

'Don't you like them?' said Dolly.

Suddenly, everyone jumped when Nancy held the box up and said, 'Absolutely and totally perfect!' with a large grin on her face.

Everyone was a little confused. *Lovely sweets*, they were thinking. But this amount of excitement over a tin of Quality Street was a bit excessive.

Nancy stepped forward, ripped off the tape, pulled the lid off and tipped all the sweets on to the table. 'Help yourselves,' she called, hurrying out of the room with her tin.

'What do you think –?' began Dolly.

But Sister Mary Joseph interrupted. 'Who cares?' she said, diving into the sweets and helping herself excitedly.

Sister Mary Joseph's mouth was still full of sweets when Nancy returned. They all looked round to see her standing in the doorway, as pleased as Punch and very full of herself.

'Look!' she said to them all. 'Just what I wanted – the most wonderful present ever.' She walked forward, placed the tin on the table and removed the lid. 'Well, what do you think of that, then?'

Everyone gathered around and looked. Packed to the top of the Quality Street tin were hundreds of little buttons.

'There, now – the most lovely button box ever. And I will never lose my buttons again.'

Nancy never did lose a button again. And, to this day, nearly sixty years later, the little Quality Street tin sits in a cupboard, full of the prettiest little buttons.

Just in case.

Fluffy Mashed Potato and Red Sauce

'Nancy, it's going to be absolutely wonderful,' said Dolly for what, to Nancy, felt like the hundredth time that day. But in all honesty, Nancy was excited too. More kindness, she thought, and hoped that the people who had given the children this holiday would be repaid somehow. Did they have any idea how much this meant to the children and the staff? Nancy hoped so. It wasn't just the holiday itself, it was the planning and looking forward to it. Sometimes it was the anticipation of an event that was the most magical part of it all. Nancy had told the children all about the beaches and sand dunes and how they would be able to run along the beach and paddle in the sea. It had been a hot summer so far and Nancy hoped the weather would hold. Not that the children would care, she thought. Susan had talked about nothing else for weeks. *I need to remember next time*, Nancy thought to herself, *not to tell the children so early on*. And definitely not mention it to Dolly – she was more excited than the children.

Most of the children going on holiday to the seaside village of Seaton Sluice were the older ones from downstairs in the junior department, but a few of the older children from the nursery had also been invited. The large hostel on the coast had six dormitories – enough to house sixty children – and there was a large marquee in the grounds with wooden tables and chairs to be used as a dining area. Large urns and enormous pots had been provided in the kitchen area of the house, with a group of volunteers happy to help make this a wonderful holiday for the children.

Well, today was the day, and along the corridors there were what looked like hundreds of bags of children's clothes, plus other paraphernalia in the parlour, waiting to be packed on to the bus. There were four double-decker buses on the driveway, and the bags of clothes, food and goodness only knew what else were being carried on to the buses by the staff and helpers.

For the first time ever in the history of Nazareth House the noise in the nuns' parlour was deafening as the children could contain their excitement no longer at the thought of riding on a double-decker bus to the seaside. The children from the nursery were brought down last of all, carrying their buckets and spades. Dolly had a smile on her face from ear to ear as she skipped across the parlour.

Nancy looked on in horror. 'Buckets and spades, Dolly? You have got to be joking.'

'Oh, but Nancy, you said to bring them one each.'

'Yes, Dolly, *bring* – not carry. Do you have any idea what –?'

But Nancy's words fell on deaf ears, so loud was the noise. Already Martha's nose was bleeding because Joseph had smacked her in the face with his spade. And Billy thought it was fun to swing his bucket round his head, nearly knocking Alison out. Robert was screaming, Janet was crying, and the noise level rose. The excitement was simply all too much for them.

Nancy stood still and surveyed the scene as Mother Superior came forward and touched her shoulder. 'God bless you all,' she said.

Nancy glared at her and strode purposefully ahead towards the parlour door. 'Let battle commence!' she shouted as she stepped outside to board the double-decker bus waiting for her.

It was to be another hour before the bus was packed and the children were, in Nancy's words, in 'some semblance of order'. Nancy, who, a few hours earlier, had got herself ready for this holiday of a lifetime, looking all cool, calm and collected in her cotton dress and sandals, was now sweating profusely, her hair was flat with the heat, and she had more cuts and bruises than she had ever had in her life. 'Dear God,' she shouted to Dolly, 'if Sir Edmund Hillary had climbed to the top deck of a double-decker bus with fourteen kids carrying buckets and spades, he would have known what climbing was.'

There was suddenly a scream of excitement as the driver turned on his engine. Nancy and Dolly smiled at each other as Susan clutched her mum's hand in excitement. 'Oh, Mum, what an adventure!' she said, looking out of the window. The children clambered over each other to look back at the house and wave as the buses made their way up the driveway.

Nancy leaned across to young Martha, who was crying. 'What's wrong, love?' she said.

'Oh, Aunty Nancy,' said Martha, 'it's just too wonderful.'

*

All the way to Seaton Sluice the children sang songs. Nancy thought her young ones might fall asleep on the bus, but there was no chance of that. They knelt up or stood on the seats, looking out of the windows as the bus drove out of town and towards the coast. If Nancy heard 'Are we there yet?' and 'How long now?' and 'When can I paddle?' once, she heard it a thousand times during the fifty-minute journey. It was Dolly who screamed 'I can see the sea' first, and all the children stood up on the seats, some trying to swing on the poles, and watched as the coast came into view.

Susan jumped into her mum's arms. 'Oh, Mum, we're here,' she said. 'Isn't it simply wonderful?'

'It is, indeed,' said Nancy. Carried away by all the excitement, she shouted, 'Who wants to paddle in the sea, then?'

There were screams from all the children.

'Oh, Nancy,' said Dolly, 'the children will never forget this, will they?'

'Oh, Dolly, I do hope not,' Nancy replied. 'I do hope not.'

The descent from the bus was worse as the children were hot and overexcited and, as Nancy would have put it, 'up a height'. Eventually, though, the bags were unpacked and the children were shown to the dormitories with all the bunk beds – yet another added thrill. By the time they were all gathered in the main hall, Nancy's young ones were tired, and she was glad to hear that they would be going straight to the dining area for a drink and something to eat. Carrying some of the younger ones, Nancy and Dolly made their way to the marquee and sat the children down at the long wooden tables ready to have their tea. Nancy looked around her. There were at least ten people who she had never seen before, obviously volunteers, with massive pans full of food all prepared for the children. Once more, she was moved beyond words. Dinner was ready, they announced. Nancy suddenly realized she was absolutely starving. 'Wonderful,' she mouthed to Dolly.

One by one, the children queued up with their plates. 'Oh my goodness,' shouted Mary at the front of the queue, looking back to all the children, 'wait till you see!'

Nancy and Dolly couldn't wait to see. Images of sausages with onions, or chips and chops with lashings of gravy were whirling round their minds. There were four massive urns full of food. 'We're in for a treat,' Nancy said, turning round to Dolly who was licking her lips in anticipation.

Fluffy mashed potato in the first one.

'Mmm-mmm,' they said.

Fluffy mashed potato in the second one.

'OK, well, there are quite a few children to feed . . .'

Fluffy mashed potato in the third.

And the fourth.

'Oh my goodness,' squealed Josephine. 'Mashed potato and as much red sauce as you want.'

'Oh joy,' said Nancy, moving down the queue. Oh joy, oh joy, oh joy.

It was too late for the beach, Nancy told the disappointed children after tea.

'I promise, tomorrow we will all go to the beach and we will run across the sand and dip our toes in the sea. But only if you are all very good children and go to bed without a fuss.' She asked Dolly to tell them a story that would help them get off to sleep whilst she got all their clothes out for the morning.

Unfortunately, an overexcited Dolly, full of fluffy mashed potato and red sauce, told them tales of mermaids, dolphins and toys that came alive when children slept. Half an hour later, they were more excited than when Nancy had left them. It was a good hour before, finally, Nancy calmed them down and they fell asleep.

'Sorry, Nancy,' said Dolly, 'it's just . . . I haven't had a holiday before.'

Nancy took Dolly's hand and they walked outside and sat on a bench overlooking the sea. 'We will make this wonderful for them, you and me, pet,' she said.

'It's been wonderful already,' said Dolly, 'don't you think?'

'Wonderful,' said Nancy, looking at the setting sun and praying there was more than fluffy mashed potato and red sauce for tea tomorrow night.

Saturday morning dawned bright and sunny, and Nancy was up early waiting for the children to wake. Bathing costumes, buckets and spades were at the end of each bunk bed. It would be an early breakfast, and then Dolly could take the children down to the beach whilst Nancy cleared up. Nancy had it all organized in her mind. Whilst the children were having fun and paddling, Nancy would clear up the breakfast things, prepare a light lunch, and then they would explore the beach together.

The children all had their breakfast of porridge and toast in the marquee and then Nancy stayed behind, sending Dolly off with the nursery children to paddle. 'There are some lovely streams along the way for the children to paddle in,' someone called after her. Dolly waved and picked up Martha, who was refusing to walk, and in twos, hand in hand, singing their hearts out, they made their way along the road to explore the coast on their very first wonderful holiday together.

They hadn't gone far when one of the children shouted, 'Look, Dolly, over there! Can we play in the water?'

Dolly gathered all the children around her and, together, they made their way down some steps to the stream below. The children ran over to the water with their buckets and spades, squealing in delight. Dresses were tucked into knicker legs, the boys all had shorts on, and the children plodged, splashed and generally had the most incredible fun as the sun shone down on them. It was an extremely happy and noisy time.

It must have been at least two hours later that Dolly realized it was probably time to return to the hostel and began gathering them all together to walk back. Every single child, and Dolly herself, was soaked to the skin, and the water was dripping off their clothes. 'Oh, well,' as Nancy was known to say, 'if they come home clean, they haven't had a good time.'

'Come on, children,' Dolly shouted, 'let's skip all the way home and dry out in the sun.'

It was a glorious sight and people in cars passing them stopped to smile and wave at them as they skipped and danced along the country road, excited about their trip down to the beach that afternoon.

Nancy heard them coming back before she saw them. She smiled as she looked up through the kitchen window where she was washing up after a nice cup of tea. The smile slowly drained from her face when she saw the state of the fourteen bedraggled, filthy dirty children coming into view.

Sister Mary Joseph looked at Nancy. 'Where in heaven's name have they been?' she said. And, 'Oh, dear God, what is that smell?'

Before Dolly and the children even got near to the kitchen door, Nancy shouted, 'Stop right there!'

Dolly's face fell. 'Is there something wrong, Nancy?'

Sister Mary Joseph began to giggle, until she received a warning glance from Nancy, so she clamped her lips together and looked away.

Slowly, Nancy walked forwards, removed a handkerchief hanging out of Billy's pocket and dangled it under Dolly's nose.

'Oh, my goodness, that is disgusting,' Dolly said.

'Dolly, love,' said Nancy, quietly, 'where exactly did you take the children?'

'To the stream. Those helpers said there were lots of them along the coastline, and I found one.'

'And did this stream come from some sort of pipe in the wall?'

'Ooh, it was bigger than a pipe, Nancy, it was huge. And the water was pouring out – the children loved it.'

'Dorothy, darling.'

'Yes, Nancy.'

'That was not a stream.'

'Not a stream! What was it, then?'

'It was a sewer. For the last two hours, my pet, you and the children have been playing in a filthy, rotten, dirty, stinking sewer.'

Dolly paused, her mouth hanging open. 'You know,' she said, a puzzled expression on her face, 'I thought there was a bit of a funny smell.'

'A funny smell, Dolly, *a funny smell*?'

It was just too much.

Sister Mary Joseph roared with laughter, and was totally unable to control herself. Nancy looked at them all standing there, filthy dirty and stinking, and suddenly she too began to laugh. Then Dolly, and finally all the children, laughed too – not knowing why but just going along with the fun – until Nancy had to spoil it all by telling them that before they could go to the beach they would all have to strip off and get washed.

'Oh, my! Whatever will she do next?' Nancy said to Sister Mary Joseph as they all made their way to the beach that afternoon.

'It would be much less fun without her, though,' said Sister.

And Nancy had to agree.

They sat on the beach and watched Dolly running round the sand with the children. Then they joined them all, and it was an extremely happy group of children that ran in and out of the water, laughing at Sister Mary Joseph who was trying to jump over the waves, carried away in all the excitement.

As the sun continued to shine Nancy thought to herself that, as perfect moments go, this was certainly one of them. 'Yes, that's just about the ticket,' she said to herself. A perfect day.

Unless, dear God, there was more fluffy mashed potato for tea.

A Sprinkle of Holy Water

Sunday morning Nancy woke at five o'clock and crept quietly down to the kitchen for a cup of tea before the children began to wake. Although it was early, Nancy opened the kitchen door and reckoned it was going to be another lovely, warm day. The children wanted to go to the beach again, so Nancy and Sister were going to go to the early service in the small church only a five-minute walk away, then make up the sandwiches whilst Dolly took the children to the later Mass. There were a few helpers going along to that Mass too, so Dolly would have help if she needed it. Nancy put her feet up, knowing she could relax a bit longer, having organized everything before she went to bed last night.

At six Sister Mary Joseph came to join her for a cuppa, knowing that the children would be waking up any time now.

Nancy was right, it was a lovely day and the sun was shining as Nancy and Sister made their way along the road to the eight o'clock service, hurrying back afterwards to help Dolly get the children ready for the 10 a.m. Mass.

Just because it was a holiday, it didn't mean the children were not to be kitted out in their Sunday best, Nancy insisted. But usually this was done without all the excitement of being on holiday. 'Honestly,' said a hot and flustered Nancy, 'next week I'm sending them all to church in their bathing costumes.'

Eventually, when they were all dressed and ready, Dolly was sent on her way with directions to the church and assurances that she 'couldn't miss it'. Nancy called out that the helpers were just ahead of her, so there would be plenty of help with the children when they got there. But Dolly couldn't hear above the noise of the excitable children, who she hoped would calm down by the time they got to Mass. Once outside, the children did begin to calm down and walked, as usual, in twos, holding hands, with Dolly at the back keeping an eye on them.

Dolly hadn't actually taken much notice of what Nancy was saying this morning and began to wonder where the helpers – who were apparently just ahead of her – actually were. It was extremely hot today, considering it was still quite early, and Dolly was just beginning to panic a little, thinking they had been walking for what seemed like at least ten minutes, when the church finally came into view.

'Quickly, children,' she said, shepherding them all in, asking them to be very good, quiet children, and taking their places in the benches at the back.

What a strange little church, thought Dolly, not at all like any she was used to. But these little villages were bound to be quite different. Dolly looked at the hymn sheet. How strange, she thought, they even sang quite different hymns. It seemed like a long service but, fortunately, two of the children had fallen asleep, for which Dolly was hugely grateful. And thank goodness the others had been as good as gold. Just as well, seeing as those helpers that were supposed to be there hadn't bothered to turn up.

'Oh, well, Nancy will be pleased to know I managed all on my own,' Dolly smiled to herself.

Nancy and Sister were sitting outside in the garden area, waiting for the children, when the helpers coming back from Mass hurried over to them.

'Oh, dear God, what now?' said Nancy, getting up.

'Nancy,' they said, 'Dolly and the children didn't arrive. They didn't get there. Do you think there has been an accident of some sort?'

'I somehow think,' said Nancy, 'that we would have heard of anything happening to Dolly and fourteen children, don't you?' Yet still she was worried.

'What on earth can have happened to them?' said Sister Mary Joseph. 'Nancy, what are we going to do?'

Nobody needed do anything. For just at that moment a very happy Dolly, with the children dancing excitedly around her, appeared through the gate.

'Hello!' she called, then saw the look on everyone's faces and her shoulders sagged. 'Oh, what have I done now?' she said, with an exasperated look in her eyes. It didn't look like anyone was pleased at how well she had managed at all.

Nancy breathed a sigh of relief and smiled at her. 'Oh, Dolly, love. Where have you been?'

'I've been to church, with the children. I don't understand.'

'Now, Nancy,' said Sister Mary Joseph, smiling at Dolly, 'I am sure she has done her best. So, where have you been, Dolly?'

Nancy was extremely puzzled but smiled at Dolly. 'Don't worry, pet. Come on now, where exactly did you go?'

'Well, just where you told me to. But it was longer than five minutes, it was right near the end of the road, and I have to say it was the strangest service I've ever been to, Nancy. Even the hymns were strange.'

'Dolly, love.'

'Yes, Nancy.'

'What was it called?'

'Church of the –'

'Dolly,' Nancy interrupted. 'That was the Methodist Church, pet.' Nancy turned to Sister Mary Joseph. 'Well, that's wiped the smile off your face,' she said, trying hard not to laugh.

There in the garden, on the coast of Seaton Sluice, as Nancy, Dolly and the children looked on, Sister Mary Joseph fainted.

Two weeks later, the children and staff once more boarded the double-decker buses, chattering non-stop about their fabulous holiday at the beach. The sun had shone, more fluffy mashed potato and red sauce than any soul on God's earth should ever be asked to eat had been eaten, and a great time had been had by all.

Mother Superior stood outside the door at the bottom of the drive, waving and welcoming the children home. She had looked forward to the peace and quiet for months. And yet, after only a couple of days, she had started counting the hours till the children came home. She was listening to the children, who were all talking at the same time, telling of their wonderful adventures.

Nancy, laden with bags, was the last off the bus.

'How marvellous to have you back, Nancy,' Mother said. 'How was it?'

'Oh, you know, the usual,' said Nancy, with a smile. 'Dolly took the children paddling in a sewer and then took them all to the Methodist Church for Mass on Sunday.'

Sister Mary Joseph scurried away, head bent, pretending she knew nothing.

Nancy rushed off to get the children back into the nursery.

Mother Superior paused . . .

Then she hurried off to the chapel to see if there was any spare holy water to sprinkle over the children.

A Bag of Kindness

Sister Mary Joseph was very excited indeed. It wasn't often she got to leave the grounds of Nazareth House but today she was going on a bus with Sister Angela to Newcastle City Centre on an errand for Mother Superior. They had talked about it for days and Nancy had laughed at them, saying they were like excited children and beginning to border on silly. They had planned exactly what they would do whilst they were there. Firstly, there were all the shop windows to look at, which Nancy had told them were full of Christmas displays. Then there were all the shops selling the most wonderful, bright Christmas decorations. There was a choir singing at the top of Northumberland Street at ten o'clock and they both agreed that was definitely something they must not miss. Of course, neither one of them actually had any money to spend – except the money for the cards and handkerchiefs Mother Superior had sent them to buy for the staff. It didn't matter in the least. The excitement of just being there, seeing and experiencing it all, was enough.

All had been well until the weather forecasters threatened snow for the weekend. Sister Mary Joseph and Sister Angela had got themselves all worked up.

Nancy had shouted at them, 'Dear God in heaven, Sisters, pull yourselves together!' Then, looking at their sad faces, she had burst out laughing. 'Oh, don't worry, I will get the spade and shovel you out myself if I have to. Just for a little peace and quiet from you two,' she had said, smiling. 'Now, go away and stop worrying yourselves into a state.'

It had been late that Friday night when the sisters lay in bed, wondering about the delights of a Saturday morning in Newcastle as Christmas 1962 approached. They had knelt beside their beds for much longer than necessary that night, praying to God for a clear start to the day so there would be no cancelling their trip out.

It was only 5 a.m., long before it was a sensible time to get up, when Nancy heard scurrying about in the corridor. She jumped out of bed and called, 'Sister Mary Joseph, if that is you up already making a commotion and waking the children, you will have more than snow to worry about!'

Sister Mary Joseph smiled as she crept along to the small kitchen to make herself a cup of tea and count the hours until it was time to go.

Nancy looked at Susan, still fast asleep in the bed next to her, and smiled at the thought of the little presents hidden at the top of the wardrobe that would be wrapped up for Christmas morning. She bent over and kissed her sleeping daughter, then looked towards the window. Nancy slowly crept across the room, almost afraid to look. 'Please, God,' she whispered, then opened the curtains and sighed with relief. No snow. 'Thank you,' she whispered to her holy pictures. *I wish I could follow them*, Nancy thought, smiling. Honestly, she had never seen such excitement, even from the children. No doubt they would hear all about it for many days to come. She wondered once more at the magic of Christmas as she sat on the edge of Susan's bed. It was children that made it so magical, she thought. On Christmas Eve the children would sing and play out the Nativity scene. It never failed to bring a tear to her eye – and a joy that touched every single part of her. Poor Joseph, the statue now had goodness only knew how much tape and glue holding it together, but Nancy had refused to buy a new one. In her entire life she would never forget that Christmas Mass in December 1945. Their first Christmas together after the war, when they were all so happy and relieved to be home once more. Joseph and the three-legged donkey had never looked so wonderful, she remembered. It would be a sad day if they were ever replaced and so, every year, ever so carefully, they were wrapped up in layers and layers of packaging, boxed up and gently placed back in the attic of treasures.

It was five thirty in the morning now and Nancy knew the sisters would both be up. She wrapped her warm dressing gown around her and quietly made her way along the corridor. There was a light on in the kitchenette and, as Nancy opened the door, Sister Mary Joseph and Sister Angela paused, their cups of tea midway to their lips, and looked up guiltily at her. Nancy smiled at them. 'Well, seeing as the kettle is singing, I might as well join you,' she said. The three of them sat together, enjoying an early cuppa, and Nancy simply sat and watched and listened once more to the plans for their wonderful trip out.

The weather did, indeed, hold off from showering Newcastle with the heavy snow that had been forecast. Nancy and Mother Superior watched as the sisters made their way up the driveway, with as much dignity as they could muster without actually screaming with excitement and running all the way.

'Look at them,' Nancy said to Mother. 'You can see their smiles from the back of their habits.'

'I am wondering, you know,' Mother said, 'whether I should have sent you with them, Nancy.'

'Heavens, Mother, they are only going into Newcastle. How much trouble can they get into?'

Yet they both continued to watch until they could no longer see them. Maybe they should pray to God to keep them safe.

Nancy looked at Mother, her eyebrows raised. 'Maybe we should pray to God to keep them out of trouble,' she laughed.

As they stepped off the bus at the top of Northumberland Street their hearts were beating fast with excitement.

'Listen!' shouted Sister Mary Joseph. 'I can hear the choir.' She pushed Sister Angela forward. 'Hurry, now,' she said.

Sister Angela almost lost her footing and complained that she did not want to spend the day in the infirmary nursing a broken foot. The mayhem would have continued but the choir began to sing again, and they both grabbed each other's hands and began to walk forward as quickly as possible without losing every ounce of dignity they had. For just over half an hour they stood with smiles on their faces that would have cheered the saddest of people and sparkles in their eyes brighter than any Christmas decorations in any of the shops. They sang along, knowing all the words to the carols, and were disappointed when it was over.

Next was Fenwick's Department Store, and it was everything they had dreamed of. It is not known how many times the words 'Oh, look at that!' were said, but it was many. Their eyes were like saucers at the displays of decorations.

'It makes our paper chains look a bit pathetic,' said Sister Mary Joseph.

Sister Angela agreed, then immediately felt guilty, thinking how much fun the children got out of making them.

They looked at each other. 'We won't tell Nancy we said that,' they said quickly to each other and moved on through the shops to buy the cards and handkerchiefs they had been sent for. They looked longingly into the many cafés they passed and stared at the cake counter, their mouths watering.

The time simply flew by and it was three o'clock before they realized just how late it was. They must have walked for miles, and it was now getting dark. It had been the most incredible day ever. They had their little packages and had seen the decorations and heard the children sing. They had stood and looked into every shop window on Northumberland Street and wondered what on earth it must feel like to go in and buy the little goodies on display. Finally, they made their way down the street to the very last shop window before they would make their way back up to the bus stop.

Suddenly, they gasped and stood still. Never had they seen the like. Such a splendid display. They walked closer to get a good look.

'Oh, my,' said Sister Mary Joseph for about the hundredth time that day.

'Pears, oranges, apples, bananas and – oh, what are they?' said Sister Angela.

Neither of them had any idea at all.

The grocer's barrel had stood at the bottom of Northumberland Street for many years and every type of fruit was displayed. There the sisters stood, staring at the rows of fruit as though they had been turned to stone, as people made their way round them and hurried along.

Finally, Sister Mary Joseph found her voice. 'Can you imagine, Sister, having all that fruit?'

'Look, Sister, can you see the juicy pears?'

'I can . . . oh, I can.'

'Red, juicy apples.'

'Yes, Sister, imagine being able to buy some.'

They both licked their lips, then looked at each other and sighed. They continued to stand and stare, much to the amusement of the barrel owner. Nancy would have been mortified and told them to stop making a spectacle of themselves. But Nancy wasn't there, so for another few moments they continued to cause an obstruction on Northumberland Street.

The sisters looked at each other and smiled. 'Can you imagine?' they said, once more, before turning to go home after what had been the most wonderful day out ever.

It was after they had turned to leave that they heard someone calling them and they both jumped, almost afraid to turn round. The barrow owner was shouting for them to come back. They stood, rooted to the spot, not knowing what exactly he wanted, or what they should do.

'What did we do?' Sister Angela whispered, but Sister Mary Joseph had no idea. He was waving at them to come back and people were looking at them. Heads bent, with a very serene and dignified slow walk and with nervous smiles plastered on their faces, they slowly turned back towards the barrel owner.

With a wide grin on his face, he shouted, 'Come over here, Sisters, and open your bags!'

They looked at each other, then stepped forward and opened up their shopping bags, holding them out in front of them. They were unable to speak and stood completely still as the barrowman tipped a bowl of oranges into the bags, followed by pears, apples and bananas, and some of the fruit which neither one of them could name.

'There you are now, Sisters,' said the barrowman. 'Happy Christmas!' And he turned back to his long queue of customers.

For a moment the sisters didn't know what to say, they were so stunned. Eventually, they managed to mumble 'Thank you' and 'God bless' before beginning their journey back to the bus stop. The struggle began about halfway up the street when the weight of the bags became heavier and heavier, and by the time they reached the bus stop it was an effort to carry them.

By half past three Nancy and Mother began to worry just a little.

'The sisters should have been back long ago, Nancy, and it's dark now,' said Mother. Put all the lights on in the windows for them, and I will put the parlour lights on so they can see their way.'

It was a little after four when, finally, Nancy saw two shapes making their way down the drive. 'What in all that is holy?' she shouted.

Both Nancy and Mother Superior pressed their noses to the window. There the sisters both were, no longer able to cope with the weight of their bags, bent double, with their arms hanging by their sides and their noses almost to the ground.

'What on earth?' said Mother, stunned.

But Nancy was gone, hurrying down the nursery stairs and up the driveway to meet the sisters. There was much hustling and bustling to bring all the bags in. Sister Mary Joseph and Sister Angela collapsed into the nearest chairs in the parlour, rubbing their arms vigorously. Mother and Nancy peered into the bags and looked at each other, unable to believe what they saw. They turned to the sisters and looked at them questioningly.

Tea was sent for and the tale of the kind barrowman was told by both sisters at the same time, talking over each other, until Nancy called a halt and said firmly, as she would have told the children, 'Right, start again, please, one at a time.' When the full story had emerged, Nancy stood up and said, 'Well, there is only one thing for it,' and, together, they all carried the bags of fruit into the kitchen to be cut up and shared out amongst the children and staff. The sisters and Nancy would have their share later on, in the little kitchenette, when the children were in bed, she told them. 'And you can tell me all about your day then,' she smiled at them.

Nancy hurried upstairs to the cupboard in her room. She had been saving something for such an occasion.

Later that evening, after Susan was tucked up in bed, Nancy took the tin of Carnation milk down from the cupboard and made her way along the corridor for the very special treat of fruit and cream. The sisters were waiting for her and their excitement went up another level, if that was possible, when they realized that Nancy had Carnation milk to pour over their fruit. They began to eat, which was difficult with the grins on their faces.

Long into the evening Nancy and the sisters sat in the kitchenette and chatted about their most wonderful day as the first flakes of snow began to fall over Newcastle.

A barrow still stands at the bottom of Northumberland Street to this day. It will never be known who that kind man was who filled the sisters' bags with more fruit than they could carry.

And filled their hearts with a kindness that would never be forgotten.

The Most Special Ice-Cream Cornet in the World

To live in the north-east is to be surrounded by strength, courage, kindness and a sense of everyone pulling together. It seems to be that it is when we are most challenged that others come forward with helping hands to hold us up, feed us when we are hungry and shelter us when we are cold. There is a friendliness about the north-east that makes people smile and feel welcomed. In all walks of life, in every corner of the world, there are those who change the lives of others by their thoughtfulness. Small, random acts of kindness, they are called, and they bring joy to the hearts of many just when they least expect it. For some, those acts of kindness will never be forgotten.

The factories of the north-east gave many parties for the children of Nazareth House which, over fifty years later, are still remembered and bring a smile to the faces of the children who got to play party games, win prizes, meet Santa Claus and – most importantly – eat ice cream and jelly. It wasn't just the time and effort that went into these treats that made them so special but the anticipation too. The children would be counting down the days for weeks, talking about who would be there, what games they would play, and what Santa Claus would bring them. They were wonderful weeks.

In the run-up to Christmas the bell on the great oak door would be rung endlessly as people came to bring gifts for the children. Many of these families were struggling themselves, yet they never forgot the children of Nazareth House.

It does not have to be a big act of kindness, even the smallest can create memories that will stay in our hearts forever.

I look back now and still remember it, that day in the summer of 1963, over fifty years ago, and smile.

Nancy looked out of the playroom window and her shoulders sagged. 'Oh, dear God, not again,' she said, hopelessly.

The children, who had been looking at her hopefully, heard the noise and ran to gather around the window on tiptoe and look out into the garden. Torrential, no other word for it. Already there were pools of water in the garden and the pond looked like it was about to overflow.

The hottest summer ever, they had predicted. Well, hot it may be, but it had been raining now for three days solid, and all the children were getting fed up. There had been tears, silly arguments and tantrums all morning. On Monday, they had put on their wellington boots when it stopped raining and had run around the garden, splashing in the puddles, and great fun had been had by all. On Tuesday, when the grass was simply too wet, Nancy had told them the rain bouncing off the ground was like dancing soldiers and they had made up a song and marched all round the playroom and down the corridors. Today, even the dancing soldiers' song was not working.

They all stood looking out of the window, hoping and praying for the sun to shine. The buckets and spades for the long-awaited trip to the seaside were all lined up against the wall and Nancy looked at them longingly. It was extremely hot today, which made things even worse. 'If that was possible,' Nancy said to Dolly.

It was late afternoon when the skies darkened and Nancy closed the curtains and put the radio on, knowing what was to come.

That summer day in July, the thunder roared and the lightning flashed across the skies for over an hour as the rain lashed against the windows, continuing long into the night.

Nancy's first thought when she woke the next morning was how quiet it was. No noise at all. 'No rain!' she shouted out loud as she jumped out of bed, ran across the room and threw the curtains open. It was still early but the clouds had gone, the rain had stopped and today the sun would shine, Nancy just knew it. She hurriedly dressed and ran downstairs to the kitchen door.

'Come in!' Cook called and, on seeing Nancy, told her she was just in time for a nice cup of tea. Cook pretended to swoon when Nancy said no, thank you. 'Nancy Harmer,' she said, laughing, 'don't tell me you are refusing a cup of tea.'

'No time,' said Nancy. 'Oh, Cook, I have to get the children out of this house today. Please tell me you have plenty of bread.'

'Indeed I do,' Cook said, understanding perfectly.

For the next hour Nancy and Cook made what seemed like hundreds of sandwiches, which were packed in many bags also full of cake, biscuits and juice.

Sister Mary Joseph had also woken early and was thrilled the rain had stopped at last. She hurried along the corridor to tell Nancy and was completely shocked at finding Nancy's room empty. Something must be wrong, she thought. After looking in the dormitories and the kitchenette, she couldn't imagine for a moment where Nancy might be. Hurrying along the corridor, she bumped into Dolly and, together, they looked everywhere, unable to imagine what on earth could have made Nancy disappear that early in the morning. The children were awake and would need to be washed, then taken for their breakfast. It had never been known for Nancy not to be here. Dolly was looking very worried and Sister Mary Joseph was clicking her rosary beads rapidly together when Nancy came through the nursery door from downstairs, looking extremely pleased with herself. She saw them standing in the middle of the corridor with shocked looks on their faces.

'What on earth is the matter with you two? You look like you've seen a ghost.'

'We were so worried, Nancy. We didn't know where you were,' said Sister Mary Joseph.

'Oh, Nancy, your room was empty.'

Nancy looked at the pair of them. 'Unbelievable!' she said. 'I go downstairs for five minutes and you two get yourselves into a proper fluster. Where exactly did you think I had got to, then?'

'Well, you might have had to dash off somewhere,' said Sister Mary Joseph, beginning to look much calmer now.

'And leave my bed unmade?' said a shocked Nancy.

Dolly began to giggle.

'I have been in the kitchen making sandwiches,' Nancy told them, and held her hand up as they both began to speak at once. 'Let's go and get the children up and ready for breakfast, shall we? I will tell you what we are going to do – and, please, no word about it yet.'

Dolly was jumping up and down and was likely to be more excited than the children. Her eyes were shining and cheeks flushed. Nancy shook her head as she walked away. There was a lot to do, but she was smiling.

There was no need to tell the children. They had seen Dolly collecting all the buckets and spades and lining them up along the corridor beside their coats and shoes. From that moment on, pandemonium ensued, and the children became excitable and impossible to organize. The wrong shoes were on the wrong feet, young Martha was screaming because Michael had taken her bucket and spade, and Dolly narrowly missed getting her head knocked off by George who was swinging his bucket round above his head and screaming, 'We're going to the seaside!'

Nancy looked at Sister Mary Joseph whose habit had been half pulled off and burst out laughing. 'Heavens above!' she shouted above the noise. 'I bet the Normandy landings were easier to organize than this.'

It was over two hours later that, eventually, after many threats of 'We'll be going absolutely nowhere if you don't behave', the children were standing in twos, all dressed and ready with their bathing costumes and trunks on underneath their clothes. It was a noisy and happy group of children that made their way downstairs to gather the food bags that Cook had ready for them all.

'I think we may have a problem,' Nancy said as they looked at the bags.

The adults were already laden down with bags containing towels, hair brushes, combs, underwear, clean clothes, ribbons and flannels. To add to this there were also six bags of food standing outside the kitchen door. Dolly, Sister Mary Joseph and Nancy all looked at each other, their hands already full.

Mother had come along to see them off. 'Can I get you a wagon, Nancy?' Mother asked, smiling.

'Really, Mother,' said Nancy, 'if you can't say something sensible!' Nancy put the bags down, looking exasperated – and they weren't even on their way yet.

'If you can wait a few moments, Nancy, I will go and get some of the older children to come with you and help,' said Mother. 'I am sure they will be delighted to come on a day out.'

This was agreed by all to be a wonderful idea. Caroline, Margaret and Jane were, indeed, very excited to be included in the nursery trip to the seaside.

'Right, could we leave now,' said Nancy, 'before it's actually time to come back?'

Mother followed them out and stood watching them walk up the driveway. Happy, excited children. And Nancy at the helm, leading them all, weighed down by her special bag for all occasions.

Not for the first time, Mother wondered where on earth they would be without her.

The sun shone and the day got hotter and hotter. Getting fourteen excited children on the bus to Newcastle, then off the bus and on the train to Tynemouth, was not a job for the faint-hearted. Sister Mary Joseph, who had been very excited about her day out at the beach, was beginning to dream longingly of her small room in the nuns' quarters and a quiet cup of tea.

'I can see the sea!' Michael screamed at the top of his voice.

The children all scrambled to the train window, and the level of excitement and noise was raised another few notches. Nancy simply sat and smiled. She was enjoying herself very much indeed.

Nancy patted Sister Mary Joseph's hand. 'Don't worry, Sister, it gets easier. I promise.'

'I was just thinking that we will all be very much gasping for a cup of tea by the time we get home tonight, Nancy,' she said, with a weak smile on her face.

'Sister Mary Joseph,' exclaimed Nancy, 'do you not know me at all? No tea for a whole afternoon! What do you take me for? There is a flask of tea in my bag.'

Sister Mary Joseph sighed. Of course there was.

Nancy's special bag was the talk of all who knew her. It sat in the corner of her room for occasions such as this. Plasters, scissors, cream for stings, bites and rashes. Then there was sun cream, hair grips, spare bags to carry wet clothes – and everything else besides. Oh, and a torch! 'Well, you never know,' was all Nancy would say to anyone who dared to ask. Nancy had been asked for many things over the years, and the bag had never let her down.

It is to be wondered whether P. L. Travers wandered along the coast of Newcastle-upon-Tyne on holiday one year and, on seeing Nancy's special bag, caught the first bus back to London with the brilliant idea of Mary Poppins' magic bag. Certainly, in August of 1964, when

Mary Poppins became the film everyone was talking about, there were many people who knew Nancy and who said her bag put Mary Poppins to shame. Nancy would simply smile, with a smug look on her face, knowing she was prepared for every eventuality.

The train eventually pulled into Tynemouth station and Nancy was very glad of her three helpers, who were doing an amazing job of assisting the children off the train, as well as carrying the many bags of food. It was a happy crowd that tramped through the sand to find a space near the wall where Nancy could set up camp. The children were stripped down to their bathers and began to play in the sand as Nancy sent Dolly to hire deckchairs for each of them. Only fifteen minutes later, a happy Nancy and Sister Mary Joseph sat sipping their cups of tea on a day that was almost 90 degrees in the shade.

'Look, Aunty Nancy!' one of the children shouted. 'What is that?'

They all looked up.

A young child not far from them was eating an ice-cream cornet. The children looked on, drooling and wondering what it would be like to eat ice cream in a cornet.

'Stop staring,' Nancy told the children, more than once. But until the ice cream had been completely eaten the children still kept glancing at it and licking their lips. To distract them, Nancy began opening the bags and feeding them sandwiches which, after only a second in their hands, were covered in sand. Unfortunately, the juice in the bags was extremely warm by now and the children didn't like it at all. The children continued, that beautiful summer day, to stare longingly at anyone eating an ice cream.

Nancy looked in her purse but there simply wasn't enough money to buy them all an ice cream. She thought about buying just a few and making them share, but she knew it would probably cause more trouble than it was worth. Even so, after being cooped up in the house for three days, the children had a wonderful day and were very well behaved. Nancy watched them making sand-castles, digging tunnels and gathering shells; it was a wonderful day and she was very happy indeed. *You don't need money to be happy*, she thought to herself, trying hard to put out of her mind the picture of all the children with an ice-cream cornet in their hands. Nancy closed her eyes, determined to think of something else and be grateful for what they already had.

Sister Mary Joseph nudged Nancy, making her jump. 'Nancy, there is a man over there.'

'Oh, yes,' said Nancy, sarcastically, 'I do believe that's what they are called,' and went back to relaxing in her deckchair, watching the children play.

'Nancy, the man is looking at us. Oh, Nancy, he is walking towards us.'

Nancy sat up. 'For goodness' sake, Sister, get a grip of yourself.' She followed Sister Mary Joseph's stare and looked towards the man who was, indeed, walking towards them.

'He has a suit on, in this weather,' Sister said.

'Ooh, he must be dangerous, then,' said Nancy, laughing.

The man called to his young daughter to take his hand, and continued to walk towards Nancy and Sister Mary Joseph. Nancy had to tell the nun to close her mouth and behave. The young child was the one they had watched eating an ice-cream cornet earlier in the day.

'Hello,' he said, smiling.

'Hello,' said Nancy. 'And who is this young lady?' she said to the child.

'This is my daughter, Geraldine, and she tells me the children like ice cream.'

Was he about to complain about the children staring?

Nancy opened her mouth but was not sure exactly what this was all about, or what to say.

The man stepped forward and pushed a ten-shilling note into Nancy's hand. 'No day at the beach is complete without an ice cream,' was all he said, then turned and left.

Nancy and Sister Mary Joseph sat like sand statues, unable to move, with their mouths hanging open. They sat silently until Sister Mary Joseph leaned towards Nancy and whispered, 'Can I feel it? Is it real? A whole ten shillings . . .' and she took it from Nancy's hand and ran her fingers over it.

Nancy suddenly found her voice and said, 'Could we please spend it before you rub the print off, Sister?' She called Dolly over, waving the ten-shilling note in her hand, and told her to go and buy an ice cream for everyone.

Dolly stood staring at the note.

'Yes, all right,' said Nancy. 'Sister Joseph and I have already done the gawping-like-idiots bit. Go on, now! Run over there and get ice creams for everyone.'

The children were gathered together for the big surprise. The ten-shilling note bought every single one of the children, the helpers and, of course, Sister Mary Joseph, Dolly and Nancy a delicious ice-cream cornet. There was hardly a sound as the children stared with big round eyes, their hands outstretched for the most wonderful ice-cream cornet they would ever eat.

It was the perfect end to a perfect day. One they would never forget.

Somewhere in the world today, I hope and pray that the man's kindness was somehow repaid. He made that day one of the happiest days of our lives. I was one of those children and, over fifty years later, I can still remember vividly the thrill and the taste of the most special ice-cream cornet in the world.

The Softest, Red Christmas
Dressing Gown

Dolly was sitting quietly in her room next to the children's dormitory. She was cold and seemed unable to get warm somehow. She wrapped a blanket around her and wondered what it would be like to own the big, soft, red dressing gown she and Nancy had seen advertised on the television last week. 'Oh, goodness,' she had told Nancy, 'it must be like walking around in a blanket. Imagine.' It was late and she should have been in bed hours ago, but she knew she wouldn't be able to sleep. She looked out of the window and her eyes fell upon the big conker tree and she felt a catch in her throat. If only somebody could tell her what to do. Nazareth House was her home where she had been secure, loved and needed. Happy – that was the word, she thought. *I am happy. In fact, I have never been happier.* Dolly switched on her little bedside lamp and picked the letter up once more. She had read the letter, over and over again, almost as if, somehow, the words might change. It was an opportunity that would change her life. Unfortunately, Dolly had no idea whether she actually wanted an opportunity – or to change her life at all.

Opportunities like this didn't come every day, the letter said. And after all, they were family. Dolly put the letter down again and whispered to herself, 'Family.'

Nancy had taught her that 'family' could also be those who stood by you, loved you, supported you, and who would be there by your side, sharing all those moments of joy, and there to redouble your strength in times of hardship and sadness. No mother could love her daughter more than Nancy did. 'You do not have to give birth to be a mother,' she had told Dolly. The bond between Nancy and Susan was as strong and powerful as the bond between any mother or daughter could be. *One day, that will be me*, thought Dolly. *I will be a mother and hold a child in my arms, and I will return and Nancy will make such a fuss of me*, she thought, smiling. Suddenly, Dolly realized that to return she would first have to leave.

The letter was offering her the opportunity of a lifetime as a dressmaker in her Aunty Lillian's business in Birmingham. Dolly was very proud of the sewing skills she had learned from Nancy and Barbara in the sewing room and, for years, had always sent little gifts she had made to her family in Birmingham. Lillian was doing very well indeed, they said, but had three young children and was struggling to manage. Dolly would help out with the children and take on some of the dressmaking. Grandma Brown was offering Dorothy a room of her own in the converted attic. This, they said, would be her very own living quarters with a bed, a small kitchen area and furniture. There would be no rent to pay and only a small donation towards the bills. You are family, after all, the letter said, and you would be great company for Grandma Brown.

Birmingham, thought Dolly. *Oh, my!* It was almost like the other side of the world and so far away from everything she knew and the people she loved. Dolly's world had been a small one so far but she loved every single bit of it.

The words of the letter had gone round and round in Dolly's mind for days now, and she had no idea what to do. Dolly had never made decisions for herself, she had never needed to. *Whatever am I going to do?* she thought once more.

Times were changing, the letter said, and Dolly should take the chance to move on with her life. Come to Birmingham, it said, the family will look after you and help give you a new start. Aunt Sylvia also lived close by and had told the children all about Aunty Dolly and Nancy. It was Dolly's gifts that the children looked forward to most each Christmas. They can't wait to meet you, the letter said.

Christmas, thought Dolly, she could not possibly go before Christmas. There was a present under the Christmas tree for Dolly from Nancy. It was big and squashy, and any time nobody was looking Dolly would have another feel of it. Nancy had caught her, the last time, and threatened to remove it if she did not leave it alone. Nancy and Dolly had been planning Christmas for weeks and the thought of not being there was too painful to consider, even for a moment.

Dolly had read the letter so many times now, she knew it by heart. One minute it excited her, and yet the next minute she was absolutely terrified of leaving behind everything she knew. 'Oh, dear God, what am I to do?'

she said, as she turned off her bedside lamp and continued to sit quietly, looking out of her bedroom window. To Dolly this had never been Nazareth House Orphanage – quite simply, it was home. Dolly sighed. She needed a cup of tea. Nobody could be expected to make decisions without a cup of tea, Nancy had told her once, laughing. She quietly made her way down the long corridor to the kitchenette. There was nobody about and Dolly made herself a cup of tea. On her way back, she paused at the television-room door and went in. Nobody would know she was there. Dolly tiptoed to the corner of the room and switched on the Christmas-tree lights and sat down on a cushion with her cup of tea. 'Oh, goodness me, what am I to do?' she asked the angel on the top of the tree.

Nancy had been watching her for days. She knew Dolly inside out, as though she was her own child. Nancy knew that a mother's instinct was always right and, whether Dolly was her daughter or not, Nancy had loved Dolly for so many years now, had watched her grow and, without a shadow of a doubt, knew there was something wrong. Dolly still laughed, but there was no sparkle. And sometimes when Nancy spoke to her, she was in a world of her own where Nancy could not reach her. Dolly would tell her in her own time, Nancy thought, but this had gone on for weeks now and still Dolly had said nothing.

Usually, Dolly and Nancy would sew together, but tonight Dolly had said she had a bit of a headache and would Nancy mind if she had an early night? So Nancy had sat and sewed alone until, realizing she was making a complete mess of everything, she had put her sewing and button box away.

Nancy now walked up the long corridor past the dormitories where the children slept and stood outside Dolly's room, but it was in darkness. 'Well, of course it is,' said Nancy to herself, 'look at the time.' Nancy's heart beat a little faster. Was Dolly ill? Had she done something wrong and was frightened to tell anyone what it was? 'I won't have it any more,' murmured Nancy. 'Poor lamb, I will talk to her tomorrow. Whatever it is, I will drag it out of her, and we will face it together. Yes, that will be the right thing.' Nancy paused, hearing something, but it was just one of the children stirring. She glanced into the dormitory, tucked the young child back in and kissed her goodnight before making her way back down the long corridor.

'What in heaven's name?' she said, seeing the dancing lights of the Christmas tree throwing their warm glow into the dark corridor. 'I switched them off. I did, surely?' she said to herself, hurrying along to the television room, towards the light.

And that was where she found her.

Nancy stopped still, and thought her heart would break at the sight of young Dolly sitting on the floor under the Christmas tree, wrapped in a blanket and sipping a cup of tea. Dolly looked up as Nancy walked towards her, then sat down beside her and put her arms around her shoulders. Dolly, Nancy knew, was going to cry – and that would never do. This had to be sorted, here and now. 'You know,' whispered Nancy, 'we must look absolutely ridiculous, sitting here on the floor in what seems like the middle of the night.'

There was a pause . . . and then Dolly began to giggle.

'There, now,' said Nancy, patting her hand, 'let's get down to business. Come along, now, no more nonsense. Tell me.'

Dolly reached into her pyjama pocket and handed the now crumpled letter to Nancy. As Dolly continued to focus on the angel and the blinking of the fairy lights, Nancy began to read. They sat there in silence, Nancy's face giving nothing away, as the angel at the top of the tree looked on. Dolly was not ill, after all, that was all that mattered. Nancy read on, her heart beginning to feel cold at the thought of losing Dolly. At the same time, Dolly's heart began to warm, knowing Nancy would know what to do. Silently, she waited. Carefully, Nancy folded the letter up and gave it to Dolly, with a smile on her face that showed none of the emotions she actually felt. Dolly shivered, and Nancy put the letter down and reached under the tree for the big, soft parcel. 'Now is the perfect time,' she said, ignoring the letter and its contents altogether for the moment. 'Happy Christmas, Dolly.'

Dolly tore open the wrapping paper and gasped out loud as the beautiful, big, soft, red, fluffy dressing gown fell out of the wrapping paper.

'Well, Dolly Marshall, I do believe you're speechless,' said Nancy, laughing. 'Come on, then, put it on.'

'Oh, Nancy, it's perfect,' said Dolly, now dancing around the room, 'and so warm. It's everything the advert said it would be.'

'Well, I'm freezing,' said Nancy, 'but then, some of us haven't had a nice warm cup of tea. Come on, let's put the kettle back on and sort everything out.'

Ten minutes later, curled up on the sofa with a nice hot cuppa, Nancy turned to Dolly and said, 'Right, this is what we are going to do . . .' and long into the night, they talked under the twinkling lights of the Christmas tree.

'This is my home,' said Dolly.

'And always will be,' said Nancy. 'Do you imagine, if this doesn't work out, that you would not be welcomed back with open arms? Of course you would be. As you said, this is your home. But imagine, darling, what new adventures await you, if you take the chance!'

'Birmingham, though,' said Dolly.

'Well, it isn't exactly the other side of the world, now, is it, pet?' Nancy said, laughing, her expression not showing in the slightest how far away Birmingham actually felt. 'You know, I do believe,' she said, rubbing Dolly's hands to cover any emotion she might be feeling, 'I do believe there is a night bus that goes from Gallowgate Bus Station to Birmingham and brings you back the next night. Think of that! I could come and visit you. We could see the sights together.'

The colour was returning to Dolly's cheeks and the sparkle in her eyes was back. 'Oh, Nancy, do you really think so?' she said.

'Why not reply to the letter and see if you can arrange a little holiday there for a couple of days? See how you feel, and then you can come home and decide about it all. Now, then, what do you think?'

Dolly threw her arms around Nancy's shoulders. 'Oh, I will,' she said. 'I will do it first thing tomorrow morning.'

'I do believe it is morning,' said Nancy as she heard the church bells ringing. 'We have been up all night.'

Dolly began to gather the cups from the many cuppas they had drunk during the night, when Nancy stopped her. 'Go to bed now, Dolly, and grab a couple of hours. Hurry along, now, I will be fine.'

Nancy washed up the cups from their all-night tea-drinking session and returned to her room, where Susan was fast asleep. Nancy sank down on to her bed and watched her daughter sleep. What was it about love? she thought. What was love, after all? It was the fear of loss. When you love someone, all you ever want is to have them close to you always, and to bask in the joy that it brings you. It was fortunate that little Susan was asleep and did not see the tears that poured down Nancy's face as she began to prepare herself for a life without her little Dilly Dolly Daydream, who was about to step out into a different world where Nancy would not be there to protect or take care of her. 'Mark my words,' she said to her holy pictures, 'they had better take good care of her, or they will have me to answer to.' Susan's night light shone on the holy pictures stuck in the corners of the mirror. Nancy straightened up. 'You listen to me,' she said, 'she is a good one, she is. So You'd better keep an eye on her, I mean it.'

Nancy closed her eyes and saw Dolly that very first day – the angry young child with leaves in her hair – then she curled up, fully clothed, on her bed and prayed with all her heart that God would take care of her little Dolly.

Dolly changed her mind every single day and walked around in a daze. Until, finally, Nancy took her to one side one evening, when the children had gone to bed.

'What is it, my darling?' Nancy said. 'What is it that is holding you back?'

'Leaving you,' Dolly said, and burst into tears as Nancy held her in her arms.

The pain in Nancy's throat was unbearable as she forced the tears back. It was strength Dolly needed now, not tears. 'Right,' said Nancy, 'this is what we are going to do. We will go together, and I will stay with you in your room for the first few days until you get settled.'

It wasn't altogether an unselfish act on Nancy's part. The thought of watching Dolly walk away up that driveway to a new life on her own was something she could not bear to even think of. But, after all, it was the right thing to do for Dolly. It was a new adventure and a life full of opportunities that she would never get if she stayed within the walls of Nazareth House.

That night, Nancy and Dolly planned their trip away together with promises of visiting and holidays together, both here at Nazareth House and in Birmingham. Nancy would be introduced to Dolly's family, and everything would work out perfectly. 'So you see,' said Nancy, 'there is actually nothing to be afraid of and everything to look forward to.'

The next few weeks passed in a blur of excitement as all the nuns prepared for Dolly's departure, giving her more gifts than she could ever possibly imagine being able to carry on the night bus. Nancy and Susan would be travelling with her, and there were promises to keep her room free in case she changed her mind. 'You will, of course, come here for holidays,' said Mother Superior, and Dolly was thrilled to know that her home would still be waiting for her if she needed it.

On a sunny yet cold morning in February, Nancy, Susan and Dolly made their way up the driveway, laden down with suitcases full of cards made by the children, little embroidered handkerchiefs that the children had spent hours making in the sewing room, and the many gifts from the staff.

Sister Mary Joseph and Mother Superior stood at the window in the nursery and watched them walk up the driveway. Dolly stopped only once to glance back and Sister Mary Joseph wept unashamedly, thinking that life in Nazareth House would never be quite the same again.

Mother Superior led Sister Mary Joseph down to the chapel where they prayed for Dolly and Nancy's safe journey. Over the years, Mother had watched so many people walk down that driveway to join them, and then leave again. She had seen so much pain and sorrow, and yet so much joy and courage. They had been blessed to have Dolly in their lives and she, for one, was grateful for her. Dolly had brought love, laughter and such an enormous sense of fun to Nazareth House.

'The children will never forget her. Nancy will never, ever forget her. And, dear God, neither will I,' whispered Mother Superior. Dolly had brought not only a heart full of love but also a great kindness and warmth. Mother was quite sure there would never again be as much laughter. How many scrapes had she got herself and the children into? And nobody could ever be cross. Dolly would be remembered for many years to come by all of them.

Mother closed her eyes and saw in her mind that last Christmas Day. The noise of all the excited children had reached new levels by two o'clock They had been up since five, had opened presents, eaten more sweets than Nancy thought reasonable, and were now tired and fractious. Above all the noise Mother Superior had heard Nancy's voice, and burst out laughing.

'Dolly Marshall, it's two o'clock in the afternoon. Will you please take your dressing gown off now and get dressed?'

Yes, altogether, it would be a sadder house without her.

Pan Lids and Silver Spoons

The storm clouds were gathering and Nancy heard the low rumble of thunder as she looked out of the window. 'It's going to rain shortly,' she said to herself. It had been a strange morning, and Nancy had felt out of sorts since waking up in the early hours. It was just the weather, she thought to herself, then wondered why on earth the weather should affect her like this. It never had before. The children had been especially good, the last few days – just the usual tears and tantrums, but nothing to speak of. Nancy had whizzed through all the chores, nothing had held her up, and yet she had this feeling. 'Goodness me,' Nancy said out loud to nobody in particular, 'what on earth is the matter with me today? Feelings, indeed! As if I have time for nonsense like that.'

Nancy heard the first splashes of rain hit the window and switched the light on as the room became suddenly dark. There was a flash of lightning and then a loud crash of thunder, which was so loud it almost sounded like it was inside the room. This was followed by the sound of torrential rain battering against the window. Nancy paused and watched it for a while, feeling a heaviness in her heart, and not knowing why. Emotions were for other people who had time for them. She certainly did not. Nancy jumped at the next flash and closed the curtains. Time to pull herself together, to go and check that the children weren't frightened by the storm.

Suddenly, out of nowhere, Nancy thought to herself: Where was Dolly when you needed her? Nancy smiled, thinking of all the fun and games Dolly would have played with the children to take their minds off the storm.

How many months had she been gone now? Nancy couldn't remember.

Too many.

Nancy sat down upon her bed, smiling at the memory of how she had scolded Dolly the last time she had been sent to help the children who were frightened of the loud thunder. It had been Sister Mary Joseph who had heard the noise first. She had run into Nancy in the corridor, with a questioning look on her face.

'I sent Dolly to quieten the children, in case they were frightened,' Nancy said to Sister, as they hurried up the corridor.

They followed the squeals and the deafening sounds of banging and clashing coming from the dormitories – noises that had never been heard inside the walls of Nazareth House for as long as it had stood. They reached the doorway together, and there was Dolly hiding under the beds with the children, banging pan lids with spoons, making their own music to drown out the sound of the thunder. To say the children were totally excited was an understatement, and Nancy had to raise her voice more than once to be heard.

One by one, the children crept out from under the beds, followed lastly by a sheepish-looking Dolly. She knelt on the floor, her face covered in dust, with a pan lid in one hand and the other hand suspended in the air, holding the dinner ladle.

'Have I done something wrong?' she asked, with an extremely surprised look on her face. 'You did ask me to distract the children from the thunder.'

'We didn't hear any thunder,' said young Martha.

'She has a point,' Sister Mary Joseph said, smiling at Nancy. 'Someone needs to tidy the children up,' continued Sister, bustling about to try and stop herself from laughing.

'Someone needs to dust under the beds,' replied Nancy, laughing at the sight of Dolly.

Nancy had never forgotten that day, and the storm outside reminded her of it now. She missed Dolly so much more than she would ever have admitted to anyone, even to herself. Dolly had a new life now, in Birmingham, and they had shared many holidays together in her little attic flat at the top of what Nancy thought was the longest and steepest set of stairs she had ever seen. Dolly loved her life as a seamstress and, in a few months, Nancy and Susan would be visiting her again for a fun holiday. Nancy was looking forward to it so much. There was another flash of lightning and Nancy jumped. There was no Dolly to distract the children today, so she had better get a move on and see to the children herself – without the need for pan lids and silver spoons, she thought, smiling.

Sister Mary Joseph entered the room quietly and tapped Nancy gently on the shoulder.

'Good heavens!' said Nancy, angrily. 'I nearly jumped out of my skin. What on earth are you doing, creeping up behind me like that?'

Sister Mary Joseph said nothing, just sat next to Nancy on the bed and took her hand. There were tears in her eyes.

Nancy took her hand away and stood up. 'What is it? Just tell me, Sister.'

'You have a telephone call, Nancy.'

Nancy never had phone calls – or at least, only 'once in a blue moon', as she would say.

'Tell me, Sister,' said Nancy, straightening up.

But Sister Mary Joseph remained silent.

Nancy left the room and began to hurry along the corridor, through the door, down the stairs and across the parlour to the telephone room. The receiver was on the seat underneath the big black telephone. Nancy slowly picked it up and put it to her ear. There was no noise in the room except for the rain battering against the windows in the parlour and the quiet voice on the other end of the telephone. Nancy had closed her eyes. If she couldn't see, maybe she wouldn't have to hear. It simply could not be. She would refuse to believe it. But the voice on the other end of the phone continued to talk, telling Nancy things she simply did not want to hear.

Finally, Nancy replaced the receiver and walked into the parlour, collapsing into the first chair she could find. Mother Superior and Sister Mary Joseph came forward and sat on either side of her. 'What have I told you about creeping up on me?' she told them, with a false laugh, before the tears began to fall. Even squeezing her eyes tight shut, the tears still fell.

Sister Mary Joseph and Mother Superior took her hands. Mother Superior would never have dreamed of making the situation worse by crying, so she sat quite still, her back straight, and closed her eyes in prayer. Sister Mary Joseph also had her head bowed in prayer, but only so that nobody could see she was crying.

'My lovely Dolly,' Nancy said, eventually lifting her head. 'Dilly Dolly Daydream. I must pack,' she said, standing up, 'she needs me.'

Mother Superior stood up too. 'I think a taxi may be necessary, Nancy. I will organize it for you. We will see to the payment of it. And, of course, we will look after Susan. Nancy, you just organize what you have to.'

Slowly, Nancy walked back up the stairs to the nursery with her head held high. There was no time for tears – not yet, anyway – there were things to do.

Dilly Dolly Daydream, with her sense of fun and adventure, her belief in happy endings and fairy tales, had suffered a massive stroke and was lying in a hospital bed in Birmingham unable to communicate with anyone.

They had made a mistake, of course – Dolly was far too young. Yes, that was the way of it. They had made a mistake.

Nancy ran up the stairs and into her attic of treasures and quickly began to gather together what she would need. 'Oh, Dolly,' she said, 'my darling, sweet Dolly Daydream!' Then, standing up, she straightened her hair, wiped her eyes on her apron and took a deep breath. There would be time for tears later. No time for silly nonsense now, she thought. She had a special job to do before catching the night coach to Birmingham.

For the next hour, Nancy pulled down boxes, old torn books, pieces of card, glue and crayons and packed them all into a bag. She took them to her room where she began throwing everything she needed into her old brown suit-case. It was a testament to how upset Nancy was that items were being packed in any-old-how and not with her usual precision and care.

Mother Superior and Sister Mary Joseph came with Nancy to the parlour door to wait for the taxi. There was not a single thing anybody could think of to say to Nancy except, 'We will pray for her.' Silently, they waited in the parlour, listening to the ticking of the clock.

They all jumped when the bell sounded. The taxi was here.

Slowly, Nancy stood up clutching her brown case. A taxi indeed, she thought to herself. Any other time, she would have been very excited at the thought of travelling in luxury, but not today. Mother Superior handed Nancy her bus tickets, which she had sent the caretaker to collect earlier that afternoon. Nancy would have thanked Mother, if it hadn't been for the fact that her throat had closed up and she herself was unable to speak.

After Nancy had left, Mother gathered the nuns, the bell was rung and they made their way to the chapel and began to pray to the God they loved that Dolly might be spared. The storm continued and the rain battered against the stained-glass windows. Sister Mary Joseph, whether it was acceptable or not, bent her head and began to cry.

Gallowgate Bus Station was never the warmest of places and the waiting room was cold, regardless of the steam from all the cups of tea that were being drunk in there tonight. *What a lonely place this is*, thought Nancy, *I never noticed it before.* The last time she had sat here with Susan, they had chatted excitedly about what they would do when they saw Aunty Dolly, where they would go, and how much Susan loved Dolly's little attic bedroom where they would all sleep. No good thinking of things like that now, Nancy decided, sitting bolt upright on a chair with a cup of tea in front of her that she was unable to drink. She needed to be busy, and she had plenty to do before she got there. Thank God for her attic of treasures, she thought, it never let her down.

Finally, the bus pulled in and Nancy took her seat on the coach. Everyone began to settle down, some closing their eyes ready to sleep, others watching the rain which had eased earlier but was once more lashing against the windows of the bus. Nancy had refused to have her case placed in the luggage hold. 'I need it with me,' she told the driver. She placed it on her knee and opened it. Scissors, books, cardboard, pens and a little battery torch. As the coach to Birmingham travelled slowly through the night due to the horrendous thunderstorm raging outside, Nancy sat quietly cutting out letters of the alphabet, gluing them on to card and making a speech board. *Unable to communicate, indeed*, she thought. *We will see about that, Dolly Marshall.*

It was many hours before they reached their destination. Nancy's eyes were so tired, she felt as though she could sleep for a week. The rain had stopped, finally, and it was daylight. Nancy packed her treasures away in her case and looked out of the window.

'I'm coming, Dolly,' she whispered. 'Just hold on, darling.' Then she closed her eyes for a little nap before arriving.

Nancy got off the bus, saying thank you to the driver and looking for all the world like she was on a wonderful day trip out. She had given herself a good talking-to and there were to be no long faces or crying. That would do Dolly no good at all. Nancy would sort it out, now she was here. Dolly would be poorly, then get better – she would see to it herself.

Another taxi took her to the hospital and it was not until she took her first step into the large, imposing building that Nancy began to feel her heart pounding. Taking a deep breath, she made her way to Dolly's ward. She was met by the ward sister, who was expecting her and explained in a very serious voice that, young as Dolly was, she had suffered a massive stroke and was being closely monitored. It was long faces and a negative prognosis.

'We will see about that,' said Nancy. 'I would like to talk to her now.'

The ward sister shook her head. 'I am so sorry, I am afraid I have not made myself clear. You don't understand, she is unable to talk.'

'Oh, no, Sister,' said Nancy, angrily, 'it's you who doesn't understand. There is more than one way to talk.' And with that, she marched into Dolly's room.

She went over to Dolly's bed, and stopped.

It took every ounce of strength not to throw herself on to the bed and gather little Dolly Daydream into her arms, march out of there and take her back home where she could look after her. Instead, Nancy stood, shocked to the core at the sight of Dolly lying there. All Nancy could think was how much she would love to have seen her running around the ward, hiding under the beds, making tents out of sheets and banging spoons and soup ladles against the kitchen pans.

Nancy sat quietly for three hours before Dolly stirred. She immediately reached out to Nancy, who sat on the bed next to her. Dolly's eyes filled with tears.

'Now, then,' said Nancy, 'no tears, Dolly. You and I are going to talk.'

The ward sister and nurses watched with simple amazement as Nancy sat with her speech board, Dolly pointing at the words and letters. Sister had never seen the like, and when Dolly managed to say she was hungry by pointing at the board, she had to admit to feeling very moved.

For the whole day Nancy was allowed to stay with Dolly, at the discretion of the ward sister, who admitted to nobody but herself that she would not have dared send her away. There was laughter on the ward that day as Nancy regaled the staff with tales of Dolly, and they promised they would hide the spoons and bed pans just in case she decided to cavort around the ward, waking up all the patients. Dolly's eyes had twinkled all day and, even though she hadn't spoken a word out loud, they had all conversed using the speech board. Until, at the end of the day, just before Nancy had to leave, Dolly managed a small grunt.

'There, you see!' screamed Nancy. 'You can do it. Now, just pull yourself together, Dolly Marshall, and no more nonsense and attention seeking.' She smiled at her friend. 'I will be back in a couple of weeks, and I will bring Susan with me.'

Dolly took Nancy's finger and pointed to the letters.

H-A-P-P-Y E-N-D-I-N-G-S
'Happy endings,' whispered Nancy.

There was no expression on Nancy's face as she hurried out of the hospital to another waiting taxi, and headed to the bus station. 'Honestly,' she said to herself, 'who on earth do I think I am? Three taxis, indeed!'

She made it with only fifteen minutes to spare and settled herself once more into her seat on the coach. She would have to wait a little longer before she could think about today, it was not yet the time. Fortunately, after such a long night and day, Nancy slept on and off all the way home and arrived in Newcastle in the early hours of the morning.

She waited at the bus stop for the first bus to Jesmond. It didn't matter how long she would have to wait, she was beginning to feel numb inside. When the bus arrived after only an hour, Nancy knew the time was coming. It took every ounce of her strength not to let go. It was as she took her first steps up the driveway that the tears began. With every step she took, she saw the young girl with leaves in her hair and a defiant look on her face, heard the sweet voice telling stories of mermaids and fairies, teaching the children about make-believe and happy endings, recalled the constant giggling, and gave thanks for one of the most beautiful souls Nancy had ever known in her life.

Sister Mary Joseph and Mother Superior watched Nancy walk down the drive, their hearts breaking for her. 'Go and open the parlour door and bring her to my room,' Mother said. 'She will need tea.'

But Nancy ran straight past the parlour door into the garden, dropping her case as she fell to her knees under the magic whispering conker tree, where she finally allowed the release of tears as she wept for her wonderful Dilly Dolly Daydream.

It was a few days later that the next phone call brought good news from the hospital: there had been a marked improvement in Dolly since Nancy's visit, and they were very pleased with her progress.

Nancy and Susan were excitedly packing for a short three-day visit to Birmingham, where they would stay in Dolly's attic room and visit her every day. Susan had made her a lovely card, and Nancy had no idea how on earth she would manage to carry all the gifts people had been giving her to take.

Mother Superior had instructed Nancy to tell Dolly that, as soon as she could travel, they would like her to come for a little holiday to Nazareth House to recuperate, where she would be well looked after.

Nancy was so excited about this, and couldn't wait to tell Dolly.

It was not to be.

In the early hours of the morning, just one week after her visit, Nancy got the phone call that she had always known deep down in her heart would come. Dolly had suffered another stroke and gone home to the God who sent her to bring unconditional love, laughter, a sense of fun, magic and a heart full of kindness to share with His world.

Nancy went to the dining room, then into her own room and closed the door. She looked at her holy pictures, refusing point blank to cry.

'She did well,' she told Him, smiling as she placed her gifts before Him and left the room. 'You take good care of her now,' she whispered.

The sun was streaming through Nancy's bedroom window and the light was bouncing off the treasures that sat there underneath the holy picture.

A pan lid and a soup ladle, with a little card.

'Happy Endings, Dolly.'

PART THREE
Full Circle

Tears and Secrets

The magic whispering conker tree had done its job well over the many years it had stood proudly in the grounds of Nazareth House. Only the tree itself knew how long it had taken to grow into the magnificent horse chestnut it was today.

Year after year, it had shed its conkers for the children to play with and heard their laughter as they gathered them. It had looked on as they attached their pieces of string to the conkers and played games happily in the shade of its branches. So large was the trunk, it had played a great part in hide and seek, seeming to lower its branches when necessary to take part in the game. It had listened to many tears being cried over the years as children had sat leaning against the tree trunk, seeking solace from their pain. It had survived the storm of bombs during the war, holding its branches totally still for fear it would be seen and destroyed.

It lifted its branches in pride, one hot summer's day, when the young child Susan told the children sitting under its shade that this was, indeed, a magic whispering conker tree and that if you placed your hands on the trunk, closed your eyes and wished, all your dreams would come true. It listened to the stories that she told them of dancing among the stars, swimming the oceans with dolphins and riding bareback on horses that ran faster than the wind.

It had also kept its secrets. It would never tell of hearing Nancy's tears as, one night, she sobbed, leaning against the trunk, praying and hoping that they would not take her daughter away. The tree had felt her pain and allowed its branches to droop slightly, comforting and sheltering Nancy. When she had finally pulled herself together and wiped her eyes, she once more touched the trunk and whispered, 'So, Susan tells me you are a magic whispering conker tree. To tell the truth, I could do with a little magic right now. But don't be telling anyone I'm talking to trees.' She smiled weakly.

Nancy need not have worried. The magic whispering conker tree always kept its secrets.

It was very proud indeed, and remembered the days when the garden was always full of children. And yet, as the years were rolling by, there didn't seem to be as many. Times were changing, it thought sadly. It missed the children.

The old laundry house had stood in the garden, unused, for many years, and the tree watched as the builders came along. It listened to the hammering and sawing and watched the old wash house come alive again as the brick-work was cleaned and painted.

It was on 21 January 1965, after many requests from the Catholic Rescue Society to accept newborn babies, that Nazareth House opened its doors to welcome the first of many. The first baby to be placed into the newly deco-rated baby home on 13 May was only twelve days old.

The tree stood tall once more. It would be needed again, it thought happily. The babies were walked around the nursery grounds in their prams. And often the young staff would sit under the shade of the tree, with the babies on blankets spread upon the ground.

The tree was happy once more, able to listen now to the sounds of young babies gurgling and laughing.

Until the first day it happened.

The tree had to stand by and watch a young mother screaming, suddenly realizing that she had handed over her daughter and was likely never to see her again.

The tree had hoped she would come to sit under its branches so that it could comfort her and give her strength, but she simply turned and left. The tree watched her go with only a battered suitcase and a heavy heart, and its branches drooped. As the gentle breeze played with the leaves, the tree seemed to sigh.

It was 1965, and times were changing.

The magic whispering conker tree was not sure it liked it one little bit.

'Hushabye'

Noreen had been sitting in her room for what seemed like hours now as the people downstairs discussed her life. She had been sent upstairs like a naughty five-year-old whilst the family decided what was best for her. With an anger she had never felt before, Noreen knew it had nothing to do with what was best for her. It was much more to do with hushing it all up. What would the neighbours think? Noreen didn't care in the least what they thought, and felt like screaming in frustration. It had been different last year when her older sister, Maureen, had announced the arrival of the first grandchild. The table in the front room had been set with the best cloth, and the china cups and saucers had been brought out from the cabinet. Mother had spent the best part of the day writing letters and letting the neighbours know of the new arrival.

Mother had sent for Maureen today and she, too, was in the kitchen downstairs where decisions were being made. Noreen had felt quite sure that Maureen would run upstairs to give her a hug first, before joining in the discussions. She had held her breath and waited when she heard the front door. But no, Maureen had gone straight through to the kitchen. How suddenly things could change – the family who had loved her all these years now looking at her like that, with disgust and disappointment, and not a shred of love in evidence.

They had been a happy family, a close family, she supposed. Her parents had dropped their first names when Maureen had been born and, for as long as Noreen could remember, she had only ever heard them address each other as 'Mother' or 'Father'. Mother could never be got round – Noreen knew better than to try – but she had always been able to talk to her father. Until today, that is. He had simply stood in front of the fire with his back to her, smoking a pipe, whilst Mother had said, 'You're in the family way, our Noreen.' A statement, not a question.

Noreen really thought she would be able to hide it for a little longer. To be honest, it was almost a relief. She had been trying to hide her feelings of nausea for days, and it was difficult to be sick in secret in this house where everybody seemed to know everyone's business. The anger was what kept Noreen going, these days. She really had believed him when he said he would stand by her. *What a fool I am*, she thought, remembering the look on Mother's face when she told her she wouldn't be getting married.

The man was from another town, and she didn't know where he was.

'I think he has simply abandoned me, Mum,' Noreen had said, taking a step towards her mother, with tears in her eyes.

It was at that point her father had turned to face the fire, and her mother had actually taken a step backwards. Noreen was shocked when her mother said simply, 'Go to your room, and we will discuss what is best for you.'

Noreen had stood still, suddenly furiously angry, and waited for her mother to look her in the eye, but she continued to study the pattern on the carpet. Noreen turned, ran up the stairs and slammed her bedroom door. It was bad enough that she had loved Paul so much and had harboured hopes of getting married and being a family. She had had it all planned in her head. How he would tell her that everything would work out all right, how they would get married and she would be just like her Maureen with a young baby, how she would sing 'Hushabye' to her child. 'How could he have done this to me?' she shouted at the walls. 'How could he just go away, knowing I was carrying his child? How could our Maureen not come and at least give me a hug? How could the mother and father I have loved all my life look at me as though I had suddenly become someone other than their daughter?'

Finally, in more pain than she had ever experienced in her entire eighteen years, Noreen curled up on her bed and sobbed so loudly that she could be heard downstairs, where the decision had been taken to send her to Aunt Elsie in Hexham until the child was born. They would say she had a job there and was living in with Elsie. The child would be sent to that new baby home in Jesmond that had just opened. It had been an orphanage up until 1965 and had only taken children from two years old. Now it had a baby home. The neighbours had been talking about it only last week, and they had wrinkled their noses in disgust, talking about unwed mothers. Well, it was sorted now, and that would be an end to it.

The thought of her daughter's pain was something Noreen's mother was fervently pushing away. Being emotional would not help anybody. When Noreen came home afterwards, they would have a little tea for her and everything would return to normal. 'I will make the arrangements,' she told Father, who stood smoking his pipe, looking at the fire.

He would have said, 'Yes, Mother,' and agreed, as always, but he was unable to speak. He continued to keep his back to everyone so that nobody would see the tears in his eyes. His little Noreen. Always been a bit of a rebel, he smiled to himself, but this. Of course, he wouldn't dream of arguing with Mother. After all, what else could they do? He relit his pipe and made his way out of the house into the back lane, pulling his cap down over his eyes. What sort of a man was he, anyway, not to have run upstairs and hugged his little girl? But Mother would never have allowed it. He stood for a moment, silently smoking, as he looked up at her bedroom window. Then, shaking his head, he made his way to the pub for a much-needed whisky.

Noreen left that evening, after watching her mother pack a suitcase in total silence as she sat on the bed, daring her mother to look at her. She was to take the bus to Newcastle Central Station for the late train to Hexham, where she would be met by Aunt Elsie. As the train slowly pulled out of Newcastle Central Station, Noreen remembered how, at the last minute, Mother had tried to place her hand on her arm, before she left, and Noreen had pulled away sharply. 'Let's not pretend you care,' she had said bitterly. Grabbing her suitcase, refusing any offers of a hand to the bus stop, she had stormed out of the house, slamming the door behind her and leaving the house in silence.

Later that evening, Noreen's mother sighed, nodding her head and wiping her hands on her apron. 'I did what was right,' she said to her husband, 'what is right and proper for this family.'

'Did you?' he said, not looking at her as he continued to smoke his pipe.

Mother, just like Noreen, turned and walked into the kitchen, slamming the door behind her. For the next hour all that could be heard in the O'Neill house was the banging of cupboard doors and the clashing of pots and pans in the sink.

There was nobody to see the tears that poured down Mrs O'Neill's face.

Noreen had never known what it was like to feel lonely. Aunt Elsie was kind enough, but her condition was not to be discussed and the farmhouse she lived in was absolutely in the middle of nowhere. Noreen had never seen darkness like it. There were no street lamps here at night, no noise of traffic. There was simply too much time to think, so Noreen distracted herself by helping with the running of the house as much as possible.

As the months passed and Noreen felt the baby begin to move, she was both fascinated and terrified at the same time. There were so many questions she would have liked answered but was afraid to ask. Aunt Elsie had no children, anyway, so it seemed pointless to ask why her swollen legs had begun to hurt so much, or if it was normal to still feel sick. And why were the persistent headaches becoming increasingly stronger by the day? Maybe this was all normal. Noreen had no idea. Today had been the worst, and Noreen hardly felt able to move. Then suddenly the pain became so intense that she could not stand up and had to lie down, praying for it to pass.

'It's too early,' Noreen cried, 'that much I do know.'

That night, when Elsie returned home from work, she found Noreen curled up on the sofa crying in pain and pleading for something to take the pain away. Thinking she was about to have the baby here and now, with all the complications of an early birth, Elsie rang her own doctor and asked for advice.

When the midwife, Mary Shaw, arrived and saw how far along Noreen was, she demanded to know why this young girl had not been seen before now. 'It's time for your baby to be born,' she told Noreen. 'Both you and the baby are in danger. Your baby could die, young lady,' said the midwife.

'That could be best all round,' whispered Aunt Elsie.

'I will pretend I did not hear that,' said Mary. 'Now please get out of my way,' she said, angrily, 'whilst I organize an ambulance to take this young girl to hospital.'

The next few hours passed in a blur until eventually, at 3.10 on a cold morning in November 1965, Noreen's daughter was born into a world where attitudes were, at long last, beginning to change. But not soon enough for the O'Neills, who still saw it as a shame and a disgrace on the whole family.

'I am calling her Catherine,' Noreen said, as she held out her arms to the nurse who turned away, hurrying towards the special care unit where the early babies were taken. Noreen cared nothing about the pain, or the others in the room and what they were doing to her. She lay back and cried, but nobody took any notice of her whatsoever.

Young trainee Nurse Robson smiled at her as she settled Noreen on the ward, ensuring everything was tidy and spick and span, before Matron did her rounds.

'Can I see her?' Noreen asked.

But Nurse Robson just smiled and continued with her duties.

Noreen became angry and shouted, but nobody was listening. 'I want to see my baby!' She shouted, then screamed, louder and louder. 'I want to see my baby!'

Matron came hurrying along, stopped at Noreen's bed and began to tell her every good reason why she was to behave and not make such a spectacle of herself, telling Noreen she would not listen to any more of this ridiculous nonsense.

It was then that Noreen instead began to sob and beg. 'Please God, let me see my child.'

'Behave yourself, and we will see,' said Matron as she turned away.

And with that Noreen had to be satisfied.

It was after 6 p.m. and tea had been cleared away. Noreen had never been to church – except, of course, for christenings, weddings and funerals – but today she sat quietly and began for the first time in her life to pray. She jumped when the young nurse she had seen earlier tapped her on the shoulder. 'I'm to take you along to the baby ward,' she said, 'but you are not allowed to touch her. She is very tiny and in an incubator. But I've been told you can look through the window.'

Down the long corridors Noreen followed Nurse Robson until she reached the big window. Finally, for the first time, she looked down upon the tiny sleeping child who was her daughter.

'I will be back in five minutes,' the nurse told her.

Noreen put her hands up against the glass to steady herself and leaned her head against the window. She studied every part of little Catherine's face, and through the glass she told her sleeping daughter how much she loved her, how she would never forget her and would pray every day that she would be happy and safe. And, one day, maybe they would meet again and she would explain herself.

Over and over, Noreen studied every single feature until she knew with certainty that she would never in her entire life forget what Catherine looked like. Very quietly, Noreen began to sing 'Hushabye' to her tiny daughter, hoping with all her heart that she could hear her. Suddenly, and very briefly, young Catherine opened her eyes, and Noreen's legs almost gave way.

'Bright blue, just like mine,' she said. 'I can't let you go,' she cried, 'I can't. Oh, dear God, I can't leave you here!'

Nurse Robson came back and almost had to drag Noreen back to her bed.

Matron told Dr Simpson that the girl was going to be trouble and the best thing for her was to be sent back to her aunt's house where she could be looked after. The child would need to stay for a few more weeks, until it was strong enough, then the plan was for it to be taken to the new baby home in Jesmond and put up for adoption.

'Best for the mother to get back to normal as quickly as possible,' Matron said, and hurried away to what promised to be a very busy day.

Two weeks later, Noreen once again found herself on the train returning to Newcastle. She desperately wanted to feel something, even anger or loss, but she felt nothing. She was numb through and through. All she wanted was to be back in her room at home and left alone forever. Quietly, as the train sped towards Newcastle, Noreen leaned her head against the window and once more hummed the tune 'Hushabye' to herself.

Aunt Elsie had warned her sister. It was all over but the girl was not pulling herself together at all. 'Keeps singing to herself,' she said.

At home, Noreen once more sat on her bed and wondered how on earth she had got into this situation. Her mind was confused and she had blanks in her memory, except for those few moments she had spent watching her daughter. For the first hour at home she had simply sat with her eyes closed, seeing Catherine's face and drawing comfort from it. Until suddenly she could no longer see her daughter's tiny features and had begun to scream.

They had given her something to calm her down and help her sleep. Now Noreen no longer knew what day it was, and cared even less. The tea that mother had prepared for her homecoming had gone cold. Nobody wanted it.

Mother had left clean towels on the chair in the corner of the room and Noreen slowly walked over to pick them up. Carefully, she rolled up the small one, wrapped the larger towel around it and cradled them in her arms, before walking over to the long mirror on the wardrobe door. She closed her eyes and pretended to rock her tiny child in her arms until, finally, she looked up and caught sight of herself in the mirror and smiled. 'Catherine,' she whispered, then closed her eyes again and began to sing

'Hushabye' to a child who was, at that moment, being carried down the long driveway towards Nazareth House baby home.

Sister Anne held her arms out for the child they told her had been named Catherine and laid her down in the cot which had been prepared for her. 'Particularly tiny, you are,' she said to the sleeping child as she reached down to hold the infant's delicate hand. Sister Anne was determined that every single child in her care would not only be looked after but loved as well. She had been thrilled to learn that she was to be sent, with a few staff to help her, to look after the babies until they were transferred to Nancy in the nursery when they were two, to be adopted or sent home to their parents. Sister Anne often wondered about each child's story and never ceased to pray that the changing world they were all now seeing would be a little kinder to them.

All over the country there would be many stories like Noreen's, and many tears would be cried. The scars would never quite heal, and the pain of childbirth would be nothing compared to the pain of loss.

For those babies who were either abandoned or orphaned – or who simply could not be accepted into the families they had been born into – the Sisters of Nazareth once more opened their doors and their hearts.

Cream Matinee Coat with the Satin Cream Ribbon

Maddy reached into the back of the drawer and took out the perfect treasure wrapped in tissue paper. Very carefully she unwrapped it and held it in her hands. It was so very beautiful. Delicately, she wrapped it up again and placed it underneath all the linen in the bottom of the drawer, then pushed it as far back as she could. It would have to remain her secret for a little longer.

Madelaine Harrison was twenty-two years old and the eldest of three girls. Her two sisters, Maggie and Lucy, were eighteen-year-old twins and had a job together as typists in Newcastle city centre. They did absolutely everything together. Maddy worked as a shop assistant in town and they often all met for lunch. They were a close family and it was a noisy, happy house when they all got home from work to eat together. Maddy had never had a secret before, and she desperately wanted to tell them all about it. But she couldn't. Not yet, anyway.

Tonight, after supper, she had hurried upstairs, wanting to be alone; she felt so desperately tired all the time, these days. Maybe that was how it was for everyone, she thought. Unfortunately, there was nobody she could ask. Maddy smiled every time she looked at her chest of drawers, which was 'full to brimming', as Mum would say. The pale blue dress and jacket were hanging on the door. The wedding was only two days away now. The dress was so pretty and still fitted, but Maddy would have to unfasten the jacket now as the material was straining ever so slightly across her stomach. Nobody would notice, she told herself again. Maddy smiled when she remembered that beautiful summer's day when they had got carried away. 'Well, so what?' Bobby had told her afterwards. 'We are getting married, after all, and you are my girl, Maddy Harrison.' Maddy had felt so proud at that moment as they lay together, making their plans for the future. They loved each other so much, nothing could go wrong. And the baby would make everything perfect.

No heartache for them, they had it all worked out. Bobby's father had died some years back, leaving him the garage business with the small flat above. It was absolutely perfect, and Maddy had been cleaning and decorating for weeks now. 'No more coming upstairs with overalls on, mind you,' she had told him, and poor Bobby was forced to strip off as soon as he walked through the door and put clean clothes on before making his way upstairs after a hard day's work. Bobby didn't mind in the least, if it meant his Maddy would be up there to welcome him home to a spotless flat and a meal on the table. Maddy and Bobby spent every spare moment they could at the flat – except, of course, for night-time. 'That is not acceptable, our Madelaine,' her mother and father had told her in no uncertain terms. 'Plenty of time for that,' they would say, nodding at each other, and Maddy was highly amused at their embarrassed glances.

*

They had met on a Saturday night at the local dance. By the end of the night, Bobby had told her that she would be going to any future dances with him and that he was going to call her 'Maddy'.

'It has a sweet ring to it,' he told her, and her heart had skipped a beat.

Only three months later, he proposed and it had not been necessary to stay overnight in the flat to do what they had promised everyone they would not do. Maddy ran her hands over her stomach, knowing that their lovemaking had brought them their first child. Nobody would know, anyway; it would be what people called 'a honeymoon baby' – although there would be no honeymoon for them. 'We will just confuse people with dates,' they laughed. Bobby was busy building up his business – 'our little empire', he called it – a holiday would have to wait, but they couldn't have cared less. All they wanted was to be left alone for a couple of days in their beautifully decorated, clean and pretty new flat. Maddy was bubbling with excitement. Never had she realized life could be so perfect.

Her family had never been well off, but they had managed. Father had worked hard all his life at the factory and was now a manager. Mum had been so proud the day she saw him off to work in a suit and tie instead of overalls. She had cried, watching him walk all the way down the back lane carrying his bait box in his hand. It was a new beginning for them, Mum had said, and they were all to be very proud of their father. Suddenly, Mum was no longer wearing her old apron but a new 'frilly pinny', as she called it. There were new posh meals cooked now. They were going up in the world, and Maddy and the twins found it all hilariously funny.

Maddy was remembering the day she came home from work after being on her feet for what felt like days. All she wanted was a cup of tea and a lie-down on her bed. She made her way upstairs and opened the bedroom door, to find her mother scrubbing the bottom drawer of her old chest of drawers.

'Mum, what on earth are you doing?' she had asked her.

'It's your bottom drawer, our Madelaine. Best be prepared.'

'Bottom drawer? Prepared?'

'It's a tradition,' Mum said. 'When you get to a certain age, people give you things to prepare for when you get married. Your Aunty Lillian has sent me some linen sheets for you and I am going to get the matching pillowcases. You won't be going into any marriage without a proper send-off, my girl, I will make sure of that.'

Maddy was trying very hard not to laugh. 'Mum, you make me sound ancient. I'm not exactly over the hill yet, you know.'

'I know what I'm doing,' said Mum, with her nose in the air and arms crossed, 'now don't you argue with me, my girl.'

Maddy smiled. 'Lovely, Mum – it's nice to know that I am all prepared to make my marital bed a pretty one.'

Mother stood up, fiddling and straightening her very new pinny, with an embarrassed flush on her face at the mention of bed and marriage in the same sentence, and hurried off, mumbling something about preparing tea.

Maddy had waited until the door was closed and then threw herself on her small single bed and roared with laughter. Wait till she told Maggie and Lucy when they came home! She lay on the bed, looking up at the ceiling and the pretty yellow lightshade with tassels hanging from it. *Married, indeed*, she thought. *I haven't even got a boyfriend.*

It was only eight weeks later that she met Bobby. And two weeks later, Maddy's bottom drawer was straining to close, it was so full. And Mum was now happily scrubbing the second drawer.

Maddy lay on her bed, thinking about Bobby. It had taken only one night for them both to realize that this was it. There was to be nobody else for either of them. And now, only a few months later, they were to be married. Bobby had been thrilled when Maddy said she thought she might be pregnant. 'We will be married in a couple of weeks,' he told her, 'nobody need know. Don't you worry, my girl,' he had said. 'It will be just perfect.'

Once more, her eyes strayed to the bottom drawer and she felt a fluttering in her stomach. Why had she done it? Hurrying home from work, just three days ago, she had passed the small shop on the high street that sold all different-coloured wools, knitting needles, patterns, ribbon, buttons, and everything else besides, necessary to make the tiny little cardigans in the shop window. In all this time, she had never noticed the shop before. How many times had she hurried past, she wondered, without taking any notice. But that day she had stopped. It had been pouring with rain and she had pretended she was sheltering under the porchway as she looked at the item displayed in the window. It was a tiny cream matinee coat with the most beautiful cream satin ribbon threaded through it. Maddy had never seen anything so beautiful. She wanted to feel it and hold it so much. She almost walked into the shop there and then, but stopped. Just because she had been feeling sick in the mornings meant nothing, it hadn't been confirmed by a doctor, and yet deep down in her heart she just knew that she was pregnant. The next night, Maddy hurried past the shop, refusing to acknowledge it even existed. But on the third night, it seemed to draw her to its window and she stood looking once more at the prettiest little baby matinee coat she had ever seen.

The bell clanged, making Maddy jump, as she walked into the shop and the lady came forward to ask if she could help.

'Erm . . . the matinee coat in the window,' she had stuttered. 'It's for a friend, you see,' she said.

The woman glanced briefly at the engagement ring on Maddy's finger, which was clearly not a wedding ring, and Maddy hadn't missed the glance. 'Of course,' was all the lady said.

Five minutes later, Maddy found herself leaving the shop with a little package wrapped in tissue paper. Hiding it under her coat, she hurried home and ran straight upstairs to the bottom drawer, pushing it as far back as she could. What on earth had she been thinking of? Suddenly, tears stung her eyes. *Oh dear God, what now?* she thought. *Why am I crying? I feel like an emotional wreck and I have no idea why.* If she had been able to ask her mother, Maddy would have understood all about the 'feelings', as Mum would call them, but she couldn't ask anyone.

It was a Wednesday evening and they had made a little leaving tea for her at work. Tea and cakes, with cards and little gifts, and Maddy had been so moved she had cried again. She seemed to be close to tears constantly, these days. There was no need to carry on working. Bobby wanted her at home, above the garage, helping him with his paperwork and keeping the house in order. At least, that is what they told everyone. In a few weeks they would announce that they were expecting their first child and then the knitting needles would come out. Maddy and Bobby would start their married life together with their very own flat. And everything in the world would be absolutely perfect and wonderful.

Maddy knelt down and reached into the back of the bottom drawer and, once more, pulled out the little matinee jacket, holding it to her cheek and feeling the softness of the wool. *One day soon, I will be putting it on my son or daughter*, she thought as she placed it carefully in the tissue paper and hid it back in the drawer amongst all the other bottom-drawer treasures.

The sun shone for them at Newcastle Registry Office, and everyone went to the local pub afterwards, where a splendid buffet befitting the daughter of a manager at the local factory took place.

Bobby had never taken his eyes off Maddy, he was so proud of her. Maddy was walking round the room, chatting to everyone, when she heard two ladies by the buffet table taking about how proud Maddy's parents should be. And then they began talking about the disgraced girls who were taking their babies to the nearby baby home in Jesmond, to be cared for and adopted. 'Expecting out of wedlock!' they said. Times might be changing but it was still a disgrace to their minds. Just for a moment, Maddy stopped and felt the life inside her move – or was it her imagination? *My child is not even born yet, or fully developed, and yet I love it so much*, she thought, unable to imagine what it must be like to have to give birth and then give the baby away. For what felt like the hundredth time that month, Maddy began to cry once more. And when the two women turned round, she gave them the most withering look she could muster.

The small incident hadn't spoiled her day and they left at 9 p.m., unable to wait any longer to get away from all the guests and be on their own. Maddy's mother, father and sisters hugged her. The newly married couple had managed to keep the baby a secret and soon, together, they would be able to make their announcement. There was a flash and their smiles in the photograph which would stand on their mantelpiece for many years to come said it all: *Life is perfect*.

Bobby carried Maddy over the threshold and all the way up the stairs to the flat. They walked together into the bedroom and Bobby kissed his new wife and led her over to the freshly made bed, with the new linen sheets and pillowcases. In the corner of the room was Maddy's bedside set of drawers, which she had brought from home. In the very top drawer, no longer hidden, lay the tiny cream matinee coat with the pretty satin ribbon.

It was only three weeks later that Maddy began to feel unwell. It was the pressure of being a new wife, people told her. 'Maybe you're not washing your vegetables properly, or cooking the meat long enough,' said Mum.

It was three o'clock in the morning when Maddy began to scream in pain and Bobby saw all the blood on the new linen sheets. The announcement of their new, impending arrival was no longer going to happen. Maddy and Bobby had lost their first child and were completely and utterly devastated. The cream matinee coat with the satin ribbon was once more pushed to the back of the bottom drawer, where Maddy wouldn't see it.

'Not to worry,' they told her, 'it's early days. You will have another one.'

'Hardly a baby at all,' said one of the neighbours, which made Maddy cry even more.

Only the doctor knew the truth about how long Maddy had been pregnant, and yet he treated them as if it was the norm. 'These things happen,' he smiled at them. 'You will be back in no time, and everything will be fine.'

Somehow, both Bobby and Maddy knew it was not going to be that simple.

Sadly, they were absolutely right.

Maddy slammed the front door and stamped up every single one of the stairs to the flat. It had been ten months now and if one more person made one more comment about when they were thinking of starting a family, she would absolutely scream.

'It's not even been a year yet,' Bobby told her.

But Maddy was not convinced. 'There is something wrong,' she said. 'I just know it.'

And yet, just six weeks later, Maddy once more began to be sick in the mornings. Life was good again, and there was hope in their hearts.

Until, three months into the pregnancy, once more Maddy miscarried.

Lying curled up on the bed, she felt totally numb. No amount of coaxing and promises of cups of tea made any difference at all. She cried most of the days and nights, not wanting any help, praying that she wasn't being punished for the first baby. Was it all her fault? A lifetime without a baby was too painful to consider.

Bobby sat downstairs, not having a clue what to do. If he went near her, she would only push him away. So he sat staring into the fire and smoked. What else was there to do?

He had dozed off when he heard the screams from upstairs.

Anger had replaced the numb feeling inside her, and his beautiful wife was on her knees ripping the tissue paper off the tiny matinee coat. It took all his strength to hold her back from tearing it to pieces. Together they sat on the floor as he held her in his arms. It was late when, finally, he got her to bed and pulled the covers up over her as she slept. There was something he needed to do.

Bobby carried the stepladder into the bedroom as quietly as he could. He picked up the little matinee coat, wrapped it back up in the torn tissue paper and carried it up the ladder, pushing it far back into the space on top of the wardrobe where Maddy would not be able to see it or know it was there. They were seeing the doctor at the end of the week, and they were going to do some tests. Bobby lay down beside Maddy and watched her sleep, then turned his face into the linen pillowcases and began to sob, praying with all his heart for the child that they wanted so very badly and would love so very much.

Maddy was only pretending to be asleep. With a heaviness in her heart that she had never felt before, she listened to her husband cry. The anger had gone and the numbness had once more invaded her heart and mind. She couldn't help him so she continued to lie silently, the pain inside worse than any physical pain the miscarriages had caused. Her mind wandered to her wedding day and she remembered the disgraced girls she had heard the neighbours talking about. The abandoned, 'unwanted' babies, they had called them. They were wrong, of course, Maddy knew that now. She had seen young Jennifer Graham last month, looking absolutely torn apart after having her baby taken away from her and adopted. Disgraced, indeed! The disgrace was in the tongues of those who had nothing better to do than criticize, condemn and judge without a sympathetic thought in their heads.

As Maddy finally fell asleep, Jennifer's words kept replaying in her head. 'Oh, Maddy, all I can hope and pray for is that someone very special can love her for me.'

Bobby had given up hoping for any sort of normal life. Maddy cried continually, and after two years of marriage there was still no sign of a baby. Nothing actually to worry about, they had been told. Miscarriage was just a sign of Mother Nature telling you there was something wrong.

'In other words, you haven't got a clue!' Maddy had said, angrily, and stormed out of the doctor's office.

Life went on. Until one day Bobby came home from a very busy day to find Maddy having a spring clean. The stepladder had been dragged over to dust the top of the wardrobe.

And she had found it.

Bobby's heart broke when he saw her sitting on the top step, her face buried in the pretty little matinee coat with the satin ribbon.

'I want a baby,' Maddy sobbed. 'Oh, Bobby, I want a baby!'

More Happy Endings

Maddy never knew what made her do such a thing. Making excuses that she had shopping to do, she made her way to the bus stop and asked the bus conductor to let her know when she had arrived. Sitting on the bus, Maddy looked around her, feeling as though everyone must know what she was up to. She clutched her handbag tightly, looked out of the window and waited. The numbness that had invaded her body for days was now being replaced by nerves. For a moment she wondered whether to jump off the bus now, run all the way home and forget about it. Yet still she sat on the Jesmond bus and waited to be told that this was her stop.

Maddy had put on her best clothes, and Bobby had raised his eyebrows. 'I may pop in to see Mum on the way home,' she had told him. But when had she ever put her best dress on to visit her mum? she thought, knowing the lie wasn't even a convincing one.

Bobby had said nothing, simply smiled at her and kissed her cheek. It was a testament to how different things were that Maddy hadn't screamed at him for coming anywhere near her with his oil-stained overalls. Bobby watched her walk away and wondered where she was actually going. Then, with a heavy heart, he returned to the broken engine he was fixing. She was a good girl, his Maddy, in time she would tell him.

Maddy jumped when the conductor tapped her on the shoulder and said, 'Your stop, love.'

This was it, then. She was here.

Maddy took a deep breath and walked purposefully along Sandyford Road in Jesmond, pretending to all the world that this was exactly what she was supposed to be doing and where she was supposed to be.

As hundreds had done before her, Madelaine stopped at the large black iron gates and saw the words 'Nazareth House'. Well, she was here now, she thought, so she might as well go through with it. She bravely took her first step on to the long driveway. Then, suddenly panicking, she ran into the wood at the side of the drive. Her hands were shaking as she hurried past the bluebells, crocuses and rhododendron bushes and found herself hiding behind the large tree at the bottom of the wood, just like a naughty child. She paused for a moment, then straightened up. 'Honestly, Madelaine,' she said out loud, using her Sunday name, 'what on God's earth are you doing?' Her heart banging in her chest, she stepped forward and turned to her right.

There she stood. Our Lady of Lourdes, smiling.

And immediately Maddy began to walk towards her, no longer caring if she was seen. There was comfort here, and a warmth began to spread through her body. Maddy had no understanding of why, she simply closed her eyes and breathed out, feeling the best she had felt in such a long time. 'Help me,' she whispered to Our Lady. Somehow, in this moment there was hope, there was a way forward, and everything was as it should be.

Maddy could never have told anyone how long she stood there.

It had been a busy day. Mother had retired to her room for a much-needed cup of tea, and maybe a biscuit, when she saw her. Mother Superior knew everyone who had been through the doors of Nazareth House and was trying to see if she knew the child. Mother watched her as she stood before Our Lady of Lourdes, as many had done before her, then placed her rosary beads between her fingers and began to pray for guidance.

Maddy jumped when she heard the cry. There was no mistaking it.

That was a baby crying.

She hurried towards the nursery garden, where she came upon the great horse chestnut tree and hid quickly behind it, her heart racing. There it was. A sweet little building with prams outside and two nuns sitting, with children on their knees, enjoying the sunshine and fresh air. Maddy had no idea how long she stood there, watching and dreaming.

A baby in her arms . . . standing at the garage door with a baby on her hip . . . chatting to Bobby as he worked . . . pushing the pram around Heaton Park . . .

It was the most wonderful dream in the world. It was all too much. Maddy leaned against the giant trunk of the magic whispering conker tree and began to cry.

Mother didn't want to frighten the child. Actually, a young woman, she thought, seeing Maddy properly for the first time. Mother was sure now that this must be a young girl who had given her baby up for adoption and was suffering, as many of them did. And so she waited until, eventually, Maddy looked over and saw her.

Mother, remembering what Nancy always told her to do with frightened children, simply smiled. Then she held out her hands.

The rush of emotion that tore through Maddy was too much to bear. She stumbled forward into the arms of Mother Superior, who simply held her and allowed the tears to flow.

Nancy had also glanced out of the nursery window and wondered who the young woman was. She incorrectly guessed she must have given her child away. Not sure whether to go and help, she stayed at the window and watched until Mother led the young girl away. 'Such a pretty girl, I would love to see her when she is smiling,' Nancy murmured, then sighed. 'Another sad story,' she said to herself, and promised to say a prayer for her. Then she returned to the unruly chaos that had broken out whilst her back was turned.

Maddy sat in Mother's room and tried very hard to drink her cup of tea with hands that would not stop shaking as she poured out the whole story. The relief of talking about it was immense, and Maddy began to feel a warmth spread through her whole body that she had not felt in such a long time. How wonderfully comforting it was to be accepted and understood.

After numerous cups of tea, Maddy left with a spring in her step and hope in her heart at what she had been told. She would be back soon, with Bobby, and this time they would walk down the long driveway together and knock at the front door. She had kept what she was going to do a secret from Bobby. 'But from now on there will be no more secrets,' Maddy smiled.

Except, maybe, for creeping through woods, talking to statues and hiding behind trees.

It was only three months later that Maddy and Bobby stood dressed in their best Sunday clothes on a Wednesday morning. Maddy had brushed Bobby's jacket so many times his shoulders hurt, he told her laughingly. They were ready far too early, that was the problem. They were due there at one and it was still only quarter past eleven. The clock had never ticked so slowly.

But finally, it was time.

'Just one more thing to do before we leave,' Maddy said, and popped into the bedroom.

The cot was in the corner of the room and there were piles of baby clothes everywhere. There had been some hasty clicking of needles in Maddy and Bobby's families. Maddy walked over to the top drawer and took out the little package wrapped in the new tissue paper they had bought.

Bobby stood in the doorway and watched with tears in his eyes as his wife opened the tissue paper and placed the matinee coat with the cream satin ribbon in the cot. 'It's time, love,' he whispered.

At 1 p.m. the paperwork was signed and, whether it was correct behaviour or not, Maddy ran to Mother Superior and gave her a hug. 'I don't know what to say,' Maddy said.

Mother patted her hand. 'Then say nothing. You will be wonderful parents,' Mother said, smiling. 'I will pray for you. Come back and see us.'

Nancy and Mother watched them walk away up the driveway, chatting happily as they pushed their new baby daughter in her pram for the very first time.

'A happy ending,' said Nancy. 'Don't you just love it when that happens?'

Mother Superior smiled. 'I do, indeed, Nancy,' she said.

'Twinkle, Twinkle'

The words didn't register. They were there in the air between them, hovering, just not quite reaching her ears. Best not listen. If you didn't hear, it couldn't be true. He was still talking but Geraldine was concentrating on the pattern of the curtains. Nice bit of quality material, she thought, trying to block out the words threatening to be heard if she turned her head to look at him. There was a photograph on his desk, a family portrait – mother, father and child – and Geraldine closed her eyes to block out the pain. She was remembering that day twenty-six years ago.

It was the most beautiful cradle she had ever seen in her life, and it was pink with little rosebuds. Geraldine loved her baby doll, Rosemary, so much and played with her every day. She couldn't wait to put her in the cradle. It squeaked every time she pushed it back and forth until Daddy put oil on the hinges, laughing and telling her it would wake the baby. It was Geraldine's sixth birthday, and life was wonderful. Daddy had been in the little outhouse in the back yard for days now, hammering and sawing, with a grin on his face and telling her to 'just wait and see'. Daddy could make anything, she thought with pride.

Never had Geraldine expected anything so beautiful, and she gasped when she saw it. 'Oh, Daddy!' was all she managed to say. Carefully, she had placed her favourite doll, little Rosemary, and the blanket into the pink rose-bud cradle. She pushed her baby back and forth, singing 'Twinkle, Twinkle, Little Star' just like Mummy, for hours and hours, perfectly content and dreaming of the day she would do this for real. Daddy would make her a big cradle with pink rosebuds on, just like this one, and everyone would ooh and aah over it. It would be a girl, naturally, with blue eyes and fair curly hair that Geraldine would spend hours brushing. And she would buy the prettiest of ribbons. Pink, of course.

Twenty-six years later, Geraldine continued to ignore the voices around her and instead began to think about her wedding day. She had smiled the whole day, knowing that her dreams were simply going to come true. *A husband, and my little Rosemary to follow.* The perfect name for a perfect child, she thought. It was definitely going to be a girl, and Geraldine dreamed about the day she would hold her daughter in her arms, wrapped in a soft white blanket, and would gently place her in the rosebud cradle, singing 'Twinkle, Twinkle'. They already had a pretty little star to hang from the ceiling above the cradle.

Geraldine knew how it felt to hold a child; her sister Linda had two children, and babysitting was one of her favourite things to do. *Now*, thought Geraldine, as she brushed the confetti off her new clothes on her wedding day, *it's my turn*, and she smiled at her new husband.

Martin winked at her and whispered, 'Well, now, Geraldine, what is it you're smiling about?' Laughing together, they made their way into the world as husband and wife with hopes, dreams and the promise of a wonderful family life together.

They rushed home that night and looked at the nursery Martin had worked so hard on. 'Nothing like being prepared,' he told her. Martin had a good job and they could afford it, so they would have a baby straight away. Naturally.

Life, unfortunately, had not exactly turned out that way. The cradle stood in the corner of the room, just under the window with the pretty rosebud curtains. Still empty, still waiting to be rocked.

'It takes time,' they said, 'just be patient, just wait. It takes time.' At first Geraldine believed them. But after a year she began to lose hope. Only a few miles away, in Jesmond, there were all those babies. 'Unwanted', people called them. The injustice of it all made her want to scream.

Three years now they had been married, and it was time to find out, people said. Geraldine had put it off as long as possible, always believing that, one day, it would happen. People were starting to ask questions: 'No family yet, then?', 'Come on, girl, you're not getting any younger.' It was amazing how you could laugh with people, smile back with some witty reply, when your heart was sinking low into your stomach.

Before this morning she hadn't been into the nursery for months. How many times, she wondered, had she stood there with her fingers resting on the door handle, afraid to go in? It used to be such a joy, sitting there sewing the rosebuds on the baby blanket, knitting, cleaning, polishing. 'Where are you, my darling?' she whispered, before taking a deep breath and pushing the door open. She gasped at the beauty of the cot, sitting there waiting, just like the one she'd had when she was six years old, so many years ago. She walked around the room, rearranging cushions, dusting, and then she made her way over to the little pink stool, sat down and reached out her hand to the rosebud cradle. With tears that she could no longer control, she began once more to sing, 'Twinkle, twinkle . . .' to an empty cradle.

Geraldine didn't hear her husband come into the room, and jumped when he put his hand on her shoulder. 'Time to go, love,' he said.

Sitting quite still now in the doctor's room, Geraldine chose to continue looking at the floor. The words had stopped now; there was silence. They were waiting for her to speak.

Geraldine took a deep breath. 'Yes, thank you,' was all she said.

No tears, just a heavy feeling in the very pit of her stomach, a pain in her heart stronger than any physical pain. Her knees were shaking but she managed to stand, refusing her husband's hand, and walked out into the street, back to a world that was normal, where ordinary things happened, where life went on as usual and people didn't tell you horrible, hurtful, ridiculous things. A few of the doctor's hurtful words had actually managed, somehow, to make themselves heard. The results showed she was unlikely to conceive.

Nothing we can do.

They were only four words, not even big words. She would block them out.

Somehow.

*

Thoughts were racing round Geraldine's head.

Look at me, my heart is still beating, my face looks the same, my feet still take one step in front of the other. There are people shopping, walking past me, not looking at me because I look perfectly normal, perfectly sane. I am not crying, although I desperately want to, and I am not screaming, because my throat hurts – there is a lump there which prevents me doing either. Why does nobody look at me? Why does nobody notice?

There is no pain, because somehow the numbness has overtaken my whole body. I can't walk, my feet appear to suddenly have become leaden. So I lean against the wall and continue to watch other people going about their daily business. Ordinary people.

Geraldine began to concentrate on the bags in the shop window and count them, over and over again. It felt like she had been counting for hours when she suddenly realized she was soaking wet from the rain that had been falling for goodness knew how long. 'I didn't notice,' she said out loud.

Now people are looking at me and I don't care, she thought. *I want to move, but I can't. I need to lift my arms but am unable to. My arms are useless, empty.*

'What is the point of empty arms?' she said, out loud, once more.

It was then that, finally, Geraldine began to cry. *Dear God*, she thought, *my hair is stuck to my head. And my face is so wet it's difficult to know where the rain ends and the tears begin.*

Maybe they were all wrong. That was the way of it, they were wrong.

Geraldine was suddenly once more able to move her arms. She made a cradle with them, then leaned against the wall and closed her eyes, imagining the child in her arms. Very gently, she began to rock her arms from side to side and began to sing, 'Twinkle, twinkle, little star . . .'

This baby is as light as a feather, she thought, *I can actually smell her.*

The lump in Geraldine's throat was beginning to subside, freeing her from the numbness that had taken hold of her. Her voice was returning and she began to sing louder, so the baby would hear. Louder and louder . . . 'Twinkle, twinkle –'

Suddenly, Geraldine's arms were pulled to her side by a concerned stranger, a kindly-looking lady who asked if she was all right.

Geraldine looked down at her empty arms. 'You took my baby,' she said, quietly. Then she sank down on to the pavement and began to scream.

This was how Martin found his wife.

He quickly took her home, having no idea what to do with her or how to help. As Geraldine slept, tucked up in bed with two hot-water bottles, Martin sat long into the night, smoking and wondering how to protect her. If he told anyone about what had happened, they might take her away. There was no way he would let that happen. They would get through this together, somehow.

Martin checked on Geraldine, who was still fast asleep, then made his way to the nursery. He wasn't actually sure whether or not to go into the room – and anyway, his feet seemed to be stuck to the spot. 'Be a man,' he said to himself, but still he waited. Eventually, he summoned up the courage to open the door. He walked over to the cradle, stretched out his hand, and paused. Then he pushed it, rocking it from side to side. There seemed suddenly to be something strange happening in his knees, which buckled, and he fell to the floor and buried his head in his hands. For the first time in his entire life Martin Brown began to cry bitterly.

His sobs disturbed Geraldine and she woke, stunned at what she was hearing. She stood in the doorway of the nursery watching her husband cry, then slowly walked over to him and placed her hand gently on his shoulder. 'I am so sorry,' she whispered. 'I should have known this was painful for you too. I didn't think, simply couldn't feel anything but my own pain.' She sat on the floor beside him. 'Look at the state of us,' she said, to cover his embarrassment.

There was very little to say so they didn't speak, they simply sat together, holding hands, comforting each other. Martin had thought of something earlier but was almost afraid to bring the subject up. Maybe it was too early.

'What are you thinking?' Geraldine asked him. 'I can see the cogs turning.' She smiled at him. 'You do that funny thing with your eyebrows when you're thinking about something serious.' She laughed.

Martin looked at her.

'Just tell me,' she said.

'Gerry, how much do you want a baby?'

'Sorry?'

'How much do you want a baby?'

'So much that it almost feels like it's not worth going on without one. I'm sorry if that hurts, but it's all I have ever dreamed of since I was six years old. I want to sit here with you, rocking the cradle and talking about all the things we will do together. What we will teach her, where we will take her. I want to sing to her, brush her hair, read her stories. And you will pick her up, toss her up in the air, and make her laugh. I will shout at you to be gentle with her and you will tell me not to worry. We will go crazy after many sleepless nights, wear out the floorboards – and our feet – walking the floor with her. Some days, I will look like a wreck and you will worry about whether or not we can make ends meet. But, most importantly, we will love every single moment of it.

'When we go out, you will carry her on your shoulders and everyone will say, "Look at the Brown family, how happy they are! Don't you just wish you were them?" Then, one day, she will get married and we will be grand-parents and the cradle will still be here and you will paint it and give it to her.'

'That much, eh?'

'That much, Martin, and so much more. What are you thinking?'

'About those babies you told me about, in Jesmond. Little ones with no one to love them. I just wondered what you thought about that, about us asking for one? You and me, Gerry, we could give a baby such a lot of love. It would be ours just the same. Well, almost.'

'Our very own baby, Martin.'

'Our very own baby, Gerry.'

The pain inside Geraldine Brown was beginning to be replaced by the one and only thing that could possibly make her feel any better on what had been the most hor-rible day of her entire life.

Hope.

*

On a beautiful spring afternoon in May, Geraldine and Martin Brown saw the tiny child in the crib and knew instantly that this was the child for them. When Sister Anne placed the child in Geraldine's arms, her knees almost gave way. Her hands were shaking so much that Martin had to put his hands underneath her arms. Sister Anne was talking to them but neither of them heard a word she was saying.

'This is it, Martin,' Geraldine said.

But her husband could not speak, so afraid was he that his voice would wobble. There were no words to describe this feeling.

The papers had been signed and little Rosemary Brown was going home. Ever so slowly, they walked through the grounds of Nazareth House carrying the tiny bundle, past the mighty horse chestnut tree and up the long driveway.

It seemed like a long journey home on the bus. Neither Martin nor Geraldine said a word, they simply stared at the child in their arms, hardly able to believe they were now parents.

Martin held out the key to open the door with shaking hands, dropped the keys and tried again while Geraldine giggled at him to hurry up. They paused at the end of the passage. Martin put his arms around his wife's shoulders and gently led her to the nursery.

Only a few miles away, in Heaton, a young girl looked out of her bedroom window and, as only a mother could, knew in her heart that her child had been taken. As Martin and Geraldine's tears were replaced by feelings of joy the young mother's tears were only just beginning. The raw pain that engulfed her would stay with her for a lifetime.

Geraldine and Martin knelt on the floor on each side of the cradle, rocking it gently and thanking God for the gift of their beautiful daughter.

The young girl was also kneeling on the floor, praying to God to take care of her baby and asking for forgiveness.

There was nothing to forgive.

The Old Battered Suitcase

It was old and torn and had seen better days. Haven't we all? thought Nancy, smiling. She ran her fingers over the lid and the handle, which seemed to be hanging on by a thread. It had served her well over the years. It had been with her on all the holidays to Birmingham to see Dolly and had carried all the treasures and gifts to the hospital when Dolly suffered her devastating stroke. Nancy closed her eyes for a moment and saw Dolly running around, making more noise than the children, splashing her feet in the pool and banging saucepan lids with the kitchen ladle. A lump formed in her throat, threatening to make her cry. Nancy stood up and fussed about, straightening her apron. This was no time for unnecessary nonsense. She had made her decision and it was time to move on. Naturally, the old battered suitcase would go with her. It had travelled on the overnight bus to the London Palladium when she had taken Susan to see *Aladdin*. What an adventure that had been! This would be a new adventure, she had told Susan, only they didn't have to go as far as London this time.

Truth is, things were changing all around them. The world was becoming a more tolerant and understanding one. The nursery was not as full these days as it used to be. The stigma faced by unmarried mothers was still very evident, but less so. The Swinging Sixties were changing all that. The young were fighting back. Quite right, thought Nancy. Her thoughts returned once more to the lady from Catholic Care who had approached her last month with the offer of a new job. It wasn't the first time someone had approached her, the last one promising a whole five pounds a week. Nancy had almost fainted. 'You mean a month, surely?' But no, five pounds a week it was. Nancy had to sit down for a good ten minutes to imagine having that amount of money.

Family Group Homes were the new thing. Ordinary houses on estates where children could be brought up in a more family-type setting, they told her. 'House Mother' would be her title, she was told. Nancy thought it all sounded rather grand. They believed it would sway her, but it didn't. Titles meant nothing to Nancy. It was when she heard the children's stories – what some of them had been through – and how much the social workers felt Nancy could help them cope and adjust. That's what did it. She would be given her own room, regular days off and, of course, her daughter would be welcome. For days Nancy had thought about it, knowing that this could be good for Susan – to be with children of her own age.

She walked over to the window and looked at the chapel bell swaying gently in the breeze, then turned and walked slowly over to her dressing table with the holy pictures that had been stuck in the corners of the mirror for more years than she could remember. This had been her home, her life for thirty-seven years, and she was not sure she could bear to leave. She remembered so well the day she had been told that, finally, she was to take her Holy Orders in preparation for becoming one of the Sisters of

Nazareth. It was what she had hoped and prayed for, and the sisters were as overjoyed as Nancy. The war had put paid to that idea and she had simply continued to look after the children – other people's children – until that special day when Susan had been placed in her arms.

Nancy had looked after little Susan for so long now that her father, Billy, could never have taken her back. 'You are her mother, Nancy,' he had said, 'and I couldn't possibly take her from you.'

Nancy had thought she would burst with happiness. Yet still, even now, she lived every day in fear that, somehow, Susan could be taken from her. 'You promised me,' she would say to her holy pictures. And so far God had, indeed, kept his promise. As had Billy.

She had seen fear in the eyes of so many little ones, and it never failed to hurt her. She could feel their terror and sometimes their anger. Her apron had wiped away rivers of tears and her knees had been the children's favourite place to sit. Already her arms felt empty at the thought of leaving them behind, and yet she had a responsibility to do what was right for Susan too. 'My daughter,' Nancy whispered to herself, never failing to feel the magic of those words. The abandoned child that Nancy got to keep as her own. Nancy had sometimes allowed herself to wonder whether or not Susan would struggle with their relationship as she grew to adulthood. She need not have worried. The child had felt the magic from the moment their fingers touched, and the bond they had would grow with every passing year.

It was almost time, and yet Nancy still wandered round her room touching everything in it. Every single inch of the room evoked yet another memory. Nancy pushed the doll's cradle that had stood at the side of Susan's bed since she was just three years old and remembered the time she had placed her tiny daughter in the cradle in the playroom and watched the baby as the cradle rocked. Susan's toys would be left for the children to play with. There was nowhere at the new home for them, anyway. The dolls had been packed away, as Susan refused to leave them behind, even though she didn't play with them any more. 'I will keep them until I can give them to my little girl, when I am a mummy,' she had told Nancy. Immediately, Nancy had caught her breath. Oh, imagine, she had thought. A grandmother – now, wouldn't that be something? *Oh dear*, she thought, *I am getting fanciful today. Considering Susan has just turned eleven years old, I think I might have to wait just a few more years. Pull yourself together!*

This move was definitely the right thing to do for both of them, but that didn't stop it hurting.

Nancy sat on the bed next to the old brown, battered suitcase. 'Looks like you and me are going on an adventure,' she told it, 'and I am absolutely terrified.'

Downstairs in the chapel Mother Superior sat quietly in the front pew, staring up at the cross of Our Lord. There was no sound except for the faint clicking of rosary beads. It was only right and fitting that there be change, she thought. People came and went. Children grew up. Like Nancy, Mother hoped they had done their best for them. *Against all the odds sometimes*, she thought. Suddenly, Mother's vision clouded. Instead of the altar steps with the clean and recently vacuumed red carpet, she saw the altar littered with straw, a stable with a wonky star of Bethlehem, Joseph with his head hanging off and a three-legged donkey. Mother thought it was one of the most beautiful and wondrous sights she had ever seen in her life. But it was time to look forward now, not back.

Mother heard the chapel doors open quietly but did not turn round. She wanted a few more moments with her memories before she had to face a life without Nancy. It was the sound of weeping that made her turn. Sister Mary Joseph did not want change if it meant a life without Nancy, and her tears were falling unashamedly. Mother beckoned her to come and sit with her.

Sister Mary Joseph and Mother Superior looked up at the cross of Our Lord, closed their eyes and prayed for Nancy. It was all they could do.

Mother patted Sister's hand. 'Calm yourself, Sister. She will come back and visit us.'

'Oh, Mother, do you think so?'

'Indeed, I do. She will be back to check up on us, to make sure we are still doing things her way.'

'We could invite her for tea, make sure all is going well for her.'

'Yes, Sister, we will ask her before she goes.'

'Mother, oh, Mother –'

'Now, Sister, we have said all there is to say. No long goodbyes. Chin up, now. I want you to be cheerful, to smile and put on a happy face to wave her goodbye as we promised.'

'Very well, Mother, I will do just that.'

They walked to the back of the chapel.

Mother turned briefly to look once more upon the cross of Our Lord. 'I just pray to God that I can do the same,' she whispered.

There was much more fuss than was necessary, Nancy was telling them all. Everyone was talking non-stop to cover their real emotions. Nancy took one look at Sister Mary Joseph's red eyes and immediately had to turn away and fiddle about with her old brown suitcase and the many bags she was carrying. If she looked at Sister, goodness only knew what sort of silly nonsense there would be.

The great oak door was opened and Nancy took her first steps on to the driveway that would take her away from the place that had been her home for the last thirty-seven years. She grabbed Susan's hand, marched out of the door and strode purposefully up the driveway, turning only once to wave furiously at the crowd of people standing in the doorway and the children gathered at the window in the nursery department.

Nancy felt as though her heart would break and had to swiftly remind herself of the exciting and challenging times ahead. The children she was going to look after needed her too.

'We need someone who understands them,' she had been told. 'Some of them have had a somewhat traumatic start in life and some of them just need a little love and attention. Some of them, unfortunately, are a little – how can I put it? – unruly,' the lady had said.

Nancy smiled. *Not for long,* she thought.

Susan was thrilled by it all. 'After all,' she had said, 'you and I will always be together, Mum,' and Nancy's heart had warmed.

Only a few more steps and she would be at the gates. Nancy was wondering if she would have the courage to actually step through them. As much as she wanted to run back to the safety and comfort of all she had known, Nancy forged ahead and walked through the large iron gates of Nazareth House.

Susan jumped as Nancy swung the old brown, battered suitcase around her. 'It's time for a new adventure!' she shouted, out loud, to the world.

Thump!

The handle had finally snapped and the old brown, battered suitcase lay broken on the ground.

Unfortunately for Nancy, it was also time for a new suitcase.

'The Times They are a-Changin''

The mood in Britain was slowly changing. The young were beginning to fight back against prejudice and Victorian attitudes. It was a time of rebellion as girls got bolder, skirts got shorter, hair got higher and Britain sang along to Bob Dylan's 'The Times They Are A-Changin''. The screams could be heard all round the city the day The Beatles played their very first concert in Newcastle, at the Majestic Ballroom on Westgate Road – or the 'Maj', as it was known by the young and trendy. It was certainly the place to be. On a weekend it was always crammed full as Newcastle danced the night away. The Majestic, so many years later, is still a music venue – now called the Academy.

As we danced and sang our way through the 1960s, it was in 1968 that the highest adoption rate was recorded: 16,164 children were adopted in England and Wales. By the end of the 1960s, the contraceptive pill had become more easily available to young women, creating a sharp decline in pregnancies. Women were able, at long last, to take control of their lives. It would be many more years before a kinder, more accepting world welcomed all children into their families without condemnation or judgement, but it was a start.

Finally, the times were changing.

Over the next ten years, housing and supplementary benefits were gradually made available to single mothers, making it possible for some of them to keep their children. It was still a struggle for a mother to bring up a child on her own, but it was becoming easier. And as the 1980s dawned, the attitudes to single parenthood were becoming even less harsh.

At Nazareth House the nursery began to fall quiet. Children were no longer brought to the nuns, and the cries outside the baby home fell silent.

Since the late sixties there had been a new system for children called Family Group Homes: large houses in residential areas where children of all ages would live together. The staff consisted of a house mother and a daily help. The Sisters of Nazareth as well as social workers were assigned to each of the houses, to help with any issues the children might have. It was a much more relaxed and easygoing life for all of the children.

There were still, however, a few of the older ones downstairs at Nazareth House. But the nursery now stood empty, until Catholic Care decided to turn the top floor into a residential care home. The baby home would become a mental health unit.

Once more, the sound of building work echoed in the halls, corridors and grounds. The long corridors disappeared and new staircases were built. As winter arrived, a new decision was made and the mighty oak door was removed to be replaced by something more user-friendly.

On a freezing-cold day in December the house stood empty as it waited for its new residents. The skies were dark and there was little or no light in the gardens. In the shadows it was hard to see the beautiful horse chestnut tree that stood silently waiting. But no matter how hard it listened, it could not hear the sound of children's voices.

Later that afternoon, snow began to fall and the storm over Newcastle became worse. The snow turned to hailstones and then suddenly, from nowhere, there was a crash of thunder and a lightning flash lit up the skies across the city. For a moment, the gardens were lit up and for the final time the magic whispering conker tree stood tall and proud and was shown in all its splendid glory.

At three o'clock on that stormy afternoon, a few days before Christmas, the skies blackened, the thunder roared and the final flash of forked lightning struck the great horse chestnut tree. It had given all it had to give. The last of the children would leave soon and its boughs hung down, heavy with sadness. It creaked, groaned and swayed. The house watched as, finally, it fell slowly and crashed to the ground.

There would be no more children to shelter and protect.

The magic whispering conker tree had done its job and would keep its secrets forever.

The Very Last Children

As so many had done before her, Mother Superior stood silently looking out of the nursery window at the driveway of Nazareth House. Her fingers, now crippled with arthritis, played gently with the rosary beads that hung around her neck. It had been a good life, after all, she thought to herself, and she had been happy to accept the invitation to join a two-week retreat. There had been a few options, but Mother knew which one she would choose. She had wanted to see the place that had been her home for so many years, one last time. Mother hadn't for a moment realized how difficult it would be to see the changes that had been made. There was a different feel about the place without the children's voices, their laughter and footsteps in the corridors, and their tears. So many tears over the years, but then so much laughter and joy too. Mother Superior had seen it all and remembered that she herself had cried more tears – in private, naturally – than she had ever imagined she would when she took her Holy Orders. Since walking through the doors of Nazareth House, the memories had begun to flood back.

She smiled, remembering the day Nancy had arrived, a quiet child wanting nothing more than to go home with her father that very moment and never come back again. Yet she had stayed and had been the very soul of the nursery department. How the children and staff had grown to love her!

Mother Superior had loved Nancy very much indeed, yet it had never been spoken of. There was no need. Sometimes, when love is that powerful, words are not needed. What would she have done without her? They would have managed, of course. But oh, my! It would have been a sadder life, she thought, remembering the sounds of laughter and the wonderful way Nancy had with each and every child they had placed in her competent hands. How many years was it now? thought Mother. She began to count back but couldn't remember. Her mind wasn't what it used to be.

As the rain began to fall heavily against the window, Mother continued to sit on her chair looking out of the window. Then she slowly closed her eyes. She could see them. Nancy walking purposefully up the driveway, pretending she was the Pied Piper, the children marching in twos behind her. It was 1939 and they were making their way to Nazareth House in Carlisle. Nancy could always make a game of anything. They had been facing a world war and they had survived. The children had returned, and life had become normal once more.

The children, Mother sighed. This house had been built for children who no longer needed it now. They were no longer taken from their mother's arms, they were brought up with the families they had been born into, regardless of the situation. Today's mothers would never have to live with the agony of loss, some spending the rest of their lives wondering what had happened to their children, their minds full of questions. Had their children forgiven them? Were they happy? Did they know who their mothers were? Sadly, for so many, their lives were lived carrying a guilt that was not theirs to feel.

Mother could remember only a few reunions, and they had been beautiful to see. Unfortunately, for most of them it did not turn out that way. Yet these brave young girls had brought joy to so many who, without their sacrifice, could only have dreamed of being parents. Mother remembered the joy on their faces as much as she remembered the tears – and sometimes the screams – of others that she could still hear to this day. There had been many children adopted from Nazareth House. Mother's thoughts wandered once more to Nancy and she smiled, remembering the first time the tiny child brought to the door, unwanted, had been placed in her arms. There was a tenderness, somehow, a knowledge that this child belonged to her.

Mother had worried – unnecessarily, as it turned out. Thankfully, Nancy had been allowed to keep Susan, and they had a mother-and-daughter relationship that was strong and beautiful and a bond that would never be broken by either of them.

Then there was Dolly, and Mother's eyes filled with tears. *I miss those days dearly*, she thought to herself. *Even now, after all these years*, she thought, *I miss them so very much*. Dolly being taken far too early had affected them all for a long time. It had been difficult, and Nancy had suffered greatly, in silence, never once wanting to talk about it, but Mother had worried. It had been a Sunday, she remembered, when she caught Nancy in the chapel late at night lighting a candle. Mother hadn't wanted to interfere with her prayers, so she knelt at the back of the chapel and waited. In the dim light of the altar steps, Nancy had stood silently looking up at the cross as Mother watched her. Nancy saw Mother as she turned. She smiled and came to sit beside her for a moment, as Mother had hoped she would.

Mother placed her hand gently over Nancy's and they sat there in silence, each with their own memories, until Mother said, 'You know, Nancy, Dolly really was the most beautiful soul. God must have needed her.'

'Oh, Mother,' Nancy replied, 'I needed her more.'

There was nothing more to be said, and Mother was remembering that moment now. *I should have found something to say to her*, she thought. Yet she knew there were no words that would have helped; the pain had been too raw.

Mother was glad she was here in Nazareth House today. It was right and fitting. The last of the children would be leaving in a while. There were no longer any children upstairs, as it was now a care home for the elderly, and the only children left were downstairs.

Tomorrow there would be none.

There was a gentle tap on the door and someone asked Mother if she would like to come back downstairs for some tea. They had been very kind to her, she thought, but she was not yet ready to leave the window.

'A little while longer?' she asked quietly. 'There is something I must see.'

Mother closed her eyes once more and began to pray and to thank God for the wonderful life she'd had. 'I wouldn't have changed it for the world,' she said to Him. Mother did not even notice when a young member of staff came quietly to her side, leaving a cup of tea and some cake on the table beside her, which would be left untouched.

Somewhere Mother heard the sound of a car door and opened her eyes. She must have courage. It was time, and she would not do this sitting down. Carefully, she held on to the table for a moment and pulled herself up. She stood still and waited.

There they were. The very last children.

With a great sadness in her heart, Mother watched them walk to the waiting cars. How far we have come, she thought, realizing that she had expected to see them walk up the long driveway. But no, it would be cars that would take them away. Her heart beat faster as young Catherine looked up to the window before getting into the last car, saw Mother and waved. Mother held her breath as she waved back, then suddenly her legs gave way and she almost fell back on to the chair behind her. Never had she realized how much it would hurt. It was right and proper that things were different – but oh, how she missed the children!

Mother bent her head and prayed for them all. Where are they now? Who are they, and what have they become? Then she wondered, as Nancy had done – and others would do in the future – if anyone would ever tell their stories.

'Did we do enough for them?' she prayed. 'I hope so. I do hope so.'

Mother held her rosary beads tightly.

'Send someone to watch over them,' she prayed.

More Farewells

Mother heard the commotion from the conservatory where she was resting. She seemed to fall asleep very easily these days and the armchair she was sitting in was so comfortable that she had dozed off for a moment. There were the sounds of hurried feet in the parlour. The voices sounded urgent, confused.

Mother waited.

Alison had been on duty since seven o'clock the night before, and it was nearly time to hand over to the day staff. It had been an unusually difficult night and many of the residents had been a little restless. Old Mrs Bell had insisted she could hear children singing at 3 a.m. and had wanted to join in. Alison had sat with her, telling her tales she had heard about the nursery and the children, then promised to play her favourite CD the next evening when she came back on duty. 'We will have a sing-along then,' she said, patting her hand. There had been a general feeling of something being not quite right, Alison thought, but put it to the back of her mind. She'd had enough to cope with on night duty – and they could be very busy nights. It had rained on and off for most of the night and Alison dearly hoped it would stop by morning. It was a long walk to the bus stop and she was dreaming of her little flat with the radiators full on and a very strong, hot cup of tea.

She hurried out of the door and stepped on to the driveway. Suddenly, she stopped. Something wasn't right. What on earth was it? Alison paused, looked around her and froze. Hardly able to breathe, Alison realized what it was and wondered why on earth her feet seemed to be suddenly stuck to the ground.

'I don't understand,' was all she could think of to say. 'Where on earth?'

Alison turned away and closed her eyes, not believing what she saw — or did not see — then turned round again and opened her eyes once more.

Sister Mary heard the frantic knocking on the door and hurried to find a breathless Alison stuttering and stumbling and looking like she had just received the most terrible shock. On hearing the commotion, other staff were arriving to see what was going on. Each one of them was trying to calm Alison down; she was making no sense whatsoever.

'Look!' she cried, pulling Sister Mary by the hand.

They all ran out and looked.

There was nothing to see.

'Look, Sister!' Alison cried again. 'The grotto.'

Slowly, unable to believe her eyes, Sister Mary walked towards the grotto as Mother Superior looked on from the conservatory in shock.

They stood in front of the grotto, unable to think of a single thing to say.

The beautiful statue of Our Lady of Lourdes — the statue that had taken part in more May Processions than anyone could remember and had stood in the grounds of Nazareth House for almost eighty years — was gone.

Parents had been comforted by her and had prayed with her. Children had played and sung alongside her. She had brought solace and comfort to many.

Our Lady of Lourdes was gone.

Nobody ever found out what happened to her, how she had been taken – or, indeed, where she is now. The grotto of Our Lady of Lourdes stands empty to this day. It is a mystery that has never been solved.

Except in the mind of Mother Superior, who leaned back in her comfortable chair with a smile on her face. Her prayers had been answered.

'Take care of them,' she whispered, and fell once more into a peaceful sleep.

Her job was done.

The Magic Begins Again

The house had fallen silent. There had never been such a silence since the war years. Even then, the Sisters of Nazareth had whispered prayers in the chapel for the safe homecoming of their staff and children. Today there was not even a whisper. A more functional and safer door had been erected. The magic whispering conker tree was gone and the nursery grounds looked sad and forlorn. The organ in the church had been dismantled and the church pews, which so many children had sat on, were all gone. The windows refused to allow the weak sunlight to stream through the stained glass showing the beauty of the small chapel. There were no ripples on the pond at the bottom of the garden, and the grotto looked sad and lonely without Our Lady of Lourdes standing at the end of the driveway ready to welcome and comfort all who came here. The grotto was now filled with leaves. The branches of the trees in the small wood to the left of the driveway refused to sway.

All was totally still.

It was December 1997 and Nazareth House was up for sale. The very first brick had been laid in 1817, making the oldest part of the house 180 years old. The Sisters of Nazareth had bought the house in 1916 and for eighty years they had cared for the children of the north-east and nursed the elderly, infirm and vulnerable. Already, parts of the land had been sold off. At the bottom of the drive – where the horse stables had once stood, behind the caretaker's cottage with the old weather vane on top – there was now a new housing estate.

Yet still, if you stood at the top of the driveway looking down towards the house, it all appeared exactly the same. The many windows looked out upon the driveway and the house waited. It had been built for children, and if you listened very carefully on a windy day it was almost as though you could hear the whispers on the wind. Echoes of Christmases past, the sounds of prayer and of children's voices raised in song as they walked round the grounds during the spring May Procession to take Our Lady of Lourdes flowers and gifts. The swings and the roundabout in the playground were also gone. It was a lonely place without the children.

The house sighed and waited.

People came and went over the next two years and there were steps that echoed in the corridors. But the house was not satisfied yet. The right people must come along; it had time to wait.

Late one morning in 1999, there were cars on the driveway and keys were turned in the lock on the new front door. The branches on the driveway began to sway, there was a rustle of leaves on the ground, and something stirred in the pool at the bottom of the garden. From somewhere in the parlour came the sound of faint ticking, although there was no longer any clock in evidence, and the weak summer sun did all it could to shine through the glass windows of the chapel. Empty or not, today it must look as beautiful as it possibly could.

The people walking from room to room were as enchanted with it as the house had expected them to be. The grounds were still enormous and would be even more beautiful when they had finished with them, they said. What exactly was its history? they wondered. What stories does this house have to tell? It was when they walked into the room upstairs – with the window which still had the original bars on and overlooked the nursery playground – that they felt it fully for the first time. There had been magic here. They walked up the little steps outside the playroom and made their way up to the small attic room above. Wow, someone's treasure trove! they whispered, pulling at the boxes to see what lay inside. There were smiles on the faces of the visitors. Aside from the financial aspects, somehow it just felt right.

The house was very pleased indeed. The sunshine streaming into the chapel became stronger so that when they eventually threw open the doors it looked as beautiful as ever. It was obvious that it was now simply used as a hall, they said. The chapel, however, had a secret yet to be discovered. They would have to wait. It would hold the secret a little longer. The keys turned in the locks and the cars made their way back up the driveway.

The house fell silent once more.

And yet, there was movement. Something in the air said the house was ready and would be prepared.

Meanwhile, it waited.

*

It was later that year when the cars returned. Behind them, furniture vans and many people were bustling about. Once more, the first pieces of furniture that were carried into the house were little tables and chairs for the children. Blackboards, bookcases, low round desks and computers. Noticeboards where pictures would be pinned were hung on the walls, and the doors were thrown open wide.

It had been worth the wait.

The name of the house was to be changed but it did not mind at all. There was only one thing that mattered. The children had returned. Once again, there would be hundreds of children passing through these doors. These children would be happy children. They would skip, dance, play music and sing. They would be taught by teachers who would guide and encourage them. It had been bought by a private girls' school. The house had gone full circle, from the first children who had arrived in 1916, to Nazareth House – private convent school.

There was no longer a magic whispering conker tree to shelter and protect the children. Our Lady of Lourdes no longer stood in the grotto to watch over all who walked down the driveway. The mermaids at the bottom of the garden had disappeared. The pool had overflowed with their tears when Dolly went home to the God who had loaned her to Nazareth House.

They were no longer needed. These children had teachers whose minds held the knowledge to give them the greatest start in life. But more importantly, from the head teacher to every single member of staff, their hearts were open to show the children love and an acceptance of who they had been, who they were and who they would become.

The children who now walked through the iron gates on to the driveway would no longer do so with sadness but with a joy in their hearts as they skipped down the driveway, happily chatting and knowing that the day ahead would be filled with fun, acceptance and new learning.

The house sighed contentedly, knowing that it still held a wonderful surprise.

Once more, the magic had begun.

I think Nancy would have been very pleased indeed. Don't you?

God's Special Souls

Walking amongst us in life are a special group of souls to whom we owe a great debt of gratitude. I believe they were born into this world with a very specific task to carry out. To nurture, support, encourage and protect. Their God-given talents include patience, understanding, acceptance and a great passion for what they do. Each person who comes into contact with them feels at some point in their life that, no matter what life throws at them, whatever challenges they face, they will be able to stand tall and overcome any obstacles with courage, a belief in themselves and a determination to succeed.

Success, of course, does not always mean superb grades, the best job or the highest wage. To be the best person you can be is simply one of the greatest successes any one of us can achieve. When we pause for a moment to hold the hand of someone in pain, bringing comfort and letting them know we believe in them wholeheartedly, we reignite the spark of hope deep inside that, one day, all will be well with their world once more. One of life's greatest successes is to give of ourselves and help to smooth the path of another person's journey.

These people walk amongst us, yet they are very rarely talked about. There will be no news reports of their greatness, their patience and the long hours they spend trying to find new ways to encourage and support those who need it most. Most of their tears will fall in private, except for those that are spilled at the gravesides of those – and there are many – who leave this world early to return home to the God who allowed us the privilege of spending part of our journey with them.

As parents, our children are everything, and it is to us they turn when they need help, encouragement, arms to comfort them, knees to sit upon and gentle hands to wipe their tears away. It is to us they come with their questions, because we are their whole world and, naturally, as parents, we know all the answers, as far as they are concerned. Of course, our own children are the most intelligent, handsome, prettiest, sweetest natured, funny and fascinating children in the whole world.

We get excited about a night out, only to discover after being away for half an hour that our arms feel empty. We wonder whether they are crying for us and then, as everyone around us becomes relaxed and enjoys chatting, we start going through the 'what if's and we only begin to relax on the way home, when we struggle to get the key in the lock quickly enough to find out whether our little ones are safe and well. Even though we are grateful that they are perfectly safe, there is a smug look on our face when we hear they cried for us when we left. We run upstairs to wake them up, cuddle them, and suddenly our hearts are more full of joy than we could ever have imagined. Yet at some point, while they are still young children, we will hand them over to a total stranger and pray to God that they will be in safe hands.

If we are very lucky, we will be handing them over to one of God's special chosen souls who have come here to do one of the most important jobs that exist. They will weave magic into the lives of our children and create a belief in each and every child that they will rise to every life challenge, meet it head on and succeed. They will know how it feels to be accepted for who they are. Their souls will sing, even when success seems a million miles away, because they have tried their very best.

For many of us that first morning comes far too soon. We wave our children off, feeling like someone has a vice-like grip on our heart and is about to rip it out. We find ourselves crying more tears than our children have ever done in their first few years. The children, of course, are usually fine and excited about their first day with this new person in their lives. However, if you are like me, I cried like a fool beyond solace as one of these gentle souls took my child from me.

They are called teachers.

From now on, for some reason, our children start coming home doing things we might have pleaded with them to do for months, but suddenly – because 'Mrs Edwards says so' – it must be done. It's Mrs Edwards this and Mrs Edwards that – and, if you are like me, I must admit to feeling a little jealous. Mrs Edwards, it seemed, was perfect. Yet, as time went on, I realized just how special she really was. There was a strength, yet a gentleness, about her that made the children feel like each and every one of them was the most important child in the class. The parents who came away from even a moment with her knew they, too, were being guided and understood. Her voice was friendly, fun and yet firm when necessary. My daughter's new start in life was in the hands of one of

God's special souls who are born to teach. To be in Mrs Edwards's class meant you were valued and special, and it was a wonderful start to my daughter's next chapter in her life. She cried more the day she left school than she had ever done in her first eleven years, because she was leaving behind a group of wonderful teachers who had done everything a parent could ask or hope for.

It is never just a job for these people, it is a vocation. And there are many of them.

Thank God for the Mrs Edwardses of this world.

A Secret Revealed

Angela paused at the large iron gates leading to Nazareth House, as many had done before her. She took her first steps towards the next chapter in her life and stopped as she saw the house in front of her for the first time. The flowers in the wood swayed in the gentle breeze, sending their beautiful scents swirling around her. The spirit of the great horse chestnut tree was still, and waited. The reeds in the pool at the bottom of the garden stirred. The sun shone on the chapel windows and bounced around the walls. The leaves rustled in the empty grotto. This was who the house had waited for as it remained empty all that time.

Angela stood at the bottom of the driveway and took it all in. 'So many windows,' she whispered to herself as she looked up. She walked into the portico, where the great oak door had once stood. There was a big old bell on the wall and she pressed it, realizing that, old as it might be, it still worked. Some things were made to last, she smiled to herself.

When the door was opened she found herself in a parlour which still held all the original features, as this part of the house was now nearly two hundred years old and a Grade II listed building. The ornately carved stairwell was absolutely beautiful. Angela began to walk up the stairs, taking in the glass dome in the ceiling, and paused before opening the door through to the next part of the building. Then she took her first steps into what had once been the entrance to Nancy's nursery department. There was no way Angela could have seen the long corridors that ran from one end of the house to the other and which seemed to stretch for miles; health and safety had insisted on more stairways, and so the corridors had been split up.

There was a small room to Angela's left, and as she opened the door there was a whiff of long-ago pots of tea and Cook's special cakes. The next room to her left had a large window that looked out on to the drive-way. There was an old radio in the corner and an enormous table covered in sewing boxes, where Nancy had sat up all Christmas Eve making rag dolls for the children, now long gone. Opposite was another room, with bars on the windows. What was this? she wondered, looking out on to the playground and seeing for the first time the enormous stump of what was once a magnificent tree.

Back in the corridor, Angela spotted another door. Goodness, she thought, there were so many doors and rooms! She walked through to find herself at the top of yet another set of stairs leading down and then some small steps up to what looked like a storage space. Something took Angela up the tiny steps, and she stood in the small cluttered space. It was crammed with what looked like hundreds of boxes, all marked with pen, and strangely, in the corner in the dim light, there was what looked like a brightly coloured bucket and spade.

'Someone's treasures,' she whispered to herself, with a smile. Nancy would have agreed wholeheartedly.

Heading back through the door, Angela continued down the corridor, turned left and then found another door to her right. There was a gentle hush, except for maybe the faint ticking of a clock coming from somewhere, as Angela held out her hand, slowly turned the door handle and walked inside. The old dressing table with the holy pictures stuck in the side of the mirror was long gone. From somewhere deep inside, Angela experienced a feeling of having made the right decision. She was here for a reason, having been chosen not only to teach but to nurture, encourage and support the people around her. Together they would make a difference.

In that perfect moment all was as it should be.

Angela walked over to the original sash windows and looked out over the chapel, with the bell that no longer rang. It really was a very special place and very soon it would be filled with smiling, happy faces and the sound of children's voices raised in song. This was what Angela had been born to do. She knew she would be surrounded by a group of people who would support her endeavours to bring all that was best in the world to the children who came here and were placed in her care.

There was something special about this room, and Angela wondered what it was. It had, of course, been a private girls' convent school back in 1916, and then an orphanage. For a moment, something reached out and touched her heart as she stood where Nancy had stood for many years of her life. Angela wondered what had happened here and what stories there were to be told.

It took Angela many days to explore the house and learn what each room was going to be. There would be classrooms, art rooms, a dining hall, music and drama rooms and staff quarters.

One day, Angela found herself standing outside yet another door. As she walked in, she discovered she was on some sort of balcony and looked up into the wooden beams of the roof. 'Oh, I know where I am,' she realized, and looked down over the balcony into what appeared to be a hall. This was the chapel, she realized, looking at the stained-glass windows. How beautiful it was, even if there was no altar. She stood for a while as the ghosts of Christmas past gave her their blessing. Innocent souls stood in line in their pretty white dresses with garlands in their hair, hands together in prayer, proud and excited to be in the May Procession. The house sighed and remembered the child who had sat in the benches praying to be a nun so she could stay and look after the children. In the end, God had other ideas for her. But she had stayed and it was a sadder place without her now. Upstairs, in the attic of treasures, lay Joseph with a wonky head, a donkey with a missing leg, and a broken star, all of which the chapel would never see again.

Angela felt strangely moved and had no idea why. It wasn't until she stood outside the chapel that she realized the chapel was actually much bigger outside than it was inside. *I must look again*, she thought. But the next few weeks and months were busy, and every moment of her time was spent preparing for the children who were arriving. The children who would walk down that driveway would be blessed to be in her care. She would know every single one of their names, she would always take the time to stop and speak to them, and she would listen not only with her ears but with her heart. One of God's special teachers, with a group of staff who would guide, protect, support and encourage every child who walked through the school doors.

Angela was hurrying along the corridor when she heard the sounds of builders at work in the chapel.

She paused. 'I wonder . . .' she said to herself, as she approached the builders.

'Tomorrow,' they told her. 'We will check it out for you.'

So it was ten o'clock the next morning when they stood in the school hall, looking at the wall in front of them.

'It's just a partition wall,' they told her. 'It's been put up some time in the last few years. It certainly isn't an original wall. What do you want us to do?'

They all stood looking at the wall, as if it would tell them its secret, but there was silence all around. They would have to find out for themselves. What should she do? Angela wondered, but there was nobody to tell her. This was a very special decision, one that could be taken only by her.

A few more quiet moments went by as the builders stood ready, hammers in their hands.

'Go ahead!' she said, praying it had, indeed, been the right choice as the hammers were raised.

Angela stood back and watched as, bit by bit, the wall came crumbling down. There was a gasp as the house finally gave up the secret it had been holding on to all this time.

'Oh!' was all Angela managed to say.

There in front of them, as the sun shone proudly through the stained-glass windows, was the original altar that had been built over eighty years earlier.

Somewhere high up in the attic at the top of the house, a dim light shone on Joseph with a wonky head, a donkey with a missing leg, and a wonky star.

The house had given up its secret and it was very happy indeed.

The Window

As soon as Angela saw the room, she knew it was perfect. Somehow, there was a knowledge that decisions had been made here, tears had been cried, many had been comforted, yet there had been much joy, even love. There were carvings on the ceilings and walls that had been created many years ago. This was one of the original rooms in the building, now nearly two hundred years old. What had taken place in this room during all those years? she wondered.

Looking around the room, her eyes fell on the large window that looked out upon the gardens. It was then that she saw it properly for the first time and wondered what it was. It seemed to be some sort of archway.

No, it was more than that.

'It's a grotto,' Angela whispered to herself. It was full of leaves and a few of the petals that had been carried on the breeze from the small wood, to land gently where once Our Lady of Lourdes had stood. Forsaken now, it stood empty. Yet still, there was a beauty about it. 'One day, I will do something about that,' she said to herself.

Angela found a seat, sat down and continued to look out of the window. 'Who sat here before me?' she asked the room. There was a feeling of goodness and, deep down inside, a feeling of being in the right place.

The large hallway outside her room had been called a 'parlour' and the original features all stood out proudly, as they had always done, looking every bit as beautiful as on the day the house had been built. The house had been an orphanage, and yet there were no feelings of sadness here. There had been tears – of course there had – yet there had been love here too, and laughter.

Magic had been created inside these walls. And if you closed your eyes, it was still there.

Every single child who went through her hands would be valued, appreciated and respected. Their imagination and creativity would be encouraged and they would feel confident in their abilities. This would be a very special place to learn, so much more than simply a school. It would be a place where each child would feel safe and supported, able to stand up and speak without fear of criticism.

Angela smiled, thinking about all the treasures she had come across in the attic. She wondered once more about the large tree stump she had discovered in the garden, which had obviously once been an enormous tree of some kind. Pushing the creaking gate open at the bottom of the garden, she had found an enchanting little pond. The water seemed to stir as she approached it. *One day*, she had thought, *I will make this area pretty again*.

There was a knock on the door. Her busy day was about to begin.

Angela turned to look out of the window. Once more, her eyes fell on the empty grotto.

'So many stories,' she whispered, as others had done before her. 'I wonder if anyone will ever tell their stories?'

Welcome Home

It was autumn once more and the grounds of Nazareth House were littered with leaves of beautiful oranges and reds. The driveway had been busy with the sounds of cars driving up and down as the school children made their way home. The crunching sounds of the leaves told the house that, yet again, autumn was upon them.

The bell on the top of the chapel stood silent, no longer required to ring out the start of a new day or announce church services. It had been more years than it could remember since it last stirred. The bell looked out over the whole of Newcastle and could be seen for many miles.

Today, there was something in the air. The breeze was playing around the bell, almost daring it to ring. The reeds in the pool at the bottom of the garden were stirring, almost as though there was something down there.

A conker appeared in the garden beside the stump of the magic whispering conker tree, and nobody could think where it could have possibly come from.

The breeze continued to push and the bell moved ever so slightly.

Today, behind what had been the nursery playground, stood a building that had once been a primary school and was now a care home for the elderly. It looked over the grounds of Nazareth House. The bell paused and the mermaids dared for the first time in many years to rise slowly to the top of the pool, where they waited.

The red car pulled slowly into the car park. Susan looked up, with tears in her eyes, and was comforted at the sight of the bell and the grounds of Nazareth House. This had been the right decision – the only one – but one of the most painful ones she had ever had to make. Nancy was suffering from dementia and needed permanent care. The fight she'd had to get her into this home, built in the grounds of Nazareth House, was worth it.

Nancy was home once more where her journey in life had begun. She had loved and cared for more children than anyone could possibly have imagined. The walls of Nazareth House held on to the sounds of the laughter she had created and the soothing lullabies she had sung. Walls did, indeed, have ears – Nancy was quite right, as usual.

As the day wore on, Susan and Gemah stayed close, settling Nancy in, chatting endlessly to cover their pain. Nancy sat quite still, smiling, watching them place photographs on the small bedside table, filling her drawers and wardrobe with all the new clothes they had bought for her. They told her about the games she would play with the other residents and read out the menu for that night's dinner.

Gemah looked out of the window. 'There seems to be a storm brewing, Mum,' she said. 'It's getting extremely windy out there.'

The breeze had turned into a strong wind. It had a purpose today and it must be carried out. It pushed the chapel bell once more.

It was time to go, and Susan knew it. 'How do I leave her?' she asked Gemah. 'Please God, how do I get up and leave her here?'

Gemah was sitting holding her grandma's hand and was unable to answer. Her throat was closing but she had no intention of crying and making things worse. She would wait until she was alone – or at least, she would try to. Finally, with promises of coming back tomorrow and how everything would be fine, and making sure Nancy understood that Susan and Gemah were only ten minutes away, they left. It was Gemah who showed the greatest strength that day, holding her mum as she broke down in tears the minute they got to the car, knowing they were leaving Nancy behind. Silent tears that would no longer wait were pouring down Gemah's face as her mum reached out to open the car door.

Gemah paused. 'Mum, what was that?' It was very faint. 'It couldn't be,' she whispered, and yet there it was again. 'Mum, listen . . .' she said, reaching out to her.

Together, hand in hand, they listened.

Nancy, at that very moment, was sitting in the conservatory of the care home that looked out over the grounds of Nazareth House. Something inside stirred, some memory. What was it?

Children, that was it! Lots and lots of children. Nancy smiled and felt comforted.

Outside, the storm continued and gathered momentum. The wind was not giving up today; it needed just one final push.

Gemah and Susan listened, and Nancy raised her head, as the chapel bell high upon the roof of Nazareth House rang out once more to welcome Nancy home.

'Oh, yes, now I remember,' said Nancy, 'it was something about mermaids . . .'

Where are the Children?

'Where are the children?' Nancy asked the nice lady who was looking after her. She was sitting in the conservatory, looking at the house and its many windows.

Susan had known her mum would somehow draw comfort from being able to see it. It was for that very reason Susan had fought to get her into that particular care home when her hand had been forced and they told her Nancy needed proper nursing care.

'Where are the children?' Nancy asked again.

The lady smiled, patted her hand and gave her a cup of tea. Nancy had been asked if she would like another cup of tea, but no matter how hard she tried she couldn't remember having the first one. She had closed her eyes and tried to remember, but it was no use, so she had simply said, 'yes, please.'

Nancy looked around the room. It was nice enough, she supposed, then suddenly felt confused, not knowing where she was. Susan had been here earlier and explained it all, but Nancy was struggling to remember what she had been told. There was music coming from somewhere. Nancy smiled and began to hum along. Maybe the children were going to sing. She closed her eyes. Ah yes, there they were, she could see them now. All their little faces beaming up at her, knowing how well they were doing, because she had told them that the louder they sang the better it sounded. It was getting harder and harder, these days, to see them and remember where they were. Surely, she should be doing something? But as Nancy looked around the large room, there were no piles of washing or ironing to be seen anywhere, just other people like herself, sitting around, doing nothing.

'Bone idle!' she said out loud, and heard a couple of the staff giggle as they came to make her comfortable and see if there was anything she wanted.

'Don't you worry, the ironing is all done,' Laura told her.

Nancy grabbed Laura's hand and looked up at her. 'It's cold outside,' she said. 'Now you make sure they have their winter coats on. They will catch their death of cold, and I don't want a dormitory full of sick children, thank you very much.'

'Of course,' said Laura and turned away, not knowing quite what to say or do.

Susan had spoken quite firmly to the staff yesterday, when they said they had tried to explain there were no children. 'They are as real to her as I am to you,' Susan said, 'and if my mother wants to talk about the children as if she can see them, she has every right to do so. Don't ever take that away from her. Imagine me trying to tell you that I don't exist, I am not here right in front of you. How would that make you feel? Frustrated, angry maybe. She has dementia, she is never going to understand, and a world without her children would be the most lonely existence possible. Leave her be. She remembers so little now,' Susan said, with tears in her eyes, as she turned to look at her mother from across the room. The pain that threatened to engulf her was greater than she had ever known in her life, worse than any physical pain.

Gemah had been heartbroken when they came to see Nancy yesterday. She had hurried over and taken her grandma's hand.

Nancy had looked up with those still-beautiful blue eyes and turned to Susan, saying, 'Oh, is this your daughter?'

Gemah's eyes had filled with tears and she had run from the room. 'It's too much, Mum,' she had said. 'I've lost her already, haven't I?' and she had cried all the way home in the car and most of the night. 'Why does she remember the children and not me?' she had sobbed.

The doctor had explained that Nancy's short-term memory was badly affected, yet her long-term memory was quite clear most of the time. 'It is normal,' he had said.

'What is normal about that?' Gemah had cried.

But Susan had no answers.

A few nights later, Nancy sat watching *Mary Poppins*, holding Susan's hand. They had been sitting together for hours but Nancy had no idea of time and no knowledge of what they were watching. This was her favourite time, when Susan came to sit with her and held her hand. Susan was her daughter. Nancy knew that, because they had told her. She liked Susan, there was just something about the way she held her hand that reminded her of a little girl she once knew.

Susan sat holding her mother's hand, wanting to simply give in to the pain and cry and scream for all the world to hear. Already the tears had begun to fall, and one of the carers had quietly passed her a tissue. *Please, God, let her know it's me*, she thought. *Please, let her remember me.*

But Nancy simply smiled and continued to watch the film. One of the staff placed another cup of tea next to Susan, with a small plate of biscuits, patted her shoulder and smiled. Just a small gesture but one which was much appreciated by Susan, and she pulled herself together. Nancy began to hum along, seeming to enjoy the film, when suddenly she sat forward and then turned to look at Susan with an excited expression on her face.

'Look at that!' she said, pointing to the television. Nancy was beaming from ear to ear. 'Look, Susan,' she said, 'up-and-down horses. Oh, Susan, do you remember?'

Susan put her head on her mum's shoulder. 'I do, Mum, I certainly do.'

Thank you, God, she thought.

Shortly afterwards, Nancy fell asleep and Susan contin-ued to hold her mum's hand, seeing nothing that was happening on the television. She was seven years old again and on holiday at Butlin's holiday camp. Susan and Christopher, another little boy at the orphanage, had become inseparable, and Nancy had brought them both on holiday. She had been saving for such a long time and Susan had never seen her mum look so proud as the day she counted the money and told them they were going to Butlin's. They had seen the fairground as soon as the coach had turned into the gates, and none of them could contain their excitement. As soon as they had reached the chalet, Nancy had thrown the cases on the bed and they had run towards the music they could hear coming from the other side of the camp, laughing all the way. Suddenly, there it was in front of them, the merry-go-round with the up-and-down horses. Nancy had picked Susan and

Christopher up and swung them up on to a horse and sat behind, holding on to them both, as they waited. The music began and slowly the horses began to move. Nancy thought it was one of the most incredibly exciting moments in her entire life as, together, Nancy and the precious daughter she loved more than anything in the world held on to each other whilst the horses continued to go round and round, up and down, and once more Nancy prayed that nobody would ever take her daughter away from her.

Susan continued to daydream until she was told they needed to get her mum ready for bed. 'Goodnight, Mum,' she whispered, 'I love you so much.'

Suddenly, Nancy looked puzzled. 'Where is Gemah today?' she asked.

Susan grinned. Her mum still remembered. She was still here with them, after all, she thought with relief. 'I will bring her tomorrow,' Susan said, with a smile, 'I promise.'

'Yes,' said Nancy, 'bring her straight from school.'

Susan laughed, Gemah was now eighteen years old. Still, all in all, it had been a good day.

Later that night, after supper, *Mary Poppins* and the up-and-down horses long forgotten, Nancy was sitting in the conservatory wearing her new blue nightgown, dressing gown and slippers that Susan had bought for her. It was a lovely summer night and there was music playing on the CD player.

Nancy was smiling as her eyes strayed once more to the grounds surrounding her.

'Where are the children?' she whispered.

Tartan Blankets and Final Farewells

It was one of those amazingly beautiful days that you sometimes get in December. There had been a crisp frost on the ground that morning, the trees were white and yet the sun was shining. Today would be perfect. Just like every other year.

Susan was remembering that first year, when Gemah had been only a few months old. Nancy had been smiling for days, planning the special trip out. It was a day very much like today – crisp, sunny, picture-card pretty and absolutely freezing cold.

It was a Sunday morning and Susan was remembering the smile on Nancy's face, because the day she had dreamed of for so long was finally here. The perfect day, she had called it. The new, warm tartan fleece was tucked around Gemah in her pram. Hat, mittens, thick coat, what looked like half a dozen blankets underneath the fleece – the poor little lamb had more chance of getting a heat rash than catching cold.

Nancy had been fussing since early morning, so excited was she about the day ahead. It was all planned down to the last detail. It was going to be perfect, she said once more.

They had been up early that morning, eaten breakfast and gone to church. When the organist began to play 'Silent Night', Nancy's favourite Christmas carol, the smile on her face said it all. 'Perfect,' she smiled as she gently rocked Gemah in her arms.

Nancy loved going to church on a Sunday, and Susan was highly amused to see her impatiently tapping her foot during the sermon that day, signalling that she wanted to be away. No tea in the church hall afterwards. Today Gemah was settled in her pram, with all the blankets tucked in, and they were ready to go. Goodbyes had been said and Susan turned to reach for the pram. It wasn't going to happen. Oh no, not that day. Nancy was already striding up the aisle, pushing her granddaughter on what was to be the beginning of a new tradition for the next eighteen years.

It was only a short walk to the bus stop and a ten-minute bus ride into town. Nancy and Susan sat so closely together that day on the bus, each of them knowing that today was simply going to be a wonderful day. And still today, Susan often closes her eyes and can see them all together on their perfect day and feel that complete and absolute joy.

They stood at the top of Northumberland Street and took in the wonderful sight of all the Christmas decorations. It was so very pretty and Nancy chatted non-stop to Gemah, telling her all about the lights, pointing out the shop displays, telling her about Santa, fussing with the blankets.

'Perfect day, Mum?' Susan asked.

'Oh, yes, Susan. Perfect!'

A happy family – grandmother, daughter and granddaughter – hurrying down Northumberland Street. Finally, they were there and could see the queue ahead.

It was Fenwick's Christmas window display.

The music was playing and then, suddenly, all the blankets were whipped off the pram and Nancy gathered Gemah in her arms, wrapping the new tartan blanket around her. All at once, without warning, her eyes filled with tears and she turned away, chatting to Gemah to hide her embarrassment. There they stood, squashed together in the crowd, hundreds of people there that day, listening to the music. Children were squealing with excitement and dancing around. Lots of people were rubbing their hands together, it was so cold. The window was amazing, as always. Santa was smiling and waving, his sack of toys beside him in his workshop, with moving toy displays, songs and jingling bells.

Above them, the many-coloured street decorations twinkled, shone and changed colour as the children all gasped in wonder.

They reached the last part of the window and Susan turned to Nancy. 'Ready for our cuppa and cake in Fenwick's warm café?'

Not yet, it would seem, as Nancy once more joined the queue. 'Just one more time, love,' she said, 'just one last time.'

Today, eighteen years later, here they were once more. A new tartan blanket had been bought in Fenwick's yesterday – only, this time, it was tucked into a wheelchair instead of a pram.

'We must keep her warm, Mum,' Gemah had said. 'It's bitterly cold out there.'

December 2005 found this happy family once more standing at the top of Northumberland Street for their traditional Perfect Day.

In Fenwick's window a big red train chuffed and tooted, little drummer mice banged their drums, and Santa sat in his workshop and waved merrily to all the children.

Today the roles were reversed and it was Gemah who pushed her grandma and pointed out all the wonders of Christmas. Susan stood back and watched them together. So much love, such tenderness, it was beautiful to see and be a part of.

'Time for tea,' Susan said, taking her mum's hand.

Nancy smiled and looked up at Gemah, then to Susan. 'Just one last time, Susan,' she said, 'just one last time.'

It was only one week later that Gemah and Susan sat all through the night with her, talking, laughing, loving.

Until finally, in the early hours of the morning, No-nonsense Nancy went home to the God who had allowed so many the privilege of loving her.

It had, indeed, been one last time.

On 6 December 2005, the softest and prettiest flakes of snow fluttered gently down to land silently upon the roof of Nazareth House.

The bell rang out once, then stopped, never to ring again.

The enchanted clock in the hallway paused, and fell silent forever.

The spirit of the magic whispering conker tree sighed as its boughs swayed and drooped.

The mermaids wept and disappeared to the bottom of the pool, never to be seen or heard of again.

A Job Well Done

There had been whispers all around, then suddenly a perfect stillness, as they waited and listened. There was a sense of increased warmth, and colours that had never been seen before merged and swirled, creating rainbows throughout the heavens and on earth.

Could it be true? they wondered.

The whispers reached the children in the garden of dreams, and they stopped and listened. Slowly, they began to gather around the young girl who looked after them and looked hopefully into her eyes. Was it true? their eyes said. The young girl was listening carefully to the breeze that carried the whispers. Her eyes filled with tears of joy and then, slowly, she began to smile as her eyes sparkled and shone. She held her hands out for the children and they came closer. It was true, her eyes told them. It was time. She was coming home. The young girl sat down amongst the children, closed her eyes and remembered.

God, of course, knew the whispers were true. It was He who had called her home. He too was remembering. It seemed only a moment ago, yet it had been eighty-five earthly years since this wise soul had come to him, pleading to go back to the place they called Earth and let the young girl go with her. 'I know she is a gentle and new soul,' she had told Him, 'but it is what she wants.' He had watched her as He made His decision.

His children were all special to Him, yet there was something about this young soul that made Him smile and His heart shone just a little more each time He heard her voice. There was a gentleness in her voice that soothed your very being. How would this beautiful and gentle soul survive leaving home for the first time? Yet it was what she wanted, the wise soul had assured Him.

Nobody knew better than God that it wasn't the easiest of places to go to, or the easiest of journeys. He had watched the people on Earth destroy themselves and the beautiful world in which they lived. In despair He had sent help, over and over again, which many times had been ignored and His heart was greatly saddened.

'She is such a gentle soul,' He had said.

Yet the wise soul had been so sure it was the right thing to do. 'She is ready,' she told Him, 'and a little kindness could go a long way down there.' She smiled at Him. 'I have done this many times before. I will go first and prepare the way so that I can protect and guide her.'

God smiled, remembering the other requests. This time she wanted to be a mother and, naturally, Tilly, her soulmate, would go with her, as always. It would be a challenging life, yet He would grant it. He thought once more about the young soul who wanted to be part of their journey, and smiled. He would allow it, He said. But as with all his most special children, He would bring her home early.

The young soul had, indeed, pleaded over and over again. 'Please ask Him to let me go. No child should be alone and unloved, and I have seen what is going to happen down there. The children must be given hope, a sense of being loved and special. They must grow up knowing that each one of them has their own special little ways and characters. Even the poorest of children can survive anything if they are loved. We can do it together. We can give them strength, courage, love, belief in themselves and a strong pair of arms to hold them. They must be taught to laugh and have fun. We can be teachers, just like we are here, only it will be even more important. Please ask Him. You have been many times, let me be the one to share your life this time.'

For a moment in time the heavens stood still, their souls merged, and the bond between them grew even stronger.

God's will had been done.

The angels gathered on earth and whispered their names to the earth mothers.

'Nancy.'

'Dolly.'

'Don't be afraid,' said Nancy, smiling as she looked into Dolly's eyes. 'I will be waiting for you.'

'What will happen when I get there? Will I know who you are?'

'You will know in your heart.'

'How will I find you? Where will you be, and who will tell me where to go?'

'You will be guided to me, God's plan is in place.'

'Oh, but what if you don't recognize me?' Dolly cried out as Nancy's soul began the journey to Earth.

'I will know you the moment I see you, my darling,' Nancy whispered. 'How could I not?'

Dolly smiled as she remembered. Now Nancy was coming home, and suddenly the silence in heaven was broken as the children raised their voices in song. Until the whispers told them she was on her way and, once more, a gentle hush fell all around. Dolly, Tilly and the children sat, silently waiting. They would know when she was home.

As the tears on Earth began to fall, God drew near and took her hand as she began her journey home. She looked so very tired. It had been her own wish to stay the longest and complete their work. 'A job well done,' He whispered in her ear as she took her last breath.

Dolly knew she was home. The children had thundered across heaven's sky the moment her soul returned. Tilly laughed when told

Nancy was demanding to know where she was, but it was Dolly who got there first.

There was a hush as the two souls merged once more, and Dolly reached for Nancy's hand.

'Oh, welcome home, Nancy,' said Dolly, her eyes shining, waiting to hear the first words of wisdom that she was sure Nancy would have brought home.

Nancy smiled.

'Any more bright ideas, Dolly Marshall?'

Echoes from the Past

There was no way of knowing as the car turned into the gates of Nazareth House how I would feel as I looked out of the car window and saw my childhood home in front of me. Large and imposing as I remembered it, today it seemed just a little smaller. The trees in the wood and the wild flowers were still there, but the little field of four-leaf clovers was gone. I felt a sadness inside and had to fight back tears.

The large oak door had been replaced and as I reached the bottom of the drive I immediately looked to my right, to see an empty grotto. The tears began to fall, unbidden. How sad it looked without the welcoming smile of Our Lady of Lourdes.

I had kindly been invited by the Head Teacher to once more step inside the doors of Nazareth House, where my own journey had begun as a tiny baby. It had been fifty-eight years since the two ladies had walked silently down the driveway, carrying the child that it was believed nobody wanted. I had dreamed about this moment for so long.

I made my way through the parlour and smiled as I looked up at the wall where the clock had once hung. I was laughing as I answered questions and told everyone the stories of my childhood. I walked from room to room, telling everyone what each space had been used for. I was loving every single minute of it.

It wasn't until I stood at the foot of the steps leading to the nursery that I had to take a moment before beginning to make my way upstairs. I paused with my hand on the handle of the door at the top of the stairs and took a deep breath, then took my first steps into the nursery and made my way to our room. I had seen it in my dreams – felt it, imagined how it would look now – and yet nothing could have prepared me for the moment I stepped inside the room I had shared with my mother all those years ago.

Immediately, tears stung my eyes as the memories came flooding back and I felt her presence so strongly, just as though she was standing next to me. My mother. This was where her story had begun eighty-four years ago when this was Nazareth House Convent School for girls. Now, the corridors and walls once more echoed with the sound of children's voices. There was an atmosphere of happiness and contentment. The teachers were kind, patient and caring, there was laughter, games in the grounds, fun learning activities, and these children smiled as they skipped to school each morning. The house had come full circle and, if you listened very carefully, you could hear the walls sigh in contentment and the very faint ticking of a clock.

As I looked around the room, suddenly I was back there. I could see the two small single beds next to each other, so we could hold hands during the night when I got too big to sleep in her bed. On my bed sat the little teddy bear Dolly had bought me for my second birthday. *It still sits on my bed now*, I thought. *Tattered, torn and so very precious.* I could see the small dressing table with the holy pictures stuck into the sides of the mirror, and my little transistor radio which Mum used to tune to Radio Luxembourg so I could fall asleep listening to music. There was a doll's cot next to my bed, with all my dolls – Caroline, Anne and Christine. Over in the corner stood an enormous wardrobe with a big mirror on the front, and in the other corner stood my beautiful red toy dresser.

I turned back to the window and felt a lump in my throat as I looked out at the chapel. It was still there, up on the roof, the bell that would ring out the dawn of a new day and announce all the Mass services. It was all as I remembered. Just the same.

My mother had loved and cared for hundreds of children, wiped their tears, sung songs, played games, soothed and comforted the most frightened of children, holding them in her arms, sitting them on her knee, bringing a little magic into their world and, if she is to be believed, ironed more children's clothes than anyone else in the whole wide world.

She had been challenged and shown great courage and strength. I could see myself sitting in bed as she held my hand and told me again about the day I had been placed in her arms and how she had fought to keep me and spent many hours in pain at the thought that she might lose me. 'Oh, but it was worth it!' she told me. 'The joy of those moments I spent with you every day overshadowed any pain or fear. You were always worth it,' she said, quite simply. 'Always.'

I smiled, remembering the many stories she had told me, each one more heartrending, fascinating and sometimes hilariously funny than the next.

I saw her opening the heavy sash window with a cloth in her hand and sitting on the window sill, leaning out backwards to clean the windows. And me, as a terrified child, hanging on to her legs, absolutely convinced she would fall out. I closed my eyes and could hear her footsteps marching down the long corridor when she was annoyed about something, remembering how all the nuns and staff would run in all directions, shouting, 'Nancy's on the warpath. Run!'

So much was the same.

I walked down the corridor, opened the door into the nursery playroom and looked around. The original window with the bars was still there. I could see us all sitting around the ironing board, singing songs, playing with the toys in the big toy box. I saw the fish tank with the catfish. And I could see Nancy standing there with a smile on her face, ironing with gusto. I wasn't even aware that tears were running down my face as I looked out of the window on to the nursery gardens below, and I caught my breath. It was gone! I felt utterly devastated.

Where was the magic whispering conker tree?

Struck by lightning not long before the last of the children left, I was told. It had been damaged beyond repair but the massive stump still sat in the garden with the roots, over many years, buried deep down in the ground. The pond was still there and I smiled, remembering the magical journey my mother had taken us all on. 'Mermaids, indeed!' I whispered to myself, smiling.

My life had been a magical journey filled with mermaids, enchantment, laughter and love, with strong and loving arms that held me and never let go. I had been truly blessed to be Nancy's daughter.

I closed my eyes and felt her standing beside me and her lips caress my cheek before she gently whispered in my ear.

'It's time, my darling. It's time to tell their stories.'

Changing Veils

In the spring of 2015, on a crisp April morning, the sun shone brightly for the bride and groom and the light bounced off the highly polished gates at the top of Nazareth House driveway. No horse and carriage had stood there for nearly a hundred years, although it was the reason the circular driveway had been built with the portico in front of the house, and stables for the horses to the left. Many cars had travelled up and down the driveway and many people had walked to and from the house. As the house came into view the window that had once belonged to the nursery bathroom could be seen. It had been Nancy's favourite place to look out on to the long driveway, where she had watched so many stories begin and end during the thirty-seven years Nazareth House had been her home. She had watched children arrive, as she prepared herself to welcome, soothe and comfort them, and she had watched them go, always leaving her feeling just a little bit sad. The long walk down the driveway on that bitterly cold morning in January 1930 was one she had never forgotten. So frightened and wanting desperately to go back home – and then, years later, fighting to stay.

Today, in a nearby church in Walker, there was joy in the air as the guests waited to see Nancy's grandchild arrive. Many of the guests had visited Nazareth House over the years.

'Nancy would not have wanted to miss this,' one of the guests whispered.

'Oh, don't worry,' another guest said, laughing, 'Nancy will have pestered the life out of God for a pass out today.'

The bride was already late but they would have to wait a little longer.

The horse and carriage paused at the top of Nazareth House driveway, and Gemah lifted her head to look at the place where so many of her grandmother's stories had taken place. 'Hello, Grandma,' she whispered. For a second she closed her eyes as her fingers tightened around the special treasures in her hands and she felt her grandmother draw near – as, of course, she had known she would.

Gemah had also had a very special bond with John's grandparents, Norma and Brian. John's grandfather had gone home to God, and she still missed him and his stories every day. She looked down once more at the treasures in her hands, and smiled. 'Perfect,' she whispered. She nodded, and the horse and carriage moved forward to complete its journey to the nearby church where everyone was waiting.

There was no need for any last words of advice or encouragement from her father. Harry knew Gemah was walking towards the kind of man her grandmother had always prayed she would marry. Kind, thoughtful, loving, fun, an incredible father and now husband-to-be. Nancy would have been very happy indeed, and immensely proud.

John stood at the front of the church and waited. Since he was fourteen years old, he had loved her. Together, they had been through all the difficulties of teenage years, growing up into adulthood and had stood strong against those who said they wouldn't make it. There had been no need to say anything, because in his heart he knew better. Even at fourteen years old he knew he would fight her battles for her, always stand by and support her – and, of course, one day they would get married. Fourteen years they had been together now, and had been blessed with two wonderful children, Séamus and Finláy. In one hour they would stand side by side as husband and wife, and John could not be happier.

He turned to look at the four men standing beside him. They had all been friends since they were young boys. Theirs was a true friendship built on support, encourage-ment – and, naturally, lots of fun. They had welcomed Gemah into their group and she was one of them. Gemah's mum had been heard to say on many occasions that she never worried when Gemah went out, she had her team of bodyguards following her everywhere she went. They were grown men now and were closer than they had ever been.

As he waited for his bride, John was remembering the day he had been asked who would be his best man. 'All of them,' he had replied. They had thought he was joking. He wasn't, and they stood proudly beside him now, wait-ing to celebrate the wedding of two of their very best friends. John briefly turned to look at the congregation, then turned back to face the altar. He would know when she had arrived.

The church was packed. There was to be no following tradition, and nobody needed to choose a side to sit on. Nancy would have liked that. Come along and celebrate with us and sit where you wish, the guests had been told. There was a definite break with tradition. Susan and Elaine, John's mum, had walked down the aisle together, holding hands, and were sitting together in the pew with their grandsons to watch their children get married. The smiles on their faces said it all. The church was full of family and friends, and behind Susan stood her great friend Eva and her husband, Maurice, who had travelled all the way from France to be there.

'She's here,' someone whispered, and Susan turned to grab Eva's hand.

There were tears in both women's eyes.

Gemah took her father's arm, ready to make her way down the aisle. 'Just as we planned, Grandma,' she whispered as the music began.

Susan stood at the front of the chapel, trying to push aside the memories of that long-ago Christmas Eve, feeling the emotion of the day begin to overwhelm her. If she started to cry now, she might never be able to stop. Gemah had brought her a world of love, she was everything a mother could wish for. She would always listen, never judge or condemn, never forget the important things like kindness, and had so many thoughtful little ways. Grandma had taught her well. *She taught me well too*, thought Susan, *only I never got away with half the things Gemah did*, she smiled to herself. *I have adored her from the moment she was born*, Susan thought, *and today the words do not exist to tell her how proud I am*. She had to stop thinking about it, feeling the tears begin to fall.

Suddenly the chapel doors opened wide, and there she was. Nancy's grandchild. A vision in ivory, looking so delicate and extremely beautiful, standing beside her father.

The music began and there was a gasp from the congregation as they turned their heads to see the bride. John smiled and turned to watch her. Gemah's eyes automatically sought him out, and as she slowly made her way down the aisle neither of them took their eyes off each other.

Gemah carried the beautiful bouquet of flowers John's mum had bought for her, but there was also something very special in her hands. People turned their heads to see what it was she was carrying. There was a sudden ray of sunlight that hit the glass windows of the chapel and then bounced off the special treasure that the bride carried. In her hands she held Brian's Bible, and delicately wound around it were her grandmother's rosary beads.

Gemah stole a glance at her mum and smiled at her.

'Love you,' Susan whispered to her, and then hastily grabbed the first tissue of the day.

Gemah walked forward to take her place beside her husband-to-be and the congregation raised their voices in song.

Harry gave his daughter to John, with tears in his eyes, which he hastily tried to conceal before leaving her to go and stand beside his wife. 'Susan, do you think Nancy is here?' he whispered.

'Oh, I do,' she smiled, then closed her eyes for a moment and prayed that God had allowed her mother to stand beside her once more.

Forever Magic

It was Christmas Eve 2015 and Susan was sitting quietly in the room with her grandsons, Séamus and Finláy, curled up on her knee. It was her favourite night of the year. Over in the corner the Christmas-tree lights twinkled and Christmas carols were playing on the television. The boys were listening to their grandma telling stories of long-ago Christmases, which Gemah had heard many times before. For a moment, she paused and listened once more to the story of the rag dolls on Christmas Eve. It was a tradition that had started many years ago, and she knew the story off by heart. Yet still she never tired of hearing it.

Gemah was smiling, remembering last Christmas when she was trying to think of something special to buy her mum. She had helped her decorate the kitchen and thought maybe a new tea service? Then suddenly her gaze had fallen upon the book Mum had written containing the story of the rag dolls. For the next week, late into the night when the children were asleep, Gemah worked with the beautiful piece of wood she had made especially, carefully crafting the words 'Nancy's Kitchen' on to it. Then two small holes and a piece of rope to hang it. It was almost finished, but the last bit must be done on the most special night of the year.

On Christmas Eve she waited until the boys were fast asleep, then began her task. It was late before she got the chance to start, but that just made it all the more special. 'Tradition, Grandma,' she whispered. Gemah opened the box in front of her, removed the tissue paper and smiled as she carefully lifted out the most beautiful rag doll and sat her upon the sign. She polished the wood and made sure it was all secure before placing it back in the box and wrapping it up with pretty ribbon and bows. 'Perfect!' she said. Gemah knew how much her mum loved anything people made themselves. Her home was filled with pictures the children had drawn, scribbles on the wall she refused to wash off, and handprints just about everywhere. Most of all she loved the picture of the children's feet when they had stood in the paint.

On Christmas morning, the boys ran to their grandma, as they always did, and Gemah hugged her mum before handing her the box. They smiled at each other.

'Now, what's this?' Susan said. 'What have I told you about spending money on me?' But she was laughing. She sat down and pulled the ribbon off, lifted the lid and removed the tissue paper. 'Oh!' she said, and then began to cry, unable to speak.

'Come on now, Mum,' Gemah said, 'what would Grandma say?'

'Nonsense!' they both said, and began to laugh.

Together, they found the perfect place to hang the very special kitchen sign and they stood back and looked at it.

'Christmas magic, Mum,' Gemah said.

Susan, as always at this time of year, was remembering Christmas Eve all those years ago. She closed her eyes and remembered it as clearly as if it had been yesterday. If she tried hard enough, she could almost see the snow falling, hear her mum talking and see once more those beautiful, bright blue eyes. Nancy had, of course, been right when her granddaughter asked her if she might, one day, be lucky enough to share the magic of *Cinderella*. Gemah had, indeed, been the most beautiful princess who rode in a crystal carriage and married the man of her dreams. Nancy would have been so proud of Gemah, John and her great-grandchildren, but she would live on in the stories she had told and in all of their hearts.

After all this time, Susan thought, *I still miss her*. Then she looked down at the sleeping children on her knee as she suddenly remembered Forever Magic. Gemah came into the room and lifted the children up into her arms, pretending not to notice the tears in her mother's eyes.

In a couple of hours, Gemah was taking Mum to midnight Mass. Susan had wanted to go early, to listen to the choir singing Christmas carols, but Gemah was worried as it was freezing cold tonight and very slippery outside. Her mum's arthritis was getting much worse, and the walking stick wouldn't help tonight – it was like an ice rink out there.

When the time came, they wrapped up warm, laughing and giggling as they always did when they were together, and Gemah helped Mum into the car. It was only a short journey, and they arrived in plenty of time. Gemah took her mother's hand and smiled as she helped her into the packed church for the carol service.

'I hope they sing Grandma's favourite,' Susan said.

Gemah gave her mum a quick hug as the choir began to sing. Susan looked around the beautiful church, seeing the candles flickering, Christmas flowers of all colours wonderfully arranged, then, finally, her eyes fell upon the altar. The Nativity scene was perfect. No statues with their heads hanging off, the donkey had all four legs, and the star stood tall and straight. *Oh, Mum*, thought Susan, *I miss you so much. Still so very much.*

Gemah moved closer and whispered in her mum's ear, 'Forever Magic'.

Susan looked up at the cross and thought about all the lives that had been touched by her mother's magic. Gemah squeezed her mum's hand as the school choir stood up and began to sing 'Silent Night', Nancy's favourite carol. Susan held on tightly to Gemah's hand and closed her eyes, hoping that if she listened hard enough she would, once more, hear her mother's voice telling her all about Forever Magic.

'As we look back over our lives and remember those we have lost, for many of us there is, and always will be, a part of us that will forever hurt. A small part of our broken heart that will not heal. We may smile and laugh at the memories of times gone by. Then suddenly, from nowhere, tears spring into our eyes and we have to close them for a moment and wait for the pain to pass. Yet I believe there is somehow a Forever Magic that we can trust in.

'Listen, what if there is a magic that exists inside every single person? A magic we carry within and around ourselves, throughout our whole lives, until we return home. It is then the magic becomes a beautiful energy to surround the ones we have left behind.

'Real magic never stops, it is always there for you to see and feel. It is when you feel at your lowest, when despair and loss threaten to break you, that the magic will be most powerful. You see, when you love someone, the magic binds you together and stays there for all eternity. Souls do not lose each other when they have shared a magical journey. It is simply just a moment in time, and then the magic is merged and we are together once more. Forever Magic is eternal.'

Is it true? Is there really a Forever Magic?

Oh, I hope so, don't you?

To the Children

Each day as you wake and remember again
Those long-ago days filled with laughter and pain,

When you hold out your hand and wonder who's there,
I always move close so you know I still care.

Those times you felt lost and cried many tears,
I held you together, calming your fears.

My children, please listen, draw near to my side
As my heart fills with joy, my soul full of pride.

I never forgot you. Believe me, it's true,
On closing my eyes I thought often of you.

I prayed you were safe, that life would be kind,
Bring love and contentment, with true peace of mind.

As I aged and grew old with the passing of years,
I remembered your laughter, along with the tears.

Each child left an imprint stamped deep in my heart,
I carried them with me when time to depart.

The clock may be silenced, the bell may not ring,
The mermaids so saddened they no longer sing,

Yet still I am near you, I watch you each day.
You're never alone, I did not go away.

God bless you, my children, your families too.
Forever, my darlings, I watch over you.

With Love Always

Aunty Nancy

Acknowledgements

To Daniel Bunyard, my publisher, and Punteha van Terheyden, Commissioning Editor of *Take a Break*, who gave me the opportunity of a lifetime and encouraged me to write my first book. It is thanks to their belief in me that my second book was ever written, finally bringing the children's stories to life.

To Fiona Crosby, Assistant Editor, who read my second book and believed in the stories to be told. I am extremely grateful for all her help with my story and her kind words of encouragement.

To Shân Morley Jones, Copy Editor. Thank you so much for all your help in making my story flow easily.

Once again, grateful thanks to Frank McChrystal for his technical wizardry and patience.

To Angela Charlton, Head Teacher of the Junior School (in what was formerly Nazareth House), one of God's special souls. Every single child in your care is honoured and valued by yourself and the incredibly dedicated teachers and staff that work there. As I walked round the school and watched the children working and playing, I saw happy, contented faces all around me. How thrilled Nancy would be.

To Mrs Lynda Edwards, to whom I handed over my young daughter, Gemah, only four years old, with tears in my eyes. I need not have worried. The children in your care had a teacher with one of the kindest and most caring souls I have ever known. To all of the staff at St Lawrence's RC Primary School, I thank you. May God bless you all. It was a wonderful start in life for my daughter. Years later, Gemah said she missed her years at St Lawrence's Primary. 'When you got reprimanded,' she said, 'it was always done in a kind voice.'

To my beautiful daughter, Gemah Louise, who, every moment of every single day, tells me how much she loves me. To love, and have that love returned, is something I thank God for every single day of my life. I think of Gemah and my heart smiles. Every day she is there with her constant support, encouragement and belief in everything I do. The poems telling me of her love for me I treasure beyond words. My daughter is one of the most beautiful and gentle souls I have ever known.

To the children, whoever and wherever you are. Thank you for your stories. I pray, as Mum often did, that your lives were blessed with love.

Finally, to my mother, No-nonsense Nancy, who, from the moment I was placed in her arms, taught me how it felt to be loved beyond measure. I still miss her every single day. I close my eyes and hear her whisper, 'Will their stories ever be told?'

Indeed they will, Mum.

God bless you.

My adopted mum, Nancy, aged seventeen. She's so beautiful and dignified; it brings a lump to my throat every time I look at it.

My birth mother, Molly. Everyone always asks if it's me in this photograph – we look so alike!

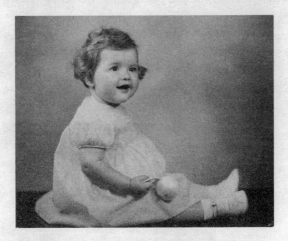

My first birthday. Every year Mum took me to Jerome's, a photographer in Newcastle, to have my picture taken.

This photograph was displayed in Jerome's shop window, and Mum was so proud. She still talked about this many years later.

Me with my doll, and the new coat Mum had bought for her.

Mum playing with the children at Nazareth House. In the background you can see the statue of Our Lady of Lourdes.

Mum, my friend Christopher and me with one of the nuns from Nazareth House, in front of the chapel.

All dressed up for a friend of Mum's wedding day, where I had the honour of being a bridesmaid.

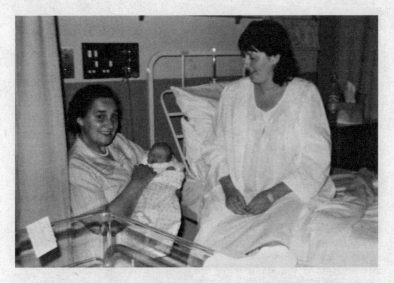

Me all grown up, and the day my beautiful daughter Gemah arrived.
I love the look on Mum's face – so very proud and happy.

Mum, Gemah and I would spend all year looking at brochures and
plan what was always a wonderful week at a holiday camp.

Me in front of the magic whispering conker tree, and the stump today.

The grotto where Our Lady of Lourdes stood.

The chapel, now a school assembly hall.